"ULSTER WILL FIGHT …"

Volume 2: The 36th (Ulster) Division from Formation to the Armistice

Everything we hear is an opinion, not a fact.
Everything we see is a perspective, not the truth.

Marcus Aurelius

David R. Orr & David Truesdale

Helion & Company

Helion & Company Limited
26 Willow Road
Solihull
West Midlands
B91 1UE
England
Tel. 0121 705 3393
Fax 0121 711 4075
Email: info@helion.co.uk
Website: www.helion.co.uk
Twitter: @helionbooks
Visit our blog http://blog.helion.co.uk/

Published by Helion & Company 2016
Designed and typeset by Mach 3 Solutions Ltd (www.mach3solutions.co.uk)
Cover designed by Paul Hewitt, Battlefield Design (www.battlefield-design.co.uk)
Printed by Gutenberg Press Limited, Tarxien, Malta

ISBN: 978-1-910777-63-3

British Library Cataloguing-in-Publication Data.
A catalogue record for this book is available from the British Library.

For details of other military history titles published by Helion & Company Limited contact
the above address, or visit our website: http://www.helion.co.uk.

We always welcome receiving book proposals from prospective authors.

The authors would like to dedicate both volumes of this history to those members of their families who enlisted as Irishmen in the Great War, 1914-1918.

Lance Corporal Albert Edward Truesdale, No.19221
D Company, 13th Royal Irish Rifles
Enlisted 19 September 1914, wounded 1 July 1916, gassed 21 March 1918
Medically discharged 26 June 1918
Silver War Badge No.423263

Captain Joseph Orr, No.2021
1st Battalion, Irish Guards
Enlisted 8 September 1904, wounded 2 February 1917
Retired due to wounds 20 March 1920
Later served as Major, King›s African Rifles

A/RQMS William John Orr, No.16395
5th Royal Irish Rifles
re-enlisted 18 September 1914 for the duration of the war.
Formerly Colour Sergeant, No.231
1st Royal Irish Rifles
7 July 1882 to 9 July 1908

Rifleman Joseph Totten, No.11/6463
11th Royal Irish Rifles
Enlisted May 1915.
GSW to face and leg, 8 August 1917
GSW to face, right arms and right thigh 21 July 1918
Transferred to Labour Corps 17 November 1918

Rifleman Herbert Totten, No.11/7550
11th Royal Irish Rifles
Enlisted 15 June 1915
Discharged 26 October 1915; aged 16 years

Lieutenant John Richard Orr
Royal Air Force, formerly Royal Flying Corps
Killed in Action 8 August 1918
Formerly 177th Overseas Battalion (Simcoe Foresters),
Canadian Expeditionary Force

Lieutenant William James Orr, No.143568
60 Siege Battery, Royal Garrison Artillery
Enlisted 8 December 1915
Transferred to Supplementary Reserve 8 March 1919
Relinquished Commission 1 April 1920

Contents

Foreword

The character and formation of the 36th (Ulster) Division is inexplicably linked to the events of the preceding years and in particular the tensions around Home Rule for Ireland. The current 'Decade of Centenaries' in Northern Ireland has encouraged many people to re-explore this period of Irish history however the roots of the events of this decade are firmly embedded in the last years of the Nineteenth Century. Randolph Churchill's call in 1886 "That Ulster will fight and Ulster will be right" was to echo in the country in subsequent years.

The actions of the Unionists in Ireland and in particular in the province of Ulster were to lead to defining moments in Irish history. Bolstered by support from the British Conservative party and key members of the British establishment they became more determined in their resistance to Home Rule. The signing of the Ulster Solemn League and Covenant in 1912 declared the signatories unswerving loyalty to the State and their determination to prevent the establishment of rule from Dublin. This stance was reinforced by the formation of the Ulster Volunteer Force to resist any attempts by the British Government to 'impose' Home Rule on Ulster.

It was these men of the Ulster Volunteer Force who would come forward as volunteers to form the nucleus of the 36th (Ulster) Division during the First World War. Those men and women of the Ulster Volunteers left in Ireland would continue their preparations to resist against the possibility of Home Rule.

In order to tell the complete story of the Ulster Division it is important to explore the Home Rule issues which led to men and women from, towns, villages and farms from all over the nine counties of Ulster and beyond, signing the Covenant and joining the Ulster Volunteers. These men were prepared to resist by force of arms if necessary.

The Somme Association is grateful to the authors for their efforts and attention to detail in explaining the issues surrounding Home Rule and the formation of the Ulster Volunteers who in turn provided the core of the 36th (Ulster) Division.

Carol Walker
Director
The Somme Association & Somme Museum
1 July 2016

Introduction

At the request of Carol Walker, the director of the Somme Museum, Newtownards, County Down, this history of the 36th (Ulster) Division has been compiled from the divisional, brigade, battalion and other unit war diaries, personal recollections and contemporary newspaper reports. A number of relevant volumes were also consulted.

David R Orr & David Truesdale
11 November 2015

The study of ancient history is as much about how we know as what we know, and engagement with all the processes of selection, constructive blindness, revolutionary interpretation and wilful misinterpretation that together produce the 'facts'… out of the messy, confusing and contradictory evidence that survives.

Mary Beard, Cambridge Classicist

Despite the history of the Great War, 1914-1918, having been recorded in fine detail, much of what Mary Beard refers to is relevant in the way Ireland's contribution has been presented. Until recently the process of selection, constructive blindness and revolutionary interpretation has been the mainstay of Irish military history. We are victims of our own propaganda and many myths and legends of the 36th (Ulster) Division, and other units, have been created.

The battles, skirmishes and patrol actions involving the division as described in this book are taken from the various war diaries, after-action reports, personal reminiscences, newspaper reports and letters from the men involved. It should be noted that these records and accounts reflect what their authors believed at the time, or wanted to record at the moment and not necessarily either fact or truth. A letter from home was always good for morale, however as the war progressed an increasing amount of mail was returned unopened and this had a detrimental effect on the morale of the home front. In many cases the letters from France or Flanders contained nothing about the fighting or the conditions and were it not for the address and man's name they could be coming from a holiday destination, *'getting plenty of rain and everything is very sloppy.'* So wrote Private Jack Anderson to his sister Susan May, Belfast.

It is not the purpose of this book to investigate why any particular action was fought, or to judge the character of anyone involved, it will simply tell what happened, based on the information available at the time.

Despite what has been written in many books and magazine articles, the Ulster Division was not formed overnight by an en bloc enlistment from the Ulster Volunteer Force and Young Citizen Volunteers [YCV], nor were the YCV the youth wing of the UVF, as some believe. Despite the surge of patriotic enlistments on the outbreak of war, by December 1914 there was still a shortfall of 1,697 men, the majority of these shortages being in the divisional troops, not the infantry brigades. It was proving difficult to fill the ranks of the Royal Army Medical Corps, Army Service Corps, Cyclist Company and Royal Engineers, in fact any unit that required a degree of mechanical skill, however small.

A member of the YCV, now
dressed in khaki.

Poster encouraging UVF
members to enlist in the
Ulster Division.

ULSTER VOLUNTEER FORCE.

➤ LORD KITCHENER'S ARMY. ◄

N O T I C E.

Members of the U.V.F. serving in any Belfast Regiment
who have not yet enlisted in the Ulster Division of
Lord Kitchener's Army can do so by applying at the

OLD TOWN HALL

ANY DAY

Between the hours of 10 a.m. and 4 p.m.

Men so enlisting will be posted to their old Battalions
in whichever Camp they may happen to be, and as far
as possible under their old Officers.

GEO. RICHARDSON,
Lieut.-General, G.O.C. U.V.F.

Headquarters, Old Town Hall, Belfast.
10th September, 1914.

> **"Quit yourselves like men, and comply
> with your country's demand."**
> —EDWARD CARSON.

GOD SAVE THE KING.

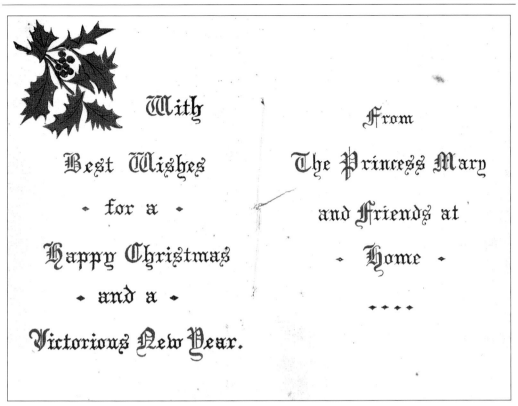

With
Best Wishes
· for a ·
Happy Christmas
· and a ·
Victorious New Year.

From
The Princess Mary
and Friends at
· Home ·
· · · ·

A Christmas card from Princess Mary, dated 2 December 1914.

The Christmas truce of 1914, a similar event was not experienced by the 36th Division while on the Western Front. (Courtesy of the Royal Irish Fusiliers Museum)

Heroes were ample on the battlefield, many being unrecognised and unrewarded, but heroic efforts away from the fighting were also commonplace. On 1 July 1915, the *Belfast News Letter* printed the following:

> The General Officer Commanding the Ulster Division has published a divisional order commending the gallant conduct of Sergeants Smith and Sadler of the Military Mounted Police and Sergeants Ennis and McGarry of the 10th Rifles. These four non-commissioned officers went to the assistance of five men whose boat had overturned in Dundrum Bay and in spite of the fact that a strong tide was running, succeeded in bringing them ashore.

Over the last number of years much has been made of those soldiers 'shot at dawn', with 21st Century minds recoiling in horror at such barbarity. This view was not shared at the time by those men who remained in the trenches holding the line and certainly not within the records of the British Army. An example of this is demonstrated by an Australian unit in 1918, shortly after the publication of Field Marshal Haig's 'backs to the wall' Order of the Day. A subaltern of the 1st Australian Division wrote the following to his section:

1. This position will be held and the section will remain here until relieved.
2. The enemy cannot be allowed to interfere with this programme.
3. If the section cannot remain here alive it will remain here dead, but in any case it will remain here.
4. If any man through shell shock or other cause attempts to surrender he will remain here dead.
5. Should all guns be blown out, the section will use Mills grenades and other novelties.
6. Finally as stated the position will be held.

This order was discovered later on the bodies of the men of that section. The Australian government may not have agreed to the death penalty during the Great War, but a certain subaltern was prepared to shoot his own men to ensure discipline. In 1914, Haig commanded 3,000,000 men, in 1916, it was 2.5 million. The war was a learning process from private to field marshal. By 1918 Field Marshal Haig was commanding over three million men in France, maintaining discipline within such numbers was not achieved by threats or rapped knuckles. The human side of war is not necessarily glorious, brave, heroic or even rational.

The image of the British Army of 1914-1918 as being inept, 'lions led by donkeys', is highly misleading.[1] While the German Army had the experience of battle schools and wargames, they had little in the way of battle experience, their last major war being against France in 1870, while the British Army had fought numerous colonial actions, the most recent being the South African War against the Boers, where "… the Boers knocked us silly at a mile."[2]

Here much experience was gained under fire, something that would benefit the officers and more senior 'other ranks' in 1914, although many of the generals seemed to learn little. The opening year of the war would prove that mass attacks against machine guns and riflemen, some of whom were capable of firing fifteen aimed shots per minute, would be carried out by both sides.

Communications were primitive, limited use of wireless and field telephone, much susceptible to shell fire. The British battlefield with a 'front' of eighty miles was controlled largely by 'runners', who spent a lot of time lying down and who were frequently killed or injured while doing so.

---

1   Gary Sheffield, *Forgotten Victory* (Headline Book Publishing, 2001).
2   From the poem *Fuzzy-Wuzzy* by Rudyard Kipling.

Communications were as fast as a man could run through narrow trenches or across muddy ground.

A continuing myth is that the Ulster Covenant was signed by many men in their own blood, there even being claims that a miniature guillotine contraption being placed on the table. Colonel Fred Crawford being one of those making such a claim, but a test carried out on his signature by Dr. Alistair Ruffell of Queen's University in September 2012, using luminal, proved otherwise.

For many years Private John Condon, Royal Irish Rifles, has been known as the youngest Irishman to be killed in the Great War, his age being listed as fourteen years. Recent research has uncovered a birth certificate showing he was born on 16 October 1896, making his nineteen years in 1915, yet, at the time of writing, the Commonwealth War Grave Commission still holds the original 'facts' on their data base.

The men of the division were sent 'over the top' on 1 July drunk! This myth stems from the issue of the rum ration. In a platoon of men where a large number would have been teetotal, as in the 14th Rifles, this meant that there was more for those that were not.

In today's armed forces there is something known as 'fragging' a word that originated with the United State military during the Vietnam era. It refers to the act of killing a comrade or superior rank. In Ulster a story is often told of a local landowner whose son had raped the sister of one of the farm workers. When the son was commissioned the farm worker also enlisted and followed the son to France. When the opportunity arose the farm worker killed the son in the heat of battle. The closest you can get to names and places is to have a particular town mentioned.

Wearing orange sashes! A small number of men have been identified as wearing either orange sashes or collarets on 1 July 1916. While widely spoken off, quite often to the extent of the entire Division of 100,000 men (sic) going 'over the top' festooned in orange, the evidence pointing to who actually wore a sash or collaret, is a lot more difficult to quantify. In a letter to his father, Private R Lavery of the 10th Inniskillings wrote:

Cover page of *The Incinerator* magazine. Jim Maulstead of the 14th Royal Irish Rifles was a major contributor.

Some of them had orange lilies in their caps, and one sergeant I saw had on his orange sash going over the parapet to meet them. He kept shouting 'Come on Ulster.'[3]

---

3   *Belfast News Letter* 29 July 1916.

Men of C Company Royal Inniskilling Fusiliers.

The pipes and drums of the Royal Inniskilling Fusiliers.

Another who reputedly wore his sash was Sergeant Samuel Kelly, of the 9th Inniskillings, was a veteran of the Boer War where he had served with the 1st Battalion, earning the promotion of being made King's Corporal for his actions in holding off a large party of Boers. For his action on 1 July he was awarded the Distinguished Conduct Medal and promoted to Sergeant. Post-war he served as a member of the Royal Ulster Constabulary.[4]

After the battle Private William Burrows wrote to his family in Prospect Road, Bangor; "…on going over the top I wore a little ivory monkey around my neck, one of our fellows wore an orange sash, while another played the bagpipes, while several manipulated the warlike mouth organ."[5]

Local street mythology would state that the division was Protestant to a man and all Ulstermen. Again this is not strictly accurate, not all members of the division were Protestant and not all came from Ulster. Private Charles Connolly, who served in the 14th Rifles, came from Drogheda, County Louth, while Second Lieutenant H De Vine, husband of Mrs De Vine of (Dugort) Doogart, Achill Island, County Mayo, died on 17 February 1919 of wounds received. His memorial is at Grangegorman Cemetery, Dublin. From 1-8 July 1916 the 11th Inniskillings had 229 men either killed or died of wounds. Of these ninety-two were born outside Ulster, mostly from the Lanarkshire and Tyneside areas.[6]

The belief that the advance of the Ulster Division on 1 July 1916 was a 'blood sacrifice' to equal, if not exceed that of Easter in Dublin is a myth manufactured by both church and politics. The division attacked in conjunction with the remainder of the British Army as part of a planned campaign; they advanced at the same rate and in the same formation as the other Kitchener divisions and suffered accordingly. Nevertheless, the date and the deed had been burned into Ulster Protestant folklore so deeply it will never been seen as anything else.

The last British soldier to die who had served in the trenches was Private 'Harry' Patch, a former Lewis gunner with the Duke of Cornwall's Light Infantry. He died on 25 July 2009 to much acclaim, gaining the sobriquet 'the last Fighting Tommy', was awarded an honorary degree from Bristol University, had a poem composed by Andrew Motion, the poet laureate, and received the freedom of the city of Wells. The last German soldier of the Great War died on New Year's Day 2008, he was Erich Kaestner, aged 107 years. It caused little comment in the German press and less in the British.

The last member of the Ulster Division to die was Thomas Shaw of Bangor, who had served with the 16th Rifles; he died on 2 March 2002.

In the Second World War the term 'missing in action' usually denoted that a man was either killed in battle, but his body had not yet been found, he had become separated from his unit and would hopefully return as things quietened down, or that he had been taken prisoner. During the 1914-1918 War things were different. Due to the conditions on the Western Front a man missing in action usually referred to his body being obliterated during shelling, sinking into the mud of the Passchendaele or elsewhere. The large number of men listed as having no known grave shows that even if a man was properly buried and recorded, successive movement of troops, weather conditions and shelling ensured that all trace of his grave would be lost.

The trenches were responsible for a multitude of health problems, but they also saved lives. When the phrase 'the horror of the trenches' is used, it must be remembered just how horrific the casualties would have been without them.[7] On 18 June 1815, the 1st Battalion Royal Inniskilling Fusiliers stood in square in the open on the battlefield of Waterloo defending

---

4   Source: Somme Museum Archive.
5   *Bangor Spectator* 21 July 1916.
6   As related by Kevin Myers.
7   Strachan, Hew, *The First World War* (London, 2003).

A message from Lord Kitchener,
which promised much.

Department of Recruiting, Ireland.

October 28th, 1915.

Sir,

Lord Kitchener sends me the attached message for YOU.

He wants 50,000 Irishmen at once for the period
of the War. You will be equipped and will start your
training in Ireland, and complete it in different
parts of the world. Wherever you go you will be
serving with Irishmen.

The relatives whom you look after will be looked
after for you while you are away. Your Wives, your
Children, or those dependent on you will receive an
allowance every week.

Every great Irishman urges the appeal. The
safety of your homes and your possessions depends on
your answer.

Sons of Farmers—whose lands are passing into
your own possession—You must come out and defend this
heritage.

Townsmen, your interests are threatened too. You
must equally respond to the call.

It is your privilege as an Irishman to come
forward voluntarily. Will you come now? Fill in this
form and post it to-day.

Yours faithfully,

Wimborne

Lord Lieutenant of Ireland and
Director-General for Recruiting.

[P.T.O.

Wellington's right flank. By the battle's end they had lost fourteen out of fifteen officers and 498 out of 670 'other ranks', killed, wounded and missing, given the choice these men would have welcomed a trench.

In November 2014, a lecture was given in St Columb's Cathedral, Londonderry, when the Very Reverend Dr William Morton spoke about composers of the Great War. He concluded his talk by mentioning an Irishwoman, Ina Boyle (1888-1967), who was the most prolific female composer in Ireland prior to 1950. In 1915, Boyle had composed a piece for organ and choir, entitle 'A Tribute To The Ulster Division', which was to have been played and sung in Derry Cathedral, but as so many of the choristers had enlisted, there were not the numbers to do it justice, so it remained unheard. Boyle also wrote a requiem for the Division, which has been held in the British Library and Trinity College, Dublin since 1915. At the time of writing plans were being made to have it performed to mark its centenary.

Unless specifically noted, the source material for this history has come from the archives of the Somme Museum, Newtownards, County Down, Northern Ireland. That men are not like that now became self-evident as the various archives and recorded memories revealed just what did and did not occur between the years 1913 to 1918. All times will be as per the various war diaries, i.e. 3:30 am, the modern rendition of 0330 hours, is not relevant to this period, the Army not adopting it until late 1918, although the Royal Navy had used it from 1915. It is best if the order of battle is consulted prior to reading the main manuscript. In this history the Royal Irish Rifles will be referred to as 'Rifles. The Royal Inniskilling Fusiliers as 'Inniskillings' and the Royal Irish Fusiliers as 'Irish Fusiliers'

Officers of the Royal Irish Fusiliers.

War

Dull, damp, desolate countryside
The sound of the rain splashing as the water approaches the muddy grass.
The shredded, begging soldiers struggle
As they trip and limp
Through the disgusting fields.
Exhausted, sweaty, pained soldiers
Sense the dreadful stench of death.
Dry, dirty smoke curls towards the sky
In the strangest colours.
The sounds of the guns – eerie like
The crying of tortured animals.
Exploding bombs erupting, scattering limbs
Across the cratered earth.
Confused, breathless, weary they drag
Themselves along the fields.
Beautiful images that grow in their minds of home;
Flaming fires, delicious smells,
Comfortable beds –
Soon swept away by the vicious wind.

Leah Donnelly, aged 9
Joint Fourth Prize: The Ulster Bank Armagh Literary Award
St Patrick's Primary School Armagh

1

Prelude

For the pace is hot, and the points are near,
And sleep hath deadened the driver's ear;
And signals flash through the night in vain.
Death is in charge of the clattering train![1]

To find a definitive reason for the outbreak of the Great War in 1914 is impossible. Personal bias in writing, depending on the author's nationality and/or beliefs, the availability of sources in the writer's own language and his or her ability to translate those that which are not. There are some factors that can be accepted and one of these is that the path to war in 1914 began in 1870.

The Franco-Prussian War (1870-71), fought with modern weapons and Napoleonic tactics, saw Germany defeat France and become a major force in the European mainland, strong economically, industrially and militarily, with her warship strength being second only to Britain's Royal Navy.

The almost beatified statesman, Prince Otto von Bismarck, had advised Kaiser Wilhelm I of Prussia to gather the twenty-five states, principalities and minor kingdoms together to create a new Germany. Once this had been achieved a succession of wars saw Denmark defeated in 1864, Austria in 1866 and France in 1871, this latter conflict in response to a declaration of war by Napoleon III.

The war had not gone well for France. Paris had been occupied and as compensation France had to surrender two provinces along the border with Germany, Alsace and Lorraine, both sources of raw material for Germany. Such was the shame felt by the French that for the foreseeable future Germany would have an unforgiving enemy on the west and a potential enemy in the shape of Tsarist Russia to the east. Germany had a loyal ally to the south in the Austria-Hungarian Empire. South of here was the Balkans, a simmering hotpot of Serbia, Bosnia, Romania, Bulgaria, Montenegro and Herzegovina, where hatred between politics, religion and race intermingled in a bewildering mixture of socialism, dissent between Catholics and Protestants and Moslems and the never-ending hatred of all towards the Jews.

In order to secure her position Germany signed a treaty with Russia to protect her eastern borders, with England to try and curb French aggression and with Austria-Hungary as a barrier with the Balkans. There was a constant fear that France and Russia would form an alliance, leaving Germany hemmed in on two flanks and it took a dazzling piece of diplomacy on the part of Bismarck to create the League of the Three Emperors: Germany, Austria-Hungary and Russia. All was well for a number of years, then Kaiser Wilhelm II came to the throne, ousted Bismarck and quickly undid years of careful diplomacy.

In 1890 the League came to an end and the Kaiser refused to renew it, cutting Russia off from financial and technological assistance. This vacuum was quickly filled by France, who saw the

---

1 *Death and his brother sleep*, by the Irish poet Edwin James Milliken, (1839-1897).

opportunity of acquiring a friend and two years later agreed to an alliance whereby each would come to the other's aid in the event of an attack by Germany or her allies.

Germany, now with potentially an enemy on either side, continued to implement a foreign policy that seemed to deliberately annoy other countries, especially Britain. The Kaiser, jealous of British overseas colonies demanded that Germany must also have 'a place in the sun' and Africa had seemed a good location to begin. Colonies were established in German South West Africa, Cameroon, Togoland and Tanganyika; they proved to be less than successful in either trade or as a supplier of raw material. However, it was all that remained, France and Britain having already secured the 'prime' locations.

Well aware that he could not match Britain in overseas territories the Kaiser embarked on bringing his naval forces into parity with the Royal Navy and so began the biggest and most expensive arms race to date. There was then the threat of German intervention in the war between the Boers and British in South Africa and the 'Moroccan Crisis' of 1905, with Germany complaining that its private companies in that country were being denied rights to establish a port by both French and British interests.

In 1912, the Balkan states went to war against their long time oppressor, the Turks, and won. Now freed of Ottoman dominion they were free to go to war with each other in a quarrel over dominion in the Second Balkan War of 1913. Both the Austrian-Hungarian Empire and Russia claimed they had a right to control in the Balkans, the former because they lay on the southern border, the latter because so many of the population were fellow Slavs.

It all came to a head on 28 June 1914, when the Austrian Archduke Franz Ferdinand and his wife were assassinated in Sarajevo. The Austrians demanded reprisals against Serbia that were well beyond compliance and Germany then confirmed support for Austria. Serbia then appealed to Russia on 24 July and Austria-Hungary declared war on Serbia on 28 July, with Belgrade being bombarded the following day. On 31 July Russia mobilised and Germany declared war the following day. On 2 August German troops entered Luxemburg, while Italy declared a state of neutrality. Twenty-four hours later Germany declared war on France and as her troops marched into Belgium the following day Britain declared war on Germany.

And so the cousins went to war,[2] Britain confident that a successful cavalry charge with drawn sabres would win the day, France depending on the spirit of the bayonet and Germany, with almost three times the numbers of machine guns possessed by France and Britain combined. However, it must be remembered, no country held the moral high ground as to the cause of the War in 1914.

Opening Moves 1914

Officers are particularly requested to pay their mess bills before leaving for the front.
Major A. Corbett-Smith, RFA, *The Retreat From Mons*

To the officers and men of the Regular Army the outbreak of war in August 1914 caused little concern. They were professionals and war was their job, to be welcomed by most as a 'picnic change' from the monotony of peacetime soldiering in England. War also offered the chance of promotion, something that had been in the doldrums since the end of the South African War.

The war against the Boers was thought by many to have been an unsporting affair, too one sided, a regular army against a bunch of farmers, although this depended on what period in the conflict was being talked about at the time! Germany on the other hand would offer much more

2   George V, Nicholas II and Wilhelm II were, either directly or through marriage descendants of Queen Victoria.

of a fair fight, with equal weapons and tactics, while experience would soon show that numbers involved were far from equal or relevant.

Actual approximate numbers as of 22 August 1914, the Western Front

Nationality	Men	Field guns	Machine guns
British	80,000	300	100
French	240,000	960	288
German	812,000	3,016	936

In order to transport the Expeditionary Force to France the London and South Western Railway was given sixty hours in which to dispatch from Aldershot to the port of Southampton 350 troop trains. Each train left five minutes ahead of its scheduled time and the operation was completed in forty-five hours! Motor lorries, each built to carry three tons, resplendent in their company livery; whiskey distillers, house movers, furniture manufacturers and makers of ladies corsets were conscripted and trundled towards the Front. It would be several months before all were coated in the universal green paint and lorries bearing company logos were a common sight in those early days, *'Johnny Walker* brings the ammunition to Belgium'. From Southampton to the mouth of the Seine was a twelve hour voyage, all ships sailed with their navigation and other lights on. The U-boat was as yet not considered a threat and escorting Royal Navy vessels kept the surface vessels of the Kriegsmarine at a safe distance. In 1914 the British Army may have saved Paris, but the Royal Navy enabled it to do so.

French and Belgian civilians swamped the columns of marching men, taking souvenirs of badges, buttons, while a special favourite was the shoulder strap of the men of the Royal Field Artillery. The letters RFA was assumed by many of the French as meaning the Triple Entente, 'Russie-France-Angleterre.' Soon tape and string was holding trousers up and coats closed.

A facet of modern warfare became quickly evident when German aircraft would fly over the British line and drop smoke markers; these would be used by the enemy artillerymen for ranging purposes. From the dropping of the marker until the first salvo landed was a mere twenty seconds. While British artillery was very good with regard to accuracy and volume of fire, they still had not learned the art of camouflage. There was also the question of quality control over the manufacture of shells and in 1915 there would be a shortage of ammunition, leading to the failure of the British attack against the Aubers Ridge on 9 May.

At the beginning of the war the British front line was about twenty-five miles long, with the town of Mons close to the centre. The Battle of Mons fought on 23 August 1914, was the first major clash between the Expeditionary Force under the command of Field Marshal Sir John French and the Imperial German Army.[3] This force fielded two corps, each with two infantry divisions plus an additional five brigades of cavalry, a total of approximately 80,000 men.

In command of I Corps was Lieutenant General Sir Douglas Haig, which was composed of the 1st Division under Brigadier General Samuel Holt Lomax,[4] while the 2nd Division was commanded by Major General Charles Monroe.

Lieutenant General Sir Horace Smith-Dorrien, a tried and tested veteran of the Zulu War of 1879, commanded the II Corps, having taken over on 21 August, four days after the death of Sir James Grierson.[5] It has been recorded that no other officer of equivalent seniority, with the possible

---

3   The Expeditionary Force would not become 'British' until the arrival of contingents from the Indian Army.
4   He was mortally wounded by an artillery shell at First Ypres in 1915.
5   He died from a heart attack in transit near Amiens on 17 August.

exception of Sir Ian Hamilton, was his equal intellectually and none could rival his ability in handling large numbers of men with economy and decision.[6]

The Corps consisted of the 3rd Division under Major General H.I.W. Hamilton, with the 5th Division commanded by Major General Sir Charles Ferguson. Each infantry division consisted of three brigades, each with four battalions. It was armed with 24 Vickers machine guns, two per battalion and was supported by three field artillery brigades totaling 54 18-pounder guns, one field howitzer brigade of 18 4.5-inch howitzers and one heavy artillery battery of four 60-pounder guns.

Smith-Dorrien's Corps, on the left of the line, occupied defensive positions along the Mons-Condé Canal, while Haig's I Corps was positioned almost at a right angle away from the canal along the Mons-Beaumont Road. I Corps was deployed in this manner to protect the BEF's right flank should the French be forced to retreat from their position at Charleroi. However, the fact that I Corps did not adopt a line along the canal meant that it played little part in the forthcoming battle and the German onslaught was faced almost exclusively by II Corps. The dominant geographical feature of the battlefield was a loop in the canal that jutted out from the town of Mons towards the village of Nimy. This loop formed a small salient that would be difficult for the British to defend and consequently this salient formed the focus of the battle.

Advancing towards the British was the German First Army commanded by General Alexander von Kluck. This was a man from a middle class Prussian family and while he had no Staff experience, he had boldness and aggression that well suited this attack. The First Army was composed of four corps, II, III, IV and IX and three Reserve Corps. The latter corps took no part in the fighting at Mons. German Corps, like the British, consisted of two divisions each with attendant cavalry and artillery. Of all the German field armies, the First Army was the strongest, with a density of about 18,000 men per mile of front, or approximately ten men per yard.

First contact between the two armies occurred on 21 August, when a British bicycle reconnaissance team encountered a German unit near Obourg. One of the cyclists, Private John Parr, was killed, thereby becoming the first British fatality of the Great War to die in action. The first substantial action occurred a day later, on the morning of 22 August. At 6.30am, when C Squadron of the 4th (Royal Irish) Dragoon Guards laid an ambush for a patrol of German Uhlans (Lancers) near the village of Casteau on the main road out of Mons to Brussels. These cavalrymen were from the German 4th Cuirassiers and despite the title, at this time all German cavalry carried lances. The Germans spotted something suspicious and fell back, a troop of the Dragoons, led by Captain Hornby, gave chase, followed by the rest of his Squadron, all with drawn sabres. The retreating Germans led the British to a larger force of Uhlans, who they promptly charged, and Captain Hornby became the first British soldier to kill an enemy in the Great War, engaged on horseback with sword against lance (The sword is today in the York Army Museum, it is a regulation '1908 Pattern' as issued to the rank and file, dress swords being very expensive they were usually exchanged from Quartermaster stores and remained in the regimental depot).

After a further pursuit of a few miles, the Germans turned and fired upon the British cavalrymen using carbines, at which point the Dragoons dismounted and opened fire with their rifles, all British cavalry being armed with the standard service rifle. Corporal Edward Thomas is reputed to have fired the first rifle shot of the war for the British Army, hitting a German officer at a range of some four hundred yards.[7] The first artillery round fired on the Western Front was at 11.15am, by No.4 gun of E Battery Royal Horse Artillery, located at Bray on the Mons to Charleroi Road.[8]

---

6   Clark, Alan, *The Donkeys* (London 1961).
7   Kenyon, David, *Horsemen In No Man's Land* (Pen & Sword 2011). However, this is the Army; claims are also made on behalf of the Royal Flying Corps and a fort in Australia.
8   Brereton, J.M., *The 4th/7th Royal Dragoon Guards 1685-1980* (Catterick 1982).

The first casualties of the war were 150 crewmen of HMS *Amphion*, sunk in the early hours of 6 August, when acting as leader of the 3rd Flotilla. She struck a sea-mine previously laid by the SMS *Konigen Luise*, which had been sunk by the flotilla the previous day.[9]

The Battle of Mons opened at dawn on 23 August with a German artillery bombardment of the British lines. Observing that the salient formed by the loop in the canal was the weak point of the British line, the Germans laid down a sustained attack at that point.

At 9:00 am, the initial German assault began, with enemt infantry attempting to force their way across the four bridges that crossed the canal at the salient. Four German battalions attacked the Nimy Bridge, which was defended by a single company of the 4th Battalion, Royal Fusiliers, commanded by Captain Ashburner and a machine gun section led by Lieutenant Maurice Dease. Advancing at first in close column of march along the road, the Germans presented a nearly unmissable target for the British riflemen, who were well capable of firing the famous fifteen rounds per minute. This fire combined with the Vickers machine guns caused horrendous casualties to the enemy close packed columns.

During the assault the machine gun section suffered heavy casualties and Lieutenant Dease was wounded no less than five times, but declined to leave his guns. The initial German attack was repulsed with heavy losses. Quickly realising the folly of attacking in close order the Germans changed to an open formation and attacked again. This attack was more successful, as the looser formation made it more difficult for the British to inflict casualties. The defenders were soon hard-pressed to hold the canal crossings. The 4th Royal Fusiliers, defending the Nimy Bridge and the Ghlin Bridge, faced some of the day's heaviest fighting, and only the piecemeal addition of reinforcements to

Lieutenant Maurice Dease VC, Royal Fusiliers, the first recipient of the Victoria Cross in the Great War.

the firing line as well as the exceptional bravery of two of the battalion's machine gunners allowed them to hold off the German attacks. At the Nimy Bridge Lieutenant Dease was eventually evacuated to an aid post, but soon after died of his wounds. Maurice James Dease, from County Westmeath, was a former pupil of Stonyhurst College and for his actions this day he was awarded the Victoria Cross, the first of the Great War.[10] At the Ghlin Bridge, Private Sidney Godley operated the battalion's other machine gun tenaciously throughout the day, remaining behind to give cover to the Fusiliers' retreat at the end of the battle. Godley surrendered after first disassembling his gun and throwing the pieces into the canal to prevent its use by the Germans. Private Godley, from East Grinsted, in West Sussx was also awarded the Victoria Cross.[11]

---

9   Added to these casualties were eighteen crew of the previously lost German vessel.
10 Doherty & Truesdale, *Irish Winners of the Victoria Cross*.
11 It is now believed that the gun did not in fact fall into the canal, but was recovered by the Germans. See the regimental history of the *84th Infanterie Regiment*.

To the right of the Royal Fusiliers, the 4th Middlesex Regiment and the 1st Gordon Highlanders were equally hard-pressed by the German assault on the salient. Vastly outnumbered, both Battalions suffered heavy casualties but, with the addition of reinforcements from the 2nd Royal Irish Regiment, part of the divisional reserve, along with effective fire support from the Divisional Artillery, they managed to hold the bridges. At this point, the Germans expanded their attack, assaulting the British defences along the canal to the west of the salient. The Germans were aided by fir plantations that lined the northern side of the canal that allowed them to advance under cover to within a few hundred yards of the canal and to rake the British defences with enfilade machine gun and rifle fire. This attack fell particularly heavily on the 1st Royal West Kent Regiment and the 2nd King's Own Scottish Borderers, but, although these battalions suffered heavy casualties, they managed to hold their positions throughout the day.

By the afternoon the weight of continuing German attacks was making the British position untenable. Most of the battalions defending the salient had taken heavy casualties; the 4th Middlesex had suffered fifteen officers and 353 other ranks as casualties. To the east of the British position units of the German IX Corps had begun to cross the canal in force threatening the right flank. At Nimy, a German private, August Neimeier, had swum across the canal under British fire to operate machinery closing a swing bridge. Although he was killed, his actions allowed the Germans to increase pressure against the 4th Royal Fusiliers.

As a result of this the British 3rd Division was ordered to retire from the salient at 3:00 pm and to take up positions to the south of Mons. This retirement necessitated a similar retreat towards evening by the 5th Division, and by nightfall the II Corps had established a new defensive line running through the villages of Montrœul, Boussu, Wasmes, Paturages, and Frameries. By this time the Germans had built pontoon bridges over the canal, and were approaching the British positions in great strength. Additionally, news had arrived that the French Fifth Army was in retreat, exposing the British right flank. At 2:00 am on 24 August, Smith-Dorrien's II Corps was ordered to retreat southwest into France with the goal of reaching defensibile positions along the Valenciennes to Maubeuge Road.

This unexpected order to retreat from prepared defensive lines in the face of the enemy meant that II Corps was required to fight a number of sharp rearguard actions against the pursuing Germans. For the first stage of the withdrawal, Smith-Dorrien detailed 5 Brigade of the 2nd Division, which had not been involved in heavy fighting on 23 August, to act as rearguard. As 5 Brigade fought a holding action at Paturages and Frameries, the brigade artillery in particular inflicting heavy casualties on the Germans, at Wasmes, elements of the 5th Division faced a heavy assault. German artillery began bombarding the village at daybreak, and at 10:00 am infantry of the German III Corps attacked. Again advancing in columns, however, the Germans were immediately met with heavy rifle and machine gun fire, and were "mown down like grass."[12] For a further two hours, soldiers of the 1st Royal West Kent Regiment, 2nd King's Own Yorkshire Light Infantry, 2nd Duke of Wellington's Regiment, and 1st Bedfordshire Regiment held off repeated German assaults on the village despite taking heavy casualties, before withdrawing in good order to St. Vaast.

A hot August day of marching on a French road, for the troops so different from British roads, thirsty and dusty, the harvest of French orchards saved the situation. But, oh, those ripened apples and pears that invited dreams of angels.[13]

On the extreme left of the British line, 14 and 15 Brigades of the 5th Division were particularly hard-pressed by the Germans, who were attempting to outflank them and were forced to call for

---

12   Atkinson, C.T., *The Queen's Own Royal West Kent Regiment* (London, 1924).
13   See relevant appendix for the Angel of Mons.

help from the cavalry. Together 2 Cavalry Brigade, 4th Dragoons and 9th Lancers, along with 119 Battery RFA, and L Battery RHA, were sent to their assistance. The cavalry in their dismounted role, protected by the two artillery batteries, successfully screened the withdrawal of 14 and 15 Brigades in four hours of intense fighting. During this time Major Ernest Wright Alexander, 119 Battery commander, realised that his detachments had suffered to the extent that there were not enough men remaining to manhandle the guns out of the action. With the assistance of volunteers from the 9th Lancers, ammunition limbers and wounded men were brought out of the line of fire to allow the horse teams and their drivers to gallop forward and remove the guns to safety. Both Alexander and Captain Francis Grenfell of the Lancers were awarded the Victoria Cross. Alexander had the good fortune to have as his mother Annie Alexander née Gregg of Belfast.[14]

By nightfall on 24 August, the British had successfully withdrawn to what was expected to be their new defensive lines on the Valenciennes to Maubeuge Road. They did not stop there, however. Outnumbered by the German First Army, and with their French allies falling back, the BEF had no choice but to continue to retire, with General Haig's I Corps retreating to Landrecies and Smith-Dorrien's II Corps to Le Cateau. The withdrawal would last for two weeks and cover over 250 miles. Throughout the withdrawal the British were closely pursued by the enemy and were forced to fight a number of rearguard actions, including the Battle of Le Cateau on 26 August, the Étreux rearguard action on 27 August, and the Action at Néry on 1 September. It was here, at Nery, that a third Victoria Cross was earned by an Irishman.[15]

On the morning of 1 September, 1 Cavalry Brigade under the command of Brigadier General Charles James Briggs, consisting of the 2nd Dragoon Guards, 5th Dragoon Guards, 11th Hussars and L Battery, Royal Horse Artillery, was located at the village of Nery. Inclement weather, in the shape of a thick mist, had delayed any movement. The men had just finished breakfast and were watering their horses when enemy shells began to fall amongst them. Within a few minures a hurricane bombardment coupled with intense machine gun and rifle fire swept the British positions. With the clearing mist it was observed that the British were under fire from three German batteries, a total of twelve guns, and that the 2nd Dragoons and L Battery were getting the heaviest fire. Almost immediately L Battery lost three of its six guns, but with great effort the

Recruiting poster dated 10 September 1914.

---

14   Doherty & Truesdale, *Irish Winners of the Victoria Cross*.
15   26 August was the 568th anniversary of the battle of Crecy, the weather being similar.

remaining three guns began to return the fire. After only firing a few rounds a further two guns were knocked out and an ever changing gun detachment kept the last weapon in action as men fell dead and wounded. One member of the detachment was a man from Monaghan, Sergeant David Nelson, who acted as range finder, despite being wounded early in the opening bombardment. Nelson was hospitalied after the battle and two days later beame a prisoner of war. However, he remained so for only a few days and soon escaped back to British lines. Sergeant Nelson was one of four members of L Battery to be awarded a Victoria Cross for their actions on 1 September. Subsequently promoted to Temporary Captain, he commanded D Battery and was again wounded on 7 April 1918. These proved mortal and he died in No.58 Casualty Clearing Station, Lillers, being buried in the Lillers Communal Cemetery.[16]

Both sides claimed a victory for the action at Mons. The BEF, outnumbered by as much as three to one, managed to hold off the German First Army for forty-eight hours while inflicting significantly heavier casualties and was then able to retire in good order, therefore achieving their main strategic objective to protect the French Fifth Army from being outflanked. Additionally Mons was an important moral victory for the British, being their first battle on the European continent since the Crimean War some sixty years earlier; prior to that it had been Waterloo in 1815. It was a matter of uncertainty as to how they would perform, having only dealt with native opponents. In the event, the British soldier came away from the battle with a clear sense that he had gotten the upper hand during the battle. The Germans, likewise, seem to have understood that they had been dealt a sharp blow by an Army they had previously considered inconsequential.

For the Germans Mons was a tactical defeat, but a strategic victory. Although Von Kluck's First Army was temporarily held up by the British and suffered heavy casualties, it still managed to cross the barrier of the Mons-Condé Canal and begin its advance into France. Ultimately, it would drive the BEF and French armies before it almost to Paris before finally being stopped, mainly by the French at the Battle of the Marne. Historically referred to as the 'retreat from Mons', it has recently been referred to as a 'rout' by some authors. The fighting skill of Sir Horace Smith-Dorrien and his men would indicate otherwise.

---

16 Doherty & Truesdale, *Irish Winners of the Victoria Cross*. Gerald Gliddon, *VCs of the First World War: 1914*. The Ulster History Circle unveiled a blue plaque to Nelson in September 2014, in his home town of Monaghan; sadly the conflict is referred to on the plaque as WWI.

2

The Division Forms

We give solemn warning to Kaiser Wilhelm:
The Skibbereen Eagle has its eye on you.[1]

On Tuesday 4 August 1914, the United Kingdom formally declared War on Imperial Germany. The following day Lord Kitchener was appointed as Secretary of State for War. Field Marshal Horatio Herbert Kitchener, 1st Earl Kitchener KG KP GCB OM GCSI GCMG GCIE ADC PC, was born in Ballylongford near Listowel, County Kerry in 1850. He was famous for his victory against the Dervish army at Omdurman in the Sudan on 2 September 1898 and had been chief of staff to Lord Roberts in the South African War (1900-1902).[2] Kitchener was one of the few who foresaw a long war and he set about raising the largest volunteer army that the British Empire had seen, as well as a significant expansion in the production of materials to fight Germany on the Western Front, which he considered would be the main battlefield. His commanding image, appearing on recruiting posters demanding "Your country needs you!" is still recognised in popular culture today.[3] It was said he never addressed a man in the ranks unless it was to give him an order and he had few married men on his staff. Two days later Kitchener met with Colonel T.E. Hickman, MP, and President of the British League for the Defence of Ulster. Colonel Hickman was also an Inspector General of the Ulster Volunteer Force and Kitchener's request to Hickman was brief; "I want the Ulster Volunteers."

Sir Edward Carson had already begun the final move that would see the men of the Ulster Volunteer Force become the basis of the new division. On 5 August he had sent a telegram to the Secretary of the Ulster Unionist Council:

> All officers, non-commissioned officers, and men who are enrolled in the Ulster Volunteer Force, and who are liable to be called out by His Majesty for service in the present crisis, are requested to answer immediately His Majesty's call, as our first duty as loyal subjects is to the King.

In effect this telegram would denude the UVF of a number of experienced officers and non-commissioned officers. At this time the strength of the UVF was some 80,000 men, although a number were underage, too old, or would prove otherwise unfit for military service. In the meetings between Sir Edward Carson and Lord Kitchener, one of the proposals from Carson was that the word 'Ulster' should follow the number to be allocated to the division when raised. After

---

1   Headline in a local County Cork newspaper August 1914, a broadsheet famous for keeping its eye on various figures, including the Czar of Russia, who really should have paid attention!
2   Dervish, Ansar and Fuzzy Wuzzy, were names used by British troops at this time.
3   Recent research would indicate this poster was not actually used during the period 1914-18.

Lord Kitchener, of whom Lady Carson had a jaundiced opinion, 'He seemed to me a grand looking sham, just medals and an (*sic*) uniform.'

some hesitation Kitchener agreed. When eventually formed the insignia of the division was the Red Hand of Ulster, the division using the 'left' hand, as opposed to the Ulster Volunteer Force, who used the 'right'.[4]

Initially Lord Kitchener asked for a brigade; however Captain James Craig, MP for East Down, veteran of the South African War and future Prime Minister of Northern Ireland, assured him that a division could be recruited without difficulty. Kitchener immediately appointed both Hickman and Craig as Chief Recruiting Officers for Ulster. Captain Craig's first duty on being appointed was to visit the London firm of Moss Brothers and order ten thousand complete uniforms.[5] The cost of these items was to be covered by a fund controlled by Oliver Locker-Lampson, a fervent Unionist supporter who was later to command a force of armoured cars in Russia fighting alongside the Czarist forces.[6]

At the beginning of September Hickman and Craig returned to Ireland to begin recruiting men for the new division. On 3 September Carson spoke at a meeting of the Unionist Council in Belfast, addressing the men of the UVF and urging them to come forward 'for the defence of the Empire, the honour of Ulster and of Ireland.'[7] Not everyone agreed with this call. In the *Irish News* a letter from an 'elderly volunteer' stated:

> The Volunteers are to be asked tomorrow if they are willing to serve abroad. It may be assumed that those who will agree to do so will be the youngest and most efficient men. It is highly probable that many of them will never return. When the War is finished, and the Home Rule situation has to be faced again, the UVF will be without many of its most useful members, and as a fighting force it will be less formidable. Therefore I ask you, is it desirable that any Volunteer should offer himself for foreign service?

4   Wheeler-Holoham, Capt. V., *Divisional and Other Signs* (London 1920).
5   Bowman, Timothy, *The Ulster Volunteer Force and the Formation of the 36th (Ulster) Division* (2003).
6   Obituary, *The Times*, 9 October 1954.
7   Lewis, Geoffrey, *Carson: The Man Who Divided Ireland* (2005).

Sir Edward Carson addressing the men and their families at Clandeboye Camp.

While these arrangements were being made a considerable number of men had already enlisted in the Army, while a much smaller number had volunteered for the Royal Navy. For the Army most had enlisted in the 10th (Irish) Division and 49 (Ulster) Brigade of the 16th (Irish) Division, while others had crossed the Irish Sea and joined battalions being formed in Glasgow, Manchester and Liverpool, many men electing to join their father's and grandfather's regiments.

As a result of Carson's speech recruiting in Belfast got underway with the full assistance of the Unionist Party and the UVF. Initial interviews and medical examinations were conducted at a building close to the Old Town Hall. Approximately 600 recruits per day attended, each man being attested and then passed to the latter building for a medical examination and issue of uniform. It was not a matter of individuals turning up as and when; specific days were set aside for volunteers from the various districts; they would assemble at their own UVF headquarters and march as a body to the recruiting office. On several occasions these marches were led by Carson and Craig, now promoted from captain to lieutenant colonel. Recruiting offices were also established through the Province where equally stringent interviews, medical examinations and enrolling were carried out. By mid-September some twelve thousand men had been enrolled, enough to form a division.

Headquarters of the division was first established at No29 Wellington Place, Belfast, at the time of writing an enquiry centre of HM Customs and Excise. It was decided that due to his seniority of rank and possibly his age, Lieutenant General Sir George Richardson would not command the division in France. George Lloyd Reilly Richardson had been born in 1847, the son of Major General Joseph Fletcher Richardson of Pinner, Middlesex. Educated at Streatham, he was commissioned into the 38th (1st Staffordshire) Regiment in 1866, first seeing action on the North West Frontier during the Hazara Black Mountain Expedition in 1869. Two years later he transferred to the Indian Army, serving with the 18th King George's Own Lancers. During 1879 and 1880, he was active in the Second Anglo Afghan War and the following year saw him involved in the

The pipes and drums of a Rifles battalion, such units made a considerable contribution to recruiting as they marched around the countryside.

Waziri expedition. By 1890 he was serving with the Zhob Valley Field Force in the Balochistan province of what is today Pakistan. He was then promoted to command of the 18th Lancers and led them as part of a flying column in the Kurram Valley expedition of 1900-1901. In 1902, he and his regiment moved to China and Richardson led his unit in the final assault on Peking during the Boxer Rebellion, when an eight nation alliance of 20,000 men defeated the Chinese Imperial Army. He returned to India and retired from the Army in 1908. In 1913, Richardson was invited to command the UVF and despite being 66 years old was described by Lord Cushendun as: "...an active little man both in body and mind, with no symptom of approaching old age."

Richardson died in April 1931 and according to his obituary in the *London Times*; "...under his command the Ulster Volunteer Force became a highly organised and perfectly disciplined body."

Despite this he was considered too old for active duty and his replacement was Major General C.H. Powell, CB, formerly of the Indian Army. Charles Herbert Powell was born on 23 October 1857; he was educated privately and entered the Army in 1876. He served in India and eventually rose to the rank of major general in 1907. During his Army service he saw action in Waziristan in 1894-95, where he received a Mention in Despatches, with the Malakand Field Force as Deputy Assistant Quartermaster General during 1897 and 1898, in Bengal with the Buner Field Force in late 1898, under the command of Sir Bindon Blood.[8]

However, General Powell was not to command the division in action. On completing a tour of inspection in France the General was informed that divisions were to be commanded by officers

---

8   Fincastle, Viscount VC, *A Frontier Campaign, A Narrative of Operations of the Malakand and Buner Field Forces 1897-1898* (London: P.C. Eliott-Lockhart,1898).

General Oliver Nugent, commander of the Ulster Division for most of the war. A man who spoke his mind.

who had experience of warfare on the continent. General Powell was awarded the KCB for his service in raising the division and was appointed to command of the British Red Cross at Vladivostok. Within the division and among local politicians, there was a degree of shame attached to this move, in that General Powell had been allowed to make the tour of the positions in France and that those staff officers with whom he made contact already knew of his replacement.

The new divisional commander was Oliver Stewart Wood Nugent. He had been born in Aldershot on 9 November 1860, the son of a serving officer. Of Norman stock, the Nugent family had owned land in County Cavan since the seventeenth century. Educated at Harrow and attending Sandhurst, he joined the Royal Munster Fusiliers in July 1882, later transferring to the 60th Rifles the following year. In 1895 Nugent saw action in the Chitral Campaign and was subsequently awarded a DSO. Nugent attended the Staff College at Camberley and married in 1899. He served in the South African War with the 60th Rifles, was wounded in action at Talana Hill in October 1900 and became a prisoner of war. Nugent was invalided home the following June and later served in Ireland, England and Bermuda. After a time commanding the Hampshire Infantry Brigade, a Territorial Force, he went on half pay to retire to his home in Cavan. On the outbreak of the Great War he was given command of the Hull defences in 1914, moving to command 41 Infantry Brigade the following year. He was then offered the command of the 36th [Ulster] Division.[9]

Major W.B. Spender was appointed as General Nugent's GSOII.[10] Wilfred Bliss Spender was born in Plymouth in 1876 and had been educated at Winchester College, later attending the Staff College at Camberley. He joined the Royal Artillery in 1897 and saw service in Bermuda, Canada, Malta, Ireland and India. He was one of the first Army officers to attend a Naval War Course and in 1909 was attached to the Imperial Defence Committee. Spender was active in the campaign against Home Rule, had signed the Ulster Covenant and assisted in establishing the Junior Imperial League. He agreed to stand for Parliament, but then withdrew when it was found that any Army officer being elected would automatically go on to half pay. In 1913 he retired

9 Carson insisted that the word Ulster would always appear as a prefix when referring to the 36th [Ulster] Division, despite objections from Kitchener, hence a trend, with Irish, Scottish, Welsh, Northern and Southern etc., added to other Divisions.

10 GSO – General Staff Officer, graded as 1, 2 and 3, Roman numeral also used, were responsible for operations, intelligence, training, personnel, logistics and equipment. It was a position, not a rank. These were usually lieutenant colonel, major or captain.

from his commission and was invited by Sir Edward Carson to help organise the UVF, becoming Quartermaster General. With the outbreak of war Spender became GSO of the division.[11] This as a result of a promise extracted from the War Officer by Carson that those regular officers who had UVF connections would be assigned to the Ulster Division. Initially the War Office would not agree to Spender's appointment, offering him instead a post with them. This decision was then reversed with the assistance of General Powell.[12] Spender and his wife, Lilian, communicated on a regular basis while he served in France, his letters giving an insight on how things were within the divisional command.

Lieutenant Colonel James Craig was appointed as Assistant Adjutant and Quartermaster General. The son of a wealthy and successful whiskey distiller, Craig had been born on the outskirts of Belfast and educated in Scotland. He had worked as a stockbroker for a time and seen service in the South African War with the 5th Royal Irish Rifles. He became a Member of Parliament in 1906, representing East Down and would continue to do so, despite his service with the division. He was well known for his ability to organise and was considered to have been the prime factor in the formation of the UVF, organising Covenant Day and the Larne gun-running. By 1914, Craig, unlike Carson, was enthusiastic about partition.

The Initial Deputy Assistant Adjutant and Quartermaster General was Major George T. Drage, a former Rifles officer. Due to illness suffered at Seaford he had to relinquish his post and after recuperation was appointed as Staff Captain to the 15th Reserve Brigade at Newtownards.[13] His position was taken by Major H.T.C. Singleton, DSO, formerly of the Highland Light Infantry and a veteran of the South African War, with some twenty years service. He had been part of the garrison at Mafeking during the siege and was wounded while serving as Adjutant of the Bechuanaland Protectorate Regiment. His family came from County Kerry.

Lord Farnham was appointed as General Nugent's ADC. Holding an estate in County Cavan, Arthur Kenlis Maxwell, 11th Baron Farnham, had succeeded to the title in 1900. Educated at Harrow he attended the Royal Military College, Sandhurst and was commissioned during the South African War as a lieutenant in the 10th Hussars. In 1908, he was elected as an Irish repre-sentative peer while in 1914 he was appointed as a major in the North Irish Horse. He would go on to command the 2nd Inniskillings later in the war and be taken prisoner in March 1918.

GSOI of the division was Lieutenant Colonel Godfrey Meynell late of the King's Shropshire Light Infantry and a former student at Winchester College, Sandhurst and the Staff College. On the outbreak of the war he had been serving at Secunderabad, India.[14] He was later replaced by Lieutenant Colonel the Honourable A.V.F. Russell, MVO, Grenadier Guards, who was in turn replaced by Lieutenant Colonel Charles Otley Place. Place had been commissioned into the Royal Engineers in 1895 and had seen service in South Africa from 1899 to 1902. He would serve in this position from 5 April 1916 until 26 March 1918 when he was wounded and taken prisoner during the German offensive.

---

11   Spender became KCB in 1929, he had been appointed CBE in 1921 and DSO in 1919, and had also earned the Military Cross. He was permanent Secretary, Ministry of Finance and Head of the Civil Service, Northern Ireland from 1925. Member of the Joint Exchequer Board from 1933, he married Lilian Dean and they had one daughter.

12   Baguley, Margaret (ed), *The Correspondence of Lilian and Wilfred Spender* (Irish Manuscripts Commission, 2009).

13   Captain Drage died in 1918, his funeral, held on 22 October, was attended by many former colleagues, including Lieutenant Colonel William Robertson, VC, OBE.

14   His son, Captain Godfrey Meynell was subsequently killed during a VC-winning action on the North West Frontier in 1935.

Men of the Division at camp in Newtownards.

In charge of musketry training was Captain R.W. Barnett, Territorial Force Reserve. Captain Barnett was a son of the late Dr Richard Barnett of Wellington Place, Belfast, and was considered to be one of the finest shots in the country, having represented Ireland in the Elcho Shield competition at Bisley on approximately thirty occasions.[15]

In September 1915, Captain H.M. Appleton, 1st (The King's) Dragoon Guards, was appointed as Assistant Provost Marshal. Captain Appleton had been serving in India since 1912 as Adjutant of Volunteers; he had served in the South African War with the Army Service Corps and as a railway staff officer. In the same month Captain J. Davies was appointed as commander of the newly formed 76th Sanitary Section of the division.

Men joined the 36th (Ulster) Division not only because they were members of the Ulster Volunteer Force, Young Citizen Volunteers or the Orange Order; there were also those who would have joined for patriotic reasons, those who were unemployed and needed a job, or those who felt they should enlist as their friends were going and it all seemed like a great adventure. While some were turned down due to being unfit, or 'unwholesome', others found themselves accepted, but sent elsewhere. Abraham Thompson Kirkpatrick was born in November 1900 and after several failed attempts eventually enlisted on 28 August 1916. He requested to be sent to the Royal Irish Rifles, but at this time, despite the losses on the Somme, men were required for the Royal Flying Corps and Abraham found himself in Cornwall and eventually France.

However, there were other ways of recruiting. On 5 November 1915, the *Lisburn Standard* reported that William Cochrane, a well built and physically fit looking young man had appeared

15   The Elcho Shield is a long distance rifle competition between England, Scotland, Wales and Ireland, shot
      over ranges from 1,000 yards to 1,200 yards; the first meeting occurred in 1862 and is still held at the time
      of writing.

in front of Lisburn Town Court the previous day to answer a charge of drunkenness and disorderly conduct. The Chairman, Sir Hugh Mack, addressed the defendant and said.

Their Worships think you are a likely looking young man for the Army; if you enlist they will let you off. The Court stands adjourned for a fortnight; but recollect if you do not enlist in the meantime it will be brought up again. The defendant turned and walked out of Court without a word. On 23 November 1917, Private William Cochrane of the 9th Rifles was subsequently killed in action; he was 20 years old.

Marches through the streets and countryside were another way of drumming up recruits. The *Lisburn Standard* told of a recruiting drive in May 1915. The band of the 11th Rifles, accompanied by No.8 Platoon had come from their camp at Clandeboye for a week of marches around the area, visiting such places at Broomhedge, Aghalee, Ballinderry and Brookhill. Some 200 men were successfully recruited for all services, the majority going to the Ulster Division. At the same time the newspaper reported that; "A goodly number of Nationalists enlisted in the Irish Brigade, and on Wednesday evening the local company of the Irish Nationalist Volunteers had a farewell route march. The company numbering one hundred and twenty strong, carrying rifles marched out from St. Joseph's Hall via the Longstone, away round by Halftowns, Blaris and then home by the Dublin Road."

Men recruited locally were mostly allowed to serve together, emulating the 'Pals' battalions being raised elsewhere in the United Kingdom. While this had its advantages regarding morale, there were serious drawbacks. On 28 June 1916, a single shell fell on a company of the 13th Rifles killing fourteen men, of these four came from the village of Hillsborough and four from the town of Dromore. There were many who enlisted under age, including George Caldwell, who eventually joined the 9th Irish Fusiliers:

> I never went to school much in those days. I went to Hemsworth School at Malvern Street, Belfast and I was a message boy for John Lennon in Queensland Street. When war broke out I was fifteen, you had to be sixteen. I went to the Town Hall, I was not in the UVF, but joined the 36th Ulster Division on 9 September 1914 and was sent to Ballykinlar.[16] They gave us a cut throat razor and a brush and soap, you had to shave every day, they were very strict.

Officers and men of the 13th Royal Irish Rifles.

---

16   Ballykinlar/Ballykinler, from the Irish Baile Cainnleora meaning 'the townland of the candelabrum'. As with many places in Ireland there are various spellings used for various reasons, the spelling in this manuscript is taken for the newspapers and accounts of the time.

The 13th Royal Irish Rifles at Clandeboye Camp, one of the first parades in uniform, rifles of unknown origin are being carried by some men, but as yet no equipment.

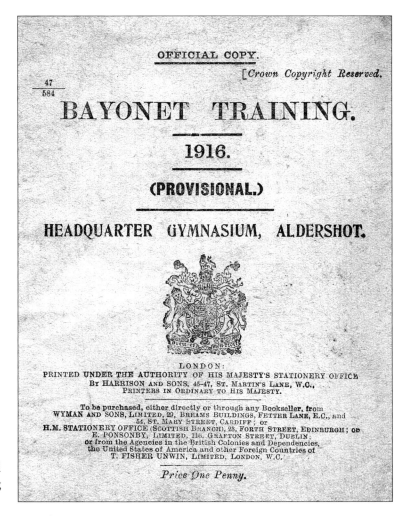

OFFICIAL COPY.

[*Crown Copyright Reserved.*

47
584

BAYONET TRAINING.

1916.

(PROVISIONAL.)

HEADQUARTER GYMNASIUM, ALDERSHOT.

LONDON:
PRINTED UNDER THE AUTHORITY OF HIS MAJESTY'S STATIONERY OFFICE
By HARRISON AND SONS, 45-47, ST. MARTIN'S LANE, W.C.,
PRINTERS IN ORDINARY TO HIS MAJESTY.

To be purchased, either directly or through any Bookseller, from
WYMAN AND SONS, LIMITED, 29, BREAMS BUILDINGS, FETTER LANE, E.C., and
54, ST. MARY STREET, CARDIFF; or
H.M. STATIONERY OFFICE (SCOTTISH BRANCH), 23, FORTH STREET, EDINBURGH; or
E. PONSONBY, LIMITED, 116, GRAFTON STREET, DUBLIN;
or from the Agencies in the British Colonies and Dependencies,
the United States of America and other Foreign Countries of
T. FISHER UNWIN, LIMITED, LONDON, W.C.

Price One Penny.

One of the many training manuals issued during the war, fighting by textbook.

Officers and men of the 15th Royal Irish Rifles, judging by the number of men displaying medal ribbons, this was later in the war.

Another messenger boy was George McBride:

> I left school at thirteen and was a message boy at the *Belfast Telegraph*. My father was an engineer and he wanted me to be one, so I started at Mackies. I was seventeen when war broke out and I was in the UVF. I enlisted in the 15th Rifles and served with them until I was captured in March 1918.

Harry Currie came from Donegall Pass, was a member of the UVF and had proudly signed the Covenant:

> I was seventeen and did not take it very seriously. I was given a lovely certificate, but it went astray. I joined because all my gang joined, we were more interested in football and billiards and we followed the bands. Our Company was No.10 and our parade ground was at the North of Ireland Cricket Ground and the headquarters the brewery at Sandy Row.

Hugh James Adams came from the village of Crossgar in County Down and prior to enlisting he worked for a short time at Crawford's Flax Mill in the village. He enlisted when he was nineteen, travelling to Lurgan to enlist in the 16th Rifles.

Sam Wallace was nineteen when he declared to his father that he was going to enlist:

> My father looked at me with a degree of shock, I am sure no nineteen years old schoolboy had ever spoken to him like that. I was about to turn away when he called me back. He told me the ranks were no place to be, people like me were needed to lead men and he would give his permission on the condition that I would apply for a commission. He said that could be sorted out by the right people and that he would sponsor me. The next day my father spoke to a Staff Captain and within a couple of hours a despatch rider had arrived with all the application forms. In the meantime I was sent to Queen's OTC and eventually my commission came through. I was interviewed by an old General and nearly put my foot in it and he gave me a dreadful time. He said the only thing against me was my age and I got fed up listening

14th R.I.R. FOOTBALL TEAM.

WINNERS OF REGIMENTAL CHALLENGE CUP.

NAMES FROM LEFT—SERGEANT POWELL, COLOUR SERGEANT-MAJOR GRIFFTH, PRIVATE KIRKWOOD, SERGEANT CLARKE, PRIVATE CRAIG, PRIVATE KYLE, PRIVATE J. MARTIN, REFEREE, QUARTERMASTER - SERGEANT J HOLMES. SECOND ROW—CAPTAIN M'KEE, LIEUTENANT WEDGWOOD, CAPTAIN HARPER, LIEUTENANT MAYES, LIEUTENANT HOOTON. FRONT ROW—PRIVATE BOYD. PRIVATE BEATTIE, PRIVATE N. DONALDSON, PRIVATE J. DONALDSON

A report in the *Belfast Weekly Telegraph* 12 June 1915, on the 14th Royal Irish Rifles football team.

to this and replied that if I lived long enough I would overcome that. He gave me a look that would kill and with an angry flourish scribbled 'I concur' and threw the papers at the staff captain. I trained at Queen's, Newtownards and at Comber, eventually joining the 9th Royal Irish Fusiliers.

Not every man who volunteered was accepted or retained. Although there was a generous leave allowance while the men were in Ulster, there were always some who considered that this was not enough and being absent without leave became a frequent charge. Those men training close to their homes could not understand why they should remain in camp doing nothing on a Sunday when they could be visiting friend and relatives. When blackguards were found in the ranks they were quickly disposed of, a sentence of discharged as incorrigible and worthless was passed, which actually had no legal standing during time of war.

On several occasions the formation of the division was considered to be complete, but then the War Office would increase the establishment figures. Originally some 12,000 men had been requested for the division. When it was obvious that there would be little difficulty in raising this number of infantrymen, to it was added three field ambulances, a divisional train and an additional infantry battalion, the Pioneers. In January 1915, the War Office added four artillery brigades to the divisional order of battle and increased the number of men in various units, leading to serious difficulties in recruiting. The *Belfast News Letter* of 4 January 1915 reported that; "…for various reasons it has been decided to increase the establishment of each battalion in the Ulster Division by fifty privates, bringing the total up to 1,150, including officers."

While it is not true that every member of the division was a member of the Orange Order, a great number were. When the division moved to England in July 1915, those men who were members of the Order were no longer able to attend lodge meetings. It followed logically that lodges would be formed within the various battalions to continue the tradition. The Military Representative of the Grand Orange Lodge of England, Lieutenant Colonel T.W. Richardson, issued the following warrants to the Ulster Division:

LOL 862, much earlier in the war.

LOL 862 October 1919.

LOL 862, 'East Belfast Volunteers' was issued to the 8th Rifles, here in Flanders 1918, complete with goat mascot.

LOL No.862, 'East Belfast Volunteers' was issued to the 8th Rifles; LOL No.863, 'South Antrim Volunteers' was issued to the 11th Rifles, the Master being D.H. Gourley; LOL No.864 'North Belfast Volunteers', was issued to the 15th Rifles, the Master being Sergeant W.J. O'Neill; LOL No.865 'Down Volunteers' was issued to the 16th Rifles, the Master being Sergeant J.W. Gordon; LOL No.868, 'West Belfast Volunteers', was issued to the 9th Rifles, the Master being Sergeant James Matthews; LOL No.869 'South Belfast Volunteers' was issued to the 10th Rifles, the Master being Quartermaster Sergeant John Wallace; LOL No.870, 'Inniskilling True Blues', was issued to the 11th Inniskillings, the Master being Sergeant J. Halliday; LOL No.871 'Young Citizen Volunteers' was issued to the 14th Rifles, the Master being Sergeant A Morgan and LOL No.882, was issued to the 110th Field Ambulance.

Within the 1st Irish Rifles, who would join the Division in 1918, were two Orange Lodges, LOL No.703, 'Rising Sons of India', Master William Windrum and LOL No.839, 'Pride of Armagh',

Lance Corporal William Barr, 8th Royal Irish Rifles.

D Company of the 7th Royal Inniskilling Fusiliers, their forebears had been the last infantry battalion to have an Orange Lodge in Europe since Waterloo.

with Sergeant D. Wilson as Master. The Canadian Expeditionary Force (CEF) also contained Lodges; the 4th Battalion of 1 Brigade had LOL No.859, '4th Canadians', with Lieutenant Bennett as Master. LOL No.880 was allotted to the Garrison Duty Battalion of the CEF, while LOL No.879 went to Mississauga, with Company Sergeant Major Hazzard, B Company, 75th Battalion, 1 Brigade, CEF. This was the first time that Orange Lodges had appeared in Europe since 1816, when the 6th Inniskilling Dragoons and 7th Inniskilling Fusiliers had formed part of the Army of Occupation after the battle of Waterloo.

On 20 November 1914, the *Belfast News Letter* printed a letter written by Sir Edward Carson to a Mrs. Clarke, of Donacloney, whose five sons had enlisted in the 16th Rifles:

Dear Mrs. Clarke – I have been told that five of your sons have joined the new battalion in the Ulster Division of Lord Kitchener's Army. It is such a splendid record for one family and such an example to others that I hope you will allow me to write you a short letter how much I appreciate the patriotism and the valour of your sons and especially your own message which you sent with them; 'that you wished you had five more to give to the King.' I know what a sacrifice this must be to you and your family, as your sons were in good positions, and of great assistance to you, but it is voluntary action such as this that is going to demonstrate to our enemies that we are determined to see this wicked war of aggression through to a finish and to put an end forever to the perpetual threatening of the peace of Europe which has emanated from the cruel and grasping ideals of the Prussian potentates. I feel certain your sons will not only add distinction to the army, but will also bring credit and lustre to the Province of Ulster, which is so devotedly attached to and proud of being a member of the United Kingdom and the Empire. I can only say may God bless them and bring them back safe to you when they have assisted in bringing to a satisfactory conclusion this detestable war.

I remain, yours sincerely (Signed) Edward Carson.

Mrs. Clarke also received a message from the King and eventually this message was read to all members of the Division.[17]

Mrs. Maurice Doherty, Sentry Hill, Letterkenny, County Donegal, also had four sons serving and a fifth was a member of the UVF, being too young to enlist in the Army. She also received a letter from Carson and a message from the King. However, the record must go to Mrs. Hawthorne of Magheragall, Lisburn, Antrim, who had eight sons serving, seven with the Ulster Division. Another such family was that of Archibald and Jane McAteer of Ballymena. They had five sons serving and also received a letter from the King. Unlike the Clarke family not all their sons came home after the war. Private Adam McAteer served with the 1st Inniskillings and was killed on 22 May 1915; he has no known grave and is commemorated on the Helles Memorial, Gallipoli. Nathaniel McAteer, was killed on 1 December 1817, while serving with the Machine Gun Corps, he also has no known grave and is commemorated on the Cambrai Memorial to the Missing.

Organisation

The organisation of an infantry battalion within the Ulster Division was the same as those of the Regular Army. The division contained three brigades, each of four battalions. Each battalion contained four companies, usually referred to as A, B, C and D, but some battalions preferred to use numbers. Each company was divided into four platoons and each platoon was divided into sections. A battalion would have in excess of a thousand men, a company approximately two hundred and twenty, while a platoon had about forty men. There was a substantial difference between a unit's 'ration' strength and 'bayonet' strength, those men who did the actual fighting, as opposed to those involved in administrative duties. Numbers varied from unit to unit and were less as the war dragged on. In 1918 brigades were reduced to three battalions due to manpower shortages, this being compensated somewhat by increased firepower.

The division also contained supporting units, the Royal Artillery, Royal Engineers, Royal Army Medical Corps, machine gun and trench mortar companies. For transport there were men of the Army Service Corps and a veterinary section to care for the horses and mules. An additional battalion was the divisional pioneers, which was not attached to any particular brigade, but was assigned where required, usually at a company level.

The Royal Artillery supplied four brigades and an ammunition column. The brigades were equipped with both 18-pounder field guns and 4.5-inch howitzers, which were capable of firing various types of ammunition, including high explosive, shrapnel, gas and smoke.

From the Royal Engineers came 121, 122 and 150 Field Companies, who would maintain roads, railways, construct bridges and ensure a supply of fresh water. They were also responsible for the running of both broad and narrow gauge railway lines, lay and maintain telephone cables, pilot canal barges, construct strong-points and artillery positions. When called upon they would also fight. The Royal Army Medical Corps would supply three field ambulances, one per brigade, along with a sanitary section and would be responsible in caring for the wounded and injured from front line to base hospital. Relatively new to the battlefield were the machine gun and trench mortar companies. Again there was one company of each allocated per brigade, although they could and were often combined and split up according to the tactical situation at the time. The Army Service Corps provided the Divisional Train, the wagons and lorries that carried the division's supplies of food, ammunition and other essentials, without which no unit could exist on the battlefield. A veterinary section was an essential component to any formation in the field. Despite the 36th Division being an infantry division, it still required almost 6,000 horses to operate.

---

17   *Belfast News Letter* 2 December 1914.

Members of the Royal Army Medical Corps on parade at Clandeboye, soon to be formed into the 108th Field Ambulance.

Buglers rehearse at Clandeboye.

Horses were needed for draft work, such as pulling the guns and supply wagons, pack horses for difficult ground and horse for officers. There was also a divisional cavalry squadron from the 6th Inniskilling Dragoon Guards and a cyclist company, whose original role was to be one of scouting. A full description of the division's order of battle is to be found in the relevant appendix.

Uniforms, weapons and equipment

The men of the Ulster Division went to France dressed in a tunic of khaki serge. The word khaki coming from Urdu and meaning 'earth or dust coloured', this in turn led to the phrase 'not so dusty', meaning to be unwell or injured.[18] This tunic had a stand and fall collar that was fastened

---

18   An alternative source quotes the word khaki as coming for the Irish word for shit, from the original description applied by the future Royal Munster Fusiliers, the first unit to use khaki. This was achieved by staining with tea or mud and from which they gained the name 'Dirty Shirts'. The Munsters were largely

Men of the Royal Irish Rifles are seen here wearing the 1908-pattern webbing equipment with two sets of pouches, thus allowing each man to carry 150 rounds of ammunition. All men wear at least one decoration, including the Military Medal, while the man front right has a wound stripe on his tunic sleeve.

by five general service pattern buttons. There were four pockets, one on each breast with a pocket flap fastened by a small button and one on each side below the waist, also with flap and button. Shoulder straps were khaki with the regimental title in brass. Each shoulder had a reinforced patch of khaki cloth sewn to the tunic. Trousers were made of the same material and worn with khaki puttees and black ammunition boots, each boot studded with seventeen studs. The uniform was hard-wearing, but when wet had the odour of a dead sheep and was an ideal home for lice. On his head he wore either the 1903 SD (Service Dress) Cap until it was replaced by the Trench Cap in 1915. The soldier's equipment was the 1908 web pattern. (Due to a shortage of this, leather equipment was also issued to a large number of men). This consisted of a waist belt with brass buckles and two cross straps. At each side of the belt was a set of five ammunition pouches, the bottom three on the left side fastening with a small strap and stud, the remainder with a flap and stud. On his back he wore a large pack and on either side his water bottle and small pack. An entrenching tool was carried in a web holder in the small of the back and the D shaped mess tin below the large pack. On the belt was a bayonet and scabbard fitted in a frog, which had a fitment to carry the handle of the entrenching tool. The original protection against gas was the Hypo Helmet introduced in August 1915, which was made from grey flannel that had been steeped in an anti gas chemical. This was succeeded by the P Helmet and later still by the Small Box Gas Mask which came into service in August 1916. This was a well designed and reportedly comfortable set of equipment, although the pack, designed to carry approximately forty pounds, often ended up

Gaelic speaking and Gaelic, as with all Celtic languages, has its origins in northern India.

with a total weight of almost seventy, especially when wet. The webbing was made by The Mills Equipment Company and was designed in collaboration with Major (Later Brigadier General) Arnold Robinson Burrowes of the Royal Irish Fusiliers.

Apart from some specialist troops the infantryman carried the Short Magazine Lee Enfield (SMLE) Mk III, a .303 rifle, introduced in 1907, of which over three million were produced. The rifle was fitted with a ten round magazine and weighed 8.8lbs (4kg). In trained hands it could fire fifteen rounds a minute and had a sighted range out to 1,000 yards. In various Marks the .303 rifle continued to serve with the Indian and Canadian forces well into the twenty-first century. While the Irish Fusiliers and Inniskillings fitted bayonets to their rifles, the men of the Royal Irish Rifles fitted 'swords', a term for the bayonet going back to the Napoleonic Wars, where riflemen are concerned.[19] The bayonet fitted was the 1907 Pattern, which was a single edge sword type with a wooden handled grip. French bayonets were of interest to some members of the division. The French Bayonet Sabre 16-inch *d'Arms de Char* 7Ba, has been identified as the first modern bayonet and was made in 1874. Some five million were manufactured and many saw service in the opening months of the Great War. Some were brought home by Irish troops and found their way into the Orange Order. Here they were painted silver and became the weapons of the banner ceremonial guards. The name on the blade is the arsenal where the bayonet was produced, while the number refers to the batch.

The term hand grenade was not widely used during the Great War, instead these were generally known as bombs and within the platoons certain men would be designated as 'bombers', usually men of good physique, with former cricketers proving to be excellent at the job. Prior to manufactured bombs being issued the infantry improvised with empty jam tins filled with scrap metal and an amount of explosive fitted with a hand lit fuze. Certainly up to October 1915, these bombs were extremely unreliable weapons. Lieutenant H. Paton of the 6th Battalion Gloucestershire Regiment wrote to his mother that while on a patrol four of his six bombs failed to explode, mainly due to being stored in damp conditions.[20] With the introduction of the Mills Bomb the British Army received a grenade that was both reliable and effective. While the German stick grenade could be thrown further due to its wooden handle, it relied mainly on blast to cause injury; the Mills Bomb had a more lethal effect. It could be thrown with accuracy up to fifty feet, but the thrower had to be in cover as its fragments were dangerous out to one hundred yards.[21]

It would be early 1916 before the men of the division were issued with steel helmets. The French Army was the first to use such helmets in 1914, coming about as a result of General Adrian of the French Army who noticed that a soldier suffering a head wound from a rifle bullet explained his survival on the fact that he had carried his metal food bowl under his cloth cap. Thereafter steel cap liners known as 'casque Adrian' were issued to French troops in 1915, which led to the characteristic French helmet being introduced in 1916. The War Office decided to design one from scratch, considering the French design to be both weak and complex. The British helmet, based on a design by John L. Brodie was specifically to provide protection against shrapnel and other falling objects. This design was based on the kettle helmet that had been worn by the army of Henry V in 1415. The bowl design provided fair coverage from above, and made production easier, being pressed from a single sheet of steel. The initial helmet was made of mild steel with a brim between one and a half and two inches wide, with a slightly flattened dome. Production had only been under way for a few weeks when, in October 1915, the specification of the helmet was changed. In

---

19 Possibly the last time the order 'fix swords' was given in an Irish regiment on active service, was that issued to the Royal Ulster Rifles on the night of 3 January 1951 during the Korean War. See Orr, D. & Truesdale, D. *A New Battlefield* (Helion & Company, 2011).
20 Letter dated 23 October 1915, held in Royal Irish Fusiliers Museum Armagh.
21 Designed and patented by William Mills of the Mills Munitions Factory, Birmingham.

LES VAINQUEURS DE LA SOMME!
THE CONQUERORS OF THE SOMME!

The victors of the Somme, French poliu and Ulster Division ally. A good view of the French Adrian helmet. (Photograph courtesy of Aribert Elpelt)

Men of the Division, after the issue of the Brodie steel helmet. This photograph was taken in the aftermath of the Cambrai battle.

A battalion drawn up to be addressed by a senior rank, steel helmets would indicate 1916 onwards.

A German steel helmet, probably the best design for protection in combat and still copied today.

future it was to be made of manganese steel and was to be capable of withstanding a shrapnel ball travelling at 750 feet per second. Helmets began to arrive in France in September 1915 and were initially issued at fifty per battalion. They were designated as 'Trench Stores', and used by each unit as they took their turn in the trenches. The issue of helmets led to an immediate reduction in head injuries and by early 1916, a quarter of a million helmets had been issued. They were painted khaki and the texture roughened with a covering of sawdust or sand whilst wet, producing an excellent non-reflective surface. Where this was not available helmets were covered in Hessian cloth. Units soon began painting divisional signs onto their helmets. Some drilled holes to affix badges, this practice being outlawed because it weakened the structure of the helmet. The general issue of steel helmets saw a seventy-five percent drop in head wounds. Ironically the German *stalhelm* of the Great War that replaced the *Pickelhaube in 1916* is deemed the best design of the twenty-first century and something similar is today worn today by the United States Army and many others and was in turn based on the *sallet* helmet of the late 15th Century. From its issue to the men of the division the helmet met with widespread approval, despite some complaints that it was heavy and uncomfortable. Private William A. Greer, 14th Rifles, wrote to his parents in Belfast, in July 1916; "It was only Providence, I think, pulled me through, I had several narrow shaves. My steel helmet saved my life."[22]

This is one of many accounts in letters home in which the helmet gets an honourable mention.

---

22   *Belfast News Letter* 10 July 1916.

3

Training in Ulster

By the latter part of September 1914, training was taking place across the Province. The 107 Brigade was in Ballykinlar and Newcastle in County Down, 108 Brigade on the Clandeboye Estate at Bangor and on the Racecourse at Newtownards, while 109 Brigade was at Finner Camp in County Donegal. All three camps enjoyed good weather for the first three weeks in October, and then it rained.

The majority of the division was under canvas at the beginning and much effort was made to construct regular barrack huts at all three camps. The provision of such huts was delayed by the discovery that Headquarters Irish Command had appointed a Catholic Q Staff Officer as liaison with divisional headquarters. Such a thing was not to be tolerated and the officer in question was sent back to England. This ensured that the huts meant for Finner, Newtownards, and Ballykinlar were not completed until the beginning of the summer of 1915; when the division was due to depart for Seaford. As a result of having to spend most of the winter under canvas and on water-logged ground men died. In Finner, exposed to the Atlantic weather as it was, seventeen men died, most of meningitis. The death tolls for Clandeboye and Ballykinlar were somewhat less.

It was not only in Ulster that training was carried out. In March 1915, a select number of officers and non-commissioned officers were sent to the Irish Command School of Musketry at Dollymount in Dublin to train as instructors. This seems to have been done on a monthly basis. Members of the pioneers also went to Dublin to take lessons in driving railway engines and learning how points operated. This training was carried out at the Inchicore Railway Works.

Ballykinlar

The military first came to Ballykinlar at the beginning of the South African War, when a rifle range was constructed on the site to enable drafts of men destined for that conflict to practice their musketry. A local unit that used the ranges was the 5th Battalion Royal Irish Rifles, commanded by Colonel R. H. 'Bob' Wallace. The Rifles' headquarters was the eighteenth century barracks located on the Mall in Downpatrick. When it was realised that the conflict in South Africa was not going to be a brief skirmish, the War Office decided to improve the ranges and purchased more land to do so. Under the Military Law Act of 1892, an additional 593 acres were purchased from local landowners, giving an eventual size of 1,200 acres. During the summer of 1901 the camp held on average some 1,600 men, infantry, yeomanry and cavalry. The Army Service Corps provided kitchens and tents, each capable of holding twenty men, along with adequate stabling for the horses. As fresh water was in short supply the ASC also provided a condenser so that salt water could be turned into drinking water. The camp benefited from having a 'Sandes' Home', at first established in a timber-framed bungalow, more suited for colonial locations than the cold misty and usually damp environs found at the foot of the Mourne Mountains. However, the Home did provide a reading room and coffee bar; there was also each evening at 8:00 pm, a session of hymn singing and a short homily. The first Home had been founded by Elise Sandes from Tralee and opened in 1869. Her care and concern for young soldiers led her to convert her home drawing-room into a coffee bar, which quickly expanded into separate premises. Soon there was not a major

Where the Mountains of Mourne sweep down to the sea, accommodation at Donard Camp, Newcastle, photograph taken on 22 September 1914.

KITCHENER'S ARMY in the Making at NEWCASTLE (South, West, and North Regiments, U.V.F.).

A postcard showing the layout of the camp at Newcastle, County Down.

At Clandeboye and elsewhere, bell tents provided accommodation until wooden huts were available. For the men at Clandeboye the late completion of hutted accommodation meant an increased amount of sickness and several deaths.

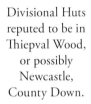

Divisional Huts reputed to be in Thiepval Wood, or possibly Newcastle, County Down.

The Heath Robinson apparatus designed to assist with bayonet fighting at Ballykinlar.

Sandes Home, a replacement building erected in 1923. It would stand until destroyed by an IRA bomb in 1974.

A S I have become a Soldier of His Majesty King George V., and have vowed to hold myself ready to serve the British Empire, so I take the Lord Jesus Christ to be my Saviour, my Master, and the Captain of my Salvation; and I promise that I shall be His good soldier and serve His Kingdom by the conquest, through His grace, of all evil in my heart and life.

I promise to take God's word as my guide, and to read a portion daily for instruction and comfort.

I promise to abstain from all intoxicating drinks, and to encourage my comrades to do likewise.

I promise to pray, at least every morning and evening, for Divine strength in such terms as follow or as the Holy Spirit may teach me—May God help me to pay the vows which my lips have spoken and my pen has signed. May He help me to live for Him day by day. Every morning may He lead me to and through the work He has given me to do. Every night may the eye that never slumbers nor sleeps watch over me for good. May He bless abundantly my home and kindred; the allied forces by land and sea, covering their heads in the battle, giving unto them the victory; and so restraining them in the hour of triumph that their acts shall bring to the people through whose lands they pass the blessings of liberty and peace.

Our Father who art in heaven, Hallowed be Thy name. Thy Kingdom come. Thy will be done in earth as it is in heaven. Give us this day our daily bread. And forgive us our tresspasses, as we forgive them that tresspass against us. And lead us not into temptation, bnt deliver us from evil. For Thine is the kingdom, and the power, and the glory, for ever and ever. Amen.

Name, *Pvt Andrew Hobbs*

Battalion, *9* Regiment, *R I Fus* Company, *C*

Camp or Station *Clandeboye*

Witness *I Nicholson* Date, *30/10/14*

A Christian pledge card in the name of Private Andrew Hobbs, 9th Battalion Royal Irish Fusiliers, while at Clandeboye Camp, dated 30 October 1914. He died on 1 July 1916.

British Army base that did not have a Sandes' Home providing not only rest and refreshment, but a 'Wholesome Christian retreat'.

Ballykinlar proved to be a popular and successful camp, and during the summer of 1903 some three thousand men attended the various courses held there. Following the South African War the camp continued to be used on a permanent basis. Elements of the North of Ireland Imperial Yeomanry[1] were quartered there and the Queen's University Officer Training Corps also made use of the facilities.

With the outbreak of war and the raising of the division, it was decided to send Brigadier G.H.H. Couchman's 107 Brigade to Ballykinlar for training. This Brigade consisted of the 8th, 9th, 10th and 15th Rifles, mostly recruited in Belfast and their discipline was not of the best in the beginning. With an influx of 4,000 recruits space proved to be at a premium and initially some men had to be housed under canvas in the grounds of Donard Lodge in Newcastle. Major Crozier, of the 9th Rifles, believed in instilling what he called 'intellectual discipline' into his younger officers, many of whom were literally teenagers, fresh from the Officer Training Corps at Queens University, Belfast or Trinity College in Dublin. Crozier himself had served in the South African War with Thornycroft's Mounted Infantry and was later commissioned into the Regular Army.

Elise Sandes, responsible for generations of soldiers receiving res, refreshment and a wholesome Christian retreat. (Source: Nigel Henderson)

---

1   Actual headquarters was located at Skegoneil Avenue, Belfast.

No.12 Platoon 15th Royal Irish Rifles. Pets seem to have been an integral part of divisional sub units. The man fifth from the left in the back row would appear to have originated outside Ulster.

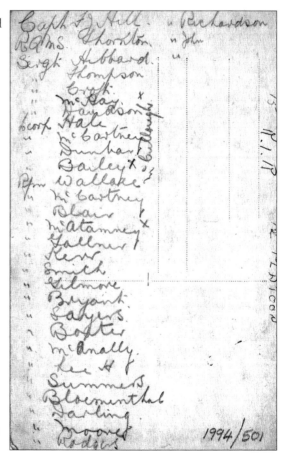

Reverse of above showing names.

The interior of a bell tent at Donard Lodge Camp, Newcastle County Down.

Crozier lectured his junior officers, for six months, five nights a week, whilst at Ballykinlar, on the process of 'hardening' that they must all undergo. The New Year period saw a rigorous stepping up of training. Crozier would later recall how in his battalion, bayonet fighting was coupled with propaganda about German atrocities and there was also plenty of martial music, as the band of each of the four battalions could be heard practising their military marches on the fife, pipe and the drum. On 5 February 1915, Private William Steward, 9th Rifles, died of illness; he was 18 years old and is buried in Lisburn Cemetery. The Belfast and County Down Railway constructed a special halt at Ballykinlar, which was opened on Sunday 28 February 1915. This was planned to continue as long as the traffic warranted it.

The winter rains in Newcastle caused not only illness, but mutiny, of a sort. With many of the tents becoming uninhabitable a number of men from the 9th Rifles walked out of the camp saying they were returning

Frank Percy Crozier, more of a soldier that he usually gets credit for.

home. The camp commandant, Colonel Wallace, accompanied by Major Crozier, rode out after the men and with some persuasive arguments and promises of better billets persuaded the men to return to the camp. No further action was taken against the men. This degree of latitude would not be extended to the men in France.

The stretcher-bearers, denoted by an armband bearing the letters "SB", had their efforts largely ignored by those who had never seen them in action. The number of lives they saved was immeasurable, the reward from a "grateful nation" meagre.

A postcard showing the layout of the various camps at Clandeboye.

Clandeboye Estate

Unlike Ballykinlar or Finner Camp, Clandeboye was not an established military training camp and this quickly became evident as the weather worsened. The home of The Marchioness of Dufferin and Ava, the Clandeboye Estate is some twelve miles from Belfast. The land was first settled in 1674, with the house of the Great War period being built in 1801. Covering some 2,000 acres the estate was an ideal training ground or so it first seemed. With hundreds of marching feet and the hooves of numerous horses the ground was soon turned into a quagmire, especially after the wet weather began in late September. A memorable feature of the estate is a stone tower, built by Lord Dufferin and Ava in memory of his mother Helen, Lady Dufferin. An almost exact replica would be built at Thiepval in memory of those men of the division who fell on the Somme in 1916. Here would be formed 108 Brigade, under the command of Brigadier Hacket Pain, CB, and consisting of the 11th, 12th, 13th Rifles and 9th Irish Fusiliers.

On Monday 14 September 1914, the men of the 1st Battalion North Down Regiment of the Ulster Volunteer Force were attested and the following day 92 men from Bangor, under the command of Mr T.E. Burroughs, Company Officer, UVF, of Bangor, and Mr J.O. Neill, arrived at Clandeboye Camp, the first of many that would eventually form the Brigade. Colonel C. Gordon, Indian Army (Ret), late of the VI King Edward's Own Cavalry, was appointed as Camp Commandant, with

New recruits of D Company, 9th Battalion, Royal Irish Fusiliers at Clandeboye Camp, displaying a mix of UVF rifles, while one man, with a flag, holds a bowl of soup.

D Company, still waiting on an issue of uniforms and that bowl of soup and flag remain important to someone.

Lieutenant C.B. Belt, late Quartermaster of the Staffordshire Regiment, acting as Camp Adjutant and Quartermaster. During this first week, the officers lived in the same lines and messed in the same tent as the Antrim Battalion, who had arrived on Tuesday 15 September. A few more recruits arrived on 17 September, along with Messrs A.C. Herdman and J.A. Craig. On 18 September there was a considerable addition to the Down Battalion, Mr G.J. Bruce of Comber, with 96 men and Messrs W.M. Wright, E. Johnston and K. Morrow of Newtownards, with 120 men marched in together, having joined forces at Newtownards. Mr Bruce was appointed as adjutant until the arrival of Mr R. Fridlington from the Egyptian Army. At this time officers were referred to as Mister as they were still considered to be members of the UVF. As of 28 September 1914 military ranks applied and Mr Bruce became Captain Bruce.

Mr R.B. Houston of Ballywalter with the Hon H.G.H. Mulholland and Mr A.H. Allen (Kircubbin) brought in 85 men of the Ards Peninsula District. Mr A. Hamilton from Killinchy came in with 197 men drawn from the east and centre of the County, while late in the evening Messrs. C.H. Murland, Castlewellan and G.W. Matthew of Newcastle brought in 100 men from their districts. Mr J.S. Davidson of Bangor also joined. Mr R.M. Erskine acted as battalion commander until the arrival of Colonel William Henry Savage, Indian Army, late of the 3rd Q.A.O. Gurkha Rifles, who was to command the Battalion. The men who came in the early part of the week were paid by money advanced from the UVF funds of the North Down district, these amounts being refunded later. Saturday 19 September, was spent in setting up tents, arranging messes, the men settling down to their new mode of life in splendid style and there being no trouble of any sort. The following day saw the first church parade of the new battalion held at 10.30am, the Reverend W. Whatham of Newtownards taking the service. Such scenes were being enacted all across Ulster.

Men of the Ulster Volunteer Force on parade at what is believed to be Walker's Factory, Newtownards. They would soon march to Clandeboye and be issued with khaki.

LINES WRITTEN ON JAMES TATE.

WHO FELL IN HEROIC CHARGE OF THE ULSTER DIVISION, ON JULY THE FIRST, 1916.

When war's dread challenge first was heard
   Throughout our Island home,
Our boys responded to the call,
   And hastened o'er the foam :

To fight for King and Country,
   A brave and noble band,
To crush out German cruelty
   From out our peaceful land.

And one among those gallant lads—
   Only a boy was he—
Left parents, all he held most dear,
   To cross the bright blue sea.

Only a boy ; but O ! so brave,
   His young heart knew no fear,
On that fatal July morning,
   Though he knew that death was near.

He nobly did his duty,
   'Mid the storm of shot and shell ;
In a hero's grave, " Somewhere in France,"
   Sleeps him we loved so well.

He little thought when he left home
   That he would ne'er return ;
But now he lies in that far-off land,
   And we are left to mourn.

God knows best, and He alone
   Can take away the pain
From the hearts he loved so dearly,
   Though he'll ne'er see them again.

Some day we shall meet him,
   In that happy home above,
When war's dread sound is heard no more,
   Where all is peace and love.
           LIZZIE SMYTH, Ballyminstra.

Writing to Mrs. Tate, under date 3rd October, 1916, the late Sergeant James Tate's platoon officer says :—

   I have great pleasure in saying that your son was in my platoon for sixteen months. He was very much liked by his comrades. He was always anxious to do his duty, and was a most capable Sergeant. He was a first-class musketry instructor and a good shot. In the trenches he was exceptionally cool and seemed indifferent to danger. On the First of July he had his section over the parapet and was keen and eager in the attack. I was always glad to have him with me.

   I can understand your feelings and sympathise with you, but pride in his sacrifice must be your consolation. With kindest regards.—Yours sincerely,
           G. T. C. ARMSTRONG.

James Tate from Killinchy, County Down was killed on 1 July 1916.

Recruits at Clandeboye, men of the *Tandragee Orange Heroes*, B Company 9th Royal Irish Fusiliers.

Each day an amount of khaki clothing was issued, along with boots and equipment. However, a great deal of the equipment was very poor and the boots in particular gave a great deal of trouble. Within the 13th Rifles a number of NCOs, chiefly from A Company, were appointed to commissions. Vaccinations were administered to all ranks and a large number of men suffered a painful reaction, exacerbated by the rifle drill. With over 1,300 men in the ranks the 13th Rifles experienced great difficulty in getting meals cooked. This situation was eased on 14 October when a Mr Savage of Bangor donated and had erected a wooden and corrugated iron cookhouse and presented it to the battalion. Mr Savage had a son who was a pioneer sergeant in the battalion. Added to this was a chimney, iron cooking plates and a large boiler for soup, provided by Lieutenants Davidson and Matthew, while Dr Connor of Newry and a group of his friends presented a set of clothing for the cooks.

One of the 36th Division's pot belly stoves in Clandeboye today, still doing an efficient job of keeping the room warm and dry over 100 years later. (Courtesy of Leanne Briggs via lady Perdita Blackwood)

The top of the working stove at Clandeboye. They are still made today, albeit in a different design and price. (Courtesy of Leanne Briggs via Lady Perdita Blackwood)

A second stove at Clandeboye, unused and badly rusted. (Courtesy of Leanne Briggs, via Lady Perdita Blackwood)

Lunch time; army food was bland, but plentiful, once the field kitchens got organised. Included in this group is a second lieutenant at rear left, next a sergeant wearing a red cross badge, a man still waiting on a tunic and a Scottish visitor? The extreme youth of some should be noted.

It is believed that the first death in the division occurred at Clandeboye Camp on 23 October 1914. Private W.J. Pritchard, B Company 13th Rifles fell ill and was sent to Holywood Hospital, where he died of pneumonia on 26 October. From Ballywalter, Private Pritchard was buried at Greyabbey two days later. There was a firing party of twelve men under the command of Captain G. J. Bruce and Second Lieutenant K. Morrow, his company and platoon commanders respectively.[2]

On 1 April Lance Corporal John Bowden, 12th Rifles, died of illness at the Newtownards Camp. His funeral took place in Ballymena on 9 April, attended by many members of the battalion. As a continued aid to recruiting on Friday 30 April the 11th Rifles marched, with full packs, from Clandeboye through Bangor, en route to Ballywalter. In the ranks marched Lieutenants Farrow, Milliken and Scott, all natives of Bangor.

Finner Camp, Ballyshannon, County Donegal, home of the 109 Brigade.

Finner Camp in 1907, then home to the 4th Royal Fusiliers.

---

2   Personal diary of Lieutenant Colonel Frank Savage, C.O. 13th Rifles (The grave is situated in the middle of the cemetery).

Finner Camp

Located between Bundoran and Ballyshannon on the coast of Donegal in the west of Ireland, the name Finner in Gaelic means fair plain or whitish place, and had been a site of military interest for many years. Archaeological research in the past has uncovered tombs, arrowheads and human bones, pointing to the area being a widespread cemetery in pagan times. The military first decided on a camp at Finner in 1890, when the Royal Engineers carried out a survey and found that the area met all the necessary criteria. There was a supply of fresh water, open spaces suitable for firing ranges, good drainage and was sufficiently distant from the civilian population. With Britain

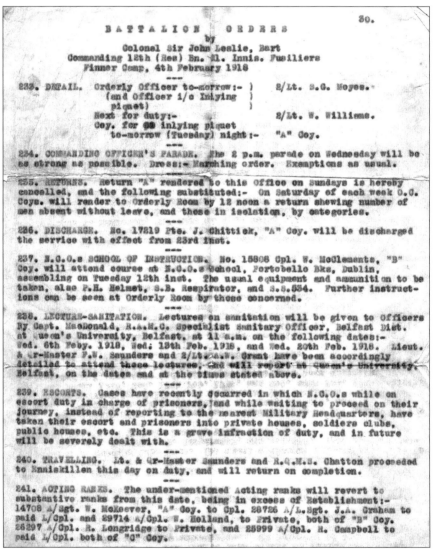

Battalion Orders as issued by Colonel Sir John Leslie, 12th (Reserve) Battalion Royal Inniskilling Fusiliers at Finner Camp, County Donegal, on 4 February 1918. Order No.241 at the bottom of the page shows that 29714 Acting Corporal W. Holland was to revert to Private and serve in B Company. William Holland was killed in action on 29 March 1918, while serving with the 9th Battalion of the Inniskillings and is commemorated on the Poziers Memorial.

preparing to go to war against the Boers in South Africa it was the Royal Inniskilling Fusiliers who were the first to make use of the camp and its facilities. In the Regimental magazine of April 1898, it was noted that; "A party consisting of Sergeant Lee, Corporal Creighton and fifteen men, proceeded to Ballyshannon on the 20th April, for the purpose of preparing the camping ground at Finner, and making some improvements to the Rifle Range. Several new buildings have been erected, notably amongst them being three new cookhouses."

Lieutenant Richard P Wright, Inland Water Transport, Royal Engineers, one of three brothers from Newtownards, County Down, who served.

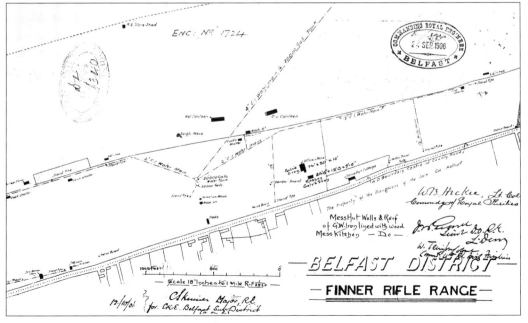

The rifle ranges at Finner Camp.

Even a cursory glance around the cemetery showed the military connection. Private Thomas McAtamney, Inniskillings, accidentally drowned at Bundoran, 10 June 1910; Private Patrick McLaughlin, Argyll and Sutherland Highlanders, died 28 June 1900; Corporal Charles Parfitt, Connaught Rangers,[3] died 4 July 1903; Private W. Prickett, Royal Fusiliers, drowned in the River Erne on Bathing Parade, 11 July 1907.

New recruits at Finner Camp, Donegal. Five men named Kyle were killed while serving with the Inniskillings of 109 Brigade.

Finner Camp, County Donegal.

---

3   The spelling Connacht is sometimes used by dwellers in ivory towers.

At Finner Camp the men prepare for a meal.

Given its location the camp suffered from severe weather during the autumn and winter months. It was a hardy environment and while ideal for training, had few comforts. With so many men gathered in one place with limited sanitary arrangements and less than skilful cooking the health of the men soon began to suffer. There were outbreaks of dysentery, influenza and cerebro-spinal-meningitis. By the time the brigade had finished its training at Finner 17 men had died.

The winter of 1914 saw the camp flattened by a severe storm that came in with great force from the Atlantic. While the Inniskillings were left with no option but to try and re-erect their sodden tents, the 14th Rifles, being more financially independent, moved into various hotels in the town of Bundoran. While at first this seemed to be a comfortable way of spending the remainder of the winter, it did not sit well with every member of the Battalion. In a letter to his sister Teenie in Rugby Road, Belfast, Private Duncan Davidson wrote; "We are sleeping in the hotel and a rotten place it is, there are eighty of us sleeping in one room, the coffee room, we are lying on top of each other."[4]

The Officers Mess was also in a hotel and this caused a problem that did not manifest itself until much later in France. In the regular army the regimental mess, officers and sergeants, served as a school for the traditions that were impossible to teach on a blackboard. In wartime the Mess became the nerve centre of the army. Within the circle of officers that gathered in the farmhouse, dug-out or barn, victory, stalemate or defeat was brewed with the tea. While the battalions of the Ulster Division were far from regular, there were still lessons to be learned by such messing and a hotel was not the place to do it. In hotels officers are no more than temporary guests, while the mess staff, cooks and waiters, had no practice in either cooking or waiting on tables.

---

4   Correspondence from Private Duncan Davidson to his sister, dated 21 December 1914.

Guarding the bread ration at Finner Camp in 1914.

9th (Service) Battalion Royal Irish Rifles

(West Belfast Volunteers).

1—It was suggested by Brigadier-General Crozier, D.S.O., when in command of the 9th Battalion Royal Irish Rifles, that steps should be taken for the maintenance of a spirit of close comradeship between all the Officers who have served with the Battalion, for so long as two such survive.

2—With this object in view, it is proposed to form immediately a Regimental Dinner Club to be called

THE WEBEL'S OWN,

and hold an Annual Dinner.

3—To cover immediate expenses such as printing, postage, &c., it is proposed to at once establish a fund and adopt rules as under :—

(a) Service with the 9th Battalion Royal Irish Rifles and clean record together constitute qualification for membership.

(b) Subject to (a) Officers become members on payment of an annual subscription of 5/-

(c) Any surplus or accumulation of the fund to be dealt with or disposed of from time to time at the discretion of the Committee.

(d) The fund will be administered by Mr. Stewart (Cox & Co.), to whom authority will be given by members to debit their accounts with the amount of subscription due. Members not having an account with Messrs. Cox & Co. will arrange to pay the amount of their subscription annually to Messrs. Cox & Co.

(e) The first subscription will become due on 1st January, 1918.

(f) The following have been constituted a Provisional Committee pending the first meeting of Club Members :—
Brigadier-General J. P. Crozier, D.S.O.
Lieutenant-Colonel G. S. Ormerod.
Major W. A. Montgomery, D.S.O.
with Major H. R. Haslett as Hon. Secretary (pro tem.)

(g) Members of the Club will, according to the state of the funds of the club, either dine free or at such reduced charge of the actual expenses of the dinner as the funds will allow and the Committee decide.

(h) There will be no guests at the Annual Dinner except those invited through the President.

It is earnestly hoped that you will allow your name to be entered on the roll of membership of the Club.

Kindly fill in the enclosed post card and post to your bankers, and send the other post card to me at the undermentioned address.

Sincerely yours,

H. R. HASLETT, Major.

Union Club,
Belfast.

Notice of the formation of a Regimental Dinner Club within the 9th (Service) Battalion Royal Irish Rifles. From the outset the social life of the division was all-important.

Royal Irish Rifles.

Sergeants and Warrant Officers of the Royal Irish Rifles.

The 14th Battalion Royal Irish Rifles on parade.

Thomas Gibson made two attempts to enlist. From his home village of Garvagh he travelled to Coleraine where the 10th Inniskillings had a recruiting office in the railway station. Here he joined a long queue and when he reached the recruiting sergeant gave his age truthfully, only to be told to come back when he was eighteen. He then moved to another queue and a different sergeant and decided to try again, possibly aging as he moved up the queue. While he was still about half way along the queue he saw the train begin to pull out of the station with many of his friends on board. Not wanting to be left behind he rushed across the platform and jumped aboard as the train left. On arrival at Finner Camp Thomas was assigned to No.15 Platoon of D Company and it was almost a month before the authorities discovered he and many others, were not actually in the Army as they had not taken the oath of allegiance. This was then dutifully carried out at a special parade. Thomas would miss 1 July due to suffering from shingles, but would be fit and well for Messines and Cambrai. Another recruit at this time was James Lancey McIntyre, who would later transfer to the Signal Company and later still the Royal Engineers.

Private Leslie Bell, serving with the 10th Inniskillings, recalled a particular route march when he and some comrades passed a farm where the farmer had left out a milk churn for collection. The men sampled the contents and quickly emptied the churn; apparently the farmer was 'quite decent about it'. The next time Bell and the Inniskillings passed the farm the farmer's wife shouted; "Johnny, bring in the dog's dinner, the soldiers are coming!"

Bell was not sure she was joking. The Young Citizens were having less luck with some of their officers. The mornings at Finner were mostly filled with platoon training, with the junior subalterns putting the men through basic foot drills such as numbering, dressing, forming fours, marching in step, saluting and signalling, and later, when rifles were available, rifle drill was introduced. Occasionally the Battalion would parade together for drill, usually under the Adjutant. Captain Bentley, who took advantage of a slight rise on the parade ground to get a clearer view, evidently enjoyed this opportunity to test the officers as much as the men and would issue his orders in quick succession. Captain Charles Owen Slacke, commanding A Company, was one of those who came under the adjutant's notice. Private George Mullin recalled such a parade when the order for the battalion to advance in column with A Company leading failed to elicit the correct response from Captain Slacke:

> He, however, instead of advancing, proceeded to retire. Thereupon the Adjutant's wrath descended on his head. 'Captain Slacke' roared the Adjutant, 'Do you not know your front from your rear?' This remark caused many subdued smiles. There were many other similar incidents.

Captain C. O. SLACKE.

Captain C. O. Slacke, missing, is the eldest son of the late Sir Owen Slacke, C.B., and was born at Carrick-on-Suir. He is proprietor of Slacke & Co., manufacturers of galvanised iron hollow-ware, and lives at Wheatfield, Crumlin Road, Belfast. He was married in 1902 to the eldest daughter of the late Right Hon. Sir Daniel Dixon, Bart. It is hoped that he is a prisoner.

Newspaper cutting regarding Captain Slacke,
then believed to be missing in action
(Courtesy of Nigel Henderson)

Captain Slacke, while commanding
A Company.

Lance Corporal John Kennedy Hope, a man who proved that the pen was sharper than the sword, also held Captain Slacke up for ridicule:

> Our soldier Company Commander is replaced by one Captain Slacke. He is a round-faced, fat bellied gentleman with a cynical smile. We have at last got something to amuse us. Slacke is a genius at drill. We like to get on a parade of this sort to see how he will unravel the company when he gets it into a mess. We snigger when he says "Carry on Sergeant Major."

Charles Slacke was the son of Sir Owen Randal Slacke and grandson of Sir Charles Lanyon, the architect responsible for so many of Belfast's striking buildings. The family owned the Wheatfield area of the city and land at Newcastle in County Down. Slacke was married to Catherine Anne, daughter of the former Belfast Lord Mayor Sir Daniel Dixon MP; and was a former leader of the North Belfast Regiment of the UVF. Neither his round face, nor fat belly would keep Captain Slacke out of battle; he would die for his faith, politics, King and country on 1 July 1916.

The Newcastle War
Memorial listing
Captain Charles
Owen Slacke, 14th
Royal Irish Rifles,
killed on 1 July 1916.
(Courtesy of Nigel
Henderson)

An officer who only spent a short time with the 14th Rifles was Captain Charles St Aubyn Wake. The son of Admiral Charles Wake, he had served in the Dorsetshire Regiment during the Nile Relief Expedition of 1885, the failed attempt to relieve General Gordon in Khartoum. He was later with the Zanzibar Protectorate Force when he lost a leg in the storming of a stockade. Wake acted for a time as Vice Consul of Mombassa, before returning to military service in 1896, serving as a captain in the East African Rifles, seeing action in the Uganda Mutiny. After this he returned to Britain and was with the Devon Militia, before retiring in 1907 and taking up the post of country recruiting officer. However, Wake was a man of adventure and from 1911 until 1912; he was on attachment to the Turkish Army in the Libyan War. With a chronic shortage of regular officers Wake was recruited by the UVF and given command of the South Belfast battalion and was subsequently commissioned into the 14th Rifles. Following a ten mile route march in County Antrim, Wake had the men 'mark time' before giving the order to 'halt'. Captain Wake's next command was "fall out the gentlemen." For some unknown reason he then fell from his horse. He lay where he fell, apparently unharmed and made no attempt to rise. He then gave the final command "battalion dismiss", whereupon the parade did a right turn, saluted and then dispersed. Only then did Captain Wake get up, and hand his mount over to the groom. Private Hope recalled the departure of Captain Wake; "There is a general reshuffle of the gentlemen and our mystery man Captain Wake departs with all his belongings on a side-car. He has had a difference of opinion with the C.O. We line the road and cheer him as he passes and wonder if he thinks it is sympathy or a soldier's farewell. It is a mixture of both."[5]

Wake was appointed to command the 18th (Reserve) Battalion Royal Irish Rifles at Holywood. He ended the war as a Major in the Royal West Kent Regiment. A brother, Major Hugh St. Aubyn

---

5   Hope, John Kennedy, quoted in Moore, Stephen, *The Chocolate Soldiers* (Colourpoint Books, 2015).

Wake, of the 2nd Battalion 8th Gurkha Rifles, had been killed in action in November 1914, and another brother, Captain D. St. Aubyn Wake, served in the Royal Navy on HMS *Jupiter*, a *Majestic* class pre-dreadnought battleship, which also acted as a successful icebreaker on the Archangel run to Russia in 1915, keeping the route for other ships clear on the way to the port.

Battalion	Officers	Other ranks
8th Royal Irish Rifles	15	1,065
9th Royal Irish Rifles	19	1,102
10th Royal Irish Rifles	17	1,119
15th Royal Irish Rifles	12	1,048
11th Royal Irish Rifles	16	666
12th Royal Irish Rifles	20	668
13th Royal Irish Rifles	23	1,246
9th Royal Irish Fusiliers	20	940
9th Royal Inniskilling Fusiliers	7	643
10th Royal Inniskilling Fusiliers	21	740
11th Royal Inniskilling Fusiliers	15	471
14th Royal Irish Rifles	17	1,038
16th Royal Irish Rifles (Pioneers)	#	#

By the beginning of October 1914 divisional strength, excluding support troops, was far from satisfactory. The difference in recruiting in rural areas and the towns and cities is evident, the 13th Rifles are shown here as being well over the prescribed battalion strength of 1,007 officers and other ranks, while the 11th Inniskillings are just over company level. The pioneers had yet to be formed. It was much more difficult to recruit in the west of Ulster due to a smaller population, much of it engaged in farming. Unlike a job in a factory or shop you cannot just walk away from a farm. In December 1914, the Division was still 1,995 under strength.[6] Things had not improved by the following year. In the local papers on 26 March 1915, Sir Edward Carson reported on the number of recruits; "From the 'six counties' thirty thousand, from Monaghan, Cavan and Donegal, two thousand, 'I regret to say…'"

Major The Earl of Leitrim, the first commanding officer of the 11th Royal Inniskilling Fusiliers.

6   Bowman, Timothy, *Carson's Army, The Ulster Volunteer Force 1910-22*, 2007

Men of the 11th Battalion Royal Inniskilling Fusiliers.

Yet Carson admits that these are agricultural areas with a smaller population. Already having a degree of drill and training instilled from their time in the UVF most recruits adapted well to the training of the regular army. Added to this was the enthusiasm shown by men who firmly believed that the war they were training for would secure their homeland within the United Kingdom and that they would be fighting for God and Ulster. With the men being recruited from specific areas it meant that those who knew each other as civilians, as members of the UVF or YCV, were now able to work together as comrades. The platoon, the company and the battalion became a close knit community, almost an enlarged family and engendered a trust that would normally have taken much longer. However, this idea of men from the same street or village serving together was to have horrific consequences when losses were suffered in battle and the news was carried home by telegram. In cases where over-familiarisation between non-commissioned officers and men caused a degree of friction changes were made and men were transferred to other platoons or companies. There was also the continuing problem of weekend leave. Apart from the 14th Rifles of 109 Brigade, which was in Donegal, the remainder of the division lived quite close to home and many men felt that as they had a free day on a Sunday why not go home and visit their families.

Throughout the division a memorial service was held on 22 November for the late Field Marshal Rt. Hon. F.S. Earl Roberts, VC who had died on active service in France. The Field Marshal was the son of General Sir Abraham Roberts of Waterford, while his mother Isabella, came from a Tipperary family. He had earned the Victoria Cross on 2 January 1858 at Khodagunge, an action of the Indian Mutiny. In 1912, Roberts had made a speech, in which he stated:

In the year 1912, just as in 1866 and just as in 1870, war will take place the instant the German forces by land and sea are, by their superiority at every point, as certain of victory

Officers and men of the Royal Irish Fusiliers in 1915.

as anything in human calculation can be made certain. We may stand still. Germany always advances and the direction of her advance, the line along which she is moving, is now most manifest. It is towards… complete supremacy by land and sea.

He was wrong by two years. On being offered command of the UVF he declined due to his age, but recommended Sir George Richardson for the post.[7] Lord Roberts' replacement was another Irishman, Field Marshal Henry Hughes Wilson, who had been born in Leinster in 1864. Wilson's support for Ulster was unequivocal, as many of his letters and diary entries show and he was MP for North Down for a time. He was assassinated on his doorstep at Eton Place by two members of the IRA on 22 June 1922, not far from the Carson family home. It was reported that he had attempted to draw his sword during the attack and should therefore be recorded as the last British field marshal to be killed in action.

In January 1915 the Brigade, less the 10th Inniskillings, moved from Finner Camp to Randalstown for further training. This was due to an outbreak of German measles and as a result the 10th Inniskillings would miss the grand review at Balmoral and the march past the City Hall in Belfast. It would be May before the battalion would rejoin the brigade and they would march across the province to join their comrades at Randalstown, taking nine days to make the journey, which also acted as a recruiting drive.

On 18 January Private T. Rowe, No.17258, 11th Inniskillings, drowned in Belfast. He was the husband of Isabella Rowe of Lisnaskea, Fermanagh. Private Rowe received a full military funeral, the cortege leaving from the Mater Hospital, the senior officer present being Major Fitzgerald while the firing party was provided by staff from Victoria Barracks commanded by Sergeant Elliott. The

7   Holme, Richard, *The Little Field Marshal: A Life of Sir John French* (2004).

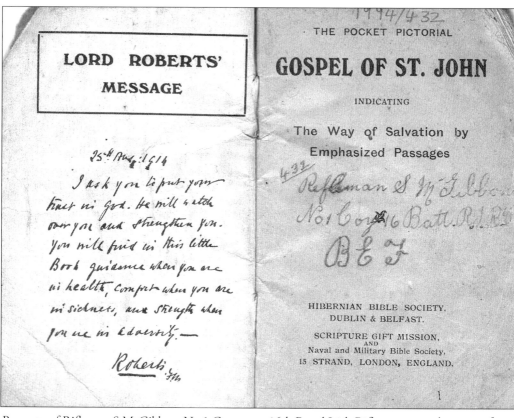

Property of Rifleman S McGibbon, No.1 Company, 16th Royal Irish Rifles, a personal message from Lord Roberts is on the back cover.

1st Platoon, D Company at Randalstown Camp.

No.5 Platoon B Company, 14th Royal Irish Rifles (YCV).

The majority of the division was under canvas at the beginning and much effort was made to construct regular barrack huts at all three camps. The provision of such huts was delayed by the discovery that Headquarters Irish Command had appointed a Catholic Q Staff Officer as liaison with divisional headquarters. Such a thing was not to be tolerated and the officer in question was sent back to England. This ensured that the huts meant for Finner, Newtownards, and Ballykinlar were not completed until the beginning of the summer of 1915; when the division was due to depart for Seaford. As a result of having to spend most of the winter under canvas and on waterlogged ground men died. In Finner, exposed to the Atlantic weather as it was, seventeen men died, most of meningitis. The death tolls for Clandeboye and Ballykinlar were somewhat less.

coffin was carried on a gun carriage and draped in the Union flag, the funeral march being played by an attendant military band.[8]

February saw the issue of the new divisional badge. With permission now granted by the War Office, the firm of Sharman D. Neill, Ltd. set about producing approximately 20,000 Red Hand of Ulster cap badges cast in bronze. This became known as the dixie badge and did not prove popular within the ranks despite its imagery. Major Frank Crozier explained:

> A single instance will illustrate the pride of regiment. Someone, I know not who, devised a Divisional cap badge, comprising the Red Hand of Ulster, to be worn by the whole of the Ulster Division. The political suggestion was approved by the higher authorities, without our knowledge. The badges arrived, were issued, and of course worn, since an order is an order; but regimental tradition prevailed over political stupidity. Protests reached Divisional Headquarters in such numbers, in the regulation manner, that within a week the Royal Irish Rifles badge was again in every cap. It is possible to play on regimental tradition to almost any extent, provided the way is known, but it cannot be cut across for apparently no good military reason.

Illness continued to afflict the men and on 2 March Private H.W. Keys of the 9th Inniskillings died in Purdysburn Hospital from suspected cerbro-spinal meningitis, most probably due to the inclement weather and overcrowding in the billets. This was the first death within the battalion. Private Keys was the son of Elizabeth Keys of Greystones, County Wicklow, he was 18 years old. He was buried with full military honours in Belfast City Cemetery.

UVF badge.

The Lagan Felt Works.

LAGAN FELT WORKS, BELFAST

ROACH ROAD WORKS, LONDON, E.

D.ANDERSON & SON.L^{TD}

FELT AND PAINT   MANUFACTURERS

LAGAN FELT WORKS   ROACH ROAD WORKS
BELFAST   OLD FORD
IRELAND   **LONDON**
                         ENGLAND

REGISTERED
TRADE MARK
FOR FELTS

CLARKE & SHERWELL, LTD, PRINTERS LONDON

The recruiting and equipping of the 16th Rifles, the pioneers of the division, was proceeding at Brownlow House in Lurgan. An article in the local press informed its readers that Lieutenant Colonel Charles Gilbert Carnegy, MVO, late of the 11th (Service) Battalion of the East Surrey Regiment, had been selected as the Commanding Officer. Educated at Clifton College and then Sandhurst, he had been gazetted into the East Yorkshire Regiment in 1884 and joined the Indian Army two years later. He had served in Burma 1886-87 and had a vast experience of pioneer work in India and beyond. His place in the East Surrey Regiment was to be taken by Major Sir Henry Blyth Hill, Bart, of the 10th Inniskillings.

However, this appointment was never filled and command of the 16th Rifles went to Major John Leader.[9] In September 1915, Major Alexander Gordon Lind, formerly of the 58th Vaughan's Rifles, Frontier Force, Indian Army, was appointed as Leader's second-in-command. Lind had joined the army in 1897 and first been commissioned in the York and Lancaster Regiment. However, little is known of this officer and Major Gardiner continued to fulfil the role of second-in-command. Under Leader's command training continued and an offer was made to the local urban council that the pioneers would carry out work on their behalf, provided that material was supplied. So it was that on 9 February 52 officers and men arrived in Keady by train from Lurgan to construct a new road in the village. While there they were billeted in local houses.

At Downpatrick Second Lieutenant A.V. Heywood, Royal Engineers arrived to assist the Signal Company in training. Here the men practised with the field telephone, basic wireless sets, heliographs, the laying and repairing of telephone wire and the care of pigeons. In the coming battles communications were vital and would prove most difficult to maintain. Among the staff was

9   *Belfast News Letter* 1 January 1915.

The Divisional Cyclist Company.

Sergeant David Stratton from Balfour Street, Newtownards. When the division moved to Seaford he would be promoted to Company Quartermaster Sergeant and despite his age, he was almost forty-one, would accompany his unit to France.

The Divisional Cyclist Company was slowly coming up to strength, mostly due to the extensive recruiting 'rides' across the Province. One of the original recruits was Private Tommy Jordan:

> I tried to get into the UVF, but they said they wanted men not boys. A few months later a man took us to an old Dance Hall opposite the Albert Clock in Belfast where a lot of men had been gathered. We were sworn in and given a shilling, I was seventeen. I was given boots, socks, riding britches and a tunic and a large white kit bag to keep them in. We were then given two days' pay and felt very wealthy. We went to the Northern Railway station and ended up in the Inniskillings Depot at Omagh. I was put into a platoon of the Cycle Corps, of which there were six."

An invitation to attend an Entertainment for Returned Soldiers, issued by the Donegal Road Presbyterian Church, on 12 November 1919 at 8:00pm. Mr George Johnston is requested to bring a lady!

On 2 March the Company, under the command of Lieutenant Warman, paraded at College Square North in Belfast to be inspected by Major General Powell. He expressed approval on the turn-out of the men and their machines, in many cases decorated with the Union flag.

There were two deaths suffered by 107 Brigade in April; Private Christopher McPherson of the 8th Rifles died in the Ulster Division Hospital on the Donegall Road, while Private Robert Bustard of the 15th Rifles died in Purdysburn Hospital. Private Bustard came from Baden Powell Street and had been a member of Foster Memorial LOL No.449. Death from disease was almost equalled by death from accidents. The 8th Rifles lost another man the following month when Private William McCall died in hospital from the effects of immersion, after a boating accident. A former guard on the Belfast and County Down Railway, his brother was serving with the Inniskilling Dragoons and a brother-in-law was also in the 8th Rifles.

The month of May saw great success for those members of the division attending the Irish Command School of Musketry in Dublin. All the officers who attended the course qualified as instructors in both rifle and machine gun training, as did a high percentage of the NCOs, several being honoured by special mention, including Lieutenant J.H. Sheehan of the 16th Rifles and Corporal W. Cochrane of the 9th Inniskillings.

Recruiting continued, both for the infantry battalions and other units, all hungry for men. In Monaghan on 8 June Lieutenant Thomas Kettle of the Dublin Fusiliers spoke to a large crowd against any attempt by politicians to interfere with recruiting for their own ends. The war was a war of 'civilisation against barbarians'. Kettle, a former barrister, member of the Irish Parliamentary Party and Irish Volunteer, was renowned for his poetry.

June also saw an incident that would be unthinkable a year later. The 14th Rifles had just completed an exercise at Drumdarragh Hill in County Antrim and had marched to Doagh railway station. From here they refused to march any further and insisted that a train be provided for the journey. This was a mutiny and a widespread mutiny, with so many men involved. Lieutenant Colonel Chichester defused the situation by agreeing to the demand and chartering a train at his own expense. No man in the battalion received any punishment, but the former Young Citizens earned the nickname Chocolate Soldiers from the remainder of the division.[10]

In July Mr R.G. Mercier-Clemente, MD DPH FRCSE, medical adviser to the Orange and Protestant Friendly Society, left Belfast to take up the post of chief surgeon at the UVF Hospital in France. In this period of extreme patriotism there was little time for 'shirkers' or other wrongdoers from either the public or the press. The *Belfast News Letter* on 4 August carried a report regarding the dismissal of two junior subalterns from His Majesty's service, the King having no further occasion for their services. Neither man appeared to have an Ulster connection.

General Powell was a firm believer in route marches as a means of toughening up his troops. At the beginning of 1915, a typical brigade route march of between twenty and twenty-five miles was the rule, with shorter battalion marches carried out on a weekly basis. As most men were still waiting for an issue of equipment a local purchase of Alpine-style rucksacks that had been manufactured in Belfast was made. These were then filled with stones or 'bolts from the shipyard' to take the place of ammunition and other pieces of equipment. However, it was not unknown for some packs to contain a straw filled pillow.[11]

As well as route marches, numerous recruiting marches were also carried out, which not only increased the fitness of the men, but allowed even the remotest village to see the division and to encourage enlistments. Despite the size of the UVF and YCV, some battalions and divisional

10   Bowman, Timothy, *Irish Regiments in the Great War, Discipline and Morale* (Manchester University Press, 2003).

11   James McRoberts diary.

Field training at Clandeboye while waiting for the issue of uniforms.

units were still finding it difficult to fill their quotas. Apart from being more than a 1,000 infantry under strength, the division also required carpenters, blacksmiths, tinsmiths, masons and bricklayers. Signallers and telegraphists were also in short supply, as were drivers, both for horse drawn wagons and motor vehicles. Given that the division had so many horses there was a great need of saddlers and farriers.

At this time the majority of rifles available were those marked 'DP', drill purpose only, which is self-explanatory. For shooting on the ranges there were only a few service rifles available and those that could be 'borrowed' from the local UVF units, to which senior officers turned a blind eye. There was much practice in the digging of trenches, by both the sappers[12] and infantry and much talk as to the advantages and disadvantages of placing them on forward or reverse slopes, although this decision was more often as not decided by the enemy, at least until late 1918.

With such a large number of men being housed in such basic conditions it was inevitable that illness would be a persistent

Rifleman Thomas Kirk, seen here armed with a Martini Henry carbine, one of the weapons supplied to the UVF. A real man-stopper if facing the 'mighty Zulu', which at least one member of the Division had done.

---

12   Within the Royal Engineers private soldiers we known as sappers, named after the sap, a narrow trench that was dug towards an enemy fortress or position. It was a medieval practice that would find a revival with the tunnelling companies of the RE.

Family members and well-wishers watching the new recruits parade at Clandeboye. Large crowds of well-wishers assembled in the camp, especially at the weekends.

The Field Ambulances of the Division pass the City Hall in Belfast on 8 May 1915.

problem. Again there were many cases of cebro-spinal meningitis, which caused a great deal of worry. This necessitated the movement of some units to other accommodation. From Clandeboye, 9th Irish Fusiliers went to barracks in Belfast and Holywood, while 11th Inniskillings went from Finner Camp to the town of Enniskillen.

While the training continued in Ulster there had been several major battles in France. The First Battle of the Marne was fought between 20 and 24 August 1914, followed by the Aisne on 13 September, 1st and 2nd Ypres on 14 October 1914 and 22 April 1915, Neuve Chapelle, in March 1915 and Loos, in May, a battle that saw grievous losses to the British Expeditionary Force.

While training and recruiting continued across the Province and elsewhere the time for moving to England came closer. The artillery had been formed in London, while volunteers had come from Scotland, Major Percy Crozier personally bringing several hundred Glasgow Orangemen who in his words; "A more drunken orgy I have never witnessed. Bands, banners, booze and blasphemy run riot."

From Tyneside, the 9th Inniskillings received a draft of men, bringing the battalion up to strength. The culmination of the preparations for departure to England was a parade through the streets of Belfast on 8 May 1915, the day after RMS *Lusitania* had been sunk by a German U-boat some eleven miles off Old Head of Kinsale with great loss of life. The entire division paraded for inspection by Major General Sir Hugh McCalmont at Malone on the outskirts of Belfast. McCalmont had previously served with the 6th Dragoon Guards in 1865 and had seen action in various campaigns including the Red River in Canada, Ashanti War, Russo-Turkish War, South African, Afghanistan and in Egypt. He was an officer of high capability and had been a member of General Wolseley's 'Ashanti Ring', a cabal of officers deemed to be of over and above intelligence and bravery. McCalmont had been elected as an Ulster Unionist MP for North Antrim in 1895. After the parade the UVF marched into the town and past the City Hall, where the general took the salute. It was a beautiful day and the streets were decorated with miles of red, white and blue bunting. A massive crowd lined the route, many of them having arrived in Belfast on special trains from across the Province. The 10th Inniskilling did not take part, having been detained at Finner Camp due to the outbreak of German measles. For troops not fully trained it was an exhausting experience; Reveille had been at 4:00 am, a quick breakfast and then the train journey to Belfast and the march to Malone Park. Then the march back in to the City, the various ceremonial duties and a return to Randalstown at 8:00 pm. According to the local press, the given length of an infantry division on the march was quoted as eight miles for its fighting elements, the infantry brigades, five miles for the first line transport and one and three quarter miles for the ambulances and train. To this would eventually be added the artillery. In June the 10th (Irish) Division Ammunition Column, which had not gone to the Dardanelles, was transferred to the 36th Division and would eventually join up with the artillery in England. One of a number of photographs taken at the City Hall on the day shows the field ambulances passing, all are horse drawn and it cannot be confirmed if the motor ambulances were present.

4

To England

Divisional Move to Seaford

On Thursday 1 July at Clandeboye, the 108 Brigade Transport and officers' chargers left camp at 3:30 pm, those belonging to the 13th Rifles under the command of Lieutenant J. Pollock, the battalion transport officer. An advance party for Seaford under Captain C.H. Murland had left on 28 June, while the brigade's heavy baggage had been shipped on 25 June under the care of the Army Service Corps. Lieutenant Pollock's command arrived at York Dock, Belfast at 8.45pm and boarded the S.S. *Archimedes*, loading being completed at 1:30 am, on Friday morning.[1] On arrival at Liverpool the transport was loaded on to a train and set off for Seaford, arriving that evening. Here they were met by Captain R. Fridlington, the adjutant, who arranged for food and accommodation. No trouble was experienced during the sea crossing or ensuing train journey and the horses quickly recovered after a short time grazing and care from the grooms.

Clinton Place, Seaford, Sussex, 1913.

---

1   The *Archimedes* had been built in 1911 and was originally named *Den of Airlie*. Requisitioned as a troop transport she served from 1914-1919, doing sterling service for the BEF. In 1941 she struck a mine and was sunk off Spurn Point near Grimsby.

The 13th Royal Irish Rifles, having marched out of Clandeboye Camp are seen here approaching Newtownards via the Crawfordsburn Road and are about to pass beneath the railway bridge on their way to the station.

The following day the 13th Rifles, 1,200 all ranks, marched out of Clandeboye Camp and made their way to the railway station at Victoria Avenue in Newtownards. The column was headed by Regimental Sergeant Major Briggs, a native of Holywood, closely followed by the battalion band. Each man carried his kitbag, although some had help from friends and family. A photograph taken from the railway bridge in William Street in the town shows the large crowd that came to wish them well; it also shows that much more practice was going to be required with regard to their marching, although given the nature of the occasion this is probably understandable. From Newtownards railway station two trains took the battalion to Belfast. Aboard the first was Colonel Savage, 14 of his officers and 509 other ranks, men of A and B Companies. The second train carried Major Maxwell with 16 officer and 514 other ranks of C and D Companies. These trains then travelled to Dublin where on arrival at the North Wall at 4:45 pm, the men were served with tea, bread and butter in a separate shed. From here they boarded the SS *Viper*, a former Ardrossan to Belfast passenger ferry, for the crossing to England.

From the diary of Private James McRoberts, 14th Rifles:

Monday 5 July 1915: – RANDALSTOWN. We were told to pack everything we possessed into our kit bags or in our rucksacks. The huts were then cleared out of everything that remained, the bed-boards and mattresses lifted so we were only left with one blanket to carry. We paraded with all our kit and the Battalion left Randalstown, County Antrim, in two special trains starting at 11:15 am and 11:45 am. I was in the first and the train went through Lisburn and quickly on towards Dublin.

Injury was also denuding the division of men. While on a visit to his home in Belfast Private William Lundy of the Army Service Corps was returning to Victoria Barracks. He was in uniform as he was a driver in that he rode the lead horse of a team, he wore spurs. At that time in Belfast there was Grosvenor Street, which was split level. While descending these steps Private Lundy caught his spur and fell, causing himself severe injury. So much so that he was eventually medically discharged and returned to his pre-war employment as a riveter in the shipyard.

On Tuesday 6 July 1915, under the command of Major General C.H. Powell the majority of the division left Belfast by train for the journey up to Dublin, travelling via Lisburn, Dundalk and Drogheda.[2] Private George Hackney, B Company of the 14th Rifles, recalled that before leaving Randalstown each man in his company was issued with a pound of bully beef, two packets of biscuits, three of nut milk chocolate, a packet of ten cigarettes, two each of bananas, oranges and boiled meat sandwiches, a packet of tea and the same of sugar. On arrival in the capital at 4:00 pm, the men were rested in one of the quay sheds and were served with tea and two bread and butter sandwiches each. Embarking from the North Wall at 5:15 pm, they sailed to Holyhead on the SS *Connaught*, leaving at 9:00 pm and arriving at 12:15 am, Irish time. Then by train to the coastal town of Seaford in East Sussex, on the journey those who possessed watches adjusted them from Irish time to English time. In 1880 Greenwich Mean Time had been legally adopted throughout Great Britain, being adopted by the Isle of Man in 1883, Guernsey in 1913 and in Ireland in 1916, prior to this Ireland had operated on Dublin Mean Time. This adoption of GMT had been the result of the spread of the railways throughout the United Kingdom with timetables having to be collated across the country.

Seaford lies on the south coast of East Sussex about half way between Brighton and Eastbourne. There were two camps, the north camp and the south camp, the 16th Rifles were billeted in the

---

2   Railways always travel up to the capital, irrespective of where they are geographically.

A section of the Divisional Cyclist Company at Seaford.

The Transport Section of the Royal Irish Fusiliers.

Cigarettes, most men smoked to try and cover the stench of the battlefield.

The Seven Sisters and Coastguard Station two miles from Seaford Camp, Sussex.

latter, mostly used for billeting troops of the Canadian Army and that also went under the name of Chyngton Camp.

This was the first time that the entire division was together in one location. It proved an excellent training area; the downs were ideal for tactical exercises and provided good practice for the digging of trenches. Brighton itself did not meet with everyone's approval; Private James McRoberts had this to say; "I went to Brighton and had a rather alarming experience. The day was brilliantly beautiful and Brighton poured forth her wealth and scum. There is an underworld in Brighton, which is appalling and disgusting."[3]

3   James McRoberts diary.

These remarks were made after having met a girl who was quite open about being involved in a back street abortion and her extremely descriptive knowledge of pornography. There were many, if not most of the division, who had never been out of Ulster and had led relatively sheltered lives. The diary of George Hackney reveals much of the character of the men. In his writing he refers to a Sunday as the Sabbath and was not taken with how some men in his barrack hut behaved:

> Reveille at 7:00 am and Church parade at 9:15 am in the open air lasting until 10:45 am. On parading volunteers were asked for the choir, but I wouldn't as Lieutenant Hanna said 'Any nightingales here?' in his usual smart way. Remained in camp after dinner time. There was a gambling school in the hut from dinner time until 10:00 pm, playing Banker, which I did not find to make the day very like the Sabbath due to the arguing and language of the players.

Due to an outbreak of German measles 9th Inniskillings had not left with the division. The battalion had therefore marched out of their camp at Randalstown and made their way north to Ballycastle to prevent any cross-infection with the remainder of the Brigade. The Inniskillings camped under canvas on the beach about a mile from the town. Some men required hospital treatment and were admitted to the Waveney Hospital, although no strict quarantine was enforced and if a man showed no sign of infection he was allowed on leave. Despite the usual discipline problems, a degree of lateness on parade, etc., the only major incident involving the Inniskillings was when three men of the battalion assaulted two members of the Christian Brothers. Taken to court the men, Privates Betts, Gillespie and Quinn, were tried, with Betts and Gillespie being sentenced to two months imprisonment, while Quinn seems to have been let off due to his 'problems with alcohol'. Quinn had previously seen action and been wounded in France while serving with the North Irish Horse. The magistrate was quick to compliment other members of the Battalion, Privates Adair, Cross and Hughes, who had gone to the assistance of the two injured priests.

The camp at Ballycastle did not allow for musketry training and when the measles seemed to have dissipated the battalion travelled to Magilligan on the shores of Lough Foyle in Londonderry to begin its introduction to shooting. Now time was of the essence and an intense programme was followed. Lieutenant Ritter and Sergeant Cassidy had attended and successfully completed a course of instruction at the Irish Command School of Musketry in Dublin and lent their expertise to the various classes. Reinforcements arrived from the 12th Reserve Battalion at Finner, but only three of the 18 men were accepted, such were the high standards set. The remainder were returned for more training.

Eventually it was time for the Inniskillings to follow the division to Seaford. On the morning of 25 August the battalion boarded their Midland Railway train at Magilligan Halt for the journey to Belfast, arriving at 4:30 pm. That evening they boarded the S.S. *Connaught*, a troopship, and sailed for Liverpool, arriving at 5:00 am, the following day.[4] The journey was described as; "Long and tiresome with no sleep on the ship and uncomfortable dozing on the rail journey to Rugby where refreshments were provided."[5]

At Seaford the 9th Inniskillings settled down in the north camp to enjoy very pleasant summer weather. The daily papers of 23 July 1915 reported that Thomas Pollock and Robert Wilson, both of the Army Service Corps, Ulster Division, were drowned on Sunday last at Seaford. A witness, Driver McClusky, stated he was with a party bathing in the sea when the incident happened. He

---

4 The *Connaught* carried men to and from France until 3 March 1917, when she was sunk by the German submarine U-48. The U-boat was in turn sunk when it ran aground on the Goodwin Sands on the morning of 24 November 1917 and was shelled by HMS *Gipsy* and accompanying drifters, before being scuttled by her crew.

5 Canning, W.J., *A Wheen of Medals* (Antrim, 2006).

An inventory of equipment held by George Hackney of the 14th Royal Irish Rifles on his admission to the 109th Field Ambulance on 1 July 1916.

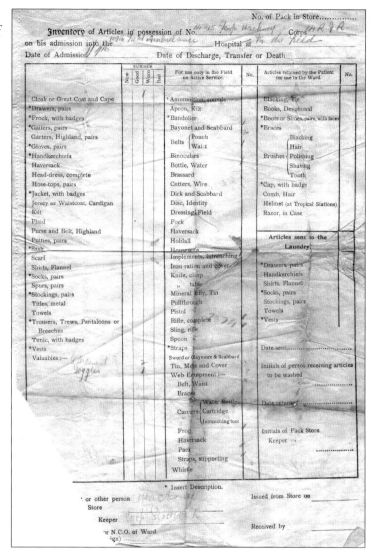

saw Wilson in difficulty and then Pollock threw off his clothes and attempted to swim out to Wilson's assistance, into a sea that was very rough. Other men made a human chain to render help and when the two men were reached it was found that Wilson's arm was tight around Pollock's neck. McClusky tried to release Wilson's hold on Pollock, but failed. When eventually Pollock was brought ashore attempts were made to revive him, but were unsuccessful. Wilson's body was not recovered until the following day. At the inquest Doctor John Charles Robb, RAMC, stated that efforts to revive Pollock went on for some two and a half hours. Also present on the beach that day were Driver John Lunday and Driver Kelly. Sergeant Archibald Pollock said that his brother had joined the Army some months previously and had left a widow and several children. Robert Wilson's parents resided at Roden Street, Belfast.

As a result of an earlier visit to the division by Lieutenant General Sir Archibald Murray, Lord Kitchener then inspected the division at 11:00 am, on 27 July. He was most impressed with the men and expressed a particular interest in the personnel of the field ambulances, who were all well mounted and in good physical shape. Kitchener then ordered that two hundred men from the field ambulances should be transferred to the Royal Artillery. This did not go down well within the division, these men had undergone intensive training in their craft and as events would prove later in France, you can never have too many medical orderlies. Despite the artillery not specifically requiring men at that time one hundred and five members of the RAMC were removed from the division and the promise that they would be used to fill the ranks of the divisional artillery was not kept.

It was after this review that Sir Archibald Murray contacted the Secretary for War and informed him that the division was not yet ready for active service. They may have looked well, but in equipment and training they were far from ready. Despite a degree of musketry training in Ireland and at Seaford, the official courses in rifle and Vickers machine gun had yet to occur. The division also lacked certain items of necessary equipment. There was the case of the divisional artillery, which was far from ready to take the field. Kitchener's response was that the firing courses should be completed as quickly as possible and the necessary equipment found and that a fully trained unit of artillery should be attached to the division. The unit selected was the 1st/1st London Territorial Artillery and while its training had been elementary, it had been intensive, with the Londoners keen to learn.

CQMS David Bell from Ballynahinch was a former member of the local UVF unit. He had enlisted on 14 September 1914, along with 33 other members of the UVF. He served in C Company of the 13th Rifles, which was commanded by Major Perceval-Maxwell and eleven weeks later was promoted to RQMS. Bell recalled:

> After a period of training in England we were ready for drafting to France, but as our UVF equipment was condemned by Lord Kitchener, we were held back until proper supplies arrived. It was fortunate for us that we did not go with the intended draft, for the Division that took our place suffered severe casualties at the Battle of Loos in 1915.

At the beginning of August the service squadron of the Inniskilling Dragoons received a new commanding officer. Major Addington Dawsonne Strong, 2nd Reserve Regiment of Cavalry, which was affiliated to the 2nd Dragoon Guards and the 6th (Inniskilling) Dragoons, was appointed to command. Strong had spent most of his twenty-one years' service in the Indian Army, having attained his commission in January 1895. Until recently he had commanded a squadron of the 10th Duke of Cambridge's Own Lancers (Hodson's Horse), formerly known as the 10th Bengal Lancers, a unit that had been raised during the Indian Mutiny in 1857. Major Strong had also served on the North West Frontier in 1897 and 1898, taking part in the attack and successful capture of the Tauga Pass, being awarded the campaign medal with clasp.

On the first anniversary of the outbreak of the Great War a service was held in the Garrison Church of the South Camp. This was voluntary and began at noon and the building, capable of holding a thousand people was full to overflowing. The service was conducted by the Reverend J Quinn, chaplain of 107 Brigade, with the special lesson being read by the Reverend C.C. Manning of 108 Brigade. Appropriate hymns were sung, the organ music being supplied by Bugle-Major Lindop of the 11th Rifles. That evening at 7:00 pm, General Nugent, accompanied by his brigadiers and a number of battalion commanders, attended a service in the Parish Church, Seaford. Here the special lesson was read by the Reverend J. Parry, Congregational minister, Seaford, while the sermon, a most thoughtful and earnest discourse, was preached by the vicar, the Reverend Canon Cremer.

There was another death at Seaford, Private Joseph Topley, 9th Irish Fusiliers, drowned on 18 August, he was 22 years old and came from Tandragee. The unfortunate private was bathing in the River Cuckmere, a tidal stream running through the valley that separates Seaford from the Eastbourne Range of the Southdown Hills. A group of men were also

The Transport Section of the 12th Royal Irish Rifles.

bathing in the river when it was noticed that Private Topley had disappeared. Privates Isaac Walker and John Allen, of the Irish Fusiliers, along with Private Robert Patterson, 12th Rifles, made strenuous efforts to find Topley and when he was discovered in about seven feet of water efforts to revive him failed. The coroner returned a verdict of accidental death. One witness, Lieutenant S.P. Rea, medical officer of the 13th Rifles, stated that Private Topley had "probably entered the water with his mouth open and was overcome at once, being unable to call out, and that death was instantaneous." Private George Hackney recollected the funeral in his diary; "Funeral today of the 9th RIF chap who dived off the wooden bridge into the Cuxmere *(sic)* river and stuck in the mud at the bottom, height 18 feet."

On 23 August there was a fire in the stables of the 14th Rifles located at Sutton Place, Seaford, and ten horses were killed, including one belonging to Major General Powell. No reason for the blaze could be ascertained, although George Hackney offered details in his diary:

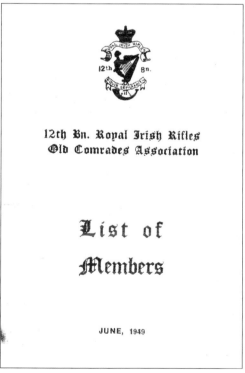

12th Royal Irish Rifles Old Comrades Association, list of members June 1949.

Early morning parade at which we heard there had been a serious fire the previous night at the Mounted Police Stables to which we should have turned out, but we were not wakened. The stables were gutted and eight horses were burned to death, some of them to cinders, and two others died later from wounds making ten in all. This big loss was due to some picket not being at his post, but sleeping, and the origins of the fire are not known – yet at any rate.

Discipline at Seaford seemed to cause little concern as reported in the various war diaries. In August Captain D.M. Wilson, 9th Inniskillings, was appointed as Acting Provost Marshal of the division. Pre-war Captain Wilson had been a well-known solicitor in County Antrim and had given up a prosperous business on obtaining his commission. Most problems concerned minor infringements and were frequently dealt with at a local level. On one drill parade when the men felt that they had done more that enough of repetitive rifle drill 'by numbers', Private George Kirkwood told Sergeant Martin to "Catch himself on." It went no further than the drill square. Later in France such a remark could lead a man to the firing squad.

Both training and sport continued to fill the days of the men. In the signals company tuition was delivered by Lieutenant Jack Moore, the former commander of the 4th South Down Battalion UVF at Kilkeel in County Down. Moore was considered an expert in signalling and his company had won second prize in a UVF competition in Belfast the previous May. In August Lieutenant J.T. Leslie of the Army Signals Service arrived in Seaford and was attached to the signals company, again bringing much valued experience and in turn being impressed with the equipment already on hand and formerly owned by the UVF. On the same day Lieutenant J. Paul of the Army Veterinary Corps arrived at Seaford, he was posted to the Royal Field Artillery camp at Lewes.

Private Simpson.

It came as some surprise to the comrades of Arthur Totton of the 14th Rifles when he was granted a commission in the 18th Battalion of the County of London Regiment. He had been a former member of the East Belfast Regiment of the UVF and came from Lombard Street. Pre-war he had been the secretary of the Irish Football league and had three brothers serving with the Colours.

Illness continued to take its toll on the division. On 27 August was the funeral of Private Robert Simpson of the Inniskillings, who had died as a result of German measles. He was 19 years old and came from Farnamullen, Tamlaght, in County Fermanagh. Within certain battalions sport was of most importance, especially the 14th Rifles, who took their running very seriously. The diary of Private James McRoberts recalls such a meeting:

Private Herbert George Holohan, known as 'Bertie', holding a signalling flag, the man with the rifle is unnamed; both members of the 9th Royal Irish Rifles. Bertie was killed on 1 July 1916, he has no known grave.

Flag of the South Down Regiment UVF, later the 10th Royal Irish Rifles, in Downpatrick Museum. (Courtesy of Downpatrick Museum)

28 August 1915: I felt in good form for the race which started at 4:00 pm from the barn on the top of the hill, north-east of Seaford. Twenty-two teams had entered and we started first, the others began, one after the other, at intervals of three minutes. The day was very sultry, while the course had not a yard of level ground but led us over hills, through hedges and across ploughed fields, being fully five miles in length. I stuck the first three miles fairly easily but the wind was collecting in my tummy and beginning to cause me considerable agony. I was with the first eleven, right to the foot of the last hill, but had then to stop running and walked in, arriving about twelfth. I felt vexed with myself for not being in the first ten, but I felt sure that our team would get a place, although I would have no share in the medals. It eventually proved that our tenth man had come in best of all the teams, his time being thirty-one minutes, forty-five seconds, beating the 8th Royal Irish Rifles by forty-nine seconds. At first there was an understanding that this Battalion had beaten us, and the virulent ridicule the 'Young Citizens' had to listen to for a time, was amusing rather than otherwise. When we reached our camp we were loudly cheered and all had our tea in the Sergeants' Mess. Afterwards I went down to the promenade.[6]

Along with training and sport, romance was in the air for members of the division. In August Corporal Gordon of the 16th Rifles married Miss Mary Adair, who had travelled all the way from Winnipeg, Canada. The service was held in the Seaford Congregational Church and was performed by the Reverend Hugh Parry, the local pastor and the Reverend Jackson Wright, Chaplain to the Forces. Special leave was granted to the corporal so that he could enjoy a short honeymoon in Glasgow, where his new bride had resided prior to going to Canada.

In the ranks of the 12th Rifles Private William Beattie received a letter from his father in Ballymena informing him that his brother Archie serving with the 6th Rifles in the Dardanelles had been wounded. Private Lewis from Linwood Street Belfast received a similar letter. His brother Lance Corporal John Lewis, also with the 6th Rifles, had been wounded and was in hospital in Cairo. Their brother, Thomas, was a well know player with Glenavon Football Club.[7]

On 1 September Lieutenant Leigh Maxwell Anderson of the 9th Irish Fusiliers, died of cerebral meningitis at Seaford, he was 36 years old. Prior to enlisting Lieutenant Anderson had been a successful land agent and stockbroker. His body was returned to his family and he was buried at St. Mark's Church of Ireland in Armagh.

On the same day a shipment of 500 Lee Enfield rifles arrived. These weapons were issued to the 10th Inniskillings, causing a degree of jealousy among the other battalions. Captain Warman of the 12th Rifles, who had temporary command of the Cyclist Company, was gazetted as a captain in the Army Cyclist Corps. Serving in the company was Private Frank Farrell, a former employee of the Textile Testing House in which he had been an expert in such work. Considered suitable for a commission he received a cadetship in the 18th Rifles and on earning his commission was subsequently posted to the 15th Rifles where he was appointed as adjutant. This seemed to happen on a regular occurrence in the company. Samuel Gatensby was also commissioned and went on to serve with the Irish Rifles as of 1 March 1917.

The RAMC put great stress on the recovery of the wounded from the battlefield. On 7 August a stretcher bearer competition was held at Seaford. Teams from the various field ambulances took part and were judged in smartness of turn-out, ability to dress wounds and steadiness of carrying a stretcher. After the initial inspection the four-man squads had to run to the other end of the field

---

6   In the published diary Young Citizens is written as Young Canadians, due to a misreading of the original manuscript.
7   *Belfast News Letter*, 31 August 1915.

Royal Irish Fusiliers with fixed bayonets, that man moved!

Stretcher bearers of the Division at the competition held on 7 August 1915, at Seaford.

where a number of 'wounded' men were lying. Here each squad attended to a patient, his wound being written on a label attached to his tunic. The man's equipment had to be carefully removed and the wound treated with the required dressings and bandages. The injured man was then placed on a stretcher and to judge the steadiness and freedom from jolting, a glass of water, filled to the brim, was placed on the handle of each stretcher. Marks were then awarded for rapidity with which the wounded were carried in, the effectiveness of the bandaging and the steadiness with which the stretchers were carried. The first prize, which was a certificate and £3, went to No1 Squad of the 9th Rifles, Lance Corporal Charles McDowell, and Privates John Mullen, John Worrell and William Whiteside.

The Royal Engineers were also had at work in preparation for their deployment to France. As per War Office guidelines, the emphasis on the campaign in France was to advance, not fortify, therefore bridging techniques were much more important than digging trenches or tunnels. The 121 and 150 Field Companies spent time on the River Thames at Henley constructing pontoon bridges, much to the interest and amusement of the local populace. At the end of the course the engineers organised a concert and a pontoon race between the two companies, which again gathered a large and supportive audience. The race was started in the traditional style by Lieutenant

The 150 Field Company Royal Engineers of the Division on parade 1915.

Officers and men of the 150 Field Company Royal Engineers, 1915.

Ferrier discharging his revolver into the air. The race steward was Lieutenant Smyth, while Major Craig, the officer commanding 121 Company, acted as judge and awarded the prizes. The winners were No.4 Section of the 121 Company, consisting of Lance Corporal Jackson with Sappers Whelan, Davison and Crawford, with Sergeant Agnew as coxswain. The band for the concert was conducted by Sergeant Major Warry and was located on a pontoon moored in the river opposite the Red Lion Hotel. Sapper J. Ledger played the accompaniment in his usual able manner. Prior to leaving for France the Divisional Engineers were inspected by Major General A.E. Sandbach, CB DSC. He congratulated Colonel Henry Finnis, CSI, on the turnout of his men and on the excellent reports he had read of their progress in training. In the training of bomb throwers it was found that former cricketers were the best when it came to both distance and accuracy. Lobbing the bomb on to the target was considered a fine art.

From 2 to15 September the companies carried out musketry training on various ranges, including Bramshott and Longmoor. By 5 September each man had been issued with his personal Lee Enfield rifle. Most of the musketry courses were shot using American-supplied ammunition, which proved to be of inferior quality. One man had previously been witnessed by Major Falls as he placed five rounds from a UVF supplied Italian Veterli rifle into the bull's eye at six hundred yards, then missed with his .303 and American ammunition. This in turn led to many men being castigated by the instructors who seemed to prefer blaming the men as opposed to the ammunition.

The move to France drew closer and things became more serious as revealed in the 17 September entry in the diary of Private George Hackney; "This evening I signed the form guaranteeing to return at my proper time. It read as follows: "I recognise that I am under orders for embarkation and that failure to return on the proper date automatically becomes Desertion, for which I am liable to suffer the penalty of Death."

A letter received from Major Falls commanding A Company 11th Inniskillings, to Mr Simpson of Tempo, County Fermanagh, brought the news that his son Private Robert Simpson had died of scarlstina and pneumonia on 25 August, while in a Brighton sanatorium. He was buried with full military honours in Seaford Cemetery. Private Samuel Maconachie, 252 Company Army Service Corps, died in Ravenscroft Hospital on 2 September 1915. This occurred while he was undergoing an operation for an internal complaint. Private Maconachie had been a member of the West Belfast Regiment of the UVF, and a former member of the 110th Field Ambulance. He was buried with full military honours in Seaford Cemetery. His family came from the Ballygomartin Road in Belfast and had only been informed of his illness by telegram a short time earlier, he was 21 years old.

From the diary of Private James McRoberts 14th Rifles:

> Thursday 30 September 1915: BRAMSHOTT: It was a dry cold day and the whole Division, including our Artillery, was reviewed by His Majesty King George the Fifth, accompanied by Lord Kitchener, Major General Sir Oliver Nugent, the new Commander of the Division and by Sir George Richardson. We marched past in double companies, with greatly reduced intervals, and it was stated that His Majesty had said this was the quickest inspection he had made since the war started."

This inspection was made at Tilford Golf Links, Hankley Common near Farnham, and by this time advance elements of the division were already in France. In the Inniskilling Dragoons, Trooper Thomas McCurry received a letter from his parents at Wall Street Belfast, telling him that his brother James, serving with the 6th Rifles in the Dardanelles, had been wounded the previous month and was in hospital in Alexandra.

5

Hullo Carson's Boys[1]

France, October 1915

On 30 September 1915, the staff members of the Deputy Assistant Director of Ordnance Services (DADOS) arrived in Boulogne, the first element of the division to land in France. In order to fight on the battlefield any unit requires to be supported, not only with food and ammunition, but all the other paraphernalia that makes life bearable. This was the responsibility of DADOS. The Ordnance Services supplied all that was needed to live and fight on the battlefield, with the exception of rations, forage, petrol and certain technical stores, which were the responsibility of the Army Service Corps. From the original eight companies of the Army Ordnance Corps of 1914 the strength had grown to 42 by 1916. Likewise the staff of 1914, one officer and one clerk had increased to an officer and 14 clerks per division, with four motor lorries as their transport element. A similar organisation was found at Corps Headquarters, while at Army Headquarters it was double the numbers. The Ordnance Services supplied ammunition for all weapons, from revolvers to siege guns; they also supplied more mundane items, bicycles, wheels of various types and sizes, horse and mule shoes, soap, kitchen utensils, boots and blankets. During the first ten months of 1916 they issued 3,500,000 yards of flannelette, 40,000 miles of signalling cable, 5,000,000 anti-gas helmets and 11,000 compasses. Workshops were established to repair stores when possible and these sometimes employed local civilian labour. The workshops themselves ranged from light mobile types to heavy repair shops, responsible for artillery pieces.

The 16th Rifles left their camp at Borden and travelled to Southampton on 1 October 1915, where they discovered that no one was expecting them and an uncomfortable night was spent sleeping at the docks. The following day the battalion sailed for France aboard the *Empress Queen*, a ferry boat. Regardless of the fact that this ship was licensed to carry some 600 persons, over 1,000 crowded aboard. Despite a severe gale blowing a safe crossing was made to Le Harve, the ship arriving just after midnight. Divisional headquarters left Bordon and sailed for France on 3 October, arriving at Boulogne at 3:00 pm the following day. General Nugent and his Staff also landed at Boulogne, but did not arrive until midnight. The following day 108 Brigade arrived, landing at Boulogne and Le Havre.

The departure of the 11th Rifles from Borden was recorded by Captain Arthur Samuels of C Company:

> We fell in at 4 o'clock on the afternoon of 4 October 1915 on the parade ground of St. Lucia Barracks, Borden. As we marched to the station we were struck by the apathy displayed by the few civilians we saw. There was no cheering, waving of handkerchiefs, or kissing of hands; even the children making mud pies on the side of the road did not trouble to look up. We were only one of many battalions that had passed down the same road during the previous fourteen months. It was almost an everyday sight for people who live there. We felt we were only going

---

1   An article in the *Belfast News Letter* of 27 October 1915 claims this was shouted at the Ulstermen shortly after entering the trenches.

One wonders what some of the French phrases uttered by men of the Division had on the French, given the plethora of accents across Ulster!

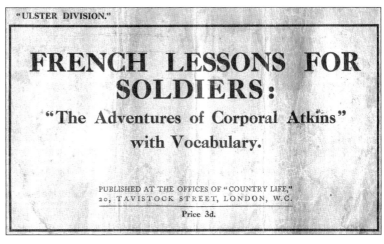

"ULSTER DIVISION."

FRENCH LESSONS FOR SOLDIERS:
"The Adventures of Corporal Atkins" with Vocabulary.

PUBLISHED AT THE OFFICES OF "COUNTRY LIFE,"
20, TAVISTOCK STREET, LONDON, W.C.

Price 3d.

on our business and that those plain-clothes civilians, many of them young and physically fit men, were going on theirs.

From Borden the battalion travelled by train to Folkestone and from there by steamer to Boulogne. The following is taken from an account by Sergeant Stephen Stone of the 110th Field Ambulance:

> The unit sailed to France on the evening of 3 October 1915 aboard the SS *Australand*. At 7:00 am the following morning the ship dropped anchor outside the port of Le Havre and we were served breakfast. This consisted of one tin of Maconochie rations per two men.[2] I was lucky in that the man I shared with, Corporal Warden, had no liking for tinned food and I being very hungry ate my fill. After breakfast the men were taken ashore by lighter and waited on the quay while the wagons and horses were unloaded. We then travelled to a rest camp some miles away, which consisted of bell tents, set up in a field that was under some twelve inches of water and mud. Three of the heavy draught horses went down with colic and had to be sent to the Veterinary Section, while replacements were fetched from the Remount Depot. Reveille was at 3:00 .am the following morning and as the horses were gathered in for harnessing it was discovered that during the night all had rolled in the mud. This involved a fair amount of swearing by the men as the animals were brushed down. The field ambulance was also supplied with mules and these seemed to have been used to pull the GS (General Service) wagons, while the draught horses pulled the ambulances.[3]

From the rest camp the unit moved to a railway station and was loaded on to a train. During the journey stops were made to feed and water the horses and on occasions a communal coffee pot was brewed for the men. On one occasion Sergeant Stone, a teetotaller, was perturbed to discover that rum had been added to the coffee and no substitute provided for men like himself, of which there were a number. Arriving at Amiens Station at 6:00 pm on 5 October, the unit received a rapturous welcome from the local populace; unfortunately they were not so lucky with rations. This shortage continued for several days and hunger was assuaged by the eating of apples from

---

2   Tinned stew of meat and vegetables, although 'meat' was something of a misnomer according to some.
3   Somme Museum Archive.

Maconochie's stew, the reality was a lot less appetising.

the nearby orchards. The unit then found itself billeted in the village of Vignicourt. After a week the men received their first pay since arriving in France, the Sergeants each being paid twenty-five francs. That night Sergeant Stone and several others went to a local bar for a drink. Beer was the equivalent of 2d a glass, while lemonade was 1/=, six times the price![4] Sergeant Stone reckoned that those who were teetotal were in for a hard time. The unit then moved to Bertacourt, here there was a plentiful supply of cheap alcohol, which in the words of Sergeant Stone; "…became the downfall of the Brigade."

From this village the unit moved to Clayrfie on the Somme.[5] Sergeant Stone's remark is not far from the truth. An examination of the courts martial records of the division shows that of the 13 battalions, seven had as their first offence, drunkenness. It would be a major cause of courts martial for the remainder of the war.

During the first two weeks of October, all elements of the division, less the artillery, had arrived in France, the advance parties having moved ahead to prepare for their arrival. The mounted portion and transport landed at Le Havre, while the infantry disembarked at Boulogne. CQMS David Bell of the 13th Rifles recorded the following:

> The advance contingent of the division consisted of the transport element, 1,000 men, 750 horses and a number of wagons. On Saturday we had arrived in Southampton by train and

4   1/= equals 5 pence at the time of writing.
5   Somme Museum Archive.

the wagons were loaded on to the steamer SS *Lapland* and crossed the Channel that night, landing at Le Havre. Still in darkness left by train arriving at Amiens on Monday morning. From Amiens the 13th Rifles advance party marched to Rainville, which was reached that evening, to prepare for the arrival of the battalion. Major Perceval-Maxwell informed me there was a luncheon basket in the Officer's Mess cart and if I fetched it we could have a meal. As I made my way through the transport lines, I saw some of the transport men eating what I took to be the legs of chickens. Sure enough, the worst had happened, for when I reached the Officer's Mess cart the basket and contents were missing.

A typical day's ration for a soldier resting behind the lines, as of 4 December 1915 was as follows; a breakfast of fried bacon, bread, jam, tea. Dinner (lunch) consisted of roast meat, potatoes, bread, jam, tea. Tea, served in the late afternoon, usually between 4:00 pm and 5:00 pm, was cheese, jam, bread, tea, dripping. For those men on guard duty cocoa was issued, while there was soup served nightly from 8:00 pm to 9:00 pm.[6] Things changed as the war progressed.

On 8 October 107 Brigade and 1/1 London Royal Field Artillery were inspected by Lieutenant General Sir Charles Monroe, commander of the Third Army, who seemed pleased enough with their turnout and equipment. Between 5 and 9 October the division concentrated around Flesselles, the location of divisional headquarters some ten miles north of Amiens. From here the sound of the guns could be heard, but strangely less than at Seaford, while during the hours of darkness Véry lights could be seen arcing into the sky.[7] To those men of the division who came from farming backgrounds the Somme seemed a poor place to try and scratch out a living,

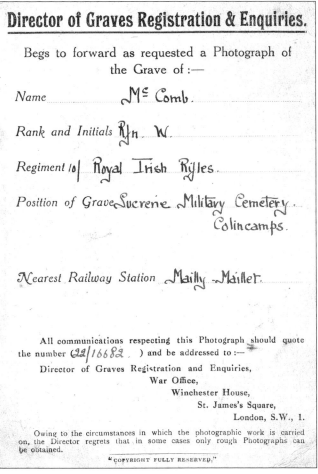

Private Thomas William McCombe served with the 10th Royal Irish Rifles and was killed on 22 December 1915, one of the first casualties to the division. He came from Coolbeg Street, Donegal Road, Belfast, and was 17 years old.

---

6   An Army Chaplain's Experiences, *Belfast Evening Telegraph*.
7   Very, also rendered as Verey, named after Edward Wilson Very, an American naval officer (1847-1910).

but the local peasants seemed to do well. Some consternation was caused by the piles of manure seen piled against the various farm houses, which it was later discovered, indicated the prosperity of the owners.

The staff members of DADOS were well on the way to establishing workshops for shoemakers, farriers and tailors. General Nugent decided that the latter was not required and tailoring should remain at brigade as opposed to divisional level. While the division was well versed in foot drill and was capable of presenting a professionally turned out appearance, it still lacked any experience in training for the front line. Therefore, on 9 October it was the turn of 108 and 109 Brigades, along with the 1st and 3rd London RFA to be inspected by the GOC. On the same day General Couchman led his 107 Brigade along with the 1st/1st (London Brigade) RFA, the light trench mortar battery and the 110th Field Ambulance on attachment to the 4th Division at Puchevillers and Herissant [Herisson] for further training and experience, this was to last for five days. They were replaced in the Ulster Division by 12 Brigade and from this unit the 2nd Lancashire Fusiliers went to 108 Brigade in exchange for the 11th Rifles, while the 2nd Essex went to 109 Brigade in exchange for the 14th Rifles. This venture lasted for five days and subsequently both 108 and 109 Brigades followed suit. In the latter cases each Brigade sent two battalions each to the 4th and 48th Divisions. A following directive from the High Command augmented this training. After the Battle of Loos, fought on 25 and 26 September across most unfavourable ground and with inexperienced troops fresh from England it was deemed that each Division from both the New Armies and Territorial divisions should have at least thirty percent of their personnel from experienced units. By 10 October 107 Brigade was in situ with the 4th Division. Due to the brigade's disciplinary problems General Nugent decided to replace Brigadier Couchman on grounds of incompetence. He wrote to his wife; "I have to write to one of my Brigadiers and tell him he won't do, so beastly, but quite unavoidable. I might have delayed it, but to what good and a good man is badly wanted at once."[8]

In war, key, and what are considered trifling decisions, are made in concert. On the same day an officer from DADOS visited the 108th Field Ambulance and arranged to replace the filter on their water cart. The following day Second Lieutenant Francis Nicholas Andrews of the 15th Rifles, died in hospital in France, he was 20 years old and the son of the Reverend I.W. Andrews of Trysull Vicarage, Wolverhampton in Staffordshire. He was buried with full military honours in Terlincthun British Cemetery, Wimille, plot VIII, row E. Two days later the Royal Engineers Headquarters and No.3 Field Company, Royal Engineers, moved to Arqueves by route march, while the 16th Rifles (Pioneers) moved to Raincheval in order to undertake entrenching work on the line and General Nugent decided to replace his GSOI; "Meynell is I am afraid a useless Staff Officer, always making heavy weather of everything and no more intelligent as a clerk. I have to think of everything in his branch and he gets on my nerves. I am afraid I shall have to get him removed."

Lieutenant Colonel Meynell returned to regimental duty and became the commanding officer of the 6th King's Own Yorkshire Light Infantry.[9] His replacement was Lieutenant Colonel Lewis James Comyn who had been commissioned into the Connaught Rangers in 1899 and was one of the first Catholic officers to be allowed to remain in the division. His family came from Ballinderry, Ballinasloe, County Galway, and on his maternal side was the great grandson of Daniel O'Connell, the 'Liberator'. Prior to joining the division he had been Deputy Assistant Adjutant & Quartermaster General (DAA&QMG) of the 14th Division. He was Assistant Adjutant and Quartermaster General (AA & QMG) from 29 October 1915 to November 1917 and

8   Bowman, Timothy, *Carson's Army, The Ulster Volunteer Force 1910-22* (2007).
9   *Hart's Army List,* July 1916.

was described as a capable staff officer. Also on Nugent's staff was Captain Robin F. Henry, acting as an aide-de-camp, having been inherited from General Powell. An article in the *Belfast News Letter* of 5 October gives his rank as second lieutenant and his home as Laurel Lodge, Strandtown. However, the divisional war diary has him listed as a captain. He seemed to have been a particular favourite and Nugent refers to him as having the enthusiasm of a schoolboy. He remained in position until late 1917.

The division incurred its first battle casualties in France on 13 October when ten men were wounded and one was reported missing from the 9th Rifles in 107 Brigade, this was Private J. Hanna. Private Hanna is today buried in Miraumont German Cemetery Mem. 6, Bucquoy. Given that Private Hanna is buried in a German cemetery it would appear he had been taken prisoner in a trench raid, injured and subsequently died of his wounds.[10]

A divisional exercise was held near Coisy on 16 October in which the 108 and 109 Brigades, the 1/3rd London RFA, 1/4th London RFA, Divisional units, the Cyclist Company and both the 108th and 109th Field Ambulances took part, it was not a success. Nor were the reports coming for the 4th Division with regard to 107 Brigade. This prompted General Nugent to write to his wife on 26 October:

> I am not too happy about the Ulster Division for it cannot be denied that some of them have very little discipline. The Belfast [107] Brigade is awful. They have absolutely no discipline and their officers are awful. I am very much disturbed about them. I don't think they are fit for service and I should be very sorry to have to trust them. Don't breathe one word of this to a living soul please. It is all due to putting a weak man in command of the brigade to start with and giving commissions to men of the wrong class.[11]

It was going to take some time to solve these disciplinary problems, although they would, like all units of the British Army, never be fully eradicated. On 18 October 107 Brigade left the trenches, having concluded its attachment to 4 and 48 Divisions. While there much experience had been gained and advice accepted. The brigade returned to its billeting area, their place being taken by 108 Brigade. Two days later the 1/1st and 1/2nd London RFA returned to their former billets in the division on completion of their attachment to 4 and 48 Divisions, their places being taken by 1st/3rd and 1st/4th.

With the continuing discipline problems within 107 Brigade General Nugent had no option but to replace Brigadier Couchman. His replacement was Brigadier W.M. Withycombe, CMG. William Maunder Withycombe was born on 8 May 1869, the son of the late William Withycombe of Gothelney, Charlinch, Somerset. In 1896 he married Cecil Mary, the daughter of the late Reverend F.C. Platts and they had one son. Withycombe was educated at Malvern College and entered the Army in 1888, being commissioned into the King's Own Yorkshire Light Infantry. He served in the South African War from 1899 to 1902, was twice mentioned in despatches and promoted to Brevet Major. He served for a time as superintendent of the Military Prison in Singapore.

The men of C Company of the 11th Rifles were attached to the 1st Battalion King's Own Royal Lancaster Regiment for familiarisation. On the night on 22 October 1915, they were in action against a dawn attack that was supported by a German artillery bombardment. During this action Private Andrew Marshall of No.11 Platoon was badly wounded in the hand and unable to use his rifle. He refused to be evacuated from the trench and throughout the action acted as a

---

10   Miraumont Cemetery has been incorporated into Queens Cemetery, Bucquoy.
11   PRONI D.3835/E/2/5/20A.

loader for those men on the firing step. Also on this day Private Samuel Hill, No.19557, serving in the 12th Rifles, was killed in action, the second death within the division that was not the result of an accident. However, accidents continued to occur and on an almost regular basis. The day prior to Private Hill's death Private Thomas Currie, from Derry Street, Belfast, serving in the 9th Rifles died of suffocation. The newspaper report gave no explanation of how this happened, but according to the battalion war diary, in October the men of the division were being trained in the use of the gas helmet. Private Currie left a widow and four young children. The local papers spell his name as Curry.

A letter from Major General E.M. Perceval, written to General Edmonds on 8 March 1925, in relation to the official history of the Great War states; "Before the first gas attack I don't think anyone realised what it would be like, and even long after the first gas attack our protective measures were very inadequate."

The division was inspected by The King, accompanied by President Poincaré and the Prince of Wales, on 25 October. As he drove by in his motor car elements of the division were drawn up on the side of the road near Beauval. In a letter home an officer of the Divisional Train told of the weather conditions:

> Winter has set in here. Our work goes on as usual; weather makes no difference. Supplies must go on. We know the gallant lads in the trenches are waiting for us. We sometimes have to dig out the leading wagon, but we always get there -- that is one comfort. Our boys are so willing and so cheery under all and every circumstance. We had a passing glance at the King when he went by in his motor. I wonder what he thought of us. We were muck to the eyes. Our cheer was none the less hearty – a good Ulster one.

The Allied Commanders; General Joffre, President Poincare, HM The King, General Foch and General Haig.

Private James McRoberts was on parade that day and recorded the event in his diary:

After dinner we were mustered and marched from the town, along the road to Amiens. The King was paying a visit to the troops in France and was passing that way, so we were turned out to do him honour. We stood two deep along one side of the road and waited there in the mist and damp. During the long wait here we pelted each other with frozen apples and Norman Paisley was heard to mutter, 'Now I realise why we are called the standing army!' Paisley was taken prisoner on the 1st July 1916 but he appeared to have had a fairly agreeable time working with a German farmer (After the war he was employed as an officer in H.M. Prison, Belfast). After two and a half hours, the first car with King George V and General Joffre passed; then came Poincaré and other cars followed. Poincaré was the President of the French Republic from 1913 to 1920. Our band played the royal salute and we, standing more or less in line, presented arms, afterwards hurrying back to our billets.

French General Joffre. "Now I realise why we are called the standing army!", Private Norman Paisley of the 14th Royal Irish Rifles was heard to mutter this remark, as they waited a long time for a visit by the King and General Joffre.

The war memorial at Castlebellingham. Some 816 men from County Louth died during the Great War.

The 14th Battalion war diary recorded that the battalion was ordered to march into trenches for instructional purposes under the 143 Infantry Brigade. This move was recorded in a letter home by Private Charles Connolly from Drogheda in County Louth:

> We get up at 5:30 am, and are in bed by 8:00 pm, when in billets. We halted for the night at one of the so called 'rest camps', some miles in rear of the firing line. We had a jolly time of it that night in the tent. We had been down to the village, and purchased some eatables from the Bucks canteen, and brought them up for supper. After getting in a supply of apples we set out for the much talked trenches. Naturally we were all bubbling over with curiosity to see what they were like. We almost crawled there in the darkness, and on the way reached a deserted village in ruins, not a house having escaped untouched. Our platoon was brought through endless communication trenches, the passage being very tiring owing to our slipping about in the mud and falling into holes. At length we reached a regular maze of trenches, following our guide like sheep. We were pushed into a dug-out, and being worn out just fell down and slept as we were. However we were knocked up to stand to arms just before daybreak. I was rather surprised to find that we were in the first line fire trench. We looked over the parapet one at a time and in the dull light could dimly discern the German lines at a short distance.

Two battalions of the 109 Brigade moved to Puchevillers en route for attachment to the 4th and 48th Divisions. At the same time 108 Brigade left the trenches on completion of the instruction. The 94th and 95th Trench Mortar Batteries joined the division.

Private James McRoberts and the 14th Rifles were in Gommecourt Wood and recorded the following in his diary for 28 October:

> I got into the working of the trenches. My experience of stand-to or the dawn mists the first morning in the trenches was somewhat of a shock. Very early, before daybreak, I had to tumble out of my bed just after I had apparently settled in. The fact that I was tired after yesterday's march did not matter in the least; this was a solemn rite in which everyone had to willingly participate. It was a wet day and they were very muddy in some parts. There were ration parties, water parties and dinner parties. The company cook house was in a ruined dwelling down in the village which is called Foncquevillers where our reserves were also stationed as well as those belonging to the Warwicks. Why the village was allowed by the Germans to exist and give shelter to our troops was a question discussed among us. It was often fired into by snipers and occasionally a shell would find its way there, but few casualties ever occurred. The Warwicks had a very neat cook house, on the right flank of our firing line, in a bomb proof dug-out, with a wide passage sloping out to the daylight. The rations came at night, right up to this entrance. Our own transport brought the stores to about one kilometre from the village, to which they were then conveyed by a fatigue party, who took the place of the mules and pulled the limbers to the Quartermaster's stores, which was situated amid the reserves in the village.

Private, later sergeant, Jim Maultsaid, also with the 14th Rifles, kept a diary and also recorded many scenes in a series of sketches. He well remembered his first breakfast in France; "It's wonderful how a drop of tea takes that low down sinking feeling from the pit of one's stomach. This was accompanied by bread that had been 'dipped in bacon fat' and made an excellent start to the day."[12]

---

12 *Cityweek*, 23 June 1966.

For the first two years of the war soldiers in the British Army received ten ounces of meat and eight ounces of vegetables per day. A combination of the size of the army coupled with the effects of the German U-boat blockade caused this to be cut to six ounces of meat per day by 1916. This was later reduced to a meal containing meat being issued on nine days per month and in 1917 the bread ration was also reduced. In theory a soldier was to receive 3,547 calories each day, although in reality a man serving in the front line required more, especially during the winter months. The rations for the men arrived each day, in theory, by the following manner. The Divisional Supply column went daily to the railhead with its trucks to meet the 'pack trains', bringing up the supplies to the refilling point. Here they were divided up into four groups, one per infantry brigade and one for the divisional troops, artillerymen, engineers etc. Then under the supervision of the Brigade Supply Officer, the supplies were loaded into horse drawn GS wagons and taken to the transport lines of the various units where they came under the care of the Quartermaster. Should the division be stationed on a very quiet part of the Front, where the railhead was far advanced, and the supply wagons would draw directly from the train, cutting out the Supply Column and saving both time and effort.

Hot food was a vital necessity for those men in the trenches. Rations were brought forward to the headquarters of the various battalions, usually after dark. Here it was heated, the actual cooking having been done at an earlier stage. Each battalion also had a stock pot and into this went ration biscuits soaked in stock, which was then put through a mincing machine and turned into cheese biscuits, sausage rolls and jam tarts. Dry rations such as tobacco, cigarettes, chocolate etc., were put into sandbags with the number of the specific section written on it. In the trenches hot food was a luxury rarely enjoyed. Cigarettes became very important to the men as time went by and eventually there were few non-smokers on the battlefield. At home a friend or family member could order from their local newsagent cigarettes directly from the factory. For the princely sum of 3/= (15p) a package of 280 Wills Wild Woodbine, or for 8/6= (42½ p) 500 Players Navy Cut. Should the cigarettes be sent for Christmas a card would be included and if they were for a man being held as a prisoner-of-war, the buyer could deduct 1/= (5p) as there was no postage on such packets.

On the morning of 30 October 1915, the *Belfast News Letter* reported that:

> Private Hugh Patton, 12th Battalion Royal Irish Rifle (Central Antrim Volunteers), is a son of Mrs. Patton, Bushmills. Mrs. Patton has received the following communication: – "I have just been talking to your son, Private Hugh Patton, who has been slightly wounded. I am pleased to tell you his wound is not serious. He is unable to write at present, but there is no need for undue anxiety, as he is cheerful. Do not write at present to him here, as he will be sent further back. – Yours sincerely, W.H. Jeffers, chaplain. Private Patton, before enlisting, was an assistant gardener in Dundarave, and was one of the first to join from the North Antrim Regiment (Ulster Volunteer Force).

Such detail referring to individual members of the division was soon to disappear as the rate of casualties increased beyond imagination. At the end of October an officer from the Divisional Train had once again put pen to paper;

> Here we are, somewhere in La Belle France, quartered in barns, stables, and other buildings, and boon companions of flying and creeping things. The men are very willing and cheery under every circumstance. I am very proud of them. We have been in touch with the enemy, and a few casualties have taken place, but nothing serious. Some of our men were under shell fire and machine gun fire on the roads. The French people are very nice with us.

Men of A and B
Companies Central
Antrim Volunteers, later
the 12th Royal Irish Rifles
at Clandeboye Camp.

The officer goes on to say that only old men and young and old women are to be seen, all the men of military age are in the trenches or undergoing training. He concludes his, rather long, letter with scathing comments on those single young fellows who remain at home and let married men fight for them.

The 121 Field Company Royal Engineers moved to the 4th Division for instruction at the beginning of November. In an issue of the *Bangor Spectator* a letter was published from three members of the Transport Section of the 13th Rifles. In it they thanked the people of Bangor for the parcels and copies of the newspaper, which were received on a weekly basis. The letter was signed by Privates O'Neill, Crozier and Beattie. William Crozier, from Castle Cottages, Bangor, had worked for Lady Clanmorris as a gardener at Bangor Castle for the last twelve years. He had enlisted in 1915 and would survive the Somme, despite being wounded on 1 July. His brother served in the 16th Battalion as a sergeant. On 19 May 1917, Private William Crozier, No.6025, would be killed in action and buried in Kemmel Chateau Military Cemetery.

On 2 November 1915, 107 Brigade was officially transferred to the 4th Division, a decision made by the War Office in that all New Army Divisions were to contain one regular brigade. Nugent explained the situation to his wife:

> The Ulster Division is being broken up I am sorry to say. That is to say we are to lose 1 Brigade of Ulster men and get another Brigade in its place of regulars. This is to happen to all the New Divisions I understand. I am very sorry and I am afraid it will cause a great feeling of disappointment and will I fear have a bad effect on recruiting in Ulster. I hope it may only be for a while and that later on the 3 Ulster Brigades will be under one roof again. It is in many ways a good idea no doubt as the new battalions will have a better opportunity of picking up useful knowledge when they have regular battalions alongside of them.[13]

Given the poor performance of the 107 Brigade there was no difficulty for Nugent in selecting which brigade was to go. He made it very clear to the officers of the brigade that this transfer, assumed to be permanent, was to be seen as a punishment. Something well understood by Lieutenant Colonel Crozier of the 9th Rifles, who by his own admission accepted that within

---

13   PRONI D.3835/E/2?5/17, dated 23 October 1915.

the 107 Brigade discipline was poor. Alcohol seemed to have been a major factor in most cases, although Crozier, being a reformed alcoholic, may have been slightly biased. Crozier stated that:

> A number of senior NCOs in the 9th Rifles became 'dead drunk' and it so happened that other unfortunate 'accidents', such as minor looting, took place in other battalions of the brigade at about the same time, with the result that Major General Oliver Nugent, the newly appointed divisional commander, begins to think one of his brigades is an undisciplined mob! General Nugent, taking the bull by the horns, assembles all the officers of our brigade in a village schoolroom where he delivers a strafe, not wholly deserved but very good for us, which I shall always treasure in my mind as the complete example of what can be said by the powerful to the powerless in the shortest space of time possible, consistent with the regulations of words and space for breathing, in the most offensive, sarcastic and uncompromising manner possible. At last the sentence is pronounced! Banishment to the 4th Division.

The above is in stark contrast to remarks written by Cyril Falls in his history of the 36th Division:

> One of the Brigadiers of the 4th Division said of them: 'the men are extraordinarily quiet, and I thought at first somewhat subdued, and put it down to the big marches they had had. But when I came to talk to them I found they were like new schoolboys, taking in everything, deadly keen, and only afraid of one thing – letting down their unit in any way. I have never seen any men with such quiet confidence in themselves, in spite of their efforts to hide it.

The 107 Brigade, two Sections of the Signal Company and the 94th Trench Mortar Battery were sent to the 4th Division on 3 November, for a period of two months, in exchange for 12 Brigade. Half the brigade moved on this date, the remainder the following day. As a result of this the 36th Division was to give up a brigade in exchange for one from the 4th Division. On 4 November, General Withycombe once again led his Brigade out of the divisional area for pastures new. Along with the brigade went its Light Trench Mortar Battery, recently arrived from England and the 110th Field Ambulance. Three days later 12 Brigade arrived from the 49th Division as its replacement. Officers from the 4th Division trained the men of the 36th in bombing tactics and techniques and had this to say; "The national sport of Ulstermen, the throwing of kidney stones in street riots, was admirable preparation for bombing."

They little realised that English cities would have their share of riots in the years to come with the introduction of conscription. There was also training against gas attacks. The gas helmets of this time were uncomfortable at best and while it was possible for the men to gain experience by passing through a gas chamber, the marching and 'double timing' ordered by some instructors added nothing to training, except to make some men violently ill. This arrangement lasted for only a month before being rescinded. It was felt that any advantage gained regarding experience was nullified by the loss of unit cohesion and the subsequent drop in morale. However, it was some three months before the 107 Brigade managed to return to the division. A letter from an unknown Lurgan soldier to his family:

> I hear accounts from Ulster that the Ulster Division had been 'cut up'. All is well with the Ulster Division. Two brigades went into the trenches during the past week. They have had a taste of fire, but no casualties to signify. One of the 9th R.I.F., Wilson of Union Street, Lurgan, is reported to have had his hand injured. I have just got Saturday's English papers, and read with horror of the butchery of Miss Cavell. When our Tommies read that, I say "God help the Huns!" Meanwhile every loyal man will 'do his bit', as will every loyal woman.

But, we shall return, many of us, to the old standard. To those who must stay at home, I say, "Be faithful unto death". Victory out here must be won, even to the shedding of the last drop of blood. The country will respond to the call of its King as it ought, or be delegated to a place in the history of nations as unworthy of the name it is supposed to have honourably born.[14]

The reference to Miss Cavell, concerned the execution of Nurse Edith Cavell by the Germans on a charge of treason. The 11th and 14th Rifles moved to St. Leger and Halloy on 6 November respectively to join 12 Brigade for training. With the cold weather food seemed to be on most men's minds. Private Duncan Davidson serving in A Company of the 14th Rifles wrote to his sister Teenie; "I received your parcel this morning, many thanks for all the good things you sent, everything was in good condition, bar the soda bread, the meat had gone bad so it affected the bread as well, hard lines as I was looking forward to having some for my tea, when sending again, don't put anything with the bread.

Sergeant William Henderson, 13th Royal Irish Rifles, who died of wounds on 25 August 1917, aged 54 years. He had a total of thirty-seven years of service and did garrison duty in the Zulu War. He came from Warkworth Street, Belfast. Buried in Rocquigny-Equancourt Road British Cemetery, Manancourt. (Courtesy of Nigel Henderson)

Sergeant Henderson's Headstone.

---

14   *Belfast News Letter* 2 November 1915, abridged.

The men of the Ulster Division listened to advice from those in 12 Brigade and in turn shared some of their own knowledge. On being told by an English corporal that a man had not experienced a battle until he had faced the Imperial German Army, a mature sergeant from Belfast replied; "You have not experienced a battle until you have faced the mighty Zulu!"

It was not only 107 Brigade that was suffering from incompetent officers. Private James McRoberts of the 14th Rifles recalled these early days in France in his diary from 8 to 13 November while at Pernois:

> We had two brigade field days also a good deal of battalion company and platoon drill. Once again we were under the control of our officers who were nearly all ignorant, conservative and bullying, to an intolerable degree. Captain Slacke was intoxicated for most of the time we were in the line. In the trenches we rarely saw even one of them. Not one was ever seen in our dug-out, not one was ever observed giving a direction of any kind, and their voices were never heard. Our lieutenant was scarcely more visible during our stay in the trenches. He never came round to see how we fared for food, he never visited our dug-outs and our rifles weren't even inspected once. But when in quarters where we had every opportunity of taking care of our equipment, then we were plagued with rifle, kit and billet inspections.[15]

Lance Corporal John Kennedy Hope, a man who wielded a pen like a rapier, had similar memories of those early days in the trenches:

> I tell very little of the nights when the sentry stood shivering on the steps for hours watching the sandbags grow a beard of frost or watching the barbed wire moving about. I tell not my thoughts as I stand on sentry and know that our fearful gas is creeping over a quick German line and carrying death to hundreds of terror stricken Huns. I tell not what I thought when ordered to present arms to a D.M.S. as he passed my post in the front line, an unheard of thing but nevertheless truth. I tell not what I thought when pulled out of a cavity in the trench, where I was sleeping, by our officious colonel and ordered to take a piece of four by two inch flannel out of the muzzle of my rifle as it might ruin the barrel. Ex-Service is one thing. Ex the trenches is the man who counts. The man who holds the front line. The man in constant danger of being blown out of the trenches or pinched by the scruff of the neck in a raid or unceremoniously shot dead.[16]

The failure to carry out regular foot inspections, especially during wet weather, could have catastrophic consequences. Trench foot, an infection that had first been noted in the army of Napoleon, is caused by prolonged immersion in water. The feet initially become numb, then swell turning red or blue. As the condition worsens the feet develop blisters and open sores which become infected and can develop into gangrene. If left untreated amputation is required, however if promptly treated complete recovery is possible, although there is severe short term pain as feeling returns to the feet. It rarely occurred in the British Army during the Second World War, but there were many cases among American troops fighting in Italy during the winter of 1943 to 1944. It was again prevalent with American troops in the Vietnam War and with the British during the Falklands War in 1982. Cases were also reported during the Glastonbury Festival of 2007. Foot care was an important part of daily trench routine. Special grease was issued, as was whale oil and some men used their rum

---

15   Truesdale, David (ed), *Young Citizen Old Soldier, The Diary of Private James McRoberts*, (Solihull: Helion & Company, 2012).
16   Moore, Steven, *The Irish on the Somme*, (Belfast: Local Press Ltd, 2005).

ration. It was the drill that each man was to rub the feet of his 'next number' once a day and it was the responsibility of officers to see that this was done. Keeping socks dry was almost impossible and drying them in the trenches equally so. Therefore wet socks were sent to the rear with the ration parties, dried during the day and brought forward the following night.

DADOS officers visited the various field ambulances on 12 November to collect small arms ammunition that had been recovered from casualties. Once inspected this was reissued to the battalions in the line. There was also a rush in supplying all units with winter clothing, with pressing requests for waterproof boots from those battalions in the trenches and DADOS sent urgent telegrams to base. Gloves were purchased locally in Amiens, as were lamps. You seemed to be able to purchase most things in Amiens. The artillery batteries reported a shortage of nosebags, DADOS ordered 2,000, but only 100 were received, they also requested that damaged nosebags be returned for repair! The winter weather appeared to have caught the army by surprise. The DADOS lorries went hither and thither delivering such things as capes Mackintosh, vests woollen and rugs horse. Keeping an army in the field was more than just rations and ammunition.

From 14 to 18 November the 107 Brigade was in the 4th Divisional Reserve, while brigade head-quarters of the 108 Brigade and the 9th Irish Fusiliers left for the 4th Division on 15 November for an additional course of instruction in the trenches. Accompanying them went two platoons of the Cyclist Company for three days of instruction. With the Fusiliers went Second Lieutenant Sam Wallace, whose youthful looks were doing him no favours at all when he had another run in with a senior officer:

> On arrival with the battalion, I, along with two others, was posted to C Company. The CO interviewed the three of us and asked who the senior officer was? When I admitted it was me and I was twenty he replied, 'My God, its men I need to lead my men, not boys. He went on to say he did not like the look of me and if I did not improve he would send me home. On the way out I said to the others that I don't think we need to unpack. I was given No.10 Platoon consisting of sixty men, but when you took the cooks and others out I have about fifty. There were four platoons in the Company and four Companies in the Battalion.

Colonel Hessey of 109 Brigade, in a correspondence with Mr WC Trimble, observed:

> The men are all very well and cheery and have now arrived at our second billets. I told all our men at Bramshott that we must never forget for a moment that a great volume of prayer goes up each day for us in Ulster and many other places, and it is, I am sure, a very great support to know that we are being prayed for in so many homes throughout the land. May we prove worthy of the trust that is placed in us when the hour of trail come.[17]

On 17 November 1915, the division was attached to the new XIII Corps, under the command of Lieutenant General Walter Congreve, VC.

> The 14th Rifles began to suffer their run of bad luck regarding officers when Major J.E. Gunning was injured in a fall from his horse on 1 December, resulting in his evacuation to hospital in England. While many newly commissioned officers in the division found them-selves on a horse for the first time at either Clandeboye, Finner or Ballykinlar, in the case of Major Gunning nature seems to have played its part. The major was riding to rejoin the battalion when his horse slipped in the wet ground and fell heavily before Gunning could

---

17 *Belfast News Letter* 11 November 1915.

take his foot from the stirrups and resulted in a broken leg. This was a severe break and he was sent to London when he was treated at the Campbell Hospital, Cambridge Square, London.

Despite only being in France for just over a month there was an indication that some of the men were becoming less than enthusiastic. Private Duncan Davidson of the 14th Rifles, who seemed to be a prolific letter writer, wrote to his sister Teenie on 20 November; "You often wonder what it will be like when we get back, well I expect it will just be the same as ever, but fonder of home, it will take more than King and country, to make us list again, no more soldering after this job is finished."

Duncan's disillusionment had not improved the following month. On 18 December he wrote to Teenie regarding his brother Norman who was serving with the 2nd Rifles and had been wounded in the leg:

I am delighted to see poor old Norman got home to England, I knew he would, I am glad he got to a good hospital and that he is having a good time, you may be sure, as he is fit, he will get his leave home, now Teenie, if you can prevent him, don't let him come out here again, if he goes the right way about it, he could manage it, I consider Norman has done his share, he could get a post about the barracks or on one of the new Battalions forming, advise him from me to do it.

Duncan did not give up and on 24 December 1915 observed:

I see Norman is still in hospital, if he is wise, he will stop there as long as he can, I supposed he exercised his leg to make the wound break out again, it is an old trick, when you think you are recovering so rapidly, tell him from me, not to come out here again, he can manage it quite easily, when he reports at the barracks at home, he can swear his leg still troubles him, they will have to take his word for it, he can get a soft job about the barracks, or go into the band again, he can manage it somehow, he has done his bit. Don't let him come out again.

A trench at Beaumont Hamel photographed after the war and 'decorated' by the photographer.

The 15th Rifles were positioned close to Beaumont Hamel on 21 November and were at that time part of 11 Brigade of the 4th Division. That night on being told that two wounded men were lying out in no-man's land Company Sergeant Major William Douglas Magookin, from York Street Mill, Belfast, along with Second Lieutenant Henry de la Maziere Harpur, went out to attempt a rescue. After making their way across some three hundred and fifty yards of open ground they found the wounded soldiers lying within twenty yards of a German listening post. Picking up one of the injured men, Private Thomas Williamson from Hazelnut Street, they began to make their way back when they were spotted and came under fire from both rifles and machine guns. Despite this the rescue was successful and the wounded man was delivered to the casualty clearing station. Sadly Private Williamson died a short time later, his wounds being too severe. They were unable to return for the second man. For their efforts Magookin was awarded the Distinguished Conduct Medal, while Lieutenant Harpur was awarded the Military Cross, the first such awards made to the division.[18] Sergeant Major Magookin had previously been a company commander in the 3rd Battalion North Belfast Regiment, UVF, and had served with the Royal Engineers in the South African War. Three of his brothers were also on active service, Alexander with the Royal Flying Corps, Daniel with the RAMC and David with the Royal Engineers, both in the Ulster Division. Magookin would later be commissioned as a Second Lieutenant. While receiving a commission was deemed a great honour for a Warrant Officer, it did produce an element of hardship. The pay of a Second Lieutenant was less than a Warrant Officer and there was the added expense of uniform, mess bills etc.

Just over a mile away on the left flank the 150 Field Company came under shell fire and Sapper Alexander McKee was killed while working in a trench. Originally from Richhill, County Armagh, Sapper McKee, was a former member of the 1st Richhill Company, Boys Brigade, and a member of Richhill LOL No.111, had travelled from the United States the previous spring to enlist, he was 20 years old.

General Nugent related to the Ulster newspapers:

> On behalf of Ulstermen in the field, I beg you will tell our Ulstermen at home that we are counting on them to keep us up to our numbers in trained men. We must not let it be said of us that we failed in the undertaking that we took on ourselves to give an Ulster Division for service of the King. Drafts are being sent out from the reserve battalions to the Division as occasion arises, and it is the duty and privilege of Ulstermen to see that these battalions are maintained at full strength. Recruits are required for the 20th Reserve Battalion Royal Irish Rifles, now being formed at Ballykinlar by Lieutenant Colonel T.V.P. McCammon, and it is hoped that its ranks will speedily be filled. Colonel Thomas Valentine Plaisted McCammon died of wound on 24 April 1917; he had been serving with the 5th Rifles at Monchy.

The 121 and 150 Field Companies returned to the division on 26 November from operating with the Third Army. They immediately began to assist and supervise the infantry in preparing rear area billets in the various villages to accommodate the troops that would take part in the forthcoming offensive. Repairs were carried out when necessary and their own sawmill provided the lumber to build thousands of bunks, benches and tables. At the same time horse lines with standings of chalk and stone were constructed.

The Headquarters Royal Artillery Ulster Division landed at Le Havre at approximately 11am on 27 November and entrained for Pont Remy. The following day the remainder of the Artillery began detraining at Pont Remy. Headquarters was located at Francieres, while the Divisional

---

18   *Belfast News Letter* 24 December 1915.

Memorial to Thomas Valentine Plaisted McCammon.

Ammunition Column went to Villers-sur-Ailly. 153 Brigade was at Lone and Loneuet, 154 Brigade was to be at Cocquerel, but had not yet arrived. The 172 Brigade was at Bouchon and Lone, while 173 Brigade was at Vauchelle and Mouflert. The accommodation at Vauchelle was considered to be very bad. By 30 November the Artillery was complete in all units, with the exception of 154 Howitzer Brigade, which was marooned in mid Channel due to engine failure on the ship carrying it across.

Second Lieutenant Stanley Hunter, 8th Rifles was wounded and taken prisoner during a trench raid by the Germans on 28 November and sent to the prison camp at Mainz, a fact not confirmed until the end of December.

By now the Vickers machine-guns and their crews had been withdrawn from the battalions and formed into 108th and 109th Machine gun Companies; with 107th being formed a short time later. An example of this can be seen from an extract fro the war diary of the 14th Rifles. On 22 January 1916, Lieutenant Clokey and Second Lieutenant Wedgewood were transferred to the 109 Brigade Machine-gun Company. Accompanying them were two sergeants, one corporal, two lance corporals, twenty-six men and four machine guns. The Vickers would be replaced at battalion level by the Lewis gun, 16 initially being issued per battalion, although by 1918 this had increased to 36. The Lewis gun was a shoulder fired air-cooled light machine gun fitted with a bipod and capable of firing 550 rounds per minute. It weighed 26 pounds and was fed from a circular magazine containing 47 or 97 rounds. The Lewis had a rate of fire that was most effective when delivered in short bursts. While the weapon could be used by one man, it was more effective when issued to a crew of two, with the second man carrying an adequate supply of

Men of the Machine Gun Corps. It was this absolute foolproof reliability which endeared the Vickers to every British soldier who ever fired one. The .455 Webley revolver seems to have been the preferred sidearm of the machine gunners.

ammunition. It was even more effective when other men in the platoon were also detailed to carry extra ammunition.

The Divisional Ammunition Column was moved to new billets at L'Etoile on 2 December, this was due to a shortage of fresh water at Villers-sur-Ailly, while arrangements were made for the construction of winter horse standings. It was important that the horses were kept fit and well, they were still the main source of motive power on the Western Front.

At home the Belfast papers printed a report concerning prisoners taken by the Germans. A Mrs Shillington of Glenmachan Towers, Strandtown, Belfast, received a telegram informing her that a notice board had been found on the Western Front conveying the information that her husband Lieutenant T. Shillington, 8th Rifles, was a prisoner in the hands of the Saxons. The notice went on to say he was in good health. Lieutenant Shillington had earlier been reported as 'wounded and missing' after he had led five other ranks out on a reconnaissance patrol on the night of 19 November. Previously Colonel Chute, DSO, had written to the Mrs. Shillington:

> Good and plucky gentleman that he was, he took all risks and went ahead on his own, leaving the remainder of his party behind. Apparently he thought all was clear, and returned some way till he found his patrol, and motioned them to come on. Almost at once rapid fire was opened, and your gallant husband fell forward. Being outnumbered the patrol was obliged to return to the trenches, when a search party was immediately sent out, and went over the same ground without being able to find any trace of Lieutenant Shillington and they surmised he was taken prisoner.[19]

---

19   *Belfast News Letter* 1 December 1915.

Whilst this news was to a degree comforting to Mrs. Shillington, other news brought tragic results. The death from wounds of Private Thomas Williamson of the 15th Rifles was conveyed to his mother at Hazelnut Street, Belfast, who a short time earlier had been informed he was seriously injured and in hospital in France. Mrs. Williamson, already in poor health, died on receiving the second telegram. Thomas was 19 years old.

In 4th Division, 107 Brigade relieved 10 Brigade in the trenches. Owing to the very wet state of the ground all battalions had a difficult time in moving into position, with several men having to be dug out of the mud. In the 15th Rifles Lieutenant Colonel Ford-Hutchinson was replaced by Colonel F.L. Gordon on 2 December 1915. According to the Army List Ford-Hutchinson held no further military command and may have been forcibly retired or dismissed due to incompetence.[20] However, his cousin, Lieutenant Stewart-Moore, then serving with the 13th Rifles, was of the opinion that he had been "…sent home because he was not sufficiently robust."

Ford-Hutchinson had seen active service in the Sudan and South Africa … and subsequently he had commanded the Connaught Rangers in India. It must have been a sad blow to him when he was adjudged too old at fifty.[21] Even a brief study of the actions in which Ford-Hutchinson had fought prior to the Great War would explain him being more worn out than incompetent, the extreme heat of the Sudan, the disease of South Africa and the prolonged wet seasons in India, all taking their toil. His replacement was Lieutenant Colonel Francis Lewis Rawson Gordon DSO; he came from a Sussex family and had been educated at Hailebury College prior to being commissioned into the 2nd Battalion Gordon Highlanders and later serving in the South African War. His father was Lieutenant Colonel F.F. Gordon of the Royal Irish Rifles. Gordon was a former member of the UVF and for a time had commanded the Special Service Force of the North Belfast Regiment. On the formation of the Ulster Division he had been commissioned into the 15th Rifles, being appointed as second-in-command in July 1915.

Over the following two days the remainder of the artillery detrained at Pont Remy and was now complete. Initial employment of the artillery was both clumsy and extravagant. The howitzer brigade was invariably split between groups and its commander func-

Lieutenant John Stewart-Moore, 13th Royal Irish Rifles.

tioned as an administrator, but not as a combatant, the system was to be modified later. The guns were dug in to pits, hidden as well as possible among trees or houses, or if in the open camouflaged to match the immediate surroundings.[22] The dug-outs of the detachments were close at hand as

20 Bowman, *Irish Regiments in the Great War.*
21 Stewart-Moore papers, National Army Museum.
22 Falls, Cyril, *The History of the 36th (Ulster) Division* London (1922).

were pits containing the ammunition, between two and four hundred rounds per gun. At dusk the guns were laid on night lines, each one set to fire on a certain target or area in accordance with a previously arranged plan. Within seconds of receiving a telephone call or an SOS rocket all the guns could open fire. To improve efficiency an Artillery Liaison officer was attached to each battalion in the trenches.

In the 4th Division, 107 Brigade was having a rough time due to rain and mud, with communication trenches virtually impassable. Despite this their bombing patrols were very active and there was little retaliation by the Germans.

Within 108 Brigade it was evident that Brigadier Hacket Pain was neither physically nor mentally fit for service in the field, nor did General Nugent rate him highly as a field commander.[23] On 4 December 1915, Brigadier General C.R.J. Griffith CMG DSO, formerly of the 1st Battalion, Bedfordshire Regiment, took command of the brigade. Charles Richard Jebb Griffith was born 4 October 1867 at Castlerea, County Roscommon, the son of Colonel Richard and Frances Griffith. After education at Clifton College, Oundle, he entered the Royal Military College at Sandhurst as a Gentleman Cadet, and was commissioned as a second lieutenant in the Bedfordshire Regiment on 14 September 1887. Spending his early career in the 2nd Battalion, Charles became a Captain on 3 June 1895, in addition to serving as the Adjutant between 16 December 1895 and 5 December 1902. As a captain, Griffith had fought in the South African War, specifically during the Orange River operation, the action at Wittebergen, the Cape Colony operations, and at Colesberg. He was mentioned in despatches on 10 September 1901, and awarded the DSO (gazetted 27 September 1901) in addition to his campaign medals with two clasps. In April 1906, he was promoted to Major, becoming Lieutenant Colonel of the 1st Battalion in October 1913. He took the battalion to the Western Front in August the following year, landing in the first wave of the original British Expeditionary Force and fighting in every single early engagement from Mons onwards. After a remarkably charmed life usually leading his Battalion from the front, Lieutenant Colonel Griffith became commander of 108 Infantry Brigade of the Ulster Division.

On 7 December 1915, on the far side of the world a British Army became besieged at the town of Kut Al Amara 100 miles south of Baghdad in Mesopotamia. While the men on the Western Front suffered cold and wet, in Kut it was heat, and thirst. They would surrender to the Turks on 29 April 1916.

The 107 Brigade was relieved in the trenches by 10 Brigade on 8 December. For the next five days they were in the divisional reserve and had to supply numerous working parties on a daily basis to work on the 2nd Division's line. The London Artillery spends the following three days entraining at Pont Remy to join the 38th Division to the north.

In mid-December the 95th, 82nd and 104th Trench Mortar Batteries left the division for the 4th, 48th and 37th Divisions respectively. In the 9th Rifles a new Adjutant was appointed on 14 December, Lieutenant E.E. Hind, who came from the East Lancashire Regiment. The 107th Machine-gun Company, which had been formed at Forceville, joined the division on 18 December under the command of Captain Woodgate, formerly of the East Lancashire Regiment, and moved into the line for the first time. On the same day a football match was played between the 14th Rifles and the 10th Inniskillings, the Inniskilling winning by two goals to one. Those who played well for the 14th Rifles were Mitchell, an ex-Barnsley half-back, McKee (Captain), former Cliftonville centre-forward and J Canning, a Distillery goal-keeper.[24]

In the artillery there were constant inspections of billets, horse standings and horse lines to ensure that both horses and men were being properly catered for. There were also tactical schemes

---

23   Perry, Nicholas, *Major General Oliver Nugent and the Ulster Division 1915-1918*, (2007).
24   *Belfast News Letter* 28 December 1918.

YCV football team with two members in YCV uniform.

in taking up battery positions and officers took part in staff rides to rehearse reconnoitring the ground.

December was a wicked month regarding the elements and many men suffered badly from the cold, some quite seriously. In the 8th Rifle Major G.E. McColl was sent home to Bloomfield in Belfast suffering from frostbite. A former member of the 6th (East Belfast) Regiment of the UVF, he had been commissioned in September 1914, being quickly promoted. A letter appeared in the *Bangor Spectator* on 24 December 1915, from the Reverend James Quinn, Rector of St. Michael's, Shankill Road, Belfast, and then serving as a Chaplain with the division. In a letter to the parents of Private Philemy, who had died of wounds, the Reverend stated; "Poor boy, he suffered a great deal and his death must have been a happy release. One could hardly die a nobler death."

Hopefully the Reverend Quinn wrote few letters like that. It was not only in France that the battalions were suffering casualties. On this date Sergeant McCarter was found lying unconscious at the head of No.3 Platform in the Great Northern Railway in Belfast. He had been travelling from the camp at Clandeboye to his home in Lisburn. The sergeant was originally from Derry and was an ex member of the UVF, and Blaris Loyal Orange Order. It was believed he had fallen from the platform; he never recovered and left a widow and nine children.[25]

James McRoberts recorded the following in his diary:

> Christmas Day in France and of course we had no parades. A prize was offered to the billet which was most tastefully decorated for the festive season and we made a noble attempt to win it in our room. With holly and evergreens, postcards and Xmas cards, our rifles and bayonets, we produced a brave and gallant show which just missed the prize by a narrow margin. For dinner we had a multitude of good things, roast fowl and meat, vegetables and potatoes with

---

25   *Bangor Spectator* 24 December 1915.

some excellent Army duff to finish off. After dinner we were engaged in an inter-platoon soccer match in which, somehow, I managed to score a goal. The evening I spent in the billet of Number 4 Section, where there were two pretty children, young girls of about eleven and twelve. At this age the girls seemed to look their best for here they were, sturdy and round of limb with pleasant faces and charming, easy manners and deportment. And they were such hard, willing little workers they touched one's heart.

While there may well have been excellent rations to celebrate Christmas, at other times the food left much to be desired both in quality and quantity. Once again Private Duncan Davidson of the 14th Rifles told it as he found it:

Well Teenie we got Xmas and the New Year over quiet, we did not know any difference, we had a better dinner that was all, if it hadn't been for the parcels we received, we would have had a poor time, these accounts in the papers of the times we have, are all rot, if I was home, I could let you know, what it is like out here, at the present time we are subscribing one franc (10d) per man, per month, to help buy us better food, what do you think of that, we can get nothing, the tunic I am wearing at present is done, I have it since I joined the army, I cannot get a new one. Then they tell

On the left James McRoberts, former 14th Royal Irish Rifles at the Armagh City war memorial with his friend Richard Bennett, Royal Irish Fusiliers. Both men were ex-YCV and members of the local Methodist Church. A rare occasion when James McRoberts allowed the right side of his scarred face to be photographed. (Courtesy of the McRoberts Family)

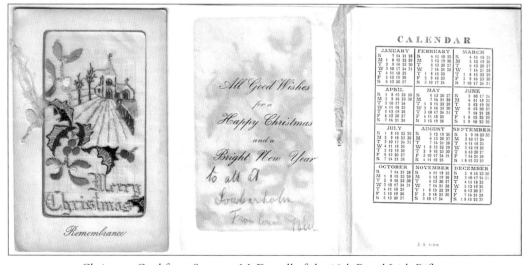

Christmas Card from Sergeant McDowell of the 12th Royal Irish Rifles.

An official 'On Active Service' envelope addressed to Mrs J McCombe, 36 Coolberg Street, Belfast. Private William Thomas McCombe, 10th Royal Irish Rifles and aged 17 years, died on 22 December 1915.

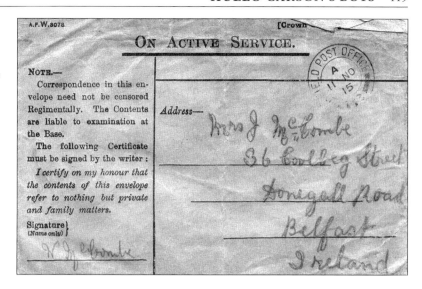

This was the Christmas card sent from Seapatrick Parish church to all the parishioners who were at the front during the Great War. (Courtesy of Seapatrick Parish Church via Peter Morton)

A Christmas card produced for the Ulster Division, the same card was used by other divisions with different wording.

the folks at home, we are treated like little Gods, all a lot of lies. It is no picnic out here. I give you my word, but I intend to stick it out."

The Reverend James Quinn wrote to Mrs Lemon of Combermere Street in South Belfast. He seems to have been a plain spoken man:

I am sorry to be the bearer of bad news, although possibly you will have heard before this reaches you. Your husband Private Samuel Lemon, No.15016, was out on duty with his officer Captain Griffith, in the early morning of the 14th. Captain Griffith, I understand, was doing some observation work in front of the front line of trenches. He was hit by a sniper and rather badly wounded, and your husband, so it would seem, went to attend to him, and I suppose to bandage him, when your husband was also hit, and I regret to say the wound proved fatal. How long he survived I have not yet been able to ascertain, or whether death was instantaneous. I feel for you greatly, as does every officer and man in his battalion. His loss will be a terrible blow to you. May God in his Mercy, comfort and sustain you, and give you grace to bear. Your husband died a noble death. He has given himself for his Country and in defence of what is right. If in the end we are victorious, and we shall be, it will be to him, and others like him, we shall owe the victory. It is a grand legacy to have left behind. If the report brought to me today by the burial party is correct, your husband would almost certainly have been decorated for gallantry in the field if he had survived. We buried him this afternoon in a little cemetery close behind the trenches.

While this letter would appear to be comforting, you must question the doubt raised regarding Private Lemon's death, instant or lingering? The newspaper report, from which this letter is taken, quotes a wrong service number, it was 15106, Private Lemon served in the 10th Rifles. The Captain Griffith mentioned above is E.W.C. Griffith, from Foster's Hill Road in Bedfordshire, he was sent home to recuperate.

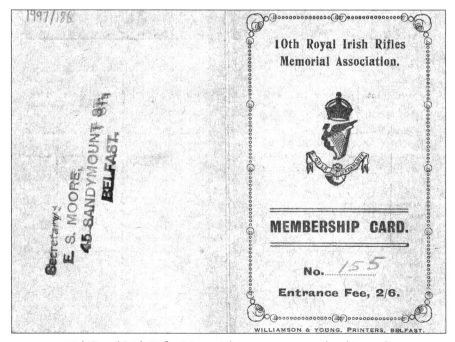

10th Royal Irish Rifles Memorial Association, membership card.

The 10th Royal Irish Rifles – in the centre seated is Sergeant George Johnston. The man seated front right wears the ribbon of the Military Medal. The man to the rear, third from the left has three wound stripes on the sleeve of his tunic.

Murals to the Division abound in Northern Ireland, while many are colourful, not all are accurate.

"The 16th Rifles had nothing much to do. So they had them build a railway from Candas to Acheux."[26]

On 26 December 1915, the 16th Rifles (Pioneers), were placed under the command of the Chief Engineer of the Third Army and are ordered to construct a broad gauge railway between Candas and Acheux. With the upcoming Somme battle there was a need for large quantities of stores, ammunition and rations. Therefore it was decided to establish a railhead close to the front line and it was proposed that this should be in the vicinity of Acheux with a station in Acheux and extensive sidings located at Belle Eglise, some two miles to the east. Acheux was approximately five and a half miles north-west of Albert and about the same distance from the front line. The line supplying the railhead was to be connected to the main Amiens-Doullens line at Candas.

The line was to be built from scratch, with officers from the battalion surveying the route and this task fell to Second Lieutenants Unwin and Slater. Given the weight the trains would pull and the soft nature of the ground, it was necessary for the line to run along the hill contours as opposed to crossing them. As the crow flies the distance between Candas and Acheux was thirteen miles, however to keep the line as flat as possible just under seventeen miles of track was to be laid.

On the morning of 29 December work on the line began at Candas with both track being laid and buildings for the new terminus being constructed. The Adjutant, Captain W.J. Allen, assisted by Captain Jewell, supervised the engineering work, while Second Lieutenant Browne was tasked with building all necessary level-crossings. Plate-laying was overseen by Captain Platt, while Captain Chase saw to ballasting, jacking and straightening. This was a major operation, not only was track to be laid, but cuttings and embankments provided, many of which were of some length. To do this required not only the men of the 16th Rifles, but outside assistance to help with the general labouring. It therefore fell to infantry battalions to supply such labour and the 9th Inniskillings, 4th South Lancashire Regiment, 4th King's Own Regiment, Seaforth Highlanders, Argyll and Sutherland Highlanders, Devonshire Regiment and 12th Rifles all supplied working parties of various sizes and for various periods. Work continued on an almost 24-hour basis, with the unloading of supply trains frequently being carried out during the hours of darkness. By 1 January 1916, the track was being laid at a rate of 1,100 yards per day, which included the claying of sidings. An example of the speed in which the railway was being constructed is shown by the following story:

> An elderly French farmer one day came upon, in one of his fields, a hole which had been dug for survey purposes. Enraged, he went off to seek retribution for this damage. Returning a few days later he found not the hole, but a brand new railway laid through his land. His comments were doubtless unprintable, even in French.[27]

A record was set in early January when some 5,000 feet of track was laid in one day. However, such a rate could not be sustained and eventually something serious was bound to occur. On 21 January the work train was reversing towards Candas when a wagon jumped the rails on a part of the track that had not been ballasted, resulting in a total of three wagons being smashed. The war diary reported that two men were killed and twelve injured. The fatal casualties came from units other than the 16th Rifles, who did suffer seven injured. All the casualties were treated by Lieutenant Dickson, the medical officer, who arrived almost immediately. A fleet of ambulances conveyed the injured to hospital, while a note in the war diary states that General Allenby "... gave

---

26   White, Stuart N., *The Terrors: 16th (Pioneer) Battalion, Royal Irish Rifles*, (Belfast: Somme Association, 1996).
27   Ibid., p. 71.

great personal assistance after the smash." Sadly no other details are given. In a letter to his wife, General Nugent wrote; "Allenby is here and no one is particularly rejoiced I can assure you."[28]

Some of those working on the railway that day probably were. As the line progressed a working party uncovered a cache of Roman coins dating from the reign of Caesar Augustus and earlier. The coins were in a typical Roman urn, which was unfortunately broken in the digging. By the end of January No.3 Company at Candas had completed the terminus, laid the necessary sidings and constructed a concrete tank capable of holding one hundred thousand gallons of water for the steam engines. At Acheux No.1 Company also constructed a terminus, sidings and a similar water tank. On 22 January it snowed heavily and no work was possible. It therefore fell to No.4 Company to organise a snow battle between No.13 and No.14 Platoons manning a defensive position, which was then attacked by No.15 and No.16 Platoons. A fierce battle ensued, which was eventually declared a draw, the whole experience being a complete bafflement to the French onlookers.

By 18 February, the final spike had been driven at Belle Eglise Farm. Four days later, in a meeting at Third Army Headquarters, it was decided that priority should be given to Belle Eglise and No.4 Company immediately began to lay sidings and build a station. Throughout this time the men had been subjected to enemy shelling, especially No.1 Company, but no casualties were reported. The major discomfort came from the noise of British guns firing from positions close to where the men rested. The station at Belle Eglise was completed on 20 March and soon a Railway Transport Officer arrived and required an office, it was build within a couple of days. From this date the line was open to traffic and quickly heavy train loads of ammunition, supplies and troops began to arrive. With this major task now finished the Battalion was allowed a degree of rest and entertainment, mostly in the form of films and the acts of the Merry Mauves, the divisional entertainment troupe. This concert party was under the control of Captain J.C. Brennan and was considered to be second to none in the British Expeditionary Force, although there may have been a degree of bias on behalf of the *Belfast News Letter*.

While there was still work to be done on the railway with the impending summer offensive two companies at a time were detailed for battle indoctrination in the trenches. On 3 June, the following article, written by Lieutenant J. Maxwell, was printed in the *Lurgan Mail* and gives his experience of a night in the front line:

> To find oneself out from the friendly shelter of sandbags and parapet on a bit of no man's land devoid of cover of any sort gives one a feeling that is far from pleasant. Leaving billets at dusk the working party stumbles along communication trenches that twist and turn in all directions until the first line is reached. A few yards off a sentry can dimly be discerned, silent but alert, keeping an unceasing watch on the German trenches. Rats scamper and scuffle about everywhere but no one worries about them; they are looked on as part of trench life, and the sentry will tell you that on quiet nights he rather likes them to be about, even although they are not the most agreeable companions one could wish for. Our party now slips over the parapet and gets silently to work, there are places where the wire protecting the trench needs to be repaired, and work of other kind claims attention. Night work requires silence – nothing can be heard save a whispered word – and every man now has a thorough knowledge of his work and does it. Up comes a star shell from the German trenches and each man throws himself flat on the ground, where he remains until the shell has expended itself. The result of these shells usually gets the machine guns busy and when they come into action the party in front begins to feel very uncomfortable. The work is pushed forward with feverish haste, the

---

28   Letter dated 31 October 1916, PRONI.

"Rats abound, and a good revolver shot can have some sport. As I have to buy my own ammunition, I don't try to bag any." From an unnamed officer.

old Hun[29] perhaps sending over a few 'whizz-bangs' to help it on, or perhaps shrapnel is the present he has selected this particular night. It cuts through the air with an angry swish and instinctively each man pulls his steel helmet well down on his head. Work continues until close to dawn and just as the first signs appear far out in the East our party is found making its way back to the billets for rest.

The rats were not everyone's friend. An officer, unnamed, from the 14th Rifles wrote a long letter home and a part of it states; "Rats abound, and a good revolver shot can have some sport. As I have to buy my own ammunition, I don't try to bag any."

Not many people know that![30] George Hackney, now a lance corporal also experienced rats; "Slept very badly as the rats were carrying on in good style and I could not get settled down. John Ewing wakened and found a rat sitting on his head, which he promptly removed. The rats annoyed us so much that John brought the dog, Billo, in, after which we got a bit of peace."

With continuing rumours of a big push preparation went ahead for the billeting of fresh troops. Brian Boyd served as a private in the 14th Rifles. Born in Swansea, he was the son of William and Lizzie Boyd and shortly after he was born the family moved to Cyprus Gardens in Belfast. Educated at RBAI, he was then apprenticed to the linen trade and became a member of the YCV. He was also a keen member of the Tenth Belfast Boy Scouts, who had sixty-five members enlist, winning two awards of the Military Cross and two Military Medals. Seven former members of the troop died on active service. Throughout his time in France Brian kept up a correspondence with a childhood friend Lily Price. In a letter dated 12 February, he told of the daily routine; "We have had a fairly decent time up to the present, sweeping roads for a good part of our time, and building wire beds into French barns to make billets more comfortable for the other troops who will come out after us, but I think all of that is over for the time being."

The *Down Recorder* carried two advertisements concerning local men serving in France and elsewhere. A dance was to be held on Wednesday 19 January 1916 in the Assembly Hall, Downpatrick,

---

29 The word Hun in reference to the Germans evolved from the Siege of Peking in the Boxer Rebellion of 1900. Kaiser Wilhelm II, speaking of the Chinese "rebels", stated 'Mercy will not be shown, prisoners will not be taken. Just as a thousand years ago, the Huns under Attila won a reputation of might that lives on in legends, so may the name of Germany in China. Taken from the *Weser-Zeitung*, 28 July 1900.

30 *Belfast New Letter* 12 November 1915.

War memorial to the men of
Strandtown and District Unionist
Club, including Second Lieutenant
Brian Boyd MM, a former
member of the Tenth Belfast Boy
Scouts, whose scout hut is nearby.
(Author's photograph)

Brian Boyd and his younger brother
Denis, both members of the Tenth
Belfast Scout Troop. (Photograph
courtesy of Andrew Totten)

Julia McMordie and representatives of the Tenth placed wreaths beneath the flags of the 14th Royal Irish Rifles in Belfast City Hall on 7 June 1920, the anniversary of the death of Brian Boyd MM. (photograph courtesy of Andrew Totten)

commencing at 9 o'clock, with admission being 3/6 for a single ticket and 6/= for a double. All proceeds in aid of the 10th and 16th (Irish) Divisions. Meanwhile Miss Miller of Killinchy was appealing through the newspaper for melodeons for the men of the 13th Rifles, which had been requested. Miss Miller would gladly receive and acknowledge such gifts.[31]

In Ireland's history from time immemorial there has always been a 'split' in the various organisations, political parties and faiths. The care for those men of the Ulster Division who had been taken or would be taken prisoner was no exception. On 20 February 1916 General Nugent wrote to Wilfred Spender:

> I fully sympathise with the desire of the Committee of the 'Ulster Women's Gift Fund' to keep in their own hands the care of the interests of men of the Ulster Division who may become prisoners of war. I understand from Lady Richardson's letter that another committee, called the 'Irish Women's Association', is working in the same direction.[32] I presume that both Committees have the same aims, that is, the amelioration of the lot of prisoners of war. I gather the Irish Women's Association is desirous of helping all Irish soldiers, whereas the Ulster women's Gift Fund wishes to confine its work to the Ulster Division. Lady Richardson asks that the Commanding Officers shall appoint the latter Committee as the Official Fund for dealing with prisoners of war of their units. In a matter of this kind, involving what appears to be a discrimination between two Committees, both presumably activated by the same public spirit and both apparently anxious to help Irish soldiers, it seems desirable to avoid any public action which could offend. I should be greatly surprised if any C.O. in the Division were to express publicly an opinion on this question without ascertaining my views.

---

31   *Down Recorder* 28 December 1915. A melodeon is a button accordion; in Estonia its high notes are used to attract ferrets.
32   Headed by Lady MacDonnell.

Men of the Tenth Scouts who died in the Great War. From top left, Second Lieutenant Brian Boyd MM, 14th Royal Irish Rifles, Lieutenant Henry Joy McCracken, 111th Squadron RFC, Lieutenant William Carlisle Hill, 2nd Royal Irish Rifles, attached to 74th Trench Mortar Battery, Corporal George Payden MM, 14th Rifles, Corporal Thomas Henry 14th Royal Irish Rifles, Private James Scott, Royal Marine Light Infantry, Sergeant James D Black, 8th Royal Irish Rifles. (Courtesy of Andrew Totten)

At present I have no views on the subject and have had no communication from any source in reference to the matter. No decision is therefore possible, but you can assure Lady Richardson that when I am in possession of the information on which to come to a decision, I shall be ready to decide in accordance with what I consider to be the interests of the Ulster Division after ascertaining the views of Commanding Officers."

According to an officer of the Army Service Corps in the division, the men of the entire division took part in an original recruiting drive. He stated; "I wonder will they get the 50,000 recruits in Ireland, I hope so. We all sent post cards home to some slackers one day last week in the hope that these might find some more to fill up. The whole Division took part in the scheme."[33]

---

33   *Belfast New Letter* 18 November 1915.

Men of the Royal Army Service Corps attached to the Division.

Officers from the divisional artillery carried out a reconnaissance of the ground south of the Ancre at the end of December, part of a tactical scheme. The officers were very professional and worked out the various fire plans from accurate maps and aerial photographs. They also rode across much of the battlefield to see and experience the lie of the land.

General Nugent, at the behest of Brigadier Withycombe, replaced Colonel H.T. Lyle of the 8th Rifles with Colonel R.T. Pelly. Colonel Lyle was given command of the 17th Rifles, a general reserve battalion in Ireland. Raymond Pelly, son of the late Canon R.P. Pelly, MA, Vicar of Great Malvern, had served in the South African War with the Worcestershire Imperial Yeomanry. Post South Africa he served with the Royal North Lancashire Regiment and the Canadian Princess Patricia's Light Infantry. He had performed well in the war so far, commanded the Patricia's at the Battle of Frezenberg and during the summer of 1915, had been responsible for the reforming of the regiment and integrating replacements with the original members. He would command the 8th Rifles until August 1916, when he once again took command of the Canadian regiment on the death of its commander at Sanctuary Wood.

It was the last day of the year and latrine buckets were urgently required by the divisional artillery. DADOS was being near constantly questioned re the shortage of grindery, tools and other equipment used by shoemakers and cobblers; the supply coming from the Ordnance Base was inadequate and the shortfall had to be purchased locally. The Ordnance Services staff made numerous trips to Amiens and Abbeville to purchase supplies.

6

Learning the Ropes

It is claimed by many writers and historians that the British Expeditionary Force of 1916 was one of the most remarkable and admirable military formations ever to have taken the field. Of the 13 attacking divisions on 1 July four were largely formed from regular, long-service volunteers. As an example, the 4th Division was composed of 12 battalions of so called 'old sweat' units. Two Irish, one Scottish, five Midland or North Country, two West Country, one East Anglian, one London, and despite losses at Mons in August 1914, many of their experienced officers and men continued to serve. Likewise, the 29th Division, apart from two battalions, was composed of pre-war 'old sweats'. The exceptions were the two war-raised battalions, the 16th (Public Schools) Battalion and the 1st Battalion the Royal Newfoundland Regiment, who would pay a horrific price on the Somme.

On 1 January orders were issued for the 36th Division to move to the Candas area between 3 and 8 January, here it would take over the former billets of the 30th Division. On Sunday 2 January, A Company of the 14th Rifles was sent to Beauval to work under the command of 122 Field Company, Royal Engineers. Private James McRoberts, 14th Rifles recorded in his diary:

> We cleaned up our billets and our company set off about 10 o'clock, to march to Beauval. It rained persistently most of the day and we had to wear our waterproofs all the way. At mid-day we halted at Berneuil and had dinner in some empty houses. We started again and as we passed by Candas the light was failing. It was quite dark when we reached Beauval and the first electric light pole in the Rue de Recque. We marched through the town in great style, singing loudly. It seemed like coming home, returning to the well-lighted streets of this shapely town. We marched up the Rue de Gasse and were put in good billets, well up on the hill. We had accomplished a long march and I felt very fit, much to my own satisfaction.

There was no accounting for the shelling. Irrespective of where you were, be it in the front line trenches, with a working party or in billets resting, the enemy shells would seek you out. On the morning of 8 January 1916, one such shell claimed the life of three men of the 8th Rifles, including the first officer of the division to be killed in action. Second Lieutenant Robert Wilson MacDermott, of the 8th Rifles had been a former member of the UVF, and was the second son of the Reverend John McDermott DD ex Moderator of the Presbyterian Church in Ireland. Educated at Campbell College and Queen's University of Belfast, he had been studying Law before the War.[1] It should be noted that Campbell College was the first school in Ireland to create an Officer Training Corps, second only to that of Queen's University. Of the more than 600 'boys' from Campbell who served during the Great War, the majority were officers. The war diary only lists two other men killed, Private George Parkinson, from Moira, County Down and Corporal Henry Murphy of D Company, possibly the third man died of wounds at a later date.

---

1   *The Times* January 1916.

Back in Ulster a draft of men in training with the Rifles at Palace Barracks, Holywood in County Down, were returning to barracks and had dismounted from the train at Kinnegar Halt. It was 10:30 pm and the platform was wet from rain, Private John Pollock, a married man from Brownlow Street, Belfast, lost his footing on the platform and fell in front of the train just as it was leaving. He was immediately taken to the hospital wing of the Barracks where it was diagnosed he had suffered a fatal injury to his abdomen, he died two days later and was buried in Belfast City Cemetery.

Captain G.J. Bruce moved from the 13th Rifles to divisional headquarters on 18 January to act as GSOIII. Two days later DADOS received 47 Lewis guns and distributed them to various units. A representative also travelled to Abbeville to purchase three sledgehammers for the Divisional Farriers workshop.

In the 4th Division the position known as the Crater was being held by the 9th Rifles and was attacked by a strong German raiding party on the night of 17 January. The raiders threw numerous bombs and killed two men, Privates Wilson and Marsden, both from Belfast, the latter serving in A Company. One man was taken prisoner before the Germans retired. Due to faulty communications between the 107 Brigade and the supporting artillery the chance to bring down fire while

Captain George James Bruce, DSO, MC and Bar, first served in B Company 13th Royal Irish Rifles, later as GSO with 109 Brigade, serving with the 16th (Irish) Division during the Battle of Langemarck. Returned to the Ulster Division and was killed in action on 2 October 1918. Born in County Cork, he was the son of Samuel and Julia Bruce of Norton Hall, Campden, Gloucester, and husband of Hilda, later of Corriewood, Castlewellan, County Down.

the retiring enemy were in the open was lost, for which the prisoner from 107 Brigade was probably most grateful.

A letter, post marked 2 January, was published in the *Belfast News Letter* on 21 January from an unnamed lance corporal writing from "somewhere in France":

Another New Year; another New Year, and here we are to our waists in filth, no hope of extrication, no hope of emancipation. Are ye folk all dead that the cry of suffering men cannot reach ye? Is there a young man capable of bearing the burden within sound of your call, tell him he is the man we want. We are tired, tired of the eternal pain of mental anguish, tired of the weariness of the flesh, tired of the bitterness of putting up with punishment, tired to death of cold, of wet, of hunger, thirst and pain. Where are the men? And politicians still argue in the 'talking shop' at Westminster; and still there is a faction of so called Irish – may they die of hunger when they are told to eat grass – who believe in Germany. Tell Ireland to denude herself of the last man, the last husband, or brother or son, but don't let us down. I cannot tell you, but I know that great times are in the making. We hear naught of home but feel that things are brewing in the vat of the incomprehensibles, the silent mob that works

Men of No.9 Platoon C Company 15th Royal Irish Rifles with two of the deadly Lewis guns, here seen without their magazines.

by back-ways and bye ways – the group of British fair-minded folk that have German gold – would it was as spurious as their silver, as a salve to conscience."

It is almost poetry and appears to be written by a relatively educated NCO given his vocabulary. Or, as has been rumoured, was it propaganda written to encourage recruiting?

In January Brigadier Hickman received the news that his brother in law, Brigadier Hugh Gregory Fitton, CB DSO ADC, had died of wounds while serving with the General Staff. Shot and shell did not differentiate between ranks.

Questions were raised by the 19th Division towards the end of the month about the quality of the iron used for making horseshoes. In the Ulster Division only old shoes were used in the remaking. There was still a shortage of nosebags within the artillery batteries and DADOS requested a supply of canvas so that they could be made locally. This shortage was not due to any carelessness on behalf of the artillerymen; it transpired that the infantry were using the nosebags for carrying bombs. When not in use they could be more easily rolled up and stored in a pack than a canvas bucket, which had a wooden rim. Eventually specific canvas bomb buckets would be introduced; in the meantime a horse could miss the odd meal.

On 26 January the 108 and 109 Machine gun Companies, which had been formed at Ribeaucourt and Fienvillers respectively, joined the division. Personnel for these units came from within the division, which was temporarily attached to the VII Corps as of 31 January, pending transfer while taking over a section of the front line from the 4th Division.

During the first week of February the division marched towards its new positions in the line. On 7 February it took responsibility for a section of the Front between the Ancre River and the Mailly-Maillet to Serre Road. The 108 Brigade was on the right flank, the 107 Brigade, recently returned from the 4th Division, on the left and the 109 Brigade in reserve. Divisional Headquarters was

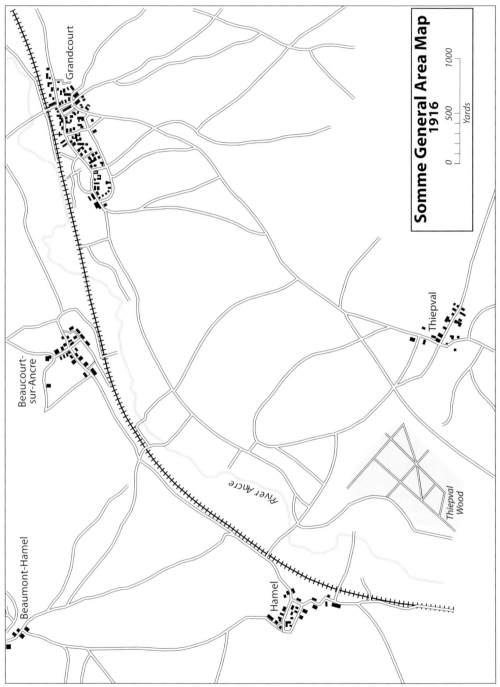

Somme General Area Map
1916

Area of operations for the Division astride the River Ancre, 1916.

The church at Thiepval.

established at Acheux, described by Cyril Falls as either a large village or small town. The division was under the temporary command of the VIII Corps.

This was a bad day for the 13th Rifles. A single enemy artillery shell exploded in the battalion area, killing four men. They were Privates David McConnell, J. Calvert, J.P.K. Tate and Bandsman Charles Newell. All four were buried together the following day, the funeral being attended by Major Perceval-Maxwell and Lieutenant M. Wright. The service was taken by the Reverend C.C. Manning, former rector of Comber, County Down. For the following six weeks the division had a relevantly quiet time, although this did include exploding enemy mines, sniping and trench raids from the enemy. The *Belfast News Letter* reported that Private Newell, from Newtownards, County Down, was the first member of the battalion to die in action.[2]

The Germans exploded a mine beneath the position known as the Redan on 13 February, killing three men of a tunnelling company who were buried when an underground passage collapsed. However, at his time the greatest enemy was the weather and life in the trenches was almost intolerable. When it had begun to rain some units had dug deep sumps in the bottom of the trenches with the intention of draining off the water. These had quickly filled and the covering duckboards would often float away from the hole, which meant many an unsuspecting individual wading through two feet of water would then suddenly find himself chest deep as he stepped into the sump. In the beginning there was a shortage of revetting material to brace the sides of trenches and

---

2   *Belfast News Letter* 17 June 1916.

this often caused sections to collapse, which in turn caused the water in the bottom of the trench to become glutinous mud. Attempts were made to drain the trenches, which included using hand pumps to move the water over the parapet, which in turn meant it slowly seeped its way back in again.

While DADOS was on occasion able to supply 'gum-boot, thigh', these were always in short supply. However, when they were available in quantity there were far fewer cases of trench foot. On 16 February the 5th Battalion Sherwood Foresters was attached to the Division for work on the trenches. They were attached to the 107 Brigade for their rations and billeted at Mailly Maillet. There was a fair degree of sniping around this time, in which the division held its own against the enemy, and that night there was a full moon that prevented any patrolling. The Sherwood Foresters continued to assist with road repairs, which were becoming quite serious.

In mid-February, 300 dismounted cavalry from the Indian Cavalry Corps were attached to the division for road work. They were stationed at Forceville. The 115th and 116th Trench Mortar Batteries were allocated to 107 and 108 Brigades. The 119th Trench Mortar Battery was sent to 109 Brigade. To add to the Indian Cavalry already serving with the Division, 300 British Cavalry arrived on 18 February to assist with the work and were placed on the divisional strength for rations. The next evening a very heavy enemy bombardment began at 6:00 pm, and lasted for approximately one and a half hours. The shells included 77mm, 105mm, 210mm and aerial torpedoes. There were also numerous trench mortar bombs and rifle grenades. Wire was destroyed and trenches knocked in, mostly on the front of the Redan and the trenches held by the men of 107 Brigade. At 6:25 pm, the barrage lifted to the rear trenches, luckily passing over the trenches holding the reserve infantry. When the barrage passed the front line the defending infantry, mostly the 9th Rifles, manned the trenches and opened a heavy fire on the enemy lines with rifle and machine gun fire. A short time later the guns of the divisional artillery replied with their own barrage pinning the enemy to their trenches. Fourteen men had been buried in a crater in the front line, but these were all safely recovered.

DADOS officers visited Amiens on 21 February to purchase canvas. This was required to make nosebags for horses, to be sewn by the Divisional tailors, which would in turn be issued to the infantry battalions for carrying bombs during any assault. It was decided by the relevant authorities that this was more effective than the infantry 'borrowing' them from the cavalry, artillery or Army Service Corps horses. Later in the day a DADOS officer visited headquarters of 108 Brigade to discuss breech-covers for the rifles. The current issue was not approved of and provision of a new cover requested, which has been sanctioned by the Government Ordnance Office, and could be supplied provided the cost did not exceed more than one franc each. It was suggested by DADOS that when a unit was using rifle grenades a specific rifle or rifles be set aside by the unit for this use. The firing of grenades fitted with a rod, such as the Hales grenade, quickly caused damage to the barrel, making it virtually useless for firing normal ammunition.

On the night of 22 February a patrol from the 9th Irish Fusiliers was sent out to the position known as 'The Mill' to the east of Hamel. This was an actual water mill that straddled the River Ancre. In command was Second Lieutenant Reginald Nixon Wood, with Second Lieutenant Arthur Carson Hollywood as his second-in-command.

Lieutenant Wood came from Dublin where had been educated at King's Hospital. He had only recently joined the battalion, having been with the Honourable Artillery Company (Infantry) where he served as a private. Wood had served in France as a lance corporal before being commissioned and transferring to the battalion. Arthur Hollywood had formerly commanded B Company of the Willowfield battalion of the UVF. As the patrol neared the Mill it came under fire from German rifle grenades that fell around it with devastating accuracy. The two leading men in the patrol, Private Samuel Forde from Portadown and Second Lieutenant Nixon, were both killed. Several other men were hit, including Lieutenant Hollywood, who received a wound to his left

The Mill on the Ancre, objective of more than one night-time patrol.

arm from a piece of shrapnel. Despite his injury Lieutenant Hollywood managed to extract the patrol and lead it back to the battalion lines, he also ensured that the bodies of both men were recovered.[3] Second Lieutenant Nixon was the first officer of the 9th Irish Fusiliers to be killed in France.

Many men of the infantry battalions came from towns and had little experience with horses and even those whose job required them to work with these animals on a daily basis risked injury. Mrs Thomas Friars of Killinchy Wood, Crossgar, County Down, received word that her husband Private Robert Friars of the 14th Rifles was in hospital at Southend, having suffered a fractured ankle after being kicked by a horse. By coincidence shoeing-smith John Hay, Army Service Corps, arrived home in Crossgar, having been discharged owing to injuries received through also being kicked by a horse.

A letter was received by the division from headquarters Third Army on the morning of 24 February. This stated that the Army Council had brought to their attention the matter of a shortage of materials for the manufacture of paper. It stressed that every economy should be exercised to reduce the use of paper and especially in the printing of orders, where undue numbers should not be ordered. Where consumption appeared to be excessive steps would be taken to establish if such use was strictly necessary and if not, further instructions would be issued, on paper. It was signed by W.N. Venning, Captain DAAG, for Adjutant General. Copies were forwarded to HQ 46th Division, OC 36th Division Supply Column, OC 46th Division Supply Column, and OC 17th

---

3   Source Battalion War Diary and *World War One Memorial Book*, compiled by Katrina Clydesdale and published by Bangor Museum in 2007.

Corps Troops Supply Column, OC 17th Corps Ammunition Park, OC 21st Reserve Park, OC 1 Section 19 Brigade, RFA, OC 21 Brigade RFA, OC 24 MMG Battery and OC No.5 Entrenching Battalion.

Towards the end of the month the winter weather set in and the first falls of snow were seen with a blizzard being reported at 9:30 pm on 25 February.

The 36th Divisional Artillery, which had been training at Cayeux, began to arrive on 27 February, taking over from the guns of the 4th Division. Movement was slow because of the inclement weather and it was only due to the good work carried out by the Field Companies that there were no serious drawbacks. On this day, a Sunday, the division saw its first execution when Private James Crozier of the 9th Rifles was shot by firing squad at Mailly-Maillet, he was 18 years old. Private Crozier had deserted on 31 January when his battalion was in position near Serre. This was his third offence and it was recorded that "From a fighting point of view, this soldier is of no value."[4]

General Nugent had recommended against commuting the death sentence because 'there have been previous cases of desertion in the 107 Brigade'[5]

On the same day Company Quartermaster David Stratton died in St. Luke's Hospital in Bradford. He had suffered from influenza several weeks before, but had recovered and returned to duty. With a second attack he was shipped back to England and his wife was informed of the seriousness of his illness and she was at his side when he died. His body was taken back to Newtownards and he was buried in Movilla Cemetery.

The 11th Rifles suffered its first death on 29 February, when Private Robert John Watt of No.12 Platoon C Company, was killed by a shell while standing by the door of his billet at Mesnil. He had stepped outside for a quiet smoke.[6]

During this first seven days of March the division extended its front to cover the ground south of the Ancre including Thiepval Wood. The Wood was made the responsibility of 109 Brigade who found it open to sudden enemy bombardment, unlike Hamel, which had been relatively quiet. Thiepval Wood had previously been held by French troops who had not left it in the best condition. The big push was near at hand and more and more artillery was positioned in the rear of the division.

The division had transferred from the Third Army, XVII Corps to the Fourth Army, X Corps as of 12 noon on 1 March. This Corps also contained the 32nd, 48th and 49th Divisions. It was commanded by Lieutenant General T.L.N. Moorland, KCB, DSO. General Nugent was ordered to extend his front to the right flank as soon as possible to join up with the 32nd Division. As of 5 March 1916, the Divisional Artillery took over completely from that of the 4th Division and was subsequently emplaced to provide support for the division.

General Nugent and his men were now responsible for the front line from the River Ancre on the left flank to the Serre Road on the right. There had been a heavy fall of snow the previous day and movement of men and animals became difficult.

4   Walker, Stephen, *Forgotten Soldiers* (2007). Private Crozier is buried in Sucrerie Military Cemetery, Colincamp, grave 1.A.5.
5   National Archives WO 71/450.
6   Stewart-Moore, Random Recollections, Somme Archive.

Recently excavated and refurbished trenches at Thiepval. (Courtesy of Carol Walker)

Battalion locations Somme March 1916

Right Sector 109 Brigade HQ at Martinsart	Right sub-sector	In Thiepval Wood on left bank of River Ancre (G1). Resting Battalion at Martinsart (½ Bn) At Authuille (½ Bn). 9th Inniskillings relieved by 10th Inniskillings.
	Left sub-sector	On west bank of the Ancre, holding Hamel (G2). Resting Battalion at Mesnil. 11th Inniskillings relieved by 14th Rifles.
Centre Sector 108 Brigade HQ at Engelbelmer	Right sub-sector	Opposite Beaumont Hamel (H1). Resting Battalion at Engelbelmer. 11th Rifles relieved by 13th Rifles.
	Left sub-sector	Resting Battalion at Hédouville [sic]. 12th Rifles relieved by 9th Irish Fusiliers.
Left Sector 107 Brigade HQ at Mailly	Right sector	In front of Auchonvillers. Resting Battalion at Mailly. 8th Rifles relieved by 10th Rifles.
	Left sub-sector	Up to Serre Road. Resting Battalion at Brausiart [sic]. 9th Rifles relieved by 15th Rifles.

Now in position a daily routine was set in motion for all ranks. Two of the brigades were in what was called the front line, with the third in reserve. Each brigade had two battalions in the trenches and two in reserve. These would change at regular intervals, but never at the same time. Within each battalion two companies would be in the line, one in support and one in reserve. From thirty minutes before dawn and thirty minutes after, all troops stood to; this entailed all men being alert and manning their relevant weapons, the hour being considered the prime time for any enemy attack. During the winter this was also the time when the rum ration was distributed, most welcome after a cold wet night. It was issued again at dusk. The ration was distributed usually by an NCO, with each jar, marked with the letters SRD, Supply Reserve Depot, and contained one Imperial gallon, enough to give sixty-four men a single tot'. In the course of a week each man usually received approximately a third of a pint. Rum was also issued to men involved in unpleasant tasks, such as burying the dead or clearing up slaughtered animals, especially horses, which caused a great degree of grief. For those men who were teetotal the rum ration could be exchanged with a neighbour for cigarettes, chocolate or some other item, while some men used it as a foot rub. Lance Corporal George Hackney recalled the experience of a platoon of the 14th Rifles and the rum ration:

> Stood to at 5:00 am, and had breakfast at 6:30 am, after which we had nothing to do till about midday when we were ordered to prepare our kits for moving up to the second line of trenches at 1:00 pm after dinner. We were duly installed in our old dug-out, eleven of us, and shortly after I went with a ration party for tea rations and tea, later on going into the village for the post, which was eagerly received by the chaps. At breakfast time we were told that we had to take rum in our tea and that every man must take his ration of it. Some of us resented being compelled to take rum when we were TT, but were told that it did not make any difference whether we tried to object or not. So we asked out ration sergeant to complain to the captain on our behalf, with the result that we managed our point and instead of two dixies being "rummed" only one was doctored so we were able to get ours free from it. When the Warwick officer came down about it and said that in his battalion only about one man in sixty would not want it.

Time spent in the front line trenches varied from four to eight days depending on the weather and the condition of the trenches. The distance back to the billets where the men rested varied according to geography and the enemy's artillery and this could vary from one to five miles. During this month the two battalions holding Hamel, the 11th Inniskillings, who were relieved in turn by the 14th Rifles, rested at Mesnil, just over a mile from the German positions.

The hours of darkness was when most trench work was carried out, the repairing or laying of barbed wire and of course patrols and trench raids. Quite often the so-called resting battalion would be involved in such work, assisting the Royal Engineer Field Company in the construction of new trenches, dug-outs and the laying of narrow gauge railways. While the constructing and laying of a narrow gauge railway was backbreaking work, it also ensured the speedy evacuation of the wounded in battle, a thought rarely far from those men involved.

Over the next few days there were patrols out all along the front of the 108 Brigade and these observed that the enemy barbed wire was very dense. Observation posts recorded that the movement of enemy trains was much greater than in the past.

At approximately 8:30 pm, on 6 March, the enemy artillery shelled the position known as the Redan and the divisional back trenches. The probable objective of this shelling was the transport lines, the tracks of which had been observed in the snow earlier in the day by an enemy aircraft. One officer and several other ranks of the 10th Rifles were wounded. Later enemy aircraft returned and dropped a number of bombs, but caused no injuries. The observation posts continued to note and record enemy trains moving behind the lines.

Enemy trench mortars fired into Hamel on 7 March, while a German aircraft strafed the observation post at Prospect Point. The division's own machine guns did some good work against enemy positions, where a great deal of movement was apparent.

Two nights later, in retaliation, the Germans shelled Thiepval Wood, which they searched and registered effectively with their guns, evidently with a view to future operations. A patrol from 107 Brigade found an enemy covering party in front of the Redan, while enemy wiring was in progress. Lewis gun fire was brought to bear on them with inconclusive results. There was more snow. The cold was becoming serious and some men were suffering from frostbite. One such was Private Robert Armstrong of the 11th Inniskillings, who had to be sent home to Carrigan, Ballyconnell, in County Cavan to recuperate.

Enemy artillery, including some heavy guns, shelled Thiepval Wood throughout 10 March. At about 11:00 am a heavy bombardment of the front line trenches and wire commenced. At the same time a barrage fell on the supporting lines and communications, including Authuille and the 10th Inniskillings battalion headquarters in Gordon Castle. Here the only occupants were Colonel Ross Smyth and two of his orderlies, none of whom were injured despite the pounding the dug-out suffered.

The communications between the front companies and the supporting batteries was cut, one line in fifteen places, which meant serious work for the men of the signals section. The 153 Battery opened fire on its own volition, other batteries joining in later. The divisional batteries were heavily shelled; approximately 400 shells landing in the area, some being direct hits, but no casualties were caused. Gas shells were fired into Authuille, while trenches in Thiepval Wood and its supporting trenches were smashed. The 10th Inniskillings opened a heavy fire, supported by machine guns and trench mortars and this prevented the enemy from leaving their positions.

After the shelling of 10 March Brigadier Hickman made a tour of the brigade's positions two days later. Of particular note were the actions of Captain Shaw in command of the right flank company of the 10th Inniskillings, who on the day in question moved his platoons about to dodge the concentration of shells

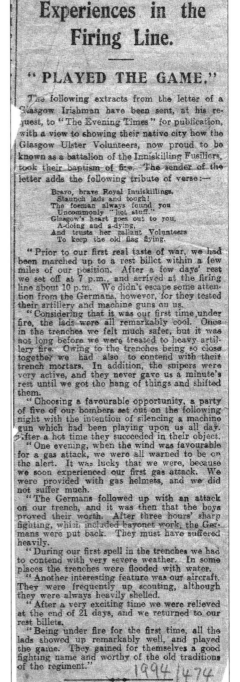

GLASGOW IRISHMEN.

Experiences in the Firing Line.

"PLAYED THE GAME."

The following extracts from the letter of a Glasgow Irishman have been sent, at his request, to "The Evening Times" for publication, with a view to showing their native city how the Glasgow Ulster Volunteers, now proud to be known as a battalion of the Inniskilling Fusiliers, took their baptism of fire. The sender of the letter adds the following tribute of verse:—

Bravo, brave Royal Inniskillings,
    Staunch lads and tough!
The foeman always found you
    Uncommonly "hot stuff."
Glasgow's heart goes out to you,
    A-doing and a-dying,
And trusts her gallant Volunteers
    To keep the old flag flying.

"Prior to our first real taste of war, we had been marched up to a rest billet within a few miles of our position. After a few days' rest we set off at 7 p.m., and arrived at the firing line about 10 p.m. We didn't escape some attention from the Germans, however, for they tested their artillery and machine guns on us.

"Considering that it was our first time under fire, the lads were all remarkably cool. Once in the trenches we felt much safer, but it was not long before we were treated to heavy artillery fire. Owing to the trenches being so close together we had also to contend with their trench mortars. In addition, the snipers were very active, and they never gave us a minute's rest until we got the hang of things and shifted them.

"Choosing a favourable opportunity, a party of five of our bombers set out on the following night with the intention of silencing a machine gun which had been playing upon us all day. After a hot time they succeeded in their object.

"One evening, when the wind was favourable for a gas attack, we were all warned to be on the alert. It was lucky that we were, because we soon experienced our first gas attack. We were provided with gas helmets, and we did not suffer much.

"The Germans followed up with an attack on our trench, and it was then that the boys proved their worth. After three hours' sharp fighting, which included bayonet work, the Germans were put back. They must have suffered heavily.

"During our first spell in the trenches we had to contend with very severe weather. In some places the trenches were flooded with water.

"Another interesting feature was our aircraft. They were frequently up scouting, although they were always heavily shelled.

"After a very exciting time we were relieved at the end of 21 days, and we returned to our rest billets.

"Being under fire for the first time, all the lads showed up remarkably well, and played the game. They gained for themselves a good fighting name and worthy of the old traditions of the regiment."

1994/474

Changed men from those brought to Ulster by Percy Crozier.

along his front trench. This resulted in his command suffering few casualties, while the company next to him had seven killed and eight wounded, mostly from shell fire on the front line trench. Brigadier Hickman also reported:

> From what I observed of the way our front line and wire was knocked about, and the obvious barrage put on our support trenches and all Avenues of approach for Reserves, I am of the opinion that the enemy evidently meant to penetrate our Front Line somewhere between Lochaber Street and Hammerhead Sap, but that they were not able to leave front line trenches owing to the effective barrage from our Artillery and the steady musketry from the infantry of the 10th Royal Inniskilling Fusiliers in our front line trench, helped by the machine guns in the same front line. Telephone wires suffered badly, most of the Company. Wires to Battalion Headquarters were cut, also from Companies to affiliated Batteries, but the Brigade line to Battalion Headquarters held out. I have taken steps to have wires buried to remedy this.

There was a concentrated bombardment of Thiepval village by the guns of the division on St Patrick's Day, along with those of the 32nd Division and other heavy guns. The enemy retaliated by firing on Albert and on the trenches at 'Tenderloin' and 4th Avenue. In the 9th Inniskillings Lieutenant Wintle celebrated the date by being wounded in the head and arm with shrapnel from an enemy shell. It would be autumn before he returned to the battalion. Armar Lowry-Corry Wintle had been commissioned in October 1915 and came from an established military family from County Wicklow. His father, Colonel Fitzharding Wintle had served with the 87th Punjabis of the Indian Army and his grandfather Major Octavius Lowry had been with the Galway Militia and 96th Regiment. Lieutenant Wintle had been educated at The College, Newton Abbot, Devon and then the Army School, Holyport, Maidenhead and the Imperial Service College, Windsor. He had applied for and received a commission in the Inniskillings on the outbreak of War, arriving in France in October 1915. While his father and grandfather had lived to a ripe old age, Captain Wintle would die for his country in 1917, two months short of his twenty-first birthday.

Attempts by the enemy to tap the communication wire to the north-west of Beaumont were thwarted by vigilant patrolling. The Germans booby-trapped a bridge near the Mill by sawing through the wooden planks; one man fell through, but was able to rejoin the patrol a little later. Private John McGuiggan of the 10th Inniskillings picked up a supposedly dud enemy rifle grenade to throw it away when it exploded, wounding him and his officer. McGuiggan suffered shrapnel wounds to his head and chest, while most of his left hand was missing.[7]

The following day the 107 Brigade was heavily shelled for about thirty minutes, especially in the area of the Redan and Auchonvillers. Communications between the front line and Headquarters were cut, but no great damage was caused. The divisional artillery continued to cut the enemy wire and during the hours of darkness this was 'searched' by machine gun fire to prohibit the enemy from carrying out repairs. There was continued shelling of Thiepval Wood and heavy projectiles were observed falling, but not always exploding. One shell that did explode fell in a trench occupied by the 9th Inniskillings, blowing the legs off Sergeant J.M. Laird; he died a short time later.[8] Enemy train movements were very active and it appeared that one division at a time was either being transferred or relieved.

Private James Templeton, aged 20 years and Private J.F. McCracken, aged 19 years, of the 15th Rifles were executed by firing squad on 19 March. Both men had a history of desertion.[9]

---

7   Letter from Stuart Hall to his mother at Castlerock, Londonderry, dated 23 March 1916.
8   Laird, Sergeant J.M., No19830, Authuille Military Cemetery, grave C48.
9   Walker, *Forgotten Soldiers*.

Officers and men of the 9th Royal Inniskilling Fusiliers in the snow, with the almost constant pet in attendance.

A divisional supply hut at Acheux caught fire and was burnt out by 7:30 pm; cause of the fire was unknown. The store-men lost all their personal belongings, however the records were saved, so what was lost was able to be fully recorded.

Captain C.A.L. Brownlow joined the artillery as a trench mortar staff officer. In 108 Brigade's area the enemy dropped eleven trench mortar shells into the area known as Q.17.D.1.1. Several did not explode, although casualties were caused. One of these was Private John Keating, of A Company 13th Rifles. He came from the Cotton near Donaghadee in County Down and had formerly worked as a farm labourer and on the railway as a plate layer. In a letter to John's parents the Reverend Gibson, Presbyterian Chaplain wrote; "...a shell came through and killed him instantaneously."

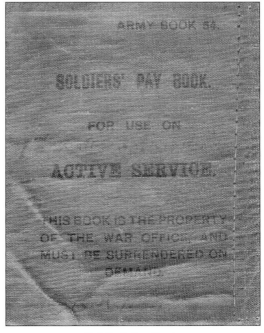

Soldier's Pay Book.

According to a battalion account a shell struck the bunker where Keating and several other men were sheltering. The bunker collapsed and he was struck on the head by one of the supporting beams. The other men were dug out unharmed. Private Keating was 21 years old.[10]

Heavy artillery shelled an enemy emplacement and a machine gun was seen to be blown into the air. Divisional patrols were kept busy with enemy patrols near the Ancre Mill. The enemy exploded a mine in front of the Redan, but no damage caused. The divisional snipers duelled with enemy snipers and there was more snow. The next few days of March are described in the divisional war diary as reasonably quiet, but the weather was terrible.

General Nugent spent the morning of 23 March carrying out a reconnaissance of ground that might be used in a future attack. The afternoon was spent with the Royal Engineers observing the effect of a flamethrower. He wrote to his wife:

> It was interesting to see the very form of attack we had to experience at Hooge (when he was with his previous division). It was most alarming to see the great sheet of flame sweep over the trenches and yet the men in the trench were perfectly safe so long as they sat on the bottom, because the flame cannot descend. If my men in 41 Brigade had only known last July and not tried to bolt from it, a good many lives would have been saved.[11]

That night a patrol from the 14th Rifles went towards the Mill and spotted a German soldier. They lobbed two bombs at him, but neither exploded. The men were adopting the thought that at night the bayonet and bombs were perhaps more effective than bullets, if you could get them to explode.

The 31st Division began sending up battalions from 92 and 93 Brigades to take over from the 107 and 108 Brigades on 27 March. More heavy snow and high winds made life difficult and DADOS had to make arrangements to re-site the Shoemakers Shop, as its present location was too dark. By the end of the month 93 Brigade had by now completely taken over from the 108 Brigade. The division's front now only covered the Thiepval Wood and Hamel sectors. Hamel was considered to be a quiet sector, with only occasional bombs from enemy long range trench mortars. While these did some damage to the communication trenches, they caused few casualties. Within this sector was a waterlogged valley, through which flowed the barely moving Ancre River. The area was filled with small lakes and the defence consisted of isolated outposts, with the forward one being on the Thiepval to Hamel Road. So quiet was it that the men were able to fish in the river and occasionally shoot game birds to supplement their rations. Thiepval Wood, on the other hand, while looking reasonably peaceful to the newcomer, was often prone to heavy bombardments, as has already been recorded.

April began with a letter in relation to some of the British airmen captured being dropped over the divisional lines. While many people assumed that the war in the air was somehow more chivalrous than that fought on the ground, combat between knights of the air, it must be remembered that for a pilot to be a good fighter pilot involved creeping up behind his opponent unnoticed and shooting him in the back.

The divisional front was extended some 300 yards to the left, reaching up to the Mary Redan and the 29th Division moved in on the left flank. At the 108 Brigade grenade school Sergeant William Magill from Hillsborough, Antrim, was demonstrating the use of the rifle grenade to a class. The grenade exploded prematurely killing the sergeant immediately and injuring three of the class. Sergeant Magill was regarded as one of the finest instructors of the Brigade and only

---

10   In an account written in the *Bangor Spectator* this name is rendered as Keatings.
11   Perry, *Major General Oliver Nugent and the Ulster Division 1915-1918.*

two days before his name had appeared in divisional orders recording an act of great courage and presence of mind.

The General Officer Commanding wishes to express his appreciation of the following act of courage on the part of No.18423, Sergeant William Magill, Royal Irish Rifles:

> At a bombing school, a live bomb failed to explode after throwing. When the grenade was afterwards moved it began to fuze and was dropped. Sergeant Magill, observing the danger picked it up and hurled it into a trench twenty yards away, thus averting a very serious accident.

William Magill was a former member of the UVF, having served in the West Down Regiment. His funeral was with full military honours and was attended by Colonel Savage and many men of the battalion. In attendance were two of the Divisional Chaplains, Reverend C.C. Manning (Rector of Comber) and the Reverend A. Gibson, (Presbyterian minister, Lurgan, County Armagh). The weather was described as a perfect spring day.[12]

About 10:30 pm on 6 April the enemy shelled Mesnil and Hamel. This went on well after midnight and at 2:30 am they scored hits on the battery position of C/153 and destroyed a gun. The 14th Rifles suffered heavy casualties under this bombardment as recorded in the diary of Private McRoberts:

> This evening while I was on sentry, our wire and front trenches were weakened a bit by a number of high explosives, these shells I am willing to admit annoyed me at the time. The bombardment was increasing in intensity and everybody was ordered by Sergeant Major J.J. Mackay to stand-to. Coming out of the dug-out into the open, the sight was terrible and the din astounding. Our ammunition was running short now but more was coming, brought by the officers' servants and bandsmen. David Paterson was among them, giving a cheerful word to everyone. 'Want any ammunition Mac?' "Yes, throw me a couple of bandoliers." "Right O", and hauling up his bandoliers he went on his way shouting, 'Here comes Gunga Din – any more ammunition for the Home Defenders?' Kipling's 'Gunga Din' was a familiar recitation by Jack Armstrong of our Company. I was up the trench several times on messages, "Pass up word to D Company to stop that machine gun, ammunition at the double for B Company", "Shovels for B Company, the ammunition is buried." I saw that the parapet had been blown in at several places and I realised that some poor fellows must have lost their lives. Meanwhile Doctor M.J.H. Garvin had arrived and I was sent down to the village to bring up the stretcher-bearers. In the firing line once more, I found we had a lot of casualties; the firing had ceased now, the bombardment having lasted two hours. Until almost daybreak, I helped to remove the wounded, first Alec Campbell, then S. McAdam and then H. Coates. Alec Campbell was usually known as 'Fatty' to distinguish him from Ronnie Campbell as they both belonged to the same Section. It was strange that they both should be our only fatal casualties in that section that night, for 'Fatty' died in the ambulance before reaching hospital.[13] Down in the Medical Officer's place the wounded had accumulated and a dead Sergeant, W. Stephenson from D Company, was laying there, his face covered with a ground sheet.[14] Returning to the dug-out I found the lads had stood down, extra sentries being posted. I was astounded to learn that Ronnie Campbell was missing, believed to be buried in the trench. Immediately afterwards a party that had been working on the place, returned to give us the news that it

---

12   *Belfast News Letter.*
13   Campbell, Private Alex, No.14173, died on 7 April 1916, he came from Nore Street, Belfast.
14   Stephenson, Sergeant William, No.19849, died on 7 April 1916, age 25 years.

was indeed Ronnie – they produced his pay-book. His rifle and steel helmet had been blown to pieces: his head could not be found."[15]

Major Spender wrote to his wife on 7 April concerning this action:

> There was another scoup [sic] attack last night, and again our men played up and the enemy failed to get in tho' it was our weakest unit, you can guess which I mean – I believe they did well.[16] For the 4th [5th?] time the Huns failed but succeeded in the next Division. I'm afraid our men will not be altogether sorry as the next Division treated us with 'marked discourtesy'. They are known as the "incomparables".[17] The GOC when they came offered to send up some of our experienced officers to teach them the line they were taking over and which we had held. Their GOC gladly accepted so our officers went up. They arrived at the front line about midnight and were sent straight back with the retort "I don't think we have anything to learn from a 6 months' division."

DADOS staff visited Acheux and purchased buttons for the tailor's shop. These were to complete the manufacture of small grenade carriers being made up. The grenade, or bomb, as it was still commonly known, was becoming the main weapon on trench raids and for night fighting.

The recent atrocious weather took its toll on many men and illness was rife. Sapper Victor Ernest Adams came from Epping in Essex and had enlisted in London in March of 1915, being posted to the 121 Field Company, Royal Engineers. He fell ill at the beginning of the month and died on 10 April, aged forty-two, his cause of death being listed as pneumonia.

On 12 April Private J. Stewart of the 14th Rifles injured himself with a revolver while on a working party. The wound was not considered to be self-inflicted and he was spared a court martial and possibly the firing squad. However, Private A. Murray, 11th Inniskillings, appeared before a Field General Court Martial on 18 April, facing a charge of Disobedience. He was sentenced to six months hard labour, which was commuted to three months Field Punishment Number 1. This consisted of the man being kept in irons, or handcuffs and secured so as to prevent escape. Often this was a post or wagon wheel, but was not to exceed two hours in any one day, nor more than three out of any four days, not more than twenty-one days in total. It was forbidden for men to be kept in direct sunlight, or within range of enemy fire, although stories abound of this happening. When not fettered the man was subject to various labouring duties.

For the following three days there was widespread shelling of the divisional positions. In Thiepval Wood the 9th Rifles suffered some twenty casualties from airburst shrapnel. The majority of these were not serious thanks to the newly issued steel helmet. Those men who cared for the division's horses found the newly issued steel helmet ideal for carrying water from stream to horse. DADOS contacted Base by telegram for a supply of 168 hand carts for the transportation of Lewis guns. These, like many other items, were eventually purchased in Amiens, where shopkeepers and small businesses were doing very well indeed.

There was no escaping the shelling, which destroyed equipment, weapons and men. Second Lieutenant Michael Richard Leader Armstrong serving with the 150 Field Company, Royal Engineers, was killed on 22 April. The following day the 10th Inniskillings had a Lewis gun destroyed and DADOS was asked to supply a new one, which they did just after providing a

---

15　Campbell, Private Randolph Churchill Bestall, No.14168, killed on 6 April 1916, age 21 years, of Ballynahinch, County Down.

16　The 14th Rifles.

17　The 29th Division had recently arrived from Gallipoli.

new weapon for the 14th Rifles, to replace a gun destroyed by shellfire. The divisional artillery supported a raid by the 29th Division on Mesnil Ridge, such cooperation now being the norm.

From the diary of Private James McRoberts, 14th Rifles:

> Easter Monday 24th April was given as a holiday to all whom it could be allowed. In the morning there was an inspection of billets, but after that the time was spent in sleeping, writing or reading as each one felt inclined, football was my choice. In the evening, because of a clear sky which promised excellent weather and with the numerous aeroplanes overhead, it was a very exhilarating and benefiting game of football in which I took part. The Irish Rebellion started in Dublin on Easter Monday, 24th April 1916, and when over three hundred lives had been lost, the rebels were forced to surrender on the 29th April. The whole uprising, when we read about it in the papers, was incomprehensible to us. That evening the two companies, A and B, left Martinsart to take up their positions as reserves, A in the cellars of Authuille, and B in the dug-outs of Thiepval Wood. The Permanent Patrol had made arrangements to be attached to B Company when, without warning, our chief Lieutenant R.L. Lack, was taken away in the ambulance, suffering from an attack of measles, the preparations were cancelled and we remained where we were. The spell was therefore spent in a fairly agreeable manner. We had little to do by day and only a certain number of us went out on night working parties, to Thiepval Wood, to assist the Royal Engineers.

The rebellion in Dublin was also mentioned by Private Norman Davidson to his sister Teenie shortly afterwards in an undated letter; "I see the accounts of the Dublin row in the papers, the number of casualties is rather alarming, I think by all accounts someone blundered as usual, by reports I think the military were rather free, in their use of firearms, they could be better employed out here."

One outcome of the rebellion was a request from the Regimental Pay Office in Dublin for a full list of all ranks entitled to service or proficiency pay. This was due to the rebels in the city having burnt down the pay office. By the end of April, the ration strength of the division was 20,822 all ranks and 5,834 horses and mules. News was received that two heavy trench mortar batteries (240mm) were to be formed, known as V 36 and W 36. The value of mortars had now been recognised within the British Army and their number increased monthly. The 11/1 Trench Mortar Battery now to be known as the 107/1 TMB rejoined the Division after training. teel helmets in possession of the division now totalled 13,524 and were most welcome by all ranks.

The pioneers suffered several non-battle casualties at this time, as well as men injured in work-related accidents. Three officers were lost to the battalion due to being thrown from their horses when startled by artillery firing close to them. These included Captain Allen who received a nasty scalp wound and required a couple of days in hospital, while Captain Jewell's injury required him to be evacuated back to hospital in England. Second Lieutenant Wilfred Unwin from Haslemere in Surrey, was also thrown from his horse, but suffered a fatal injury. He is remembered as a 'capable and efficient officer'. He was 39 years old and died on 5 May 1916.

The pioneers were engaged with laying many miles of tramway, building gun pits and digging communication trenches, while the 122 Field Company was tasked with constructing two causeways across the Ancre and the marshes. Prior to this there existed only a ramshackle wooden foot bridge that had been built by the French. With the assistance of working parties from various infantry battalions the causeways were built using sandbags filled with chalk. Initially there was some protest from the 32nd Division when the water rose behind their lines, but this proved to be only temporary. The work was carried on throughout the nights and many casualties were suffered from enemy machine gun fire, especially in the location of the northern causeway.

On Mesnil Ridge the divisional artillery constructed an observation trench and named it Brock's Benefit in honour of their commander. It contained a series of observation posts ideally suited for the coming battle.

The enemy shelled Thiepval Wood on 6 May and a great many casualties were caused. A machine gun in Hammerhead Sap was buried by an explosion. It was recovered the following day and found to be undamaged. The 14th Rifles lost another Lewis gun to shellfire when shrapnel tore it to pieces. This was most likely in D Company who received a fair degree of enemy shelling, as recorded in the diary of Private James McRoberts; "However, on the right D Company came in for a terrible mauling from shrapnel and trench mortars, entire platoons were buried and put out of action."

Again communications suffered due to the enemy shelling. Lance Corporal William John Gibson, serving with the 14th Rifles as a signaller was awarded a divisional certificate for the constant repairing of telephone wires running between his Battalion Headquarters and that of 109 Brigade, a distance of about 500 yards. Gibson came from Ainsworth Avenue, Belfast and had worked for the Singer Sewing Machine Company before the War and had been a member of the YCV.

According to a letter written by General Nugent to his wife the division lost nine men killed and about twenty wounded.[18] So severe was the bombardment that it generated a Special Battalion Order, issued on 10 May:

> The Commanding Officer, while deeply regretting the death of the following Officer, NCOs and Men, who were killed in action during the bombardment of the front line trenches on the morning of 6th May, and wishes to place on record his high appreciation of the great gallantry and devotion to duty under very trying circumstances.

> Killed
> Second Lieutenant J.L. Walker
> No.2907 Private McBratney, J.
> No.16158 Private Adams, E.
> No.17242 Private Beattie, A.
> No.18109 Lance Corporal Lowe, J.
> No.16869 Private Martin, T.
> No.18780 Private Sloane, T.G.
> No.6744 Private McKeown, D.T.
> No.6050 Private Tollerton, J.
> Died of Wounds
> No.4642 Private Walker, J.W.
> No.15085 Private Kirkwood, G.
> Killed in Action prior to the bombardment
> No.15443 Lance Corporal McLaughlin, W.[19]
> No.14730 Private Grainger, W.[20]

On 7 May a series of divisional moves was carried out as the brigades were positioned for the coming battle. The 108 Brigade was designated as the forward Brigade and would take over the

---

18   Perry, *Major General Oliver Nugent and the Ulster Division 1915-1918*.
19   CWGC quotes date of death as 2 May 1916 and spells his name as McLauchlan.
20   Died 3 May 1916.

Thiepval Wood sub-sector from 109 Brigade. Elsewhere 107 Brigade was the support brigade located at Martinsart, a place described as a 'shell wrecked village'.[21] In reserve was 109 Brigade which was also to carry out special training. In turn 107 Machine Gun Company relieved 109 Machine Gun Company in the Thiepval Wood sector. They would be under the command of Brigadier Griffith's 108 Brigade while in the line. The division launched its first raid against the enemy, one of many. While any sabotage to the enemy trenches and dug-outs was perfectly acceptable, prisoners were a priority, along with any captured documents and maps.

A large number of rifles were being received by the armourer's workshops, many from wounded men and most of these were repairable. There were many reasons for weapons being damaged; a chief one at the beginning of the war was men leaving their rifles lying on the lip of the trench during bombardments, where they were damaged by shell fragments and machine gun bullets.

At midnight on 8 May, a raid was carried out on the enemy trenches by a unit of the 9th Inniskillings. Major W.J. Peacocke led five officers and 84 other ranks out on to no man's land and into the enemy trenches. Warren John Richard Peacocke was born about 1889, came from Innishannon, County Cork, and was a cousin of Lady Carson. He had joined the Inniskillings as a Lieutenant on the outbreak of the War and would eventually command the battalion as a Lieutenant Colonel and later be awarded the DSO with Bar and the Croix de Guerre (first class). The path towards the enemy positions had been cleared by accurate artillery fire from B Battery of 153 Brigade RFA, under the command of Captain W. Mc C Cowan, which had completely destroyed the enemy barbed wire, therefore making both entry and egress that much faster. Six dug-outs were successfully bombed and a machine gun blown up. Casualties were caused resulting in the sound of shrieks and moans being heard from the various dug-outs. It was believed that between fifty and sixty of the enemy had been killed. The blocking detachments of the raiders ensured German attempts to counteract the raid were thwarted by lively bombing. On completing the raid the party halted in the sunken road to take stock and found that two men had been wounded, while one NCO had been killed. However, before they could move off the enemy opened a tremendous barrage on the area, which resulted in a further nine men being killed and twenty-two wounded. Eventually the raiders returned to their trenches, bringing all dead and wounded with them. Those batteries supporting the raid were heavily shelled in turn by the enemy.

As this raid was in progress there were developments on the right flank of the division. The 1st Dorsets of 14 Brigade of the 32nd Division were under considerable pressure and three companies of the 10th Inniskillings and part of the 109th Machine-Gun Company quickly moved up through a heavy barrage to assist in the defence. Two machine guns, under the command of Lieutenant Holt Hewitt, were set up between Hammerhead Sap and Foxbar Street. Such was the weight of enemy fire that the two teams, along with several members of the Dorsets, were forced to take shelter in a dug-out. Under this covering fire a large number of Germans entered the trench at Queens Cross Street, here nineteen year old Second Lieutenant Vere Talbot Bayly of the 1st Dorsets and Corporal W. Millar of 109 Machine Gun Company, who were somehow still out in the trench, put up a fierce resistance and were later found dead, having suffered many bayonet wounds. The enemy lines were watched constantly and no detail was deemed to insignificant to report. The divisional war diary for 7 May 1916 reported; "A man carrying a plank was seen at Q24.b.2.1."

Information is power. The divisional cavalry and divisional cyclists were to be withdrawn from the division and incorporated into corps organisation. General Nugent wrote to his wife in connection with the rebellion in Dublin; "I hear a battalion of my reserve brigade came down from Belfast and were rather happy in having the chance of meeting their natural enemies."

---

21   Divisional Headquarters War Diary.

This remark was in relation to the 18th Rifles, under the command of Colonel R.G. Sharman Crawford, CBE, who was sent to Dublin where they reoccupied the damaged Liberty Hall. Prior to the rebellion the hall had reportedly been used in the manufacture of weapons. During Easter Week it had remained empty of any insurgents, but was one of the first locations to be fired on by British forces. The firing had come from HMY *Helga*, a former fishery and protection vessel that had been equipped with two 12-pounder guns.[22]

The thrift of the Ulsterman shown through when the tailor workshops, who had been instructed by DADOS to make new putties from old ones, were now engaged in making bomb carriers, flags and nose bags. There seemed to be an increasing number of special and odd things required to be made due to the continuous and developing nature of trench warfare.

The division had lost men to drowning in Seaford, both in the sea and in rivers while relaxing. Here in France another was fated to die in water during an afternoon's rest. On 17 May Sergeant Henry Corkin, along with Privates Hillis and Wright, members of a party were bathing in the waters of a marsh, although only the sergeant was a swimmer. Suddenly the sergeant got caught in a bed of weeds and while Willis ran for help, Wright did his best to assist the struggling NCO. Private Lamont and Corporal Dunlop arrived and both swam out to the weeds where they recovered the sergeant from some ten feet of water. The medical officer arrived and did all was possible, but to no avail. Sergeant Corkin came from Gregg Street, Lisburn, Antrim, and was a former member of the UVF.[23]

The local papers of 22 May 1916 carried an article regarding recruits for the division. There was still a need for men to serve in the mechanical transport branch of the Army Service Corps and the 14th Rifles were reported to be 300 men under-strength. Sapper John Malone, No.64005, of Church Street, Downpatrick, was killed on 23 May 1916; he was 22 years old. His comrades erected a much-engraved Celtic cross to mark his grave. It resides in the Down Museum today.

There was a shortage of magazines for the Lewis guns due to many being faulty and DADOS was inundated with requests for new ones. The 15th Rifles required 55, while the 13th Rifles asked for 39. Within 24 hours the 9th Inniskillings had asked for 27 and the 10th Inniskillings required 35, the 11th Inniskillings 28, 9th Irish Fusiliers 40, 9th Rifles 49, and 12th Rifles 34. By the end of the month the 16th Rifles had requested 26. It would appear that a defective consignment had been delivered to the division, the magazine of the Lewis gun was of an intricate design.[24]

Between 31 May and 1 June 1916, the Royal Navy's Grand Fleet gave battle with the German Navy's High Seas Fleet at Jutland. The result was a tactical victory of the Germans in that they sank more ships, but a strategic victory for the British as on returning to their bases the German Navy never again ventured out to sea to meet the Royal Navy, at least not on the surface. Within the division men from Bangor read of the death of Commander Barry Bingham, the third son of the fifth Baron Clanmorris, who had been lost with the sinking of HMS *Nestor*, one of the 5,570 Royal Navy personnel to die in that battle.[25]

Within the division this day saw the break-up of the divisional cyclist company. Half the personnel went to the Tenth Corps Cyclist Battalion, the others to the 15th Rifles. The month of May also saw the reorganisation of the divisional artillery. In order to take advantage of the howitzers, it was decided to share them out among the other brigades. Therefore 153, 172 and 173 Brigades now held three four-gun 18-pounder batteries and a four-gun 4.5-inch howitzer battery each, while the 154 Brigade, the former howitzer brigade, received guns in exchange for

22   HMY, His Majesty's Yacht, later purchased by the Irish government and renames *Muirchu*, the first Irish Naval Service vessel.
23   Letter in the *Belfast News Letter* dated 24 May 1916. The CWGC lists Corkin as a Lance Corporal.
24   Skennerton, Ian, *Small Arms Identification Series 14: .303 Lewis Machine Gun* (1988).
25   Bingham was not dead, but a prisoner-of-war and would later be awarded the Victoria Cross.

The 'knuts' of No.9 Platoon C Company, 15th Royal Irish Rifles.

its howitzers and was of the same organisation. The Brigade Ammunition Columns were abolished and the Divisional Ammunition Column was increased in size.

Brigadier General Hickman returned to England at the end of May 1916 and the 109 Brigade received a new commander. Hickman had mentioned at a dinner with Nugent and Haig that he felt he could do better at home as a Member of Parliament than commanding a brigade in France. Haig advised Nugent to "… put no obstacle in his way of returning to his parliamentary duties."[26]

Hickman's replacement was Brigadier General R.J. Shuter, DSO, late of the Royal Irish Fusiliers. Shuter brought with him his own Brigade Major, Captain A.W.C. Richardson, late of the Bedfordshire Regiment. He would remain in post until February 1917, when he was appointed as a GSO to another division.[27]

Sapper John Malone, the Celtic Cross that marked his grave can today be seen in Down Museum.

---

26 Perry, *Major General Oliver Nugent and the Ulster Division 1915-1918.*
27 *Belfast News Letter,* 23 February 1917.

Men of the Cyclist Company advancing through a captured village.

At the beginning of June the divisional front was held by 107 Brigade, supported by 108 Brigade, which was located in and around the area of Martinsart. In training was 109 Brigade. It was then decided that both 108 and 109 Brigades would train together, so the 147 Brigade from the 49th Division was brought forward to take over the duties of 108 including all working parties. The 108 moved to the area of Varennes, Harponville and Lealvillers, a series of small villages. Here at a place called Clairfaye Farm an elaborate series of dummy trenches had been marked out that replicated those German trenches soon to be attacked.

Described as a fairly quiet day in the divisional war diary, 2 June bore ominous signs. A report from the Commander Royal Artillery stated that the pattern of shellfire received on the divisional positions indicated that the enemy was registering the fire of a new battery under cover of an existing one.

Well to the west of the Somme off the Orkney Islands the British armoured cruiser HMS *Hampshire* hit a sea mine at 7:40 pm on 5 June. On board were Field Marshal Lord Kitchener and his staff, making their way to the Russian port of Archangel. All but twelve of those on board were killed, including the man who had originally asked for the Ulster Volunteers from Carson. According to subsequent rumours twenty-four hours before the ship sailed a German spy in Scotland had sent a telegram to Holland that read; "Shall Herbert enter the legal academy next December."

Which of course spells Shetland; the conspiracy theories continue to this day, including one that lays the blame on Boer 'bitter-enders'.[28] Among the dead was Surgeon Hugh Francis McNally,

---

28   *Bangor Spectator* 24 August 1918

The iconic recruiting poster of the Great War featuring Kitchener still has a visible impact today.
(Author's photograph)

RN, from Portaferry, County Down, he was twenty-four years old and is remembered on the Portsmouth Naval Memorial. General Nugent had written to his wife regarding this incident on 7 June and seemed to have been aware of these rumours:

> Yesterday afternoon we heard the news of the tragedy of the Hampshire. It is a tragedy indeed. 'K' was such a personality and one feels there was not lately the loyalty to him that was his due. He no doubt made many mistakes, but it was he who realised at the beginning that this war was going to be and who taught the country to think in vast numbers. He was a great man and a very great loss to the Empire. What I cannot help thinking is that the Germans may have known by some means or other. It cannot be only a coincidence. I think so important a mission should never have been allowed to go in a ship unattended by another. If there had been a second ship, 'K' might have been saved and most of the crew too perhaps.

Not everyone had a positive view of Kitchener; Lady Carson wrote in her diary after attending the memorial service held on 11 June; "He seemed to me a grand looking sham, just medals and an [sic] uniform."[29]

During the hours of darkness on 5 June the division in concert with the 32nd Division carried out a series of raids. The 12th Rifles put their training on hold as they were brought forward to carry out a raid on the Railway Saps that ran parallel with the main railway line north of the

---

29   Lewis, Geoffrey, *Carson The Man Who Divided Ireland*, London 2005.

River Ancre. The smaller party, which was to enter by the sap head found the wire too thick for the available cutters and could not get in. The second party, under the command of Lieutenant McCluggage, was able to enter successfully when the enemy wire was blown by Lieutenant Fawcett of the Royal Engineers using a Bangalore Torpedo. This was a zinc tube some six feet long, three inches in diameter and filled with ammonal explosive. It had been invented by Captain McClintock of the Madras Sappers and Miners of the Indian Army in 1912, a Donegal man from Dunmore House in Carrigans. The torpedo had originally been used to clear booby traps and barricades that remained after the Boer and Russo-Japanese Wars. The method of use was that the first tube, containing the explosive, was attached to other tubes by means of a bayonet type fitting or screw thread until the required length had been reached. A rounded nose cone was fitted to the explosive tube to prevent snagging on the ground or wire and the whole thing pushed through or over the obstacle. When detonated a gap some five feet was created in barbed wire.[30] The torpedo was usually assembled and fired by an accompanying sapper, in this case Lieutenant Fawcett. On this raid the enemy had retired to their dug-outs under the fire of the British artillery. These dug-outs were then bombed and an enemy officer who appeared was shot. In the German trenches two tunnels leading towards the British lines were discovered, one of which contained fourteen high tension copper wires, which apparently pointed to the use of a mechanical digger. Lieutenant Fawcett got to work and soon the saps had been blown in rendering them useless for a time. Several sentry posts were bombed, but these were only lightly manned. Two tunnels were found leading towards the divisional lines and these were blown in, along with a supply of trench mortar bombs. Lieutenant Fawcett, acting as rearguard, shot a German as the raiders left the trench. A supply of copper wire was found and a sample brought back for examination by the Intelligence officer. Artillery support for this raid lasted approximately one and a half hours.

During the night of 10 June the enemy made a strong raid against the division, the main focus of the attack falling on the William Redan defended by the 15th Rifles. After a terrific bombardment a large party of enemy attempted to rush the position, but due to the weight of fire put out by the defenders only three or four enemy actually made it into the trench. The officer leading the assault was shot at point blank range and the others made a hasty escape, taking their wounded officer with them. Attempts by some of the Riflemen to take the officer prisoner were thwarted by the amount of debris filling the trench. The defenders suffered many casualties and much damage was done to the trenches. A wiring party of five men was out in front of the Redan when the bombardment began and three of these were blown to pieces, a fourth was reported missing. The 15th Rifles lost nine men killed, only one does not have a grave, Private

Thiepval Memorial to the Missing.

---

30 Miles, Captain Wilfred, *Military Operations, France and Belgium 1917, Vol. 3* (1948).

Schloß Thiépval nach der Erstürmung durch Inf.-Regt.180 (28. Sept. 14)

Thiepval Chateau after it was stormed by I.R.180 (28 September 1914).

William McCartney is listed on the Thiepval Memorial and may be the man who was initially listed as missing.

Arrangements were made to wash out petrol cans for issue to the trenches as water carriers. The importance of water to men in combat cannot be over-stressed. Combat breeds thirst, not only in the men, but also for the machine guns, both of which require copious amounts in action. While the Vickers machine gun was happy with water in any condition, even urine was used in emergencies, men preferred something purer for their tea and cooking. Sadly on many occasions the petrol cans were not that thoroughly cleaned leaving the tea with a distinct flavour. It rained all day on 12 June, as it had rained for almost a week and the ground had become very soggy, a foretaste of things to come. Any movement on foot was nigh impossible as cross-country tracks disappeared in the mud and the carrying of ammunition to the new artillery positions became a major operation.

In the 11th Inniskillings Colonel Hessey was promoted to command 110 Brigade in the 21st Division, his replacement as commanding officer being Lieutenant Colonel George Howard Brush, on transfer from the 10th Inniskillings. Brush was the son of Augustus E. Brush from Drumabreeze, Maralin, County Down, and had served in the South African War from 1899 to 1900 with the King's Regiment. The Reverend Alexander Spence arrived with the Inniskillings on the same date. Spence had previously been curate of Christ Church, Londonderry, and would earn the Military Cross in October 1917.

The rains continued for several days. Working parties were active throughout the division and on 14 June orders were issued that all watches and clocks were to advance by one hour. A detachment of tailors arrived from outside the division to assist in the manufacture of pennons for signalling to aeroplanes. It was again decided that petrol cans could be washed out to enable drinking water to be carried to the trenches. This made for some strange tasting cups of tea.

On 24 June the divisional artillery opened fire on the German defences. This was U Day, the first day of the Battle of Albert, or as it would become known, the Somme, and all along the front the British guns were firing. The bombardment would continue intermittently for the next twenty-four hours. There was little reply from the enemy until 8:30 pm, when they opened a severe fire on Thiepval Wood, although not much damage was done. There was an arrangement to discharge gas, but this was cancelled due to lack of wind. While wind was required to deliver gas towards the enemy positions it had to be blowing at less than seven miles per hour and would not be effective if it was raining heavily. The bombardment was to last for five days, U, V, W, X, Y, with the attack launched on Z Day.

Thiepval Chapel, late 1914.

The bombardment of the enemy wire and trenches continued. It was V Day, and numerous gaps, some up to eighty yards wide, had been cut and many sections of trench knocked in. Those gaps in the wire that had been cut during the day were kept open at night by the fire of light howitzers and 18-pounders. The enemy replied most vigorously with weapons of all calibres and trench mortars. Two German observation balloons were brought down in flames by being bombed from above according to the divisional war diary, however the records kept by the CRA stated three. A German Fokker aircraft was brought down by shelling and was seen to fall by Shaving Brush Tree. At 2:30 pm, British gas was released from Thiepval Wood, accompanied by a terrific bombardment. Enemy infantry and machine gun teams were observed moving across the open to support their D Line and fire from British 60-pounders was opened up on them.

At the morning parade on W Day, 26 June, the officers of the division were given a severe dressing down, as the result of a letter from G.H. Fowke, the Adjutant General to all units of the Fourth Army, which stated:

> During the period from the 1st to the 16th June, three cases in which Officers have disclosed their location or movements have been referred to this Office by the Chief Censor, and eight similar breaches by the rank and file have been referred to the Headquarters of Armies. The Censors are only able to examine a small proportion of the total outgoing mail, and this therefore probably represents a considerable leakage. The attention of all ranks is drawn to the necessity for secrecy being maintained at whatever cost to individual interests. The present facilities which all ranks enjoy for communications with their friends at home can only continue as long as they observe the regulations. Cases of disclosure of information, which

Thiepval Chateau following its destruction by French artillery, October 1914.

Grandcourt

may endanger the success of operations and cost the lives of many comrades, will be most severely dealt with.

In the afternoon there was a further discharge of gas towards the German lines accompanied by a heavy bombardment. The enemy was seen to reinforce from east of Grandcourt. Enemy artillery retaliation during the day was considered 'very poor'. That night there was a heavy German bombardment and many of the British gas cylinders were damaged and casualties were suffered by the men of the Special Brigade who were handling them and by those infantry who had been detailed to assist.

A party, some 100 strong, from the 8th and 13th Rifles, raided the German trenches opposite Thiepval Wood and penetrated as far as the second line. Among them were Corporal William 'Jack' Peake of B Company 13th Rifles, from Downpatrick and Lieutenant Morgan Moore, from Letterkenny, County Donegal. Moore had been educated at Trinity College, Dublin and Cambridge, being commissioned into the Rifles in the autumn of 1914. The trenches were found to have been badly knocked about and a German officer, two NCOs and ten other ranks were taken prisoner. Two men died on the raid, Lance Sergeant William John Brown, aged 20, of B Company 13th Rifles, from Comber, County Down, and Private J.H. Cunningham, aged 32, of A Company 11th Rifles, from Carrickfergus, County Antrim.[31]

---

31 *Newtownards Chronicle.* Corporal Peake's brother, Private Reuben Henry Peake, was killed on 8 August 1917,

Thiepval.

That same night another trench raid was carried out by the 13th Rifles, this time under the command of Captain Elliott Johnston, a 28-year old from Deramore Park, Belfast. The route into the enemy trench was marked out with white tape that had been laid a short time previously by Lieutenant Moore. On this particular night, between 11:00 pm and 2:30 am, Moore laid tape for several raiding parties, at times cutting his way through the enemy wire and again marking the gaps with tape. Due to random enemy shelling the tape was occasionally cut and had to be laid again. The men went forward with blackened faces and after a bout of fierce hand-to-hand fighting in the enemy trench succeeded in capturing a German officer, fourteen other ranks and a machine gun. On the return journey the Rifles were forced to take shelter in the Sunken Road and here most of their casualties were suffered, losing six men killed and nine wounded by enemy shelling.[32] The last raider to be carried back to the Rifles' trench was a wounded man, brought in by Lieutenant Moore. For his actions on this night Moore was awarded the Military Cross, as was Captain Johnston.[33] Interrogation of the prisoners and an examination of their respirators revealed no word or sign of the gas that had been released earlier. Corporal Peake was awarded the Military Medal for his actions during the raid. He had successfully searched several enemy dug-outs and taken two prisoners and then commanded a blocking party as the main body withdrew. Corporal William John Peake, always known as Jack, and his brother Reuben, came from Ballywalter on the Ards peninsula; both men had enlisted on the outbreak of war. Jack joined the 13th Rifles, while Reuben, who was only seventeen, had grown a moustache and eventually succeeded in being posted to 7th Rifles.

The bombardment intensified on X Day, with shells falling through driving rain. Gas was used by the 32nd Division. Again the enemy counter-bombardment was considered to be feeble, a view not shared by those men in the forward trenches. German prisoners reported that they had received no food for three days due to the shelling and the destruction of supplies. Given the weather, it was decided by the High Command to postpone the attack for two days. Z Day was to

aged eighteen, while serving with the 2nd Rifles.

32   CWGC list only four men from the 13th Rifles killed that night and, it is probable that the others died of wounds at a later date.

33   Captain Johnston was killed on 1 July 1916.

Advanced trenches in the park at Thiepval.

have been 29 June and this was then changed to Y1 Day and the following day Y2 Day. The opportunity was then taken to provide inter-brigade relief to give some rest to those troops that had been under the enemy bombardment. Unfortunately this rest was in huts located at Martinsart, with their next-door neighbour being a battery of siege howitzers that was firing both night and day.

The German retaliatory bombardment on Y Day was equally as serious and in the divisional area it was concentrated on Thiepval Wood. Large quantities of shells also fell in the Marsh, with the obvious intention of destroying the crossings. The divisional trench mortar batteries, engaged in cutting the German wire, came under particularly heavy fire. In the late evening, approximately 10:00 pm, on 28 June the 13th Rifles were in the process of relieving the 11th Rifles at Thiepval Wood. They had left the village of Martinsart, marching by platoons spaced at 200 yard intervals, the order of the march being D Company, followed by A Company and then C Company. On arrival A Company took over the front line from the 11th Rifles and remained in the assembly trenches. D Company went into the left of the line and C Company into Antrim Villas. As No.11 Platoon of C Company and Battalion Headquarters, a total of 58 men, left the village a single shell landed in the middle of the group, killing 14 men immediately and mortally wounding a further ten. Almost everyone else was injured including Major Perceval-Maxwell, the second-in-command, and Major Wright, the Adjutant. Among the wounded was Private Andy Bell, brother of RQMS Bell. After treatment in hospital Bell was offered a commission and posted to the 12th Rifles, he was taken prisoner on 22 March 1918. Major Perceval-Maxwell was injured to the extent that he had to be sent home; his place was taken by Major Lloyd.[34] One of those killed was Private Richard Crawley, originally from Larne, but then residing in Hillsborough. He left a widow, Edith, from Larne.

Bad as this shelling was, a more serious result would have been the shelling of Lancashire Dump on the Albert-Hamel road in Aveluy Wood during the hours of darkness on any night. This was the rendezvous point for the transport bringing up supplies of ammunition, food and other necessities

---

34   Those killed were, RSM Beatson, CSM McCoy, Privates Crawley, Heenan, Mercer, Crangle, Bell, Martin, Hamilton, Thompson, Darragh, Jones, Carson and Dale. Of these four came from the town of Banbridge and four from the village of Hillsborough.

for the forthcoming offensive. On the river bank dug-outs had been specially constructed to hold these supplies and the work of the divisional train was overseen by Colonel Bernard, 10th Rifles, who ensured the smooth running of the re-supply missions. Such was the proximity of the dump to the enemy trenches that the most extraordinary measures had to be taken to prevent discovery. Wagon wheels were wrapped with straw and disused motor tyres, while chains were replaced by leather straps. Special boots were designed and fitted to the hooves of the horses and drivers were constantly on the alert to stop their charges from neighing a greeting to other horses, something they were prone to do on a regular basis.

Through the bombardment an officer from DADOS made his way forward to the 15th Rifles and delivered a new Lewis gun to replace one damaged by shrapnel. He then delivered some harsh words about the future care of the weapon during enemy bombardments and a warning not to leave it on the lip of the trench.

It was Y1 Day and again Thiepval Wood received concentrations of enemy artillery, leaving the front line and support trenches in a very bad way. It was noticed that when a British bombardment began the enemy

Lieutenant William M Wright, 13th Royal Irish Rifles, was wounded at Martinsart and later served as a captain with the Royal Dublin Fusiliers.

immediately put down a counter bombardment on the River Ancre crossings. This made the crossing, even for individual runners, nearly impossible. The wire cutting continued at a satisfactory rate and the postponement meant that more gaps were cut. According to the artillery observers all the wire that had been required to be cut had been cut. Although according to General A.R. Cameron, writing to Brigadier General James Edmonds in May 1930, as he compiled the *Official History*; "I presume in the preliminary account of the battle you have dealt with the bombardment which certainly to an onlooker seemed rather inadequate and ineffective. It is of course obvious that everything depended on the result of the bombardment as exemplified by the difference in results obtained by the 36th and 32nd Divisions."

This view of the artillery preparation was shared by General Sir A.A. Montgomery-Massingberd, who wrote to Edmonds in January 1931:

> It is interesting that the only ground we were able to hold on to was on the front where distant objectives were given to the troops, in spite of the greatest gallantry and very heavy losses, not only failed to get to distant objectives (except in the case of the 36th Division), but failed in all cases to hold the near ones. We had not yet the guns to deal with such deep objectives and, as the narrative shows very clearly, the ground was, as a result, not sufficiently prepared for the infantry advance.

Nach erfolgreicher Verteidigung
des Eckpfeilers der Sommeschlacht, „Thiépval“,
abgelöfte Kampftruppen des Inf.-Regt. 180 in Achiet le Grand (Sept. 16)

Park von Thiépval im Sept. 16

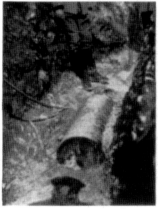

Blindgänger einer engl. 38-cm-Granate
in Thiépval

Top: members of I.R. 180 in
Achiet le Grand following
their successful defence of the
cornerstone of the Somme
positions at Thiepval.
Centre: The park at Thiepval,
September 1916.
Bottom: at unexploded British
38cm shell, Thiepval.

Thiepval
Chateau.

Dawn of Y2 Day was fine, with good visibility and some sunshine. A heavy British bombardment was fired in the morning and another in the afternoon. By this date a French artillery brigade of 75mm guns was attached to the division for counter-battery work; and was assigned to fire gas shells in the opening hours of the battle. This brigade had arrived almost at the last minute and required gun pits. The pioneers, with the assistance of the 11th Inniskillings set to work immediately and soon had the required gun pits dug, along with dug-outs for ammunition storage completed.

In the 10th Inniskillings Colonel Ross Smyth had a serious fall from his horse and broke his leg. This was a severe fracture that saw him sent home and he was not to serve with his battalion again.[35] Command of the Inniskillings devolved to Major Francis (Frank) Samuel Needham Macrory, who came from Limavady and was to earn the DSO.

Probably the first inclination that the general public in Ulster had regarding the events in France was the publication of a letter from General Nugent to General Richardson, published in the *Belfast News Letter* on 4 July 1916:

> June 30th 1916
>
> Dear George,
> Before you get this we shall have put the values of the Ulster Division to the supreme test. I have no fears of the result. I am certain no General in the armies out here has a finer Division, fitter or keener. I am certain they will be magnificent in attack, and we could hardly have a date better calculated to inspire every national tradition amongst our men of the North. It makes me very sad to think what the price may be; but I am sure the officers and men think nothing of that. They only want to be let go, – Believe me, yours sincerely.
> O.S. Nugent

By the end of the day, the officers, the men and the Ulster public would be thinking a lot about that!

---

35 Colonel Smyth did not have much luck with horses and died in a fall from his pony and trap on 27 September 1917, aged 55 years. Both father and son are listed on the Londonderry War Memorial, despite not residing within the county borough boundaries, most likely due to previous service.

7

Battle of Albert
1 July 1916

The Somme, both the glory and the graveyard of 'Kitchener's Army', those citizen volunteers who, instantly answering the call in 1914, had formed the first national army of Britain.[1]

The Battle of Waterloo had been fought on Sunday 18 June 1815. Then the British had held their ground until the arrival of their German allies, thus ensuring victory against the French on a European battlefield. One hundred and one years later and 108 miles away, again on a European battlefield, a British army, with French allies faced a German army. While the action fought in 1815 was settled in a single day, thanks to the Prussians, that of 1916 would take somewhat longer, again due to the Prussians.

The battle that would be known as the Somme would last from July to November 1916 and traced its origins back to the Chantilly Conference of 6 to 8 December 1915. Here French General Joffre met with the Allied commanders, including Sir John French, to discuss the war so far. Joffre considered that the autumn offensives in Champagne, Artois and Loos had achieved brilliant tactical results, which could have been expanded into strategic success but for the weather and a temporary shortage of ammunition. Due to the question of ammunition it was decided that any future operations could not be mounted for at least three months. However, by February Joffre realised that the date must be postponed further if the Russian offensive was to take place simultaneously and the British were to play their part with the new Kitchener armies.[2]

Given the importance of this action in Ulster's history this chapter will cover not only the action on the day and days after, but will go back in time slightly to cover the intensive preparations made by the division.

The forthcoming attack by the British Fourth Army had been preceded by a five-day artillery bombardment of the enemy positions. The objective of the bombardment had been to kill as many of the enemy as possible, to blow in his trenches and machine gun emplacements, to cut his wire, destroy his morale and pave the way for the infantry assault. Supporting the division's attack was their own 36th Divisional Artillery, a brigade from the 49th Division and a regiment of French artillery. This support, on the day, would be directed by a forward observation officer attached to the headquarters of each battalion. These observers were under the sole command of the artillery liaison officers located at the relevant infantry brigade headquarters and would only advance when told to by him. Each observation officer was to be accompanied by three telephonists, one a linesman, two miles of wire, two telephones, flags, discs and lamps. The artillery liaison officer was to have one officer with him to send forward as he required, obtaining information on the progress of the attack. If any re-bombardment was ordered during Z Day or afterwards, it would

---

1   Liddell Hart, Basil, *History of the First World War* (1970).
2   Ibid.

last for 30 minutes, the last five minutes of which was to be intensive. Serving with the French artillery on 1 July was Private R.T. 'Bob' Grange of the 35th Divisional Signals Company, who came from Ballyclare, County Antrim:

> I was attached to a brigade of French artillery and looked after their communications up forward. I remember reading some years ago that a French war correspondent described the Ulstermen as entering the battle as enthusiastic young sportsmen and emerging as professional soldiers. He was correct as this was our first engagement and we learnt from it.[3]

The orders issued to the infantry were emphatic and detailed, with the following points stressed. It was important that the utmost cooperation with the artillery was achieved. Each night the artillery was to shell enemy communication trenches, approaches, roads, railways, etc., to stop the replenishment of ammunition, food and water to the enemy's front-line trenches. In this machine guns were to cooperate by intermittent fire throughout the hours of darkness. Gaps in the wire cut by the artillery were to be covered by machine gun fire to prevent it being replaced or repaired.

From the opening of the preparatory bombardment to the end of the battle, the British artillery suffered a loss of twenty-five percent of their guns due to design faults and inferior material. Of all shells fired some thirty percent failed to explode.[4]

At Thiepval, 1st July, 1916.

Charge of the Ulster Division.

"When I saw the Ulstermen emerge through the smoke and form up as on parade, I could hardly believe my eyes. Then I saw them attack, beginning at a slow walk over no-man's land, and then suddenly let loose as they charged over the two front lines of the enemy's trenches, shouting 'No Surrender!'"—*The Times.*

'The charge of the Ulster Division', by William Connor, taken from a newspaper clipping.
(*Times*, 7 July 1916.

Both 108 and 109 Brigades were to arrange to keep at least six machine guns from their brigade machine gun companies in action in the Thiepval Wood sub-sector and the Hamel sub-sector respectively throughout this period. Each gun was allotted certain communication trenches or other approaches as its defined targets. During the Y/Z night these guns were withdrawn and made available for use in the attack as required by the brigade commanders. To support those troops attacking north of the Ancre, machine guns of the 107 Brigade, four from Thiepval Wood and four from Hamel, were to enfilade the German trenches on the north bank of the Ancre. In order to register and ensure accuracy the guns were to occupy their position during the five days of the bombardment, and as their task was directly concerned with helping the assault, these guns

---

3   Private Grange gives no source for this.
4   Strachan, *The First World War.*

had to have choice of position. The guns of the 108 and 109 Brigades would not therefore take any emplacements required by 107 Brigade.

The Lewis guns of the battalion in the line during the bombardment were to be used for opening bursts of fire on the gaps in the enemy wire to ensure that these were not repaired, and would also fire surprise bursts on concealed approaches where reinforcements and ration parties might be congregated. The 2-inch trench mortars would take every advantage of the bombardment to cut wire and destroy machine gun emplacements. The rate of expenditure of ammunition was never to fall below that of 50 rounds per mortar daily. The Stokes mortars were to open a deliberate fire on any targets within their range, but would not employ very rapid fire and care was to be taken that the detachments were kept fresh for the hurricane bombardment on the day of the assault.

Gas canisters had been installed at certain positions on the front line in order to inflict losses on the enemy by taking him by surprise at night. Canisters were installed in the Thiepval Wood sub-sector, approximately from Inverness Street to Thurso Street, and in the Hamel sub-sector along the new trench at the extreme left of the line. The gas was to be discharged at any favourable hour and was the responsibility of the Special Company, Royal Engineers. The noise created by the discharge was to be covered by rapid rifle and machine gun fire and be maintained with the view of killing Germans who were forced to get out of their trenches. Divisions were to be ready to let off gas from the night U-V inclusive. If the wind was favourable a wire would be sent by the corps after 5:00 pm, as follows: 'WARN ROGER'. If the wind continued favourable a fixed hour would be sent by corps headquarters giving zero hour, at which gas would be discharged, as follows: 'ROGER TONIGHT' (Time). On conclusion of the gas discharge a raid would take place on each flank of the trench onto which the gas had been discharged and the raiding parties would turn inwards along the gassed trench. To support this raid a barrage was to be put up on each flank of the gassed trench. As it was impossible beforehand to tell the two points on the German front trench between which the gas would take effect, a message was to be sent to the supporting artillery as soon as this had been established. The supporting barrages would then be supplied using four 18-pounder batteries and one 4.5-inch howitzer battery. The front and support lines would not be fired on; the 18-pounders would concentrate on the reserve lines, while the 4.5-inch battery would shell the communication trenches. A steady rate of fire was to be used for this barrage during the entire period of the raid.

On the morning of 1 July 1916, 36th Division was on the extreme left flank of X Corps. On its right flank was 32nd Division; this was a New Army Division and consisted mainly of service battalions with a few regular battalions included, one of which was 2nd Inniskillings. The 32nd Division's objective on 1 July was the village of Thiepval.

On the left flank of 36th Division was 29th Division comprising of 86, 87 and 88 Brigades. Two Irish battalions served with this division, the 1st Inniskillings and 1st Royal Dublin Fusiliers. The 29th Division had recently fought in Gallipoli and had earned a reputation second to none; their nickname was the 'Incomparables'. Its objective on 1 July was the capture of Beaumont-Hamel, a German strongpoint manned by the German 51 Reserve Brigade, consisting of Reserve Infantry Regiments 119 and 121. To assist the attack the British had dug a mine below Hawthorne Ridge, timed to be detonated ten minutes prior to zero.

Running almost up the centre of the division's front was the Ancre, its marshy banks precluding any direct advance along there. The right flank boundary of the division was from the north-east corner of Thiepval Wood to the position known as D8. The left boundary ran from the Mary Redan to a bridge across the Ancre approximately halfway between Beaucourt-sur-Ancre and Grandcourt. The objective on the right flank was the German D Line, their fifth line of trenches. On the left the objective was a triangle of trenches just beyond Beaucourt railway station. The divisional frontage was 2,800 yards.

On either side of the bed of the Ancre the ground rose steeply. On the north it was cut by a gorge running down from the village of Beaumont-Hamel at right angles to the river and parallel with the German trenches. On the southern side the ground rose up in a rising convex curve, rising 250 feet in a thousand yards. The crest of this hill, known as Hill 151, was crowned by a parallelogram of trenches extending from the enemy B Line to the C Line.[5] This position would become known as the Schwaben Redoubt (*Fest Schwaben*).[6] As well as numerous machine guns, the trenches were defended by masses of barbed wire. A British artillery officer located in Brock's Benefit on Mesnil Ridge had counted sixteen rows of wire placed in front of the line facing the river. The majority of the German dug-outs were at least thirty feet deep and practically impervious to all but the heaviest of shells. They were also spacious enough to hold the entire trench garrison. It was the belief of the Germans that if this strongpoint was taken it could endanger the entire German position to both the north and south and it was imperative that this position be held at all costs.

The divisional attack was divided into four sections, defined as right, right-centre, left and left-centre. The right section was allocated to General Shuter's 109 Brigade, while the right-centre section was the responsibility of General Griffith's 108 Brigade. The left-centre section, which ran from the north east corner of Thiepval Wood to the River Ancre, was not attacked directly due to the ground conditions. The left section was also the responsibility of 108 Brigade, which was reinforced by the 15th Rifles from Brigadier Withycombe's 107 Brigade, with the remainder of the brigade in support. It was fully realised that these dispositions left nothing in the way of a divisional reserve (Divisional war diary, after action report).

36th Division 1 July 1916

LEFT	LEFT-CENTRE	RIGHT-CENTRE	RIGHT
Griffith	Not attacked	Griffith	Shuter
108 Brigade	waterlogged ground	108 Brigade	109 Brigade
Left of the Ancre		13th Rifles	10th Inniskillings
12th Rifles		11th Rifles	9th Inniskillings
9th Irish Fusiliers		15th Rifles	14th Rifles
		(From 107th)	11th Inniskillings

Withycombe
107 Brigade in reserve, less 15th Rifles

The role for 109 Brigade was to assault the German A and B lines (This second line was also known as the A.I. line) and advance to a line between C8 and B16 on the Grandcourt to Thiepval Road, a frontage of some 400 yards. Here they were to halt and consolidate. The brigade advanced on a two-battalion front, 10th Inniskillings on the left and 9th Inniskillings on the right, with the 14th Rifles and 11th Inniskillings forming the second line. In keeping with the tactics of the time the battalions would advance in waves consisting of two platoons per wave on a 400 yard front with five yards between each man. Each battalion would advance in eight waves at 50-yard intervals with additional waves for headquarter troops and stretcher bearers, all advancing at a steady walking pace of 50 yards per minute. The individual soldier was carrying approximately 70 pounds

---

5   A parallelogram is a simple, non-intersecting, quadrilateral with two pairs of parallel sides. The opposite or facing sides of which are of equal length and the opposite angles of a parallelogram are of equal measure. Simple!

6   Schwaben; or 'Swabia' in English, is one of seven regions of Bavaria. It lies in the south-west area of the state. It is very rich in cultural and architectural history that spreads far beyond the borders of modern-day Bavaria.

of equipment, but this included his uniform, boots, rifle, bombs and ammunition. Added to this was an entrenching tool, a number of empty sandbags and wire cutters. Successive waves carried rolls of barbed wire and screw stakes to help build defences in captured trenches, which would now be facing the other way. Much criticism has been levelled at the directives that said men should walk at this rate and carry so much equipment. Given the intensity of the pre-attack bombardment, it was supposed that enemy resistance would be negligible and it should be known that in 1916 the basic tactical unit of manoeuvre was the company, approximately 100 men, under the command of just one officer. The vast majority of the New Army divisions, of which the 36th was one, had been given little in the way of tactical training and its battlefield experience was limited. The first day of July 1916, was the first time the division, in common with others, would fight as a single formation.

The first two battalions were to take and hold the final objective, while the following up battalions would hold the A and B lines and send out liaison patrols to maintain contact with the leading battalions. The prime objective of the 11th Inniskillings was the capture and subsequent fortification of the position known as the Crucifix on the Thiepval to Grandcourt Road.

In the right-centre section 108 Brigade was to clear the A and B lines within its section and then advance to the C line where it would consolidate on the salient formed by C9, C10 and C11, which was the north-east corner of the Schwaben Redoubt. Here a special detachment of one Stokes mortar, one Vickers machine gun and a Lewis gun was to act as left flank guard, to clear the communication trench from B19 to C12 and hold the latter as a defensive post. They would also send a detachment to C13 to act as observers for fire directed on to the Grandcourt to St Pierre Divion Road. In addition, two officers' patrols, each of platoon strength and equipped with a Lewis gun were to carry out a reconnaissance and clear the left of the A and B lines up as far as St. Pierre Divion. In this section General Griffith was attacking with the 11th Rifles on the right, the 13th Rifles on the left and the 15th Rifles from 107 Brigade in support.

Second Lieutenant Mathew John Wright served in C Company of the 14th Royal Irish Rifles and was killed in action on 1 July 1916. He was the son of the Reverend William and Charlotte Wright of Newtownards, County Down.

Sergeant David Harkness Blakey MM, No.18634, 11th Royal Inniskilling Fusiliers, whose body was found at Connaught Cemetery in October 2013. Previously listed on the Thiepval Memorial as missing, he was the son of Henry and Isabella Blakey and left a widow Sarah, he was 26 years old. Today buried in grave V.A.13.

In the left section north of the Ancre, the 12th Rifles on the left flank and 9th Irish Fusiliers on the right, were tasked with assaulting the German trenches from A27 opposite Mary Point and clearing them down to the railway, establishing strong-points at B26, B24, B21 and occupying Beaucourt Station and the trenches behind it. They would then occupy the Mill on the river-bank and two houses located just beyond the railway station. One platoon of the 12th Rifles was detailed to attack the railway sap, while another patrolled the marsh.[7]

When 108 and 109 Brigades had completed their tasks up to the D line, 107 Brigade, moving in artillery formation, was to pass through them, attack the D line from D8 to D9, from where they would extend their left flank to D11. The brigade was to deploy the 10th Rifles with their right flank on D8 and the 9th Rifles with their left flank on D9. When this position had been captured the 9th Rifles would extend to D10 and the 10th Rifles to D9. The 8th Rifles moving up in support were to occupy and hold a line running from D10 to D11.

Sergeant Wesley Jackson was killed in action on 1 July 1916, while serving with the 9th Royal Irish Fusiliers.

From the divisional observation posts all barbed wire that could be seen was apparently effectively cut and the enemy trenches were pulverised beyond recognition. Artillery fire to support the attack was not a creeping barrage, as would be employed in later attacks, although such a barrage was in fact used by the French on their front.

For the British attack there was a final intensive bombardment of 65 minutes when it fell on each German line in succession. It lifted from the A line to 'AI at Zero', from the AI at Zero plus three minutes, from the B line at Zero plus 18 minutes, to a line 400 yards east of this objective. Then at Zero plus 28 minutes it would move on to the C line and at Zero plus one hour 18 minutes from the C line to the D line. There would then be a halt to permit the passing through of 107 Brigade. At Zero plus two hours 38 minutes the barrage would move up to a line 300 yards east of the D line. At each lift, sections of 18-pounder field guns and 4.5-inch howitzers 'walked up' the communication trenches to the next barrage line. The Stokes mortars were to fire in a final hurricane bombardment just prior to Zero, while the medium mortars of Z/49 Trench Mortar Battery, on loan from 49th Division and heavy mortars would also be used. The Stokes mortars were to concentrate on specific targets, while the heavier mortars would accompany the artillery barrage to the extent of their range.

The brigade of French 75mm field guns assisted with the wire cutting, using high explosive as opposed to shrapnel according to its custom. The British preferred to use shrapnel, which cut wire without causing shell holes. However, for 1 July the main role of the French guns was to

---

7   In the official summary written just after the battle it states that the 9th Irish Fusiliers and 12th Rifles were on the 'right' bank of the Ancre, a mistake that has been repeated by subsequent writers, the latest in 2013.

smother the Ancre valley with gas shells. In the preparation of the official history, Captain Cyril Falls later wrote; "You might add that the Corps had a French artillery regiment attached which used gas during the preliminary bombardment. I fancy the gas was useless, but the seventy-fives did wonderfully good work with their H.E. flanking barrage when the 36th Division was 'out by itself.'"

In the assault each battalion was to be accompanied by two Vickers machine guns from the relevant machine gun company, the remaining eight guns of the company being in the brigade reserve. Eighteen Stokes mortars were to go forward; the detachments of the remaining 18 weapons were to act as carriers of ammunition and other supplies.

The 109 Brigade was allotted two sections of 150 Field Company, while one section of 122 Field Company went with 108 Brigade; the remaining companies being held in the divisional reserve.

There were two main dressing stations for the division. The first at Forceville, was manned by the 108th Field Ambulance, a second at Clairfaye Farm was under the control of 110th Field Ambulance, while the advance dressing station was located close to the Albert to Arras Road in Aveluy Wood. The evacuation of wounded from the regimental aid posts located in Thiepval Wood and Authuille was via the Authuille Bridge, or by the trench tramway which crossed the River Ancre to the north of it. The vehicles of the field ambulance were parked on the Martinsart to Albert Road, south of the former village, while a collecting point for walking wounded was located to the west of Martinsart. Here horse-drawn wagons would carry the wounded along a cross-country track through Hédouville to Clairfaye Farm. From Hamel the wounded were to be evacuated through a specially dug trench from the village to a point on the Hamel to Albert Road that was screened from enemy observation.

Memorial to Sergeant Samuel Bond YCV, killed on 1 July 1916, while serving in A Company of the 14th Royal Irish Rifles. His parents lived at Manor Drive, Belfast, his late father having served in the Royal Navy.

Saturday 1 July saw a day of bravery and death, but even before the men left their trenches both would be fully evident. At 6:45 am, in a crowded assembly trench known as Elgin Avenue in Aveluy Wood, the men of the 14th Rifles were preparing for the forthcoming attack. Private William McFadzean, from Lurgan, County Armagh, employed as a bomber, was opening a box of bombs when it slipped from the trench edge and two fell to the ground, their safety pins coming loose. As a trained bomber, McFadzean knew the effect this would have and immediately threw himself on top of the two bombs. They exploded almost simultaneously and he was killed instantly. Due to his swift action only one other man was seriously injured, Private George Gillespie, his leg so shattered it had to be amputated. For his actions Private McFadzean was the first man of the division to be posthumously awarded the Victoria Cross, the first member of the division to be so. Three more VCs would be awarded within the next forty-eight hours, while a further five would be awarded by the end of the War. The award of the Victoria Cross has long been contentious and many more were earned

Private William McFadzean VC, 14th Royal Irish Rifles.

than were awarded. An example of this can be found in a letter from Stuart Hall to his mother at Castlerock, Londonderry, dated 7 March 1916; "I saw young Hollinger who got the DCM, he is a perfect gasbag and there was a corporal telling me one McGuiggan ought to have got the V.C. at Richenburg, but there was no one to recommend him."

Elgin Avenue was also the location of the regimental aid post of the 11th Inniskillings, under the command of Captain D.E. Crosbie, RAMC. At Lancashire Dump, Tommy Jordan of the Cyclist Corps, now a lance corporal, was assisting Sergeant Cassidy, Privates Crawford, Cunningham and about 40 others, to lay a rail track from the dump to Peterhead Sap; "It seemed to go on for miles. Lancashire Dump was near Albert. We had quite a few Roman Catholics, Sergeant Tommy Cassidy for one."[8]

Battle: 1 July 1916

The *Belfast News Letter* of 1 July 1916 in its 'Ulster and the War' column, was simply that, a single column, and carried news of the current operations in East Africa, also that Brevet Lieutenant Colonel Louis J Lipsell, CMG, had been promoted to the temporary rank of major-general, whilst commanding the First Canadian Division. Lipsell was a member of an old Ballyshannon family. There were also notices of casualties and decorations including one awarded to Mrs George King of Newry, who was made an Associate of the Royal Red Cross by the King at Buckingham Palace, for meritorious service. In most newspapers the War news merited a third of a column. The entry in General Haig's diary for 1 July 1916 reads; "Reports up to 8:00 am most satisfactory. Our troops had everywhere crossed the Enemy's front trenches."

---

8   Taped interview in the Somme Archives.

The attack of the Ulster Division on 1 July, by J.P. Beadle, the original can be found in Belfast City Hall. It shows men of the 11th Royal Irish Rifles (South Antrim Volunteers) leaving the 'A' line of trenches, with 'bombers' in the vanguard, their bombs carried in horse nose bags. The man leaving the trench with the bloodied bayonet is from the 15th Royal Irish Rifles, his unit distinguished by the Scarlet triangular shoulder flash. The officer depicted is Francis Bodenham Thornely, the nephew of Major Blair Oliphant, the second-in-command of the 11th Battalion. While recuperating after being wounded Thornely advised the artist on the composition of the painting. (Courtesy of Belfast City Council)

Such was the speed of communications in the third year of the war. Within 24 hours General Haig had a better understanding of the situation along the front line and the troops would have been committed to a second day of battle; it would take until 7 July before the people of Ulster began to comprehend the full horror of the day. The single column of 1 July would in many cases grow to a double-page spread and would continue as such for some time.

On 1 July dawn came early. It was high summer and between one day and another there was approximately four hours of darkness. The opening hours of this Saturday saw some rain, but it was light and by mid-morning the sun was blazing in a cloudless sky with all ranks feeling the heat. Zero-hour was at 7:30 am, and daylight had been some four hours earlier; there were those that felt the attacks should have been launched at this time.

Between 5:00 am and 6:00 am, the men had hot tea for breakfast and a rum ration was issued. At 6:30 am the 13th Rifles paraded and in single files moved up to the three gaps in their parapet. Being located on the steep hillside they were under cover from both view and fire there were no casualties at this time. Private Jim Brown was a scout in C Company of the 13th Rifles, commanded by Major 'Bertie' McCreedy. The battalion had a total of 15 Scouts prior to the battle, but in the hours before Zero two were killed and four wounded, leaving only two per company. The task of the scouts was to remove all papers from the enemy dead, wounded and prisoners, also

'The ration party', a famous and often used image, reported to be at the Somme.

to note their regiment or unit. Brown had been taught basic German by Major McCreedy to help in this task. In B Company Corporal Jack Peake from Ballywalter, County Down, who had previously been awarded the Military Medal, saw his platoon sergeant killed just before the advance started. As the next senior rank Jack took command of the platoon, leading it towards the first line. The platoon was about 20y yards from that line when Jack was seen to fall fatally wounded. Like many on the Somme, he has no known grave. Two other men from Ballywalter were killed while fighting alongside Corporal Peake; they were Privates Edward Curry and Robert Regan.[9] Jack's brother, Reuben, was wounded during the Third Battle of Ypres while serving with the 7th Rifles in the 16th (Irish) Division and died on 8 August 1917, when as a patient in hospital it was bombed by enemy aircraft. Like his brother, Reuben has no known grave, he was eighteen years old.[10]

At 7:15 am, the leading troops had moved out of Thiepval Wood and the trenches in front of Hamel, passed through the gaps cut in the British wire, extended into line, two paces between each man, and moved forward to within 150 yards of the barrage, where they lay down, this position marked by tape that had been laid out previously. The casualties suffered in this deployment were light, being mostly concealed by the smoke from the barrage which was terrific. The Stokes mortars were hurling bombs at the enemy lines at their highest rate of fire and there were a 100 bombs in the air at any one time.

At Zero the British barrage lifted off the enemy front line and the Stokes mortars stopped firing. To the sound of many whistles the men got to their feet and advanced at a steady pace towards the German trenches. From the trenches those commanding officers forbidden from accompanying

9   Private R Regan is buried in the AIF Burial Ground, Flers, grave X.A.2. There is no Edward Curry listed, but a William Curry, 11th Rifles (killed 1 July 1916) is commemorated on the Thiepval Memorial.
10   Down Museum archive.

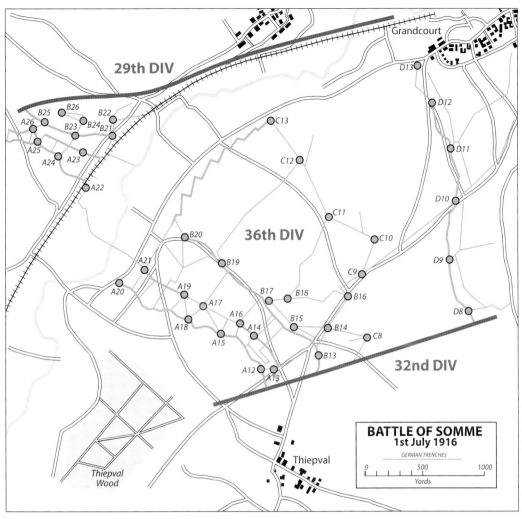

Divisional objectives on 1 July 1916.

their men saw 'powerful and enduring impressions'. Colonel Macrory of the 10th Inniskillings spoke of "…lines of men moving forward, with rifles sloped and the sun glistening upon their fixed bayonets, keeping their alignment and distance as well as if on a ceremonial parade, unfaltering, unwavering."

Colonel Ricardo, 9th Inniskillings observed:

> I stood on the parapet between the two centre exits to wish them luck. They got going without delay; no fuss, no shouting, no running, everything solid and thorough, just like them themselves. Here and there a boy would wave his hand to me as I shouted good luck to them through my megaphone. And all had a cheery face. Most were carrying loads. Fancy advancing against heavy fire with a big roll of barbed wire on your shoulder!

As these men moved forward from Thiepval Wood in the succeeding waves, they were emerging from the trees that were being rocked by exploding German shells. According to 107 Brigade's war diary it was the commanding officer's view that due to the heavy weights carried by the men, weapons and ammunition, when they arrived at the top of Thiepval Wood they were in an exhausted condition, which made the task of keeping together and in touch with the battalions almost impossible with the congestion of wounded and prisoners in the trenches. A casualty in the leading lines of the Inniskillings was Lance Corporal Richard Phillips from Fintona, County Tyrone. On the formation on the division he had successfully managed to enlist, despite being only fifteen and a half. He was a tall, strapping lad and had been appointed as a bomber. Shortly after the advance began, Phillips was hit by shell fragments that had lacerated his right arm and blown off his left hand. He was initially reported as having been killed, but this was later amended to wounded in action. His brother also served and had been reported as missing in the Dardanelles the previous August.

Colonel Ambrose St. Quentin Ricardo DSO, 9th Royal Inniskilling Fusiliers. Post-war he took a great interest in the Boy Scout movement and was Ulster's Chief Scout.

Major George Horner Gaffikin, a 30 year old from King's Castle, Ardglass in County Down, was the commander of B Company, 9th Rifles, and he led his men on waving an orange handkerchief.[11] Gaffikin had been educated at Uppingham and Clare College, Cambridge, and prior to being commissioned he had commanded the Ardglass district contingent of the UVF.

Captain Hubert Mulkern, RAMC, was attached to the 9th Inniskillings this day. He was the son of a doctor and came from Kingstown-on-Thames. Captain Mulkern was last seen at about 8:00 am in the aid post and was believed killed at this time. His place was taken by Captain Grimstone who came up from the collecting post at about 8:30 am. He remained treating the wounded and there were many, until approximately 10:30 am, when Lieutenant G. Lindsey of the 109th Field Ambulance came forward to relieve him and he returned to the collection post

In the 10th Rifles Private Richard Henry Thompson, from Belfast, was an acting lance corporal, giving him a little more responsibility than just looking out for himself. It made little difference. Like so many others he was hit quite quickly during the advance, a shell splinter lodging in his head. For the following three days he would lie in no man's land until recovered by the stretcher bearers. He survived the war, eventually reaching the rank of sergeant, but for the remainder of his life only his wife was allowed to cut his hair.[12]

It was at this point that the management of the battle was taken from the command of generals and colonels and devolved into the hands of subalterns and NCOs. Colonel Savage of the 13th Rifles reported; "Directly the start was made the German machine guns could be heard firing at once. From this time I received no messages and the companies were lost."

The leading troops reached the German front-line trench and moved straight across it, having suffered few casualties. As they moved towards the next line the German barrage fell on no man's land, decimating the following units. From positions concealed in Thiepval Cemetery, German

---

11   Anon, *The Great War 1914-1918'* (Belfast 1919).
12   Letter from Richard Wallace, Sergeant Thompson's grandson.

Believed to be stretcher bearers from the Ulster Division on Pilcken Ridge, August 1917, the man third from the left has been identified at Private James Coates from Belfast.

machine guns fired into the right flank of units that emerged from Thiepval Wood, the 11th Inniskillings and 14th Rifles being badly hit. In no man's land the garrison consisted of the dead and wounded.

The death of Captain Slacke of the 14th Rifles was witnessed by both officers and other ranks, albeit with some confusion. One report stated that together with a mere handful of men, isolated on the fringe of Thiepval village, the gallant captain held out long into the night, fighting against enormous odds, preferring to die rather than surrender. Another report stated that Captain Slacke was last seen side by side with Captain Willis, also killed, in the midst of a counter-attack "… fighting with his naked fists, being ultimately beaten to the ground under the rifle butts and bayonets of the attacking Hun."[13]

However, the testament of Private Irvine, also in A Company, stated that Captain Slacke was killed at 7:45 am while the company was crossing no man's land immediately after leaving the trenches and that death had been the result of a high explosive shell. On the other hand, Private George Courtney stated that Captain Slacke had led the company as far as the third line of German trenches and was proceeding to the fourth line when he was wounded. On attempting to return to the dressing station he was killed by a high explosive shell sometime between 10:00 am and 11:00 am. A further version came from Sergeant Adams and Corporal Doherty of the Royal Irish Fusiliers, erroneously reported as the battalion supporting the 14th Rifles. Both men stated they saw Captain Slacke at the third German line at 3:30 pm.[14]

---

13 Moore, Stephen, 'The Chocolate Soldiers', at the time of this writing an unpublished manuscript.
14 *Belfast News Letter* 5 December 1916, a report of the court case brought by Captain Slacke's widow in the Probate Court, Dublin.

Captain Charles Owen Slacke in uniform and now known to have been killed on 1 July 1916. (Courtesy of Nigel Henderson)

The stretcher bearers were hard at work across the battlefield. Private Joseph Short, serving with the 108th Field Ambulance, was making his way from shell hole to shell hole when he came across his brother Robert, a corporal with the 9th Rifles. Robert had been seriously wounded and Joseph carried him back to the dressing station, but it proved to be a mortal wound and he died that evening. The brothers came from Dundee Street, Belfast. Two other brothers were acting as stretcher bearers that day; George and Richard McCracken from Annsborough, County Down, serving in the 13th Rifles, were both hit while removing wounded from the battlefield. George died on 3 July, while Richard would eventually recover from what was a very serious wound.

(Left) In the ranks of the 108th Field Ambulance Joseph Short was again instrumental in recovering wounded men from the battlefield and was recommend for the Victoria Cross. This was rejected and no award was made. However, the incident, along with the actions of other members of the party were not forgotten by the officer commanding the unit, post war he paid tribute to the men with the presentation of silver medals in the shape of a VC. The medal was hallmarked by the Birmingham Assay Office in 1919 and is inscribed B3 1SB. (Right) Reverse. (Courtesy of Jeanetta Harper)

Private Joseph Short, serving with the 108th Field Ambulance, was making his way from shell hole to shell hole when he came across his brother Robert, a corporal with the 9th Rifles. Robert had been seriously wounded and Joseph carried him back to the dressing station, but it proved to be a mortal wound and he died that evening.

German machine guns firing from Beaucourt Redoubt on the north bank of the Ancre caused severe casualties to the 13th Rifles, who were on the left flank of 108 Brigade. At 7:30 am the 13th Rifles had advanced out of Aveluy Wood. Leading No.3 Platoon was Second Lieutenant Ernest George Boas, assisted by Sergeant Arnold. Lieutenant Boas had only been with the platoon for some three weeks, but, according to Sergeant Arnold, seemed a competent leader. The two men became separated and when Arnold reached the ground between the second and third enemy trenches he found the officer lying in a communications trench. It was the sergeant's opinion that Lieutenant Boas had been hit by enemy bombs, as these were falling thick and fast at this time. At approximately 11:00 am, Lance Corporal Watterson had watched as Lieutenant Boas, armed with a rifle and bayonet, had attacked the enemy with some ferocity, but was then wounded and he saw no more of him. Later in the day, when forced to retire, Sergeant Arnold passed the same spot where the officer had been lying and saw no sign of his body and reported; "He was not lying where we left him, and the trench had been blown

Robert Short, brother of Joseph, died of wounds received on 1 July 1916.
(Courtesy of Jeanetta Harper)

in, in two places; he could not have been taken prisoner as no Germans except prisoners under escort got through and I firmly believe he was blown to pieces by a shell."

This description of the lieutenant being armed with a rifle was not uncommon. Experience from the war in South Africa had taught the infantry officer that it was safer to blend in than be conspicuous. Private Matthew Brown was also there and wrote a letter to the lieutenant's father on 25 July:

> I'm sorry I cannot inform you as you would like, I saw the young Lieutenant before we mounted the parapet but never since. I heard some of the men in his platoon, those who returned safe, saying Lieutenant Boas knocked a German to the ground with his fist and after that he was killed. They surely have saw [sic] it happen or they would not say that, I know his platoon got badly cut up. Sir, it may be wrong, but I believe he is dead. The papers only reported him missing. It is hard, yes cruel to think of all I saw on that day. The Germans didn't take many prisoners, they would rather kill. At one time I gave up all hope and when I think today of July 1st it's a mystery I'm living.

Private Jim Brown, one of the scouts of the 13th Rifles, arrived at the first enemy trench. Here Brown had called out in both English and German for the enemy to surrender and five men did so. Once Brown had removed all the relevant papers the prisoners were handed over to the infantry to be escorted to the rear. Later Brown was wounded by a gunshot to the knee and was one of the lucky ones recovered quickly from the battlefield. While in hospital he wrote home asking that a copy of the *Bangor Spectator* newspaper be sent out to him. His sister bought a copy first thing on Friday morning and it was delivered to him in the field hospital in France the following day.[15]

The battlefield on this day was also a place of serendipity. Advancing towards the German lines was Private Truesdale of the 13th Rifles, who had previously worked in the Slieve Donard Hotel in Newcastle, County Down.[16] As he moved forward he met a group of German prisoners being escorted to the rear and immediately recognised one of them as his best friend from pre-war days in Newcastle when they had both worked in the hotel kitchens. There was a brief exchange of greetings, but they did not meet again.

Also in the brigade sector the 11th Rifles, the right-hand battalion, was equally successful, reaching part of the Hansa Line under the cover of a smokescreen provided by the Stokes mortars. Here Second Lieutenant C.G.F. Waring, commanding A Company scouts, ensured that the men, identified by their white brassards marked with a black I, removed papers and maps from the bodies of dead Germans. Within the 11th Rifles, German prisoners were escorted to the rear at a ratio of one guard per seven prisoners.

Captain Charles Craig, with B Company, 11th Rifles, reached the German C Line where he was hit in the leg by shrapnel. He lay in a shell hole for some six hours before a German counter attack was launched at 4:00 pm. Captain Craig was then found by advancing enemy troops and taken prisoner, when he was moved to a nearby trench where, such were the number of wounded, he waited until 9:00 pm, before receiving any medical treatment. A contemporary photograph shows the captain being taken from the battlefield in a wheel barrow; this was due to his size, attempts to carry him on a groundsheet proving impossible given his weight. Captain Craig was fortunate in that he was later transferred to Holland in 1918, where his wife came out to join him in October of that year. He returned to the United Kingdom, landing at Boston, Lincolnshire, with other

---

15　*Bangor Spectator* 21 July 1916.
16　No relation to the author.

Entitled 'The Glorious First of July 1916', this *Daily Mail* image shows the initial batch of German prisoners being escorted to the rear.

Newcastle memorial; on this side we have Private Herbert Cooper, killed on 28 August 1916, aged 22 years, while serving with the 10th Royal Irish Rifles. He was the nephew of Margaret Browne of Newcastle, County Down. (Courtesy of Nigel Henderson)

returning prisoners of war.[17] Also wounded was Major A.P. Jenkins, commanding A Company, 11th Rifles, he was hit in the head by a bullet and later taken prisoner.[18] An officer mortally wounded was Captain Oswald Brooke Webb, from Randalstown. He would die on 3 July.

The remainder of the brigade, on either side of the bemired Ancre valley, came under very heavy machine gun fire from St Pierre Divion.

An objective of the 10th Inniskillings was a strongpoint labelled B.16 on the map and known to the Inniskillings as 'Dungannon', which was to be consolidated once captured. An error perpetrated by the leading companies during the advance was to twice ignore the timetable of the supporting artillery barrage and, in consequence, through their eagerness to advance they ran into the barrage before it had lifted to the next target. This had come about due to the loss of many of the senior officers during the early stages of the attack. Cyril Falls wrote in the preparation of the official history; "Largely owing to the lamentable (underlined) decision that no C.O. should go over. We had a very small proportion of officers

Captain ENF Bell, VC, 1 July 1916: ... on no less than three occasions when out bombing parties, which were clearing the enemy trenches, he went forward alone and threw trench mortar bombs.

with any training among the company commanders, but some absolutely first-class soldiers."

This point was also strongly made by the then Major Frank Crozier, writing to General Edmonds in March 1930; "But Nugent had lain down that no C.O. should go any further than his battle H.Q. Had this been acted upon I do not think 9th or 10th Rifles would ever have deployed or got going."

When the German support trench was reached prisoners came out of the deep dug-outs. Most were anxious to surrender and seemed dazed by the barrage. These were then gathered up and sent back under escort, in this case one Inniskillings Fusilier to every 16 Germans. The first batches of prisoners began to move back across no man's land and they were most anxious to reach the safety of the British trenches. The prisoners ran so fast that they outstripped their escorts and met reinforcements coming forward. In the heat of the moment and faced with what was assumed to be a German charge the Inniskillings met them with levelled bayonets. The survivors managed to reach the British line and were conveyed to the rear. This was not the only instance of this happening, the confusion of the battlefield being manifold. Some wounded of the 10th Inniskillings were brought in by James McIntyre, by then a sergeant. Among the injured was Lance Corporal Robert

---

17   Craig was subsequently awarded the Croix de Chevalier of the Legion of Honour, *Belfast News Letter* November 1918.

18   Adam Primrose Jenkins had previously commanded the 1st Lisburn Battalion of the UVF and when this unit enlisted he felt obliged to go with them despite his age. Due to the severity of his wound he was transferred to Switzerland in January 1917, where he was interned until the end of the War. His son, Garret Primrose Jenkins, C Battery 75 Brigade, RFA, was killed on 7 September 1917.

Bacon from Portstewart, who died of his wounds and Captain Lindsay who survived despite having a shell land between him and Sergeant McIntyre, which thankfully did not explode. The sergeant brought in a third man and, as a result was awarded the Military Medal.

Despite the abundance of enemy fire the advance continued. The plan had been that the German B line was to be reached at 7:48 am. Even without the majority of their officers the leading battalions crossed it at precisely that moment. Here a large number of prisoners were taken and these were immediately sent to the rear under guard. From the North Irish Horse, No.2 and No.4 Troops had been attached to the division for this attack and their primary task was to escort these prisoners back to the divisional lines, in this case with one guard per seven prisoners.

The 15th Rifles, the supporting battalion of 108 Brigade, had a fierce fight with enemy troops who emerged from dug-outs in the A line after the leading waves had passed. The bombing squads of the leading battalion that should have dealt with these positions all had been killed or wounded by machine guns firing on them from both flanks. Maintaining their pace behind the barrage, the leading battalion reached the C line, including the north-east corner of the Schwaben Redoubt at 8.48am. Here the advance came to a halt. Even in the cover of the German trenches they suffered from the machine gun fire and artillery which ensured that any movement from front or rear was all but impossible. Those survivors of the supporting battalion had also reached their objectives, but were going no further. All reports from this part of the front indicated that the wire had been well cut by the artillery.

In the 108th Trench Mortar Battery Company Sergeant Major John Croft, from Railway View Street, Bangor, was well aware that the enemy were closing in on all sides. Realising that capture or death was almost inevitable, he and his officer destroyed their mortar to keep it from falling into German hands. Such was the ebb and flow of the battle that he was eventually able to return to the brigade positions. For his actions John Croft was awarded the Distinguished Conduct Medal; he would continue to serve and was taken prisoner in March 1918.

At 7:30 am the bugles had sounded the advance throughout the 9th and 10th Inniskillings of 109 Brigade, situated on the right flank of the division. Second Lieutenant William Arthur Hewitt of the 9th Inniskillings led his platoon over the top. Almost immediately they were hit by the concentrated machine gun fire and both Hewitt and Sergeant Lally were wounded. Colonel Ricardo later wrote to Hewitt's father; "Your little lad Willie led his platoon over our parapet and the last I saw of him was his happy smile as I wished him good luck."[19]

Hewitt's wound did not preclude him leading his men on towards the German line. The Inniskillings advanced at a steady walk, laden as they were with equipment. After crossing 300 to 400 yards of no man's land they found that the enemy wire had been successfully cut by the artillery and both battalions continued to advance through to the German reserve trench, some 500 yards inside the Schwaben Redoubt, an advance of almost a mile from their starting position. By 8:30 am, the advance had reached the Mouquet Switch and the eastern salient of the Redoubt.

The attack by 107 Brigade had begun by its moving out of Aveluy Wood, crossing the River Ancre and advancing to the western side of Thiepval Wood, almost at the bottom of the valley. Here they had assembled at 6:30 am, in the area of the track known as Speyside, and waited for zero. During the hour spent under shellfire they suffered, few casualties. Such was the steepness of the hill that most shells passed over their heads and exploded in the marsh behind them. They were joined just before Zero by Second Lieutenant Thorpe and 25 men and two mortars of the 107th Trench Mortar Battery. Thorpe and his detachment joined the 10th Rifles in Aveluy Wood. Loaded with their weapons and 50 mortar bombs they accompanied the battalion as it moved up to the line. After crossing Ross Castle the rear half company of the battalion was held up by machine gun and trench mortar fire from Thiepval village. Lieutenant Thorpe and two of his

---

19 *Bangor Spectator* 14 July 1916.

NCOs went forward in an attempt to bring fire down on these positions, but the lieutenant and one NCO were wounded, while one of their mortars was knocked out by shellfire. As a result of this none of the mortars was able to make it out of the woods. A second section of mortars, led by Lieutenant Lloyd Dodd had joined the 9th Rifles and had followed this battalion to the top of the wood. However, due to the confusion caused by numerous wounded men and returning enemy prisoners, the section became separated and lost touch. Lieutenant Dodd and his remaining detachment with their mortars pressed on forward and eventually joined up with Lieutenant J.B. Brown's section, also of two mortars, that had been attached to the 8th Rifles. The mortars were brought into action near the position known as Omagh. Here they were of great assistance in breaking up a later German counter-attack. Lieutenant Brown had been wounded earlier in the action, but Sergeant Brown, of the lieutenant's section, took command and all ranks performed well. When the ammunition was expended Lieutenant Dodd withdrew his mortars to the A line and later to Gordon Castle, which was 107 Battery Headquarters.

At Zero, 107 Brigade, led by the 10th Rifles, had moved back east for a short distance in order to reach the paths through Thiepval Wood to the front line. The path being used by the 10th Rifles had been stripped of its foliage by the enemy bombardment and the men were in full view of the Germans as they advanced. They came under machine gun fire from their front, right and right rear almost simultaneously. As the battalion reached the position known as Ross Castle, Colonel Bernard was struck by a shell splinter in the head and killed, one of many to fall within the first few minutes. Command of the battalion then devolved to Captain J. Sugden, the adjutant, and the advance became a series of short rushes towards the front line, the men clearly being able to see the muzzle flashes of the enemy guns firing on them. An attempt was made to bring forward the Lewis gun teams to try and counteract the enemy guns, but each was shot down before coming into action. The other battalions in the brigade suffered fewer casualties as the wood rides were still well screened by trees and were further from batteries firing from Thiepval. At 9:15 am, the brigade, acting in support, crossed no man's land, suffering considerable losses. They pushed on and got within 100 yards of the Grandcourt Line, where they ran into their own artillery barrage and were forced to ground in the open, taking whatever cover was available, including shell holes. Added to their discomfort was machine gun fire coming from Beaucourt Redoubt and Grandcourt. At 10:10 am, however, some fifty men of the brigade entered Stuff Redoubt and discovered it was unoccupied. Another group of men entered the Redoubt some 300 yards to the north, working their way along the trench towards Grandcourt and eventually blocking it. On the left 200 men reached a German artillery battery position in the upper sector of Battery Valley.

Just before 10:00 am, some runners, with a combination of skill and good luck, had returned to report that the C line had been reached. Ahead of the 8th Rifles the artillery had done an efficient job of cutting the wire, apart from just in front of the Grandcourt Line where there were only a few gaps. Several casualties were suffered from 'friendly fire' while waiting for the guns to lift from here.[20]

Private Andrew Ranson, from the Ravenhill Road, Belfast, served in A Company of the 8th Rifles and was the acting orderly to the battalion commander, Colonel Pelly. Private Ranson was reported to have been killed in sight of the German D Line at the top of Grandcourt Road at Thiepval. Andrew is listed on the CWGC site as dying on 2 July 1916 and it is possible that he died later of wounds received. His brother Thomas, also a member of the battalion, was wounded on 1 July and evacuated to hospital in England. Andrew Ranson was posted as missing in action and his death was only confirmed in April 1917.[21]

---

20   Letter from Major J.D.M. McCallum, 8th Rifles to official historian Sir James Edmonds.
21   *Battle Lines* article by Jim Loughran.

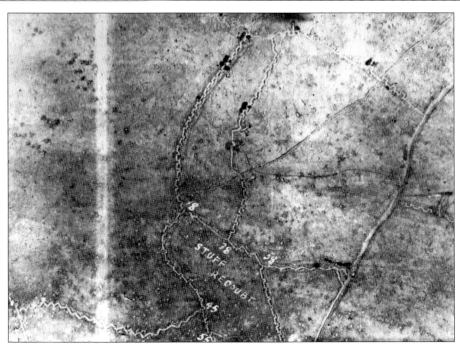

Stuff Redoubt: At 10:10 am, on 1 July some fifty men of 107 Brigade entered Stuff
Redoubt and discovered it was unoccupied. (Courtesy of Michael LoCicero)

At his headquarters General Nugent knew from the positions marked on his map that any additional advance by the division would see them going into an exposed salient, as neither the 29th
Division on the left, nor the 32nd Division on the right had been able to advance at the same rate
due to ferocious resistance and very heavy casualties.

On the right flank the 32nd Division, tasked with capturing Thiepval village, had faced uncut
wire, which prevented both 96 and 97 Brigades from getting beyond the German front line. In 14
Brigade the 11th (Lonsdale) Battalion of the Border Regiment was ordered to advance despite the
obvious lack of movement to its front and they suffered 500 casualties just getting from Authuille
Wood to the Leipzig Redoubt. The Redoubt was eventually captured by the 17th Highland Light
Infantry (Glasgow Commercials), who had crawled to within forty yards of the German front
line prior to Zero. However, the casualties and the wounds had been horrendous. Major J.R.
Meiklejohn, serving with 1st Border, 87 Brigade, described how he came across;

> One officer, who had been hit by eighteen bullets from a machine gun, yet was still alive.
> Within the 1st Battalion Border Regiment, only one small party, under the command of
> Captain Fraser, reached the front of the German wire and were there all shot down. No
> members of 87 Brigade were taken prisoner; all casualties occurring within their own wire or
> in no man's land. The entire Battalion Headquarters, with the exception of the Intelligence
> Officer, fell in their own wire, this included runners, servants etc., complete. The Battalion's
> commanding officer, Lieutenant Colonel A.J. Ellis was found by me after a long search, he
> had been severely wounded through both thighs."[22]

---

22   Letter from Major Meiklejohn to General Edmonds, author of the *Official History*, dated 27.12.29, and
     written from Roberts Barracks, Rawalpindi, India.

North of the Ancre

The 29th Division, on the left flank and north of the Ancre, had performed well during the Gallipoli Campaign. It was commanded by Major General H. de B-de-Lisle. On 1 July the 29th Division's objective was the capture of the village of Beaumont-Hamel, a German stronghold that was positioned on the left flank of the Ulster Division. British Sappers had placed a mine beneath the Hawthorne Redoubt, which was to be detonated at Zero hour minus ten minutes and hopefully breach the defences of Beaumont-Hamel. At 7:20 am the mine under the Hawthorne Redoubt was detonated and sent a sheet of flame 100 feet into the air, but despite this and the artillery barrage, the German machine gunners were able to man their positions when 29th Division went over the top. A smokescreen was laid down on the left of the division, but even so, the troops were cut to pieces. The fighting was so fierce that the 1st Newfoundland Regiment sustained 600 casualties out of a complement of 800 men. It was also north of the Ancre that two battalions of 108 Brigade made their attack.

The "action on the north side of the Ancre was separate from the other and of lesser importance…" Thus Cyril Falls discounts the actions of the 9th Irish Fusiliers and 12th Rifles north of the Ancre. The line occupied by the two battalions ran from the Mary Redan on the divisional boundary with 29th Division to the north bank of the Ancre. To their front was a ravine, the map showing contours running from 80 beside the railway line to 130 on the divisional boundary with 29th Division. This was a deep ravine with steep sides! Dug in on the other side was the German 119th Reserve Infantry Regiment. From 6:25 am, the German trenches and machine gun posts had come under an even more intense bombardment, which lasted until 7:30 pm. According to several accounts much of the wire remained uncut and most of the machine gun positions remained intact. The two battalions were basically on their own, no support could be had from south of the River, while on their left 87 Brigade had their own problems to deal with. According to a letter written by Major A.H. Burne, DSO, B Battery, 154 Brigade, commenting on a draft of the official history:

> There is an impression that the failure north of the river was because the wire was not cut so well as it was south. This is incorrect. I don't consider the wire was as well cut behind the front line as south of the river (owing to more difficult observation), but the failure came before ever our infantry reached the wire. Our barrage on the front line was too thin. The fastest rate I fired was only three rounds per gun per minute, and it did not prevent their machine guns opening on our people going through our own wire before even our barrage lifted. Considering we had been in position for months and knew every inch of the ground, we could have supported our infantry better by 'observed' fire than by a fixed timetable of lifts. As it was our successive lifts left our infantry miles behind, and when I asked for leave to bring my fire back it was refused (so I then did it without permission)!

The plan of attack was that A, C and D companies of the 12th Rifles would advance in conjunction with 87 Brigade, while the Irish Fusiliers would advance on the right flank of the Rifles, supported by two platoons of the Rifles' B Company, while the remaining two Rifles platoons attacked along the northern bank of the Ancre.

The Irish Fusiliers deployed as follows: on the right flank A Company, commanded by Captain C Ensor; right-centre B Company, led by Major T.S. Atkinson; left-centre C Company, commanded by Captain T.M. Johnston; left flank Captain J.G. Brew's D Company. Each company was on a platoon front, resulting in four waves, each with 60 yards between each platoon. The two leading waves assembled in the front-line trench, with the third, supporting platoons, in the communications trenches, while the fourth wave, the consolidating platoons, were in the second-line trench.

The second wave was accompanied by two Stokes mortars, while five Vickers machine guns were attached to the third wave. All units were in position by 3:00 am and between that time and zero, the battalion suffered some 50 casualties from a single high explosive shell.

At Zero the leading wave of the Irish Fusiliers made it into the ravine without serious loss, mainly due to the smokescreen provide by the Stokes mortars and the time taken by the artillerymen of the German 26th Reserve Division to prepare their guns for firing on predetermined map coordinates that were now covered with the smoke.[23] Not with them at this time was Second Lieutenant Sam Wallace. It was the practice in each battalion that a certain number of officers and other ranks be held back to ensure there was a cadre on which to rebuild the battalion in the event of heavy casualties. Such a practice was needed this day. Wallace recalled; "At the start I was not in the front line, two days before word had come down that certain people were to be held back and I was put in B Company, which was commanded by Captain Shillington. There were about a dozen of us."

While the five-day bombardment may have done little to destroy German machine gun posts, it did have one benefit. It was observed that men of the German I/R119 had left their trenches and stood on the parapet to fire their weapons, something noticed elsewhere on the battlefield that day. While this allowed for better aiming and did permit bombs to be thrown further, it also exposed the men against the skyline, making them excellent targets. It was later agreed by the German High Command that these actions were the result of the stress induced by the British bombardment.[24]

The second wave of the Irish Fusiliers was met by a virtual hail of machine gun fire and was practically wiped out. This fire was not only from their front, but from machine guns firing from St Pierre Divion. Survivors of B Company managed to get further forward than the remainder and were observed in and around Beaucourt Station. One of the casualties was Lieutenant Arthur Carson Hollywood. Hollywood, from Helen's Bay, was a former pupil of the Friends School, Lisburn, RBAI, and the Royal University of Ireland.[25] He had been promoted as a result of his actions on 22 February 1916, when he had brought back a night patrol and recovered the bodies of two men killed. Private Charles Stewart of A Company was taking cover close to the enemy line when he saw Lieutenant Hollywood hit by a burst of machine gun fire as he left the German first-line trench. Private James Nelson had also been wounded and would lie beside the dead lieutenant for the following two days and a night before being able to crawl back to his own lines. Lieutenant Hollywood's brother, Second Lieutenant James Hollywood, was serving with the 12th Rifles on the right flank of the Irish Fusiliers and he was also killed this day. Their parents would receive the telegrams 24 hours apart. Lance Corporal William Stringer served in A Company and was a Lewis gunner. He came from Milford, Armagh, was eighteen years old and had worked in McCrum's factory in the village, as well as being a prominent member of the UVF. The Lewis gun Section Officer stated:

> He got as far as the German wire, and got his gun alone into action, but the Boches apparently concentrated machine guns on him and he could hardly have survived many minutes. Considering the terrific fire of the Boche machine guns and artillery, which so few of our men survived, his performance was absolutely magnificent. He must have known it meant certain death, and yet he never hesitated a moment.

---

23   Ralph Whitehead, *The Other Side of the Wire, Vol II* (2013).
24   Ibid.
25   Later Queen's University

Lance Corporal Stringer has no known grave. Second Lieutenant Sam Wallace and Captain Shillington were sent forward along with several others, but they made little difference.

From the German first line the crew of machine gun No.7 had been observing the advancing Irish Fusiliers using a mirror that allowed them to see over the trench without exposing themselves. Despite this occasionally a crewman would peer over the edge of the position to get a clear view across no man's land. On one occasion a shell exploded and Schutz Vogt was killed. However, the MG08 had an immediate crew of four while other men were detailed as ammunition carriers. During the attack, from beginning to end, this gun only fired ten belts of ammunition, a total of 2,500 rounds, very few compared to the ammunition expended by other guns that day.[26]

William and Ellen Turkington of Brownlow Terrace, Lurgan, County Armagh, gave three sons to the army. Sergeant Bertie Turkington had served from the beginning of the war, surviving the retreat from Mons in 1914, having been wounded on several occasions and going on to serve in Salonika. Ernest and Alfred had both enlisted in the 9th Irish Fusiliers. During the advance Alfred saw his younger brother Ernest lying wounded, but was unable to stop. Alfred survived 1 July and on the following two nights he roamed the battlefield searching for his brother among the dead and dying. Ernest was not to be found by his brother, but Alfred did find his own officer lying dead. As the latter was beyond all aid, he searched him and brought away all his personal belongings. Among these were some very important documents that would have been of value to the enemy. For his actions Alfred was promoted to sergeant the following day. Ernest was found by the stretcher-bearers later and is today buried in the Ancre British Cemetery at Beaumont Hamel.

It was a bad day for brothers. The four Hobbs brothers from Lurgan, Armagh were all in the ranks of the Irish Fusiliers on 1 July; Andrew, David and Robert served in C Company and all died. A fourth brother, Herbert George, was severely wounded, and returned to his home in Lurgan the following month. He was subsequently discharged due to his wounds in July 1917. Two other brothers who died were George and William Larmour from Fitzroy Avenue, Belfast, serving in the 14th Rifles; both are listed as having no known grave. From Bangor, County Down, the Angus family lost three sons, they are detailed later in the history.

When the survivors of the two battalions reached the far side of the ravine it was found that here the German wire was not completely cut and those gaps that did exist were now covered by enemy machine guns. In the final ten minutes of the bombardment No.8 Platoon, C Company, of the 12th Rifles, under the command of Sergeant Hoare, had moved out from the Crow's Nest, a forming-up point in the trenches, and lay outside the wire. At Zero a smokescreen was laid by the brigade trench mortars and the platoon began its advance, splitting into three sections, that on the left under Sergeant Hamilton, the centre under Sergeant Hoare and the right under Sergeant Benison. As they moved forward they came under heavy machine gun fire, Sergeant Hoare's section being particularly badly hit.

To the left Sergeant Hamilton's party was also badly hit, but the sergeant and three or four men managed to get into the enemy sap where they were pinned down by heavy machine gun fire. To the right Sergeant Benison and his group were stopped, the sergeant was killed almost immediately and the Lewis-gun team silenced by machine gun fire coming from the right flank. This fire was coming from machine gun positions at St Pierre Divion on the south bank of the River Ancre firing in enfilade. With such a high casualty rate, Sergeant Hoare sent back a runner to request orders from Lieutenant Colonel Blacker, who was in command of this section.

The British shellfire caused a large number of German casualties despite support having to be called for using coloured flares as the land lines had been cut by the British barrage. Many of these were repaired by the signallers, only to be cut again by shells falling short.

---

26 Whitehead, *The Other Side of the Wire, Vol II.*

The three Angus brothers from Bangor County Down.

It is a common misconception that the German Army of the Great War was an automotive organisation, hidebound by rules and regulations. This was far from the truth. Once it was realised that the British had penetrated their lines the German troops did as they had been taught, taking control of the situation facing them without having to consult with senior commanders. Within each company sector the commander and his non-commissioned officers were all quite capable of assessing the situation and taking the necessary action.

Lieutenant Lemon's No.6 Platoon of the 12th Rifles had been briefed to assault the position known as the Railway Sap. Archie Dunlap Lemon was forty-one years old and came from Strandtown in Belfast. They moved out of their trenches at the same time as the remainder of the Irish Fusiliers, but before moving into the ravine all but the lieutenant and twelve other ranks had become casualties, mostly from the fire of two enemy machine guns, No.7 and No.9 located in the German front and second-line trenches. Added to this a piece of shrapnel had put their Lewis gun out of action. On arriving in the ravine the lieutenant sought out support from other platoons, but none was available. Pushing forward to the Railway Sap cost the group another three casualties. Once inside the lieutenant detailed Lance Sergeant Millar and three men to move to the right down the sap, bombing as they went. However, it was an unequal fight and soon the sergeant and all his men had become casualties.

Lemon, with the remainder of his platoon, then moved up the main sap, Private J.M. Gamble, the lead bayonet man, cutting wire entanglements as they advanced using the wire-cutter on the end of his rifle. As they moved forward they came across a machine gun that was firing across the sap from a small tunnel mouth and directing its fire towards the infantry attacking the enemy line south of the Ancre. It is most probable that this was Machine gun No.7, still under the command of *Unteroffizer* Kaeser.

Lieutenant Lemon climbed above the tunnel armed with some bombs to use on any enemy that might emerge and sent the remainder of the men on down the trench. Before he could take any action the lieutenant was shot and killed by two German officers who fired at him with rifles from the top of a dug-out. These two men were in turn killed by a well thrown bomb. What remained of No.6 Platoon was now cut off between the first and second German lines. Eventually only two men managed to make their way back to the start line, Corporal Burgess and Private McNeilly. The remainder were either wounded, killed, or had been taken prisoner. The redoubtable wire cutter Private Gamble was a prisoner, but his efforts had earned him the Military Medal. The other two platoons, under the command of Captain C.S. Murray, fared no better. No.7 Platoon of the Rifles had advanced behind the Irish Fusiliers, but like the Fusiliers got no further than their own wire. Designated as the 'carrying platoon', they did not advance beyond the wire and Captain Murray was wounded almost immediately.

At Zero No.10 Platoon had advanced followed by No.11 Platoon and found their way barred by enemy wire, which had only two small gaps cut in it. The leading platoon immediately split into two, each going for a gap, but as each was covered by an enemy machine gun the casualties were very heavy. Subsequent investigation showed that these gaps had been cut by the Germans to funnel attacking troops into killing zones. With No.11 Platoon acting as reinforcements and following immediately behind they also suffered while going through the gaps and few made it into the enemy lines.

Captain Griffiths took command of No.9 and No.11 Platoons and ordered them forward, but was killed even as he spoke. There was no option but to order the men back; the casualties suffered were horrific and the enemy fire too strong. As the survivors of C Company filtered back Sergeant Cunningham, with the assistance of Corporal Herbison, Lance Corporal Jackson and Private Craig, remained to fire at the enemy who were by now standing on their parapet openly shooting and throwing bombs. Private Craig used his Lewis gun to good effect, despite the others in his team having become casualties. Lance Corporal Harvey was then seen to rally what men were in his immediate area and attempt for the third time to rush the gaps in the German wire, but was again forced back. Eventually all ranks retired to the Sunken Road, where Sergeant Cunningham and Corporal Herbison assisted the wounded to cross the road, which was under near continuous shellfire.

Also in the Sunken Road was Lance Corporal Edward Scott who was attending to the wounded and under severe machine gun and artillery fire managed to bring ten injured men to safety. A former member of the UVF and employee of Dunbar, McMaster & Co. of Gilford, County Armagh, Edward Scott later received an illuminated certificate signed by General Nugent. His brother, CSM James Scott, was killed on 1 August 1917. Another brother, Private William Scott, who served with the Inniskillings, had been discharged.

Private Andrew Moore was a member of the platoon commanded by Lieutenant J. E. Furniss.[27] As he went forward Private Moore was wounded by a shell splinter that caused a severe wound. On being forced to return he was wounded for a second time and then came across a wounded officer and several men sheltering in a shell hole. Doing his best to treat the wounded, he then went back to the lines and directed stretcher bearers to the location of the injured men, his actions that day earning him the Military Medal. Lieutenant Furniss would later also be severely wounded and earn the Military Cross.

As D Company advanced it was led by No.16 Platoon, commanded by Second Lieutenant Sir Harry Macnaghten. Sir Harry, who came from Dundarave, Antrim, had been commissioned into the Black Watch and was attached to the 12th Rifles. His batman, Private Robert Quigg, had come with him, having worked for the family at home in County Antrim.[28] The platoon advanced in extended line with Sir Harry on the right and Sergeant McFall on the left and on reaching the German front line, the sergeant immediately detailed two bombers to deal with each dug-out. Fire from the German second line caused heavy casualties and the remaining platoons of D Company took heavy casualties as they closed with the enemy. These men suffered severely

---

27   His brother Second Lieutenant James Furniss, 1st Rifles, was killed on 31 July 1917. He has no known grave.
28   In many sources the name is spelt as Macnaughten. Sir Harry's brother, Sir Arthur Douglas, aged 19 years, was killed on 15 September 1916 whilst serving with the Rifle Brigade.

[*This paper is to be considered by each soldier as confidential, and to be kept in his Active Service Pay Book.*]

A personal message from Kitchener that was kept inside each soldier's pay book.

You are ordered abroad as a soldier of the King to help our French comrades against the invasion of a common Enemy. You have to perform a task which will need your courage, your energy, your patience. Remember that the honour of the British Army depends on your individual conduct. It will be your duty not only to set an example of discipline and perfect steadiness under fire but also to maintain the most friendly relations with those whom you are helping in this struggle. The operations in which **you** are engaged will, for the most part, take place in a friendly country, and you can do your own country no better service than in showing yourself in France and Belgium in the true character of a British soldier.

Be invariably courteous, considerate and kind. Never do anything likely to injure or destroy property,

W 12373—1596   500ᴍ   2/15   H W V (P 951)
   7607—2528   500ᴍ   8/15

1997/20

2

and always look upon looting as a disgraceful act. You are sure to meet with a welcome and to be trusted; your conduct must justify that welcome and that trust. Your duty cannot be done unless your health is sound. So keep constantly on your guard against any excesses. In this new experience you may find temptations both in wine and women. You must entirely resist both temptations, and, while treating all women with perfect courtesy, you should avoid any intimacy.

Do your duty bravely.
Fear God.
Honour the King.

KITCHENER,
Field-Marshal.

Second page of above.

as they approached the German wire and many casualties were caused with No.14 Platoon losing half their men before No.16 Platoon had gained the German front line. With such a high casualty rate there was no option and the order to retire was given. However, in No.16 Platoon Macnaghten did not agree, and jumping out of the trench, he called to his men not to retire, but to come on. He was then hit in the legs by a burst from a machine gun and fell back onto the parapet of the trench. Private Kane, who was quite close to the lieutenant, bayoneted the machine gunner, but was killed by three Germans who then took Macnaghten prisoner. The last view his men had was the wounded officer being carried to the rear.

Both D and A Companies fell back behind the rim of the ravine and here Second Lieutenant Dickson formed up the survivors for another charge against the German line. As they moved forward Dickson was hit almost immediately and command devolved to Sergeant McFall. The attack failed due to the weight of enemy fire and again the men were forced back.

All along the line it was a similar story; those gaps in the wire that existed were well

Private Thomas Joyce, 9th Royal Irish Fusiliers, killed in action 1 July 1916 and commemorated on the Thiepval Memorial.

covered by machine guns and if any advance was made close to the enemy lines it was met be rifle fire and bombing parties. Lieutenant William McCluggage, a twenty-three year old from Ballyboley, Larne, was killed leading his men towards the first line. Lieutenant Thomas Haughton, aged twenty-five, from Cullybackey, Antrim, was wounded in the leg as he led his men out of the British line, but continued forward. He was killed during the retirement. The Lewis gun teams suffered as much as the infantry, but when the gun was brought into action it proved its value beyond measure. Private McMullen, the sole surviving member of his team, entered the German trench and proceeded to empty two magazines at the second-line trench, firing from the shoulder. When his company withdrew, he went with them bringing his gun back safely.

At 10:12 am, Lieutenant Colonel Bull received an order to attack once again. Major Cole-Hamilton DSO was given command and managed to gather approximately a hundred men in the New Trench. In preparing for this next attack the major had able assistance from Sergeant McFall, Sergeant Smith of D Company and Lance Corporal Harvey of C Company. From the outset the attack came under heavy fire from shrapnel shells and machine gun fire and once again was driven back. In the retirement Lance Corporal Harvey brought in a wounded man on his back.

At 11:00 am, another attack was ordered, to be launched at 12:30 pm, in conjunction with 29th Division. Once again the men were assembled in the New Trench, a total of 46 officers and other ranks. Major Cole-Hamilton took the men out into no man's land prior to the attack time and waited for the 29th Division to move. As 12:30 pm, passed and there was no sign of movement from the division, the major sent back a runner for new orders. Colonel Bull told the men to retire and by 2:00 pm, they were all safely in their own lines. Sentries were posted and the remnants of the 12th Rifles held their ground until relieved by the York and Lancaster Regiment at 6:30 pm.[29]

As the result of a rumour in the early hours of the morning of 2 July a member of the 12th Rifles climbed out of his trench and made his way out into no man's land. This was Private Robert Quigg, a native of Antrim and loyal family servant. Quigg had been educated at the Giant's Causeway National School and later worked on the Macnaghten family estate. A former member of the Bushmills Volunteers, UVF, he had subsequently enlisted in the 12th Rifles. From before midnight Quigg had made several trips out into no man's land to search for Second Lieutenant Harry Macnaghten, his platoon commander, but without success. The officer was last seen alive sitting in an enemy trench having been wounded in the legs.[30] Each time Quigg returned he brought in an injured man, on one occasion from within a few yards of an enemy position, dragged to safety on a groundsheet. After seven hours, exhaustion forced him to give up without finding

Robert Quigg VC.

the lieutenant's body, which was never found and to this day Macnaghten is one of the many with no known grave.[31] For his actions Quigg was subsequently awarded the Victoria Cross, it being presented by the King on 8 January 1917. Hope that the officer was still alive was reported in the local papers as late as 15 July. A letter to Lady Macnaghten from Colonel Bull stated; "The young soldier baronet was observed sitting wounded in the leg in one of the captured front trenches. His subsequent whereabouts cannot yet be traced, but as the search for his body has so far proved unavailing, there is reason to hope that Sir Harry may be a wounded prisoner behind enemy lines."

Another Victoria Cross was awarded for actions north of the Ancre. From 7:00 pm, until midnight on 1 July, Lieutenant Geoffrey Cather, the Irish Fusiliers battalion Adjutant, along with Captain W.J. Menaul, the Fusiliers' Intelligence and Sniping Officer, searched no man's land and had successfully brought in three wounded men. The two officers were helping a fourth injured soldier when a burst of machine gun fire hit both of them. Lieutenant Cather was killed and Menaul wounded. As a result of their actions Cather received the Victoria Cross, while Menaul was awarded the Military Cross.[32] Not far away Lieutenant Cather's cousin, Lieutenant Thomas Shillington, from Portadown, also in the Fusiliers, was lying wounded. He would survive this battle and be promoted to captain, only to die at Langemarck on 18 August 1917.

On the left flank of the Irish Fusiliers and 12th Rifles, the battalions of 29th Division were also held up by uncut wire and the casualties were horrendous. On the right flank small groups of

---

29   Most of these details are taken from a report written by Lieutenant Colonel Bull after the battle.
30   *Belfast News Letter* 15 July 1916.
31   Second Lieutenant Sir Edward Harry Macnaghten, Black Watch (Royal Highlanders), attached 12th Royal Irish Rifles, Thiepval Memorial, Pier & Face 10A, he was 20 years old.
32   Post-war Captain Menaul would gain recognition as a painter of scenes of his military service.

Robert Quigg brings in another injured man in his search for Lieutenant Macnaghten. A postcard showing Lieutenant Cather rescuing men from no-man's-land on the evening of 1 July 1916. (Courtesy of the Royal Irish Fusiliers Museum and AJ Clarke)

A postcard showing Lieutenant Cather rescuing men from no-man's-land on the evening of 1 July 1916. (Courtesy of the Royal Irish Fusiliers Museum and AJ Clarke)

Rifles and Irish Fusiliers were still holding out near the railway station, using shell holes for cover. They were under continuous machine gun fire from the German positions near the Grallsburg and *Feste Alt Wurttemberg*, located north of the Station Road and from shells fired by several *Erdmörsers*, a type of mortar that lobbed large shells filled with high explosive. By 9:00 am, reports from the German positions were saying that their sectors were quiet.

On the other side of the ravine a report made at 8:00 am, stated that the attack by the two battalions of the division had failed, as had that of 29th Division.

With his flanks insecure General Nugent realised that any further advance was going to waste lives. At 8:32 am, at the general's behest Colonel Place, the GSOI, had contacted X Corps Headquarters and asked if 107 Brigade might be stopped from advancing on the last enemy line. The answer from headquarters was that a new attack was being made on Thiepval and also by VIII Corps on the north bank of the Ancre and that 107 Brigade must play its part by continuing its advance. Forty-five minutes later an order was received from the corps headquarters to say that the brigade must hold its position until the situation on the flanks had become clearer. The message was quickly passed to General Withycombe to hold his brigade and he employed every means in his power to do so. The telephone lines that had been carried forward had all been cut by shellfire and the distance to be covered by a runner through still-falling shells and machine gun fire offered little hope of success. The message did arrive, but it was too late and the brigade went forward.

Throughout the day communication via land lines proved virtually impossible to maintain. A post-battle report, written by Colonel Savage, 13th Rifles and dated 7 July 1916 to headquarters of the 108 Brigade states:

> Very little information was sent in, this was due in the first place to most of the officers becoming casualties, and the difficulty of getting men across the fire swept zone of no man's land. Signalling wire had been laid out by the Signalling Officer of the 17th, but all attempts by the signallers to take a line forward were useless. I had ten signallers killed and wounded. Second Lieutenant Fullerton of D Company is the only officer who went over who has come back unwounded and has very little information about his company.

The attempts to keep communications open meant almost constant repairs to field telephone lines. Corporal Edward Quinn DCM, despite being a member of the RAMC, was active throughout the battle in such attempts and was subsequently awarded the Military Medal.

After crossing about 1,000 yards of shell and machine gun swept ground, some men of 107 Brigade actually made it into the enemy trenches, only to find them full of German reserves. There was some desperate hand-to-hand fighting before the men were forced back to the next line.

The enemy came swarming up the trenches from St Pierre Divion led by bombing parties, the German stick grenades being used in copious numbers, However, the men of the 8th and 15th Rifles, along with the few surviving men of the 13th Rifles, beat them off time and time again. Among the dead of the 13th Rifles was Private Blair Angus, from Albert Street, Bangor, one of three brothers all to be killed within a few weeks of each other. On 9 July Lance Corporal Robert Angus would be killed serving with the Royal Scots Fusiliers, while Private James Angus, serving with the 29th Battalion British Columbia Regiment, Canadian Infantry, would be killed on 11 September. There was also Corporal John O'Neill, second son of Samuel O'Neill of William Street, Newtownards, County Down, who was also killed. William, his eldest son was killed on 3 September 1916 while serving with the 2nd King's Own Scottish Borderers. A third son, Lance Corporal James O'Neill, also with the 13th Rifles, was wounded in September 1916.

(Top left) Private John Blair Angus, A Company 13th Royal Irish Rifles, killed on 1 July 1916, aged 19 years. One of three brothers from The Cotton, Donaghadee, to be killed in the Great War. Known as 'rat killer' within his platoon due to his expertise with a shovel against the vermin, he was initially listed as missing in action, his death not being confirmed until June 1917.
(Top right) Lance Corporal Robert Angus was killed on 9 July 1916, while serving with the 2nd Battalion of the Royal Scots Fusiliers. The second of the Angus brothers to die, he had worked as a farm labourer prior to moving to Scotland, where he enlisted.
(Left) Private James Angus was killed on 11 September 1916, while serving with the 29th Battalion British Columbia Regiment, Canadian Army.

Company Sergeant Major William Taylor was killed as he attempted to assist one of the battalion officers. The Reverend W.J. McConnell, Presbyterian chaplain reported "…the Sergeant Major was killed as he stopped to attend to Major Uprichard in the latter's dying moments."

The previous March Major Henry Albert Uprichard had in turn written to Mr F.H. Mullan of Newry saying; "There is no one to touch Taylor; he is the cheeriest and best sergeant major not only in the battalion, but in the brigade."

Sergeant Major Taylor was a time-expired soldier and had been a drill instructor of No.1 Company of the South Down Regiment of the UVF. One of his sons was then serving with the Royal Irish Fusiliers.[33]

An unidentified Sergeant wrote to Major Uprichard's parents:

> The Major and I were almost always together in the trenches and patrolling no man's land, as I was his Bombing Sergeant, in fact, the Major, Lieutenant A---- and I were always the first three to go out on patrol in the battalion. I cannot express my feeling by letter, but he was so good and kind to me that I had grown to love him, and I often told my mother that we had the best and bravest officer in France. He was a model officer to his men, and did more than his duty for them in looking after their needs and making them comfortable. I can say on behalf of D Company that Major Uprichard was loved and esteemed by all his men.[34]

Private Robert Stewart of Church Street, Bangor was badly wounded when a German explosive bullet hit his Brodie helmet and sliced into his neck and shoulder causing quite a serious wound.[35] Stewart was quoted as saying: "They are not allowed to use these bullets, but we bayoneted a terrible lot. The Ulster Division fought well, but the machine guns mowed us down fast."

Stewart lay in a shell hole from 7:30 am, until 11:00 pm, some 16 hours. He had no use of his right arm and had lost a lot of blood. As he was only 30 to 40 yards from the German trenches he considered surrendering and consequently disposed of his bombs and rifle. However, before this happened he was found by a team of stretcher bearers and taken back to the divisional lines.[36]

On the right flank the attacks did not occur so soon. Lieutenant Sanderson of the 9th Rifles carried out a reconnaissance of the trench known as Mouquet Switch, located in front of 32nd Division and found it unoccupied. This trench led down to Mouquet Farm. To try and bring forward men to garrison it was impossible; the German machine guns of Thiepval still reigned over no man's land.

Captain Davidson and his machine gunners of 108 Brigade had been held in reserve for some thirty minutes after the initial assault. At 8:06 am, a runner delivered a note from Captain Matthews of A Company 13th Rifles, to say that he was held up in the A line and was asking for a Vickers gun. A few minutes after that Captain Davidson and his men moved forward. At 10:20 am, a report was received from Davidson stating that he and what remained of his command were in the B Line, with two machine guns and approximately 30 men of the 11th, 13th, and 15th Rifles. He also stated that any further advance was impossible and reinforcements were urgently required, as was ammunition, water and bombs. Shortly after this message was despatched Davidson was seriously wounded in the knee, but refused to be evacuated. He sent a second message back to battalion headquarters stating that his small command was being pressed on all sides and were virtually surrounded:

33   Bangor Museum Archives.
34   *Belfast News Letter* 19 July 1916.
35   The German 'explosive bullet' was the *Luft Einschiess*, (aerial ranging). The explosion occurred at 300 yards, producing a puff of white smoke utilised for ranging purposes.
36   *Bangor Spectator* 21 July 1916.

I am holding the end of a communication trench in A line with a few bombers and a Lewis gun. We cannot hold much longer. We are being pressed on all sides and ammunition almost finished.

Colonel Savage did what he could to assist the machine gunners:

At 12:50 pm, I then sent up the few remaining battalion staff, the orderly room sergeant, two officers' servants, two company quartermaster sergeants with ammunition, these men were unable to cross no man's land. Two were killed, three were wounded. At 1:05 pm 270 bombs were also sent up with a party and a man who knew the way. Second Lieutenant Findlay went out about this time for information and returned wounded later on. At 1:40 pm Second Lieutenant Dale sent in a note to say he was installed in a German trench 50 yards or more to the left of Captain Davidson, firing on a German bombing party. This officer returned later on, gallantly saving his two guns and bringing in an extra tripod which he found.

Captain James Samuel Davidson, 108th Machine Gun Company, killed in action 1 July 1916.

Captain Davidson's Vickers guns were no longer operable and they were holding the end of a communication trench in the A Line with a few bombers and a single Lewis gun. Eventually there was no option but to retire. Two men picked up the wounded captain and began to make their way back to the British front line through a barrage of small arms fire and exploding shells. They had reached to within 20 yards of the British wire when Captain Davidson was hit in the head by a single bullet and died instantly.[37] The captain's batman, Private Hugh Wilson of Abbey Street, Bangor, had accompanied Davidson across the battlefield. Having worked for the captain's father as a gardener, it was only natural that he should have followed him into the Army. He was mortally wounded on 1 July, dying five days later. The news of Captain Davidson's death came to Colonel Savage via Private J. Blakely, who arrived in from the sunken road and reported that the captain had been wounded in the knee and while he and another man were carrying him out, he was shot dead between them.

In 109th Machine Gun Company the casualties were equally heavy. Second Lieutenant Noel Duncan Edingborough who had transferred from the 15th Battalion Middlesex Regiment, was killed, and has no known grave. Lieutenant Holt Montgomery Hewitt, formerly D Company UVF, the son of James Hewitt of Mornington Park, Bangor, was also killed. He had originally enlisted in the 13th Rifles and was later commissioned into the 9th Inniskillings; he then transferred to the 109th Machine Gun Company. Two of his brothers were also killed in action: Lieutenant Ernest

---

37   In many accounts of this action it is claimed that the captain was killed by a 'sniper'. Given the volume of fire reported on the day it is inconceivable that anyone could distinguish a single aimed rifle shot above all else. A stray bullet will kill just as easily as an aimed shot.

Henry Hewitt of the King's Own (Royal Lancaster Regiment) had been killed on 15 June 1915, at Festubert and is commemorated on the Le Touret Memorial, while Second Lieutenant William Arthur Hewitt also died on 1 July, serving in the 9th Inniskillings. Two Donegal men were among the killed that day, they were Lieutenant Andrew Chichester Hart from Kilderry and Private Joseph Atcheson Crockett from Burnfoot. A lethal burst from a German machine gun brought down Sergeant Alfred Owens and Lieutenant Gilbert Wedgwood. Lieutenant Clokey had spoken to the Sergeant just before leaving the trench at the start line; "He was in great spirits. He was a very fine chap and was looked upon as our best sergeant."

Lieutenant Wedgwood's brother Philip was also killed while serving with the 16th Rifles. Captain Eric Norman Frankland Bell, serving with the 109th Trench Mortar Battery, had brought his command as far as the Crucifix where they came under enfilading machine gun fire from the right flank. Bell was able to locate one machine gun and using a borrowed rifle succeeded in killing the gunner. With his mortars now in position and engaging the numerous enemy targets Bell then went to the assistance of the bombing parties who were in the process of clearing the enemy trenches, and throwing trench mortar bombs by hand, assisted in clearing enemy barricades. After Bell had exhausted all his own bombs he stood on the parapet and used the rifle to good effect against the infantry that were gathering for a counter-attack. When it was reported that the mortars were out of ammunition Captain Bell organised a carrying party to fetch more and led them back towards the British lines. As they moved across no man's land they were spotted by the German machine gunners firing from enfilade in Thiepval village and Bell was shot, dying almost instantly. His batman remained with him until the end and then managed to return to his own lines despite injuries. For his actions in and around the Crucifix Captain Bell was awarded a posthumous Victoria Cross. In September 1918 his brother Lieutenant A.G.F. Bell, Inniskillings, attached to the Irish Fusiliers, was wounded in action.

The Crucifix saw some of the fiercest fighting by the 9th Inniskillings. Lance Corporal Dan Lyttle, from Ardstraw, County Tyrone, found himself isolated and then stumbled onto an abandoned Vickers machine gun and a Lewis gun. With the enemy in sight he picked up the Lewis gun, firing it until the ammunition was used up. Then, not wanting the weapons to fall into enemy hands, he made both unserviceable, before picking up his rifle and making his way back to the main position, using bombs to clear his way. Private J. Gibson had reached the German wire and saw a machine gun firing from the parapet. Without waiting for any assistance he entered the trench and ferociously attacked the gun crew, killing all three men using the butt of his rifle.[38] Killed at this time was Private John Henry Lowin, from Killala, County Mayo, one of a small number of men from that county who died in the ranks of the Ulster Division. Sergeant Samuel Kelly, a veteran of the South African War with the 1st Inniskillings, made several dashes across machine gun swept ground to try and contact other members of the battalion on the right flank. He was successful in this and would eventually be in overall command when all the officers had become casualties, until he himself was hit. For his actions he was awarded the Distinguished Conduct Medal. Sergeant Kelly is believed to be one of the few men who wore his orange sash that day.[39]

The pioneers were tasked with digging a communication trench across this area to enable ammunition and water to be brought up. At 8:40 am, No.2 Company began to dig their way forward, but machine gun fire cut them down every time they left the sap. After suffering about 20

---

38   Battalion War Diary.
39   A report in the *Belfast News Letter* on 29 March 1917, stated this to be the case, the award of the DCM being made by Captain H.C. Gordon. This also may be the same Sergeant Kelly as mentioned in the letter from Private Laverty regarding 1 July 1916.

casualties Colonel Leader ordered the digging to be abandoned. A further attempt was to be made about 9:00 pm, with No.3 Company assisting, but just before digging began it was announced that those men of the division in the enemy first line had fallen back. The pioneers also assisted the 9th Irish Fusiliers north of the Ancre, recovering wounded men from no man's land while under a severe fire. They brought in about 60 to 70 wounded, but at a cost of 12 of their own men.

The 11th Inniskillings closed with the A line, with A and D Companies in the lead. They immediately came under the intense machine gun fire which was lacing the front line, most coming from the direction of Thiepval village. These companies and those following suffered heavy casualties, including most of the officers. The battalion pushed on to the A line and successfully crossed it, with Captain W.T. Sewel out in front.[40] At this point the captain was seen to fall and only Lieutenant Gallaugher remained on his feet. In the B line there was not a great deal of opposition was encountered, with most Germans throwing up their hands all too willing to surrender.

As the only remaining officer of the Inniskillings Lieutenant Henry Gallaugher,[41] from Manorcunningham, County Donegal, ordered Sergeant Major Stephen Bullock to take a party and continue to the C line, while he and the remaining men went to assist in consolidating the Crucifix.[42] Having barricaded the communication trenches leading to the Crucifix, the lieutenant then began making fire steps from which to shoot. With this completed, he returned to the A line to collect men and material. On arrival Gallaugher found part of the line occupied by the enemy. Quickly organising a bombing party the Germans were soon cleared out of the trench, forcing them towards the right flank. Gallaugher then erected a barricade and left it under the control of a lance corporal and six men. From that position Gallaugher sent a message by runner reporting the situation so far. The runner became lost in the maze of shell holes and drifting smoke and the message was actually delivered to the 9th Inniskillings. Gallaugher then collected all the available men in the A line and surrounding shell-holes and led them forward to the Crucifix. Here, in conjunction with Lieutenant McKinley of the 9th Inniskillings, they placed themselves under the command of Major Peacocke.

Major Peacocke and the remnants of C Company had managed to cross no man's land at about noon and had entered the front line close to A.12. They had encountered some German infantry bombing their way up from Thiepval village and these had been beaten off. Collecting what men he could they had made their way to the Crucifix and quickly discovered that holding it was impossible while the Germans held Thiepval. Despite this the men were putting up a dogged resistance although there was a shortage of ammunition and water for the Vickers and all ranks were suffering from heat and exhaustion. Given that German machine gun and artillery fire still dominated no man's land, it was all but impossible to send any relief. One of those who had attempted to follow Major Peacocke was Sergeant Mark Magonagle, a Catholic from Newtownstewart, County Tyrone, who had enlisted in the 9th Inniskillings at Omagh in 1910, being first posted to the 5th Inniskillings, the old Donegal Militia. He had advanced about 200 yards from the start line when he was hit by a burst of machine gun fire. The bullets ripped into both his legs, penetrated a lung and tore the knuckle from the third finger of his right hand. For the following four days and nights he would attempt to crawl back to his own lines, surviving on water taken from the canteens of dead comrades. He was eventually recovered and taken to the regimental aid post, where prompt treatment saved his life.

In the trenches held by some men of the 11th Rifles, Major Blair Oliphant, the second-in-command, had successfully sent a runner back to Brigadier Griffith informing him of a shortage

---

40   As per the CWGC, listed as Major William Tait Sewell, KIA 1 July 1916, from Sunderland.
41   Spelt as Gallagher in some other sources.
42   Company Sergeant Major Bullock was awarded the DCM.

of ammunition, water and bombs. Just as darkness was falling a train had come into Grandcourt station and disgorged fresh German troops. They immediately launched a counter-attack and drove the remaining defenders from the B line. The fact that this runner got through is extremely lucky. The after-action report of the 11th Inniskillings states; "The signallers who went forward with the battalion with telephones etc., were almost immediately knocked out and during the day I tried continually to get in touch with the battalion by runners, scouts and signallers, but all were wounded except one."

In the 11th Rifles, Colonel Pakenham had instructed every officer and NCO above the rank of lance corporal to carry three flares for signalling purposes. Given the losses sustained in the advance few if any of these appear to have been used during the attack.

Lieutenant Fullerton and his platoon of the 13th Rifles went over the top and by the time they had reached the German trench only the lieutenant and 12 men of the company were still on their feet. Fullerton, Sergeant James McCleery and the remaining other ranks were cut off and managed to hold out for the next six hours. When they eventually ran out of bombs the enemy began to close in. By this time only the lieutenant, McCleery, and three men remained. Fullerton then ordered the sergeant and remaining men back to a sunken road, about halfway between the opposing trenches. On reaching the road they noticed that the Lieutenant had failed to follow them and Sergeant McCleery sent two men back for him. As the men returned with the officer the sergeant moved forward to assist them and a shell exploded, killing him instantly. James Moor McCleery was the son of the Reverend John R.M. McCleery of Killyleagh County Down.[43]

Falling back from the Crucifix Corporal John Conn, 9th Inniskillings, came across two abandoned Lewis guns, both damaged. He was able to effect repairs on one and as it was fixed he spotted a group of German infantry on the flank. With the devastating fire that the Lewis was capable of delivering he made short work of any attempt by the enemy to advance further. He then placed both guns on his shoulders and continued to fall back towards his own lines. However, the Lewis gun weighs twenty-six pounds and the weight of both weapons was too much and he had to leave one behind.[44]

In the German B line Second Lieutenant Spalding of the 10th Inniskillings was engaged in clearing German dug-outs with bombs. He had just emerged from one dug-out, suddenly appearing in front of a member of the 14th Rifles, who mistook him for a German and shot him dead. The 10th lost more officers as the advance continued. Captain Miller of D Company was severely wounded in the face by shrapnel and had to be evacuated. The remnants of C Company were being led towards the Crucifix by Captain Proctor when a shell landed close by and exploding shell fragments shattered his leg. He lay in a nearby trench for many hours, it being impossible to get him back through the shell and machine gun fire. It was not until 5:00 pm when, Captain Knox having come forward with reinforcements, it was able to take the wounded officer back to the A line, but no further. Captain Proctor died soon after. James Claude Beauchamp Proctor came from Limavady, County Londonderry, he was 31 years old.

At about noon Captain Robertson of B Company had been studying a map with Lieutenant Wilton of A Company, as they attempted to ascertain their position in the maze of trenches at and around the C line. Some alert Germans spotted them and a fusillade of rifle fire struck both men. Robertson was hit on the chin and shoulder, while Wilton was struck in the chest. Sergeant Porter from Londonderry and serving in B Company assisted the wounded subaltern to his feet and then proceeded to make their way back to the battalion lines. They had only gone a short distance when a shell burst close by and Sergeant Porter was killed.[45] Lieutenant Wilton[46] survived his wound, while Captain Robertson, aged forty-two died leaving a widow Ethel, in Wickham, Hampshire.

As mentioned earlier, Captain Knox had come forward at about 5:00 pm, bringing much needed supplies and reinforcements. The reinforcements were some hastily rallied stragglers and amounted to some 30 men. There were also six four-gallon petrol tins full of drinking water carried by a separate party. This group was to rendezvous with Lieutenant Ernest McClure, the water being needed to quench the thirst of both men and machine guns. While crossing no man's land the party suffered several casualties and when the survivors arrived in the C line, they were unable to find the lieutenant; so distributed the water to men of the different battalions in the C line. Captain Knox and his men were also unable to find Lieutenant McClure due to the enormous confusion in the area and the constant shelling and machine gun fire from Thiepval. After incurring many casualties retirement was inevitable, and late in the evening a withdrawal was made. One of those who remained behind was Lieutenant McClure, killed at the Crucifix. Ernest McClure, from Beechwood Avenue, Londonderry, aged thirty-two years and, according to those men who had been there with him, well deserved a Victoria Cross for his actions. This did not happen and he was posthumously awarded a Mention in Despatches, he has no known grave.

Lieutenant Albert Stewart, a former pupil at RBAI, had been a top-class rugby player winning three international caps. He had first been commissioned into the 10th Rifles before transferring to their machine gun company. For his actions on the Somme on 1 July he was recommended for the Victoria Cross, but it was not awarded. A fellow officer wrote to his father; "I saw him on the night of 1 July when he came back having been over all day in the German trenches, where he had done such splendid work. He was completely worn out, as he had a terrible time all day, but he was himself again the following morning."

After the Somme Stewart was promoted to captain and transferred to the 22nd Machine Gun Company and was killed on 4 October 1917 at Glencorse Wood, being awarded the DSO, which was gazetted the following December. He was one of eight Irish Rugby internationals to die in the Great War.[47]

The French guns supporting the division were ordered to provide a barrage on the right flank, which was done quickly and with accuracy. There was also superb support from the

Lieutenant Ernest McClure from Beechwood Avenue, Londonderry, was killed at the Crucifix on 1 July 1916, and according to those men who were with him, well deserved a Victoria Cross for his actions. This did not happen and he was posthumously awarded a Mention in Despatches, he has no known grave.

---

45 Sergeant Porter's nickname within the battalion was 'Fadeaway', due to his parade dismissals with the phrase 'fade away boys, fade away', rather than routine words of command.

46 Lieutenant Wilton was later awarded the Military Cross and post-war became Mayor of Londonderry.

47 The DSO cannot be awarded posthumously; it would appear there was an administrative error in the relevant paperwork.

The memorial at the Ravenhill rugby grounds. The stadium opened in 1923 and has an ornate entrance arch that was erected as a memorial to those players who died in the Great War; later a second memorial was added to cover the Second World War.

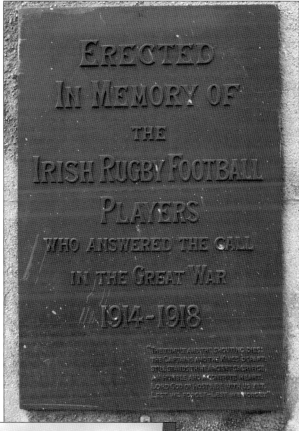

Ravenhill rugby grounds. The arch is a memorial to both World Wars and is in the process of restoration. (photograph courtesy of Nigel Henderson)

guns of 172 Brigade located in Hamel. Despite being in full view of the enemy the 18-pounders and howitzers were able to enfilade the enemy positions across the Ancre with devastating effect.

At approximately the same time the enemy launched a counter-attack against the left flank of the division. Two companies of German infantry emerged from the trees of the Ancre valley and advanced on C11. As they advanced up the open hill they were hit by the combined fire of the divisional artillery and the Lewis guns of the 8th Rifles. The attack melted away due to very heavy casualties.

Throughout the day the wounded had been streaming back to the various aid posts. The experience of Captain Crosbie, Medical Officer to the 11th Inniskillings is probably typical. Prior to the battle he had taken over the regimental aid post at Ross Street and Elgin Avenue, a busy place at the best of times, in conjunction with Lieutenant John Gavin of the 14th Rifles and Captain Picken of the 10th Inniskillings. Samuel Ernest Picken came from the Antrim Road in Belfast and was the son of the late Dr James Picken of Randalstown.

Here nothing of note had occurred until the night of 30 June when almost 100 wounded passed through the aid post. On 1 July the stretcher-bearers were to remain with their companies until the attack started, but once it had got going they were ordered to pick up casualties from any unit and take them to the nearest dressing station. This was carried out and the stretcher-bearers worked continuously night and day bringing wounded in from the Sunken Road, no man's land and Thiepval Wood, under continual shell and machine gun fire. There were wounded recovered from shell holes, dug-outs and half buried under the battlefield dead. The greatest difficulty was in keeping the aid post clear of wounded men. As stretcher-bearers became casualties, they were not bullet-proof and the red-cross armband was no defence against shot and shell, it was then proving difficult to move the wounded on to the advance dressing station. On several occasions the medical officers had to resort to using the regimental stretcher-bearers to evacuate the wounded to the collecting post, which was a great hardship to them having to carry the wounded for such an extended distance. While in the aid post all wounded, where possible, were given hot cocoa or soup and cigarettes. This went on for a total of six days and nights as the wounded continued to be recovered from the battlefield.

In places where the trench tramway was being used to evacuate the wounded things went reasonably smoothly and the injured men were transported in some comfort. However, when this tramway was damaged by shellfire, as it frequently was, then the stretcher-bearers had to carry the wounded down from Thiepval Wood, across the Ancre at Authuille. Some of these men dropped from sheer exhaustion, others refused to be rested, even when relieved. The drivers of the Army Service Corps kept their ambulances on the road for 36 hours, transporting the constant stream of wounded back to Forceville and elsewhere.

Second Lieutenant Cole's squad of the 16th Rifles was located on the north bank of the Ancre to maintain the tramway and had been badly hit by a shelling and among the survivors was Private Hugh Adams:

> We were not thinking about medals. My officer was Lieutenant Cole and a staff officer came up and it was very bad, bodies were lying scattered everywhere. He said the squad would be recommended or medals. But he was hardly out of sight when another shell landed about six feet away and killed Lieutenant Cole who was in front of me and the fella behind and it blew my gas helmet off. The officer's heart was torn out. I don't know who buried them. I left them lying there and went back to the Wood across the river where they gave me another officer, that was the way it was, it was tough.

The Colonel, Adjutant and Sergeants of the 14th Royal Irish Rifles (Young Citizen Volunteers) at Randalstown Camp on 28 January 1915.

The brigade war diary records the death of Second Lieutenant Cole occurring on 3 July. The war diary of the Commander Royal Engineers contained a note recording the actions of Second Lieutenant Cole:

> I desire to bring to your notice the work done by the late 2/Lt D. Cole, 16th RIR (Pioneers). This officer was in charge of the tramway maintenance and traffic during the preliminary bombardment and during subsequent operations until he was killed on the tramway on the morning of 3 July 16. During this time 2/Lt Cole ran his job without a hitch in spite of considerable difficulties. By his personality and example he got his repair gang to a high state of efficiency and pluck. The numerous breaks in the line caused by shells were repaired rapidly and in consequence a great number of wounded were brought down the tramway and a large amount of ammunition and stores got up. Whenever there was confusion or danger 2/Lt Cole was there putting things straight. He was a fine officer and his death was a great loss. The entire credit of what I consider to have been the success of working of the tramline belongs to him.

This was signed by Captain R.N. Burns, Adjutant, RE. On the reverse of this report the Commander Royal Engineers wrote:

> I cannot speak too highly of the cool, deliberate and clear-headed manner in which the late 2/Lt Cole 16 RIR (P) carried out the duties close behind the front-line trenches. Whenever and wherever any difficulty or confusion occurred in connection with his work, especially the trench tramway, whether it was sending up ammunition or evacuating wounded, 2/Lt Cole would go there and smooth it out no matter what unit was concerned. He was possessed with an unusual personality which impressed all who came in contact with him. He though only of his duty regardless of the danger always surrounding him. He impressed his men with confidence and fell gallantly carrying out his duties under heavy shell fire, at Authuille, 3/7/16.

WHAT IS THE GREATEST DEED OF VALOUR?   587

MR. H. B. MARRIOTT-WATSON.

I BEGIN by frankly confessing my inability to answer this question. But I can respond to it. In looking back over our island story, recorded now over many centuries, certain deeds of valour, certain episodes of undying fame, pick themselves out and shine lustrously. This is because they are naturally fine, but also because they have the advantage of advertisement. Many deeds have doubtless taken place of equal glory, but they have been unregistered, they have had no historian. There are incidents distinguished in our history which it is impossible to read without emotion. You will find them scattered along the pages of our annals, where they glow and incite us by their example. Whether it be the story of the *Revenge*, or of Balaclava, of the Heights of Abraham, of Corunna, of Waterloo, of the Indian Mutiny, of Crécy, of Trafalgar—you have a vast field and can make your choice without risking a mistake. But which will be the bravest deed?

It seems to me that when the curtain has been rolled up which now obscures our view of this present great war, and when we are allowed to know and to talk about it, it will be found to have been marked by deeds as great, as valorous, as immortal as any inherited from the past. At present we have received details of many isolated acts of gallantry, the work of individuals, but we have few particulars of concerted action. Even the terrible retreat from Mons is still veiled in some mystery. Yet one has glimpses here and there of things that have happened, things that indicate great and tragic issues, things which may be equalled by scores of other happenings so far unrevealed to us. I can think of one or two with which I have become acquainted, and I am going to mention one, not because it is the most valiant deed I know, but because I know it, and it is worth recording in a symposium such as this, and because it has great and tragic issues.

On June 30th, 1916, the Thirty-sixth Division lay in the trenches which lined Thiépval Wood, in Artois. Thiépval is (or was) a little village on rising ground from the Ancre, a brook rather than a river, which flows sluggishly through marshy ground into the Somme. The Thirty-sixth Division, otherwise known as the Ulster Division, had been established in Thiépval Wood for some time, and it was known to all what work was before them, and what was expected of them. In this first of the Great Pushes of the now matured war each division had its objective settled by headquarters, and by each the operations of the advance had been studiously rehearsed. On the left of the Thirty-sixth was the Twenty-ninth, which had covered itself with glory in Gallipoli, and on the right was the Thirty-second. To each its particular aim and objective was allotted. The wood of Thiépval is just to the east of the Ancre, which, flowing west-south-west from Miraumont, just below Beaucourt, takes a twist due south and so passes on by Hamel, Mesnil, and other villages into Albert. The British front line was on the north-easterly border of the wood, and the advance on July 1st was made in that direction.

The composition of the Thirty-sixth consisted of seven battalions of Royal Irish Rifles and four of Enniskillings. They were the flower of their age from the northern counties of Ireland—Down, Derry, Antrim, Armagh, and others. They had most of them been known before the war as volunteers in a domestic difficulty which we all hope is now in process of solution; and here on the Somme they were to give their lives, as did the Sixteenth Division at Ginchy, in the cause of civilization, freedom, and their common country. They were mill-hands and factory-hands and farm-hands, all gathered without the constraint of conscription, and they were to die for Ulster, for Ireland, for Great Britain. On

"MEN FELL IN DOZENS, IN SCORES, BUT THE ADVANCE KEPT STEADILY ON."

First page of an article about the Division on 1 July 1916.

the night of June 30th young officers were busy in front of the trenches marking the line from which the start was to be made on the morrow.

In the grey chill dawn of a midsummer day the men rose for an hour or two of anxious waiting before the attack. Our artillery had thundered all night, breaking a way for the infantry. But in those days was it a sufficient preparation? We have learnt much since then, and the affairs at Vimy and Messines and on the Menin Road have been much more successfully managed. The hardest time of all, soldiers will tell you, is the hour before zero. On this occasion zero—that is, the hour when the men go over the top—was seven-thirty, seven-thirty of a perfect summer day.

The main objectives of this attack were Grandcourt and Beaucourt, villages on the high ground in front, fortified to the full by the Germans, about a mile and a half from Thièpval Wood, to the north-north-east and north-east. Between, of course, lay the German trenches the other side of No Man's Land, which had to be penetrated before the objectives were attainable. Were the objectives attainable? As I have said before, we have learnt much since then, and it seems that on parts of the Artois line in July, 1916, some units were given tasks which were beyond their strength. Not beyond their courage and determination, but beyond their numbers. These places had been in possession of the Germans for two years and were highly fortified, as subsequent observation, when they *were* taken, demonstrated. The land rose slowly at times, and at times swiftly from the marshes of the Ancre to the heights of Thièpval, of Grandcourt, which are some three hundred feet above. Patrol officers, scout officers, intelligence officers had their doubts. Had they sufficient numbers to carry their objectives? The doubts increased and spread, and eventually reached a brigadier. His answer was: "We are instructed to attack, and we must do it." They attacked.

Across No Man's Land from the verge of the wood the German trenches were visible, and known, an intricate criss-cross. Beyond were second-line trenches, and third line, and fourth line—and beyond all the objectives. At seven-thirty in the morning the division marched into the front trenches and went over the parapet. What was before them?

The comparatively short distance between them and the German positions was the field of Death. From the moment that the parapet was crossed the advancing battalions became the mark of shot and shell. Our own artillery rended the air with deafening sound, so that it was impossible for our men to hear another. They opened out and spread and went forward steadily, punctuated with the "crump" of the five-niners. Thièpval Wood was being stripped to pieces by the bombardment. With bayonets fixed the troops kept steadily on, saved often from serious injury by their steel helmets. And presently the machine-guns of the enemy came into play upon them. With the continuous crr-ump of the five-niners and the incessant mowing of the machine-guns all in No Man's Land and beyond it became a wild and disorderly welter of confusion. But the advance kept on.

Men fell in dozens, in scores. The machine-guns like scythes mowed them down in swathes. They fell and were engulfed in shell-holes. They still advanced with constantly-lessening numbers, gained the German first lines with bayonet and bomb; passed out, moved on, and penetrated to the second line. Down on the ground to avoid enfilading fire. Forward again. The terrible machine-guns from ambuscade poured a ceaseless swish of bullets. The grasses on the earth were cut as evenly and as regularly as though by mowing machines. Dug-outs were captured and bombed. Still the gallant tide rolled on until in some cases the fourth and fifth German lines were occupied.

But, alas! the German bombardment went on—the terrible machine-fire went on. We have changed all that; for one shell the Huns send us we return them ten. Not so in the old days of the Somme. Grandcourt was reached but by a remnant of the battered division, and this handful of men were unable to hold on to their gain. Night fell, and in the night the retirement was made. Thièpval, Grandcourt, Beaucourt Hamel —all these villages were not to pass into our hand just then—not for some months. The forces were not sufficient to hold the objectives. Back into the reeking, blasted wood crept the remnants of that gallant assault, an assault worthy of record with that of the Light Brigade. Out of ten thousand fighting effectives there were seven thousand casualties. And the fight was so determined that practically no prisoners were taken by the Germans.

On the right the attack of the Thirty-second on Thièpval had failed, and on the left the attack on Beaucourt Hamel. The Ulsters were thus left with both flanks in the air, which accounted for their terrible losses.

There is a little blood-stained pendant to this brief story. On the east bank of the Ancre stood a small village, called St. Pierre Divion, and it was necessary that this should be taken. Two platoons were detailed to storm it, and over the parapet a young subaltern waved them good-bye—"God be with you." A young captain in the twenties led the brave boys, and very soon they were lost to view in the "brown" of the general advance. Not one of these returned. They were wiped out of existence, and the good-bye was indeed "God be with you." I quote the simple lines in remembrance of a young officer who watched them go:—

"Upon the parados a scarlet poppy grows,
　　Symbol of oblivion—
Scarlet as the blood that flows
　　By St. Pierre Divion.

"Only the north wind sighs
　　Over the stricken brave;
Far in the wood there lies
　　An unknown soldier's grave."

[*Next month we shall publish replies from Mr. Max Pemberton, Mr. Edgar Jepson, and Mr. Morley Roberts.*]

Second page of above.

Despite such testaments to his behaviour no award was made to Second Lieutenant Cole, proving, if proof were needed, that most deeds of valour on the battlefield go unrewarded.

Among those who were also attempting to keep the causeways across the Ancre open were men of 150 Field Company, Royal Engineers. In their ranks was Sapper Robert Burrows, from Ballygowan, County Down. Sapper Burrows was one of the nine men in the company who became a casualty that day and is one of the many who has no known grave, being commemorated on the Thiepval Memorial. Others who were killed included Sappers D. Fulton, William Dempster and Andrew Walker from Elswick Street, Belfast, while in 122 Field Company Sappers James Hughes, William Molloy and Daniel Davidson from the Donegall Road, Belfast, were killed.

At 4:00 pm, General Nugent was informed by Corps Headquarters that 146 Brigade of 49th Division was at his disposal. The situation was recalled by Major General Perceval in a letter to official historian Edmonds dated 29 July 1930:

> On the 1st July when I heard of the initial success of the Ulster Division I thought that Corps reserve would be used on that divisional front. I went to the headquarters of that division to find out all I could about the situation. I saw Nugent and his staff. The impression I got after talking to them was that there was not a moment to be lost and that it might be too late to do more than secure what had been gained. I therefore went straight to the corps headquarters where I found Cameron. He agreed with me that the matter was urgent and asked me to go to Moreland who was at a sort of O.P. from which he tried to observe the situation for himself. I went on there and told him that I did not think the Ulster Division would hold what it had gained unless it were given assistance at once. I was doubtful whether it was still possible to exploit its success. It is not for me to criticise the way my division was used when in reserve. Of course it seemed to me to be frittered away.[48]

The 146 Brigade, consisting of four battalions of the West Yorkshire Regiment, was given to General Withycombe, the senior brigadier in Thiepval Wood. He was then ordered to send two of its battalions to reinforce the Schwaben Redoubt where the Ulstermen were on the verge of being forced back. However, two of the West Yorkshire battalions were already committed to an attack on Thiepval, while the other two had moved up behind them into trenches of the 32nd Division. It was not until 7:18 pm that six companies of the Yorkshires, led by the 1/6th Battalion, began to move up towards the C line, under the cover of an intense bombardment, but by then it was too late and as the battalion strove to deploy it was cut to pieces by the seemly indestructible German machine guns firing from the village. By 10:00 pm, it appeared to observers that no troops of the division remained in the German lines, although this was not the case.

In the late evening the divisional front line from Elgin Avenue to the River Ancre was being held by the 16th Rifles, the 5th West Yorkshire Regiment and a few companies of the 2/5 West Riding Regiment.

In the Irish Fusiliers' position north of the river Second Lieutenant Sam Wallace received some surprising news:

There would be a sentry in each fire bay and another sitting beside him and if the sentry saw something he would kick him to call a sergeant. The sergeant would have a look and if necessary he would call the platoon commander who would have a look. He then decided if the company commander should be called. Early on 2 July the second-in-command came along and could not find anyone and I was told I was now commanding C Company! All I could do was salute and say "Yes Sir."

---

48   Somme Museum archive.

A sentry on guard duty using a periscope to keep watch. On the ledge can be seen a pocket watch, used to note the time of any enemy movement and the remains of his lunch. The butts of the rifles may be splattered with mud, but the working parts are impeccable; also note that both rifles are cocked.

All day the wounded had been streaming back from the battlefield, some on stretchers, some walking wounded and some being carried by German prisoners under escort. In the 110th Field Ambulance Robert Doggart was on duty and recalled that his unit deployed three aid posts. Close to the front line were Thompson Post and Craigmore, with the third, The Bluff, located to the rear. Robert was at The Bluff and acted as a stretcher-bearer carrying men back to the Dressing Station in Aveluy Wood, he worked constantly for three days. Lance Corporal Tommy Jordan remained on the Somme until 6 July:

> A relief party came and I guided them up to the line. A shell burst and my ears were bleeding and an officer gave me some rum and I was taken up a communication trench named Ulster Avenue, where I fell unconscious. A new officer told me off for poor dress and I told him I had not had my boots off for weeks. This cost me my stripe and now I can't hear a thing!

According to the war diary of A and Q Branch, the entire 36th Ulster Division suffered losses of 214 officers and 5,210 other ranks on 1 July. The heaviest losses within the division were the 13th Battalion Royal Irish Rifles, which reported 595 casualties, followed by the 11th Battalion Royal Inniskilling Fusiliers, reporting 589, and then the 9th Battalion Royal Irish Fusiliers with 532. Over the next few days these figures would be slightly amended.

Total British losses for that day amounted to 19,240 dead, 35,493 wounded, 2,152 missing, and 585 men taken prisoner. It is purported to be the greatest ever number of casualties for any one single day.[49] However, any attempt to give a totally accurate number of casualties is impossible to

---

49   The losses of 1 July 1916 are overshadowed by the 82,000 men lost with the fall of Singapore in the Second World War, which few remember.

HE whom this scroll commemorates was numbered among those who, at the call of King and Country, left all that was dear to them, endured hardness, faced danger, and finally passed out of the sight of men by the path of duty and self-sacrifice, giving up their own lives that others might live in freedom. Let those who come after see to it that his name be not forgotten.

Pte. Thomas Joyce
Royal Irish Fusiliers

The Death Scroll of Private Thomas Joyce, No.16114, killed on 1 July 1916 and commemorated on the Thiepval Memorial.

do. Men who fought on the Somme and were wounded continued to die for days, weeks, months and years later.

Today the losses suffered on the Somme are considered appalling, but compared with the major battles of the Franco-Austrian, Austro-Prussian and Franco-Prussian Wars fought between 1859 and 1871 the *rate* of casualties was actually quite normal. It must be stressed, not the *numbers*, but the *rate*. For the first time in her history Britain was experiencing as a nation what war was like as Europeans had known for centuries.

Now it was time for officers and padres to write letters to the next of kin, while many of those in the ranks also put pen to paper. Within the division numerous brothers were in action on 1 July, Second Lieutenant Philip Wedgwood served in the 16th Rifles, while his brother Gilbert was with the 109th Machine Gun Company. They came from Bloomfield, Belfast, and were the sons of the Reverend George Wedgwood. In a letter written to the family Canon R.G.S. King[50] wrote:

> I write to tell you of my deep sympathy in very great sorrow. I know your sons well. I saw a great deal more of the younger because he remained with the battalion. When the 14th endured a terrible bombardment on 6th April, he spent the night digging out the killed and wounded.

The Canon went on to describe the events of 1 July;

---

50 Canon King's son, Lieutenant Robert F King, Royal Dublin Fusiliers, had died of wounds on 23 May 1915.

Comber post office, how many letters to France passed through here? (Courtesy of Laura Spence)

He was in the German trenches and was taking prisoners in the dug-outs. He and his party had bombs with them, and the Germans were at their mercy. He came to a dug-out where there were some twenty Germans. He might have killed these, but, instead, offered them their lives if they would come out and surrender. They did so, and all came out. He turned his back for a moment, and one of them treacherously shot him dead. I do not know the particulars of his brother's death. I am sure Captain McConachie, CO of the Brigade Machine Gun Company, will write you all the particulars that are known.

Captain McConachie, commanding 109th Machine Gun Company, also observed:

It was with much sorrow that I had to report your son, Lieutenant G.C. Wedgwood as killed. From all information I have gathered I find he was killed instantaneously while leading his teams across no man's land. His death is a great loss to me and my company. He has done some excellent work in the months he was with us in the trenches, and in the face of the enemy he has always shown the coolness and courage which are expected of British officers. During the seven days bombardment he was in charge of four guns which fired on the enemy all night. The enemy were very much annoyed at this firing and searched for his guns every day with heavy shells, but your son had selected the positions for his guns and men so carefully that none of them was hit during this period. As a companion in the Mess he was full of good spirits. My sole remaining officer and myself send sincere sympathy to you and your family in your hour of sorrow.

Captain McConachie wrote many letters during the first few days of July; another was to William Kennedy of Coleraine, concerning his son William Robert:

I have officially reported your son as wounded, missing and believed killed. I regret that I cannot hold out much hope of his being found alive. He was severely wounded when in the German trenches. All near him were put out of action. I cannot find words to express my feeling at this time; I have lost so many comrades that I feel dazed. I can only say that your son fell like a true British soldier by his gun with his face to the enemy.

Like so many others, Lance Corporal Kennedy has no known grave.

Lieutenant S.H. Monard, of D Company 14th Rifles, in a letter to Mr David Williamson, of Market Street, Tandragee, County Armagh, on the death of his son David on 1 July wrote:

Your loss is greater than mine, but to me Davy was a great friend, and I find it impossible to realise that his absence is permanent. During the battle he never left my side, and he was with me in the fourth line of the German defences. We were the only two of the battalion to get to the fourth line. Here we met a party of six Germans, who pretended to surrender. One of them, however, had a bomb, and he was making to throw it at us when Davy shot him dead. The others commenced to run, but we shot them all except one, and a bayonet thrust from Davy accounted for him. Our troops had all retired, so we made out way back to the third line, and joined our company again. We stayed in that line six hours under heavy shellfire, although tired, the men were in the best of spirits. Davy was cracking jokes with everybody, and was very cool and happy. Towards dusk a strong counter-attack by the enemy made it necessary to fall back to a stronger position, and a rearguard of a few men kept up a heavy fire on the enemy to cover the retirement of our troops. Davy was one of this rearguard, and, while exposing himself to get a better view of the enemy, a bullet went through his head, and he died instantly. You have every reason to be proud of your son.

A letter from Colonel Ricardo to Mr Alexander Weir of Convoy, County Donegal, concerning the death of Captain Jack Weir, appeared in the local papers; "John fell gallantly leading his platoon, who would have followed him anywhere. He was just at the German wire and was killed instantly. He has consistently done splendid work, and whenever there was a special difficulty we always consulted him, and he usually found a way out."

The Reverend W.J. McConnell, Presbyterian chaplain, wrote to Mr and Mrs McCracken of Annsborough, on behalf of Colonel Savage and the remaining officers of the 13th Rifles:

It is with much sorrow that I write to express our deepest sympathy with you in the loss of your son, who was killed during the recent attack in which Ulster played so brilliant a part. With many of his brave comrades he fought a good fight, and made the greatest sacrifice a man can make. Today your home and many homes are darkened. Great-hearted Ulster is sore stricken because so many of her bravest and worthiest sons who covered her name with glory in the day of battle shall return to her no more. Their loss to us is heavy also, and we mourn with you for them. We cannot, however, but believe that those at home will manifest in their day of grief the same high courage and strength of soul as sent and sustained their beloved to do their duty in the day of trial.

A letter from Captain W.R. White to George and Eliza Morrison of Lisbane, Comber, County Down, in regard to their eighteen year old son Private James Morrison, 16th Rifles, appeared in the *Belfast News Letter* on 7 July:

It is with great sorrow that I have to inform you of the death of your son, which occurred last night (29 June 1916). He was in the trenches with the rest of the company working when a shell exploded near him and killed him instantly.

We all feel his loss very much because he was a fine soldier, who always did his best and performed his duty uncomplainingly. My sympathy and the sympathy of all his comrades is with you and all his relatives. We can only offer you the consoling thoughts that he died, as we should all wish to die, fighting for his country, and that he died suddenly and painlessly.

1 July took a terrible toll of stretcher bearers and another who died was Corporal James Weir of the 16th Rifles. His father, whose home was at Ballyward, Banbridge, received a letter from Captain Chase, a former master at Campbell College, Belfast. The letter described how Corporal Weir was one of a party carrying a wounded man to the dressing station when a shell burst among them killing him and three others. His brother William was also serving with the pioneers.

Private Andrew Stephenson of the 14th Rifles was badly wounded on1 July and wrote to his father at Fitzwilliam Street, Belfast from Salisbury hospital:

Our division went over the top at a part called Thiepval, about five miles north of Albert. We had no difficulty in taking the first three lines of German trenches. It was just like as if we had been out on an ordinary manoeuvre, except that they shelled us something awful and the bullets were hissing all over the place. I had one or two very narrow escapes. While we were advancing I was carrying my rifle over my right shoulder, and a bullet hit the butt of it and shattered it to pieces. A bit of luck wasn't it? Another time my shrapnel helmet saved me from what would have been a very nasty wound. But it only put a big bruise in it. I got a German rifle with five cartridges in it. I took the cartridges out and kept them, and left the rifle where I got it. I have got one of the cartridges yet as a souvenir. I also got a belt and two helmets. We took an awful crowd of prisoners, and I think they were glad to get out of it."

Private Stephenson's brother, Sergeant William Stephenson, had been killed the previous April when the 14th Rifles suffered heavily under a German artillery bombardment.

A letter from Lance Corporal William A. Greer to his parents at Stranmillis Road, Belfast, was published in the *Belfast News Letter* on 10 July:

Our division has made a name for itself these past few days. We knew that something big was coming off soon, and on the 1st July we got the order to attack, and take, if possible, four lines of German trenches opposite the line we had been holding since we came out. The German lines were bombarded for almost a week before we went over the parapet. On 1st July the boys were all very cool about matters, but we had to face a very heavy fire from machineguns, though our artillery had accounted for a big lot of them in the bombardment. We reached the first line of the trenches alright and pushed on to the second and third without meeting very much resistance, as any Germans who survived the preliminary bombardment were almost demoralised by the shellfire. We held on to the four lines of trenches until nightfall, we had to temporarily fall back to our own lines owing to our right and left flanks not being able to push forward with our division at the time. However, they were regained later, and as I write, we still hold them – not our division, of course, but another relieving one. The bombardment just before we attacked was terrible. It developed in intensity an hour before the infantry started operations, and how any living being in the German lines could survive it is a mystery. Certainly, they were very glad to be taken as prisoners, and were all very much shaken. We took a big lot of prisoners during the day – some of them big, strong-looking chaps, but a good lot of them young and middle-aged. We ourselves, unfortunately, lost fairly heavily, as you will see for yourself later on. It was only Providence, I think, pulled me through; I had several narrow shaves. My steel helmet saved my life.

Private William Burrows wrote to his father at Prospect Road, Bangor, beginning his letter with the famous quote from Shakespeare's Henry V.

"We few, we happy few, we band of brothers. For he today that sheds his blood with me, shall be my brother." I have come through the attack and am still alive and smiling. I shall not try to tell you what it was like, that is beyond my powers of description, and I think everyone who was there would see it in a different light. But I think each one would agree that a scrap between the Shankill and the Falls is tame compared with it, no matter how serious you would think it. Our fellows fought splendidly, we absolutely walked through them. The rush I used to remember [sic] to the German trenches would be like a forward on the ball, but we went much steadier than that. We lost a great many, of course, but we gave a great deal more than we got. Looking back I think it was a miracle that any of us escaped. When we were in the scrap I could not eat, for the awful sights turned my stomach, and I would have given anything for a drink of cold water. What must have the wounded have suffered when I felt the thirst so severely? Do you remember the little ivory monkey Aunt Nena gave me as a mascot, which she bought when she was in Alaska? Well I wore it around my neck going into action. One of our fellows wore an Orange sash, and, as Mickey Free would say "by the same token" came out unscathed, another one played bagpipes, while several manipulated the warlike mouth organ. There was no fear in anyone, but I cannot tell you enough, you will have to wait until I get home, which won't be very long now.

While the wearing of the orange sash has taken on almost mythical proportions, actual accounts are few. The *Belfast News Letter* published a letter on 29 July from Private R. Laverty of the 10th Inniskillings:

The 10th have made a name for themselves and old Derry. When we got the order to charge on the glorious 1st of July every man went over the parapet as light-heartedly as if on parade. A lot of our chaps went down before we got far, but seeing them fall only made us more eager to get at the Germans. Nothing could stop our men. Our officers acted magnificently, every one of them. Captain Wilton fearlessly led us over, keeping in front all the time, encouraging us as we went forward, and exposing himself to the very heavy fire. At length he got wounded, but still on we went, some of the boys shouting 'No Surrender' and 'Good old Ulster'. Some of them had orange lilies in their caps, and one sergeant I saw had on his orange sash going over the parapet to meet them. He kept shouting 'Come on Ulster.' I heard an officer of the Irish Rifles, and a fine chap he was, shouting 'Come on Derry, and remember your watchword is still 'No Surrender.' And away we went again to meet the foe."

Private Jim Brown, the scout in C Company of the 13th Rifles was wounded on 1 July and while in Milton Hill Hospital in Berkshire wrote a long letter to his mother at Church Street in Bangor, County Down:

My leg is near all right again. You will see by my address that I am in another hospital. This one is situated in the country, in a gentleman's estate. Have you seen the official casualty list for my battalion yet? It will likely be in next week's *Spectator*'. Will you please post it to me? I saw last week's, the 7th. There were some of our names on it. It was a lucky thing for me that I joined the scouts or I might not have been here to tell the tale today. You see it was this way, we had to take three lines of trenches. It was 650 yards to the first, 250 to the second, 300 to the third and that made the whole distance twelve hundred yards and each trench full of Germans. Well, now, to tell you my job, there were fifteen scouts to the battalion, but before the attack came off six got put out of action, two killed and four wounded. That left nine of us, so two were put to each company. I was in C Company (Bertie McCready's company). My job was to get information from the Germans. I was to strip them of all papers and take the numbers of their regiments, be they dead or alive. So Saturday morning came and a lovely morning it was, the sun was shining and our big guns were sending the shells over to the enemy in thousands and the Germans did not forget to send a few back and I tell you they did some damage. Over a hundred of our fellows were knocked out before we got at them. Half past 7 o'clock was the time and over we went. At the first trench there was a group of Germans and my mate and I made them all prisoners, and stripped them of all their belongings, papers, watches, money, and took the numbers of their regiment. We handed them over to our fellows to take back to our lines and they were only too pleased to go for they all said they were fed up. Now all we scouts wanted was to get back to our lines, but how were we to get back? The machine guns of the Germans were firing like mad, and they were shelling our first line where we had to go, but we had to get there somehow or fall in the attempt. So my mate and I set off, but before we got five yards, they saw us and turned a machine gun on us, but we got into a shell hole just in time, and had to lie there for three-quarters of an hour. They keep firing at the hole all the time, for they knew we were there. Well, time was going on, and one of us had to get back some way. That was our orders before leaving, so I asked my mate was he going to make a bid for it. He said he would get hit if he did so, and he was going to say there until things quietened down a bit. I told him the longer he stayed the worse it would be, but he would not come with me. I can't tell you how I got in, but I did, only getting hit in the knee. I haven't heard how my mate fared, but I believe he got killed, poor fellow. If he had come with me he might have got in all right.

In a later letter Private Brown reminded his mother to post the local newspaper to him:

Don't forget about Friday's *Spectator*. Get it early on Friday morning, and if you post it at once I will have it on Saturday morning first thing. It is getting a bit lonely in hospital as there are none of the Bangor boys with me. They are all I think down London way, but you know George McGee, of Church Street. Well, one of his brothers is in the same ward as me. They call him James. He is in the Royal Horse Artillery. He is a very nice chap, he asked me if I knew George and I told him I used to be in his battalion. I suppose there is no more word of the missing Bangor boys?"

Wilfred Spender, General Nugent's GSOII, wrote to his wife from Hédouville on 2 July and set in motion the myth that the division had been 'let down' on the previous day:

I am not an Ulsterman, but yesterday as I followed their amazing attack I felt that I would rather be an Ulsterman than anything else in the world. My position enabled me to watch the commencement of their attack from the wood in which they had formed up, but which, long prior to the hour of assault, was being overwhelmed with shellfire so that the trees were stripped and the top half of the wood ceased to be anything but a slope of bare stumps with innumerable shell holes pitted in the chalk. It looked as if nothing could live in the wood, and indeed the losses were heavy before they started, two companies of one battalion being reduced to a fourth in the assembly trenches. When I saw their men emerge out of the smoke and for up as if on parade, I could hardly believe my eyes. Then I saw them attack, beginning at a slow walk over no man's land, and then suddenly let loose as they charged over the two front lines of the enemy's trenches shouting 'No surrender, Boys.' The enemy's gunfire raked them from the left, and machine guns in a village enfiladed them on the right, but battalion after battalion came out of that awful wood as steadily as I have seen them at Ballykinlar, Clandeboye or Shane's Castle. The enemy's first, second and third lines were soon taken, and still the waves of men went on, getting thinner and thinner but without hesitation. The enemy's fourth line fell before these men who would not be stopped. I saw parties of them, now much reduced indeed, enter the fifth line of the enemy's trenches, our final objective. It could not be held as the Division had advanced into a narrow salient. The Corps on our right and left had been unable to advance so that the Ulstermen were the target of the concentrated hostile guns and machine guns behind and on both flanks, though the enemy in front were vanquished and retiring. The order to retire was given, but many parties preferred to die in the ground they had won so hardly. My pen cannot describe adequately the hundreds of heroic acts that I witnessed nor how yesterday a relieving force was organised of men who had already been fighting for 36 hours to carry ammunition and water to the gallant

William Moore had been a member of the YCV and had served as a CQMS with the 14th Royal Irish Rifles in 1916. He was commissioned the following year and earned the Military Cross for his action during a wiring party. He survived the war.

garrison still holding on. The Ulster Division has lost more than half the men who attacked, and in doing so has sacrificed itself for the Empire which has treated them none too well. The much derided Ulster Volunteer force has won a name which equals any in History. Their devotion, which no doubt has helped the advance elsewhere, deserves the gratitude of the British Empire. It is due to the memory of these brave heroes that their beloved Province shall be fairly treated.

The myth was further generated by his wife's reply of 4 July, with her use of the word "failed":

Your two scraps of July 2 have come, and I can think of nothing else. I never dreamt I should hear yet. It must have nearly broken your heart to watch such things, but oh how proud I am. I can't write about it. My heart is too full. It seems so cruel a thing to have happened that the flanking divisions should have failed to come up. I ask nothing better than to spend my whole day if necessary at our work of helping the wounded. It isn't much to do, and oh how I wish one could do more. It is so glorious to know that our men are all and more than we thought them. Words are simply useless, as you will understand. And yet, I don't know how to write or think of anything else. Thank God so few shells came your way. But to be watching it all must have been awful. Oh it's hard to sit at home with such things happening to you and our splendid men. But I can't be too thankful that I choose this work, and not the Laboratory work. I couldn't have borne not to be in touch with it all now. I mean to try and get to see some of the men in London hospitals, so as to be more in touch with them. One wrote to me the other day and said that the chief thing he wanted was 'to get back for a good roll on the drums on July 12th!' A true Orangeman, that!"

Spender wrote again to his wife on 6 July:

Our men are quite cheery and saying they don't want any Derby recruits. The General wrote an excellent order of the day and made a very nice speech to all the brigades, nearly breaking down. Somehow he fails to strike the spark, so the officers say, tho' it is absolutely genuine. I think he cannot quite forgive himself. I have written to Mrs Davidson of the Sirocco works whose son was killed after earning the VC, and to Jenkins of Larne who was wounded; also briefly to Craig about his brother of whom we have still no news except for his gallantry. Some of our men returned yesterday after having held a post in the distant lines nearly 2,000 yards beyond our lines for 36 hours: eight men against an army.

Captain James Davidson may well have earned a Victoria Cross on 1 July, but no such award was made. Major A.P. Jenkins had been wounded by a bullet to the head and was a prisoner, as was Captain Craig. The reference to 'Derby' recruits was a scheme introduced whereby men could continue to enlist voluntarily or attest with an obligation to join if called upon at a later date. Eventually these recruits would make up a large part of the division. Spender's letter to Mrs Davidson was later published in the local press and this caused some consternation as other letters he had written to various people contained some very personal remarks and there was a fear these would also appear in the papers. He vowed to his wife to be circumspect in his future epistles.

The part played by the division on the Somme may have been over, but men continued to die. On 10 July two members of the 13th Rifles were killed. They were Privates W.J. Johnston from Hillsborough and N. McCready from Bangor. Nathanial McCready was 30 years old and lived in Ballymagee Street with his wife Elizabeth. Prior to the war he had worked as a plumber and also been a member of the local fire brigade. He had been wounded and taken prisoner on 1 July.

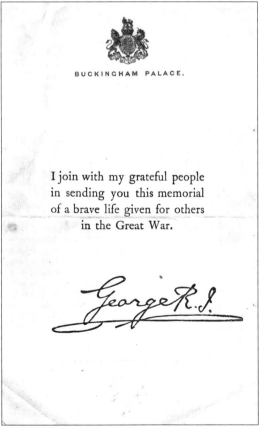

BUCKINGHAM PALACE.

I join with my grateful people in sending you this memorial of a brave life given for others in the Great War.

George R.I.

A short note from the King, which was sent out with each Death Penny.

Captain James McKee was Private McFadzean's company commander, and his letter to McFadzean's father tells of what happened that night:

I wish you to accept my sincere sympathy in your great sorrow caused by the death of your son. You will have great satisfaction in knowing that he died a hero's death. Our men were in the assembly trenches and bombs were being distributed. Your son had a box passed to him, and in the passing some bombs dropped out. In falling, the safety pins fell out; and your son, realising the danger to his comrades, flung himself on top of the bombs. He was killed, and two others were slightly wounded. He saved the lives of a number of his comrades by his action and we are proud of him. His name has been sent forward to higher authority, with recommendation for a decoration. I was not in the fight on July 1, as I was then at the Army School. I am sorry I was not there, as I believe our attack was magnificent. Our boys did exception-ally well. Corporal Dave Marshall was standing beside McFadzean and tells that by his heroic self-sacrifice saved the lives of his comrades around him, earning their admiration and grati-tude, which will never be forgotten by them.[51]

The King commands me to assure you of the true sympathy of His Majesty and The Queen in your sorrow.

Kitchener

Message from Kitchener on the death of a loved one.

Corporal James Hogg, from Ballymoney, in a letter home observed:

After we had taken the first line of German trenches I received my first wound on the side with shrapnel, but after having it hurriedly dressed I managed to keep on. Before I got into the next trench I got a bullet through my left leg, which dropped me. When I was lying the Germans were bombarding for all they were worth, so I got it again by shrapnel in the back, followed by another bullet through the same leg. Lieutenant Moore, who brought in a great many under fire, then came out and lifted me. When he saw me safe he returned and continued at the work until he got wounded himself. I saw him in the dressing-station, and certainly he done a lot for the poor fellows who were lying exposed to fire.

This is Second Lieutenant J.R. Moore, younger son of William Moore, KC, MP. Lieutenant E.W. Crawford, Adjutant to the 9th Inniskillings wrote to the father of Holt and William Hewitt on 6 July 1916:

My Dear Mr Hewitt,
I suppose you will have heard that both Holt and Willie fell in the attack we made last Saturday. Your loss is so terrible that any words of mine are of little worth. Poor Holt, the most loveable and cheerful of souls! His Sergeant says he was killed outright. He was one

---

51 _Belfast New Letter_ 13 July 1916.

of my closest friends and although he had gone to the Machine gun Corps, we of the 9th Inniskillings consider him ours. Willie led his platoon over the top. One of his men told me he was wounded, but still carried on, but had to stop, from loss of blood. After that the only thing I can gather is that a Sergeant Lally of his battery (*sic*), who himself was wounded, said he saw him die. He was a grand boy, one of the finest characters I have ever seen. He acted as Adjutant to me, and no more conscientious and better boy ever lived. The whole attack was the most heroic thing possible. The divisional commander, speaking of it, said it was the most gallant and heroic incident of the War. The pity of it was we lost our best, both officers and men. Nothing on this earth can atone for your losses, but you have the certain knowledge that this was a fine and fitting finish to a fine life. Personally I cannot tell you how I feel. I have lost two of the best friends. I am sending you Willie's kit. If I can do anything for you, please do not hesitate to let me know. With much sympathy and kindest regards, I am yours very sincerely.

Lieutenant E.W. Crawford, Adj.

This family had already lost a son when Ernest Hewitt, serving with the King's Own (Royal Lancaster) Regiment, was killed on 15 June 1915 at Festubert.

On 1 July, Private Duncan Davidson had transferred into 109th Trench Mortar Battery and the events of that day affected him as it did most other men, although he still took the opportunity to mention the small things in life when writing to his sister Teenie:

At last, a few lines, forgive me for not writing sooner, but Teenie this last three weeks have been hell, firstly I must thank you, for the splendid parcel you sent me, the parcel had one fault Teenie, it was too expensive firstly a cheaper class of shaving soap would have served, secondly I could have done without a hair brush and comb, I will not go over the different articles, I

(Top) Lieutenant Holt Montgomery Hewitt was killed in action on 1 July 1916, while serving with the 109th Machine Company.
(Middle) Second Lieutenant William Arthur Hewitt was killed in action on 1 July 1916, while serving with the 9th Royal Inniskilling Fusiliers.
(Bottom) Lieutenant Ernest Henry Hewitt, brother of Holt and William, killed in action on 15 June 1915, while serving with the King's Own Royal Lancaster Regiment.

thank you very much for all you sent, especially were the cigarettes, pipe tobacco welcome, I was clean out of smokes, the eatables were a veritable God-send, the bread you sent, was the first I had tasted for three weeks, we had been living on Bully Beef, biscuits and black tea, I got the parcel on 30th June, a night I will never forget, the 1st July we started the big attack, I must tell you, our Battery was in the trenches, ten days before the attack came off, five days of those ten, our Artillery kept up a heavy bombardment of the enemy lines, the roar of the guns, was like heavy thunder, we lost thirteen men with shell shock, before we attacked. Well now for July 1st it was a glorious morning, very warm, and sunny, for ninety minutes before we topped the parapet, our guns doubled their fire, it was a fearful, and yet a grand sight, the morning was just breaking, for miles the sky was lit up with the flash of the guns, the roar was fearful, you couldn't hear the chap beside you speak, one had to shout, at 7:30 sharp the advance began my old Brigade, led the way. I wish you could have seen them, they advanced under a heavy shell and machine gun fire, as steady as if on parade, it was marvellous, immediately the first line advanced, we followed with our guns, we got it hot, before we had advanced one hundred yards half the Battery was killed or wounded, I lost my chum Teenie, shot dead beside me (I avenged him), we took the first line trench easily, the second line we had some hot work, there we didn't bomb or bayonet, we took prisoners (our Brigade took over six hundred prisoners). The third line, we took at the bayonet point, there was no stopping our fellows, hell itself wouldn't stop an Irish Division, so determined were our fellows, that we actually reached the fifth line, but we paid the cost, as the flanking Divisions, failed to level up with us, this allowed the Allemande, to get us on the front, rear, and two flanks with machine guns, and he played fair hell with us, but withal he couldn't beat us, we held the third line, for seventeen hours, and repulsed two counter attacks before we were relieved, the 36th Division has made a name that will live forever, especially our Brigade, we were thanked personally by the General, he said we done deeds that would live forever in history, we lost heavily, in fact the Ulster Division is no more, I daren't tell you, the numbers, God knows, you will all know soon enough, our Battery was wiped out, we went into action with one hundred and eleven men and six officers, we came out with twenty-seven men and two officers, out of eleven men on our gun two of us are left, the Corporal and myself, I had some marvellous escapes, got my rifle carried out of my hand with shrapnel, a machine gun bullet through my pack and hit in the arm, I thank God I am alive and well today. At present we are proceeding down the line, in easy stages for a rest, God knows we need one, I expect when we get settled down, leave may start again, I trust it does, as I stand a good chance, I am praying to seeing you all I trust DV before summer ends.

Elements of the division had held parts of the German lines throughout 1 July, but a shortage of small arms ammunition and bombs coupled with manifold enemy attacks from three sides forced them to withdraw. By 10:30 pm on that day, only a few scattered small parties of men still held out in the Schwaben Redoubt and original German front line. The 49th Division, acting as corps reserve, sent two companies of the 1/7th West Yorkshires to support the troops attacking the Schwaben Redoubt; however, the Yorkshires wandered too far to the left and took possession of some trenches in the enemy reserve line, north of the Redoubt.

For those men left wounded on the battlefield a terrible thirst tormented them for the remainder of the day and into the night. During the hours of darkness the stretcher-bearers and others had searched no man's land for survivors. These searches would continue up until 5 July.

By 7:00 am on 2 July the ground mist had been burnt off by the sun and observers on Mesnil Ridge could see that there were still scattered groups of British troops in the first two lines of enemy trenches. That afternoon at 2:00 pm, the supporting artillery put a box barrage around Thiepval village as, from 107 Brigade, General Withycombe ordered Major P.J. Woods of the 9th Rifles to take 360 reinforcements from its various battalions and carrying parties to bring forward supplies of ammunition, bombs and water. Along with these went two machine guns of 107th Machine Gun Company. On crossing no man's land, despite being in 'artillery formation', this force lost a third of its strength to enemy fire. Near their objective Major Woods of the 9th Rifles, came across Corporal George Sanders of the 7th Battalion West Yorkshire Regiment and his command of some 30 men, who had been holding off enemy attacks since the previous day. Sanders, from Leeds, also had in his care several members of the division, all of whom were wounded and had been taken prisoner by the Germans, before Sanders and his men had rescued them. The West Yorkshires had advanced at 9:00 am, on 1 July to act as support on the attack against the Schwaben Redoubt. Overnight Sanders and his men had held off repeated enemy bombing attacks and on occasions had resorted to the bayonet. Corporal Sanders was a remarkable man; he was later commissioned and in April 1917 at Mount Kemmel was awarded a Military Cross while a temporary captain.

That afternoon, two small groups of men from the 16th Rifles crossed no man's land carrying much needed supplies of ammunition, water and bombs. After 6:00 pm the Germans made repeated attacks on the remaining positions held by the division and the Leipzig Redoubt. The 29th Division took over from the 36th north of the Ancre, while the 49th relieved the remainder of the division at dusk.

Cyril Falls, in his history, lays the blame for failure on 1 July on lack of support to the flanks. This is clearly nonsense and a slur on those men who fought on the right and left of the Ulster Division. To the north at Beaumont Hamel the 29th Division suffered 5,240 casualties, while to the south at Thiepval the 32nd Division had 3,949 casualties.[52]

Total prisoners taken by the division over the two days were 543. Many others had been taken, but were either killed on the journey back to the British lines by their own artillery and machine gun fire, or escaped in the confusion of the near constant shelling:

SPECIAL ORDER OF THE DAY

LIEUT-GENERAL T.L.N. MOORLAND KCB, DSO
3rd July 1916

On the withdrawal of the 36th Ulster Division into reserve after the desperate fighting of the last few days, the G.O.C. X Corps wishes to express to the G.O.C. and all ranks his admiration of the dash and gallantry with which the attack was carried out which attained a large measure of success under unfavourable conditions.

He regrets the heavy and inevitable losses sustained and feels sure that, after a period of rest, the Division will be ready to respond to any call made upon it.

(Sd) G. Welsh, Br. Genrl.
D.A.& Q.M.G., X Corps

SPECIAL ORDER OF THE DAY
By
Major-General O.S.W. Nugent, DSO
Commanding 36th (Ulster) Division

---

52   The losses on 1 July have overshadowed the fact that this battle was a British victory, ending as it did on 18 November 1916. It must also be remembered that the British suffered more casualties in the Normandy campaign of 1944 than they did on the Somme. Figures are Normandy 6 June-25 August 1944, 100 men per division per day, the Somme 1 July -18 November 1916, 89 men per division per day.

The General Officer Commanding the Ulster Division desires that the Division should know that, in his opinion, nothing finer has been done in the War than the attack by the Ulster Division on the 1st July. The leading of the Company Officers, the discipline and courage shown by all ranks of the Division will stand out in the future history of the War as an example of what good troops, well led, are capable of accomplishing. None but troops of the best quality could have faced the fire which was brought to bear on them and the losses suffered during the advance. Nothing could have been finer than the steadiness and discipline shown by every Battalion, not only in forming up outside its own trenches but in advancing under severe enfilading fire. The advance across the open to the German line was carried out like the steadiness of a parade movement, under a fire both from front and flanks which could only have been faced by troops of the highest quality. The fact that the objects of the attack on one side were not obtained is no reflection on the Battalions which were entrusted with the task. They did all that man could do and in common with every Battalion in the Division showed the most conspicuous courage and devotion.

On the other side, the Division carried out every portion of its allotted task in spite of the heaviest losses. It captured nearly 600 prisoners and carried its advance triumphantly to the limits of the objective laid down. There is nothing in the operations carried out by the Ulster Division on the 1st July that will not be a source of pride to all Ulstermen. The Division has been highly tried and has emerged from the ordeal with unstained honour, having fulfilled, in every particular, the great expectations formed of it. Tales of individual and collective heroism on the part of Officers and Men come in from every side, too numerous to mention, but all showing that the standard of gallantry and devotion attained is one that may be equalled, but never likely to be surpassed. The General Officer Commanding deeply regrets the heavy losses of Officers and Men. He is proud beyond description, as every Officer and Man in the Division may well be, of the magnificent example of sublime courage and discipline which the Ulster Division has given to the Army.

Ulster has every reason to be proud of the men she has given to the service of our country. Though many of our best men have gone the spirit which animated them remains in the Division and will never die.

Signed L.J. Comyn, Lt-Col. A.A.&Q.M.G. 36th Division

Dawn on 4 July and Second Lieutenant Sam Wallace celebrated a date he never thought he would live to see:

My birthday was on the 4th of July, but on the night of 1st July I had told Captain Shillington that I would never be twenty-one, because we had been lifted off our feet by the blast of a 5.9 and thrown into the bottom of a trench, which saved our lives because some of the shell fragments were like a scythe and if they hit your arm or leg you would lose them. That was when I said I would never be twenty-one! For the week prior to the Somme we had been well fed as the rations came up, but of course they were rough and ready. Bully beef stew out of a tin, with any amount of strong tea and white bread. The Cook back at base was eventually decorated for the way he did the rations and all the white bread was baked at base. We started to march off to Belgium and we only marched about ten miles that day. They wanted us to get out of the battle area as quickly as possible and, rather than march north, we started out towards Amiens. Before we started north we slept out in the open as the weather was lovely. There weren't so many of us anyway, the only officers were only the company commander, Captain Shillington and myself. We began marching at 9:00 am and stopped for lunch from the travelling kitchen that accompanied us. It was pulled by two mules and the stew was being cooked as we marched along, you followed the smell. We marched for three miles then halted

Headstone of Private A J Dempster
13th Royal Irish Rifles from
Moneyrea, Comber, County Down,
killed on 1 July 1916, aged 25 years.

Helen's Tower, Clandeboye Estate, County
Down, on which the Ulster Tower at Thiepval
was based.

(Above) The inauguration
of the Ulster Tower in
France included a dinner.
(Right) Reverse of the
above.

Mr McMaster of Lambeg,
Lisburn, the first caretaker of
the Ulster Tower in France,
circa 1928.

for five minutes and the day ended at 4:00 pm. When the post arrived there was a parcel for me, it was a birthday cake from my sister, who had baked it at school. There were so few officers left that each one had a piece. We heard that Captain Shillington's nephew had been killed and I remember the Captain saying 'his mother will not thank me for this'. This was Lieutenant Cather who was posthumously awarded a Victoria Cross. That night I cleaned my revolver. You had to buy your own and mine had cost three guineas.

The rations were mostly prompt, the postal service second to none and the Division's administration worked smoothly. There was a request to DADOS to supply five Vickers machine guns to replace those lost on 1 July, mostly destroyed by enemy shellfire. Four Lewis guns were required for the 14th Rifles, to replace those destroyed in the battle, while other battalions made similar requests. The following day DADOS was running out of springs for the Lewis guns, many requiring replacements having been weakened by so much firing on 1 July. The new springs supplied gave much trouble, possibly being a poor batch from the factory.

The division moved back to Rubempré on 5 July, where it bivouacked for the following five days. While the divisional artillery remained in position the division then moved to Bernaville. Replacements then arrived prior to the move to Flanders. A report was submitted to Army Command on 6 July, an analysis of the effects of artillery in cutting barbed wire.[53] A sample of German barbed wire was attached and it was noted that it was very strong and had mainly been attached to iron uprights, although wooden posts had also been observed. Where wire was under direct observation it had been successfully cut and the majority of reports from the infantry had

---

53   Headlam, Major General J., *Notes on Artillery Material in the Battle of the Somme.*

Inscription on the Tablet in the Memorial
Chamber of the Tower at Thiepval.

 1914 1918

THIS TOWER IS DEDICATED
TO THE GLORY OF GOD IN
GRATEFUL MEMORY OF THE
OFFICERS, NON-COMMISSIONED
OFFICERS AND MEN OF THE
36TH (ULSTER) DIVISION, AND
OF THE SONS OF ULSTER IN
OTHER FORCES WHO LAID
DOWN THEIR LIVES IN THE
GREAT WAR, AND OF ALL
THEIR COMRADES-IN-ARMS,
WHO BY DIVINE GRACE WERE
SPARED TO TESTIFY TO THEIR
GLORIOUS DEEDS.

IT IS ERECTED ON THE SITE
OF THE FAMOUS ADVANCE OF
THE ULSTER DIVISION
ON THE 1ST JULY, 1916.

"THROUGHOUT THE LONG
YEARS OF STRUGGLE THE
MEN OF ULSTER HAVE
PROVED HOW NOBLY THEY
FIGHT AND DIE."
16TH NOVEMBER, 1918.   KING GEORGE V.

"THEIR NAME LIVETH FOR
EVERMORE."

UNVEILED 19TH NOVEMBER, 1921,
BY THE RIGHT HON
LORD CARSON OF DUNCAIRN.

Helen's Tower here I stand,
Dominant o'er sea and land,
Sons' love built me, and I hold
Ulster's love in letter'd gold.
Tennyson.

(Above) Programme for the dedication of the Ulster Tower, which took place on Saturday 19 November 1921, being unveiled by Field Marshal Sir Henry Wilson, Chief of the Imperial General Staff. (Right) Reverse of the above.

Dedication at Thiepval
36th (Ulster) Division

PROGRAMME FOR THE DAY.

9 a.m.
Motors leave Amiens for Thiepval.

11 a.m.
The Prime Minister of Northern Ireland receives the Visitors on behalf of the Committee, and asks Field Marshall Sir Henry Wilson, Bart., G.C.B., to unlock the Memorial Tower (handing him a presentation Silver Casket containing the Key). The Field Marshall will make a speech (in French) welcoming the French representatives who are present, and open the Tower.

Lord Carson of Duncairn will unveil the Tablet in the Memorial Chamber.

The Dedication Service will be performed by the Primate of All Ireland, the Moderator of the Presbyterian Church, and the President of the Methodist Church in Ireland.

The Visitors will then file outside, and Her Grace the Duchess of Abercorn will unfurl the first Union Jack, presented by the Women of Ulster; and the French National Flag, presented by Messrs. Samuel Wilson & Co.

The Prime Minister of Northern Ireland will address the Representatives of the Ulster Patriotic Fund, handing over to them the Trust of the Memorial.

The Prime Minister of Northern Ireland will then ask those present in a representative capacity to plant trees which have been brought from Ulster.

General Nugent, C.B., D.S.O., who was in command of the Ulster Division on the 1st July, 1916; Captain Charles Craig, M.P., and other Officers who took part will describe the memorable advance of the Division.

Visitors will inspect the Tower.

of the Memorial to the
19th November, 1921.

12-30 p.m
Leave in motors for Albert, where déjeuner will be served at 1 p.m. at the Salle des Fêtes (by kind permission of the Mayor of Albert).

DÉJEUNER :
A
SALLE DES FÊTES, ALBERT.

TOAST LIST.

" THE KING."	Proposed by The Préfet of the Somme.
"THE PRESIDENT."	Proposed by Lord Carson of Duncairn.
THE ALLIED FORCES.	Proposed by The Prime Minister of Northern Ireland. Responded to by Field Marshal Sir Henry Wilson, and The Senior French Military Representative.
THE 36th ULSTER DIVISION & OTHER ULSTER FORCES.	Proposed by Lord Carson of Duncairn. Responded to by Major-General O. Nugent, C.B., D.S.O.
THE ARCHITECT.	Proposed by The Marquis of Dufferin & Ava. Responded to by Major A. L. Abbott, M.S.A.

told of no obstruction from the enemy wire. Shrapnel shells from the 18-pounder field guns were the most effective in clearing wire; "…it sweeps the wire away completely without damaging the surface of the ground and so substituting another obstacle."

It was found that the 2-inch mortar shell fitted with the Newton fuse was adequate, but in places had heaped the wire, creating further obstacles. In several cases fire from the 18-pounders had in turn been used to sweep away these heaps. Wire cutting was found to be less effective on forward slopes and practically impossible on reverse slopes. In these circumstances howitzers were used; however the 4.5-inch appeared to have too small a bursting charge, while the 6-inch simply piled the wire to either side of the shell crater, therefore increasing the obstacle. It was discovered that iron uprights were the easiest to separate the wire from, mainly due to their rigidity; wooden stakes remained attached. The most difficult wire to deal with was that attached to iron knife-rests, as there were simply blown aside by the explosion without being broken up and could easily be replaced.

On 7 July a final estimated casualty list for the division was prepared.[54]

107 Brigade

8th Royal Irish Rifles	17 officers	350 other ranks
9th Royal Irish Rifles	19 officers	300 other ranks
10th Royal Irish Rifles	17 officers	400 other ranks
15th Royal Irish Rifles	15 officers	260 other ranks
107th MG Coy	5 officers	30 other ranks
107th TM Bty	3 officers	20 other ranks

108 Brigade

11th Royal Irish Rifles	12 officers	500 other ranks
12th Royal Irish Rifles	14 officers	400 other ranks
13th Royal Irish Rifles	18 officers	470 other ranks
9th Royal Irish Fusiliers	16 officers	520 other ranks
108th MGC	7 officers	50 other ranks
108th TMB	2 officers	30 other ranks

109 Brigade

9th Royal Inniskilling Fusiliers	18 officers	400 other ranks
10th Royal Inniskilling Fusiliers	11 officers	420 other ranks
11th Royal Inniskilling Fusiliers	14 officers	580 other ranks
14th Royal Irish Rifles	16 officers	300 other ranks
109th MGC	6 officers	100 other ranks
109th TMB	4 officers	70 other ranks

Divisional Troops

Royal Engineers		9 other ranks
16th Royal Irish Rifles	1 officer	32 other ranks
Royal Artillery	1 officer	15 other ranks

---

54   TNA WO 95 2491.

The above table shows a total of 216 officers and 5,266 other ranks reported as casualties including dead, wounded and missing, which would include the small number taken prisoner. However, such a list does not give a true picture of how many men were lost. Private John Wilson from Holywood, County Down, served with the 8th Rifles and died on 13 July, of wounds received on the first day of the battle, one of many that would die in the days, weeks and months to come. This was also the day that the local newspapers brought home to the people of Ulster just what had happened on 1 July.

Wilfred Spender, writing te to his wife from Rubempré, remarked on the political situation in Ireland:

> If you are staying with the Carsons, try to cheer him up with an account of how the Division has behaved. Not even he could have expected such heroism from our men. I wonder if you gave him my message the other day. I look upon it as important that he should know, in view of his apparent intimacy with Lloyd George now. Sir Edward will trust my word in this I know. I see that Sinn Feiners are all being reinstated now, and have little doubt that Casement will not be executed and will be feted in less than a year. The 'loyal rebels' are apparently not to be amnestied or Harrel and myself might find ourselves in a very different position.

Spender was incorrect with regard to Roger Casement; he was hanged for treason on 3 August at Pentonville Prison. In Ulster on 12 July, the usual parades or celebrations had been cancelled and at noon all traffic across the province came to a standstill as a five-minute silence was observed. This cancellation, however, had not been instigated because of the actions on the Somme. The following paragraph taken from the local press of 12 July 1916 and shows how Belfast and the people of Ulster paid a tribute to their glorious dead:

> This year, for the first time in the history of the Orange Institution, the celebration of the anniversary of the Battle of the Boyne was abandoned, while the customary holidays were to a great extent postponed until next month, to enable the shipyards and 'munition works to complete immediate orders. At the suggestion of the Lord Mayor, all work, business and household, was temporarily suspended for five minutes following the hour of noon to-day, as a tribute to the men who have fallen in the great British offensive. Viewed from the City Hall, on the steps of which the Lord Mayor and Lady Mayoress were standing, the scene was most impressive. On the stroke of 12 all traffic came to a standstill, men raised their hats, ladies bowed their heads, the blinds in business and private houses were drawn, and flags were flown at half-mast. The bells at the Assembly Hall tolled, and after the interval of five minutes chimed the hymn 'Abide with Me.' Intercessory services were held in the Cathedral and other churches. Shortly before noon the following telegram was received by the Lord Mayor from Sir Edward and Lady Carson: "Our prayers and solemn thoughts will be with you all at 12 o'clock, in memory of our illustrious dead, who have won glory for the Empire and undying fame for Ulster. May God bless and help their sorrowing families."

On same day 107 Brigade marched from the railway station at Thiennes towards Blaringhem. According to Cyril Falls:

> The sun was shining on the old Flemish village. Officers and men wore marigolds in caps to honour the day; the bands played *King William's March*. The least practised eye could tell that to these men confidence was returning; that the worst of the horror they had endured had been shaken from their shoulders. They marched like victors, as was their right.

In the House of Commons on 10 July the Prime Minister, H.H. Asquith stated: "The gallant Ulster Division has covered itself with undying fame."

There was no doubting the gallantry, but the horror 'shaken from their shoulders' was far from over and much worse was to come. The division moved into a training area to the west of St. Omer, with General Nugent's headquarters being established at Tilques on 13 July. The brigades were located at various villages in the area. At Bayenghem was 107 Brigade, 108 at Eperlecques, while 109 was at Boisdinghem. This was a time of reorganisation and training as replacements were received and integrated with the various battalions. During the month of July the division received one 193 officers and 2,182 other ranks as reinforcements, mostly from the reserve battalions in Ulster. Despite this the division still remained well under strength. This was a relatively quiet area in which they had little to do but hold the front line and carry out trench raids, of which they did many. Here the division remained until the summer of 1917, although it would seldom hold the same section of front for more than a few weeks at any one time.

The divisional artillery re-joined on 18 July; it had remained in the line providing support for the 49th Division. Now its headquarters was located in a chateau at Recques, where they too received replacements and some much needed equipment.

Again divisional headquarters moved, this time to Esquelbecq, on 20 July, occupying a chateau surrounded by a moat and whose grounds had once provided grazing for the cavalry of the Duke of Marlborough. General Nugent now occupied rooms that had housed

ULSTER DIVISION'S FURIOUS ONSLAUGHT.

GENERAL NUGENT'S ORDER OF THE DAY

Sublime Courage and Discipline.

DID EVERY PORTION OF ITS TASK.

Tribute by Sir George Richardson.

THE TOLL OF DEAD AND WOUNDED.

Special Order of the Day by Major-General O. S. W. Nugent, D.S.O., Commanding 36th (Ulster) Division.

The General Officer Commanding the Ulster Division desires that the Division should know that, in his opinion, nothing finer has been done in the War than the attack by the Ulster Division on the 1st July.

The leading of the Company Officers, the discipline and courage shown by all ranks of the Division, will stand out in the future history of the War as an example of what good troops, well led, are capable of accomplishing.

None but troops of the best quality could have faced the fire which was brought to bear on them and the losses suffered during the advance.

Nothing could have been finer than the steadiness and discipline shown by every Battalion, not only in forming up outside its own trenches but in advancing under severe enfilading fire.

The advance across the open to the German line was carried out with the steadiness of a parade movement, under a fire both from front and flanks which could only have been faced by troops of the highest quality.

The fact that the objects of the attack on one side were not obtained is no reflection on the Battalions which were entrusted with the task. They did all that men could do, and in common with every Battalion in the Division showed the most conspicuous courage and devotion.

On the other side, the Division carried out every portion of its allotted task in spite of the heaviest losses. It captured nearly 600 prisoners and carried its advance triumphantly to the limits of the objective laid down.

There is nothing in the operations carried out by the Ulster Division on the 1st July that will not be a source of pride to all Ulstermen.

The Division has been highly tried, and has emerged from the ordeal with unstained honour, having fulfilled in every particular the great expectations formed of it.

Tales of individual and collective heroism on the part of Officers and Men come in from every side, too numerous to mention, but all showing that the standard of gallantry and devotion attained is one that may be equalled, but is never likely to be surpassed.

The General Officer Commanding deeply regrets the heavy losses of Officers and Men. He is proud beyond description, as every Officer and Man in the Division may well be, of the magnificent example of sublime courage and discipline which the Ulster Division has given to the Army.

Ulster has every reason to be proud of the Men she has given to the service of our country.

Though many of our best Men have gone, the spirit which animated them remains in the Division, and will never die.

L. J. COMYN,
Lt.-Col. A.A. and Q.M.G. 36th Division.

A cutting from the *Northern Whig* dated 15 July 1916.

General John Colquhoun Grant, commander of the 5th Cavalry Brigade at the Battle of Waterloo just over 100 years earlier. Grant would have well needed the rest, having had five horses shot from under him during that battle. The 108 Brigade were fortunate in that when ordered forward to Kortepyp Camp, south of Neuve Eglise and Red Lodge on the southern slopes of Hill 63, that they were provided with bus and lorry transport. They were now to the west of the Bois de Ploegsteert, more commonly known to the British soldier as Plugstreet Wood.

Once again divisional headquarters was on the move, on 23 July General Nugent and his staff moved to a chateau on Mont Noir, several miles north of Bailleul. That same night the 108 Brigade moved into the line providing relief for two battalions of the 20th Division. By the month's end

109 Brigade had moved on the right flank of 108 Brigade relieving part of the 41st Division. At the same time 107 Brigade relieved the 108. The division's front line now ran from Anton's Farm, a ruined building on the Neuve Eglise to Warneton Road, on its right flank, and to Boyle's Farm on the Wulverghem to Messines Road on the left flank. This gave a frontage 'as the crow flies' of three thousand yards, but actually involved some two and a half miles of trenches. Some miles to the east lay a ridge on which were two villages Messines and Wytschaete, this was to be the division's next major battlefield.

A letter from Private Duncan Davidson to Teenie regarding the replacements the division was received on 26 July:

> We are up the line again, of some hot fighting, we did not get a rest, why I don't really know, it is the usual thing for a Division to hold a line for a certain period, then go back, we held our line from last March, made an attack, now into the line again, I guess we made such a fighting name for ourselves, they want us to do some more, wouldn't mind so much, if we had the old boys amongst us again, the reserves our Battalion are getting seem to be of a poor class, conscripts most of them, damned hard lines having to fight with such, however anything more we may have to do, we will do, and do well, we may go into the trenches any time, however don't worry, as it seems to be, quiet around here.

The end of the month saw several gas warning issued. On 29 July a red paper balloon fell into a field at 9.20am, close to divisional headquarters. These balloons were apparently being used by the German to gauge wind strength and direction and signalled the enemy's intention to release gas at the earliest suitable opportunity. All units were warned of the probability of a gas attack and a special inspection was carried out on all gas helmets. These included not only the men in the front line, but other divisional units, working parties, officers' servants, trench mortar detachments and those men in charge of the horses.[55]

On 27 July a notice had appeared in the *Belfast News Letter* headed 'Tidings Wanted'. In this the Reverend John Pollock of St. Enoch's Church, said he would be glad to receive any information regarding his son, Lance Corporal Paul G. Pollock, Scout, B Company, 14th Battalion Royal Irish Rifles (YCV), who was engaged in the advance of the Ulster Division on 1st July last, and has been 'missing' since that date. Lance Corporal Pollock was 21 years old and has no known grave. Private James McRoberts knew Lance Corporal Pollock:

> A sister of Pollock's wrote to my mother asking for my photo which was sent to her, and in due course there arrived a picture of Mr. Lack surrounded by his twenty scouts. This picture is in my possession. Pollock's father was the Presbyterian minister in charge of St. Enoch's Church in Belfast. The previous summer he had spent a month with his family at Seaford and preached to the troops one Sunday."

Second Lieutenant R.L. Lack had died from wounds on 18 July and was buried in Thames Ditton (St Nicholas) Churchyard, Surrey. On the last day of this fateful month Private Alexander Lionel Adolphus Sproule, 9th Irish Fusiliers, from County Monaghan, was killed.

---

55 'A' & 'Q' War Diary 31 July 1916.

8

Still Fighting

In 107 Brigade the 15th Rifles relieved the 8th Rifles in the trenches on 8 August. Private D Tulloch of B Company, the 8th Rifles, took the opportunity to write home:

> Dear Dad, Just a few lines to let you know I received your ever welcome letter and am glad to hear you are all in good health. It is useless thinking that I will get the parcel now, it must been wrongly addressed or I would have got it in four or five days. We are having very fine weather out here now so that is one consolation as it is very nasty when it rains. I think a month's holiday for Mary and Martha would do them all the good in the world as it is not weedy people we will want after the war. I think that is all at present, hoping this finds you all at home in the best of health as it leaves me the same at present. With love to all. Good night. Private D. Tulloch.

Despite the horror of the previous month his letter could well have been coming from someone on holiday.

The Somme losses were slowly being replaced, but the battle continued to take its toll in both men and officers, not all wounds were caused by shot or shell. While General Nugent showed patience with some individuals, he showed less with others. On 10 August he wrote to his wife:

> I got a letter from the Grand Master of Belfast Orangemen saying the brethren were proud of the Division and that their hearts went out to them. I thought this was about the limit, considering that none of them are enlisting, so I replied that if their bodies accompanied their hearts, it would be much more to the point. I think it is sheer impertinence to write flapdoodle of that kind at the present time. I did not visit the trenches today but went to the 2nd Army school of instruction near St Omer instead to see what I could pick up in the way of hints for my school. I have got Colonel Pakenham staying here for a couple of days which I think is very nice of me, but he has not been well and may have to go home, at any rate for a time.

On the afternoon of 14 August 1916, Lieutenant Godson of A Company, 9th Irish Fusiliers, made a telephone call from company headquarters and announced in a clear voice that an officer and three other ranks would leave the trench at midnight and move on the right of the Le Rossignol to Messines Road in order to carry out a reconnaissance at the clump of willows in no man's land. This telephone call was a subterfuge, brought about by the ability of the Germans to 'tap' the British land lines. This had first come to notice on the Somme when it was discovered that conversations carried out between the various units could be heard by special listening devices that worked surprisingly well in the chalky ground. The British-issued field telephone relied on a ground return system. In this the phones were connected by a single wire with the second wire of the circuit being a short wire connected to a spike in the ground. Unknown to the British the AC current was creating a signal through the ground that could be picked up by the enemy using devices known as Moritz Stations. The British answer to this was to introduce the Fuller phone.

The Fullerphone. This was the invention of Captain A.C. Fuller and came into widespread use in 1915. It could transmit Morse code over a twenty mile long single wire and voice over a shorter distance, even at the same time.

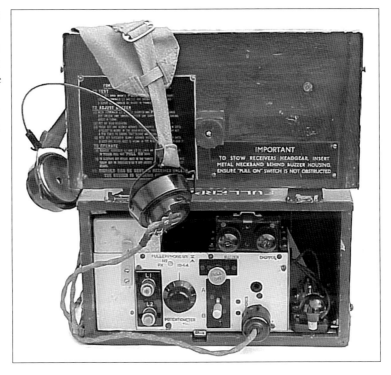

This was the invention of Captain A.C. Fuller and came into widespread use in 1915. It could transmit Morse code over a twenty mile long single wire and voice over a shorter distance, even at the same time. As it used a DC signal as opposed to AC, it made it more difficult for the enemy to listen in. An added bonus was that Morse code could be transmitted over damaged lines and even between the gaps in a broken line, provided that each side of the break was in contact with the ground and the space was not too great.

Now the Germans were going to be caught out as a result of their own technology. At 9:30 pm Lieutenant Godson, accompanied by Lieutenant Wingfield and 14 other ranks moved out of their trench and crawled into the ambush position. It took 30 minutes to reach the stand of willows and then the men settled down to wait. After some two hours lying in cold damp grass a German patrol was sighted and Godson's men opened fire at a range of some five yards. Immediately after the initial volley they rushed forward and after a brief struggle the enemy patrol surrendered. The Germans had lost two men killed and four were taken prisoner, including the patrol commander. It was never proved conclusively that the bogus phone call had caused the German patrol to appear, but Lieutenant Godson was convinced it did and recovered intelligence was worth the effort for the cost of three Irish Fusiliers slightly wounded. For his actions Lieutenant Godson was awarded the Military Cross, the first of two he would earn, while Corporal Clements, a member of the patrol, received the Military Medal.

The 107th Trench Mortar Battery was hit by a shell on 28 August and Private William Kincaid from Glasgow was killed. This fact would not be known to his family until a year later.

It was forbidden to give wounded soldiers alcohol while they were on sick leave and they were not allowed to enter public houses while wearing their hospital blues, a uniform named for its colour, blue trousers and jacket, with a white shirt and a red tie. In Bangor, on 21 August, Constable Donnelly, Royal Irish Constabulary, had summoned Mr Charles Cribben of Carrick House, Belfast, for giving intoxicating liquor to wounded soldiers in the town. At Bangor Petty Sessions a witness testified that he observed the defendant speaking to three wounded soldiers who were in hospital dress, the blue uniforms specifically issued to wounded soldiers. The defendant then left them, went towards Quay Street and shortly afterwards returned and crossed over towards the lavatory in Mill Lane. The witness followed and found three bottle of stout. The defendant's excuse was that he considered he had done no harm, but when questioned by the magistrate as to why he had not taken the men to a public house replied that they were wearing their blue uniforms. The defendant was fined 5/=, but warned that any further occurrences could see him fined the maximum penalty of £100 or six months in prison. Bangor people were very observant.

This incident led to a letter from E. McKitterick, Matron of Bangor Hospital, being published in which she craves publicity regarding members of the public giving 'drink' to wounded soldiers:

> It is a serious offence under the Defence of the Realm regulations to supply intoxicating liquor to wounded soldiers. The practice of obtaining liquor for some of the soldiers who from time to time have undergone treatment in this Hospital has, I regret to say been prevalent in Bangor to the detriment of the soldiers themselves, as their progress to recovery is retarded, as well as which it has been found necessary to curtail their freedom, which means that the innocent must suffer with the guilty. For the same reason it has been found necessary to send some of the wounded from here to the Victoria Barracks Military Hospital, where they are under strict discipline. This course, which is resorted to only with reluctance, the men regard as a severe punishment, but however much it is to be regretted, it is essential to the maintenance of discipline, and it is directly due to the unpatriotic conduct of civilians supplying them with liquor, which far from being a kindness is little short of positive cruelty. I hope the matter has only to be ventilated to secure the co-operation of the townspeople in protecting the welfare of the men sent here to recuperate. Thanking you in anticipation for inserting this letter, I am yours etc., E. McKitterick, Matron Bangor Hospital. 14 September 1916.

There were some very alert members of the public in Bangor in 1916.

It was during the month of September that Captain McConachie of the 109th Machine Gun Company was able to write a letter that was not to a grieving parent or widow. The addressee was Mr James Fisher of Carrigart, County Donegal, and concerned the award of the Distinguished Conduct Medal to his twenty-three year old son, Lance Corporal James Fisher:

> In the attack on 1st of July young Mr Fisher brought a machine gun into action in a shell hole in front of the German third line trenches. Although wounded in the face early in the fight he continued with his gun, and drove back several counter attacks, and must have accounted for several hundreds of the enemy. I am proud of having had him in my company, and send you my heartiest congratulations. I hope he will live many years to wear the honour the King has conferred on him.[1]

However, the letters of commiseration had not yet finished. Private John and Florence Murphy of Newry Street, Rathfriland, were officially notified that their son, Corporal William Lindsey Murphy, 108th Machine Gun Company, had been listed as wounded and missing in action on 1 July. In a letter, perhaps a little premature, to his father, Lieutenant W. Woolsley Ashcroft stated:

> You have no doubt long since heard of your son's death, and knowing him as I did, I fear it will be a very sad blow to his mother and yourself. At the same time I hope you will both find some consolation in the fact that he was killed at the very point of duty and whilst making

---

1   *Belfast News Letter* 6 September 1916. Lance Corporal Fisher survived the War.

a very gallant charge, and no man can do more. He died with the flower of Ulster, and as a NCO, he proved himself as worthy as the wortherist (sic). I can hardly tell you the admiration I had for your son. Always keen on his duty, resourceful and obliging, popular with everyone with whom he came into contact he, indeed, set a great example, and had he been spared I feel he would have had a great future in the Army if he had stuck to it. The Lieutenant then added a postscript, "I need not mention that there may be some small hope even yet that your son might after all be wounded and a prisoner in Germany, but from all the evidence I can obtain I dare not suggest that you should build too much hope on that possibility."

Today Corporal Murphy lies in Heath Cemetery, Harbonnieres. Lieutenant Ashcroft also wrote to Mrs William Brown of Jervis Street, Portadown, County Armagh, on the death of her husband, Sergeant Major William John Brown, 108th Machine Gun Company:

> Your husband died a noble death, and although this is but small consolation to you I fear, I am happy to be able to tell you that he was held in the very highest respect by all ranks in this company. Always at his duty and always ready to help wherever he could, it will be difficult to fill his place, and all those left behind feel we have lost a ready, worthy friend and soldier. He was awaiting orders with a reserve gun in his dugout when a German shell made a direct hit. I fear all were killed, at any rate your husband was recovered, but I regret to say only lived about five minutes. This was on the night of the day the attack was launched.[2]

With the losses being suffered on the Western Front and elsewhere, at home there was a concentrated effort to round up shirkers. After a football match in London one Saturday men of military age were stopped when leaving the grounds and required to produce registration or exemption cards. About 250 failed to do so and were marched to the police station where their details were recorded. At the local music halls in Bermondsey and Rotherhithe only a few men were found in the audience, while in Glasgow several tea-rooms were raided and a number of names taken. These raids and inspections were carried out across Britain and included 'gipsy' camps. In one dawn raid on Exmoor one man fled wearing little clothing and was found to have grown a beard to make him look older, claiming he was forty-two. However, his mother said he was only thirty-seven! He was taken to court, fined £2 and then handed over to the military authorities. Similar raids are rarely reported in local papers.

In Ulster the various regiments continued to raise both funds and men for the division in France. In the west of the Province at Bundoran, Omagh and Fivemiletown concerts were held which featured 'The Inniskillings Nigger Minstrels' from the 12th Battalion.[3] This troupe had been organised in March 1916 under the leadership of Mr Egbert Trimble and had done much to raise the profile of the Inniskillings and much needed funds, this last tour raised £200. Nevertheless, such was the call for men in France that the troupe was to be broken up, temporarily it was hoped, and the men sent to the Front.

In France the division moved to the north occupying a new position, its left flank being Piccadilly Trench, south of the Kemmel to Wytschaete Road, its right being the River Douve. The brigades were located with 109 Brigade on the left, 107 Brigade in the centre and 108 Brigade on the right.

A cliché of the Great War is that of waterlogged trenches and men often wading up to their knees in liquid mud. The ground now occupied by the division aptly fitted this image. August had been a wet month and as a result of the near constant rainfall the valley of the Douve River from

---

2   *Portadown News*, 5 August 1916.
3   *Belfast News Letter*, 9 December 1916.

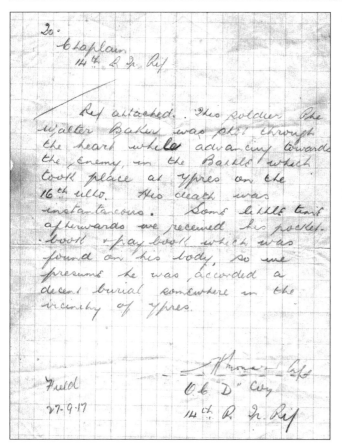

A letter to the chaplain from OC D Company 14th Royal Irish Rifles concerning the death of a soldier and dated 27 September 1917: Ref attached. "This soldier Private Walter Baker was shot through the heart while advancing towards the enemy, in the Battle which took place a Ypres on the 16th***. His death was instantaneous. Some little time afterwards we received his pocket book & pay book which was found on his body, so we presume he was accorded a decent burial somewhere in the vicinity of Ypres." (Killed on 16 August 1917, buried in Bridge House War Cemetery , grave C1, no family details listed)

Wulverghem to the front line consisted of a muddy swamp.[4] While the Somme had consisted of white chalk, here the ground was 'dirty, mournful, and disconsolate; haunted by the evil stench of blue clay, and brooded over by an atmosphere of decay.' The British trenches, unlike those of the Germans, were never defensive. Not for the British deep dug-outs with various comforts. Given the wet conditions of the ground the fighting trenches were constructed everywhere, except on the highest ground, of parapets built of sand bags filled with clay. Along certain lengths a parados was constructed. The parados not only defended the men from shells that exploded behind them, but prevented the defenders from being outlined against the skyline. However, for long stretches the only cover the men had was the front wall of sand bags and they had no protection from the back blast of shells.

With the high water table present just below the surface, communication trenches were usually no more than a foot deep with the spoil and other earth piled high on the sides, giving adequate cover from view, but vulnerable to shell fire. The communication trenches were much longer than they had been on the Somme and there was an absence of dug-outs. Instead there were baby elephants, arched steel shelters that were covered with a thick layer of sand bags, giving a degree of shelter from enemy shelling. Along the parapet were small wooden framed shelves that would hold one or two men. Back from the front line those officers and men attached to battalion and

---

4   Widespread shelling resulted in the destruction of an efficient drainage system that had been in existence since medieval times.

Tents in Thiepval Wood 1916, painted to blend in with the surrounding trees.

battery headquarters had it slightly easier. These were usually housed in the ruins of farms where the cellar was intact and where the remains of outbuildings could disguise the construction of concrete bunkers.

For the Germans life was much easier. On the ridge to the east their four lines of barbed wire protected trenches were interlinked with the fortified villages of Messines and Wytschaete, with many small concrete forts also protected by wire. Being situated on the higher ground they were also dry. From the British lines the view of the enemy positions was negligible, with the exception of observations posts on Kemmel Hill and to a lesser degree on Hill 63.

In autumn 1916 Colonel Savage of the 13th Rifles was sent home on retirement and Major Waring took command while Captain Belt became adjutant. From the 9th Irish Fusiliers Major Pratt moved to the 9th Inniskillings on promotion to lieutenant colonel and took command of the battalion from Lieutenant Colonel G.H. Brush, who had held the command since the promotion of Lieutenant Colonel Hessey to brigadier.

Divisional headquarters moved again on 1 September, this time to the village of St Jans Cappel, near Bailleul, close to the Belgian border, just over seventy miles north of Thiepval Wood. They were now part of the Second Army under General Sir Herbert Plumer. This area was to be the division's home for the next year, although it would only hold the same sector of the line for a few weeks at a time.

The army front was lightly defended even at Ypres, which was considered quiet as of late. Some preparations had been made for an offensive in the summer of 1917, but these had been largely abandoned due to a lack of labour. Despite this General Plumer insisted on continuing with his mining operations, in which he had great faith and in which he would be proved right. Throughout the winter and following spring the division furnished large work parties to assist the various tunnelling companies in driving shafts forward under no man's land towards the enemy lines. At times there was combat underground. One instance was at La Petite Douve Farm, located on the Ploegsteert to Messines Road. Here a British tunnelling unit had succeeded in pumping a large amount of the River Douve into the German shaft, where it took them many nights of pumping to get it clear. The enemy did enjoy several successes against the British tunnels, but not enough to stop progress. Within the division the work of the 171st Tunnelling Company was applauded by all ranks.

Victory against the Germans located on the Messines Ridge would depend on the success of these tunnels in getting beneath their strong-points. On the Ridge the German line consisted of four lines of fully wired trenches and superbly placed concrete machine gun block houses capable of withstanding anything up to an eight inch shell. On 1 September the war diary of 109 Brigade recorded; "Enemy's artillery reply was feeble, chiefly on our support trenches, CURRIE AVENUE in particular."

However, even feeble artillery fire can be fatal, one officer was killed and six wounded, whilst 20 other ranks were killed and 101 wounded in the 11th Rifles. The officer who died was Second Lieutenant William Nicholas Sheridan, a twenty-five year old from Mournview, Banbridge. Among the other ranks was Private David Drennan, who before the war had been a well-known footballer in Belfast. Employed by the GPO he had enlisted in the 18th Rifles, trained at Clandeboye and then been posted to the 11th Rifles in France. He left a widow and four sons who resided at Vernon Street, Belfast. A second officer was lost to the Rifles when Second Lieutenant H.A. Sandys, 3rd Royal Dublin Fusiliers, on attachment to the 11th Rifles, faced a court martial on a charge of drunkenness, he was found guilty and dismissed from the army.[5]

It was not only on the battlefield that men of the division were showing their courage. The *Belfast News Letter* of 11 September tells the story of Second Lieutenant John Brown, MC, of the 8th Rifles. Brown, from the Holywood Road, Belfast had been commissioned in the Rifles in November 1914 and had been wounded in the shoulder on 1 July when he had been awarded the Military Cross. While home on leave Brown was crossing the Albert Bridge in a tramcar when he noticed that a young boy was in the river and in danger of drowning. Brown quickly dismounted from the tram and throwing off his overcoat, he leapt into the water and brought the boy to the bank despite being hindered by the thick mud. With the assistance of some members of the public and the police the boy was safely brought ashore.

During August and September a limit was placed on the number of shells that could be fired per day, usually between one and two rounds per 18-pounder, with heavier guns similarly rationed. This rationing should not be confused with the so-called shell scandal of 1915, when the failure at Aubers Ridge (9 May) was blamed on the shortage of artillery ammunition. At that time the munitions factories were not operating on a full War time schedule and the fact that in the opening barrage the British guns fired more shells than had been expended in the entire South African War was bound to lead to inevitable shortages. Rationing at this time was on the rate of fire, not on ammunition available. Gun pits and rear echelons had ample supplies and when required adequate fire could be delivered on the enemy.

On first arriving in Flanders the division had noticed that enemy shelling was comparatively light compared to the Somme. However, this was offset by the fire delivered by enemy trench mortars and as they held the high ground it was extremely effective. With Teutonic efficiency the enemy bombardment would begin each day at 3:30 pm, and was particularly heavy in the Spanbroek salient. A quote from one of the machine gun officers in the divisional history states; "In this sector I have seen five or six large 'minnies' in the air at one time, really fearsome things. You could see the fuses of the bombs alight in the air and follow their flight most of the way, only to lose it when straight overhead; and then there was nothing to do but wonder where it would fall!"

---

5   Just over 3,500 British officers were sent for court martial during the war, of these six percent were charged with desertion while thirty-seven percent were convicted of drunkenness, few were executed.

During the first few weeks the division found itself at a disadvantage in the exchange of mortar bombs and steps were taken to rectify the situation. The first step in this process was to observe, identify and mark the emplacements of the enemy mortars; this was achieved by direct spotting from the front line and the use of photographs taken by reconnaissance aircraft. Maps were then drawn with the enemy positions named, the names beginning with the letter of the map square. Therefore all those in square U would be such as Una, Ursula, etc. Feminine names appeared to be the most popular. A specific number of these emplacements were then allocated to each howitzer battery in the divisional artillery and to the 6-inch howitzers of the corps heavy artillery. When an enemy mortar fired it was only necessary for the artillery observer to state via field telephone 'Ursula active' to bring down counter-battery fire. In order to catch reinforcements moving into the emplacement or crews evacuating, any machine guns within the area also opened fire. Experience showed that an enemy mortar position could be knocked out within fifteen minutes of opening fire.

The British also deployed their own trench mortars, the heaviest of which threw a bomb weighing 180 pounds. One such weapon was located at R.E. Farm on the Wulverghem – Wytschaete Road, and from here numerous bombs, nicknamed flying pigs, were launched towards the German lines. Added to this was the fire from the medium mortars with their 60-pound plum puddings and the lighter Stokes mortars, capable of firing between 20 and 25 rounds per minute.

German retaliation was swift and deadly and it took a special kind of individual to be a mortar crewman. Heavy and medium mortars were manned by detachments of artillerymen, the Stokes mortars were served by the infantry, but whatever branch they came from, these men were a breed apart.

In the beginning mortars were a trifle uncertain in their launching capability and the first fired from RE Farm caused a degree of worry. As the bomb launched the charge did not ignite properly and the bomb landed after only 300 yards, just behind British front line, exploding to leave a huge crater and also demolishing a company headquarters. Thankfully a sense of humour prevailed over any panic. This humour was common to all ranks. An intelligence summary issued by IX Corps, commanded by Lieutenant General Hamilton Gordon, stated that "...a German cemetery behind the Ridge appeared to be filling up nicely." This remark that was greeted as 'the joke of the season.

On arriving in France during the previous December, the divisional artillery had been organised as three 18-pounder and one 4.5-inch howitzer brigades. In May it had been reorganised with the howitzer batteries being divided among the other three brigades. Now in September it was again reorganised. The four gun batteries were increased to six, although slow supply meant that the howitzer batteries did not receive their extra guns until early 1917.

The 154 Brigade was broken up and in February 1917 the 172 Brigade was renamed the 113 Army Brigade and transferred out of the division. This was as a result of a decision to form army brigades to be used to increase the artillery at the disposal of divisions in attacks or in particularly threatened sectors of the front. While this produced some tactical advantages, it was far from popular with the artillerymen concerned. The division was now left with only two artillery brigades, the 153 and 173, still under the command of General Brock.

While bombardment of the enemy lines and rear areas continued, another weapon designed to harass the Germans was the raiding party. First conceived by Indian Army units in November 1914, these were later refined by both Australian and Canadian units, but British troops were never keen on this activity. Raiding had as its objective the gathering of enemy intelligence through the taking of prisoners and recovered documents, while at the same time causing the enemy to be constantly on the alert. While most raids were useful and often necessary, it was the opinion of many that the British raided too often.[6] While those raids designed to identify the troops opposite

---

6   Falls, Cyril, *The History of the 36th (Ulster) Division* (1922).

and to keep the enemy on his toes were justifiable, those whose object was to raise troop morale were not. Cyril Falls quotes a 36th Division brigadier:

> No doubt a successful raid had a good effect in a unit, but not always among the raiding party. The meticulous preparation made the waiting for the dentist period hard and trying. And the raiders were always picked men, who in a battle were of inestimable value. Many units had to deplore the loss of the very cream of their officers, NCOs and men in raids. And the cold-blooded courage demanded of all concerned took heavy toll of the nervous energy of even the biggest thruster.[7]

Falls' remarks regarding men, who in a battle were of inestimable value, is borne out by the losses suffered by the 11th Inniskillings on the night of 15 September; of the three men lost, two were holders of the Military Medal. Another drawback was when the high command ordered troops recently new to an area of the Front to raid immediately, before they had time to find their way about by dint of normal patrolling, or had yet to recover from an attack delivered elsewhere on the battlefield.

Of the two raids carried out on 15 September, the first was by the 9th Rifles just to the east of the Wulverghem to Wytschaete Road, the second by the 11th Inniskillings some five hundred yards to the north of this position. The 9th Rifles were to ascertain the identification of the unit facing them and this was best done by taking a prisoner. As the raiding party entered the enemy trench the leading officer shot two Germans, while the flank guard accounted for a third. As the party got to work searching for a prisoner and any other valuable pieces of material Private Kidd, well known for his long distance bomb throwing, kept enemy reinforcements at bay and accounted for a further three enemy killed. On returning to their own lines it was discovered that three of the raiding party had been injured, having suffered minor wounds, they were able to remain on duty.

Meanwhile the 11th Inniskillings were not having such good luck. Part of the British line opposite Kruisstraat Cabaret jutted out into a field-work known as the Bull Ring, which overlooked some slight high ground about 70 yards from the enemy trench. Just to the north of this work the raiders crossed into the enemy trench while supported by machine gun fire. At the same time the divisional artillery put down a box barrage around the raiders, protecting them from outside interference. In the ensuing melee over 30 enemy soldiers were reported killed and one taken prisoner, but unlike the Rifles, the Inniskillings did not escape unscathed. As well as ten walking wounded, three other wounded subsequently became missing. The term missing can mean several things. A man reported as missing may have been taken prisoner, or have gone into hiding or been injured and would and later return to his lines, he may even have deserted. Soldiers killed by a direct hit from a high explosive shell could be vaporised, in certain weather conditions bodies would sink into the mud and disappear. In this case the three wounded men left behind may have died from their wounds. The CWGC shows that Lance Corporals Charles Wray, MM, Alexander McKay and Private Robert Taylor, MM, all died on this date and have no known grave. Once again experienced men were being lost for little return. However, the raid was considered very successful, which pleased both General Nugent and the men concerned; "We killed a lot and took prisoners and only lost two men. The men were very pleased in consequence."

General Nugent took exception to one particular section of enemy trench:

> I had every big gun I could borrow 9-inch, 6-inch, and 4.7-inch. I looked on and it was most pleasing to see the German trenches and dug-outs going up into the air, trenches and beams

---

7   Ibid.

and corrugated iron and one German who went up like a Catherine Wheel and came down more or less in pieces on to their wire where he was hanging all day yesterday.[8]

Gas cylinders had been installed on the fronts of both the 107 and 108 Brigades on 18 September and were due to be discharged on the night of 19 September. This was to be carried out by K Company, No.3 Special Battalion, Royal Engineers, the party to be under the command of Major Knox, 10th Inniskillings. Wind reports were to be sent from the trenches every 30 minutes from 7:00 pm, onwards. The gas was to be discharged at full density from midnight on 19 September and would last for 15 minutes. If at any time prior to the discharge the weather conditions were deemed unfavourable a telegram was to be sent to divisional headquarters reading; "The answer is No."

This message would cancel the attack. All troops not directly involved in the discharge of the gas were to withdraw some 250 yards to the rear and wear their gas respirators. At midnight plus four minutes the Artillery was to bombard the enemy front line, support and communication trenches for 36 minutes. The Stokes mortars, machine guns, Lewis guns and rifle grenade batteries were to cooperate in the bombardment under Brigade arrangements. A strong patrol from the 10th Inniskillings was then to enter the enemy trenches at 1:15 am and ascertain the effects of the gas and to procure unit identification from any bodies found. A box barrage to support this patrol would be available if required. There may be no connection, but the 108th Field Ambulance reported an increase of gas case treatment during September.

The raids carried out on 30 September involved all elements of IX Corps, within the 36th Division one battalion from each brigade raided. On the right flank of the division the 11th Rifles raid had to be cancelled when several bombs exploded as they were being issued to the raiders. Approximately twenty men were injured in the incident, none fatally.[9] The incident was blamed on faulty fuses. In the centre the raiding party of the10th Rifles consisted of 70 other ranks commanded by Lieutenant Hackett, assisted by Lieutenant McKee and Second Lieutenant Haslett. They left their trenches in good order at 9:30 pm, and moved towards the German trenches, which they were due to reach at 10:00 pm. Second Lieutenant Haslett led the way forward with accuracy and soon reached the exact spot in the enemy wire, which was found to be well cut. The Germans appeared to have been alerted by a raid further to the south that had begun before time and were 'standing to' in their trenches in large numbers. As the party reached the wire the enemy opened a rapid rifle fire and threw bombs. A salvo of bombs was returned which fell with accuracy in the German trench. CSM Whelan and Sergeant McCune performed sterling service in this bomb throwing. However, it appears that the three men, Whelan, McCune and Sergeant Shaw had gotten too far ahead of the remainder of the party and consequently were not in sufficient force to rush the trench. While all preparations for this raid had gone without a hitch, its failure was due the following; The raid on the right beginning too early, while the party was too big for the purpose intended and could not be handled properly in the darkness. It was the opinion of Colonel Bernard that the officers and NCOs concerned did all in their power during the raid to ensure its success. He described them as "… a most determined set of men."[10]

On the left flank there was more success. Here the 10th Inniskillings entered the German positions after having blown the wire, but only when the accompanying Sapper had replaced a faulty fuse on their Bangalore torpedo after the first one failed to ignite, all this under the noses of enemy sentries. Once into the trenches the Inniskillings set about destroying dug-outs, killing any enemy

---

8   Letter from General Nugent to his wife, 17 September 1916.
9   Brigade War Diary.
10   After action report, 108 Brigade War Diary.

that appeared and withdrawing with a captured machine gun and a number of rifles and other equipment.

It was five days since 8th Rifles had relieved the 15th Rifles in the trenches. The war diary reported that all was quiet except for about one hour each evening when the trench mortars and supporting artillery exchanged fire with their German opponents. One casualty to the 8th Rifles on 21 September was Private D. Tulloch of B Company.[11] It was a week later before Lieutenant Wellington, his platoon commander, was able to write to Tulloch's father:

> Sir, I regret to have to inform you of the death in action of your son No.19/310 Private D. Tulloch. He was a promising young soldier, popular with his comrades, and his death will be felt by us all. I hope that it will be some small comfort to you that he died in the execution of his duty, and that his death was painless, being instantaneous. With unreserved sympathy…

The month was almost over when on 28 September Captain John Sugden, adjutant of the 10th Rifles, was killed by enemy shellfire. He had taken command of the battalion on 1 July when Colonel Bernard had been killed and for his action on that day had had been awarded the DSO. He was 38 years old and left a widow at Harrogate in Yorkshire.

At 1:30 am on 9 October, gas was released from the trenches of the 14th Rifles. Within a very short time there was a response from the German artillery that resulted in the deaths of six men, including two of the Royal Engineers operating the cylinders. The Rifles' casualties were Lance Corporal Samuel Ferris, MM, and Privates Fred Greer, William McIvor and James Robinson. Two days later, another man, Private George Paysden, MM, died from his wounds. Lance Corporal Ferris, from Dromore, County Down, had been awarded the Military Medal for his actions on the Somme on 1 July. His brother was serving with the Canadian Forces. Private Paysden was another holder of the Military Medal and was the son of Captain J. Paysden of Connsbrook Avenue, Belfast, who commanded a transport ship. An older brother was an assistant scoutmaster with the 10th Belfast Scouts. The funeral for these men was held at Pond Farm Cemetery. As no coffins were available the men were simply sewn into blankets and then placed in a shallow grave. The cemetery was approximately a thousand yards behind the front line and in full view of the German positions. The burial service was carried out by Canon King, dressed in his full surplice and, despite the shells falling around the party, he read from the Bible and conducted a full service.[12]

On the night of 12 October all three brigades again furnished a battalion each for raiding purposes. The 108 Brigade had no luck against the strongly wired Petite Douve Farm, the numerous thick coils of barbed wire proving impossible to cut through in the time allotted. The

---

11   Listed on the CWGC website as Tullock.

12   See *The Chocolate Soldiers*. Canon Richard G. S. King, a son of the cloth, would have been well known to many of the Ulster Division before the war as he was an outspoken opponent of Home Rule who regularly had articles published in the local newspapers. He had been chaplain to the 2nd (Roe Valley) Battalion, North Londonderry Regiment of the UVF. His eldest son, 19 year old Lieutenant Robert Andrew Ferguson Smyly King, 2nd Royal Dublin Fusiliers, was severely wounded on May 10 when a 'Jack Johnson' mortar blew in his dug-out at La Bassee, smashing both legs and his right hand. Although one leg had to be amputated two days later, the lieutenant showed signs of recovery until tetanus symptoms appeared. With Canon King and his wife by his bedside, the teenager died at No.7 Stationary Hospital, Boulogne, on Whit Sunday, 1915. His funeral service was read by the Reverend Lowry Hamilton, Chaplain to the Forces and an old family friend. A nephew, Sub-Lieutenant H. S. King, Royal Navy, was killed at the Battle of Jutland in May, 1916. Canon King resigned his commission as Senior Chaplain of the Division in November 1916, earning a mention in the Haig's dispatch of January, 1917. A Jack Johnson was the nickname given by British troops to describe the impact of a German 150mm shell and named after the well know American world heavyweight boxer of the same name.

107 Brigade had a successful raid. At 2:00 am supporting artillery and trench mortars opened an intense bombardment of the German trenches, being joined by the Stokes mortars that fired 1,123 rounds rapid fire. The 9th Rifles then entered the enemy trench at 2:15 am, much damage was done to equipment and a prisoner was taken.[13] In 109 Brigade the raid was carried out by a party of the 9th Inniskillings, commanded by Second Lieutenant William Boyd, assisted by Second Lieutenants Kempston and Lavelle, along with 62 other ranks. William Boyd came from Lifford in Donegal and had been educated at Foyle College in Londonderry, St Columba's and Trinity College in Dublin. He had originally served with the 2nd Canadian Contingent and on receiving a commission had been posted to the Inniskillings. Noel Kempston had previously served with the Connaught Rangers and came from County Roscommon. The force was divided into two groups and were protected by a box barrage as they approached the German wire. Here one of the Bangalore torpedoes failed to explode and a section of the wire remained intact, delaying the left-hand party. Up to this point the raiders had not been observed by the Germans and Kempston continued to lay out the marking tape, despite only being a few yards from a large group of Germans who were carrying out repairs to their wire. Kempston then attempted to cut his way through the wire, but the supporting artillery was falling short and both he and his party were caught in the blast of the shells. The officer was killed and eight of his men wounded. In the right-hand party Second Lieutenant Boyd was mortally wounded and two of his men wounded. Once inside the German trenches the remainder of the raiders spent up to 40 minutes searching for mines, machine gun positions and any sign of new work to the defences. A German counter-attack was beaten off, mostly by using bombs left behind by the enemy when they had first withdrawn. Eventually the raiders were able to make their way back to their own lines, carrying with them the wounded, including Second Lieutenant Boyd. Sadly he died the following day while being cared for by the 108th Field Ambulance.

While this raiding was going on a 'battle' was being fought by the administration staff and the men. Brigade Order No.90, contained, amongst other things, specific instruction that; "The Lewis Gun handcarts must not be used for carrying men's packs, etc. Proper transport must be provided under Regimental arrangements."

It was also stressed that men marching to and from the trenches must be marched correctly as a formed party under an officer, NCO, or senior soldier.

Thursday 24 October to Sunday 29 October 1916: BAILLEUL. From the diary of Private James McRoberts:

> The battalion came out of the trenches and we continued our practising for the raid. The weather got colder and wetter and we were served out with strong, leather jerkins, gloves and extra blankets. One day the battalion marched into Bailleul; we piled arms in a field and went to the Picture House where the French picture of the Battle of the Somme was demonstrated. We were all delighted with it, for what it showed was the real thing; the surrender of the Germans in their own trenches being portrayed as it could only be done by photographs taken on the spot. Then there was a good performance given by the Merry Mauves after which a short ramble was allowed round the town and then we marched back to Dranoutre. The Merry Mauves was only one of the numerous amateur concert parties organised by the military to entertain the troops when they were 'resting' behind the lines.

On the night of 30 October 107 Brigade again prepared to raid the enemy trenches. A party of 15th Rifles consisting of sixty men crossed no man's land at 2:10 am and successfully entered the

---

13   107 Brigade War Diary.

German positions. The enemy was quick to react and after an exchange of bombs the Rifles were forced back with two men killed and an officer and two other ranks wounded. The men who died were Privates William McReavie and William Parry, both from Belfast.

That following night a raid was carried out by the 108 Brigade against that part of the German line manned by the men of the 26th (Wurttemberg) Division. The raiding party came from the 11th Rifles, was commanded by Second Lieutenant S. Waring and consisted of three officers, 72 other ranks and three Sappers of the Royal Engineers. The objective of the raid was to take prisoners, examine the enemy trenches and search dug-outs, to kill Germans and to damage the enemy defences. The raiders were divided into five groups, a blocking group to secure the ends of the enemy trench, a search and demolition party, prisoners' escort, signallers and stretcher bearers. There was also to be a covering party consisting of a Lewis gun detachment under an officer. At zero, 7:00 pm, the artillery placed a barrage on the enemy front line, while howitzers blocked neighbouring communication trenches. The 18-pounders ceased firing at zero plus 28 minutes. Acting as a feint a dummy raid was carried out by the 13th Rifles, supported by the 108th Stokes battery. Added to this was covering fire from the guns of the 108th Machine Gun Company who swept the enemy front line and saps at pre-timed intervals. The party left their trenches at 6:30 pm and safely made their way across no man's land until meeting a large deep and wide ditch filled with barbed wire and covered with matting, making it impossible to either see or cross. By 8:30 pm the party had safely returned to their on lines having suffered three other ranks slightly wounded. According to Cyril Falls the raid failed due to the prowess of the bomb throwing "Swabian peasants".

The 14th Rifles had little more luck on 1 November when they raided a position known as "Cooker Farm". This extract from the diary of Private McRoberts recounts the story:

Wednesday 1 November 1916: WYTSCHAETE (COOKER FARM)
I went first, laying down a white tape. It was after 2am and the night was dry and quiet but the ground was very wet. Fritz was throwing up very few lights and it was hard to tell the proper direction to go. Twice Mr. J.D. O'Brien told me to keep more to the right and I did not understand why but went on blindly as I was directed. I was perfectly cool, but I knew I was out of my way. Then after a long time Mr. O'Brien came up to me excitedly, "McRoberts", he said, "where are you going? You will soon have us back to our own line, there's the German part, we want to enter that way", and he pointed much to the left. To myself I blamed him for putting me wrong but went as directed. After a little distance there were numerous, big shell-holes and next the German wire appeared right in front. Mr. O'Brien came and said, 'It is almost 4 o'clock, we are not the proper spot, but put in the tubes.' I crawled round the huge shell-holes, the three other chaps coming up with the three tubes, or Bangalore torpedoes as they were called. All at once there was a flash and shot from the German parapet high up in front. I knew we were suspected and rushed up to the wire – there was no creeping any longer. I pushed in the first tube and the other chap helped me with the second. We drove the first two home through the wire right up against the parapet; we did not require the third. My companion, who was a Royal Engineer, quietly fitted the detonator to the fuse and set off the patent lighter. I scrambled back, about fifteen yards and lay down, fingers in ears and mouth open. There was silence for a few seconds, then a terrific explosion, the flame dazzling our eyes. Our first party rushed the place but I stood by, for I was to enter the trench with the last or search party. Our chaps, however, their eyes dazed by the bright flame and now in complete darkness again, did not rush exactly at the right place and came up against some wire. Bombs were flung and shots fired from the German parapet. I saw our chaps kneeling and feeling their way. "Rush them, Rush them!" I shouted. "Show us the way", said someone. I ran forward to the German parapet, the others beside me, and I tried to fire my revolver but

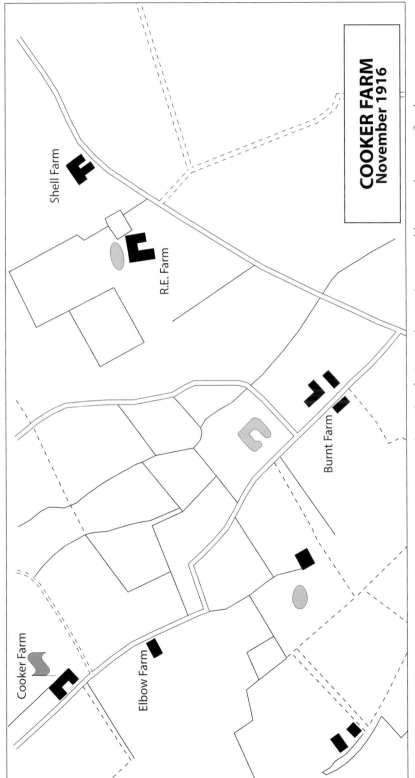

COOKER FARM
November 1916

The raid on Cooker Farm was carried out on the night of 1 November 1916, it was cold, wet and very confused.

it wouldn't work, it had fallen in the mud when I was laying the tube. I drew out a bomb, and was just about to pull the pin when there was a great flare of light in my eyes and I must have fallen back, although I do not remember doing so. I next found myself in one of the shell-holes, up to the neck in water. There were still shots and the bright explosion of bombs. The water was red and there were bits of flesh floating in it. My mouth was full of blood and shattered flesh, the right side of my head seemed a blank and there were painful places in my right leg. I thought of my first aid bandage but realised it was useless and that the only thing for me to do was to hurry back to my trenches while I could. I scrambled out of the hole and turning my back to the firing and bomb explosions, I ran across no man's land, got through some wire and scrambled into the trench. No one had observed me and curiously also, I had seen no one. I even thought I had entered some Boche line and was only reassured when I saw an ammunition box of ours with the figures 'VII' on it. Doctor Garvin was soon found and I had a dressing put on my face. Then I started off, running down King's Way, staggering all the time and accompanied by Alec Flynn, who was also wounded; eventually I reached our First Aid station. My face was again bandaged, also my leg at the knee and I was put on a stretcher and felt myself being carried for a long time. I had frequently pictured myself as being killed and imagined the scene at home when the news arrived. The greatest disability I could conjecture was being blinded in both eyes. I pictured myself with my eyesight gone, typing for a firm to whom I would be particularly valuable because of my knowledge of French! It was getting clear and I could see now, but I was feeling in a bad way, chiefly from the wetting I had got and my knee was paining me a lot.

On 11 November the *London Gazette* published notification of the award of the Military Medal to Lance Corporal Robert Craig, 109th Field Ambulance. Craig came from Dunmoyle Street, Belfast, and was also awarded an Ulster Division Certificate of Gallantry for his actions on 1 July. The next day a party of the 11th Inniskillings was in no man's land carrying out a reconnaissance of the German wire prior to a raid planned for two nights later. Having the state of the wire for a considerable length and noted its thickness the party return to their lines. The last two men to leave were Sergeant A.W. Gailbraith, from Ballyshannon, County Donegal and his platoon commander. Seeing that the men had gotten safely away the officer and Sergeant had just begun their own journey back when the area was illuminated by German rockets and both men sought shelter in a shell hole. However, the shell hole was of shallow draught leaving both men exposed to enemy fire and Sergeant Gailbraith was mortally wounded.

On 16 November a raid was carried out by the men of the 11th Inniskillings against the Spanbroek Salient, on a frontage of two hundred yards. Their opponents were from the 104 Saxon Regiment who had replaced the Wurttemberg troops and had only recently arrived in the trenches and were still unfamiliar with the routine. At 10:00 pm, the raiding party of four officers and one 184 other ranks from G Company, crossed no man's land and into the German trenches. There had been no earlier artillery barrage; instead trench mortars had provided an intense barrage for several days prior to the raid. The raiders were well prepared, having been given training in the use of German bombs with their distinctive wooden handles and the enemy machine guns. They also took with them a large supply of their own Mills bombs. The raiders were divided into four separate groups and torches covered in coloured paper were used for identification. Working from aerial photographs the plan was to be carried out in two distinct phases. Initially the first, second and third line trenches would be attacked. Then on the launching of two green Very lights, the fourth line would be assaulted.

Exactly on time the raiding parties moved forward, led by those men carrying the Bangalore torpedoes. The group led by Second Lieutenant Strong exploded their torpedo and rushed through the gap blown in the wire and into the enemy trench. Any resistance was met with the

An enemy trench captured by men of the Lincolns. They are waiting on the inevitable German counter-attack with their Lewis gun in position. Such was the success of the Lewis gun that the Germans paid a bounty for each one captured.

bayonet. Moving along the trench they met four Germans, who attempted to bomb them, but the Inniskillings were quicker and all four were killed. The trench was then blocked to prevent any enemy counter-attack. A second group from D Company was shot at by a private and a member of the party was wounded. An accurately thrown bomb settled the matter. So it went on, much more bombing than shooting on the part of the raiders. Enemy soldiers were killed and a machine gun position destroyed. It was reported that in excess of 300 bombs had been used by the raiders, while the Lewis gun had proved its worth on more than one occasion. In one instance a German counter attack had been beaten off by the sole use of the Lewis gun that had expended 11 drums of ammunition in doing so.

The raiders remained in the enemy trenches for an hour, killing at least 23 enemy and taking three prisoners. The veterans of the Inniskillings in action against these green troops caused mayhem and the terror-stricken Saxons deserted their front line on a wide front. The Inniskillings had their pleasure with it for half an hour, looting everything which they could carry back, blowing up all the dug-outs, to the accompaniment of tunes played in no man's land on mouth organs.[14]

Three prisoners were taken and losses to the Inniskillings were two men killed and 14 wounded. The two men killed were Privates William Orr and Thomas Young. Private Orr is listed as having served in D Company and was reportedly killed by a German officer, who was in turn killed by the man following Orr.[15]

Horses played a large part in moving the division throughout the war, as it did in all units of the British Army. Unfortunately not all those men assigned to the care of these animals were that

14   Falls, 'The History of the 36th (Ulster) Division.
15   *Belfast News Letter,* 30 November 1916.

experienced. On 20 November a confidential memo was sent from Captain G. Leslie DAA & QMG, of the Division to the IV Corps commander:

> Out of forty-one recent cases where men have been charged with trotting horse on paved roads, twenty-four men have been admonished, and in other cases, punishments have been awarded which are not sufficiently severe to act as a deterrent. The Divisional Commander wishes all Commanding Officers to be informed that, unless they recognise that they are dealing with direct disobedience of orders and punish men accordingly, it will be necessary to order that all such cases be tried by FGCM.[16]

Elsewhere discipline was causing concern. A letter marked 'Secret' was distributed on 14 October 1916, stating:

> Those who when engaged with the enemy fail to maintain equilibrium do so either –
> 1. Because they are lacking in the nerve stability which must be assumed to be inherent in all soldiers, or –
> 2. Because they have been subjected to some extraordinary exposure not incidental to all military operations.
>   Those who have committed themselves for the first of the above reasons cannot be allowed to escape disciplinary action on the grounds of a medical diagnosis of "Shell Shock" or "Neurasthenia" or "Inability to stand shell fire."[17]

However, the cases of men suffering from 'shell shock' were on the increase and causing a degree of anxiety in the higher echelons of the British Second Army. On 23 November a secret report regarding this condition and suggestions as to how it was to be treated, coming into effect as of 1 December 1916. The report highlights the following and was copied to all Divisions and Brigades:
Officers and other ranks reporting as:-

a) Suffering from Shell Shock
b) Suffering from Gas
c) Suffering from Nervous Breakdown, inability to stand shell fire, or neurasthenia,

Were to be sent to No.12 Casualty Clearing Station and not to be evacuated to the Base, unless:-
i)   In the case of (a), there are definite lesions and symptoms which justify the classification of the case as a battle casualty.
ii) In the case of (b), it is proved that the patient has been gassed.
   Cases that came in under (a) and (b) will not be reported by units as battle casualties until they have been diagnosed at No.12 Casualty Clearing Station as genuine battle casualties. Cases coming under (c) were not battle casualties and would be evacuated under the orders of the D.M.S.
   The medical officer of the unit would immediately report any case coming within the above categories to the commanding officer, who would carefully investigate the case and in order that it could be decided whether disciplinary action was necessary, a statement of the facts

---

16   A&Q Branch War Diary.
17   TNA WO 95 2493.

(marked confidential) of each case would be forwarded as early as possible by the CO direct to the officer of the A.A.G.

General Nugent wrote to his wife on 24 November commenting on his reinforcements; he was decidedly unimpressed:

The new conscript army is beginning to roll up. I got about 300 or more this week and inspected them yesterday. I found artisans of all sorts, cooks of all kinds, entrée cooks, pastry cooks, plain cooks, and one great find, a music hall comedian. I asked him what line he did and he said "I'm versatile, sing, dance or juggle", so I have said he is to be marked down for our Follies. I gave them an address and good advice and said I hoped they would be very happy and well looked after and at the end they called out "Thank you Sir!" I nearly fainted. Such want of discipline, on parade too. Besides the idea of the British soldier thanking one for anything was too much."

Three days later Nugent wrote to his son St George and held little back concerning battlefield brutality:

We did a highly successful raid the other day, broke into the German trenches in 3 places, took several prisoners and killed nearly fifty. I was rather annoyed that the parties did not take more prisoners, but our men wouldn't trust them. They had been had before by Boches holding up their hands and shouting "Kamerad" while another man took a pot shot from behind him, so they killed everyone that they met. They left behind a number of booby traps for the Boches when they returned. They pulled the pins out of Mills grenades and put them under the dead Boches in the trenches, so that the weight of the body keeps the lever down, in the hope that when the Boches come back and lifted up their defunct comrades, they would explode violently. I did not hear whether the traps worked, but they deserved to.
   Barring weekly bombardments and occasional raids times are fairly quiet, but I never trust the Boche. He is full of fight yet and I see no end in sight yet."

The 12th Rifles saw a change of command. Lieutenant Colonel George Bull, DSO, was promoted to brigadier as of 3 December and given command of 8 Brigade in the 3rd Division. While on a tour of inspection of the division's trenches three days later he was shot by a sniper and died of his wound on 11 December. His place in the 12th Battalion was taken by his former second-in-command, Lieutenant Colonel William Richard Goodwin. A former Adjutant with the South Belfast Volunteers of the UVF, Goodwin had seen action on 1 July and was rated by General Nugent as a capable commander.

The 109 Brigade was relieved by 49 Brigade, 16th (Irish) Division in the Spanbroek Sector on 5 December. In turn 109 were to relieve 76 Brigade in the Douve Sector. Earlier there had been advice issued in connection with possible gas attacks and 'Instructions for Wind Dangerous Period and actions during a Gas Attack' had been issued. However, this instruction had raised the question, should a telephonist, on his own initiative send the message 'Gas Attack Trench -----', or whether he should do so only on the orders of an officer. It was decided that a telephonist who had detected gas or had heard the gas alarm on his front should send the message 'Warning Gas Trench -----'. The message 'Gas Attack Trench-----' would only be sent on the approval of an officer once he had assured himself that an actual gas attack had been launched, irrespective of any previous warning. The artillery support would act on receipt of the 'Warning' message if satisfied of its genuineness.

A 1916 Christmas card carrying the name
Captain B Flood. There is no B Flood listed,
however, Captain Robert Samuel Flood MC,
9th Royal Irish Fusiliers, aged 26 years, was
killed on 5 December 1917. He was the son of
Robert Flood of Milhale, Tullyvin, Cootehill,
County Cavan.

A homemade Christmas card for 1915 – The first
Christmas in France, from William to his mother,
Sadie and Edie – did he ever see them again?

The first man of the division to be awarded a Bar to the Military Medal was Staff Sergeant R.S.
Gillespie, of the Royal Army Medical Corps, so reported the *Belfast New Letter* of 12 December.
Staff Sergeant Gillespie lived at Mayo Street, Belfast, with his wife and family and had served in
the South African War with the Inniskillings. The newspaper does not state which field ambulance
he served with.

Christmas Eve for the 15th Rifles saw the death of Bugler James Baird. The previous day Baird
had been fatally wounded while attempting to rescue his friend Corporal Thomas Bradshaw, who
died shortly after being recovered from the battlefield. James Baird came from Arlington Street,
Belfast, while Corporal Bradshaw had resided at Upper Townsend Street, Belfast, the two friends
were 19 and 18 years old respectively.

On 20 December the 14th Rifles relieved the 11th Inniskillings, who were in brigade reserve
and were to be inspected by General Haig. The occasion was recorded in a letter from General
Nugent to his wife:

> Well, the C-in-C (D Haig is his name. He's in the Army. He's had a brilliant career) came this
> morning and saw some of my men. I rode with him for three or four miles while he was going
> through my area. Nothing could have been more charming. He said "I must thank you for
> all the splendid work done by your Division since it came out. You did magnificently on the
> Somme and I always think with regret that we failed to give you all the support we ought to

have done." I thanked him and said I thought that perhaps we had all been rather optimistic as to what was possible to do. He replied "Well, we are all learning." Anyhow that was really very nice saying [sic] and so far from my back hair standing up. I was almost purring.

This was also the day that Haig met with General Nivelle, the new French commander-in-chief who mentioned that he had met David Lloyd George at Verdun. Nivelle added that he had been informed by the prime minister that the British were not 'a military people'. General Haig replied with the observation that Lloyd George had never studied British military history.[18]

---

18   Sheffield, Gary & Bourne, John, *Douglas Haig; War Diaries and Letters* (London 2005).

9

Like the end of the World

The year 1917 will always be remembered as the year of Passchendaele, not so much a single battle, but a great campaign fought between June and November of that year. This was also the year of the Russian Revolution, with the Tsar's abdication and the Bolsheviks coming to power.

General Nivelle's Chief of Staff was Colonel d'Alencon, who at this time was suffering from terminal consumption. Knowing he had little time left and convinced that the French Army was only capable of one more major effort, he helped propel Nivelle into the disaster that was the April offensive and subsequent mutiny of the French Army.

The winter months would see the division supplying men for numerous working parties. A Works Battalion, with a nucleus of 100 trained pioneers, was formed on a temporary basis, each brigade supplying a company. It proved to be extremely unpopular with those concerned and was of limited value. Possibly the only exception to this was the famous underground barracks built by the Australian Tunnelling Company on the southern slope of Hill 63, this was proof against artillery, illuminated throughout by electric light and capable of holding two battalions of infantry.

Born in Waterford, the son of a Surgeon General, Major Horace Sampson Roch was appointed as ADMS of the Division. He had been ADMS with the 2nd Cavalry Division and been awarded a DSO while there. Before that Roch had been DADMS with the 7th Division. Post-war he would

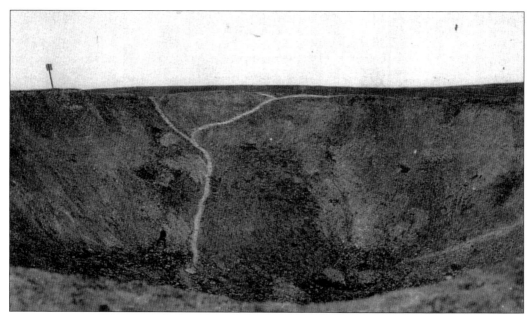

A post war photograph showing the aftermath of a mine explosion at La Boisselle. Visitors have left a well trodden path.

go on to serve in Russia with the White Russian forces and be made an honorary Colonel in the Imperial Russian Army.[1]

In the midst of all this scenes of normality still occurred. A *Belfast News Letter* clipping, dated 15 January 1917, stated; "At a local camp somewhere in France a new YMCA hut was officially opened."

Accidents in wartime are also the norm and on 3 February Second Lieutenant Alfred Nicholl, aged 27, from St. Jude's Avenue Belfast, who was a bombing instructor with the 13th Rifles, died as a result of an accident during training at the Brigade Bombing School, where he was the officer in charge. Also killed in this incident was Corporal Charles Graham, 9th Irish Fusiliers, with a further five other ranks being wounded.

Much has been said regarding the myth of the relaxed life of staff officers, the misconception of their easy life in the various headquarter chateaus, long lunches and evening soirees to the local nightspots. The truth was somewhat different. Staff Officers worked long hours as they copied orders, marked maps and kept the various war diaries up to date. An example of work carried out by these staff officers is the following 109 Brigade order, as issued on 5 January 1917:

1. In the left sub-sector the 14th Rifles will relieve the 9th Inniskillings on Saturday 6th Instant. Relieving units will not pass Ration Farm until 5:00 pm. Relief will take place via Plum Duff Trench and Calgary Avenue. With the exception of half a company at Stinking Farm which will use Currie Avenue. Units after relief will use Currie Avenue. The relief of the Company in Winter Trench will take place by Gas Trench and Regina Cutoff. From 1:00 pm until 3:00 pm Plum Duff Trench will be reserved for 'In' traffic. From 3:00 pm until 4:30 pm it will be reserved for 'Out' traffic, after that time until the incoming battalion has passed through, it will be reserved for 'In' traffic.

    O.C. 9th Inniskillings will arrange to post sentries at each end of Plum Duff Trench to enforce this order.

    This will not affect working parties of the 9th Irish Fusiliers and 13th Rifles who are working on the front line.

    No transport will pass the Shrine before 5:30 pm. The 9th Inniskillings after relief will withdraw into Brigade Reserve at Red Lodge relieving the 14th Rifles.

2. In the 'Right' sub-sector the 11th Inniskillings will relieve the 10th Inniskillings on the same day. Relieving unit will not pass Hyde Park Corner before 2:00 pm.

    Gas Trench and Annscroft Avenue will be reserved for 'In' traffic, and the 'Only Way' for 'Out' traffic. The 10th Inniskillings, after relief will withdraw into Brigade Reserve at the Catacombs, relieving the 11th Inniskillings.

    Transport will not pass Hyde Park Corner till 5:00 pm.

3. All Specialists may be relieved during the day under orders from O.C. Battalions. They must be marched as formed parties under an officer or NCO.

4. All movements will be by Platoons at 200 yards interval. Each Battalion will detail an officer to patrol the routes by which the relief will take place to ensure that there will be no straggling. Movement by day must be carefully regulated and supervised owing to the fact that our lines are under such close observation from Messines. Details of relief, guides, etc. will be arranged directly between the Battalion Commanders concerned.

5. All units will take over the same tactical dispositions which were in force in the Battalion they relieve.

---

1   *British Medical Journal* 25 June 1960.

6. All Trench Stores, log Books and programmes of work, etc. will be taken over by reliev-
    ing units. Lists will be forwarded so as to reach Brigade Headquarters before 6:00 pm on
    the day of relief.
7. R.E. Working Parties now found by 11th Inniskillings and 14th Rifles will cease after
    work on the night of the 5th/6th instant and will be found on the night of 7th/8th by the
    9th and 10th Inniskillings.
8. Completion of reliefs will be wired in code to Brigade Headquarters.
9. Acknowledge.

The above document was signed by Captain A. C. Richardson, Brigade Major of the 109
Brigade and was distributed to 21 separate locations. A similar order was issued eight days later
and again eight days after that and would continue as long as the brigade was in the front line; the
paperwork battle was unending, tedious, tiresome, draining, but vitally important. In October
1918 General Haig would acknowledge the great assistance given to him by Lieutenant General
the Honourable Sir Herbert Lawrence, KCB, whose cool judgement and unfailing military insight
was of the utmost value. Sir Herbert was the son of Lord Lawrence of Indian Mutiny fame and
came from Londonderry.

The Merry Mauve Melody Makers, the Pierrot troupe of the 14th Rifles, returned home to
Ulster and appeared in Bangor, County Down on 26 January, to help raise funds for the UVF
Patriotic Fund.

The month of February saw practically all other work stop within the division as the men were
deployed in stringing barbed wire over a wide area and in considerable depth. Plug Street Wood
was remembered as being in such a tangle that it has always been a mystery to those who saw it
how the Germans passed through it in 1918'.[2]

At this time the division was without its pioneers, the 16th Rifles were away working under the
command of Sir Eric Geddes, also known as the railway king. Geddes, a civilian, had been granted
the honorary rank of major general and was responsible for the improvement of communications
and transport behind the lines. The 16th Rifles, now part of X Corps specifically worked on a
narrow gauge railway running between Ouderdom, which was south of the Kemmel and between
Busseboom and Dickebusch. They also worked on a broad gauge line running to Ouderdom.
Despite most of this work being 'behind the lines', casualties had been sustained; on 30 January
Private A. Lynn, from Belfast, was killed. The following day a working party was sent to Ypres to
collect bricks and lost Private G. Cope, from Skipton Street Belfast, killed, while another man was
wounded, the result of enemy shelling.

A successful German raid on the divisional trenches occurred on St Valentine's Day 1917. The
division's trenches on the Wulverghem to Messines Road were obliterated by German artillery and
two men were lost as prisoners. At 7:00 am on 18 February, the weather was misty and Captain
J.A. Johnston, 9th Irish Fusiliers, had just climbed on to the fire step to examine the barbed wire
in front of the position, when he was shot through the heart by a sniper. In this case it was a single
shot fired from the enemy lines in what was barely daylight. His funeral was held later that day at
St. Quentin Cabaret. Previously on 7 February, Private William Hickey, also 9th Irish Fusiliers,
had been killed by a sniper in the same area.

As the war dragged on the letters home continued to carry more bad news than good. Mr
J.A. Williams of the Londonderry Savings Bank received news that his son Lieutenant Earnest J.
Williams Royal Irish Rifles had been accidentally wounded in France. Earnest had been in the
service of the Bank of Montreal when war was declared and had joined the Canadian Expeditionary
Force and after a winter's service in France had been granted a commission in the Rifles in August

---

2   Falls, *The History of the 36th (Ulster) Division* (1922).

A section of infantry entering a captured German trench on a tour of duty, the spade being almost as important as the rifle in the Great War. These men are from the Irish Guards.

1916. His only surviving brother, Temporary Captain H.B. Williams, served in France with the Inniskillings, while two other brothers, Captain Charles Beasley Williams and Second Lieutenant Alfred Williams, both serving with the Rifles, were killed in action, Charles with the 2nd Rifles on 28 August 1915, at the time of writing the CWGC holds no record of Alfred.

The division found one advantage to holding the same part of the front for a considerable time and this was in the provision of some comforts and recreation for the troops. Both football and boxing competitions were organised as was a horse show and several other types of sporting activities. A large hut was erected at Dranoutre, which was used for concerts and other entertainments. A bus service was introduced running from Hyde Park Corner, just outside Ploegsteert village to Bailleul, a place still containing a fair number of shops, cafes houses of ill repute and bars all centred on the square that held the Hotel de Ville. Despite these comforts there was still the numbing cold and many men preferred to sleep in the trenches than suffer the bare draughty wooden huts with a temperature of 15 degrees below zero and insufficient fuel for the stoves.

In March the division's front ran from the Wulverghem to Wytschaete Road on the right to a point opposite Maedelstede Farm on the left. The frontage was held by a single brigade, with the second in reserve back in the area around Fletre, while the third brigade was training in the neighbourhood of Lumbres, west of St. Omer.

The month of March saw the 14th Rifles receive a new commanding officer, the ninth to hold this position since coming on service. This was Captain George Ronald Hamilton Cheape of the King's Dragoon Guards, who was given the temporary rank of lieutenant colonel, having lately command the 7th Battalion Black Watch. Cheape was the son of the later Lieutenant Colonel George Clerk Cheape of Gateside, Fifeshire, and was married to Margaret Bruce Ismay, eldest daughter of J. Bruce Ismay of the White Star Line, a man vilified for his behaviour on the sinking of the Titanic.[3] Cheape's brother Captain Leslie St Clair Cheape had been killed while serving with the 1st (King's) Dragoon Guards in the Middle East in April 1916.

On 16 March Colonel Blacker left the 9th Irish Fusiliers and Colonel S.J. Somerville took command of the battalion. The previous evening there had been a farewell dinner at the Café Francis in Caestre, the colonel, at fifty-two years of age, was to return to Ireland to command the 20th (Reserve) Battalion of the Royal Irish Rifles, which he would command from April until May the following year, when he transferred to the reserve of officers.[4] Stafford James Somerville was the youngest and only surviving son of the late Reverend Dudley Somerville, Chaplain to the Forces, and had been educated at Wellington College. He was later commissioned into the Inniskillings and had served with their 2nd Battalion on the North West Frontier under Sir William Lockhart in the 1897 to 1898 campaign, including operations in the Bara Valley and the occupation of the Khyber Pass. Prior to joining the Irish Fusiliers he had served with the 1st Inniskillings at Gallipoli, where he had been wounded. His elder brother, Lieutenant Stafford Dudley Somerville, of the 5th Battalion King's Own Yorkshire Light Infantry, had been killed on 5 July 1915, near Thiepval while leading his company into action.

On the same day there was a meeting of the Young Citizens' L.O.L. 871, with Br. G. Uprichard, W.M. presiding.[5] After the meeting was declared open the members proceeded to elect officers in place of those who were made casualties since the last meeting. The following officers were elected; Deputy Master, CQMS J. Keating; secretary, Br. Lieutenant T.H. Mayes; treasurer, Br. Sergeant Minnis. Members of the committee; Br. Lance Corporal Burns (foreman), Br. W. Condell, and Br. CSM J. Nevins. Br. Corporal Agnew was admitted on certificate from L.O.L. 428 Star of Down. Congratulatory messages were ordered to be sent to Brs. Captain Lewis, MC, and Sergeant Neely, DCM; and votes of condolence were passed to the relatives of Brs. CSM J. Scott and Private S. Boyd, killed in action. The treasurer reported the finances of the lodge in a flourishing condition, and after several names had been proposed for membership the meeting stood adjourned until the following week.

The distribution of shamrock to the Irish regiments was a tradition that dated back many years. That for the Ulster Division was in this year to be supplied by the Ulster Women's Gift Fund. However, an announcement from Buckingham Palace that the Queen, following past precedent, had undertaken to supply all Irish units in the British Army with shamrock, made the offer redundant. Still, this did have an unfortunate consequence for the Ulster Division as a letter from General Nugent to his wife shows, after discussing the Russian Revolution and its potential effect on the war, he says; "I had no shamrock today and no one had any. The supplies either were not sent off or they have failed to get here on time."

With the coming of the spring months all ranks noticed a new activity as the rear area became packed with troops and a new railhead appeared at Haagedoorne outside Bailleul. Ammunition and supply dumps sprang up almost overnight, as did new communication trenches and narrow gauge railways. With so much going on and despite camouflage it was not long before the Germans became aware that something serious was about to occur.

The Kemmel area, held by the 12th Rifles along with the 108th Trench Mortar Battery and Machine Gun Company, came under accurate enemy shelling on 22 March, causing seven casualties, two of whom were fatal. Private William Beers, of the Mortar Battery, had been on sentry duty. He came from Comber, County Down, and had first enlisted in the 11th Rifles. The other was Private R. Magee from Ballymena serving with the 12th Rifles. Two days later German

3   This was mostly in the American press and his positive role in later years is largely ignored, even today.
4   Details provided by Professor Timothy Bowman.
5   Br. Brother, W.M. Worshipful Master.

artillery fell on the right flank of 107 Brigade and on the New Zealand unit on their right. The bombardment lasted for an hour and a half. At daybreak German infantry swarmed towards the Brigade lines, but the counter barrage and intense machine gun fire from both Vickers and Lewis guns brought them down in droves.

In conjunction with his battles on the Western Front, General Nugent had to contend with battles on the home front and even within his own headquarters. A extract from a letter home written on 21 May 1917:

> I got a parcel of socks from Mrs Blackley in Cavan for the division, 100 pairs. But it is such a waste to send them. They are not wanted and the men can get all the socks they want by asking for them, but the scream of the matter is that Mrs Blackley sent them out through Lady MacDonald's Committee instead of the Ulster one. The dear ones of Ulster will become purple with indignation. The socks of course are contaminated and infected and unfit for an Ulsterman to wear so I must give them to the Englishmen who compose nearly half of the 'Ulster Division'! I sometimes feel that I should like to attend one of the meetings and just tell the committee my most inward views of them.

The pace began to quicken on this front in spring 1917. A decision had been made to conduct an operation that had been in the planning for well over a year, as a large preparatory operation to a larger attack from the Ypres area. The Second Army, of which the Ulster Division was currently part, arranged for two overwhelming advantages in the attack, the purpose of which was the capture of the long ridge running south from Ypres to Armentieres, through the villages of Wytschaete and Messines. Firstly, the most intensive concentration of artillery managed by the Army in the entire War so far was assembled. Secondly, the blowing of 19 of 21 immense mines under the key German positions would precede the attack. These mines had been prepared many months before, at an immense cost in terms of labour, by the tunnelling companies of the Royal Engineers, assisted by many working parties from various infantry battalions.[6] Training was also to be more intense and thorough than anything that had gone before and staff work was to be meticulous. The preliminary bombardment would be opened on 31 May 1917. Fully aware that the British were preparing for a major offensive the Germans concentrated a lot of their artillery fire on the rear areas, shelling billets and horse lines. The guns of the 107th Machine Gun Company were positioned on the Wulverghem to Wytschaete Road close to Spanbroekmolen. An enemy shell landed at Thatched Cottage on 7 May, burying a number of men. Lieutenant Barker was instrumental in digging out several of those who had been trapped under the rubble and as a consequence was awarded the Military Cross. John Barker was perhaps a typical Machine Gun Officer. He had been born in Lincolnshire in December 1895, one of three children and was considered to be "… the black sheep of the family."[7]

Barker had been a member of the Inns of Court OTC and later joined the Territorial Force as a private. He was commissioned as a second lieutenant in the Worcestershire Regiment in February 1915, transferring to the Machine Gun Corps on 13 March the following year and was attached to the 107th Machine Gun Company as of 12 July 1916.

At 10:00 pm, on the night of 19 May, a raid on the German lines launched from the Bull Ring. The raiding party consisted of one officer and 12 other ranks from the 12th Rifles who crossed into the enemy trenches at N. 30.c.55.10. Six of the raiders managed to enter the enemy trench,

---

6   Information provided by Stuart Eastwood, Border Regiment and King's Own Royal Border Regiment Museum.
7   Letter from his son Richard, who also has a note from his aunt that states "John – a bit of a problem."

but were forced out after a brief exchange of bombs. The entire party returned having suffered no casualties. At 1:50 am, the Germans launched a counter raid and began to bomb their way to the Bull Ring. The Rifles replied with a shower of bombs, rifle and Lewis gun fire, which resulted in two of the enemy being killed. These bodies were recovered the following evening and proved to be from a Saxon Regiment. A further raid by five Germans was beaten off at N. 36.a.6.3, and at 2:30 am a party of 15 Germans again assaulted the Bull Ring. These were also driven off, the entire night costing the Rifles four casualties. Throughout the following night more raids were beaten off and some heavy shelling experienced. Intelligence reports indicated that these determined enemy raids were designed to find and destroy the mine shafts in the Divisional area.

The 14th Rifles launched a raid on the enemy trenches on the Kemmel to Wytschaete Road on the night of 23 May, capturing a prisoner and confirming intelligence reports that the German had reinforced their lines. The following day news came through to the division that Lieutenant Colonel T.V.P. McCammon, former 5th Rifles, who was on attachment to the 2nd Battalion Hampshire Regiment, had died. He had been heavily engaged in the original formation of the UVF.

At 2:00 am, on 29 May, German artillery and trench mortars fired on the front line and communication trenches of the 108 Brigade. Fifty minutes later they delivered a box barrage on Piccadilly-Ulster Road-George St, while two parties of enemy infantry approached the north side of the Bull Ring and yet a third came from the south, each comprised of some 20 men. Defensive fire from the brigade's Lewis guns, bombers and rifle fire drove them back and when a second attack was launched a few minutes later, it was in turn driven back. The cost to the brigade was 14 casualties and three Lewis guns destroyed. Between 12:30 and 1:00 pm, approximately 100 rounds of high explosive shells from German 150mm guns fell on the Regent Street dug-outs area; British artillery was not able to give accurate counter-battery fire due to bad visibility. This same lack of visibility allowed a party of two officers and 40 other ranks from the brigade to cross no man's land then enter the enemy trenches and remain there for some 45 minutes. No Germans were encountered.

Casualties were also suffered by 107 Brigade. In the ranks of the 10th Rifles Lance Corporal Samuel Gregg was mortally wounded. Samuel came from East Street, Newtownards, and left a widow, Margaret, and son Alexander. His pre-war employment was given as tailor and given his age, forty-one, would probably explain his position within the battalion.[8]

During this time the divisional artillery of the 32nd Division plus four army artillery brigades had been brought into the 36th Divisional area, all movement being made under the cover of darkness. There were now 192 guns and howitzers arranged along the divisional front. These positions had been constructed by the 36th Division artillerymen and reserve stocks of ammunition had been placed ready for use, all under the direction of the redoubtable General Brock and his staff.

A further large number of guns, under the direct command of IX Corps, had arrived and was in the process of bombarding the Messines Ridge. The enemy concrete bunkers, of which there were many along the Ridge, were being systematically destroyed. It should be noted that German bunkers at this time were used to provide cover for infantry and gun crews during bombardments. They were known as MEBU (*Mannshafts-Eisen-Beton-Unterstand* or reinforced concrete for troops to stand under); they were not usually fitted with any sort of firing slit, having only an entry/exit opening on the side away from the enemy. The idea was that when the shelling stopped the men would emerge from the bunker and take up firing positions, either on the roof to take advantage

---

8   Switzer, Catherine and Ken, 'Remembering the Fallen' in *Newtownards Chronicle*, 26 May 2011. It is believed that the oldest British soldier to die on the Western Front was Lieutenant Harry Webber, 7th South Lancashire Regiment, at 68 years of age.

C Company of the 10th Battalion Royal Irish Fusiliers at the Newtownards Camp, 1917. Men from here would be sent to France as reinforcements.

of the extra height or into old shell holes that had been prepared as such.[9] However, where specific machine gun emplacements were encountered they proved incredibly difficulty to attack and knock out. Eventually specific tactics evolved incorporating the accurate fire of the Lewis guns, generous use of bombs and when available tanks.

The British did not have it all their own way and German counter-bombardments were effective. They made very effective use of a railway gun, which being mobile, was difficult to locate and this weapon fired with considerable accuracy on horse lines, tented encampments and supply dumps.

During the night of 27 May divisional headquarters moved to a new position known as Ulster Camp, just to the west of Dranoutre. Here they came under fire from a German 100mm gun and over the next two hours several hits were made on the Headquarters, including one direct hit on an office that killed one and wounded four other clerks. General Nugent's ADC was slightly wounded by a splinter, but 'nothing to speak of'. It became necessary for the staff to disperse into the surrounding fields to obtain whatever cover was available. In doing so another shell killed Lieutenant Colonel W.A. De Courcey King DSO, the Commander Royal Engineers, which was a great loss. General Nugent rated him as first rate at organisation and a good friend.[10]

The following morning it was discovered just how accurate the shelling had been. Seventy horses had been killed and between 60 and 70 men injured. Convinced that the location of divisional headquarters was now known to the enemy Nugent ordered that the headquarters be split into smaller camps, while he and his advance headquarters moved from Dranoutre on 28 May to his command post that had been prepared on the western slope of Kemmel Hill.

---

9   The authors are grateful to Jack Sheldon for explaining the difference between Messines and Normandy beach bunkers.

10   Perry, *Major General Oliver Nugent and the Ulster Division 1915-1918* (2007).

The preliminary bombardment of the Battle of Messines opened on 31 May and from then day and night firing was carried out by the artillery on an extensive scale targeting enemy communication, fire and support trenches, while the divisional trench mortars bombarded enemy trench mortar positions.

Units of 108 Brigade in the line were thinned out as arranged, while machine guns and Stokes mortars took their allotted places in the line. All infantry working parties ceased work at midnight and became available to their respective battalion commanders for training. The bombardment continued and by 9:45 pm on 2 June, the heavy trench mortars had fired 183 bombs, the 2-inch mortars 1,000 bombs and the machine guns 6, 900 rounds in the past 24 hours.

The following 24 hours the divisional artillery's 18-pounders and 4.5-inch howitzers again carried out a night bombardment and at 11:00 am a concentration of all available heavy batteries were turned on Wytschaete with very good effect. A practice creeping barrage followed during which smoke shells were used to gauge the speed of the lifts. At 3:00 pm, a second practice barrage was fired and under cover of this a raiding party entered the enemy lines. This group consisted of three officers with 70 other ranks from the 13th Rifles and after crossing no man's land they entered the enemy trenches at Peckham. There followed a brief, but fierce exchange of bombs in which the Mills outperformed the *Stielhandgranate* in effect if not in range, resulted in 19 prisoners. On returning to the divisional lines three of the prisoners gave trouble and were killed. On questioning it was revealed that the prisoners were from the 4th Grenadier Regiment of the German 2nd Division. During the hours of daylight the heavy trench mortars fired 327 rounds, the 2-inch mortars 2,012. Enemy retaliation to the divisional bombardments was considered slight.

On 4 June yet another practice barrage was carried out at 2:00 pm. Behind this went another raiding party from B Company of the 9th Irish Fusiliers, entered the Spanbroekmolen Salient and captured a German officer and 30 other ranks, again from the 4th Grenadier Regiment. This time there was no trouble from the prisoners and all were returned to the divisional lines. For a daylight raid this was a remarkable achievement, although the raiding party suffered six men wounded and two killed. These were Private William McIlroy, from County Antrim and Lance Corporal J Scott

Cigarette cards describing the three divisions, 10th (Irish), 16th (Irish) and 36th (Ulster).

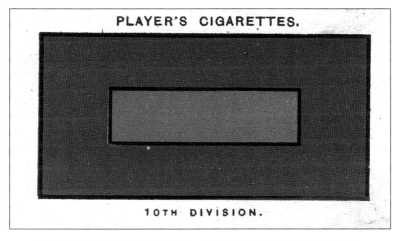

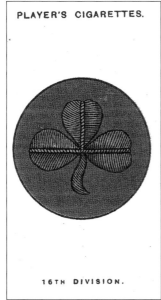 

(Top) Face of the 10th (Irish) Division card. (Above left) Face of the
16th (Irish) Division card. (Above right) Face of the 36th (Ulster)
Division card, the Division used the left hand, the UVF the right.

from County Cavan. Later the enemy shelled Daylight Corner and the Lindenhoek Road, N 33, with gas shells. The shelling continued, the 4.5-inch howitzers concentrating on those parts of the German line that still appeared undamaged, while the heavy trench mortars fired repeatedly into L'Enfer Wood, doing it much damage. On the night of 5 June the Vickers guns of the 108th Machine Gun Company fired a total of 110,600 rounds, experiencing no stoppages or other difficulties and delivered a literal rain of bullets on the German positions. During the night of 6 June the 107 and 109 Brigades moved into their assembly positions together with the two Battalions of the 108 Brigade allocated for the attack. This assembly being completed by 2:30 am on the morning of 7 June. While the preliminary bombardment was in progress the divisional front had been held by the 9th Irish Fusiliers and 13th Rifles and theses units were now placed in reserve in the vicinity of Fort Victoria, awaiting further orders.

Battle of Messines and Capture of Wytschaete (7-14 June 1917).

> Gentlemen, I don't know whether we are going to make history tomorrow, but at any rate we shall change geography.

Major General Charles 'Tim' Harington, Plumer's Chief of Staff (Not Plumer as is so often reported, and an Irishman to boot).

Divisional Order of Battle June 1917

Field Artillery
36th Divisional Artillery Group
Commanded by Brigadier General H.J. Brock, DSO, R.A.

36th Divisional Artillery
153rd Brigade, RFA Lieutenant Colonel R.G. Thompson, DSO, RFA
173rd Brigade, RFA Lieutenant Colonel H.C. Simpson, DSO, RFA

Army Field Artillery Brigades
76th F.A. Brigade, Lieutenant Colonel F.C. Bryant, C.M.G., RFA
84th F.A. Brigade, Lieutenant Colonel H. Cornes, DSO, RFA
108th F.A. Brigade, Lieutenant Colonel W.H. Drake, C.M.G., RFA
282nd F.A. Brigade, Lieutenant Colonel A.F. Prechtel, DSO, RFA

32nd Divisional Artillery
161st Brigade, RFA, Lieutenant Colonel A.S. Cotton, DSO, RFA
168 Brigade, RFA, Lieutenant Colonel R. Fitzmaurice, DSO, RFA

36th Division Trench Mortar Batteries
Divisional Trench Mortar Officer; Lieutenant (A/Capt.) A.F. Gimson, M.C.
V/36 Trench Mortar Battery
2/Lieut. (A/Capt.) M.C. McPhee
X/36 Trench Mortar Battery
2/Lieut. (A/Lieut.) R.P. Nathan
Y/36 Trench Mortar Battery
2/Lieut. (A/Lieut.) T.E. Cocker
Z/36 Trench Mortar Battery
2/Lieut. (A/Lieut.) J. Cuthbert

32nd Division Trench Mortar Batteries
Divisional Trench Mortar Officer, Captain A.L. Woods, M.C., 4th South Staffs
V/32 Trench Mortar Battery
2/Lieut. (A/Capt.) R. Whinyates, 8th Hussars
X/32 Trench Mortar Battery
A/Lieutenant J.G. Harrison, RFA
Y/32 Trench Mortar Battery
2/Lieut. A. Guthrie, RFA
Z/32 Trench Mortar Battery

2/Lieut. (A/Lieut.) J. Gillies, 16th H.L.I.

Royal Engineers and Pioneers
Commanding Royal Engineer
Major (Temp.Lieut.Col.) A. Campbell, DSO, R.E.
121st Field Company, R.E.
Lieut. (Actg. Major) R.A.H. Lewin, R.E.
122nd Field Company, R.E.
Temp. Major C.C.A. Hardie, R.E.
150th Field Company, R.E.
Temp. Major J.C. Boyle, R.E.
16th Battn. Royal Irish Rifle (Pioneers)
Lieut. Col. C.F. Meares
(Note. 100 infantry were attached to each Field Company, R.E.)

Machine guns (attached)
32nd Machine Gun Company
33rd Machine Gun Company (less 2 sections)
19th Motor Machine gun Battery
Under the command of the Divisional Machine Gun officer – Major J.S. Miller, DSO

INFANTRY

107 Brigade
Brigade Commander
Brigadier-General W.M. Withycombe, C.M.G.
8th Battn. Royal Irish Rifles
Lieut. Col. C.G. Cole-Hamilton, DSO
9th Battn. Royal Irish Rifles
Lieut. Col. P.J. Woods, DSO
10th Battn. Royal Irish Rifles
Lieut. Col. N.G. Burnand, DSO
15th Battn. Royal Irish Rifles
Lieut. Col. F.L. Gordon, DSO
12th Battn. Royal Irish Rifles
Lieut. Col. W.R. Goodwin,
(This Battalion was attached to this Brigade from the 108 Infantry Brigade)
107th Machine Gun Company
Captain R.H. Forbes
107th Trench mortar Battery
Captain I. Grove-White

108 Brigade
Brigade Commander
Brigadier-General C.R.J. Griffith, C.M.G., DSO
13th Battn. Royal Irish Rifles
Lieut. Col. R.P.D. Perceval-Maxwell
9th Battn. Royal Irish Fusiliers
Major J.G. Brew

108th Machine Gun Company
Major J.S. Miller, DSO
108th Trench Mortar Battery
Captain M.H. Browne
Lieut. Col. S. J. Somerville, Commanding 9th Battn. Royal Irish Fusiliers was kept back under the provision of SS.135, Section XXX
(Note. 11th and 12th Battns. Royal Irish Rifles were detached from their Brigade temporarily during the actual attack, and attached to 109 and 107 Infantry Brigade respectively).

109 Brigade

Brigade Commander
Brigadier-General A. St. Q. Ricardo, C.M.G., DSO
9th Battn. Royal Inniskilling Fusiliers
Lieut. Col. W.J. Peacocke, DSO
10th Battn. Royal Inniskilling Fusiliers
Lieut. Col. F.S.N. MacCrory, DSO
11th Battn. Royal Inniskilling Fusiliers
Lieut. Col. A.C. Pratt, DSO
14th Battn. Royal Irish Rifles
Major E.F. Smyth
(This Battalion was attached to this Brigade from the 108th Infantry Brigade)
109th Machine Gun Company
Captain P.D. Mulholland
109th Trench Mortar Battery
Captain J. Allen
(Lieut. Col. P.K. Blair Oliphant, DSO, Commanding 11th Battn. Royal Irish Rifles, was kept back under the provision of SS.135, Section XXX.

It has been argued by many that the Battle of Messines was the most successful self-contained battle of the Great War, at least on the Western Front. Considered as a forerunner of the blitzkrieg of 1940 this attack, carried out by General Herbert Plumer's Second Army and was launched on 7 June 1917 with the detonation of 19 mines beneath the German front line trenches. The objective of this attack was the capture of the Messines Ridge, a natural strongpoint southeast of Ypres and an enemy salient since late 1914. Such was the degree of planning associated with this action that many have said it was won, not by firepower, but with pen and paper.

The date of the attack, 7 June, was designated as Z Day, with the five days preceding this during which the bombardment was carried out being coded as U, V, W, X, and Y Days. While there had been a considerable bombardment delivered prior to U Day, it had become more intense since then.

In order to effectively damage or destroy the German concrete pill-boxes it required a direct hit from an 8-inch howitzer. The buildings of Wytschaete were bombarded with shells from 12-inch and 15-inch howitzers, while innumerable 18-pounder guns and trench mortars made efforts to cut the enemy barbed wire. Shelling of communications and billets was also carried out and gas shells were fire throughout the bombardment, these targets being selected from photographs taken during reconnaissance flights by the Royal Flying Corps.

The Second Army was to assault the Messines – Wytschaete Ridge and beyond as far as the Oosttaverne Line. The IX Corps frontage was 6,400 yards, from the Wulverghem to Wytschaete Road and as far as the Diependaal Beek. It would attack with three divisions in line; from right to left were 36th (Ulster) Division, the 16th (Irish) Division and the 19th (Western) Division. These

OFFICIAL PHOTOGRAPH,
CROWN COPYRIGHT RESERVED.   63. TOMMY AT HOME IN GERMAN DUG-OUTS.

German front line trenches with new residents, crowded, unsanitary, uncomfortable, necessary.

troops were to advance to the Black Line, east of the Messines to Wytschaete Road, after which the 11th Division, from Corps Reserve, would pass through to the final objective. On the right flank of the 36th Division was the 25th Division of the II Anzac Corps. The frontage of the attack narrowed with every 1,000 yards of the advance.

The artillery support for the attack consisted of a creeping barrage of 18-pounder shrapnel shells that would move in advance of the infantry, lifting 100 yards every three minutes. There was one gun for every 20 yards of frontage and each would fire at its maximum rate of 20 rounds per minute. In each section one gun was designated to fire smoke shells to help screen the infantry. The planning of this barrage was a complicated affair as the German line was far from straight and there were varying times for the barrage to lift of one objective and moving on to the next. Added to this was a standing barrage of shells from 18-pounders, 4.5-inch howitzers and medium and heavy howitzers that would concentrate on trenches and strong-points. The attack was also a precursor to the much larger Third Battle of Ypres, more commonly known as Passchendaele, decided upon by Haig following the collapse of the Nivelle Offensive in May 1917.

The plan for the attack on the Ridge included the detonation of a number of mines located beneath the enemy trenches. Twenty-two mines were dug, the work having begun in 1915. On moving into the area the division had supplied a large number of men to work with the tunnelling companies who were driving shafts out into no-man's-land and under the German positions. The division was most closely associated with the 171st Tunnelling Company. German miners dug counter-mines, but on all occasions were out-fought and out-manoeuvred. In one instance, at La Petite Douve Farm, the British tunnellers pumped a large amount of water from the Douve River into one of the German shafts and for many nights after could be heard the sound of enemy pumps as they attempted to empty it.

Some mines were up to 2160 feet (658 metres) long and up to 125 feet (38 metres) deep. One mine (at Petite Douve Farm) was discovered by German counter-miners on 24 August 1916 and

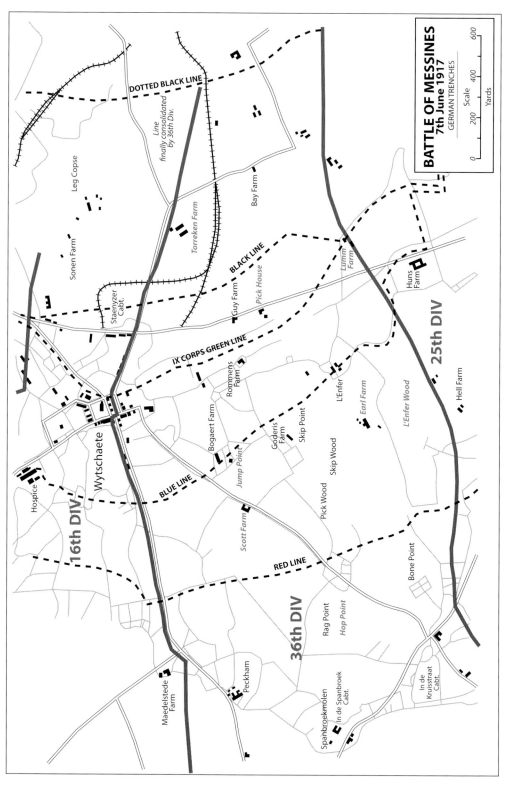

BATTLE OF MESSINES
7th June 1917
GERMAN TRENCHES

Scale

0   200   400   600

Yards

DOTTED BLACK LINE

Line finally consolidated by 36th Div.

Leg Copse

Torreken Farm

Bay Farm

Sonen Farm

BLACK LINE

Lumm Farm

Pick House

Guy Farm

Huns Farm

Staenyzer Cabt.

25th DIV

IX CORPS GREEN LINE

Rommens Farm

Hell Farm

L'Enfer

Earl Farm

L'Enfer Wood

Bogaert Farm

Goderis Farm

Skip Point

Jump Point

Skip Wood

Hospice

16th DIV

Wytschaete

BLUE LINE

Scott Farm

Pick Wood

Bone Point

RED LINE

36th DIV

Rag Point

Hop Point

Maedelstede Farm

Peckham

Spanbroekmolen

In de Spanbroek Cabt.

In de Kruisstraat Cabt.

Messines

destroyed. Two mines close to Ploegsteert Wood were not exploded as they were outside the attack area.[11]

The two unexploded mines were planned to be dismantled by the British but with the impending start of the Third Battle of Ypres, there was always something else to do. When the Germans launched their Lys Offensive in April 1918, the British headquarters was overrun and the documentation relating to these two mines was lost and they never were dug up. The precise location of them was not known and they were forgotten until during a thunderstorm on 17 July 1955, one of them exploded. No one was killed but the explosion did some slight damage to some distant property. The other mine as far as anyone knows, is still lurking under the Flanders countryside.[12]

General Plumer had begun plans to capture the Ridge in early 1916. Meticulous in manner, Plumer preferred to plan for a limited success rather than gamble all on a significant breakthrough. In preparing for the battle he had authorised the digging of 22 mine shafts under the German positions along the Ridge. The plan being to detonate these at zero hour, which was to be 3:10 am on 7 June. This was to be followed by an immediate assault by infantry and tanks ably supported by aircraft and artillery.

It is the very nature of mining that it requires an ample amount of time to prepare. Of the 19 mines exploded under the Messines Ridge, some had been started as early as August 1915, others in December, in expectation of action that year.

The actual process of mining itself was difficult, but here the topsoil consisted of sand or sandy loam, which rested on a layer of semi liquid slurry, which in turn sat on a seam of blue clay. Early mining equipment confined those men employed in digging the tunnels to the top layer, but by 1916, new technology such as the mechanical diggers being used to construct the new London Underground, enabled digging in the clay seam. The mechanical digger quickly proved to be a disappointment, manual labour was much quicker, but technology proved to be useful in other ways. Silent air and water pumps, better survey and listening equipment, better rescue apparatus and steel tubing for sinking shafts through the wet slurry.

The final hazard in the tunnelling was the disposal of the spoil. Any sign of the blue clay would immediately alert the enemy as to the British intentions. It was therefore necessary that every shovelful of clay was carted a long way to the rear and then hidden from aerial observation, usually by being buried!

The furthest reaching mine was the Kruisstraat No.3 Mine; this had a gallery of 2,160 feet and was packed with 30,000 pounds of ammonal. The Petit Bois No.1 Right mine gallery stretched for 2,070 feet and had a charge of 21,000 pounds of ammonal and 9,000 pounds of blasting gelatine. Seven more galleries were in excess of 1,000 feet long. The total explosive charge under the Messines Ridge was 1,000,000 pounds. When detonated it was said the noise could be heard as far away as Dublin, yet by a trick of acoustics the noise passed over the men in the trenches, adding to an already eerie experience.

There were three mines on the divisional front. The first was at Kruisstraat Cabaret, the second at Spanbroekmolen, while the third was at Peckham. The mines at Spanbroekmolen and Kruisstraat Cabaret were under the command of Major H.M. Hudspeth, 171st Tunnelling Company, while that at Peckham was in the hands of Major H.W. Laws, 250th Tunnelling Company. Instructions were issued regarding what men were to do when the mines exploded. Regarding debris, a radius of two hundred yards from the mine was considered to be safe, with all debris falling back to earth with 20 seconds of firing. Men were told to avoid sheltering close to old brick walls, buildings and

---

11 Ferguson, R. & Truesdale, D., *And the Dragon Sleeps, The Battle of Messines, 7th-14th June 1917*. Written on behalf of Ards Borough Council (1997).

12 Barrie, Alexander, *War Underground: The Tunnellers of the Great War* (2006 reprint of 1961 edition).

trees with damaged trunks within 500 yards of the mine, to vacate all dug-outs and tunnels within 400 yards and to extinguish all candles and oil lamps to prevent fire. After the crater was formed men were not to go to the bottom, but consolidate within ten feet of the lip to avoid the poisonous fumes that would still be gathered there. If a mine had not exploded within ten seconds of zero, it was to be assumed that it would not be fired at all.

The training for this attack was thorough in the extreme. The various battalions had practiced their advance over ground that had been marked out to represent the German defences, including trenches and pill-boxes. Officers from the flanking battalions of the 29th and 32nd Divisions attended each other's field days to ensure that every detail of the attack could be duplicated if necessary. An elaborate model of the Messines Ridge was constructed by the Royal Engineers on the slopes of the Scherpenberg Hill, between the villages of Locre and La Clytte. The model was surrounded by a wooden catwalk, which allowed a view of the Ridge from all directions and had space for a company at a time to visit.

Another innovation was the message-map, which was issued in large numbers to officers and NCO's. On one side of the paper was the map of the German defences, while on the other was a skeleton message-form, which was marked clearly with the relevant important information that should be transmitted back to headquarters.

Rations, water and ammunition were stored in huge amounts, beginning with the divisional dumps at Lindenhoek cross-roads and at Daylight Corner, located on the Lindenhoek to Neuve Eglise Road. This was followed by advance dumps, a further dump for each of the attacking brigades, six battalion dumps and many smaller dumps in the trenches. Within the division an elaborate system of pack transport was devised. Two hundred extra pack-saddles were issued along with 250 Yukon packs, a Canadian invention that allowed a man to carry a heavy load. Rations were deemed important and arrangements were made to serve a hot meal in the trenches at midnight prior to the attack. There was also a special ration of oranges, Oxo cubes for hot drinks, chewing gum and lime juice for every man. A tin of solidified alcohol was issued between every four men for the purposes of cooking only.

A huge amount of planning and preparation was put into the establishing and maintaining of communications for the battle. Signalling, as always crucial in any combat situation was to be carried out using flags, carrier pigeons, wireless, and where available, Fullerphones and rockets for emergency SOS calls, and the ever available runners. It was stressed that runners were not to be employed if other means of communications were available. Runners soon became exhausted and their casualty rate was very high. They were to be used only when all other methods failed, or when an important sketch or report could not be transmitted otherwise.

For the Fuller phones, two lines of cable were buried with the cable heads ending in the forward trenches. Forward stations were selected in the enemy lines at Spanbroekmolen and Peckham and when suitable armoured cables were to be laid across no man's land from the cable heads to the brigade forward parties. As soon as the final objective had been reached, these forward stations were to move to the crest of the Ridge. For visual signalling a divisional signal station was established on Kemmel Hill, which had a clear view to the brigade forward stations, with messages being passed by use of the Lucas Lamp.

Within the division two wireless sets were made available and these would enable communications between divisional headquarters and the 107 Brigade on the right, which would in turn transmit messages for the 109 Brigade on the left. The artillery liaison officers would also have use of this means to transmit to artillery groups and batteries. Ample pigeons were made available to maintain a daily supply of four pairs per battalion in the attack, four pairs per brigade forward station and four pairs with selected forward observation officers. The pigeons would fly to Dranoutre where the messages were forwarded by telegraph wire. From zero onwards 28 pairs of pigeons were transported by car every evening to Lindenhoek Cross Roads. Here one "pigeon man" or "pigeonier" from each brigade took the birds to the trench tramway and from there to Regent Street dug-outs. From here they were distributed as necessary. It was stressed that empty pigeon baskets should be returned to the car at Lindenhoek, or the service would have failed due to lack of baskets.

Working independently from these means of communication was the brigade and battalion intelligence sections. At brigade level the sections would establish observation posts at Spanbroekmolen and Peckham, while the battalion intelligence sections followed up their respective battalions, selecting observation posts to enable their movement to be followed and to cover their final positions. They were also responsible for sending out scouts to maintain contact with flanking battalions and to bring back information as to their progress. Prisoners taken on the field were to be escorted back to the divisional collecting cage at a rate of one sentry per ten prisoners, with officers and NCO's being kept separate from the other ranks. Maps and papers taken from the prisoners were to be put into sand bags and handed over to the intelligence officers. All weapons would be removed from prisoners, but no other searching was to be permitted.

The final objective of the division was a line running from Lumm Farm to a cutting on the Wytschaete to Oosttaverne Road, east of Staenyzer Cabaret. Lumm Farm was a ruin that had concrete pill boxes and bunkers incorporated. This attack was to be made by two brigades forward and the third in reserve. On the right flank was 107 with the 109 on the left, each brigade having a battalion from the 108 Brigade attached.[13]

Each brigade would attack with two battalions in front, which would advance to the Blue Line, the ground behind being mopped up by the attached battalion from the 108 Brigade. The remaining two battalion of each leading brigade would then pass through the Blue Line and advance as far as the Black Line, but had to provide their own mopping-up parties.

The attack formation was as follows:

107 Brigade

9th Rifles	8th Rifles
10th Rifles	15th Rifles

12th Rifles from the 108 Brigade as 'moppers'

109 Brigade

11th Inniskillings	14th Rifles
10th Inniskillings	9th Inniskillings

11th Rifles from the 108 Brigade as 'moppers'

The boundary line between the 36th Division and the 16th Divisions was the main street of Wytschaete.

Within the division Stokes mortars and machine guns were assigned to specific targets for the opening of the attack. Each brigade was to give up four mortars to be taken forward with the attacking troops, while the remainder where to open a 'hurricane' bombardment for three and a half minutes at zero. A battery of Stokes 4-inch mortars that had been specifically attached to the division was to shell the Spanbroek Salient with two lifts, using thermite incendiary bombs, which had a highly demoralising effect on the enemy.

A similar plan was made for the machine gun companies. Six guns were to go forward, while the remainder, along with those of the 108th, 32nd, two sections of the 33rd and six guns of the 19th

---

13   The author is grateful to Dr Michael LoCicero for assistance with this section.

Men of the 16th (Irish) Division after the battle of Messines, June 1917.

Motor Machine gun Battery, a total of 66 guns, were employed in providing a creeping barrage to support the infantry. Like the artillery they would also provide a standing barrage and bring fire onto strong-points, wood and ravines. These guns were liberally supplied with ammunition, 3,500 rounds per gun in belt boxes at the gun position, 8,000 per gun at the belt filling centre, 8,500 per gun at the reserve dump and 4,500 per gun in the limbers. The guns going forward were each issued with 5,000 rounds of ammunition and extra ammunition carries were allocated to the gun teams.

One section of four tanks was allotted to the division for assistance in assaulting from the Blue to the Black line. It was impressed on all infantrymen that the tanks were present to assist in their advance if possible, but they should not forget for one moment that success was not dependent on their presence. The men were not to wait for them, but to push on to objectives irrespective of whether tanks came forward or not. There was a great danger of the attack being held up if this was not thoroughly realised by all ranks.

All the successive lines, with the exception of the Green Line, were to be consolidated, with strong-points to be established at various positions, including L'Enfer Farm, Skip Point and Jump Point on the Blue Line, while on the Black Line there was Lumm Farm, Pick House and Torreken Farm. The infantry would begin the work of consolidation and once the Black Line had been taken the 121 and 150 Field Companies RE would move up to work on the principle strong-points.

After dusk on Z Day the 122 Field Company was to move forward and construct a wire entanglement along the entire length of the Black Line. Once this was all in place the Germans would have little opportunity for any sort of counter-attack.

The Royal Flying Corps was to provide two aircraft to fly over the division throughout the battle. The infantry would mark their progress by the firing of green flares, these to be fired in bunches of three and by the use of Watson fans. A Watson fan was literally a fan, sometime made from canvas and was about twelve inches in diameter when opened. It was painted white on one side and black on the other. It was described as being lightweight, but cumbersome to operate. It was claimed that when used properly its ripple of white could clearly be seen from a height of between one and two thousand feet. The aircraft would signal to the infantry by the use of klaxon horns.

An advanced dressing station, manned by 109th Field Ambulance was established at Lindenhock, situated close to the main road. Here the wounded would be carried from the trench tramway into the station from the north side and given what treatment was necessary. From here they would exit via a door on the west side to be picked up by the motor ambulances of the division that had arrived on a specially constructed semi-circular road that allowed them to sweep around without turning. The wounded were then to be driven to the main dressing station located just east of Dranoutre, which was manned by 108th Field Ambulance. Meanwhile walking wounded would be sent by a specially marked track to another main dressing station a mile east of the village and manned by 110th Field Ambulance at Hell-Fire Corner. From these locations the motor ambulance park had the task of carrying the wounded to the two Casualty Clearing Stations in Bailleul. Robert Doggart was here:

> I was at a first-aid post known as Hell-Fire Corner, because it was always being shelled. Well, it turned out to be a cushy number for me, from 3:00 am until 8:00 pm; I had only one casualty to dress. He was a soldier from the British West Indies Regiment. I dressed his wound, gave him a cup of tea and sent him on his way.

Private Jack Christie came from Belfast and had been educated at Agnes Street Central National School, which he left at twelve years of age to work in the Ulster Spinning Company mill on the Falls Road, a truly dreadful experience:

> Sir Edward Carson was holding a series of meetings and Unionist Clubs were meeting and there was great excitement and tension. Then the UVF were formed and are not in any way to be considered anything like the UVF today, they were very responsible people. I was only fourteen at the time, but we drilled as a member of the Church Lads Brigade belonging to St. Luke's Company in Northumberland Street. There I did courses in First Aid and I became a First aid man in the UVF because I could put on a bandage to make a sling and things like that.

At Messines Jack was in charge of a party of stretcher bearers, men recently joined from the Base Depot:

> I was given a group of newly arrived stretcher bearers and we were on the St. Jean Road, which was paved and if a shell landed on it, it did not penetrate like in the mud, but exploded immediately. The new stretcher bearers were very frightened, we all were, but you paid attention to what you were doing and that helped you survive and not panic. I told them to follow me and get in groups of four, twenty paces apart, so that one shell would not get the whole lot. So we started off and we had not got a hundred yards when a shell exploded and they went in all directions, they were conscripts and I did not blame them, but they were foolish. Fortunately I got them together again.

On several occasions during the Messines battle Jack had come in contact with men of the 16th (Irish) Division; "We should not allow politics to blind us to the truth about things, bravery and loyalty is not all on one side. We had the greatest respect for the 16th except maybe for the odd hardliner, but great regard for the 16th."

The men were warned regarding the misuse of white flags and signs of surrender by the enemy. In the past it was not unknown for German soldiers to sham death and then to shoot into the back of the assault. The possibility of the enemy using ruses, such as giving the order to retire, was impressed upon all ranks. All commanders down to platoon commanders were to keep in touch throughout with the commander of the similar formation on their flanks. They had to know the disposition and action being taken by their neighbours and the more particularly so when he units on the flanks belonged to another division.

The necessity of pushing forward to their objective regardless of the progress of units on either flank was stressed to all ranks. It was also made known that the care of the wounded was not their responsibility; the medicals orderlies and stretcher-bearers would follow up the advance and care for the injured.

Should movement be made on a moonlit night great care was to be taken that bayonets did not 'flash' in the moonlight. In the event of enemy aircraft flying overhead to ascertain if the trenches were more strongly manned than usual, all ranks were warned to keep absolutely still and under no circumstances to look up. A face, like a Watson fan, could be seen from a great height. The crews of Vickers and Lewis guns on anti-aircraft mounts were to be particularly on the alert to deal with such aircraft from 29 May onwards.

It was decided by the high command that a specific policy was to be implemented regarding captured enemy artillery. This was that any enemy gun that would be of use was to be saved. The gun teams were to be killed and the breech mechanism with any removable sight removed if necessary. Destruction by explosives was not to be resorted to unless it was evident that the Oosttaverne line could not be gained and held. In that case the officer on the spot was to use his own judgment as to destroying the guns. Explosives for that purpose were to be carried forward. Breech blocks and sights removed from the guns were to be retained near the guns by the parties who were to remain in charge of them until it became evident that no use could be made of the guns by the British, in which case parts removed were to be carried back to the relevant battalion headquarters or destroyed.[14]

The morning of 7 June dawned clear, warm and dry, ideal for observation. All units that were to make the attack were in position from 2:50 am, having used earlier prepared tracks to avoid congestion. East of the Neuve Eglise to Lindenhoek Road there were no less than four tracks available for each Brigade. It had been 11 months since the division had fought on the Somme and in the intervening time replacements had been integrated, wounded men had returned to the ranks and what had been an untested volunteer force was now a professional body. In its efficiency the division was war-tried, but not war-weary and in the early hours of that June morning was probably at the highest pitch it would ever attain.

To cover this assembly of attacking troops over Y/Z night patrols had lain out in no man's land to intercept any incursion from the enemy. At midnight two German soldiers ran into one of these patrols, one was killed and the other captured. On being returned to the lines and questioned by a member of the intelligence staff, it was discovered that the soldier belonged to the 23rd Bavarian Division and that a relief was in progress in the German lines just opposite the Ulster Division's front.

Zero was at 3:10 am, considered to be that time of day when men should have been able to see just 100 yards ahead. Normal artillery operation had continued throughout the night, anything less would have warned the enemy that something was afoot, although to some men in the trenches

---

14   TNA WO 95 2491 G.S.2/21/9 Part 1 note 57 (IMG 0720).

it seemed unnaturally quiet. Precisely at Zero every British artillery piece on a ten mile frontage fired with one gigantic roar, while at the same time the huge semi-circle of mines exploded. Tall columns of earth rose into the dawning sky with pieces falling as much as half a mile away. It was said the noise could be heard in England, some claimed Dublin. Into this man-made cloud of dust and debris the first wave of infantry rose from their trenches and advanced. The second wave followed at 25-yard intervals to avoid the German barrage. The mine at Spanbroekmolen detonated 15 seconds late and some men of the 109 Brigade became casualties due to falling debris. Brigadier Ricardo estimated that from the explosion of the first mine to the last was some 20 seconds. Lieutenant Witherow witnessed a lance corporal of the 8th Rifles being killed by a stone thrown out from the explosion. In the 10th Inniskillings Private Thomas Gibson, along with the remainder of his company, waited in silence for the mines to explode; "As soon as the mines went up we went over the top…the whole place was devastated."

Sergeant Robert Grange from Ballyclare, County Antrim, and a veteran of the Somme battle, was almost knocked off his feet by the blast so close was the 12th Rifles to the Spanbroekmolen mine.

Given the available amount of daylight, the smoke and dust from the barrage and mine explosions, it would have been impossible to maintain any forward movement if it were not for the use of compasses by the platoon commanders and NCOs, although the SOS rockets being fired by the Germans did also assist. As the advance continued men from the 25th Division on the right flank began to drift over and at least two companies swung across the division's front. Later the body of an officer from the 25th Division was found in the bed of the Steenebeek at L'Enfer Wood, some 200 yards within the division's boundary. Enemy resistance was spasmodic and there was no difficulty whatever from the wire. "All wire was cut to shreds, not merely gaps, and caused absolutely no obstacle."[15]

By 3:45 am, the majority of messages being passed back to headquarters reported resistance to be negligible. The 14th Rifles had at this time only one man injured and suffered sparse enemy shelling. Given past experience no time was lost in digging new positions and clearing out the old German dugouts. The war diary of the 14th Rifles reveals a late Edwardian penchant for paying a compliment with offhand racism; "After a restless night owing to frequent shelling of the Boche we awoke to start work building dugouts, clearing out old German dugouts etc. This went on all day long under the supervision of Major Vivian, who worked like the proverbial nigger."

In 107 Brigade's area the first obstacle encountered by the 9th Rifles was at Hop Point. Here B Company, under the command of Captain C.H. Harding, MC, made short work of the position with accurate bombing under covering fire from the Lewis guns. On the front of the 109 Brigade two enemy machine guns fired through the barrage. The first was knocked out by a section using rifle grenades, while the second fell to the fire of a Lewis gun from the 11th Inniskillings. The enemy barrage was negligible, with the 109 Brigade reporting that a ten-minute barrage fell on some of the reserve trenches.

At 4:30 am, Brigadier Ricardo telephoned divisional headquarters and reported that the attack was progressing very well. His men were facing practically no machine gun fire, hardly any barrage and not many prisoners were being taken. The mine at Peckham had exploded at Zero and his brigade intelligence officer reported that visibility was poor due to the dust from the British barrage. No dug-outs had been found and great numbers of German dead were lying everywhere.

The troops advanced straight to the Red Line, following close behind the barrage, in some cases men had to be restrained from running into the British shells. The moppers-up had little difficulty in dealing with any resistance and this was quickly dealt with by a combination of rifle grenadiers

---

15   11th Inniskillings War Diary.

Abide With Me, a prayer postcard, popular during the war.

(Below) 'On Active Service' this small booklet carried the name Lance Corporal E. Atwell of the 9th Royal Irish Rifles.

and the accurate bursts from a Lewis gun. The Red Line was reached at zero plus 35 minutes (3:45 am), and here there was a halt in the barrage of 15 minutes. It was also here that the third and fourth companies of each battalion leap-frogged the first and second companies for the assault on the Blue Line.

The 14th Rifles were hit by machine gun fire as they closed with the Red Line, but this was quickly dealt with. There were few casualties, one being Captain James McKee, who was shot in the arm. He refused to be evacuated and led his men on towards the Blue Line. As the battalion advanced several machine guns opened fire from Skip Point and Scott Farm, the bullets convening on the men from both flanks. Here Captain McKee was hit again, this time a more serious wound to the leg, the bullets breaking the bone. He eventually allowed himself to be treated, but only after his men had been cared for. Captain McKee, who had been Private McFadzean's commanding officer, came from Cyprus Park, Belfast and pre-war had been a popular and prominent figure in the Boys' Brigade and association football circles. The wound would cost him his leg and in exchange a grateful government awarded him the DSO for this battle.[16]

The advance continued, those men on the right flank moving into the marshy bed of the Steenebeek. Here they came under fire from German machine guns located at L'Enfer Wood, Earl Farm, Skip Point and Scott Farm. From Skip Point two guns in particular caused a great deal of annoyance and although this position was outside the 109 Brigade boundary it was captured by Lieutenant John Dwyer O'Brien with a mixed force of 14th Rifles and 9th Rifles from 107 Brigade. O'Brien came from Skibbereen in County Cork, had joined the Ulster Division in 1916 and would go on to win the Military Cross. At Scott Farm, D Company of the 14th Rifles had assaulted the machine gun post, killing the crew and then sending the weapon back to their own lines as a trophy.

Just before reaching the Red Line the 11th Inniskillings had their share of enemy machine guns. A casualty was Captain Henry Gallaugher DSO, of B Company, the man who had done so much at the 'Crucifix' on the Somme the previous July. Initially hit in the arm, he dropped the rifle he was carrying and proceeded on armed with his revolver. Despite his wound he was able to exert the required command of his men, on occasion stopping them from advancing too close to the falling British barrage. On reaching the Blue Line Captain Gallaugher saw to it that his men were properly positioned before agreeing to go back and have his wound dressed. It was during the return journey that he was shot and killed instantly. He was subsequently recommended for a posthumous Victoria Cross, but this was denied. Captain Gallaugher was buried just outside the Bull Ring, a position he had often led the defence off in times past.[17] By 5:35 am the 11th Inniskillings were consolidating their objectives and it was safe enough for Captain Crosbie RAMC to move up and set up an advanced regimental aid post beside Scott Farm.

In the ranks of the 121 Field Company, Royal Engineers, 2nd Corporal R. Beeby was killed. Sapper Beeby came from Newcastle-on-Tyne. Also within the ranks of the Field Company Sapper Samuel Irvine from Ballyboy, County Monaghan, earned the Meritorious Service Medal.

In practically every battle of the Great War it was the German machine gunner who provided the stoutest resistance. Here on the Messines battlefield while the enemy artillerymen, under near constant shell fire were concerned about saving their guns, the machine gunners remained, fighting to the last. Some men of the 11th Inniskillings reported finding a German machine gunner chained to his weapon. Unable to free the man from his gun, one of the Inniskillings

16 Captain McKee relinquished his commission in October 1918. His brother Lieutenant W.D. McKee, 12th Rifles, had been killed in action on 11 August 1917.
17 His brother, Corporal W. Gallaugher, served with the Canadian Expeditionary Force and was awarded the Military Medal for his actions at Vimy Ridge.

placed the muzzle of his rifle against the chain and fired, cutting the link. However, this was the only instance of this being found by the Inniskillings and was, according to the brigade after action report, not confirmed. Many stories, both during and after the war, relate how German gunners were found in this manner. It is more likely that the chains were mistaken for the carrying harness, which included chain like steel hoops, worn by the crew to assist in moving a weapon that weighed almost 150 pounds, across the battlefield.

This collection of farms and strong-points formed a veritable fortress and it required a fair degree of bombing to clear the dug-outs. Eventually approximately one 150 prisoners had been taken and a large number of machine guns either captured or destroyed. At Scott Farm a German officer was seen standing on the roof of the pillbox and by his gestures seemed to be encouraging his men. One of the divisional snipers shot him at a range estimated to be 400 yards, after this resistance within the complex appeared to slacken.

The position regarding Jump Point was still in question until an intelligence officer from the 109 Brigade located on the high ground beyond Peckham noticed what he thought was a yellow flag flying from that location. Calling headquarters he spoke to General Ricardo and told what he saw. Ricardo at once realised that this was in fact the orange flag of the 14th Rifles and passed the information immediately back to divisional headquarters. In fact the YCV flag had been raised at 5:07 am, despite the position not being entirely secure. An enemy machine gun was still firing from behind Jump Point and it took a few minutes to kill the detachment. Attempts were then made to get the captured gun into action, but in his dying moments one of the crewmen had managed to throw away the lock.

By 5:35 am the 11th Inniskillings were consolidating their objectives and it was safe enough for Captain Crosbie RAMC to move up and set up an advanced regimental aid post beside Scott Farm. Lieutenant Ivan Henry McCaw, a 19 year old former medical student serving with the 14th Rifles was badly wounded that day. He had been commissioned on 8 January 1916 and had formerly served as transport officer for a time. An entry in the battalion war diary timed at 8:00 am, quotes a report from Captain Lewis stating that Lieutenant McCaw was wounded at Jump Point, along with Second Lieutenant H.S. Kennedy and Captain J. McKee. Lieutenant McCaw was brought into the dressing station suffering from a severe haemorrhage and an extensive brachial-plexus injury, which would leave him with long-term partial paralysis in his right arm. He had been shot while advancing with the battalion flag. The staff at the dressing station remembered the lieutenant making several suggestions that others were in much greater need of treatment.[18] Second Lieutenants J. Downey and Brian Boyd were also killed at this time. At 6:00 am, the war diary of 108 Brigade recorded that "... a high velocity armour-piercing shell fired probably from a naval gun got a direct hit on Brigade Headquarters tunnel dug-out and almost succeeded in collapsing the Staff Captain's office."

Some two hours later the headquarters was relocated in the Regent Street dug-outs. Along the front the leading waves of infantry, well closed up to the barrage, reached the Blue Line. On the right flank the 25th Division had reached its objective, while on the left, the 16th (Irish) Division was also in its prescribed position. Here there was a halt of two hours, which was spent in consolidating the captured positions. Those battalions tasked with attacking the Black Line, 15th and10th Rifles, 9th and 10th Inniskillings, moved up in artillery formation, the two former battalion experiencing a light enemy artillery barrage as they crossed the valley of the Steenebeek, but suffering few casualties. At 6:50 am, the British barrage moved forward again, closely followed up by the fresh battalions. The Green Line was passed and the Battalions had almost reached the road that ran north to south from Wytschaete to Messines when they came to Pick House,

---

18   Unable to perform surgery, Dr McCaw became a dermatologist of some renown; he died on 17 March 1961.

a strongly defended position. While attacks were made using rifle grenades a captured German machine gun was brought into action from the flank in lieu of the supporting Vickers gun teams, these having fallen behind during the advance. While the average infantry-man was carrying about 60 pounds of equipment, those men of the machine gun companies had to carry guns, tripods, ammunition boxes and water for cooling the weapons. Not the easiest load over ground cut to pieces by shell fire. Eventually, after some fierce fighting, the garrison of Pick House surrendered; the bag of prisoners included a regimental commander and 30 other officers. It was here that 107 Brigade lost its first and only officer of the day. Lieutenant Robert McLaurin of the 10th Rifles was 31 years old and came from Omagh in County Tyrone.

The problem of crossing ground churned up by shellfire was being addressed by the men of the 16th Rifles. The pioneers had been hard at work from 6:30 am clearing the roads leading towards the German positions and, where these had ceased to exist, creating new ones. This required a considerable amount of work as the ground was a mess of shell holes that made wheeled transport impossible. By early afternoon two tracks had been completed and were marked with white posts and tape. Added to this a large number of wooden direction boards had been erected and where the tracks crossed enemy trenches, the name of each trench was displayed.

North of Pick House the 10th Inniskillings got held up by a machine gun nest, the crew and weapon well ensconced in a fortified shell hole, but this was quickly neutralised by thrown bombs, while a Lewis gun team closed in and killed the crew. Further north still one of the supporting tanks was just in front of the Inniskillings when they came under more machine gun fire, but the tank crew had not noticed the gun. A sergeant ran to the tank rapping on its side with a Mills bomb and having gotten the attention of the crew, was able to direct them towards the enemy gun. The tank made short work of this position by simply driving over it. This incident is an example of the difficulty in communication between tanks and infantry once the attack has begun. It would be more than 25 years before this problem was resolved.

With each yard of advance it seemed there was another machine gun or group of determined riflemen. A platoon of the 10th Inniskillings was stopped by a trench full of German infantry. Corporal Clarke (No.17614) led his section forward and, outflanking the position, attacked killing three and making the remainder prisoners. On reaching the Black Line, Corporal Clarke pushed forward for another 500 yards, bombed several dug-outs and took 40 prisoners, including two officers.

Within their half of the village of Wytschaete the remainder of the 9th Inniskillings carried out some mopping-up and took a further 50 prisoners. In the other half of the village the 9th Royal Munster Fusiliers carried out a similar task, although village was an erroneous term for what was now a pile of shattered masonry, bricks and smouldering wood, none standing more than a few feet high.

In the ranks of the 16th (Irish) Division Major William Redmond was leading his men of the 6th Royal Irish Regiment across no man's land towards the enemy lines. 'Willie' Redmond was a Nationalist MP, his brother John being leader of the Irish Parliamentary Party. Redmond was 56 years old and had begged for the opportunity to lead his men into action. As they closed with their objective Major Redmond was hit, first in the wrist and then the leg. He was seen to fall by Private John Meeke, a stretcher bearer with the 11th Inniskillings who had been scouring the battlefield for the wounded of his own division. Despite the heavy machine gun and artillery fire, Meek, using shell holes and debris as cover, made his way to the fallen officer. As he finished applying a field dressing to the injured officer Meeke was himself wounded. Within a few seconds he was hit for a second time, but despite this and disobeying a direct order from Redmond to leave him, Meeke struggled across the battlefield until he met up with Lieutenant Charles Paul and a party of the 11th Rifles who were escorting prisoners to the rear. Together they managed to get the wounded Redmond to the casualty clearing station located in the Catholic Hospice at Locre,

Private John Meeke, Royal Inniskilling Fusiliers from Benvarden, Ballymoney, wounded in action and awarded the Military Medal for attending to Major Redmond under fire at Messines.

Major Redmond, 6th Royal Irish Regiment, killed at Messines.

The temporary headstone of Private John Meeke MM.

The CWGC headstone of Private Samuel Meeke, Royal Inniskilling Fusiliers who died of wounds received on 19 January 1919. The headstone also mentions his brother John, who was the first man to find Major Redmond on the Messines battlefield.

Major William Redmond, mortally wounded at Messines, cared for by Private John Meeke, a stretcher bearer with the 11th Inniskillings.

but he died later that afternoon, most likely of shock.[19] For his actions Private Meeke was awarded the Military Medal.[20] Private Robert Doggart had witnessed this and knew of two other soldiers buried in the convent grounds at this time. "I knew one of them, a young man called McCracken, who was serving with the Canadians; he was from the Donegal Road in Belfast."

Private William George Hamilton aged 33 years, from Lurgan, County Armagh, also served in the 108th Field Ambulance both as a stretcher bearer and nursing aid, being present at the forward field dressing tent when Major Redmond was brought in. The major was being treated by Captain John Dunlop, MC, and was heard by Hamilton to say; "Do you know who this is over here on the table? This is Major Willie Redmond and I can do nothing for him!"[21]

---

19   *Irish Times*, 7 March 1985.
20   In October 1918 Private Meeke received a serious wounded to the leg from an explosive bullet. Discharge, he returned to his home near Ballymoney, Antrim and worked as a gardener. He died on 7 December 1923 and was buried in an unmarked grave. It was not until 2004 that a headstone was erected, funding obtained from public subscription.
21   Source: Somme Archive/2005/09/010.

Hamilton and Dunlop had served together since the outbreak of the war and would continue to do so until the Armistice. Captain John Leeper Dunlop had been born in the village of Keady, County Armagh in 1883. He had attended Queen's University, worked in the Royal Victoria Hospital and been commissioned into the RAMC on 9 October 1914. Dunlop had earned his Military Cross the previous year, the citation stating in part; "... fine service rendered since coming to France, but especially by excellent work at Forceville, 1-5 July 1916."

In the ranks of the 108th Field Ambulance Joseph Short was again instrumental in recovering wounded men from the battlefield and was recommend for the Victoria Cross. This was rejected and no award was made. However, the incident, along with the actions of other members of the party, were not forgotten by the officer commanding the unit and post-war he paid tribute to the men with the presentation of silver medals in the shape of a VC. The medal was hallmarked by the Birmingham Assay Office in 1919 and is inscribed B3 1SB. Joseph Silas Short, No.41122, was a former member of the South Belfast UVF, his lapel badge number being 3257 Cs. Both he and his brother Robert had signed the Covenant.

In the ranks of the 14th Rifles, Private Fred McKee from Court Street, Newtownards, was going into action for the first time. A former labourer, Fred had enlisted in the 18th Rifles, one of the reserve battalions of the division and had arrived at the Front in April as a much needed reinforcement. This was Fred's first and last major action and he was killed during the advance. His platoon commander, Lieutenant R.C. McCrum wrote a rather brief note to Fred's mother; "It is with extreme regret that I have to inform you of the death of your son in action on 7 June. He was in my platoon, and although only with us for a short time he had shown himself to be a capable soldier. He is buried at Spanbroekmolen. Accept my sincere sympathy in your bereavement."

The Presbyterian chaplain, the Reverend John Knowles was a little wordier in his letter to Mrs McKee:

> I am very sorry to have to tell you that your son, F. McKee (No.1542) of this battalion was killed in action in the attack of 7 June. We found his body on the battlefield and buried him next day. I was present and conducted a service at the grave. The place is marked with a cross and will be enclosed and carefully tended. We are all deeply grieved for the loss of your son. He was a good soldier and has been faithful unto death. Our heartfelt sympathy is with you in your bereavement. I pray God may comfort you in your great sorrow.[22]

While Lieutenant McCrum's letter can be criticised for its brevity, the number of similar letters he would have to write can only be guessed at.

Second Lieutenant George Wilmer Devitt from Toronto had enlisted in the Eaton Machine gun Battery of the Canadian Expeditionary Force and came to France in May 1915. He had transferred to the 36th Division the following December, was wounded in the Somme battle, gassed at Kemmel in April 1917 and now lay wounded close to his machine gun section. He had been in the process of bringing forward his gun when he was hit by a shell splinter, but despite this he brought the gun into action and laid out the line of fire. His was a serious injury and he was invalided back to England. He was awarded the Military Cross for his actions at Messines. Casualties were overall light to the machine gunners. Lieutenant Herbert Newton Walker of the 107th Machine Gun Company was killed prior to the attack, while Sergeant James Irwin from Lambeg, Lisburn, County Antrim, of the 109th was wounded. Lieutenant Walker, like George Devitt, had come from Canada to serve, his home being in British Columbia and like his fellow Canadian he was 27 years old.

---

22   Switzer & Switzer, 'Remembering the Fallen', *Newtownards Chronicle*.

On the extreme right flank the 15th Rifles came under heavy machine gun fire some two hundred yards short of the Messines to Wytschaete road. Captain P.K. Miller, commanding B Company, had crawled forward and crossed the road, in the midst of the still falling British bombardment and spotted the enemy position. He then returned to his company and ordered Lieutenant Falkiner to take his platoon, less the Lewis gun team and assault the position. The Lewis gun was put into position where it could spray the objective, but keeping it in action cost the lives of three of the five men in the section. Meanwhile Captain Miller went along to the left flank and ordered forward B Company to attack another strong-point that was causing problems. It was then he discovered that the company commander had received a Blighty wound on the way up the Ridge. His place was taken by Lieutenant Frank Farrell, a former employee of the Textile Testing House and now acting as intelligence officer in brigade headquarters. On returning to the right flank Miller discovered that Lieutenant Falkiner had successfully captured Lumm Farm. This had involved some nasty close quarter combat and the almost surgical application of the rifle grenade in lobbing them through the firing slits of the bunker. At one emplacement Private Aicken, with the assistance of Private Cochrane, had forced the surrender of one bunker after several accurate shots. A short distance away Lieutenant Falkiner and a German officer had engaged in hand to hand combat before the Lieutenant has used his revolver to good effect. At the end of the skirmish only 15 of the enemy remained alive to be taken prisoner.

Captain Miller then pushed his company forward for approximately another 100 yards and had them dig in. A while later the A Company commander of the 8th Battalion South Lancashire Regiment, 75 Brigade 25th Division, on the right flank, arrived and requested the use of Lumm Farm as a headquarters as there were no suitable dug-outs in his sector. Captain Miller gave him one of the rooms in the dug-out, of which there were three or four. Given that the demarcation line between the two divisions bisected the Farm it is not surprising that some confusion arose. In the regimental history of the 25th Division it is claimed that No.2 Platoon of A Company 8th Battalion, under Second Lieutenant Stowell, captured Lumm Farm.[23]

The division consolidated on the Black Line and at 8:40 am was able to send forward patrols in concert with those of the 16th and 25th Divisions. These patrols advanced 1,000 yards on to what had originally known as the Dotted Black Line, but was later known as the Mauve Line. Here the patrols dug in and established a series of outposts.

While the majority of the artillery moved forward to the old British front line, those of the 36th Division, the 153 and 173 Brigades, crossed no man's land and took up positions on the Red Line. By 10:05 am Lieutenant Colonel Simpson reported that 173 Brigade was ready to open fire and a few minutes later Lieutenant Colonel Thompson reported his 153 Brigade was also ready. At 10:20 am, Captain Mulholland, commanding the 109th Machine Gun Company, reported British cavalry patrols advancing and he then sent three of his guns forward with orders to go into Wytschaete if possible.

For the following two hours all was quiet and the infantry took the opportunity to enhance their defences and where possible brew up some tea. It is a misconception that the British Army was always stopping for tea, something it gained notoriety for from American troops in the Second World War. The truth is that when the British Army has to stop, for whatever reason, its takes the opportunity to brew tea, which is a totally different matter. As the Black Line became consolidated the Engineers from the 121 and 150 Field Companies had constructed strong-points to the rear of the Line. In conjunction with stringing their own supply of barbed wire, which had been brought forward by a train of pack mules led by Lieutenant Haig, MC, of the 107 Brigade, the Engineers had come across a large dump of German wire, most of it near Guy Farm.

---

23   Kincaid-Smith, Lieutenant Colonel M., *The 25th Division in France and Flanders* (1918).

Men from the Royal Irish Fusiliers in 1917, note the number of men swearing wound chevrons.

From Jump Point Colonel Cheape, 14th Rifles, had sent a runner back to headquarters at 9:35 am, to report that he had reorganised the position and had a garrison of about 100 'YCVs', including eight officers. All ranks were exhausted, but digging in. He was short of barbed wire and tools. Many stragglers from other units were about and he was co-operating with the OC of the 9th Irish Fusiliers on his right flank and the 11th Inniskillings on his left. The runner had arrived at 10:35 am and given the condition of the ground this was good going. By 10:38 am a runner had arrived at 10th Inniskilling headquarters from the 10th Rifles, the runner having gotten lost in the maze of shell holes. In some cases the use of valuable runners seemed to be trivial. A runner from the 11th Rifles took an hour to cover the battlefield to deliver a receipt for 80 picks and 160 shovels that had been handed over to an officer on the Black Line.

At 11:55 am, reports were received from Corps headquarters that there was movement in the Germans lines indicating a counter-attack from the direction of Houthern. However, this caused no concern to General Nugent, 107 and 109 Brigades were well ensconced and there was no cause for anxiety.

In the forward position were located twelve Vickers machine guns, three were dug in to the north of Lumm Farm, three located between Guy Farm and Staenyzer Cabaret, three more approximately 100 yards to the west of the main road and the remainder in reserve.

The 108th Machine Gun Company's 16 guns had taken up positions further to the rear. Eight guns were located to the east of L'Enfer Wood, four at Jump Point and four on Hill 94, on the south-west corner of Wytschaete village. Ammunition for these guns had been brought forward from the old front line by pack mules, arriving at 5:40 am, the ground being unsuitable for the two-wheeled limbers. Now well stocked the guns prepared to put down a protective barrage on the Black Line. Later these guns were repositioned to enable them to put down a protecting barrage in front of the Mauve Line. This barrage opened at 2:40 pm, the guns opening a traversing and searching fire from the positions known as 0.28.c.90.80 to 0.21.b.50.25 to a depth of 1,000 yards

A German trench on Messines Ridge after a British bombardment.

making lifts of 100 yards every three minutes. This lasted for some 30 minutes and for those 30 minutes it rained bullets on the enemy positions.

The redoubtable pack mules brought forward all munitions required, machine gun belts, small arms ammunition, Mills bombs and water. Water was required for the Vickers guns and also for the men, combat breeds thirst. At 7:50 am 109 Brigade had requested such supplies for its two battalions in the Black Line and these had included ten mules each carrying six full petrol tins of water, hopefully well rinsed.

While it was possible that a major German counter-attack would have driven in the outposts on the Mauve Line, it was doubtful that any attack on the Black Line would have been successful. An intelligence report from IX Corps reported that long columns of infantry and supply wagons had been observed from balloons and aircraft, moving west from the canal at Houthern. These troops eventually launched an attack, which fell on the right flanking 25th and New Zealand Divisions and was beaten off by the defensive artillery barrages.

The day had now become very hot and the stench from the horses and men killed by the British bombardment during the preceding week was almost overwhelming. The men were tired, the adrenalin having worn off and even the mugs of strong sweet tea were having little effect. Added to this was that the villages of Messines and Wytschaete now begin to receive an inordinate amount of shelling from the German artillery. At 12:20 pm orders were received from IX Corps that the Mauve Line was to be consolidated and held in force. This was in order to provide a firm second line of defence once the 11th Division had captured the Oosttaverne Line.

The first contact between the 36th and 16th Divisions was recorded as happening at 12:45 pm, with patrols for each division meeting on the Black Line. At the same time some 900 German prisoners were escorted back, while an enemy observation balloon appeared behind Wytschaete.

The two forward Brigades, 107 and 109, were both ordered to provide a battalion to garrison the Mauve Line and both commanders opted to use the attached battalion from the 108 Brigade. These had previously been used as moppers-up and were therefore fresher than the other battalions. Just before 3:00 pm the 11th and 12th Rifles arrived in the Mauve Line and had begun the process of fortifying it.

At 3:10 pm 34 Brigade of the 11th Division advanced through the Mauve Line following up a tremendous barrage and being supported by four tanks. While fewer British guns were firing the barrage was even thicker than before, due to the frontage of the advance being reduced by more than 50 percent.

As the day wore on the task of collecting the wounded and burying the dead continued. Near Wytschaete Sergeant Ernest Barrington-Palmer, a medical orderly, saw one such working party come under heavy German shell fire. Collecting a number of stretcher bearers from the regimental aid post he recovered the wounded men applying first aid on the field. The training he had received at Newry in 1914 being put to good use. For the following three days the sergeant was rarely off the battlefield and the number of men he recovered and treated is unknown, but for his efforts he was awarded the Military Medal.

As the 11th Division reached the Oosttaverne Line it came under intense German artillery fire, all of which was now east of the Canal. The IX Corps Cavalry went forward at 6:00 pm, but it was too late to exploit a breakthrough. Once again the sluggishness of communications was to blame and the cavalry suffered casualties from machine guns and artillery.

All this time the 16th Rifles were carrying on with their pioneering duties. Two companies were hard at work clearing a road, removing rubble and filling in shell-holes. There were also the all-important mule tracks to be marked out and by evening a practical road for wheeled traffic had been cleared across no man's land as far as the Spanbroek Crater, a distance of approximately 1,350 yards in all. Two mule tracks had also been cleared and marked, one of 2,500 yards and a second of 3,400 yards. Added to this was the manufacture and erection of numerous sign boards to direct the various units across a most confusing landscape. Once again use was made of German barbed wire, with the 122 Field Company sowing a barricade of wire along the entire length of the Black Line. By 3:00 am on the morning of 8 June all the new defences had been put in place.

With the enemy now pushed off the Messines Ridge no further enemy observation could be made on the British positions and as they also had command of the air, it was now relatively safe to move about in the open. The division made much use of pack mules and horses and even before the Black Line had been fully captured the transport officers were making great headway in bringing forward supplies of ammunition, water and rations.

The Messines Ridge itself was a total shambles of destroyed buildings and ploughed up ground. L'Enfer Wood had all but disappeared, only a few tree stumps marking its location. Several of the concrete pill-boxes has been totally destroyed, many others damaged. The Steenebeek no longer flowed as a stream, but had been churned to liquid mud. Most of the enemy dead lay facing the top of the Ridge, having been killed by the British creeping barrage as they attempted to escape.

That night, 8 June, 108 Brigade came forward and relieved 107 and 109 Brigades, who moved back into the relative comfort of the old British trenches. The Ridge was now subjected to very heavy shelling from the German guns on a near continuous basis and the 150 Field Company had a terrible time as they strung barbed wire along the Mauve Line. A strong-point on the Blue Line that had been known as Unnamed Wood was subsequently officially named Inniskilling Wood to reflect the achievements of 109 Brigade.

At 4:00 pm, the following day General Griffith handed over command of the front line to the 11th Division and that night 32 Brigade relieved the 108 Brigade in the Mauve, Black and Blue lines and the men moved back to positions on the slopes of Kemmel Hill.

Within the division various reports were compiled to access the success and failures of the day. The Lewis gun had proved to be of immense value in dealing with hostile machine guns and

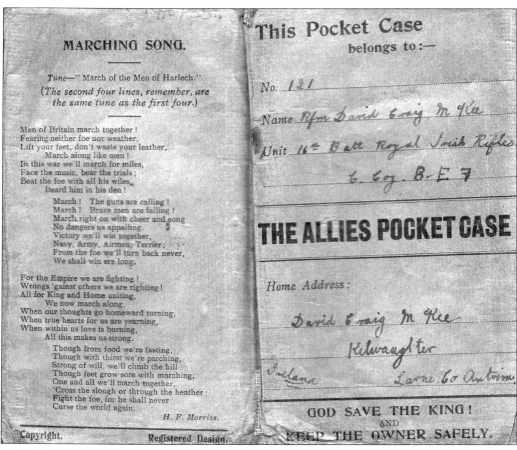

The Allies Pocket Case belonging to Sergeant David Craig McKee, 16th Royal Irish Rifles, killed on 19 August 1917. The son of Robert James McKee of Kilwaughter, Larne, County Antrim.

snipers operating from shell-holes. The rifle grenade, both No.20 and No.24, was rarely used, but proved to be effective on several occasions when dealing with enemy machine guns and snipers. The Yukon packs proved extremely useful, allowing a man to carry a box of small arms ammunition or five boxes of bombs. Likewise the mule packs were successful. The Lucas lamps worked very well in providing communications from front to rear. The success of the operation was attributed chiefly to the platoon system of training, to thorough organisation and to the dissemination to all ranks of information they should know. Every man entered the battle knowing what to do and how to do it. The lessons learnt from the Canadians at Vimy Ridge as regards dealing with enemy machine guns was acted upon with excellent results and it was confirmed in the operations that the platoon, as now organised, has at its disposal all the arms necessary to deal with any enemy machine gun which may come into action at close range. In the operations under review, pack animals were invaluable, for immediately the enemy had been dislodged off the Ridge pack trains with ammunition, bombs, water, barbed wire etc., were sent up without interference from the enemy's artillery. Battalion carrying parties were fully justified with supplies of water and ammunition reaching the various lines within ten to 20 minutes after the objectives had been taken. Likewise, the provision of carrying parties from the support battalion with tools for the Blue Line and Black Line was also satisfactory. The parties dumped the tools at selected points and returned to their headquarters practically without suffering any casualties. The arrangement made for communications worked out to all intents and purposes exactly as laid down in instructions. Telephone lines were cut occasionally but were quickly repaired and brigade headquarters was on telephonic communication with the forward brigade station and forward battalion command posts, when these latter were established, without any serious lengthy interruption throughout the operation. The card message forms with maps printed on them were a constant source of information and it was strongly urged that these should be an issue for all future operations. It was felt that their value could be over-estimated.

Brigadier Ricardo attributed success to the platoon system of training, thorough organisation and the dissemination of information to all ranks. The troops also enjoyed four days rest under canvas in ideal weather in the back area and were issued with a hot meal about 7:00 pm on Y/Z night and on passing their battalion headquarters to the assembly positions were issued with hot tea, rissoles and whatever else the cooks could manage to concoct.

On the downside there appeared to be more abandoned British material strewn about the battlefield than the casualties warranted. It was suggested that in future the stores sent forward should be marked with the name of the unit carrying them, with a view of identifying those responsible for undue waste. Evidence within the division showed that articles carried in the hand were more likely to be discarded than those carried attaché to the body in sand bags or haversacks. A great number of boards with rifle grenades attached were lying about and the number of canvas carriers for drums of Lewis gun ammunition was considerable.

In the after action reports the following points were stressed: There was also the question of Zero, many felt it was too early, although not by more than a few minutes at most. It was felt that men still did not use their rifles sufficiently in the attack; they still require very considerable training to make them accustomed to using their rifles. There was an absolute necessity of immediate and energetic wiring and consolidation of captured positions, no matter how tired troops may be. There does not yet appear to be sufficiently grasped by junior commanders. There also seemed to be a want of initiative in making use of the enemy's tools and stores that could be collected with a little energy and enterprise. The whole subject of consolidation needed practice; the effort of some parties merely resulted in a safe and inconspicuous shell-hole being converted into an insecure and very obvious target, with a few sand bags to give it a home-like appearance.

The total number of prisoners that passed through the divisional cage was 29 officers and 1,039 other ranks, all but 11 of the other ranks being captured on 7 June. Nine were taken on 8 June and two on 9 June. Additionally, two officers and 169 other ranks that had been wounded were admitted to the divisional dressing station, giving a grand total of thirty-one officers and 1,208 other ranks.

A considerable number of field guns were abandoned by the enemy as they retreated over the ground taken by the division, but only a few were brought back before the division was relieved. The following were handed over to the Ordnance Branch, two 77mm field guns, eight trench mortars, including one heavy, twenty-eight machine guns and one Stick Gun.

36th Division Casualties

109 Brigade

9th Inniskillings	6 Officers	122 other ranks
10th Inniskillings	2 Officers	59 other ranks
11th Inniskillings	10 Officers	103 other ranks
14th Rifles	4 Officers	178 other ranks
109th Machine Gun Company	1 Officer	4 other ranks
109th Trench Mortar Battery	Nil	Nil

From the German point of view the battle had cost them dear, approximately 25,000 casualties and a huge amount of material. While aware that an attack was imminent the Germans expected it on 9 June. Knowing that the troops in the front line trenches were not up to maintaining a strong defence, they had undergone a terrific bombardment, incurred heavy losses and were suffering a shortage of food, the High Command was in the process of replacing them when the attack occurred. Given that on this occasion the British artillery had the high ground, their firing was excellent and it was estimated that one German gun in four was destroyed in the pre-attack bombardment, as were a large number of horses.

The headquarters of the division moved back to its former location in the village of St. Jans Cappel on 16 June. A post-action report showed that the division had captured 31 officers and 1,208 other ranks. Casualties suffered by the division between 7 and 9 June 1917, when it was relieved, were 61 officers and 1,058 other ranks, many more than during the actual assault on 7 June, the majority being suffered during the subsequent German bombardment. The flanking divisions, especially those of the II Anzac Corps did suffer more casualties.

On the night of 19 June, the 107 Brigade on the right flank and 109 Brigade on the left relieved the 11th Division and took over the Front now held by the IX Corps. This stretched from the Blauwepoortbeek at Deconinck Farm located to the north of the village of Gapaard on the right flank to Rose Wood north of the Roozebeek on the left, a distance of some 3,000 yards. Headquarters of 107 Brigade was located in the old British trenches, while that of 109 Brigade was in abandoned enemy dug-outs in the northern part of Grand Bois (The Oosttaverne Line).

On 20 June divisional headquarters began to operate from Ulster Camp. The holding of these new positions was not going to be an easy job. The German artillery was present in great numbers and contained many heavy guns, all aligned behind the Canal d'Ypres. The barrage fell on the divisional positions during both day and night. Such was the fierceness of the German artillery on the headquarters of 109 Brigade in the Grand Bois that General Nugent ordered them back to a company headquarters position in the old lines on 21 June.

Those troops in the front line trenches on the forward slope of the Ridge had a particularly bad time. Directly exposed to observation they suffered a high number of casualties, the average being approximately 00 per battalion per day. Even during the hours of darkness the pressure did not let up and the ration parties experienced their share of dead and wounded. Nor was it safe on the western side of the Ridge and in the rear areas. While the British had controlled the air during the battle, now many of the squadrons had been moved north to the Salient, while the Imperial German Army Air Force had in turn been reinforced.

Apart from strafing the trenches with machine guns the German aircraft also targeted the British observation balloons. One of the most effective units at this was *Jagdgeschwader 1*, a group of four squadrons commanded by Manfred von Richthofen, popularly known as the Red Baron. However, no matter how many the Germans shot down and on 23 June they destroyed three in succession, replacements were in position very quickly. As the observers in the balloons were equipped with parachutes they generally survived these attacks and were soon back in action spotting for the artillery and others. Von Richthofen was killed on 21 April 1918, and evidence from his post mortem pointed to a bullet fired from the ground as causing the fatal wound.[24] Most of the enemy infantry was now located east of the Canal d'Ypres, with only isolated posts held on the west bank and these were of a nature that indicated they were not going to be held for any length of time.

The war diary of 107 Brigade contains a revealing report (28 June 1917) entitled "Enemy Attitude during the Tour":

24 Kilduff, Peter, *The Red Baron, Beyond the Legend* (1994).

For the first three days of the tour the enemy was apparently only spasmodically active, and contented himself with holding a line of posts some 250 yards behind. It was not until the night of 22nd/23rd that work to any extent was reported in the groups of trees in 0.29.d and in the wood 0.29.b. Since then he has apparently been endeavouring to make something like two strong-points at these places and the fact that there is not much sign of completed work on recent aeroplane photographs at these points is due to the harassing fire of our artillery. On the 24th, 25th/26th the enemy apparently discontinued their activity at work, perhaps owing to our artillery activity, but on the night of the 27th stronger working parties then ever were discovered. A conformation of this is found in the decrease of enemy artillery activity (thus encouraging our artillery to be quieter) in proportion to the increase in his work.

Another strong-point outside our sector has been made and is garrisoned at 0.29.b90.63. From this part of the ridge all the front part of our sector is under observation and the trenches will be correspondingly unhealthy until the enemy is driven from this part of the ridge. The enemy's delay in starting to work at these places may be explained by his waiting to see what our policy would be. Of this he must have been fully and accurately informed by the constant and close patrol work of his air service.

The division was relieved by 37th Division on 29 June and the following day all units, with the exception of the artillery, engineers and pioneers moved to the Merris area. Divisional headquarters and that of the 108 Brigade were located in the village of Merris, while the 107 Brigade was in Outtersteene and 109 Brigade was in Strazeele. The divisional artillery remained in the line until 5 July, all the time under very heavy enemy fire and in bad weather. The pioneers and the field companies were given only one day's rest before being moved to the Salient to take up new duties there.

On 30 June the *Belfast News Letter* printed an account that Captain Charles Bernard Tate, aged twenty-seven, serving with the 15th Rifles, missing since 1 July the previous year was now officially presumed dead. A former officer with the Whitehouse Company of the UVF, he had served in the Motor Car Corps before receiving his commission with the division. In the same paper it was reported that Corporal James Long, Royal Engineers, attached to the divisional signals company, had been awarded the Ulster Division certificate for gallantry in laying and maintaining telephone wires under shell fire during the attack on the Ancre on 1 July. Prior to enlisting Corporal Long, one of three sons of John Long, North Street, Lurgan, had been a member of the Armagh Post Office.

On 1 July, a year after the cataclysmic first day of the Somme battle 109 Brigade was encamped at Strazeele. Here all units were engaged in refitting and taking advantage of the opportunity to avail of hot baths. For most of the month the brigade was engaged in training, although on 25 July this was cancelled due to torrential rain.

On 3 July, as per Army Order No.51, the 36th Division was transferred from the Second Army to the Fifth Army and would form part of the XIX Corps, commanded by Lieutenant General Herbert Watts; described by General Haig as "...a plucky hard little man, with no great brains, I should judge from his doing at Ypres last November."

It was Haig's impression that Watts' staff did all the work.[25] The Fifth Army was commanded by General Hubert de la Poer Gough, a product of Eton and Sandhurst. Born in County Waterford, he was the eldest son of General Sir Charles Gough, VC, the brother of Brigadier General Sir John Edmund Gough, VC, and nephew of General Sir Hugh H. Gough, VC, the Goughs being the only family ever to have the Victoria Cross awarded three times. Gough was educated at

---

25   Sheffield & Bourne (eds), *Douglas Haig: War Diaries and Letters, 1914-1918*.

The East Wing of the Curragh Camp.

Eton, where he was abysmal at Latin, but excelled at sports, before gaining entrance to Sandhurst in 1888.[26] In March 1889 he was commissioned into the 16th Lancers, serving with them in the Tirah Campaign of 1897-1898. By 1902 he was a lieutenant colonel, having campaigned across numerous racing, polo and hunting fields. He attended the Staff College at Camberley, but was sent on active service to South Africa before completing his course. During the Boer War Gough enjoyed a reputation as a dashing cavalry commander, in spite of several reversals due to his ignoring of intelligence reports. In one instance of such behaviour Gough suffered a defeat at Blood River Poort on 17 September 1901; he was briefly captured but escaped on the same day. On returning to England he was appointed to the staff College as an instructor. Despite being involved in the Curragh Mutiny[27] Gough served as a brigade commander quite successfully in the opening weeks of the war. He was promoted to Major General and commanded the 2nd Cavalry Division during the First Battle of Ypres and in March 1915 took command of the 7th Division. In July 1915, he was again promoted, to Lieutenant General and given command of I Corps, a rank and position for which he seemed unsuited.[28]

The division, less pioneers, artillery and engineers, moved to a training area to the south west of St. Omer, with General Nugent's headquarters being established in the town of Wizernes on 7 July. Much smaller than that occupied the previous summer after the Somme battle, it was in fact the southern part of the latter. This was not an ideal area for training, extremely cramped for any exercises, with billets being inadequate and having to be augmented by tents. Although given the weather this was no great hardship. For the following twelve days the men of the division would enjoy rest and relaxation to a degree not experienced since they came to France. There was ample sport for the men and the officers enjoyed a gymkhana, with horse racing, mule racing, jumping,

26   Gough, Sir Hubert, *Soldiering On* (1954).
27   See Volume I.
28   Sheffield, Gary & Todman, Dan (eds), *Command and Control on the Western Front* (2004).

transport competitions and finishing with a divisional drag. At this time the divisional artillery, engineers and 16th Rifles were detached, coming under the command of the 55th Division. Here the artillery would provide support for the coming attack, while the pioneers and field companies dug new wells to improve the water supply for the large number of troops that would be engaged in the coming offensive. This seems somewhat ironic; water was something there would be no shortage of in the coming weeks. Once the wells had been dug there were roads to repair and the construction of cross-country tracks for men and pack animals.

On 18 July a brigade commander's conference was held and various items came up for discussion. It was decided that there should be systematic and frequent practice in the use of the Yukon pack and that the provision of a long stout stick or Alpen-stock was an absolute necessity in helping a man maintain his balance while carrying such a load. There were several suggestions on the carrying of entrenching tools and the merits of wearing it to the front of the body to provide a degree of protection, first used by Australian troops. It was agreed that nothing should be decided until after the next field firing exercise. Intelligence reports indicated that the Germans were using a new type of gas. This was mustard gas, which attacked not only the lungs and eyes, but any exposed skin and all units were advised on what precautions to take in the event of an attack.

A request was made to DADOS, for 900 feet of rope in order to construct carrying slings for the divisional pack transport, while the quartermasters were reminded to ensure an adequate amount of oil be available for the cleaning of all rifles and machine guns. The brigadier stressed that the list of questions a platoon commander should ask himself on reaching the objective must include "*are my rifles and machine guns cleaned and oiled*?" It was decided that battalion and company flags were very useful, but their adoption was optional for commanding officers. All units were to submit a table of ammunition regarding the different specialists etc., for the information of the GOC. The minimum requirement for hot food containers was 16 per battalion, four for the machine gun company and two for the trench mortar battery. For the removal of surplus kit to Bailleul, each battalion was allocated five lorries, while the machine gunners and trench mortars detachments would share one.

10

Langemarck

The Third Battle of Ypres started on 22 July when 3,091 British guns commenced a lengthy bombardment of the German positions that lasted until 31 July, by which time some 4,250,000 shells had been fired, the terrain transformed into a quagmire.

On 28 July 1917, the 36th Division was first informed of its role in the forthcoming campaign. The Fifth Army, in conjunction with Second Army and First French Army, was to attack the enemy to its front on a date to be notified later, which was to be known as Z Day. The XIX Corps would attack with the 15th Division on the right and the 55th Division on the left, and the 16th (Irish) and 36th (Ulster) Divisions in reserve. The 8th Division of II Corps supported by the 25th Division was to be on the right of the 15th Division, and the 39th Division of XVIII Corps was on the left of the 55th Division.[1]

According to Allied intelligence sources the enemy opposite XIX Corps consisted of two regiments of the 17th Division and one regiment of the 233rd Division. Each regiment had one battalion in the front system, one battalion in the Stutzpunkt Line and a third battalion in the Gheluvelt – Langemarck Line. Each division had a further regiment in reserve.

The attack had three objectives, the capture and consolidation of the enemy's front system of trenches, to continue on to take the *Stutzpunkt* line and finally the third line of defences at Gheluvelt – Langemarck. The attack was to be preceded by an artillery bombardment that had already begun on 18 July. On paper all so neat and tidy, the reality would be somewhat different, small gains for heavy casualties.

On the night of 30 July 1917, 109 Brigade moved to the Watou area in preparation for the forthcoming attack. This movement was carried out by motorised transport, a combination of lorries and omnibuses, which required the introduction of a special drill for both loading and unloading having to be put into practice. The officers commanding the various units were instructed to have their men deployed on the right-hand side of the road, the troops to be distributed in six groups per 80 yards of road, with groups of 20 for each lorry and 25 for each omnibus. No baggage of any kind was to be carried, although two camp kettles were permitted aboard each vehicle. Officers were to be distributed among all vehicles and a specific 'officers only' vehicle was not permitted. There was to be a gap of 500 yards between each unit and all units would provide aeroplane sentries. A mounted officer was to precede each unit at a sufficient distance to give adequate warning to traffic control points of the approach of these units. The movement of infantry on this night was to take precedence over all other units. On the division's right flank the 16th (Irish) Division was undergoing a similar experience.

---

1   36th (Ulster) Division Order No.123, dated 28 July 1917.

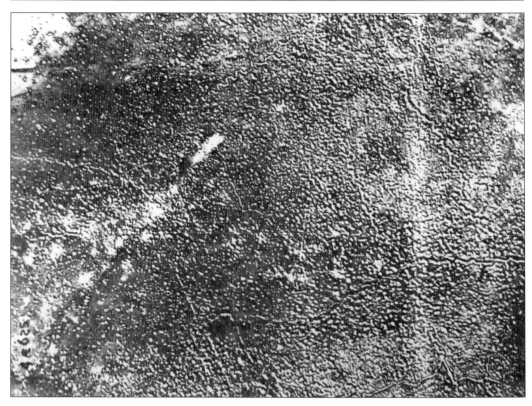

The Western Front, a myriad of shell holes obliterating all but the most prominent landmarks.
(Courtesy of Michael LoCicero)

Mud, water and barbed wire, typical conditions of Langemarck, August 1917.

The Third Battle of Ypres – 36th (Ulster) Division Order of Battle

Divisional Troops
Field Artillery
36th Divisional Artillery Group
Brigadier General H.J. Brock, DSO, R.A.

36th Divisional Artillery
153 Brigade, RFA Lieutenant Colonel C.F. Potter, DSO, RFA
173 Brigade, RFA, Lieutenant-Colonel H.C. Simpson, DSO, RFA

61st Divisional Artillery
306 Brigade, RFA, Lieutenant Colonel F.G. Willock, RFA
307 Brigade, RFA, Lieutenant Colonel S.P. Morter, RFA

Army Field Artillery Brigades
108 F.A. Brigade, Lieutenant Colonel W.H. Drake, C.M.G., RFA
150 F.A. Brigade, Lieutenant Colonel V.H. Dickson, DSO, RFA

Royal Engineers and Pioneers
Commanding Royal Engineer: – Major (Temp. Lt. Col.) A. Campbell, DSO, R.E.
121st Field Company, R.E., Lieutenant (A/Major) R.A.H. Lewin, R.E.
122nd Field Company, R.E., (Temp. Major) C.C.A. Hardie, R.E.
150th Field Company, R.E., Captain (A/Major) H.M. Fordham, R.E.
16th Battalion Royal Irish Rifles (Pioneers) Lieutenant-Colonel C.F. Meares
(Note: 100 Infantrymen were attached to each Field Company, R.E.)

107 Brigade
Brigadier General W.M. Withycombe, C.M.G.
8th Battalion Royal Irish Rifles
Major J.D. McCallum, DSO
9th Battalion Royal Irish Rifles
Lieutenant Colonel H.C. Elwes, M.V.O.
10th Battalion Royal Irish Rifles
Lieutenant Colonel N.G. Burnard, DSO
15th Battalion Royal Irish Rifles
Major WA Montgomery, DSO
107th Machine Gun Company
Captain J.S. Cressale
107th Trench Mortar Battery
Captain I.A. Grove-White
(Note: Lieutenant Colonel C.G. Cole-Hamilton, DSO, was wounded on 2 August)[2]

---

2   Cole-Hamilton vacated command of the 15th Rifles on 28 January 1919.

108 Brigade

Brigadier General C.R.J. Griffith, CMG, DSO
11th Battalion Royal Irish Rifles
Lieutenant Colonel P. Blair-Oliphant, DSO
12th Battalion Royal Irish Rifles
Major G. Thompson
13th Battalion Royal Irish Rifles
Lieutenant Colonel R.P.D. Perceval-Maxwell
9th Battalion Royal Irish Fusiliers
Lieutenant Colonel S.J. Somerville
108th Machine Gun Company
Lieutenant G.S. Moorhouse
108th Trench Mortar Battery
Captain M.H. Browne

109 Brigade

Brigadier General A. St.Q. Ricardo, C.M.G., DSO
9th Royal Inniskilling Fusiliers
Lieutenant Colonel W.J. Peacocke, DSO
10th Royal Inniskilling Fusiliers
Major R.S. Knox, DSO
11th Royal Inniskilling Fusiliers
Major J.E. Knott, D.S.O
14th Royal Irish Rifles
Major The Hon. O.R. Vivian, M.V.O.
109th Machine Gun Company
Captain P.D. Mulholland
109th Trench Mortar Battery
A/Captain R.A. O'Neill
(Note: Lieutenant Colonel A. C. Pratt, D.S.O. was killed just prior to the attack and Major J.E. Knott, DSO took over command of that unit. Lieutenant Colonel G.R.H. Cheape, M.C., commanding the 14th Battalion Royal Irish Rifles, was kept back under the provisions of S.S. 155, Section XXX)

On 31 July at 3:50 am, in torrential rain, 12 British divisions made their attack on an 11-mile wide front against the Pilckem Ridge and Ghelveult Plateau. Initially, on the left flank, some ground was gained, but on the right the attack quickly bogged down in the gelatinous mud. From here on little would move, the torrential rain continued day after day and created a nightmare for men, animals and machines. Initially the attack seemed to go well, but the Germans, despite holding the line lightly, were in depth and fierce counter-attacks soon retook the captured ground. One success was the Pilckem Spur, which remained in British hands.

While conditions for the British were terrible, for the Germans it was equally bad. Max Osborn, an official German observer at Ypres recorded the following; "Never-ending howls and piercing screams are rending the air from the sea to the River Lys, while accessory noises like growls and blows seem to spring from everywhere on the Yser, in front of Dixmude and Langemarck around Hollebeke and Warneton." Osborn went on to describe the West Flanders war zone as one large, steaming pot, in which death and devastation were brewing.

The 36th Divisional Artillery, Royal Engineers and 16th Rifles were serving with the 55th Division for this attack and suffered accordingly. The troops had gone forward with great dash and in practically all locations had reached their final designated objective, known as the Green Line, which was to the east and just south of St. Julien. However, the leading battalions had suffered high casualties from German machine guns firing from positions in depth and had consequently not had the manpower to resist the inevitable counter-attacks. Forced back to the Black Line their advance had been some 1,500 yards. Further to the south the attack had not been so successful and here the Black line remained to be taken. While it had been the intention to keep the assaulting troops in the line after they had made their attack, this did not happen. The 55th Division had suffered a huge number of casualties and its infantry were so worn out that it was decided to withdraw it immediately. This decision would have severe consequences for the 36th Division.

In the German command General Ludendorff reported; "…the English, assisted by a few French Divisions on their left, had attacked on a front of about 31 kilometres, but beside the loss of from two to four kilometres along the whole front, it caused us heavy losses in prisoners and stores, and a heavy expenditure of reserves."

The Ulster Division was located in and around the area of Watou, west of Poperinghe, with Headquarters in Poperinghe itself as of 1 August. From Corps headquarters General Nugent received orders to move forward one of his infantry brigades to the 55th Division, which was at that time holding the left sector of the XIX Corps front. The following day General Withycombe's 107 Brigade left Poperinghe by train and travelled to the famous Goldfish Chateau, some 2,000 yards to the west of Ypres Railway Station. It was here on 22 April 1915 that the Germans had launched their first major gas attack against the French. At the Chateau the brigade came under the command of the 55th Division and was placed in reserve, but was almost immediately sent to take over from the 164 Brigade. At 12:45 pm General Withycombe reached Wieltje, the headquarters of 164 Brigade and established his own headquarters in the Wieltje Dugouts. He later received a telegram from the 55th Division telling him to continue on and relieve both the 165 and 166 Brigades, who were occupying the captured German trenches. Withycombe's men had a long tiring march in pouring rain through thick clinging mud that was up to 18 inches deep and had not completed the relief of the 164 Brigade until 3:40 pm. Besides the weather the men of 107 Brigade had dealt with heavy fire from large calibre enemy howitzers and had been involved in bombing attacks against the right flank of the 55th Division. It was 6:00 am the following morning before the relief was completed. The Brigade had suffered heavy casualties, especially the 10th and 15th Rifles, who had taken over the defence of the Black Line. Such were the losses that there was no possibility of these two battalions being used in any forthcoming attack.

In the continuing toil of collecting the dead and injured Private William James Cranston, 109th Field Ambulance, was killed. From Boundary Street, Belfast, he had been an original member of the Field Ambulance.

The 1st Irish Fusiliers, a regular battalion, joined the division on 3 August, coming from the 4th Division. They initially served in 107 Brigade, as of 24 August, before moving on to 108 Brigade on 8 February 1918. Losses suffered at and after Messines by the brigade had not been made up by recruits from Ulster and this regular battalion had been brought into the division to bolster the division's Ulster identity. The following day the two brigades were ordered to withdraw their remaining battalion to the same area. From the 108 Brigade the 13th Rifles and 9th Irish Fusiliers were sent to relieve 165 Brigade, which had moved back to the former British front and support lines. The 109 Brigade supplied the 11th Inniskillings and 14th Rifles to relieve the 166 Brigade, all these battalions now under the command of General Withycombe from his headquarters at the mined dug-outs at Wieltje. These dug-outs had 13 different entrances and while they gave cover from the shelling, they were dismal, with poor light emitting from the strung electric lamps. The air was fetid, water flowed along its main passages and the smell was overpowering, a mixture of sweat, damp, fumes from the generators, cigarette smoke, stale food and dead rats. The dug-outs provided a place of rest, albeit temporary, but most men could not wait to leave. In

Captured German artillery pieces, most are marked with chalk, identifying the unit that captured them.

the main side corridors were a series of offices, with the click of typewriters mingling with the sounds of coughing, spitting, farting and snoring. While the dug-outs were deep and relatively safe, both entering and exiting was most hazardous, the tracks leading to the dug-outs were known to the enemy and artillery fire was a constant danger. The tracks were shelled continuously by the German artillery with every calibre available to them, including the mighty 8-inch howitzers.

While most men accepted and endured the sights of the front line, wreckage and dead bodies rarely caused a comment, there was one sight close to the dug-outs that was remembered by all the men that saw it; "… the mangled remains of a complete party of artillery carriers, six men and twelve horses."[3]

Somehow it was always the sight of dead horses rather than soldiers that created the deepest impression on the men.

Divisional headquarters were at Mersey Camp, situated north of the Poperinghe to Ypres Road, about midway between the two towns. The 36th Division officially took over the line from the 55th Division at 4:00 am on 4 August. On reviewing the current situation General Nugent decided that due to the appalling weather and ground conditions the line could be held with fewer men and subsequently issued his Divisional Order No.126, which directed that two of the supporting battalions should return to camps at Brandhoek and Vlamertinghe. These battalions were replaced by companies of 107 Brigade, who were in reserve. The following day the remaining battalion of

3   Falls, *The History of the 36th (Ulster) Division.*

A much battered front line trench.

the two brigades were also withdrawn. Other relief work was carried out during this period, but the six battalions that were to lead the attack on 16 August were spared where possible.

This was now the period of total war, men in the rest camps as far back as Vlamertinghe and Elverdinghe were subjected, night after night, to bombing from enemy aircraft and the use of gas shells from German artillery became more common both in the trenches and rear areas. Casualties caused to the horses were most severe, horses being much more vulnerable than men to wounds from shrapnel and bomb fragments. The casualty clearing stations were constantly overworked and despite suffering the highest casualty rate among their own personnel, somehow managed to cope with the unending flow of wounded and injured.

All ranks were suffering in the horrific conditions. General Nugent wrote to his wife;

> The weather conditions are simply indescribable. My Headquarters are in a grove of trees about a quarter of a mile off the main road, and there is only one track to it. The mud in the camp is only surpassed by the mud in front. I met Audley Pratt looking rather curious up in front. He had not had a wash or his clothes off for three days, nor shaved and was caked in mud, but still cheerful.

For the artillery counter-battery work was non-stop. The gun positions had little in the way of concealment, while the artillerymen and horses lacked all but the most basic shelter. The divisional artillery had already been in action for a month and was suffering such strain and discomfort that it seemed a miracle that they were able to remain in action. Added to all this was the rain, which fell ceaselessly. For the artillery detachments the nightmare seemed unending, the constant fatigue and difficulty in handling mud-splattered shells, while keeping an eye on the gun to stop it disappearing into the morass. Each gun became a small island in a sea of mud, the men clustered around the weapon precariously balanced on the wet duckboards and all the time under German counter-battery fire.

The greatest enemy was the combination of the ground and enemy artillery, there was little to fear from the German infantry, who were finding the conditions just as debilitating. On 8 August the Germans, supported by a bombardment of gas shells, launched a minor attack on the left flank of the division. The recently formed bombing squads moved up and drove the enemy infantry clear of the line.

As well as their pioneering role some men of the 16th Rifles were given other duties prior to the battle. The problem of stragglers had increased over the past months and detailed instructions were issued regarding their collection. Within the 36th Division there was to be a divisional stragglers post. It was to be manned by an NCO of the Military Police and three members of the 16th Rifles. A straggler was defined as a man who leaves the trenches ostensibly wounded, but without a field medical card or other evidence of being wounded or gassed. Superfluous assistants to wounded men, such as carrying a wounded man's rifle and or pack, or any man who could not give evidence of being on duty when leaving the trenches. Any man stopped by the NCO, as defined above would have his name, rank, number and unit recorded, be he armed or unarmed. When a convenient number of stragglers have been collected they were to be forwarded under escort together with their details to the nearest stragglers collecting station. A report dated 5 August stated the following; "The senior rank at each Straggling Post was to ensure the following equipment was at hand. Lamp, drinking water stored in petrol tins, spare gas helmets, iron rations, field dressings, picks and shovels, sandbags and empty SAA (small arms ammunition) boxes for grenades etc." Also, at the divisional stragglers collecting station a rather large supply of the listed equipment was to be kept in order to replenish the forward posts as necessary. There was also to be the means of giving a hot meal to stragglers before returning them to first line transport. It would appear that not every straggler was to be treated as a potential deserter.

Instructions were also issued regarding trophies of war. These trophies, usually enemy artillery pieces or machine guns, could be claimed as a trophy if captured by a unit in the attack. The unit had to prove that the gun was in action at the time of capture and not that it had been simply abandoned in the enemy's retreat. A trophy, properly captured, was to be marked in some way with the code letters of the unit. Paint was preferable, but if this was not available then the letters were to be cut into some part of the leatherwork. Captured trophies were also to be removed from the battle area as soon as possible as there could be subsequent difficulties later once the enemy had time to settle into his new positions. Claims by units were to be submitted to the GOC of the relevant division who, after investigation, would forward the claim, through corps headquarters to the headquarters of the Fifth Army. Eventually, after much paperwork, if successful, the trophy would be transported to the relevant regimental depot or other suitable location. It was stressed that captured guns, arms, ammunition, equipment, vehicles and other stores were the property of the Government and were to be handed over to the nearest ordnance or transport officer for conveyance to a railhead for carriage to the nearest base. In the case of special articles such as anti-gas appliances, letters, identification marks and discs were to be sent at once to headquarters of formations, as they would be required by the Intelligence Branch. Disciplinary action would be taken against anyone found in possession of these articles.

Sergeant R. McKay served with the 109th Field Ambulance and recorded in his diary the days leading up to the division's assault:

> Today awful: was obliged to carry some of the wounded into the graveyard and look on help-less till they died. Sometimes we could not even obtain a drink of water for them. Working parties are repairing the road so that the ambulances will be able to go right up to the Mine

Shaft. Yesterday and today have been the most fearful couple of days I ever put in. We are waiting every minute until a shell lights among us. We would not mind so much if there was no wounded. Went up to Wieltje at night: ambulance now going right up, one at a time. As a rule I am not very nervous, but I don't wish to spend another night at St. Jean Corner.

In one of the field ambulances Captain Richard Robson died of his wounds. He had been hit by multiple shell splinters close to the position known as Capricorn Support, and despite prompt removal from the battlefield there was nothing to be done. Born in Belfast and educated at Blackwood's Preparatory School in Northamptonshire, Barton was an excellent shot, having won the Ashburton Shield at Bisley. Formerly a company commander with the Bangor UVF, he had joined the 13th Rifles as a sergeant, prior to being commissioned as a lieutenant with the 15th Rifles. He had served on the Somme and at Messines, being awarded the Military Cross the previous spring. Captain Robson left a widow and four children.

This day, 6 August, the 15th Rifles lost two valuable members of the battalion. They say an army marches on its stomach and the supply of rations, especially hot food, is an important factor for those men in the front line. Company Quartermaster Sergeants Robert Ernest Toye and George Frank Newel, died while bringing forward rations that evening. Regimental Quartermaster Sergeant W. Thornton, a good friend of Sergeant Toye, wrote a letter to Mr John Toye of Garvagh, County Londonderry and explained what had occurred:

> Bob Toye has been killed. He was up with rations on the night of 6th August, and while at the ration dump a shell exploded close to him and killed him instantaneously, along with another, Company Quartermaster Newel, from Antrim Road, Belfast. These two were my best friends. Bob joined with me, and was in stores with me almost all the time, so I can feel a little of the sorrow that his mother will feel. Will you please tell her that her grief is shared by the men of D Company, and by many others in the regiment who, like me, knew Bob to be a straight man and a good friend. We are having crosses made, and later on, when they are erected, I will let you have all particulars.

Throughout this period there was active patrolling by elements of the division and by 7 August there was definite evidence that the enemy were located in the positions known as Iberian, Hill 35, Somme, Pond Farm and Don Trench. Iberian was actually in the 16th Division's sector, but such was the state of the ground that patrols often crossed boundary lines without knowing it.

The107 Brigade was relieved in the front line on the night of 7 August by the 11th and 12th Rifles of 108 Brigade and by 9th and 10th Inniskillings of the 109 Brigade, all moves being completed by 2:00 am. The 107 Brigade would then rest until the night of 12 August.

Private James Ailinne Gray, 108th Field Ambulance was killed on 9 August, he was 17 years old. Private Gray had three years' service to date, which gives his enlistment age as being 14.[4] He was the son of Robert and Agnes Gray of Belfast.

The II Corps, on the division's right flank, moved up to attack the Black Line on 10 August, the 36th Division's supporting artillery lending its fire to the assault. The attack was reasonably successful and preparations were made for a further advance. At 6:00 pm, the headquarters of 109 Brigade relieved headquarters of 108 Brigade at Wieltje. This was a change of headquarters only, the troops in the line remained as they were. At 4:30 am, the II Corps attacked the German lines, the XIX Corps artillery lending support. Enemy guns retaliated on XIX Corps front, the heavy shelling continuing until 5:00 am. For the remainder of the day the shelling was described as light

---

4   Local newspapers spelled his name as Grey. See *Belfast News Letter*, 7 May 1919.

as the enemy guns turned their efforts on to the II Corps. The relief did not last long and on 11 and 12 August the Division's position at Plum Farm, Bank Farm and Call Reserve were all heavily shelled. Among the casualties was Lieutenant Colonel Macrory of 10th Inniskillings who was wounded by a gunshot to the knee.[5] Command of the battalion was assumed by Lord Farnham.

On the night of 12 August 107 Brigade again took over the front line. Owing to the continuous shelling of the Blue Line, that area was left unoccupied from the night of 12 August for the following 48, hours and the two supporting battalions being disposed entirely in the old British trenches during that period. During the night Lance Corporal Hill Dugan, Army Cyclist Corps, was killed; he came from Lisburn, County Antrim. The brigade was then relieved on 14 August and those of the 108 and 109 Brigades who were to make the assault moved up, the platoons advancing in single file and collecting bombs and other special equipment at designated dumps that had been established as far forward as possible. The carrying of battalion and company flags had proved successful in the past, but for this attack their adoption was left to the discretion of individual commanding officers.

The contact patrol for the 36th Division was an RE8 aircraft from No.21 Squadron, Royal Flying Corps, although this aircraft had also to provide cover for other divisions. Contact between the aircraft and the infantry was to be by klaxon horns and Very lights from the aircraft, while the infantry were to use flares and/or Watson fans, 40 of which were issued to each battalion. A section of tanks from F Battalion, 3 Brigade, Tank Corps, was allocated to the division, but they were too far back to assist with the assault and it was hoped they could by employed in the mopping-up phase. The weather would dictate otherwise.

All officers were ordered to dress as per the men and no sticks were to be carried, it was strongly suggested they substitute a rifle. Packs were to be carried by all ranks with the exception of the men in the Lewis gun sections, who were equipped with the web pattern magazine carrier. Each Private would carry 200 rounds of ammunition and the normal issue of two No.5 Mills bombs would not be carried on this occasion. Half of each company would carry full-sized entrenching tools, the proportion of picks to shovels being one to five. Each bombing section and mopping-up squad was to carry four MSK grenades filled with KJ, or if these were not available, P grenades.[6] Experience had taught that the ordinary Mills bomb had little effect inside a concrete bunker, so if the blast would not kill or incapacitate the enemy, suffocation would suffice. The effective Yukon packs were issued with 16 going to each machine gun company, eight per battalion and six to the men of the trench mortar batteries who were acting as carriers.

While preparations were being made men continued to be killed and wounded. Sergeant R. McKay of the 109th Field Ambulance wrote on 14 August:

> Bombardment by British heavy, enemy retaliating; many casualties. We can only get up to the First Aid Posts early in the morning (3-4 o'clock am) and at twilight (8-10 pm). One party of stretcher bearers was bringing down a wounded man when an airman swooped down and dropped a bomb deliberately on them. The enemy shells the stretcher bearers all the time.

The following day he again recorded his experiences:

> Sometimes the gas does not affect the men until three or four days have elapsed when they suddenly collapse. Some of my stretcher bearers have no fear; one man, Corporal Service, was

---

5   *Belfast News Letter* 17 August 1917.
6   Grenades filled with phosgene gas, phosphorous, etc. In an underground bunker this gas and smoke would not disperse, as it did in the open air and bunkers could remain uninhabitable for up to twelve hours.

taking a wounded man down when a gas shell came over and burst just in front of the party. 'Hold your breath and come on,' Service said, as he covered the wounded man's head with a blanket, and he walked on unconcerned. The same man, Service, was with me one morning when we volunteered to go up at 4 o'clock am, and take forty-eight men along to bring six seriously wounded from a pill box known as 'Scottish Post'. The Germans had a barrage on round the house when we got up but we got through it and got the wounded out, seven cases altogether. As soon as we managed to get out through the barrage the artillerymen followed us with shells all the way down. The German gun had fired ten or twelve 5.9's at us when he placed one just to the left of our stretcher. Mud was flying everywhere when we heard the gun go again and I could have sworn the next shell was coming fair down my back. Luckily it just missed the stretcher and only covered us with more mud. The position was too hot and was getting on our nerves, so we just grabbed the stretcher and ran for it.

It was some compensation to the stretcher bearers and others that the soft mud caused the shells to bury for a considerable depth before exploding, which cushioned many of the shell splinters. With the coming attack it was obvious that more stretcher bearers would be required and soon 100 men from the Liverpool Scottish had arrived for duty. These men, along with the 200 of the 108th and 109th Field Ambulances, were catered for in the mine shaft, with all cooking being done on two Primus stoves. Each man was lucky if he got one cup of hot tea in 24 hours. Sergeant McKay also recorded; "The smell of the place is abdominal, as one staggers along the shaft splashing through the water, tripping over equipment and perhaps one of the stretcher bearers who in spite of the discomfort is sleeping soundly, exhausted too much to care about anything."

The local papers in Ulster carried the story of the erection of a brass memorial tablet to the late Captain Oswald Brooke Webb, late of the 11th Rifles. He had died on 3 July 1916, from wounds received on the first day of the Somme battle. The service was held in Drumaul Parish Church; his widow was present and saw the tablet placed in the chancel, just above where her late husband sat when he was a member of the choir.

Headstone of Captain Oswald Brooke Webb, 11th Royal Irish Rifles.

The Germans called them MEBUs, *Mannschaftseisenbetonunterstand*, a blockhouse built of reinforced concrete. This one, much overgrown, remains almost intact. (Courtesy of Jack Sheldon)

A close-up of the building showing the steel reinforcing.

Battle of Langemarck (16-18 August 1917) – "A dolorous affair"

The 36th and 16th Divisions of XIX Corps were to attack towards the Zonnebeke Ridge, which ran out as a spur from the village of Zonnebeke towards St. Julien. The artillery preparation had been completely inadequate and scores of cleverly sited machine gun posts in solid concrete pill-boxes were waiting almost unscathed on the slopes of the Ridge.[7] It must be remembered that the majority of the MEBU pillboxes and bunkers were provided to shelter machine guns and their crews from artillery fire and few were built to allow the machine guns to fire from within. As a rule they only had one entrance, on the side away from the enemy. Rarely were proper foundations laid and in the waterlogged ground of the Ypres salient it was not beyond the bounds of possibility that a blockhouse would subside to one side or the other and a near miss from a heavy calibre shell was more than capable of turning the blockhouse on its side. Should this be the side with the door then there could only follow a slow death to the occupants, from suffocation, thirst, drowning or starvation.

The conditions on the battlefield were terrible, with large areas flooded. No shell hole was dry, all contained water that could and often did conceal barbed wire and the decomposing bodies of animals and men. Movement across the ploughed-up ground was via duckboards, where an unwary footstep could send a man into liquid mud with drowning a real possibility.[8] There were no trees, just stunted trunks and everywhere could be seen the remains of corpses unearthed by the torrential rain and constant shelling.

As stated earlier, if Passchendaele had one saving grace it was the fact that the gelatinous mud ensured that many of the shells buried themselves deeply prior to exploding. However, quality control in British factories was still poor, Major Ralph Hamilton of the 106 Brigade, RFA, recorded; "We have been shelled off and on the whole time. In addition one of our own 6-in batteries has been dropping its shells on our heads; fortunately they have not exploded."[9]

The lines to be consolidated were the Red Line, a series of strong-points from Deep Trench to Aviatik Farm, the Dotted Red Line, which was the line of Don Trench and Deep Drive and the Dotted Green line on the British side of the enemy wire running from D.7 Central by Green House to D.20a.2.8.

The division's final objective was a point on the Zonnebeke – Langemarck Road close to Gallipoli Copse on the right, to Aviatik Farm on the left flank. The 16th (Irish) Division was on the right flank, the 48th (South Midland) Division, a Territorial force division, on the left; these men were recognised by the white diamond on their sleeve.

The 36th Division was to attack with 109 Brigade on the left, 108 Brigade on the right and 107 Brigade in reserve. Each brigade would attack with two battalions in the front line, with the third in support and the fourth in reserve approximately 1,000 yards behind. A half-section of a Royal Engineers Field Company was attached to each attacking battalion to provide technical assistance in the consolidation of the forward points. Each battalion would advance on a two company front, in four waves. The second and fourth waves were to be only half the strength of the first and third, due to the companies having been reduced to three platoons. Given the casualties suffered so far, approximately half the division's battle strength was now lost.[10]

---

7 Steel, Nigel & Hart, Peter, *Passchendaele, the Sacrificial Ground* (2001).
8 On 22 August the 6th Battalion Cameron Highlanders were making their way up the C Track to Cambridge Trench, moving in single file, wearing respirators and under shellfire. An NCO leading a platoon slipped off the track into a large shell hole filled with water and disappeared, attempts to pull him out were impossible as the crater interior was just glutinous mud.
9 Steel & Hart, *Passchendaele, the Sacrificial Ground*.
10 Ibid.

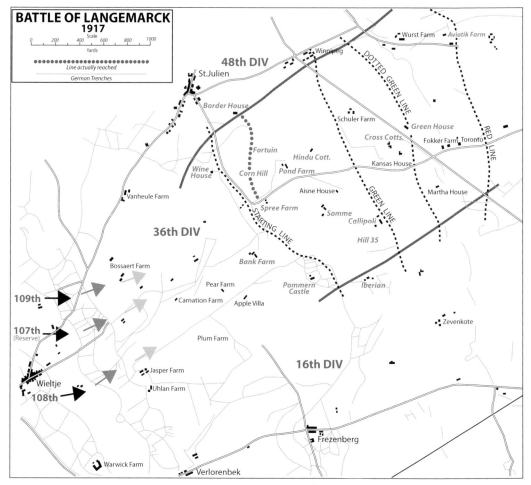

Battle of Langemarck

The objective of the leading companies was the line Gallipoli to Schuler Farm, this being on the old Green Line of the first offensive and still bearing that name. When on this line the rear companies were to pass through and advance on the final objective, with the leading companies then providing close support. The supporting battalion would then move up and take over the Green Line. One company from each of the supporting battalions was allotted to the leading two battalions on each brigade front to act as moppers-up. Nominated platoons were allotted as their specific objectives. These were concrete strong-points, most if not all sheltering one or more machine guns and their crews. On the right flank the 108 Brigades would attack the dug-outs at D.19.b.6.8, Gallipoli, Somme, Martha House, Cross Cotts and Green House. On the left flank the 109 Brigade was responsible for Pond Farm, Hindu Cott and Schuler Farm. The divisional machine gun companies would each supply four guns to accompany the advancing infantry. However, the ground was considered unsuitable for the carrying of the Stokes mortars and these remained behind, the crews being employed as carriers.

Several mopping-up squads were detailed to deal with hostile machine guns and other detachments hiding in shell holes, dug-outs and such that might be overrun by the attacking troops. One company in the supporting battalion in each brigade would furnish these squads.

The task of the field companies from the Royal Engineers was the consolidation of the Dotted Green Line. Here a defensive system was to be created on the British side of the wire that would run from Gallipoli Copse through to Green House, incorporating that position into a strong-point. From the pioneers a small party of one officer and twelve other ranks was detailed to clear the Wieltje to Gravenstafel Road where it crossed the Black Line. This was later altered to the provision of two companies.

The field artillery, under the command of General Brock, consisted of the 36th and 61st Divisional Artillery and the 108 and 150 Army Field Artillery Brigades. There were 14 18-pounder batteries allocated to the creeping barrage, which worked out at roughly one gun per 20 yards of frontage, similar to those at Messines. A further four 18-pounder batteries were made available for a distant barrage that would search out hidden ground and deal with any strong-points beyond the creeping barrage. Six 4.5-inch howitzer batteries were to fire 100 yards ahead of the distant barrage, concentrating on all known strong-points and machine gun emplacements. The pace of the barrage was set at 100 yards in five minutes, with a pause of 35 minutes in front of the Green Line. While this was considered a slow pace, events and ground conditions would prove it was too fast. There were to be three gas shell bombardments prior to the attack, the final one being on the night of 15 August, which was Y/Z night. For these a total of 100 rounds per 18-pounder and 50 rounds per howitzer were allocated. While a section of tanks was allotted to the division, there was absolutely no opportunity for the vehicles to reach the front line in time. Zero was to be at 4:45 am.

The concealment of artillery at Passchendaele was nigh on impossible given the terrain, it being little more than a swathe of mud. One option was to keep the gun position in a state of untidiness, a view reinforced by advice from the pilots carrying out aerial patrols:

For God's sake don't have any kind of order! Have your battery positions as untidy as you can make it and that will do more to defeat the Germans than anything else. Never allow men to approach the guns the same way all the time or they will make a track and that will be visible from the air.[11]

On the night of 14 August, the Black Line was taken over from 107 Brigade by two companies of each of the attacking battalions of the 108 and 109 Brigades. As soon as it was dark on the night of 15 August the remaining two companies of these battalions moved into the Black Line; the supporting battalions moved to between the Blue and the Black Lines and the reserve battalions occupied the old German front and support lines. The assembly of the two attacking brigades was complete by 3:00 am on 16 August. The 107 Brigade in divisional reserve moved into its positions in the old British front line system and the trenches just to the rear a short time later. The enemy's artillery was active throughout the night, increasing in volume from about 2:00 am. Most of the shells fell between the Black and the Blue Lines. The Black Line itself up to Zero was more or less free from shelling except around Spree Farm. Fairly heavy casualties were incurred by the attacking brigades when moving into their positions of assembly. The 11th Inniskillings being unfortunate in having their headquarters signallers and equipment knocked out. In the 14th Rifles the headquarters staff suffered heavy casualties just prior to Zero. This was just after 3:00 am, when a German shell scored a direct hit on the headquarters dug-out near Spree Farm. At least six men were killed and many more wounded. However, the dug-out did not collapse, bearing testimony to the skill of German engineers and the quality of their concrete. The battalion war diary recorded; "Dug-out full of wounded, can only bandage a few of them as we have no more dressings. Their sufferings are terrible and we cannot move."

---

11 Ibid.

The Attack of 16 August

The leading waves moved forward on time and the German barrage began. However, the majority of this fire came down on the assembly trenches in the Black Line and rear areas, leaving the assaulting troops relatively untouched. The enemy machine guns were a different matter. From the strong-points identified as Gallipoli, Somme, Aisne House, Hindu Cott, Schuler Farm, Border House and Jew Hill, a devastating hail of fire met the leading waves, and it was obvious these positions were being held in strength. The British barrage seemed to have little effect on the German machine gun fire.

As the assault commenced, Lieutenant Colonel Audley Pratt DSO, commanding 11th Inniskillings, stepped out of his command post and was mortally wounded by the blast from an exploding shell. Despite almost instant medical treatment he died 15 minutes later, Major Knott, DSO, took immediate command of the battalion.

It seemed that the preceding week's barrage had little or no effect on the enemy bunkers, the German concrete being able to withstand the heaviest pounding. Added to this were masses of uncut wire entanglements and those lanes that had been successfully cut by the supporting artillery were now covered by numerous enemy machine guns. The wire running from Capricorn Keep to Gallipoli was of considerable depth and in two distinct lines in most places, with a few gaps cut in it. The assault was no charge, more a case of the men struggling through a quagmire of churned mud and water, in many places deep enough to have barbed wire hidden under the surface. In some cases it was observed that men who fell or ran into a deep shell hole were unable to climb out due to the near liquid mud.[12] It was quickly discovered that the usual method of bypassing the strong-points and letting the moppers-do their job, was not possible and each bunker had to be fought for. This had the added difficulty in that as the men stopped to fight the bunkers the British barrage continued on without them. Nor were the Germans just ensconced in the bunkers, units had come forward and were holding various shell holes that had been prepared as strong-points and were consequently able to fire into the backs of the assaulting troops.

This battlefield was no place for a bicycle, but the men of the cyclist company were present, acting mostly as runners, attempting to carry messages back and forth between the lines. Private John Pace, a twenty-two year old from Belfast, was one of those killed. Another man killed while attempting to maintain communications between the front lines and headquarters was 20 year old Sapper Henry Victor Barr of the 36th Signals Company, he came from Twickenham Street, Belfast. Among the many wounded were Signaller Edward Cunningham, an RBAI old boy, who suffered a shattered wrist when hit by a shell fragment and Private Mark Crossey from the Ormeau Road, who received shrapnel wounds to his leg and arm. Private Crossey's brother Lieutenant W.E. Crossey, was serving with the 107th Machine Gun Company.

By now the number of men attacking was totally inadequate for the task in hand. Casualties from the machine guns, coupled with the previous losses suffered since the division took over the line, meant that the average strength of a company at the beginning of the attack was about 70 men, far from the number necessary to cover a frontage of 1,500 yards. A sergeant recorded; "It looked more like a big raiding party than anything else."[13]

On the right flank the 9th Irish Fusiliers advancing from the Pommern Redoubt drove the Germans off Hill 35. Reported initially as missing, Second Lieutenant Bristow Malone from Fortwilliam Park, Belfast, of the Fusiliers, was killed. His brother, Second Lieutenant W.A. Malone, had been taken prisoner the previous May while serving with the Cheshire Regiment. Corporal Archibald McCammond was killed; he was the son of Mr W.J. and Jane McCammond

---

12   TNA WO 95 2492 36th Division Headquarters War Diary.
13   Falls, *The History of the 36th (Ulster) Division.*

of 16 Monaghan Street, Milford, County Armagh. Another to die was Private William Greer from Newtownhamilton, Armagh; he was 26 years old and has no known grave. The Jones brothers went into action on this day, they came from Annagh Hill, Portadown, and four would survive the battle. The loss to the family was Private Edward Jones who served in C Company; he was 38 years old. In the Irish Fusiliers Private W.J. McCoy, a medical orderly on attachment from the RAMC, was in the process of winning the fifteenth Military Medal for his town of Lurgan. This was not the first time his actions had come to notice. On 1 July 1916 he was one of a party of strong men who had been sent by the field ambulance to Hamel to collect wounded and for seven days and nights had worked continuously, without sleep and little food or rest. Then again at Messines his conduct on the battlefield had caused much comment as he recovered and treated the wounded in the most trying circumstances. Now, here on the battlefield of Langemarck, he was to receive due recognition.[14] Listed as missing this day was Second Lieutenant William Matthew Seymour from Marlborough Park, Belfast. He served in No.8 Platoon of B Company and was still listed as such in January 1919, when his brother made an appeal through the pages of the local papers.[15]

The 13th Rifles on the left flank of the Irish Fusiliers also advanced and by-passed the strongpoint known as Somme, reckoned to be one of the strongest bunkers on this section of the front line. A platoon from the 13th Rifles was detailed to take and hold the bunker, but was unable to make any headway, despite some very accurate shooting from the rifle grenade section, who attempted to outflank it. Captain Belt, the battalion adjutant, with a small group of men, attempted to dig in to the front of the bunker. He was almost immediately hit, a serious bullet wound and only with good fortune was he able to crawl back to his own lines, having refused any assistance, he would later be awarded the Military Cross. This day saw the death of Corporal David John MacAuley of the 13th Rifles, his brother Marshall, also serving in the 13th Rifles, had been killed the previous February. David was a member of the Orange Order and Masonic Order in Belturbet.[16]

As the 11th Inniskillings advanced they were supported by the 9th Inniskillings, the leading Company moving out of Capricorn Trench at 4:45 am. They were met by a heavy barrage of artillery, but casualties seemed to be slight, the deep mud cushioning most of the shell fragments. Given that the ground was pockmarked from the bombardment the advance slowed as men stumbled into shell holes and around wire obstacles and they lost their own barrage as it crept ahead. This left them open to enemy machine guns which seemed to be plentiful, and the Inniskillings were forced to take cover in the shell holes and dig in. Shortly afterwards Lieutenant Wintle of the 9th Inniskillings received a bullet wound and then almost immediately a second, this proved to be fatal and despite medical treatment he would later die of his wounds in hospital on 22 August. Later General Nugent wrote to Captain Wintle's mother; "He showed the greatest courage and gallantry, and even after he had been wounded at once insisted on carrying on until he fell mortally wounded. I have recommended him for a Military Cross, which he richly deserves."

A fellow officer wrote:

> I must tell you how proud I am of his conduct before and during the battle. His men were greatly encouraged by his bravery and courage, and he has added new laurels to a name well

---

14 *Belfast News Letter* 15 October 1917.
15 As of April 2014 the CWGC lists him as having served with 10th Royal Irish Fusiliers.
16 Both men are commemorated in the private chapel of Castle Saunderson in Belturbet, Cavan, and their father being the land steward of the Estate.

Masonic jewel as issued to the 16th Royal
Irish Rifles (Pioneers).

A newspaper cutting dated 5 April 1919 putting
the blame for the Great War squarely on the Grand
Lodge of Orient for starting the conflict.

SATURDAY. APRIL 5. 1919.

Kaiser and Freemasons.

GRAND LODGE OF ORIENT BLAMED FOR STARTING WAR.

Professor Theodore Schiemann, a journalistic and confident of the ex-Kaiser, has been showing to a correspondent of the "Chicago Daily News" some letters he recently received from William Hohenzollern. The letters were sent by courier from Holland. During his exile the Kaiser has been studying the causes of the war, and he has arrived at the curious conclusion that it was not he but the Freemasons who started it. He declares that through the machinations of the Grand Lodge of the Orient a pact was made by which America, England, and France were bound up together, and that there never had been any question about American participation, as America was pledged to fight when called upon. The Kaiser wrote to Professor Schiemann a few weeks ago as follows: "It was not the Lusitania, it was not the U-boats, which caused America to come in. These were only incidents raised and magnified by Wilson as excuses. Wilson was merely carrying out his part of the programme." The Kaiser added characteristically: "I learn from a source in Switzerland that the Americans were going to withdraw their forces from the front on January 1, 1919, because of the terrible losses they were suffering, and there I stood with my victorious armies ready to reach out and grasp the fruits of our struggle. But no! Had I returned to Berlin a conqueror, the programme of the Social Democrats would have been set back years at least. They would not have it so."

known for its soldierly deeds, and I can assure you his death is very keenly felt by us all. Even when mortally wounded he would not allow the men to carry him in, fearing harm should come to them in doing so, and remained out until dark as the place was swept by machine gun fire.

Lieutenant Wintle's MC was gazetted on 18 October. The Inniskillings lost another officer when Lieutenant Fred Irwin was killed. The lieutenant and his men had advanced and were occupying a German dug-out equipped with a lookout position in the roof. Fred Irwin was looking through this watching the Germans prepare for a counter attack from the hill opposite. The position came under accurate small arms fire, possibly from a sniper and Irwin ordered his men to take cover. Before he himself could withdraw he was shot between the eyes and killed instantly.[17]

---

17   Letter from Reverend J.G. Paton, MC, Battalion chaplain, to the deceased officer's sister.

In the 10th Inniskillings a man from Mayo was killed. Sergeant Joseph William Shaw from Ballysakerry was 26 years old and like so many other on this battlefield, he has no known grave. In the 11th Inniskillings Sergeant Richard Owens was killed, he was 25 years old and came from Fountain Street, Londonderry. Owens had been wounded while serving at Gallipoli in 1915.

From 6:00 am it was noticed that men were beginning to fall back. Colonel Perceval-Maxwell, 13th Rifles, now recovered from the wounds he had received at Martinsart in July the previous year, attempted to stop this withdrawal by leading forward his battalion headquarters in a desperate attack on the Somme bunker. As with the other attacks, this failed and Perceval-Maxwell was wounded for a second time when a bullet smashed his thigh. It would be the following year before he was again fit for active service. In the ranks Lance Corporal Hans Morrison was killed, he was 32 years old and the son of Francis and Agnes Morrison of Meeting Street, Ballynahinch. One of the few Catholic officers in the division was killed here, Captain John Nugent Cahill, also with the 13th Rifles came from Kilkenny and had joined the battalion in July 1916, shortly after the Somme fighting. Fellow officers remembered him as being brave, keen and mindful of his duties. Despite the difference in religion Cahill got on well with his fellow officer, their mutual interests being hunting and horses. The 13th Rifles had moved forward only a short distance when Captain Cahill was wounded. He was carried back to the dressing station, but was found to have died on the way. A fellow officer wrote; "His stay with the 13th Royal Irish Rifles was a short one, but a pleasant one for those brought into contact with him, his courage and happy spirit will keep his memory green amongst us."

With the failure of this attack, any further assaults by 108 Brigade came to a halt. There were just too few men and the loss in officers had been high. The 9th Irish Fusiliers had lost their commander, Colonel Somerville, mortally wounded while attempting to rally his men and organised a line. While the brigade would move no further forward, were still able to hold their positions on Hill 35, their right flank protected by the 16th.Division. In the 12th Rifles Captain William Stuart, from Mount Earl, County Antrim, was in the process of earning his Military Cross. With great dash and personal bravery he led his company in capturing many prisoners and doing excellent work in consolidating his positions, although his men were on the point of exhaustion. Despite Stuart's encouragement it wasn't enough and the assault here came to a halt.

Across the battlefield the men of the various trench mortar batteries, acting as carriers, were doing their best to bring forward ammunition, water and other supplies. They were paying a heavy price as they slogged through the mud. Private William Tosh, from Windmill Terrace, Londonderry, served with the 109th Trench Mortar Battery and was an 'old soldier' at 40 years of age. He was killed and like so many others, has no known grave. Private John Stewart from Templepatrick, County Antrim, was another who fell; he had originally enlisted in the 14th Rifles in 1914. Also with the 109th was Second Lieutenant Alexander McCullough from the Antrim Road, Belfast. He was 21 and had been a student at Connell's Academy, Belfast, studying for a career with the Civil Service. He was initially reported as missing, then wounded and finally the dreaded telegram bearing the fateful news was received by his family. Another man killed from the 109th was Private John Campbell from Aghadowey, Couny Londonderry.

Second Lieutenant John Alexander Paterson Bill of the 12th Rifles died this day. The son of missionaries in Southern Nigeria, John was born in Edinburgh and was a former pupil of Inst and Queen's University. His initial intention was to follow his parents as a missionary, but with the outbreak of War he joined the Royal Army Medical Corps, before transferring to the Rifles in 1915. He served firstly with the 18th Reserve Battalion before being attached to the 12th Rifles. His final moments were witnessed by two fellow officers. Second Lieutenant Branningan, a close friend, confirmed that Bill was hit just in front of the British wire; "Mr Bill was hit before he got right over and his body was seen in front of our wire. Mr Bill was a great friend of mine."

Second Lieutenant Stokes observed:

> This officer was last seen about map ref. D 19 b 10 90. He was lying on the ground apparently wounded in the groin or lower abdomen. Private Matthews went out to dress him but was himself killed in the act of doing so, and it is supposed that the same bullet also hit Mr Bill. The men had by this time started coming back and Mr Bill was left behind apparently very seriously wounded.[18]

The location identified is very close to Gallipoli Farm, just to the south of the Wieltje – Gravenstafel Road. The lieutenant's body was lost and he is commemorated on the Tyne Cot Memorial. To the stretcher bearers of the field ambulances the mud made their job nigh impossible. Robert Doggart had one abiding memory of Langemarck:

> The Engineers had lifted most of the duck boards, making it very difficult to walk along the trenches. When we had to carry a wounded man through the trenches, we had to carry the stretcher on our shoulders; it took at least four of us to do this task. Well, I remember one case in particular, as we made our way to the dressing station, the man on the stretcher toppled off; right on top of my head and onto the ground. Of course we apologised to him, but he said not to worry because if it hadn't been for us he may still have been lying out in no man's land.

In the 109th Field Ambulance Private James Graham Currie from Northumberland Street, Belfast, was wounded. His comrades brought him to the aid post, but despite treatment he later died, he was 31 years old. Private Richard O'Brien had formerly worked as a gardener for the Davidson family of Seacourt, Bangor. He was a stretcher-bearer in the 13th Rifles and was killed as he attempted to bring the wounded off the field. The Reverend Robert Kelso, padre of the battalion wrote to the family:

> Your brother was acting as a stretcher-bearer and was killed late in the day. Before the end came he had behaved in a most gallant and courageous manner, and all who saw him at work amongst the wounded are loud in their praises and unanimous that his conduct deserved the Victoria Cross. All over the battlefield regardless of personal safety he attended the wounded, dressing them and getting them back to the medical aid post. By his splendid example, coolness and endurance he inspired all around him, and no doubt saved many lives by his labour. His conduct has been the talk of the battalion since he came out and should a posthumous honour be awarded him all his comrades will be rejoiced.[19]

On the right flank of the 109 Brigade, the 14th Rifles were faced with the worst terrain of the assault. Here the men literally waded through water that ranged from knee to waist deep; every step forward was an effort as the mud threatened to suck men under. As they slowly moved forward, the machine gun fire from Pond Farm to their front laced into them and Lieutenant Ledlie, with a small number of men made a gallant effort to capture this strong-point. He managed to surround the bunker on three sides and any enemy that showed themselves was quickly killed. However, with so few men an actual assault was out of the question and Ledlie twice sent back a runner to ask for reinforcements, but none came. It was impossible to make any further attack, losses to the terrific machine gun fire and the enemy artillery being just too much. Deciding that the position

---

18 Believed to be Private Samuel Matthews, 11th Inniskillings.
19 No award of any kind appears to have been made.

was hopeless Lieutenant Ledlie ordered his men back to another position some 150 yards away, this move being covered by fire from the ever dependable Lewis guns. Even in the fall-back casualties were suffered. Lance Corporal John Harvey Dixon, a veteran of the Somme and Messines, was in charge of a Lewis gun section in B Company. A former member of the YCV, he was 25 when he was killed. The Reverend John Knowles, Presbyterian Chaplain, wrote to his father; "We are all deeply grieved for the loss of your son. He was a good soldier, faithful in his duty, and has been faithful unto death."

It was now 8:00 am, another casualty here was Second Lieutenant James Wilson McBurney, a former pupil of RBAI and Queen's University OTC. He had been commissioned in September 1916 and arrived with the division in December. James came from Moatville, Comber County Down and was 19 years old when he was killed. Second Lieutenant McBurney was just one of 23 second lieutenants of the Rifles to be killed between 1 and 31 August and one of many who has no known grave. Lieutenant J. Riddy wrote to McBurney's parents on 19 August:

> It is with deepest sadness I write to express my sympathy and regret at the loss of your beloved son Jim. I cannot find the words to express my feelings of regret and sorrow. He was a brave and good comrade, and most cheerful under all circumstances. Since I joined the regiment, we were the closest friends and a truer friend I never wish to have. Jim and I slept in the same tent before the attack; he seemed to know something would happen to him for he asked me to write, and if I could, to bring him back to a dressing station in case he was hurt, but I thought he was joking. He was in good form before the attack; I was on his right flank. He went forward at the head of his men, and did splendid work. A fine example of Irish pluck leading and cheering his men on against fearful odds and machine gun fire. He was first at the enemy strong-point, but got shot in the chest before getting in. Although dying fast, he urged his men on, and his last words were 'Tell my father and mother I died at the head of my men fighting for my country.' I afterwards took charge of part of his men, who spoke in the highest terms of his valour and coolness. After the attack my men searched for his body, but could not find him, sorry to say. Every effort is being made to recover our dead, and I hope he will be found. You cannot imagine how lonesome and sad we feel without him. Everyone who knew him loved and respected him and his men would do anything for him. A more noble or gallant boy never died for his country. I hope you will not worry too much, but I know it is a heavy blow; the dearest must part and one day we must all pay the price. I hope poor Jim is much happier now. As you will have seen, our losses were awful. Please accept my most sincere sympathy.[20]

Second Lieutenant McBurney's parents also received letter from Lieutenant McGhie who informed them that that their son had been shot through the heart and died painlessly. Something he had in common with the majority of men killed between 1914 and 1918.

The converging fire of three separate enemy machine guns had stopped the company of Lieutenant John Dwyer O'Brien, the man from County Cork. Having successfully located their positions the lieutenant directed Lewis gun fire and rifle grenades against the enemy guns. O'Brien then made several dashes against the positions, setting a splendid example to his men, something he had been doing since his arrival with the division; he had a considerable reputation earned during trench raids. Sadly on this day dash and courage were not enough and the Lieutenant fell mortally wounded and died the next day. For his actions he was award the Military Cross. Another who died and has no known grave was Private James Harper. The *Belfast Evening Telegraph* of

---

20 Clarke, Alan, *Over The Top,* newsletter of the Western Front Association, N Ireland Branch (Winter 1999).

March 1918, reported the unveiling of a plaque to the Ulsterville Harriers, on it he is listed on it as having served in the 10th Rifles.

In the ranks of the 11th Inniskillings casualties had been heavy and the survivors were pinned down in front of the Green Line. From their left flank machine guns fired on them from Border House and Fort Hill. One officer and seven men ran forward as the barrage lifted and actually reached the Green Line, but no others were able to move forward to support them and they were later forced to withdraw. Fort Hill was rushed by men from the support companies who attacked it with bombs and the bayonet. A number of the enemy were killed and several taken prisoner.

It was here that the only appreciable gain was made in the entire attack, with an advance of some 400 yards on the left flank in the area of 109 Brigade. At this point a position running from C.18.a.2.6 through Fort Hill to Corn Hill and Strong-point 66 was held by the men of the 109 Brigade who had dug in and consolidated. The reserve battalion of each brigade, the 12th Rifles on the right and the 10th Inniskillings on the left, moved into the Black Line where preparations were made against any counter-attack. Observers noticed that the Germans were moving reinforcements into position behind Pond Farm. An SOS rocket, bursting into two red and two green lights, was launched and the British barrage quickly fell on the enemy platoons as they formed up, causing heavy casualties and spoiling any planned attack on this front.

On the division's left flank, the 48th Division of XVIII Corps also suffered from inadequate artillery support. Pill boxes were not suppressed and counter-battery fire was ineffective. While they could only manage a meagre advance they did manage to capture St Julien and Border House later in the morning despite horrendous casualties. On the right flank the 16th Division was also having a bad time. The diary of Captain Arthur Glanville Royal Dublin Fusiliers recorded prior to the action;

Hell all the time, mud awful, no trenches, no shelters, no landmarks. All movement by night, shellfire all the time and everywhere casualties enormous! Several killed every day and wounded every hour. Anxiety for officers who do not know what time attack starts until late at night. Impossible to get into position in dark under hellish shelling. Attack at dawn – given away by Sergeant Phillips. Boche puts up terrible barrage before zero as we are moving into position.

The reference to a Sergeant Phillips was due to a rumour throughout the army at this time that an NCO had deserted to the enemy and took with him maps and orders pertaining to the attack. The 16th Division saw fierce resistance from machine guns firing from Potsdam, Vampire and Borry Farms. These had not been cleared by the leading companies due to the severe shortage of infantry. As a result of this the men of 48 Brigade found themselves being shot in the back. The division's 49 Brigade made several costly attacks on Borry Farm, but without success. The brigade eventually got within 400 yards of the top of Hill 37, their furthermost point forward.

The Germans counter-attacked at approximately 9:00 am, the infantry assault being preceded by a crushing artillery barrage consisting of both high explosive and smoke shells. The 36th and 16th Divisions were attacked by the reserve regiment of the 5th Bavarian Division, supported by elements of the 12th Reserve (*Eingreif*) Division, part of the VI Reserve Corps. An *Eingreif* division was responsible for engaging in immediate counter-attacks against any enemy troops who had broken through a defensive position; these units had only been formed in 1917 and were self-contained with its own artillery, machine gun, pioneer, cavalry and medical units. Despite the British having air superiority preparations for this counter-attack had not been spotted by the patrolling aircraft.

In the Ulster Division at 3:30 pm, a conference was held at headquarters, attended by all brigade commanders and it was decided that 107 Brigade would relieve 108 and 109 Brigades that evening. Further progress, if any, was to be decided at a later time.

The 16th Division was badly hit and they had no option but to execute a fighting withdrawal. It was 10:00 pm that night before the last man had returned to their original start line. In the early hours of the following morning the 16th Division lost one of their most revered characters. The Reverend William Doyle, MC, the chaplain of the 8th Royal Dublin Fusiliers, was killed. He was as well known in the 36th Division as in the 16th, a report in the *Glasgow Evening News* on 1 September 1917 from a member of the Ulster Division stated:

> We couldn't possibly agree with his religious opinions, but we simply worshipped him for other things. He didn't know the meaning of fear, and he didn't know what bigotry was. He was as ready to risk his life to take a drop of water to a wounded Ulsterman as to assist men of his own faith and regiment. If he risked his life looking after Ulster Protestant soldiers once, he did it a hundred times in his last few days. The Ulstermen felt his loss more keenly than anybody and none were readier to show their marks of respect to the dead hero priest than were our Ulster Presbyterians. Father Doyle was a true Christian in every sense of the word and a credit to any religious faith.

In the ranks of the 2nd Royal Irish Regiment Lance Corporal F.G. Room, a stretcher bearer was awarded the Victoria Cross for his actions on the battlefield. There are those who maintain all stretcher bearers should have been so awarded.

At Bank Farm a captured pillbox had been utilised as a dressing station by the 109th Field Ambulance who were treating men from the 13th Rifles. A drawback of using such positions was that the entrance to the pillbox then faced enemy lines. In conditions where it took up to eight men to carry a stretcher, quite often literally up to their knees in mud, exhaustion was the order of the day. Added to this was the necessity to attempt to ignore shell bursts, bullets and writhing swirls of gas. At noon a team of stretcher-bearers were resting at the door of the pillbox when an enemy shell exploded just inside the entrance. Among those killed was Corporal John Edwin Greenwood MM, from Newington Avenue, Belfast, Private William McCormick MM, Beverley Street, Belfast and Private John Henry Barrett, Carnan Street, Belfast, all of the 109th Field Ambulance. Also among the casualties was 24 year old Private John Graham Savage, 13th Rifles, the son of Councillor James Savage and Mary Savage of Ballyholme Road, Bangor. In a letter to the Savage family, Padre Robert Kelso told of how Private Savage, rated highly as a medical orderly, had been assisting the medical officer at the battalion first aid post when the shell had landed.[21] Lieutenant S.P. Rea, RAMC, also wrote to the Savage family; "… the blow was a hard one, but he fell at the post of duty."[22]

Corporal John Greenwood also had connections to Bangor and like the others has no known grave. All are commemorated on the Tyne Cot Memorial.[23] Another casualty was Captain Horace Dorset Eccles, RAMC; the 13th Rifles' medical officer.[24] Eccles was a man of exceptional courage, he was a veteran of the war in South Africa where he had served with the 8th New Zealand Contingent RAMC, and had been mentioned in despatches. He had entered Guy's Hospital in 1888 and qualified in 1893. He then practiced in South Africa for about three years, subsequently migrating to New Zealand where he established himself in a practice on the North Island.[25] With

---

21   *Bangor Spectator* , 24 August 1917.
22   *Belfast News Letter,* 25 August 1917.
23   In a local publication, dated 2011, John Greenwood is misidentified as having served in the 9th Field Ambulance.
24   The son of Gregory William and Ann Hyde Eccles of Southfields, London, New Irish Farm Cemetery, grave XVI. C. 20
25   Guy's Hospital Medical School Records, King's College London, Archives.

the destruction of Bank Farm, except during quiet intervals, the wounded requiring stretchers were collected in the trenches in the vicinity prior to removal.

Approximately 433 stretcher bearers had been made available for the attack. Of these 260 were RAMC and the remainder were tunnellers, divisional salvage and burial section members. They were absolutely necessary as east of the advance dressing station at Wieltje the ground was impossible for any sort of wheeled transport. Further to the rear from Zero plus four hours, a half-hourly train service was provided for the walking wounded on the light railway as far as St Jean, until the line was knocked out at midday. Lorries ran from 300 yards west of St Jean to the corps walking wounded dressing station. These arrangements proved more than adequate for all requirements and could have efficiently dealt with a very much larger number of walking cases.

By the second day of the battle the Mine Shaft was worse than ever, if such a thing were to be possible. Sergeant McKay stated:

> There is a heap of dead lying up at the entrance where they have been thrown out. I was told by Captain Johnston that the division was being relieved tonight and to warn the men of the 109th Field Ambulance that they could make their way down to headquarters. One man, B. Edgar, asked me when I was going down, and I said in the morning between two and three o'clock. Edgar then said he was going to have a sleep and not to go down without him. I looked at him and said, "Where in Heaven's name are you going to sleep here?" and for an answer was told that there were two dead men at the entrance with a blanket thrown over them and I would find him in under the blanket, and he would not be disturbed, as all three were lying in the open above ground.

When Sergeant McKay was eventually able to take his boots off, after five days, he claimed his feet looked parboiled. In those five days he had little food or water and even less sleep. The recovery of the wounded from the battlefield had required Herculean efforts on the part of the stretcher-bearers. From the regimental aid posts at Bank Farm, Rat Farm and Plum Farm to the dressing station was at a minimum a distance of 2,000 yards over shell torn ground sometimes knee deep in mud. In most cases it took eight men to carry a laden stretcher for any length of distance. Battlefield evacuations were made under shellfire and the deeds of valour were countless and generally unrewarded. Among those comforting to the wounded was the Assistant Chaplain-General of the division, the Reverend F.J. Halahan MC, who spent hours on the field encouraging the men to even greater efforts. At Rat Farm the medical officer of the 14th Rifles, Captain John Gavin, MC, promoted since the Somme and succeeding Captain W.R. Mackenzie, carried out magnificent work and was subsequently awarded a Bar to his MC.[26] Here two other medical officers were killed. Records show that from 16 to18 August, some 58 officers and 1,278 other ranks passed through the divisional dressing stations.

Captain Samuel Picken made numerous trips out into the battlefield to assist in treating and recovering the wounded, much of it under shellfire. Moving from shell hole to shell hole he treated men where they lay and then ensured that they were recovered by the stretcher-bearers. Like Captain Gavin he would also earn a Military Cross. One of those who succumbed to his wounds was Sergeant William Henderson of the 13th Rifles, who died on 25 August. He came from Warkworth Street, Belfast, and was one of the oldest men to serve in the division, he was fifty-seven. A veteran of the Zulu War of 1879, he had been a previous member of the Bangor Regiment of the UVF and was one of the first to enlist on the outbreak of war. His only son,

---

26   Gavin, Captain Noel John Hay, MC & Bar, RAMC, *Belfast News Letter* 3 October 1917.

Lance Corporal Hermon Henderson was killed in the Dardanelles serving with the Inniskillings. Sergeant Henderson left a widow, Annie and three daughters.

Between midnight and 2:30 am on 18 August, the four leading battalions of the division suffered approximately 50 casualties apiece. All were suffering from shell and gunshot wounds and from the effects of gas. Not included in this total are those men from the attached artillery batteries.[27]

At divisional headquarters General Nugent was contemplating a new attack to try and again capture the Green Line. On advice from those staff officers who had visited the line and from his brigadiers, it became evident that any such attack was totally out of the question. A considerable number of officers and NCOs had either been killed, wounded or were missing. All units were thoroughly disorganised and exhausted and neither 108 Brigade nor 109 Brigade could field more than 500 men capable of making any assault. General Nugent therefore cancelled any plans for an attack and instead ordered 107 Brigade to relieve the other two after darkness had fallen. This relief was carried out under the most difficult circumstances and the relieving units struggled to find those men still in the line, or lying out in no man's land. Eventually the exhausted survivors of the two assaulting brigades were brought back to Winnizeele by omnibus. Later that night 183 Brigade of the 61st (2nd South Midland) Division relieved 107 Brigade, which then moved back to Brandhoek. The final command of the line was handed over to the GOC 61st Division at 3:00 pm on 18 August.

The division had suffered terribly during the month. A high ratio of men was lost considering how few had actually been involved. The total number of casualties suffered between 2 August and 18 August was 144 officers and 3,441 other ranks. It was in this action that the division lost its highest number of pack animals, again something that seemed to cause more concern among the handlers than the loss of their fellow men.[28]

A post action report highlighted the difficulties of procuring rations and how this added to the overall exhaustion of the men. Owing to the very heavy rains during the first two days of August and the occasional showers during the days that followed the ground was in a very boggy condition and in places was impassable. Rations were taken forward by road as far as Wieltje where they were offloaded and taken up to the line by carrying parties; the personnel for these carrying parties having to be supplied by the infantry battalions. The conditions of the ground meant that the use of pack animals was impossible for this work forward of Wieltje and it had to be done by men. The constant and at times very heavy shelling by the enemy increased the difficulty of movement. The state of the trenches and the bad weather made frequent relief essential if the men were to be kept even reasonably fit. To cope with the work in the forward area, principally the making of tracks, roads and gun emplacements etc., large working parties running into almost a 1,000 men per day had to be furnished. Given this number it proved impossible to keep any troops fresh for the attack and all had to take their turn in the line and do their share of the work, time for resting was sparse. As a consequence by the time the attack was launched the men were already exhausted.

In the after action report five reasons were given for the failure of the attack:

1. The divisions were holding the line for 13 days prior to the attack. They were under near continuous shelling and had to supply from their 'resting' battalions to various working parties, sometimes up to a 1,000 men a day, again these had to work under fire from enemy artillery.
2. The water-logged ground; many areas were under water that was up to knee deep. This water also concealed shell holes, barbed wire and decomposing bodies of men and animals.

---

27   Falls, *The History of the 36th (Ulster) Division.*
28   War Diary A and Q Branch.

A dressing station near Zillebeke on the Menin Road. A member of the Division gets his leg wound dressed as the prisoner he was escorting to the rear waits patiently. The RAMC lance corporal had a particularly nasty dent to the top of his steel helmet.

3.   The machine guns in pill boxes, the vast majority of which were undamaged by British guns and a defence that had been organised 'in depth' as opposed to linear.
4.   The British were outgunned in artillery, both in numbers and in firepower
5.   The failure of the British guns to cut the wire as effectively as it had done at Messines.

One of the obvious lessons learnt was that, given the ground to be crossed, the barrage moved too quickly. In future it had to be slower and of greater depth. After the battle General Nugent had access to captured German orders from the Fourth German Army and these revealed some interesting points and brought up others for discussion. The Germans were now unable to shell the area over which the British advanced as their own troops were distributed in depth over it. The enemy was still capable of causing damage to the British support lines, but counter-battery fire was more important in supporting the advance than protecting the rear. In future attacks the creeping barrage would have to be slowed down and with frequent pauses. During these pauses a sweeping barrage and a 60-pounder barrage in front of it might sweep and search. It was also suggested that the infantry might somehow take charge of the speed and direction of the barrage, but as of this time the difficulties of doing so were insurmountable. Given that the Germans were now fighting using new defensive tactics, it was suggested that the attacking tactics should also change. Long lines of attack present difficulties of command and control and lacked manoeuvrability. New tactics and formations could and would be adopted.

The end of the day saw more letters being written by officers, men and the ever dependable padres. With the death of Sergeant Fraser Douglas Mann, 13th Rifles, Lieutenant Harold Hardy wrote to the family on 27 August:

> I am very sorry to have to tell you that your son, Sergeant Mann, was killed in action on the 16th inst. Your son was a very gallant soldier, and not only in his last battle, but in the raid before the Messines battle he did splendid work. He will be greatly missed in the battalion. Please accept my deepest sympathy with you in your great loss.

Sergeant Mann has no known grave. Once again the padres put pen to paper. The Reverend Samuel Mayes with the 9th Irish Fusiliers wrote to the mother of Private William Campbell:

> Your gallant boy has not been heard of since 16th of August. On that day our brave lads were driven from a position they had taken early in the day, and some of the wounded were left in German hands. I hope your son is still alive as he was such a gallant soldier and beloved by all.

Private Campbell is buried in Bedford House Cemetery, Zillebeke. Private Edward Jones was old for frontline service, being thirty-eight when he was killed on 16 August, his being a stretcher bearer in C Company may well explain this. The Reverend Mayes wrote to Mrs Jones:

> I most deeply sympathise with you on the death of your gallant husband. He was killed instantly while carrying a wounded man back from the line. He died the death of a hero and Portadown has every right to be proud of such sons. We miss him very much in the band, and as a stretcher bearer. He nobly did his duty, and died like a man at his post.

General Nugent wrote to his wife:

> It has been a truly terrible day. Worse than the 1st July I am afraid. Our losses have been very heavy indeed and we have failed all along the line, so far as this division is concerned and the whole division has been driven back with terrible losses. Audley Pratt is gone, Somerville another of my colonels also gone, Bob Maxwell I grieve to say was last seen wounded and lying out in front and we have been driven in since then and he was not brought back. Blair Oliphant another of my colonels has not been heard of for several hours. Peacock another commanding officer has not been seen or heard of since early morning and his whole battalion has disappeared. We don't know where they are but we hope they may be holding out in shell holes in front and will get back after dark. Tomorrow we have to make another attack at dawn and I have no men to do it with. It is a ghastly business. Our failure has involved the failure of the divisions on both sides of us and that is so bitter a pill. In July last year, we did our work but failed because the division on either flank failed us. This time it is the Ulster Division which has failed the Army. I am heartbroken over it and I fear we shall be absolutely wiped out tomorrow. We have not enough men left to do the attack or to hold the line we are to hold, even if we get it. My poor men. Now I mustn't go on like this. It isn't fair to you. I have no time for more. Bless you all my dearest. How I wish I could have given you a more cheering letter.
>
> P.S. Just heard that Bob Maxwell has been got in and is in the Field Ambulance, shot through the thigh but nothing serious."

As already stated Colonels Pratt and Somerville had been killed, but both Peacock and Blair Oliphant were unharmed. General Nugent was also mistaken in his belief that the flanking divisions were let down on 16 August. Given the terrain and casualties suffered on that day no division could have succeeded. Likewise given the strength of the Ulster Division and the German positions on the Frezenberg Ridge, the outcome could not have been otherwise.

On 17 August, a Friday, Field Marshal Haig visited General Gough and was told that both the 16th and 36th Divisions had gone forward, but failed to keep what they had won. The men are Irish and do not like the shelling, Gough said. Haig then visited General Watts at XIX headquarters, who also gave a bad account of the two Irish divisions. However, Haig also listened to the opinion of others and wrote:

> But I gather that the attacking troops had a long march up the evening before the battle through Ypres to the front line and then had to fight from zero 4:45 am until nightfall. The men could have had no sleep and must have been dead tired. Here also a number of concrete buildings and dugouts had never really been destroyed by artillery fire, and do not appear to have been taken. So the advances made were small.[29] General Gough also seems to have been unaware on the make-up of the two divisions and just where the reinforcements were coming from. These were no longer "Irish" divisions.

In the 109th Field Ambulance a medical report dated 22 August stated; "Williamson very sick, evacuated…with Typhoid Fever. Several men have already gone away with the same disease."

Given the circumstances, unburied bodies, lack of sanitation and rats, this was not unexpected. It took strenuous efforts to ensure that this outbreak did not become an epidemic.

Transferred from 4th Division, the 1st Royal Irish Fusiliers arrived and was posted to 107 Brigade on 27 August. In order to facilitate this transfer it was necessary to amalgamate to of the existing battalions. Therefore the 8th and 9th Rifles became the 8th/9th Rifles, which was greeted with some dismay with those few original officers and men who had survived the war so far. There were other changes within the division. A draft of some 300 men from the North Irish Horse, recently dismounted, arrived and was posted to the 9th Irish Fusiliers, which was subsequently known as the rather convoluted 9th (North Irish Horse) Battalion Royal Irish Fusiliers. From the 16th (Irish) Division came the 7th Rifles, along with the 2nd Rifles from the 25th.Division. The 7th Rifles strength was just under 400 men, some of whom were volunteers from the Channel Islands. The men from Jersey and Guernsey had originally been allocated to the same battalion until it was pointed out to the authorities that traditional rivalry would see the two bailiwicks spending as much time fighting each other as the enemy![30] The 7th Rifles men were transferred to the 2nd Rifles, which was then allocated to the 108 Brigade. Again space had to be created so the 11th and 13th Rifles, who were both under strength, became the 11th/13th Rifles.

The division, again less its artillery and pioneers, had four days' rest in the area around Winnizeele, before moving south by railway. The troops that detrained at Bapaume and Miraumont were faced with a totally devastated landscape. The scars of previous fighting were largely hidden under a carpet of coarse grass, while traces of buildings were difficult to discern, the ruins had been blown flat and the rubble removed to repair and maintain the excellent roads that now traversed the countryside. Even the location of villages presented a difficulty and the site of the church at Le Sars was only found due to a sign that had been placed in its original location.

---

29   Sheffield & Bourne, *Douglas Haig: War Diaries and Letters*.
30   Ford, Douglas, Jersey Museum Service, April 1990.

Men of the 2nd Royal Irish Rifles wearing the leather issue of equipment. This battalion joined the Division in 1917.

This was the area that had been evacuated by the enemy on his retreat to the Hindenburg Line, known to the Germans as the *Siegfried Stellung*. The Germans had evacuated all the local population, demolished every building, blown up every bridge, destroyed fruit trees and left few comforts for any advancing troops. There were some advantages to the area. There were few shell holes and the coarse grass provided fodder for horses and other pack animals. The woods had survived and the ground was dry, a vast improvement on life in the Salient.

Having relieved the 9th (Scottish) Division between 28 and 30 August, the division had taken up its new positions in the line. On the right flank this was marked by a communications trench called Queen Lane, situated on the Beauchamp to Ribecourt Road, 1,000 yards north of the former village. The left flank was on the Demicourt to Graincourt Road, giving a frontage of approximately 6,000 yards, a considerable distance considering the manpower available.

All three brigades were in the line; 107 Brigade was on the right in the Trescault sector, the 108 Brigade in the centre, in the Havrincourt sector, and the 109 Brigade on the left in the Hermies sector. The principle feature of this front was the Canal du Nord, which had been designed to link up the Canal de la Sensee with the Canal de la Somme at Peronne. However, on the outbreak of the war the Canal du Nord had only been partially completed and was in most places dry, with its depth varying from 15 to 100 feet. The canal ran due south to the northern outskirts of Havrincourt Wood and it was dry where it crossed the Bapaume to Cambria road, but with a few feet of water lying in it further south. North of Havrincourt Wood it turned west along the Grand Ravin, then south again, disappearing at Ruyalcourt and reappearing a couple of miles further on north of Etricourt. At the destroyed railway bridge between Hermies and Havrincourt it formed a barrier between the British and German lines.

The Hindenburg Line, as it was known to the British was a masterpiece of defence. The German trench system ranged across the entire front and varied in distance between 500 and 2,000 yards

Belts of barbed wire on the Hindenberg Line 1918.

apart and both consisted of front and support trenches. With ample time to prepare and with the assistance of numerous Russian prisoners-of-war and forced civilian labour, the most formidable fortifications had been constructed. The trenches were both wide and deep, with well revetted sides and contained numerous dug-outs. These had all been built to a pattern; with the stairways and supports being built from timber cut and shaped in the many German sawmills behind the lines, probably the first recorded use of mass production in the construction of defences.

The barbed wire fortifications consisted of between three and four deep belts of wire at least 20 feet apart, covered in all places by numerous machine guns. There had previously been one occasion when the wire had been penetrated; this was at Bullecourt on 10 and 11 April 1917. Here, despite the support of the new tanks, casualties had been very heavy and by attacking into a re-entrant, the assaulting troops came under fire from three sides.

From the village of Moeuvres the Hindenburg Line followed the western bank of the Canal du Nord for a distance of some 4,000 yards, before crossing the Canal to sweep around to the west of the village of Havrincourt and then south to Ribecourt. However, this was not the actual line of defence as the Germans had established strong-points up to a 1,000 yards ahead of this line. These were well constructed and had their own barbed wire entanglements to provide an independent defence.

Added to this were a number of spoil heaps of the chalk dug from the bed of the Canal that dotted the banks at intervals. Two of these were of particular interest to the division. The first, on the west bank of the Canal, was to the front of Brigadier Ricardo's 109 Brigade. It stood some 60 feet in height, was ensconced in thick entanglements of barbed wire and had machine guns mounted on its flat top that were able to sweep the brigade's trenches, it was marked on maps as the Spoil Heap.

Another spoil heap to the south was smaller in size and was located at a sharp bend in the Canal to the west of Havrincourt, where the Canal turned west along the Grand Ravin. This southern spoil heap was known as Yorkshire Bank. On top of this position was a British trench, while the Germans had established some posts on the eastern rim. This heap had been the scene of some fierce attacks and counter-attacks prior to the arrival of the division, with the Argyll and Sutherland Highlanders of the 9th Division being engaged with the enemy on several occasions, the last of which had been on 30 August.

In the 36th Division history, in fact in the history of the British Army in both world wars, there have been men blessed with an abundance of courage whose service is associated with a particular trait. One such man was Sergeant Major Robert Selkirk Whelan of the 10th Rifles. A former member of the Willowfield Detachment of the UVF, he came from the Ravenhill Road, Belfast. For his actions on 1 July 1916, he had been awarded the Military Medal and in June 1917 at Messines he had received the Military Cross. A man such as this was destined to gain the Victoria Cross; Sergeant Major Whelan's only bar to this was death, which he suffered on 29 August. There was no major action reported that day in the war diary, possibly a random shell of bullet was responsible.

On 30 August a memorandum, numbered Q.66, was issued, which discussed ways of providing comforts for the troops in the coming winter months:

> The question of providing comfort and recreation for all ranks during the winter months is one of more than usual importance in an area such as the present one where the troops are thrown absolutely on their own resources. Men will no doubt feel the loss of the Estaminets which in other areas provide them with warmth and the cheery companionship of the local inhabitants, amounting almost to a 'home from home. It is all the more necessary that nothing should be left undone which we can possibly do to make the winter months as cheery as out circumstances will permit. The Divisional Commander hopes that all officers will give this matter their closest attention. Any suggestions which officers or other ranks wish to bring forward will receive most careful consideration.

> 1. One of the first and most important things is to ensure that before winter really sets in all officers and other ranks have a good roof over their heads. The supply of huts is 42 per week at present for the whole Division and it can be increased at any time if it can be shown that a larger number can be erected. There is no shortage of huts; the governing factor is the amount of labour available for erecting them. This must be provided by the Division. If Brigade or Divisional troops will guarantee to erect the huts they can be provided in increasing numbers.
> 2. The comfort of a Nissen hut can be immensely increased by building a good brick fireplace at one end as was done by the 16th Division in some of their camps near Locre last winter. This should not be a difficult matter as the bricks are at hand. Such a fireplace is infinitely preferable to a stove.
> 3. More urgent even than living huts at the present moment is the question of recreation rooms. This matter has been represented to the Corps who have promised to provide one large recreation room hut immediately for each Brigade Area. It is proposed to erect one each at Equancourt, Ruyaulcourt and Bertincourt. Work on the first hut is already in hand.
> 4. As soon as these three huts have been provided it is proposed to erect a similar one for a Divisional 'Officers' Club' at Ytres. It is considered that there would be great scope for such a club and Ytres seems to be, on the whole, the best centre for Brigades and Divisional Troops. A good hot bathroom might be added to the Club and possibly a golf

course.

5. Once these 4 large huts are erected it will be possible for Brigades to get more benefit from the 'Merry Mauves', cinema and Divisional Band, all of which are handicapped at present by the fact of there being no hall of any kind in the new Divisional Area.

6. It is not at present possible to judge to what extent the ground will be suitable for football in the winter months. If it is suitable the men themselves may be relied upon to play, no doubt the game will be properly organised by officers and a liberal supply of footballs maintained. A supply of footballs can be supplied by the Divisional Canteen if units wish to purchase them through that agency. It might be worthwhile to consider the question of starting a Football League Competition and the formation of a committee to deal generally with sport in the Division.

7. If, however, football and hockey are not possible later on, it should always be possible by means of a little clearing of debris to provide good handball alleys in each village. This is a very popular game with Irishmen and there is no better form of exercise. Officers may also find it possible to make squash racquet courts in certain places.

8. The scope of the Divisional Canteens is being very much enlarged as it is realised that the comfort of all ranks will depend very much on the Canteen Service. Arrangements have been made for one railway truck daily from Amiens for the Divisional Canteen. Goods will be delivered the second morning after the order is received. In order to obtain the best results units are recommended to give standing orders.

9. As already notified a contract has been made for the supply of beer which promises to be satisfactory both as regards the quality and the quantity of the supply.

10. The current edition of the Paris *Daily Mail* will be obtainable in Divisional Canteens. A limited number of copies of the *Daily Mirror* and *Daily Sketch* will also be supplied. Orders for other papers will be accepted in the Divisional Canteens.

11. Fresh fruit and vegetables and possibly a limited amount of fresh milk can also be supplied for Messes and Canteens.

12. A Divisional Soda Water Factory will be established at an early date.

13. It is hoped it may be possible to arrange later on for an excursion train to run as often as possible to the Ancre Valley battlefields, passengers at first being limited to those who took part in the Somme offensive 1916."

August had been a wicked month for the division. Total casualties amounted to 159 officers and 3,574 other ranks, of which 523 had been killed, 2,685 wounded and the remainder reported as missing.[31]

General Nugent had established his headquarters in Little Wood, just outside the village of Ytres on 31 August. On that evening there was a bombardment of Yorkshire Bank and a German attack drove in the picquets of the 12th Rifles. At 4:15 am the following morning they were ejected, but the following night they again attacked, two parties bombing their way forward from either flank. At 1:00 am the 12th Rifles again captured the post using a combination of bombs and Lewis guns. The Germans had not gone very far, that evening as dusk fell an officer was doing his rounds when he saw the heads of some Germans looking over the rim of the bank. An immediate attack was made, which drove them out forcing the Germans to leave behind one wounded man who was made a prisoner. However, this was a persistent enemy and two nights later they tried again, but the Rifles were ready and a shower of bombs from the top of the spoil heap drove them off, they being harried during their withdrawal by fire from the Stokes mortars. The Germans tried one

---

31 A & Q War Diary.

more time, again without success. In the 109th Machine Gun Company Gunner David Dalton of Lurganure, the Maze, County Antrim, was killed, he was 25 years old.

Back in Belfast Mr H. Blackburne, secretary of the East Antrim Unionist Association received a letter from Brigadier General McCalmont, MP. It made a point with regard to recruiting that was a little less forceful than that made by General Nugent:

Dear Mr Blackburne, Having read newspaper reports of the recent annual meeting of the East Antrim Unionist Association, I take the opportunity afforded by a short leave to write my thanks to the members of the Association, not only for their continued confidence, but for their kind personal references both in the annual report and at the meeting. A few weeks ago I had the privilege of visiting the battalion which I had the honour to raise and command, and which has again recently done its part in making a glorious name for the Ulster Division. They appear to lack nothing except a large proportion of Ulster recruits, and may I perhaps be allowed to join in the thanks of the East Antrim Unionist Association to those ladies and gentlemen who have so generously maintained a regular supply of comforts for the battalion.

Yours very faithfully, R. McCalmont, Brig. General.

11

September 1917

Field Marshal Haig and his generals assumed the German withdrawal to the Hindenburg Line was a sign of weakness – a mistake Napoleon made during the Waterloo campaign – so they attempted to break through the new enemy defences as part of the Anglo-French spring offensive. The result was General Gough's Fifth Army, of which V Corps and I ANZAC Corps was attached during spring 1917, suffered enormous losses during subsequent costly fighting at Bullecourt.

The present divisional area was rolling, well-watered and fairly thickly wooded countryside. Havrincourt Wood, which had originally covered some four square miles, had suffered from German saws and axes, much of it having been felled for construction of the Hindenburg Line. Despite this there still remained ample trees to provide ample cover. General Nugent describes this area as 'well-watered', although there were numerous reports of the Germans having poisoned the wells.

The Hindenburg defences were admirably sited and gave excellent observation of the British positions, especially from the Bourlon Wood located on the top of the 100 metre contour north of the Bapaume to Cambrai Road. There was however ample good ground and the British also enjoyed excellent observation posts located at such places as Hermies Ridge, the Trescault spur and from Havrincourt Wood itself. On the other side of the German lines could be seen intact villages and at some eight miles the steeples and roof tops of the city of Cambrai. The trench system in Trescault and Havrincourt consisted of a series of lines which was so vast that they had to be occupied and defended at intervals only, each manned in general by no more than a platoon. In the Hermies sector defences were at a minimum, consisting of little more than some trenches that had been dug around the village. Unlike the tactics of the 9th Division, the previous unit that relied on counter-attacks as a means of defence, 109 Brigade began at once with a full programme of trench digging and wiring.

The divisional artillery, 16th Rifles and the mobile veterinary section, still positioned in the Salient, had experienced a terrible time. The artillery had gone into action on 14 July in support of the 55th Division and had remained in action ever since. On 21 August they had supported an unsuccessful attack by 61st Division. It was not until the night of 23 August that they were eventually relieved. This period of six weeks had seen a huge expenditure of ammunition, near constant heavy and accurate counter-battery fire, the shelling of the wagon lines and the bare minimum of shelter and rest. The 16th Rifles spent even longer in the Salient. Two companies were engaged in repairs to the infantry barracks in Ypres, while the remainder of the battalion were employed in screening the Menin Road, building a trench tramway from a point north of Hellfire corner to Railway Wood. This was laid on top of the old railway track and ran for a distance of about one seventh of a mile, the work much interrupted by shell fire and gas that caused some casualties. No.2 Company was engaged on the construction of three new strong-points on the Westhoek Ridge. This lasted until 30 September when the pioneers rejoined the division. From 1 June until now the pioneers had suffered 217 battle casualties of all ranks, representing one quarter of their strength.

Another month on the Western Front and again there was action at Yorkshire Bank. At 4:15 am, on 1 September the 12th Rifles counter-attacked and re-established their posts. That night the Germans attacked again, two separate attacks, the raiders working their way up either side of the heap and using bombs in great number. A large party of enemy infantry emerged from Wigan Copse at approximately the same time and these were dealt with using Lewis guns. During the action the Rifles had seven men wounded.

An adjustment to the front held by each brigade was to be carried out on 2 September. The left brigade sector was the widest by far and required a great deal of work to make it defensible. At 1:00 am, the 12th Rifles again attacked and retook the positions with a finely combined assault using bombs and Lewis guns. Another enemy attack began at 8:15 pm, this was quickly repulsed and a seriously wounded German was made prisoner, he later died. He was identified as belonging to the Ersatz Battalion of the 86th Fusilier Regiment, although according to other papers and marking on his haversack, he belonged to the 84th Jäger Regiment, 54th Division, which hailed from Schleswig Holstein.

A day of shelling was experienced on 3 September along the Yorkshire Bank. The following day the Germans attacked again, only to be driven off with well-aimed bombs. As they withdrew a bomb from a Stokes mortar was observed falling in the centre of a group and causing casualties. One more attempt was made that night, which also met with failure.

At 3:15 pm, on 6 September, a German aircraft bombed the area of the 109 Brigade and a single bomb landed on brigade headquarters, no damage was caused. In the 107 Brigade the 15th Rifles lost an officer when Captain Robson died of wounds received. Richard Ivan Robson came from the Princetown Road in Bangor, County Down, and had been educated at Blackwood's Preparatory School in Northamptonshire, followed by Oundel and Peterborough. Remembered as a popular student and keen sportsman and an excellent shot, he was attending Dublin University when war was declared. Robson enlisted as a private soldier in the 13th Rifles, but given his background and education was soon commissioned and received rapid promotion to Captain in the 15th Rifles. He had served at the Somme and been awarded the Military Cross in late 1916, later serving at Messines.

Also serving with the 15th Rifles was Captain J.H.A. Patton, who was attached to brigade headquarters. From Wellington Park in Belfast, he had been a student at Trinity College, Dublin, before receiving his commission in August 1914. For his actions in this battle he was awarded the Military Cross. A younger brother, Second Lieutenant Alex D. Patton, served in the Royal Field Artillery.

The village of Havrincourt was subjected to an artillery concentration in conjunction with the heavy trench mortars on 13 September. The machine guns fired some 8,000 rounds into the village between 11: 00pm and 2:00 am. It was on this date that the 2nd Rifles were transferred in to the 36th Division and not without complaint. Two days before, after the fighting at Westhoek, the battalion had moved by bus to Caestre and then continued on foot to Steenbecque. They had then moved to Raimbert, a mining village, for training, arriving on 13 September. It was here that the battalion was informed that they would become part of the 36th Division. Father Gill was far from pleased:

> Our repose was disturbed by some bad news which reached us. We were to be transferred into the 36th (Ulster) Division. This news came as a surprise and disagreeable shock to almost everyone in the battalion. The prospect of a change into a political division was not pleasant, nor did the outlook appear very bright. Everything possible was done to have the decision changed, but without success … there were not many Catholics in the other battalions except the 1st R.I.R.[1]

---

1   Gill, Major Fr. Henry Vincent, DSO, MC, MA, SJ.

The division saw the operation and effect of the Livens Projector when 600 of these weapons were dug in at the bend of the Canal and on the night of 14 September and fired into Havrincourt at 11:30 pm. The projector consisted of a simple metal pipe that was buried in the ground at a 45° angle. The calibre was eventually standardised as eight inches and the ammunition either gas or oil, was discharges electrically. They had previously been used on the Somme, Messines, Vimy Ridge and Langemarck, rarely with success. On this occasion the projectors were loaded with gas and a favourable four mile per hour westerly wind was blowing. The Germans retaliated at 12:15 pm, shelling the right sector with a combination of 77mm and 105mm guns firing a 50-50 mixture of high explosive and gas shells on to the southern edge of Yorkshire Bank. It was later ascertained that the effect of the Livens Projectors had, for once, been effective. The interrogation of prisoners revealed that losses had been so heavy the defending battalion had to be relieved and in one dug-out 20 men had been killed by the gas.

At a meeting of the Londonderry Corporation on 17 September, a letter was read out from General Nugent in which he offered a number of trophies to the city. These had been taken at Messines the previous June and included a German 77mm field gun, a light *minewerfer* and a *granatenwerfer*. General Nugent added that he understood several individual units of the division proposed presenting to the city other trophies captured by them on the same date; but he hoped those enumerated would be regarded as presented by the division as a whole, and accepted by the citizens as mementoes of a brilliant success in which the division took no mean part, acquitting themselves like men.

All deaths in wartime can be viewed as a tragedy, those on the Western Front occurred in great numbers, on the home front the deaths may have been fewer, but were no les tragic. On 24 September, the death of Lance Corporal Richard Quinn, was not only tragic, it was both 'shameful and painful.'[2] Quinn, a 40 year old member of the 17th Rifles, had joined the army on the outbreak of war. Some months previously he had been taken ill at Holywood Barracks and was hospitalised for nine weeks in Belfast. On 24 September, Quinn, along with several other men, was selected to be transferred from Victoria Barracks, Belfast to Londonderry. Quinn declared he was too ill to travel, but despite this he was conveyed to York Road railway station by motor ambulance. During the journey he lay on the floor of the vehicle and on arrival at the Station was carried into the buffet when he again lay on the floor writhing in agony. He is reported to have said; "As sure as there is a God in Heaven I am ill and am not malingering; but they won't believe me." Despite his protestations and concern expressed by waiting passengers he was placed on the train and died before reaching Ballymena.

The North Irish Horse had been raised as a Yeomanry Regiment in 1902 and after the Haldane Reforms of 1908, became a Special Reserve cavalry regiment. It was mobilised in Belfast in August 1914 and the squadrons split up, being mainly employed as divisional cavalry until 1916. Post 1916 they became corps cavalry and finally, in 1918, as corps cyclists and infantry. On the second day of the Somme battle they were engaged in helping to bury the dead of the division. On both occasions the men were heavily shelled and casualties occurred.[3] On 25 September 1917, the 9th Irish Fusiliers absorbed 304 men of the NIH Squadrons, adding (North Irish Horse) to its battalion title.

As September turned to October the divisional pioneers continued to be paragons of their craft. At the village of Hermies the 16th Battalion dug a trench that was to all intents and purposes a model of excellencesuitable for a school of engineering. In the pioneer's honour it was named Lurgan Switch. When it came to dug-outs, again these were superb. Excavated into the chalk,

---

2   *Belfast News Letter,* 13 October 1917.
3   Doherty, Richard, *The North Irish Horse* (2002).

under the supervision of the field companies, they were up to 30 feet deep, dry and comfortable. There were also positions known as champagne dug-outs, as they were vaguely in the shape of such a bottle and ideal for holding the crew of a machine gun. For accommodation behind the lines there was the Nissen hut. This building was the brainchild of Major Peter Norman Nissen, Royal Engineers, and comprised of corrugated tin bent in a half moon shape and attached to a wooden frame. A former mining engineer, Nissen had worked on three prototypes prior to his hut going into full production. Available from September 1916, some 100,000 were built during the Great War and continued to be produced in the Second World War. For his service Nissen was awarded a DSO and received a cash payment of £13,000 for post-war sales, having refused royalties for any huts produced from 1914 to 1918.

General Nugent wrote to Mr J.F. Wray, chairman of the Enniskillen Urban District Council, offering on behalf of the division trophies forming part of the booty captured by the division at Messines the previous June. Similar to the offer made to Londonderry, these consisted of a field gun and a canister bomb thrower, according to the newspaper. While General Nugent understood that individual units of the division had also proposed to present to the town other trophies captured that day, he hoped that the trophies mentioned might be regarded as being presented by the division as a whole and that they would be accepted by the people of the town as mementoes of the brilliant success in which the Ulster Division took no mean part and acquitted themselves as men. The letter was read to the Council on the Monday night meeting and on the motion of Mr W. Copeland Trimble, JP, seconded by Mr Thomas Gordon a vote of thanks was passed to General Nugent for his thoughtfulness.

Lieutenant Alexander Charles Paul, 11th Rifles, from Clontarf, Dublin, died on 2 October of wounds received earlier, he was 20 years old. It was he who had assisted in recovering Major Redmond's body from the battlefield at Messines.[4]

At the beginning of October the division was encamped in the area of Ytres, Neuville and Bertincourt, an area devoid of any of the local inhabitants. The Divisional Provost Staff reported that in their experience there was less crime and unrest among the troops when they were billeted in inhabited areas. This 'Teuton-made' veldt, while dry and comfortable, offered little in the way of distraction to the men.[5] At this stage in his Divisional history Cyril Falls states that; "There was among the men of the Ulster Division little crime at any time, but undoubtedly they also were in some degree a prey to the inevitable nostalgia born of desolation."

This statement by Cyril Falls was either naivety, wishful thinking or simply a desire to brush over what would then have been considered an unattractive side to the division. On the other hand Falls may be drawing a line between crimes such as theft and problems of discipline. When men were charged with a disciplinary offence it was often possible that this could be dealt with by the relevant commanding officer, such offences as dirty equipment, being unshaven, or being late on parade. The 14th Rifles had a particular reputation for dealing with most misdemeanours 'in-house'. Should the offence be considered too serious to be dealt with in the manner, such as desertion, cowardice and sleeping at his post, the man was then sent for a court martial.

The 8th Rifles had 40 men face a court martial between October 1915 and April 1918. Of these two men received death sentences for 'sleeping at post', Private McConnell and Rea. In both cases the sentences were commuted to hard labour, one and two years respectively, with both sentences suspended.

In the 9th Rifles 73 men were tried by court martial resulting in the award of seven death sentences, Privates Carson, desertion, Prior, desertion, Crozier, desertion, McFarland, quitting

4   *Irish Times*, 7 March 1985.
5   Falls, *The History of the 36th (Ulster) Division* (1922).

post, Tighe, sleeping at post, Bright, desertion. Private Deuchart, desertion for a second time, all but one of these were commuted to various punishments ranging from hard labour to penal servitude, the exception was Private James Crozier, shot on 27 February 1916.

The 10th Rifles sent 90 men to face a court martial, the most from any battalion in the division and three received a death sentence; Private Tootle, sleeping at post, Private Barr, desertion and Private Power, also desertion. These were all commuted to five years penal servitude, ten years penal servitude and sentence not confirmed, respectively.

Thirty-five men from the 11th Rifles were sent for court martial, none received a death sentence. There were three cases of desertion, two were found guilty of absence only and received 56 days field punishment No.1, while the third was judged to be insane. There was one case of 'quitting post' and this earned the man concerned two years hard labour, which was in turn reduced to six months, the sentence being suspended.

In the 12th Rifles Sergeant Butler was the first man to face a court martial on 9 October 1915, when he was charged with 'drunkenness'. He was reduced in the ranks and awarded two months Field Punishment No.2. Another 55 men faced a court martial, there were no death sentences.

The 13th Rifles had 17 men face a court martial, the least number in the division, with more than half of these cases being for 'drunkenness'. Again there were no death sentences.

Within the ranks of the 14th Rifles there were 27 men sent for court martial, none faced a death sentence.

The next men to be shot came from the 15th Rifles, a battalion that sent 72 men to a court martial. The four men sentenced to death were Privates Waterworth, Beattie, McCracken and Templeton, all for desertion. Waterworth and Beattie had their sentences commuted to five and 15 years penal servitude respectively, McCracken and Templeton were shot on 19 March 1916.

The Pioneers (16th Rifles) saw 52 men face trial, almost half of the cases being for 'drunkenness'. There were no death sentences. Within the ranks of the 9th Inniskillings there were 68 men that faced a court martial between October 1915 and September 1917. Of these only one man received a death sentence, Private Speers for 'sleeping at post'. His sentence was commuted to five years penal servitude. Of the 55 men from the 10th Inniskillings who faced a court martial, none received a death sentence. The 11th Inniskillings saw 65 men face trial, of these none received a death sentence. Private Murray was charged with murder and manslaughter, but found guilty of manslaughter only and received ten years penal servitude. The 9th Irish Fusiliers sent 37 men for trial, none received a death sentence. The 1st Inniskillings joined the division on 5 February 1918, from that date until 28 September 1918, the battalion sent 43 men to trial. Two men were sentenced to death, Private Miller, for desertion and Private Walsh, for offences against civilian inhabitants. In both cases the sentences were commuted to ten and fifteen years' penal servitude respectively.

On 3 February 1918, the 2nd Inniskillings joined the division. The first court martial after this date was 24 May 1918, when Private Duffy was charged with desertion and sentenced to 56 days Field Punishment No.2, the charge of desertion being reduced to absence only. A further 17 men faced trial, no death sentences were passed. The 1st Irish Fusiliers joined the division on 3 August 1917, being sent to 107 Brigade. From this date until 10 August 1918, 45 men were sent for court martial. Of these two received a death sentence, Privates Hanna and Gerraghty, both for desertion. Private Gerraghty's sentence was commuted to two years penal servitude, Private Hanna was shot on 6 November 1917.

The 1st Rifles joined the division on 3 February 1918, seeing a court martial happen on that very day. Private Quirke received three months Field Punishment No.1 for offences under S40 (Conduct, disorder, or neglect to the prejudice of good order and military discipline). Another 51 men would go to trial, but no death sentences would be passed. The 2nd Rifles also joined the division on 13 November 1917, being posted to the 108 Brigade. A total of 82 men would face a court martial from this date until the end of the War. No death sentences were passed within these dates.

Within the division the majority of all ranks continued to perform their duty to the best of their ability. On the night of 5 October, according to a report submitted by Major Holt Waring of the 12th Rifles, Lieutenant James Gibson, from Coleraine, showed great determination and presence of mind in avoiding a bombing incident, although no further details are given. However, on this night at 10:30 pm, some 596 out of 600 Livens gas drums were launched towards the enemy lines at Havrincourt, this in conjunction with concentrated artillery and machine gun fire. By 11:00 pm, the Germans retaliated with their own artillery, interspersing high explosive with gas shells. Raids were carried out from within the division and German prisoners from the 413 Infantry Regiment (204th Wurttemberg Division) reported at least 20 men killed in their dugouts from the gas.

The Germans defended the Hindenburg Line with a series of forward outposts, some a fair distance in front of the main positions. They were not always strongly defended and many were manned during the hours of darkness only. This situation left ample opportunity for raiding, following in the Canadian style, which was known as winkling. The division's first raid was a large-scale operation, employing some 60 officers and men from the 12th Rifles against what turned out to be an enemy force almost equal in number. This raid was carried out at 10:00 pm, on 6 October at Wigan Copse, just to the north of Yorkshire Bank. The raiding party of two officers and 57 other ranks was divided in three, the first under a Warrant Officer, the second and third under officers, all three parties being protected by a screen of scouts. The leading party proceeded to the German wire at K.26.d.4.32 and formed the right covering party. The second party, one officer and twelve other ranks went through the wire at K.26.d.10.35, moved towards the north-west corner of Wigan Copse and formed the left covering party. The third party then went through the wire at the same place and proceeded to search the Copse. There was no opposition until 10:27 pm, when the left covering party, was fired on and bombed by a strong enemy post located at K.26.d.10.50. The officer and four of the other ranks were wounded. The remainder of the party returned a rapid fire, but were not strong enough to rush the post. The officer leading the patrol reinforced them, but by this time the occupants had fled. By 10:39 pm, the main party had searched Wigan Copse and found it unoccupied. They then moved to the north end of the Copse and lay down to await developments. From 10:45 to 11:30 pm, all was quiet, then two strong groups of enemy were observed leaving the trenches at K.26d.20.90 covered by a screen of scouts. Two of these scouts came towards the raiders until they were within 30 yards. Here they halted and listened, but the raiders held their fire. On receiving the all clear from the two German scouts the main bodies of the enemy infantry, estimated at about 70 men, then approached the British position. Fire was opened at about 20 yards and the officer and two men rushed out to grab the scouts. One was taken, but the other escaped. Rapid rifle fire and bursts from the Lewis gun must have inflicted several casualties, going by the noise heard from the German positions. A further search of the Copse ensured no enemy wounded were present and the raiders returned to their own lines. On interrogation it was discovered that the prisoner was from the 413th Regiment of the 204th Division. Casualties to the patrol were one officer and five other ranks slightly wounded.[6]

At 4:00 pm on 9 October, a party from the 10th Rifles, consisting of Lieutenant Gibson and seven other ranks, was able to cross no man's land and cut the barbed wire surrounding an outpost on the eastern arm of Havrincourt Wood, known as Femy Wood. The raiders entered the outpost and lay in wait for the enemy garrison to arrive. When the party of 11 men arrived shortly after 6:00 pm, the leader, a lance corporal of the 3rd Battalion 84th Infantry Regiment, was taken prisoner, while the remainder were killed by close range rifle fire. The party then safely returned

---

6   TNA WO 95 2492 (DSC6652).

The original caption states 'A church service before battle', given the countryside, this is well behind the lines.

with the captured corporal, who had been slightly wounded in the ambush. In this same action Lieutenant Gibson was seriously wounded.

According to the local papers of 20 October Second Corporal A.H. Jackson, Royal Engineers, and an ex motor cycle despatch rider in the UVF Signalling Corps, had recently been awarded the Military Medal. From Loughgall in County Armagh, Jackson was one of four brothers, two of whom had been decorated for their service in the War, so far. Sergeant G.A. Jackson had also received an MM for his actions the previous April, Sergeant J.E. Jackson, another UVF despatch rider, had received the DCM in June. The fourth brother, Victor, had been wounded while serving with the Canadians at Vimy Ridge.

The divisional war diary describes 21 October as an uneventful day. For the 9th Irish Fusiliers it was a day of church parades and rugby football, the first practise of the season. There was also the announcement of awards made for the fighting of 16 August. The Military Cross was awarded to Captains T.F. Given, R.S. Flood, O.V. Burrows, RAMC and RSM C.H. Turner. The Distinguished Conduct Medal went to Sergeant S. Carvell (17545), while the Military Medal was awarded to Sergeants J. Adams (Later to be awarded a Bar) (13971), J. McCullough (14555), A. Turkington (14720), Acting Corporal R.W. Knaggs (16117), Lance Corporal S. Whiteside (14748) and Privates C. Shanks (23926), J. Rodgers (20353), Lance Corporal E. Jackson (24174) and Privates G. Steele (22562), J. Elliott (14154, R.J. McCormick (14566), W.J. Lynn (15864) and J. Morton (14447).

At 4:00 am, on 24 October, a party of the 11th Rifles was out covering work being done on the British wire when a patrol of six enemy infantry were observed approaching. Splitting into two the covering party was able to close in on the Germans from either flank and took all six men prisoner without a shot being fired. The prisoners were from the 84th Regiment of the 54th Division. Around the same time the 1st Irish Fusiliers had both a success and a failure on the battlefield. A sap north of Trescault was assaulted by the enemy, but was driven off, losing Fusilier taken prisoner. However, later, a patrol of one officer and nine other ranks of the Fusiliers were out examining the result of trench mortar fire on the German wire when it was ambushed by approximately 30 enemy soldiers. After some fierce fighting in which several enemy infantry were killed, the Fusiliers were forced to withdraw, having to leave behind three of their men who were wounded and then taken prisoner.

Raids from both sides of the wire became numerous, developing into small intimate struggles of life and death, when subterfuge became as deadly a weapon as the revolver or trench knife. On one occasion four men from the 15th Rifles were holding a sap when a party of nine men approached calling out in English; "It's all right. We're coming to visit you."

This ruse allowed the Germans to come within bombing range and immediately a shower of bombs fell in and around the sap, quickly followed by the enemy soldiers. With one of their number wounded and the explosions of the bombs ringing in their ears the three remaining defenders had an instant decision to make, fight or flight? In this instance the response was to fight and with fixed bayonets the men immediately charged the German raiding party. Before actual contact could be made the enemy fled, quite often it was the perceived threat of the bayonet that was more effective than its actual use. One man was too slow to escape and was taken prisoner. As dawn broke the body of the officer was found lying outside the sap, he had been killed by a bayonet thrust.

The divisional artillery, located in the area of Ytres Wood and, unrestrained by ammunition supply, was in near constant action. Headquarters of IV Corps directed that two thirds of all firing was to be carried out at night, directing harassing fire on support trenches, roads and suspected supply dumps. Given that most batteries lacked any form of cover, the muzzle flash made German counter-battery fire very accurate. From 1 October onwards night firing had been carried out by single guns, these being brought forward at dusk and withdrawn again before dawn. This was not wholly effective. On the night of 5 October two guns were brought forward, but almost immediately were engaged by the enemy, one gun being completely destroyed.

There seemed to be greater attention being paid to the gun batteries than to the infantry. During daylight hours enemy aircraft would spot an individual battery and direct fire on to it. However, the artillerymen became adept at disguising their positions and creating dummy batteries, causing the enemy to waste ammunition on more than one occasion.

Active on the battlefield was the Reverend Alexander Stuart, Presbyterian chaplain to the 12th Rifles. From Bessbrook, he had arrived in France only two weeks earlier, having seen service in Egypt. In a letter to the Reverend T.C. Stuart, Alexander's brother, Padre James Gilbert Paton MC[7] wrote:

> Poor old Alex was killed by a shell. He was going up the line to see his boys when the shell came. It gave him no chance at all, and he was killed on the spot. He was only ten days with the battalion, but even in that short time they had learned to love him. He died as he lived, and by his death he has shown his devotion to his God and his country, and proved that his religion was no cant, but the real thing.

October 1917 had been a month of major events elsewhere on the European battlefield. In Italy the Battle of Caporetto, also known as the Twelfth Battle of the Isonzo, began on 24 October 1917, it would last until 19 November of the same year. The action, fought between Austro-Hungarian forces with German reinforcements and the Italian Army, saw the widespread use of Storm troopers and poison gas, along with the newly devised infiltration tactics devised by General Oskar von Hutier, something the British would experience in March of 1918. The resulting battle was largely responsible for the collapse of the Italian Second Army.

On the night of 25 October a patrol of one officer and nine other ranks went out to the enemy wire at K.33.d.5.1 to observe the effect of the divisional trench mortar fire. It was discovered that

---

7   By the end of the war Padre Paton would have earned two MC Bars and a MID.

the wire had suffered little damage and there were no complete gaps. The patrol then moved to K.33.d.6.2 when between 20 and 30 of the enemy appeared on the parapet of their outpost trench. The patrol fired a couple of volleys of rifle fire and threw some bombs. There was instant retaliation in the form of rifle fire, bombs and machine gun bursts. The machine gun was spotted firing from K.33.d.70.25 and was silenced by bombs and rifle fire at close range. The patrol then withdrew through gaps in the wire, eventually making their way back to their own lines. It was then discovered that three men were missing, having last been seen in the scrub close to the enemy trench. The officer and one other rank immediately returned to search for them, but they could not be found. A further patrol searched the scrub the following day and found evidence of a struggle at K.33.d.8.2. A satchel of British bombs and a German letter card dated 17/10/17 was found and it was presumed that the men had been taken prisoner.

Captain W.A. Foley, 1st Irish Fusiliers, died of his wounds at No.48 Casualty Clearing Station on 1 November. The 12th Rifles were resting at Ruyaullcourt before moving off at 5:30 pm to the trenches located to the south-west of Havincourt, where they relieved the 9th Irish Fusiliers. This was completed three hours later and the 12th Rifles settled into their positions, with the 11th Rifles on the right flank and the 14th Rifles on the left. At 9:45 pm, the enemy artillery opened fire and approximately 20 rounds of 7.7cm fell on the old battery position on Cheetham Hill, the majority of the shells being gas. At 11:10 pm, a similar salvo landed on the same position, while German machine guns were active on Yorkshire Bank throughout the hours of darkness. In the Divisional Artillery Headquarters a fire broke out in the offices and destroyed the bulk of the records that had been accumulated since their arrival in France. There was heavy shelling of the forward areas and the battery located at Q1a 32 was badly damaged by 105mm shells, but no casualties were reported.

The funeral of Captain Foley was held on 2 November and was attended by 15 officers and 50 other ranks of the battalion. The 1st Irish Fusiliers relieved the 10th Rifles in the line and proceeded to the trenches by train. Relief was completed by 8:00 pm. Enemy artillery caught the relieved troops on their way out. A German patrol attempted to bomb a C Company outpost and in the ensuing melee one wounded enemy soldier was taken prisoner. Identified as belonging to the 84th Infantry Regiment, he died while being transported back to the Field Ambulance.

In the 14th Rifles Captain Gavin, the Medical Officer, was thrown from his horse, suffering a fractured skull. He was immediately taken to No.21 Casualty Clearing Station, but died several hours later without regaining consciousness. In the 20 months that Captain Gavin had been with the battalion he had earned the Military Cross and Bar, along with the grateful thanks of every man he had come in contact with. In the *Belfast News Letter* of 8 November a letter written by a member of the battalion to his mother summed up how the men felt:

> As I write, I hear that the battalion is the poorer, and very much poorer, by the loss of one of the best men I have ever met. I mean our doctor, who has done so much for us all. He was thrown from his horse last night, sustaining such severe injuries that he died this morning. We may get the best doctor in the army, but never will we get one to come up to Dr Gavin's standard. He was so gentle always, and paid the greatest attention to the meanest soldier in the battalion, listening to every complaint, no matter how small, and doing his best to fix it up. After telling you so much about him in days gone past, I felt it would not be out of place to write these few words in passing, as I know both you and E looked on him as a sort of personal friend.

On the evening of 3 November, at 7:30 pm, three raiding parties from the 9th Irish Fusiliers (NIH) left their trenches and advanced towards the enemy positions to the south of the Hermies – Havrincourt Road and east of the Canal. This force consisted of four officers and 67 other ranks, including Sappers and stretcher-bearers. The parties moved out from Yorkshire Bank and made their way through gaps in the enemy wire. Once through they sent up a red flare which brought down a protective barrage on all enemy approaches to the trench. Only one party had any difficulty in entering the enemy position when they came up against wire that, although previously cut by the British artillery, had been effectively repaired by the Germans. They were eventually able to make their way into the position, but suffered heavy casualties in doing so. These raiders, mostly men were mostly men who had recently transferred into the battalion from the North Irish Horse and in the words of Cyril Falls; "Had the men not been more eager to kill than to capture, a considerable number of prisoners might have been taken."

As the enemy had tried to escape through their own wire they had been ruthlessly bayoneted in the back, their screams plainly heard in the British lines. Total casualties to the raiders were one other rank killed, three others missing presumed killed, with an officer, 13 other ranks and one Royal Engineer wounded. These were Sergeant R. Irwin and Privates J. Ford, John Donaldson King and Robert Heathwood. At a later date five of the raiders received the award of the Military Medal; they were Corporals Henry Mackinson, George Craig and Privates John Morrison, Thomas Chambers, and Robert Averall.

On 5 November winter fog was thick around the area controlled by 109 Brigade. Such was the limited visibility that artillery firing on selected targets could not be observed and only indiscriminate fire from the enemy was received. The brigade trench mortars fired on the enemy wire and no fire was received in return, while the brigade's machine guns fired 2,500 rounds without seeing any significant enemy reaction. While observation of the German trenches was impossible due to the fogreconnaissance patrols were able to ascertain that new barbed wire had been strung up to six coils deepand the sound of working in the enemy trench was heard during the hours of darkness.

Private G. Hanna, 1st Irish Fusiliers, was shot by firing squad at 6:40 am on 6 November. He had been sentenced the previous day, the first time a death sentence had been ordered to be carried out in this battalion. Private Hanna had only served with the battalion for some five hours, having gone absent from his post shortly after arriving with a draft of reinforcements. Also on this day the General Court Martial of Second Lieutenant R.G.H. Mansfield commenced.[8] It was a one-day affair and the officer was cashiered.

Shortly after 6 November 1917, Teenie Davidson received a letter from Private Scott of 7/8th Inniskillings:

> Just a few lines to say how sorry I am about Duncan. I spoke to Norman a month ago about him, but he did not know.[9] Do not take it to heart too much old girl, he died for a good cause and I am sure it is the way he would have wished. I am sure you are all cut up about him, kindly convey to your father, Tommie and Aunt Grace my deepest sympathy, also let Norman know that feel deeply for him. I had no idea he was gone until this morning when I saw it in the paper. I wonder how many of our old school chums will come out of it, I hope and pray that Norrie will be spared to you. When I think of the happy days we spent together at school, I can hardly realise that he is gone. In our boyhood days we often wanted to be soldiers, and often played at being so, little did we know that we would in future years be playing the game in earnest. I know it is hard on you dear but it was duty to the flag he died for. It may be my turn next, but please remember he will never be forgotten by an old chum in our school days and comrades in battle. Hope you are keeping in good health. God bless you all.

---

8   1st Royal Irish Fusiliers War Diary.
9   Private Norman Davidson, Duncan's brother, served in the 2nd and later 7th Rifles.

Duncan Davidson had been killed on 16 August; he was 26 years old and has no known grave.

While this was going on the last British cavalry charge was being made half a world away. At Huj, on 8 November 1917, a small township some ten miles east of Gaza in Palestine, Lieutenant Colonel Gray-Cheape led a squadron of the Warwickshire Yeomanry, along with a squadron of the Worcestershire Yeomanry, commanded by Major William Wiggin, as part of General Allenby's advance through Palestine. A total of 18 officers and 172 other ranks charged across virtually open ground without any supporting fire and captured three 105mm howitzers, four 75mm field guns, four pack guns and four machine guns. Ninety Turkish and Austrian soldiers died under the swords of the Yeomanry, 70 were taken prisoner and a further 2,000 were routed. Losses to the British were three officers killed and six wounded, with 33 other ranks being killed and 51 wounded. Over half the Yeomanry horses were killed or had to be destroyed. General Allenby's message read; "Brilliant action in which you have upheld the finest traditions of the British cavalry."[10] It was a scene that was rarely enacted on the Western Front.

The 2nd Rifles, absorbing the remnants of the 7th Rifles on 13 November, were attached to the 108 Brigade. Behind the lines the men were enjoying entertainment in the form of a cinema and concert parties from the Merry Mauves. There was also football and boxing competitions, horse shows and race meetings. Workshops supplied necessary equipment, often at short notice, rations almost always arrived on time and there was a post office that was described as a marvel. With regard to intelligence matters, up-to-date maps were produced on a regular basis and recent aerial photographs, vital for planning raids were available at 24 hours' notice.

Each day two lorry loads of beer, 90 barrels, were delivered to the division from a brewery in Amiens, being sold by the various canteens in an attempt to make up for the loss of estaminets. Also sold was a selection of tobacco, biscuits, chocolate, tinned foods, books, candles, eggs, cake, bread, fresh fruit and on occasion oysters. All this was made available through the efficiency of the Quarter-master General's Staff. Throughout the division's time in France it had always been well supported by this branch, first under the command of Colonel Comyn and later his successor, Colonel S.H. Green who took command when Colonel Comyn was posted to the War Office. The Staff were also able to arrange transport to take both officers and other ranks on a day's leave to Amiens. A combination of lorry and train ensured that six hours could be spent in this city doing whatever soldiers did. A soft drinks factory. established on the banks of the Canal de Nord, supplied soda water, the bottle being labelled Boyne Water were sold at a penny a bottle to raise money to buy comforts for the men. While popular within the division, it did not go down well with some of the neighbours. The 7th Rifles were close by and one evening a ration party was sent to the Ulster Division to collect canteen supplies. A short time after their return the acting battalion commander Major Deneys Reitz, a South African officer, heard an unholy row coming from the marquee being used as a store. On investigating Reitz discovered the men smashing bottles of the said Boyne Water and uttering threats against the Ulstermen. Major Reitz made a quick telephone call to the Ulster Division Headquarters who turned out a guard of several 100 men to surround the 'malcontents', and with the assistance of Lieutenant Hartery of the 7th Rifles, who understood Irish politics better than Reitz, was able to calm the situation without bloodshed. The following day there was a football match between the two sides as if nothing had happened.[11]

All of the above had a cost and this cost was in manpower and at a time when manpower was at a critical level. A typical example of a battalion with a paper strength of 600 men had its numbers reduced considerably by the following; A number of men were employed in battalion headquarters, in the transport line and at divisional headquarters as clerks, draughtsmen, orderlies, a cook,

10   Information related by Jerry Wiggin.
11   Reitz, Deneys, *Trekking On* (1933).

a further number attached to the Signals Company, some at brigade headquarters, traffic control, working party attached to a tunnelling company, camp wardens, guards for the coal, straw and ration dumps, men on leave and men sick. This left a grand total of 147 available for duty in the trenches.

A number of men would also be attending schools. While considered a vital necessity in training, so many schools being run at the same time soaked up men. The schools were run at GHQ, Army, Corps, Divisional and Brigade level and included, infantry schools, artillery, trench-mortar, machine gun, Lewis gun, bombing, gas, horsemanship, shoe making, brick laying, carpentry, sanitation, butchery and cooking. For a division weak in manpower such schools became a nightmare. One interpretation of such a school was that it "…is a plot of ground traversed by imitation trenches, where officers who have never been near the line teach war-worn veterans their business."

The 11th Inniskillings mounted a raid on the night of 14 November. This was carried out by a force of four officers and 180 other ranks, the officers being Second Lieutenants Strong, Johnston, Malseed and Talbot. The force was identified as G Company, although it contained men from all four companies of the battalion and a number of Royal Engineers who were experienced in tunnelling. The party was well equipped with Bangalore torpedoes, a plentiful supply of bombs, axes for smashing enemy apparatus and Lewis guns. Each member of the party was ordered to blacken his face with burnt cork, steel helmets were worn and gas masks carried. The raid was rehearsed, as was training in the use of German hand grenades and machine guns, while the company was divided up into squads of three to five men. For a number of days prior to the raid trench mortars fired into the area in the hope of cutting the wire and while there was no preceding artillery barrage, a box barrage could be called down in an emergency. No details of the outcome of the patrol are recorded in the brigade war diary, apart from the fact that the white boards previously placed at each gap in the enemy wire were still in position. Nor had any attempts been made to fill the gaps.

12

Battle of Cambrai

The Battle of Cambrai was fought between 20 November and 7 December 1917 and was carried out by the British Third Army under the command of General Julian Byng. While the 36th Division would play a minimal part, it was nevertheless an important role. The town of Cambrai acted as a key supply base for the position known as the *Siegfried Stellung* and also the capture of the Bourlon Ridge would be an excellent position from which to threaten the rear area of the German line. Despite what many books have stated this was not the first use of massed tanks in action, the French having used over 100 the previous May, whilst the British had deployed some 200 in Flanders during Third Ypres. However, it was the first British use of a predicted artillery barrage.[1]

Downpatrick War Memorial – the ninth name, Private John Clydesdale, who lived in Church Street, was killed at Cambrai in November 1917, while serving with the 15th Royal Irish Rifles.

---

1   Terraine, John, *The Smoke and the Fire* (1980).

Cambrai: The plan

Until this time the Cambrai Front had been relatively quiet and there had been more than adequate time to prepare defences. The trenches were in depth and much wider than elsewhere, allowing the swift movement of troops both forward and back. On the other hand there was a shortage of artillery shells and armoured piercing ammunition for the machine guns was also in short supply. These were known as K bullets and consisted of Mauser 7.92x57mm armour piercing rounds that had a steel core and were designed to be fired from a standard Mauser rifle or machine gun. The K bullet had a probability of penetrating approximately 12 to 13 millimetres of armour at 100 yards. In February 1918, the Germans would field the only specific anti-tank rifle of the Great War with the introduction of the Mauser 1918T-*Gewehr*, with a calibre of 13.2mm.

For the attack at Cambrai the British tanks would advance driving through the German wire of the Hindenburg System, creating gaps through which the infantry would follow. It was then intended that the enemy holding the line between the Canal du Nord and the Canal de l'Escaut, which runs parallel to it at a distance of six to eight miles, would be overrun. It would then be possible to secure the area between the Canals and also clear the ground west of the Canal du Nord.

British artillery was silently registered to prevent the enemy from knowing just how many guns were present, which would in turn achieve instant suppression on enemy positions. The attacking tanks would clear gaps in the barbed wire, both by driving over it and by the use of the No.106 fuze, designed to explode the shell on contact and not to crater the ground. Some tanks would carry fascines, large bundles of brushwood that could be dropped into the wider trenches to allow the tanks to drive across. The tank's guns and machine guns would assist in neutralising enemy positions. German generals had originally scoffed at the idea of tanks, calling them a useless weapon, but that did not fool the common soldier.

The 36th Division was part of IV Corps, which also contained the 62nd (West Riding) Division and the 51st (Highland) Division. It also had under command the 56th Division to the north

Waiting for the advance, the men on foot, the officers on horseback.

and the 6th Division of the III Corps to the south. The right boundary of the IV Corps was the Trescault to Ribecourt Road, the left the area just beyond Noyelles. The order of attack was the 51st Division on the right, the 62nd in the centre and the 36th on the left. The 51st and 62nd was to advance north from the outskirts of Havrincourt Wood, their objective being the Bapaume to Cambrai Road. If there was little resistance they were to proceed on to take the high ground on Bourlon Ridge.

The 107 and 108 Brigades would meanwhile move parallel with them east of the Canal, forming a flank guard facing west and capturing the Canal crossings at Moeuvres and at Inchy-en-Artois. The primary task given to the 36th Division was the capture of the German trenches west of the Canal de Nord and south of the Bapaume to Cambrai Road, and responsibility for this was given to General Ricardo and his 109 Brigade.

The 109 Brigade would be supported by three Field Artillery Brigades; the division's own 173 Brigade and the 280 and 93 Army Brigades, RFA. The division's other artillery brigade, the 153, was lending support to the 62nd Division. General Ricardo worked closely with Lieutenant Colonel H.C. Simpson, DSO, and had the almost unique opportunity of planning his own battle in his own fashion.

Communications across the canal was to be established by the construction of a bridge on the Demicourt to Flesquieres Road that would be capable of carrying wagons and artillery pieces. Material for this bridge and several others capable of carrying infantry and pack mules was stored close by.

The German defence line began just west of the canal at a position known as the Spoil Heap. From here to the Bapaume to Cambrai Road they consisted of two main lines of trenches, except for the stretch between Lock No.6 and No.7, where they were three deep, this was for a length of some 1,500 yards.

As no tanks had been allocated to the division a frontal attack without artillery preparation was out of the question. It was therefore decided to capture the Spoil Heap, whose defending wire had been cut by a long period of artillery fire and the judicious use of a 6-inch Trench Mortar that fired bombs fitted with an instantaneous fuze. This weapon was, in the opinion of those who operated it, the best wire-cutter ever discovered. Once the Spoil Heap had been taken the brigade would then work its way along the enemy trenches from south to north. Given the maze of trenches to be cleared it was decided that Zero for the division should be 8:35 am, while the remainder of the force began at 6:20 am. That way the defenders would already be partially outflanked and would have in sight the mass of attacking tanks moving past their flank. Soon after meeting these armoured monsters on the battlefield the German infantry were calling the tanks *Deutsch's Tod*, Germany's Death.

The assault carried out by 109 Brigade was later described as a bombing action. However, it was not a conventional bombing action. In discussion General Nugent and Brigadier Ricardo decided that if the attack did develop into the conventional bombing action, an action that was slow at best and required a huge supply of bombs for each yard of ground gained, it would soon grind to a halt. The area to be taken was some 4,000 yards, consisting of two or three parallel lines of trenches intersected at frequent points by numerous communication trenches at right angles to the attack, all of which had to be cleared. Speed was of the essence and an order was issued that there was to be no bombing until all other methods had failed. The plan was that at the head of each platoon the bomber was to be replaced by a Lewis gunner and his ammunition carriers. While the Lewis gun was at its most accurate when fired from a prone position using its bipod, it could be fired from the hip. This required a man of large physique and the use of a sling and while a degree of accuracy suffered, this meant little in the confines of a trench. Brigadier Ricardo had seen this method used by Canadian troops at Vimy Ridge where it had been most successful. This method would spearhead the attacks along the trenches and where possible riflemen would advance on top

Cadets of the 19th (Reserve) Battalion Royal Irish Rifles.

outside the trench. Within the 14th Rifles the Lewis gunners were ordered to load their magazines with two armour-piercing rounds and one tracer for every ten rounds. The tracer would assist with aiming from the hip, while the armour-piercing rounds would account for those enemy soldiers availing of body armour or gun shields.

Artillery support would be controlled by Colonel Simpson directly from Brigadier Ricardo's headquarters, established in the sunken Demicourt to Havrincourt Road, just short of the British front line. Simpson had a reputation for being one of the more scientific and least conventional artillery commanders in the British Army. Within Havrincourt Woods, sited along the rides, the guns stood almost wheel to wheel. It had been impossible to register the guns and so the barrage was kept further in front of the advancing tanks as would normally have been the case.

The 18-pounders were supplied with some 500,000 shells, these being brought forward during the hours of darkness by train. For a number of reasons these trains were often late, necessitating a long cold wait at the sidings for the working parties supplied by the division. On some occasions common sense prevailed and the working parties were kept at their billets until the trains actually arrived and were then shipped to the sidings by lorry. The casualties suffered in the Somme battle had mostly been replaced from the division's own reserve battalions and these had fought with success at Messines and Ypres. However, much of the spirit of the original division had disappeared into the Flanders mud.

The tanks, which in this case would be the main wire-cutters, had moved into position on the night of 19 November and were position approximately 1,000 yards from the German outpost line. The noise of their engines as they came forward had been covered by long bursts of machine gun fire.

Battle

The attack began at exactly 6:20 am on 20 November, the guns firing their various barrages and the tanks trundling towards the German wire followed by the infantry in columns. Surprise on the enemy was complete; he had no idea of the numbers of guns firing on him, nor of the presence of the tanks. It would appear that those British taken prisoner in previous trench raids had said little or nothing. At 7:15 am, divisional observers on the ridge east of Hermies could at last see through the early morning mist and the advance of the tanks was all too obvious. They crossed the ridge north of Havrincourt keeping well up with the barrage, but stopping and waiting for each lift. Behind them the men of the 62nd Division met little resistance and suffered few casualties. German shelling appeared desultory and by 8:00 am, the first objective, Havrincourt, Ribecourt, Couillet Wood and the front system of the Hindenburg defences were all taken, although there was continued fighting in and around the buildings of Havrincourt and its chateau until 10:00 am.

Now there was a pause while fresh troops passed through to take the next objectives. At 8:35 am the advance began again along the front and once more little resistance was met, except in one position. Those men defending the village of Flesquières seemed to be both brave and stubborn. The Highlanders of the 51st Division found themselves in a bitter fight. Here the garrison was the German 84th Infantry Regiment, reinforced by the 27th Reserve Infantry Regiment, recently arrived from Marcoing. Despite there only being 600 infantry there was also in and around the village a high concentration of field artillery, almost two regiments, plus a battery from a third. Despite losses from the British bombardment and an air attack, many of these guns were still in action and had been dragged out of their emplacements into the open ground where they had a much wider field of fire. When the tanks of D and E Battalion arrived at the top of the Ridge they made excellent targets for these guns. Within a short time 28 tanks had been lost to the German artillery and the attack by the Highlanders faltered.

The position known as the Spoil Heap was the first objective of 109 Brigade and the attack would be led by the 10th Inniskillings under the command of Major E.W. Crawford. The 10th had spent an uncomfortable night in the assembly trenches crowded in among the men of the Machine Gun Companies and Trench Mortar Batteries. Only No.4 Company had a relatively peaceful night being billeted in the village of Demicourt, although they did have a dangerous journey coming to the assembly trenches just before dawn along a road being heavily shelled, however no casualties were suffered.

Prior to the attack all companies visited the battalion supply dump at the Chinese Wall and here picked up their allocation of bombs, rifle grenades, Lewis gun magazines and rifle ammunition. During the night there had been spasmodic enemy shelling and Sergeant D. Griffith of No.2 Company was killed with several men being wounded. A hot breakfast was served to all ranks, but No.1 Company's cookhouse was hit by a shell and about half the men had to go without.

For the attack on the Spoil Heap support came from a battery of four 4-inch Stokes mortars firing thermite shells, these had been used to great effect at Messines the previous June. For four minutes these mortars and the supporting artillery bombarded the south-west side of the Spoil Heap. Instantly it stopped the 10th Inniskillings rushed the enemy position, entering it at Slag Street and after a brief flurry of action the defenders withdrew and made their way northwards up the trenches. Several of these were killed by the Lewis guns, while 70 prisoners were taken, along with two machine guns. The prisoners were identified as belonging to the 20th *Landwehr* Division, which had only arrived in the position two days before. At this time the Intelligence Branch considered that *Landwehr* troops were of low quality, in fact there was little difference between them and regular infantry. On entering the German defence system the Inniskillings were quick to continue up the German trench, clearing communication trenches and dug-outs as they went. One company of the 14th Rifles, attached to the Inniskillings, entered a communication trench on the Demicourt to Flesquieres Road some 1,500 yards to the north and here they proceeded with their own clearing. This clearing was done in a systematic manner. The leading platoons dropped a man at the entrance to each dug-out, to be picked up by the section following in the rear, whose job it was to mop up. As each dug-out was cleared, usually with several bombs, it had a wooden notice board set up at the entrance bearing the significant inscription 'Mopped'. When the vanguard platoon had exhausted its men, another moved through to the front, the

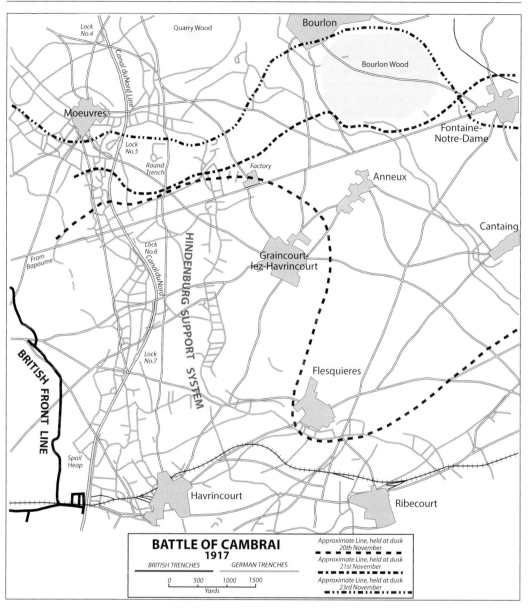

BATTLE OF CAMBRAI
1917

BRITISH TRENCHES   GERMAN TRENCHES

0   500   1000   1500
Yards

Approximate Line, held at dusk
20th November

Approximate Line, held at dusk
21st November

Approximate Line, held at dusk
23rd November

The battle that was almost a victory.

first platoon forming up behind it. A single flag bearing the battalion colours was carried by the leading platoon and was only displayed at the head of the advance, being passed to each platoon in turn. The flag of the 10th Inniskilling being blue and yellow verticals equally divided on the field. The Inniskillings reached their objective, named 'Hill 90', just to the north of the Demicourt to Flesquieres Road at 9:30 am

Meanwhile the 9th Inniskillings, who were responsible for the next phase of the attack, moved forward. While No.2 Company moved along the dry bed of the Canal, supported by a Platoon of B Company of the 11th Inniskillings, the remainder of the battalion came forward along the trenches, their extra width making it easier for one group to pass through another. There was some resistance encountered from German machine gun nests that had been established in shell holes on the Demicourt to Graincourt Road and this was dealt with by No.1 Company. The assault was led by Second Lieutenant J.J. McNamee and two sections in the forward line, while Second Lieutenant G.M.K. Martin and six sections were in the front line. During the attack the company had the misfortune to lose one of their bravest men, Private Joseph M. Buchanan, MM, who came from Aughlish, Dromore in County Tyrone. He was shot down as he made a valiant attempt to close with an enemy position. A little later Major Crawford came forward and by his example encouraged the men to a superb effort that successfully carried all before it. The attack swept some two to 300 yards beyond the objective and there it halted. Once the 11th Inniskillings had passed through the 9th moved back and consolidated the original objective. They brought back with them 16 enemy[2] machine guns and 160 prisoners, most having been taken by No.1 Company.

The 11th Inniskilling had followed closely on the heels of the 9th, with A Company under Captain William Knight leading up the C Trench, with, as previously mentioned, a platoon of B Company moving up the dry bed of the Canal. Second Lieutenant R. Barrowman led his D Company up the B Trench (the German support line), while C Company commanded by Captain W.H. Wagentreiber, known to the men as Willy Wag, advanced up A Trench (the German front line). Held in battalion reserve were two Lewis gun teams from B Company. This company, less the two teams and the platoon advancing up the bed of the Canal, acted as a carrying company for the remainder of the battalion, bringing forward ammunition, water and rations. There was considerable resistance encountered in several positions along both the A and C trenches from both machine guns and bombers and the battalion lost four men killed for eight of the enemy. Eventually the battalion passed through the 9th Inniskillings at their objective and both A and D Companies arrived at Lock No.6 at 1:10 pm. Here, through the pouring rain, they were stopped by machine gun fire. However, Captain Knight pressed the enemy and with clear and complete orders his company was responsible for the capture of two German machine guns. William Knight had practised as a solicitor before the war, having an office in Lisnaskea, County Fermanagh, and was the son of George Knight of County Meath. For his actions on this day he was subsequently awarded the Military Cross.

On the eastern side of the Canal the 62nd Division was also held up by the same machine gun fire. Second Lieutenant Finney crossed the Canal and arranged with the 62nd to send on two tanks. Once these had appeared the German garrison at the Lock withdrew over a spoil heap located at E.27.c.5.1. They were fired on by the Lewis guns of A Company, which inflicted a number of casualties. By 3:30 pm C Company had leap-frogged the 9th Inniskillings at their objective and joined up with the remainder of their battalion. By 4.30 pm, with darkness falling, the battalion reorganised in depth and consolidation commenced.

Also in the 9th Inniskillings Captain Edward Marshall was making the acquaintance of a tank. When his company became held up by a particularly well-sited machine gun, the captain ran across the fire-swept ground and attracted the attention of the tank commander. Within a few moments the target was identified and the tank's 6-pounder gun made short work of the position with several well placed high explosive shells. For his actions Captain Marshall, from Craigavad, County Down, was awarded the Military Cross, the first of two he would be awarded in the war.

By 3:30 pm, 109 Brigade had crossed the Cambrai to Bapaume Road and had consolidated their position, with their outpost some three or 400 yards north of it. The road bridge across the Canal had been demolished some time earlier, as part of the German defensive plan.

---

2   Wagentreiber had been a company commander in the Lifford UVF and a veteran of the Somme campaign where he had been wounded on 1 July.

An advance dressing station during the initial advance at Cambrai, German prisoners are being utilised as stretcher bearers, while two German medical orderlies are also present.

On the left flank of 109 Brigade the 56th Division had taken up a position along the Bapaume to Cambrai Road. On the right flank 62 Division had met with complete success. Graincourt had been captured at 1:30 pm, and the long communication trench north of the Bapaume to Cambrai Road was consolidated at the same time as the final objective of the 36th Division.

While this independent action was being fought in the Hindenburg System, the 107 and 108 Brigades had moved forward at 1:30 pm, 107 Brigade going to the northern slope of the Grand Ravin, close to Square Copse, while the 108th went to Yorkshire Bank and the old British trenches south of it. The rain had begun and those men without shelter, especially those in 107 Brigade, suffered a miserable time. This lasted until 8:00 pm, when 107 Brigade was ordered into Havrincourt and those trenches and dug-outs around it. It was 3:00 am before the men finally had the chance to rest.

The personnel of the 110th Field Ambulance were busy dealing with the wounded and Robert Doggart was told that a wounded man with the same name had been recovered from the battle-field. When he went to see if the man was related he found that the casualty had just been driven away by ambulance. One of the stretcher bearers who had helped bring in the other Doggart was Sergeant Edwin Crothers from Groomsport, County Down, but he was unable to give Robert any further information.

The 10th Inniskillings were moved across the Canal to a location known as Kangaroo Alley, which was south of and parallel to the Bapaume to Cambrai Road. On their left flank patrols from the 11th Inniskillings advanced to within 500 yards of the village of Moeuvres before being driven back by machine gun and mortar fire.

Throughout this time the Royal Engineers had made excellent progress with the construction of the bridge across the Canal. By 4:00 pm, a bridge capable of carrying infantry and pack animals had been completed about 1,000 yards north of the Hermies to Havrincourt railway line. Thirty minutes later the Engineers were able to report that successful repairs had been made to the Demicourt to Flesquieres Road causeway and that it was now capable of carrying field guns and wagons.

The Divisional Signal Service, under the command of Major Vigers, was not resting on the laurels won at Messines and had quickly established communications. By utilising the Canal bed to lay wires it was soon possible for telephone communications between headquarters at Ytres to those units in position at Lock No.6.

With darkness on 20 November operations came to a halt. The division held a line 500 yards north of the Bapaume to Cambrai Road and was in contact with the 56th Division on its left flank. To the east of the Canal the 62nd Division held the trench north of the road and the position known as the factory. From here it continued to the west of Anneux to Graincourt and ended just west of Flesquieres. The III Corps continued this line to the north of Noyelles, leaving a German salient containing Flesquieres and Orival Wood, from where, it was reported, enemy guns were still in action.

The artillery was repositioned during the hours of darkness. The majority of the IV Corps heavy artillery was positioned around Hermies and Demicourt, positions where it was easy to re-supply them with ammunition. The 153 Brigade, then positioned in Havrincourt Wood, had provided support for the assault of the 62nd Division and once this was complete it had moved to a new positions in the former no man's land east of Demicourt. Given the condition of the roads and the weather, it was 7:30 am, on 21 November, before the guns of the 153 Brigade were in action. They were then joined by the 173 Brigade, who also experienced great difficulty in moving, with road congestion being added to the problems of nature.

During the fighting of 20 November the IV Corps had taken over 2,000 prisoners, of these 109 Brigade's share was 509. They had also been fortunate in securing a large supply of stores at Lock No.6, it having been used as a general store-house for the German forward area.

At the end of the day there had been success mixed with failure. There had been a penetration of three to four miles into the enemy lines on a six-mile front. The Germans had suffered tremendous losses and in places the surprise of the tank had been tremendous. In Britain there was the pealing of church bells and many considered the war was as good as over. Not so for those officers peering over situation maps in various headquarters. With Flesquières still in German hands, and with the failure to capture Bourlon Wood, the promised breakout by the cavalry had been denied. Now, with surprise lost it was to be a race between further advances and the arrival of German reserves. As for the 36th Division, they had done all that had been asked and had done it well.

The second day of the battle and the 51st Division found that Flesquieres had been abandoned by the Germans. The advance moved on and Cantaing was taken by a combined attack by the division and 2 Cavalry Brigade, after some stiff fighting in the early morning. Later the 51st took Fontaine-Notre-Dame, just two and a half miles from Cambrai. The 62nd Division also met with success and Anneux was taken after heavy fighting, followed by Anneux Chapel, on the edge of Bourlon Wood, but were unable to take the Wood itself.

On the western bank of the Canal du Nord the attack was led by the 109 Brigade and the 9th Inniskillings. They reached a point where the enemy trenches turned west, 1,000 yards north of the Bapaume to Cambrai Road, and here were stopped by heavy machine gun fire from Lock No.5 and east of the Canal. It was not until noon that the attack could be resumed and the 10th Inniskillings in company with the 14th Rifles faced increasing opposition as they closed with the outskirts of Moeuvres.

There was a machine gun position to the east of the village that pinned B Company of the Rifles. They managed to link up with the 9th Inniskillings, but they also were under intense machine gun fire. By 3:00 pm, A Company of the Rifles had managed to enter one of the trenches and was working its way along the Canal in an attempt to meet with B Company. For a distance they had to work around an enemy outpost and later were shot at from a position known as the Slag Heap, which caused further delays. Enemy shells were falling on D Company and they sent an urgent message for artillery support. Eventually it was apparent that the village was just too heavily defended and both C and D Companies fell back. They were rallied by Second Lieutenant Reddy, who then reported to battalion headquarters that the enemy appeared to be preparing for a counter-attack, which did not materialise. The casualties to the 109 Brigade were much heavier than the previous day and the advance had been less than 1,000 yards. The division dug in and waited.

In 107 Brigade three men were killed on 21 November; Private Patrick Blunden, Lance Corporal Vazey Holden and Private Frederick Bryans. All men are listed as having no known grave; Blunden and Holden are listed on the Thiepval Memorial, Bryans on the Cambrai Memorial. Frederick Bryans was 19 years old and the son of Samuel and Rachel Bryans of Cambrai Street, Belfast.[3]

While on paper the day appeared to be a success, the advance had fallen short of the planned programme. The intention had been that the 62nd and 51st Division should reach Bourlon, while the 1st Cavalry Division would follow through and seize the Canal crossing running from Sains-lez-Marquion and on to the north. The 107 and 108 Brigades were then to have advanced on the side of the Canal and held a line from Moeuvres to Sains-lez-Marquion. This had not happened.

Corporal Glass of C Company, 10th Rifles recoded in his diary on 22 November:

> We left the reserve trench about 8:00 am and went right up into the front line. At this time John (the enemy) being in possession of it so he had to clear out in quick time as bombs were thrown into it very freely. Our lads were close at his heels and kept up the Iron rations for him going steady in pursuit for almost two miles when our bombs were exhausted so we had to cease the chase for want of bombs. He made several counter-attacks during the day all being fruitless and very costly to him. Dead bodies were lying very numerous all over the place. He made a rush on us late in the evening when the trench was choked up with men. The word being passed along to move back but one of our Officers took it upon himself to stop the message with the result that some of our men got the wind up when they saw that no-one was moving back, to ease the pressure they got out of the trench and made a present of their lives to Johnny's machine gunners.

The intention for 22 November were that the 51st and 62nd Divisions were to improve and consolidate their positions, while the 36th and 56th Divisions attempted to gain ground on the left flank. Within the division 109 Brigade would rest, having accomplished so much in the previous two days. It was relieved in the early hours of the morning and by 7:00 am; the 12th Rifles had taken over its advanced position supported by the 9th (NIH) Irish Fusiliers. 109 Brigade then moved back to the old British trenches at Hermies.

On the eastern bank of the Canal General Withycombe had established his headquarters in an old German dug-out to the west of Graincourt. His 107 Brigade was tasked with clearing the first and second lines of the Hindenburg Support System up to the actual Canal, while 108 Brigade were responsible for the taking of Moeuvres. For the clearing of the trenches the 15th Rifles were

---

3   Cambrai Street, Leopold Street and Brussels Street had derived their names pre-war from places and people in Flanders and Belgium where the flax from which linen was woven had originated.

selected. The 10th Rifles would then pass through and continue the attack towards Lock No.4, which was opposite Inchy. From the 107th Machine Gun Company eight guns would assist in covering the attack. The rate of the barrage was to be 50 yards in five minutes east of the Canal and 50 yards in seven and a half minutes to the west of it. There was further support from four Siege and one Heavy Battery and one 9.2-inch howitzer, this to be opened at 11:00 am.

By now the element of surprise had been lost and the German were well aware of what was to happen. At 9:20 am, they counter-attacked on the front of the 51st and 62nd Divisions. While the 62nd was able to hold its ground on the right flank it was forced back on the left, further east the 51st Division was driven out of Fontaine.

In 36th Division a battery of guns from the 108th Machine Gun Company had been pushed too far forward and was in action half-way between Lock No.5 and the factory on the Bapaume to Cambrai Road. The guns were rushed by a strong party of German infantry who engaged them at close quarters. Lieutenant I.C. Macintyre and Private A. Bee were killed and the guns surrounded. Observing this incident was Major Miller, the Divisional Machine Gun Officer who immediately ordered two guns of another battery into action. At just over 100 yards the two Vickers tore into the enemy infantry causing them to scatter and seek cover in nearby ditches and shell holes. Later that day 42 German dead were counted in the immediate area.

At 11:00 am, the division's attack was launched after a 40-minute bombardment. On the right flank the leading company of the 15th Rifles reached its objective, gaining some 500 yards of enemy trench, mostly through ferocious bombing. The 10th Rifles following up found that the continuing German trenches were only half complete and this was working well in favour of the defenders who were generously armed with machine guns. As dusk fell one last attempt was made to rush the barrier, but it cost too many casualties and the battalion was forced to withdraw. Losses for the two battalions had been heavy. Among those in the 15th Rifles who were killed was Private Thomas Dalzell, from Belfast, a former member of the Army Service Corps, and Private Thomas Black from Whitehouse, Belfast. There was Sergeant Thomas Stead, DCM, Private William Fletcher from Blackburn in Lancashire and also Private John Clydesdale from Downpatrick. Lance Corporal Herbert Horton was a 19 year old from Chelsea in London who was one of several men transferred from the King's Royal Rifle Corps, as was Private Harry Lane-Verral from Eastbourne, who had formerly served with the Royal Sussex Regiment. The 10th Rifles had also suffered heavily, losing among others, Private John Baker, Private Samuel Bradshaw from Courtrai Street, Belfast and Private Robert Shaw.

The Rifles had particularly heavy losses in officers in charging that last barrier and among the dead from a single burst of enemy machine gun fire were Lieutenant Thomas Haslett, MC, from Ballymena, County Antrim, Lieutenant George York Henderson, MC, from Belfast, and Lieutenant Alexander McKee, Antrim Road, Belfast. McKee had been an original member of the YCV, but on the outbreak of war had enlisted in the Black Watch, before being granted a commission in the Rifles. He had served in Dublin during the rebellion in April 1916, before moving to France and was a member of Ekenhead Presbyterian Church and Ulidia Masonic Lodge. Lieutenant Henderson, a former pupil of Methodist College and Trinity, had originally been commissioned into the Army Service corps and was appointed as Adjutant of the 36th Divisional Train. Prior to 1 July 1916, he had transferred to the 10th Rifles and had been awarded the Military Cross for his actions at Messines in June. Three of his brothers also served.

Other officer casualties were Captain James Jamison of Belfast and Second Lieutenants Thomas McCay, Walter Scott of Botanic, Belfast. and Hugh Atkinson, MID, from Camden Street, Belfast. Atkinson had been educated at Wesley College, Dublin, and Methodist College, Belfast, before entering the Board of Works. On the outbreak of War he had enlisted in the 6th (Territorial) Battalion, Black Watch, serving with them in France for a year. He then obtained a commission in the Rifles on 22 November 1915 and was appointed as intelligence officer for the battalion and later as a brigade intelligence officer. Colonel Burnand wrote to the family; "At the time he was shot he was ahead of my battalion, endeavoring to find out how the situation lay. He located the enemy sniper who was doing considerable damage and proceeded to stalk him. In doing so he was shot through the head and died instantly. Your son always showed great fearlessness."

Acting Brigade Major Ronald D. Williams observed:

> Hugh was sent up with a party of the Brigade Intelligence section to keep in touch with the attack on the Hindenburg support line and to send us back news of what was happening. He was in the best of spirits, he always was, and was joking with me before he left about a pair of German boots which he had been wearing while his own dried. He got among his own battalion (10th Rifles) when he was up in the line and found that the attack was being held up by some German machine guns and snipers. He immediately got out of our trench and got out to some bushes in front and tried to pick off the Boche snipers with a rifle. Unfortunately, he was hit through the head by one of the enemy's shots and died almost instantly.

When the lieutenant was hit Lieutenant T.S. Huslett ran forward to assist, but was shot and wounded a few seconds later.

West of the Canal things went a little better at the outset. On the left of the division the 56th Division bombed their way up the Hindenburg Front System and captured Tadpole Copse. Colonel W.R. Goodwin, commanding the 12th Rifles, had established his headquarters near the Canal on the Bapaume – Cambrai Road, with his forward command post under Captain A.H. Hall located at E2.C.6.2. The Rifles, with the 9th (NIH) Irish Fusiliers in support, attacked Moeuvres under cover of an artillery barrage at 10:30 am, with three of its companies in line, the centre and left-hand companies managed to penetrate the village, but on the right flank A Company was held up by machine gun fire from the Hindenburg Support System and suffered heavy casualties. This was due to 107 Brigade having been held up on its own front and the Germans being able to traverse their machine guns across the System. Colonel Goodwin then ordered his right flank company to bomb its way up the trench leading from the sunken Moeuvres to Graincourt Road to the Hindenburg Support System, while the other companies exploited their partial success in the village. Initially the right-hand company had success and soon reached the front line trench of the Support System and cleared it of enemy. However, the next line was crammed with Germans and there was no possibility of taking it. Meanwhile in the village the centre and western side had been cleared and many Germans had been killed in dug-outs and cellars. Pushing on through the village the Rifles took the trench on the western edge, fringing the Cemetery and began to consolidate it.

Then, it seemed from nowhere, came the German counter-attack. Between 3:30 and 4:00 pm, it had been observed that the enemy was assembling in great force in Hobart Street, half way between Moeuvres and Inchy and also in the Hindenburg Support System north-west of the former village. Messages were sent back for support and for an artillery barrage. Both requested were answered, support from the 9th (NIH) Irish Fusiliers and shelling from the guns of the divisional artillery. Unfortunately neither arrived in time.

As dusk fell the Germans attacked with what appeared to be two battalions, one advancing parallel with the Hindenburg Support System and the second coming down the Canal, in several waves. Initially the Rifles east of the cemetery were forced to withdraw to stop being surrounded, this being done in an orderly fashion. The Lewis guns again proving their worth as they covered the rifles' section and then each other. They also accounted for a large number of enemy casualties. A, C and D Companies fell back, but only across that ground already taken and fighting every inch of the way, they also brought with them two prisoners. Two company commanders fell in this action; Captain William Stuart, MC, from Ballymena, County Antrim, with his men, refused to retire and despite a bullet wound to the throat. Stuart continued to command until he received a fatal wound to the head. Captain David McCausland, from St Johnston, County Londonderry, had previously served with the North Irish Horse in the South African War. He was 38 years old and despite his age always insisted in leading his men from the front, he too died during the withdrawal.[4] In C Company Sergeant William Beattie of Lisburn, County Antrim, died. Other casualties included Private Albert Nelson from Comber, County Down, and Private George Alder, from Stonehouse, Gloucestershire. The vast majority of the men who died here are listed as having no known grave.[5]

In the 12th Rifles Lieutenant Edward McDonald, from the Antrim Road Belfast, was killed. A fellow, unnamed, officer wrote to McDonald's family:

> We were forced to withdraw, the Boches advancing in eight waves and completely encircling us. He formed a strong-point at the sunken road and gave the order to advance again to the attack. I worked my way forward till I got in touch with another division; came back and found him still in possession of the village, and being driven back foot by foot, but still fighting and cheering on his men. I reinforced him; we filled that village with dead Boches. Two platoon held up roughly one thousand enemy for almost three hours, mainly through McDonald's hard work, control and cheerfulness, who had he lived, would certainly have had a decoration for that night's work.

The delay in British artillery support was simply down to the primitive communication of the day. The support for the Irish Fusiliers was slowed by a German artillery barrage that fell south of Moeuvres and the interlocking machine gun fire from either flank. This action again demonstrated the disadvantage of attacking on a narrow front. The Hindenburg trenches to the west of Moeuvres were on higher ground, overlooked the village and permitted intense machine gun fire to be concentrated on it. There had also been machine gun fire delivered from the German trenches to the east of the Canal, both this position and the high ground being outside the area of operations and had not been dealt with. It had not been dealt with due to the lack of artillery preparation and support of tanks, neither of which was available.

On the right flank the cavalry breakthrough had not happened. Fresh German reserves had now arrived and resistance all along the line was very strong. The 40th Division had relieved the 62nd, now badly exhausted. While much had been achieved, there was still the matter of the Bourlon Ridge. While it remained in German hands all the British positions were overlooked and it was imperative that it be captured.

Haig called with General Nugent and discussed the situation, recording the following in his diary; "Today had been hard fighting at Moeuvres. He (Nugent) thought that Enemy had no infantry on their front only machine gun companies. Several of these machine gunners fought like fanatics and instead of surrendering blew out their brains."[6]

The weather was turning. Adding to increased German artillery fire and numerous skilfully and well sited machine guns, the rain was turning to snow as the temperature dropped. This would in turn affect the lines of communications. While the light railways were able to handle some traffic, they had not come up to expectation and as for the roads, they were practically non-existent. The main route of supply for the division was the Hermies to Graincourt road and for the greater part of its length it was sunken. This meant it was impossible to widen it and flooding or snow drifts

---

4   Captain McCausland had been wounded at Messines in June 1917. *Belfast News Letter,* 3 December 1917.
5   12th Battalion war diary and after action report.
6   Sheffield & Bourne, *Douglas Haig: War Diaries and Letters.*

could cause delays. A more frequent delay was caused by a wagon suffering a broken axle or losing a wheel and due to the narrowness nothing being able to pass in either direction. Eventually the road was abandoned and all traffic used the ground on either side, running repairs being made to any deep wheel ruts and shell holes that appeared.

IV Corps plans for 23 November were ambitious enough, yet more modest than the previous day. On the right flank the 51st Division was to re-capture Fontaine and then move on to secure the high ground east of Bourlon Wood. The 40th Division was to capture the village of Bourlon, while the 36th and 56th Divisions were to advance up the Canal and roll up the Hindenburg Support System. For the first time in this battle the 36th Division was to have the support of tanks.

Unknown to most men in the division a former member of the 8th Rifles was aboard one of the tanks. Lieutenant T.P. McConnell from Cranmore Park, Belfast, had been wounded on 1 July 1916. Now this ex-member of the YCV was in command of one of the supporting tanks and by the day's end would be evacuated suffering from severe wounds to his chest and knee. He would survive these wounds and be promoted to acting captain and adjutant in February 1918.

Once again the division would advance on both sides of the canal, 107 Brigade on the eastern side, supported by 93 Army Field Artillery Brigade and 16 tanks. The 108 Brigade on the west would have the support of the divisional artillery, while 109 Brigade was to be in reserve.

At his headquarters near Graincourt General Withycombe held a conference of his commanding officers and the officers of the tank battalion at 4:00 am. The forthcoming attack was to be in two phases. The first was the capture of the Hindenburg trenches up to the canal, then Round Trench and finally Lock No.5. The second phase was an advance northwards to Hobart Street from the canal to the north corner of Quarry Wood and a position held here. For the first phase 11 tanks were allocated, for the second five, plus any survivors of the first phase! Ninety minutes was deemed adequate time for phase one; there would then be a pause of one hour before phase two. On the west bank of the Canal the capture of Moeuvres was to coincide with phase one; the second was to be the capture of the trench running westward from Lock No.4 to the Hindenburg Support System. Zero for the first phase was set at 10:30 am, the earliest moment possible, seeing that General Withycombe had not been able to issue his orders due to the difficulty in the tank officers attending the briefing.

The objective of the 15th Rifles was the rolling up of the Hindenburg Support System and on the success of that the entire plan of 107 Brigade rested. The Rifles advanced, led by two of the tanks, one of which promptly broke down, while the second turned to the right and departed on its own business. The Rifles continued their advance alone and were met with ferocious machine gun fire. One company made an advance of 100 yards, while one of its platoons successfully rushed a machine gun post located in a crater on the road running north from the Factory. Despite this the company had to withdraw when the men ran short of ammunition and rifle grenades. The 8th Rifles with the assistance of a tank captured and consolidated around Lock No.5 and succeeded in taking several prisoners. This was the sum total of success for the division. A frontal attack was totally out of the question. Only two of the 11 tanks had succeeded in their tasks, the remainder either having broken down, or been put out of action by the German artillery fire, which was extremely heavy. Without tanks any further movement forward was impossible.

On the left bank of the Canal the attack on Moeuvres by the 12th Rifles and the 9th (N.I.H.) Irish Fusiliers had made some progress, which was increased when the fresh 2nd Rifles was sent in to support them. The fighting in the village lasted all day and by dusk three quarters of the building had been cleared and four machine guns captured. While the Hindenburg trenches on either side of the village remained untaken, it was impossible to consolidate the position. As darkness fell the troops were withdrawn to the southern edge of the village and took up positions in the houses there. During the night 108 Brigade was relieved by 109 Brigade.

Elsewhere the 40th Division had captured Bourlon, while the 51st Division had again taken Fontaine. Heavy German counter-attacks drove the 40th from the village, but was unable to penetrate the Wood, while the 51st were forced out of Fontaine.

A planned attack by the 107 Brigade was cancelled, Lieutenant Colonel Lucas-Clements, 1st Irish Fusiliers, taking full responsibility in ordering his men not to advance, a decision fully justified given the lack of available artillery support. Previously on 18 November Nugent had written to his wife complaining bitterly about the 1st Irish Fusiliers and had ordered Lucas-Clements to be replaced, although this did not occur prior to the battle. The reason for his replacement was a successful German trench raid;

> I am furious; the Germans raided me last night and walked off with a Sergeant and five men, belonging to the 1st Battalion R. Irish Fusiliers, one of the regular battalions that have been recently sent to me. It was most important that the Germans should get no prisoners to question. I should like to shoot the whole party. Goodness knows how much the men taken prisoners knew, but the Germans will get everything out of them they do know, I am quite certain.
>
> We have lost no more than three or four men as a result of German raids since we came to France and this wretched regular battalion which ought to be an example has let us down.[7]

Shuckburgh Upton Lucas-Clements, DSO, had a family home at Rathkenny, Coothill, County Cavan. He had attended Trinity College, Dublin graduating BAI, and then been commissioned into the 4th Irish Fusiliers, seeing action in the South African War. He died in February 1960, aged 76 years.

On 24 November, General Nugent informed his corps commander, Lieutenant General Woollcombe, that he was not prepared to attack again unless adequately supported by artillery and tanks. Woollcombe saw the sense in Nugent's comment and on the night of 26 November the division, exhausted by the fighting and atrocious weather, was withdrawn.[8] The previous day Second Lieutenant R.G.H. Mansfield, Royal Irish Fusiliers, had been cashiered by Field General Court Martial.[9]

To many men of the division the night of 26 November was the most miserable night of the war. The persistent rain had turned to snow and with the strong east wind swept almost horizontally across the battlefield. The relief took much longer than usual, the snow and wind making marching in any order almost impossible. The assigned billets were far from satisfactory. The 108 Brigade was placed in Beaumetz, the 109 Brigade in Doignies and its surrounding trenches were allocated to 107 Brigade. Nowhere was there sufficient space, especially in Doignies, where troops from other units were vying for any available space, and many men spent what was left of the night in the open snow-covered ground.

The division, less its pioneers, artillery and engineers, moved to the area of Barastre-Rocquigny-Beaulencourt the following day, which contained more suitable billets and the men had a chance to sleep in some comfort. There was also time for reorganisation, refitting and the cleaning of weapons and equipment.

Two days later, with the 121st Field Company once again attached, the division was transferred from the IV Corps to the XVII Corps, under the command of Lieutenant General Sir Julian Byng, which was in position holding the line east of Arras. The intention was that the division's infantry

---

7   There is no evidence that the capture of these men made any difference to the battle.
8   Perry, *Major General Oliver Nugent and the Ulster Division 1915-1918.*
9   *London Gazette,* 23 February 1918.

would move by train to Ytres and Bapaume, the transport moving by road to Gomiecourt, Achiet-le-Petit and Courcelles-leComte, three devastated villages in the Somme area, but where shelter for horses and men had been erected. The Staff of XVII Corps assured General Nugent that the Division could expect to spend some weeks, at least, out of the line. This was not to be the case and the ongoing battle at Cambrai would be the cause of it.

On 27 November the British IV Corps had made another attack against Bourlon. With the assistance of tanks the 62nd Division had taken half the village, but was unable to hold it against powerful German counter-attacks. At Fontaine three battalions of the Guards Division attacked, but with no available supports they had to be withdrawn at dusk. The Third Army was now almost used up; the Guards were relieved by the 59th Division, while the 62nd was relieved by the 47th, giving three comparatively fresh divisions to the corps as of the morning of 30 November.

This was also the morning that the Germans launched their major counter-offensive. Subsequent intelligence revealed that this was in fact the biggest attack made by German forces on the Western Front since the assault on Verdun, some 18 months previously. While counter-attacks had been expected and arrangements made to meet them, this was something much more serious. The Germans had made a deliberate attempt, heavily supported by artillery, to apply pincers to the left and right flanks of the large salient created by the earlier British attack. On the northern flank the attacks fell mainly on the 47th, 2nd, and 56th Divisions. Given that the 2nd was a Regular division and the others London Territorials, it says much in that they lost so little in the way of ground. Throughout the day there were repeated attacks, each heavily supported by artillery of all calibres. Between eight and ten separate waves of infantry threw themselves at the British positions and while some were lost on a temporary basis, the line held. The fact that the British IV Corps Heavy Artillery had not moved forward, but was still at Doignies and Demicourt, with Divisional Royal Artillery Headquarters, established at Little Wood, Ytres, was a tremendous advantage and it took little time to engage the designated targets. The guns were able to take the advancing enemy in enfilade, while the guns of the field artillery were also blessed with numerous targets in the open.

The Potter medals, held by the Somme Museum.

Supporting the 2nd Division were the 153 and 173 Brigades of the divisional artillery under the command of Colonel Simpson, who was sharing a headquarters with the Infantry Brigadier in the former Headquarters at Scotch Street. During the day 153 Brigade fired 10,000 rounds, in many cases finding and destroying large parties of the enemy as they crossed open ground. Observers noted German batteries coming into action and several sections of 18-pounders and 4.5-inch howitzers of the 173rd Brigade were run forward to the crest of the Demicourt Ridge to engage them. This was witnessed by Colonel Claud Potter from his position close to Lock No.7:

> The Huns came on in dense masses, wave after wave of them in full view in the open and accompanied by guns. Our artillery had fine targets and fairly strafed them. A very large number of his men were bowled over. It is impossible to estimate the size of the attack, but I myself have seen many thousands. I've never seen anything like it before in the war. The whole thing was thrilling and when I saw our infantry up and counter-attack, I could scarcely contain myself and longed to pick up a gun and bayonet and go after them.

By nightfall the situation had been restored. On the southern flank it was a different story. The Germans broke through the British lines at several places. La Vacquerie was retaken, also Villers-Guislain, Gonnelieu and Gouzeaucourt, although Masnieres, defended by a brigade of the 29th Division, held out. Numerous prisoners were taken, estimated at several 1,000 and many guns lost. At noon the Guards Division attacked Gouzeaucourt and drove the Germans out of it and back for a 1,000 yards. There were other attempts to retake Gonnelieu and La Vacquerie, but these were not successful. The Germans also held Welsh Ridge.

At about the same time as the Guards were attacking Gouzeaucourt, the Corps staff officers were reconnoitring camps in the area of Arras, when the division received the news that the Germans had broken through and it was to retrace its steps. Given the now-congested railways there was no option but for the troops to march on foot and by 2:30 pm, they were making their way back. Members of the divisional cyclist company were sent ahead to turn back the division's horse-drawn transport. Eventually both men and animals were gathered in the area of Lechelle-Bancourt Rocquigny. Both were exhausted, the men of the division had fought for the last ten days followed by the marching and counter-marching, while the horses and mules had dragged heavy loads over miles of atrocious roads. Added to this was the accommodation in the area which was scarce for both men and animals.

From 23 November the division had been under the command of the British III Corps and in the course of this 108 Brigade was placed at the disposal of the 61st Division and positioned in and around the village of Beaucamp.

The 36th Division artillery battled hard in the forlorn hope of saving a beleaguered and desperate company of the Essex Regiment. This action took place at Lock No.5 on the Canal de Nord, on 1 December, between one and two miles from Moeuvres. Here the artillery brigades were under the command of the 2nd Division. Despite some accurate and heavy shelling the efforts of the artillery were in vain and the company was wiped out. 173 Brigade lost ten men that day, including Major Robert Lloyd Thompson MC, the commander of C Battery. All the casualties were buried in the cemetery at Hermies Hill.[10] The major had been conversing with the colonel of another brigade shortly before he was fatally injured in the head by a piece of shrapnel from an enemy shell. He had been one of the most popular officers in the brigade, Brigadier Brock wrote to the family:

---

10   *Over the Top*, journal of the Ulster Branch, Western Front Association (Autumn 1999).

I am sending you a few lines to try and express my very deep sympathy with you in the loss of your gallant son. He had been in the divisional artillery since I took over command in 1915, and had acted in various capacities, and gained general and constant promotion. He had invariably carried out his duties with keenness and capacity. He was a great friend of mine, and I cannot tell you how I feel his loss. I know his battery and brigade feel the same, as he was universally popular. I was up at the observation post shortly after the sad event. He was unconscious from the moment he was hit and died almost immediately afterwards. You will always have the consolation, though a poor one, for his loss, that he set a fine example to all ranks under him in an endeavour to best the most brutal race alive.

The 16th Rifles were occupying a camp to the south of Hermies on 2 December and came under heavy enemy shellfire. The outcome was seven men killed and 22 wounded. Those killed were, Corporal E. Holmes, Lance Corporal W. McConnell and Privates W.G. Horne from Surrey, F.R. Hedges, James Neill from Lurgan, A. Shorter and William Maurice Stringer, also from Surrey. Captain Oscar Henry Macready was seriously injured and died from his wounds the following day in No.29 Casualty Clearing Station. A newspaper dated 3 December recorded that Company Sergeant Major James Cullen, from Portadown, Armagh, serving in the 1st Irish Fusiliers, had received a permanent commission for service in the field. Twice wounded, he had served from the outbreak of War.

On 4 December 107 and 109 Brigades moved from Lechelle and Bertincourt, 107 Brigade was placed in the old British trenches between Beaucamp and Villers-Plouich, while 109 Brigade moved into the old German front line to the north of the 107 Brigade and in reserve to the 6th Division. The two field companies of Royal Engineers remained behind, while the pioneers rejoined the division moving into a camp near Dessart Wood. General Nugent established his headquarters at Sorel-le-Grande, an infantry camp that provided what was necessary in the form of shelter and communications. That evening 108 Brigade relieved 88 Brigade in the line that was situated in the Couillet Valley.

The success of the German attack on the southern face of the Bourlon-Noyelles-Masnieres Salient had made that Salient so narrow in proportion to its depth that its maintenance would be a constant source of attrition. Therefore, a considerable portion of the captured ground was given up, including Bourlon Wood, Cantaing, Noyelles, Graincourt and Marcoing, with all dug-outs within the area being destroyed.

The new line held by the division faced east and ran from the south-west at Villers-Plouich to the north east just before Marcoing. The former was a ruined village, the latter bearing little damage. Marcoing had been captured by the British in the Cambrai battle, but was now again in German hands. Between these two points ran the densely wooded Couillet Valley, on either side of what were on the south-east Welsh Valley and on the north-west Highland Ridge. Across these, at right angles to the valley, ran the two Hindenburg Systems, which on Welsh Ridge were within 200 yards of each other, forming a single system of defence. To the men of 108 Brigade it was just as important a position as it had been to the Germans.

The front line from R4 to R10 was taken over by 109 Brigade on 5 December, with the 9th Inniskillings on the right, the 10th on the left, the 14th Rifles in support and the 11th Inniskillings in reserve. Just prior to this the enemy had broken through part of the line and were now well ensconced. Brigade headquarters came under heavy shellfire the three hours from 9:00 pm, until midnight, and a number of casualties were suffered, including the indomitable brigade quarter-master Sergeant Craig.

From the 9th Inniskillings two companies were sent to support 182 Brigade then on Welsh Ridge. Second Lieutenant Emerson led No.2 Company and Captain Douglas commanded No.4. As the Inniskillings arrived the Germans were laying in a terrific bombardment and those old hands of the Inniskillings recognised with some dismay the sound of exploding 18-pounder shells, obviously coming from captured guns, there being no British artillery support available at this time. On arrival at the Ridge the Inniskillings were told that the Germans were advancing up the Hindenburg Support Systems and had already advanced a considerable distance. The few survivors of the Warwick Battalion, 182 Brigade, having undergone this shelling for many hours, were in the process of retiring. The Inniskillings, having advanced in open order due to the shelling had their platoons well spaced out and the leading platoon, No.10 Platoon, was at once ordered into the front line. The men were short of bombs and as there was no artillery support, it fell to the riflemen to hold back the enemy. Three times the enemy attacked and three times they were driven back. A report was received that an enemy force had been observed advancing on the second line, and ten men from No.10 Platoon, all that could be spared, were sent to assist.

Eventually the remainder of the battalion arrived and by 4:00 pm, the battalion held 200 yards of the front-line trench. The dispositions were No.3 Company on the right, with No.1 Company in support and No.2 Company on the left, with No.4 In support. Thankfully the night passed in relative quiet and there was ample opportunity to re-supply the men with ammunition and rations.

On 6 December the 9th Inniskillings were again in action on the Hindenburg Line north of La Vacquene, which was described by Captain Densmore Walker of the 109th Machine Gun Company as 'a filthy place. So many unburied corpses were present they were touching and lay along the fire step, all casualties of the 61st Division.

The bank guard, Dublin, April 1916, back row; Rifleman T. Heatley, Lance Corporal D Lehane, Sergeant W. Morris, Rifleman J. Luby Kneeling; Rifleman J. Emerson, Rifleman J. Burton, Rifleman P. Hughes, Rifleman T. Barr. Rifleman Emerson would later become Lieutenant Emerson VC.
(Courtesy of John Emerson)

Temporary Second Lieutenant
James Samuel Emerson VC,
9th Royal Inniskilling Fusiliers,
killed in action 6 December 1917.
(Courtesy of John Emerson)

At dawn the 9th Inniskillings, reinforced by a platoon from B Company of the 14th Rifles, attacked and drove the enemy from the line. Nine prisoners were reported to have been taken and seven of these may have been captured by Lance Corporal Hope of the 14th Rifles. He had just jumped into a trench when he was faced by a group of Germans; "vAnother gesture and I'm pushing them all into our line at the end of a bayonet. I take the lot as far as Brigade Headquarters, one of them can speak good English. I get a 'bite' and some tea at Headquarters and up again I go."

Again the Inniskillings had no artillery support and suffered heavy casualties from the enemy shelling. This attack had only been possible due to the magnificent efforts of the brigade transport officer, Lieutenant Vaughan. During the course of the night the lieutenant had organised 14 limber loads of ammunition, grenades and Stokes mortar bombs. These had been assembled and then brought forward by road through Villers-Plouich, which had been reported impracticable for any transport, but not for Lieutenant Vaughan and his men; not forgetting their trustworthy and loyal pack horses and mules.

Second Lieutenant James Emerson, from County Louth, was leading his No.2 Company of the Inniskillings through the trenches and had been stopped by a strong party of the enemy who were 30 yards away using bombs in great number.[11]

James Emerson had enlisted in the 3rd Rifles as a Private and served in France. He was wounded in the wrist and ankle by gunshot wounds and reportedly spent eight months in hospital at Hoige. On recovering he then returned to the 3rd Rifles and was in Portobello Barracks, Dublin, in April 1916, when the rebellion began. Under the command of Sergeant Morris and Lance Corporal Lehane, he and five others garrisoned the Bank of Ireland for the duration of the fighting.[12] As a reward the bank presented Sergeant Morris with £5, Lance Corporal Lehane £3 and the other men £2 each.[13] On returning to France Emerson was posted to the 9th Rifles and fought on the Somme in July. He was then selected for officer training and was posted to Finner Camp in Donegal, being commissioned into the 9th Inniskillings on 1 August 1917.

---

11   Some battalions appear to have numbered companies; others A, B, C, D.
12   The others were Privates T. Heatley, J. Burton, P. Hughes, J. Luby and T. Barr.
13   Hughes, Gavin, *The Hounds of Ulster* (2012).

As Emerson passed along the trench, Captain Walker noticed that the subaltern had been wounded; there was a shrapnel hole in his helmet and blood was covering part of his face. Emerson and his men continued their advance and had soon cleared some 400 yards of enemy trench. The Germans then made a strong counter-attack and Emerson, accompanied by only eight men, held them off for three hours and in the course of the fighting took six prisoners. With all the other officers of the company now casualties Emerson, despite his head wound, refused to be evacuated to the dressing station. As each enemy bombing attack occurred Emerson, by his personal example, inspired his men to beat them off, until inevitably he received a mortal wound. For his actions on 6 December Lieutenant Emerson was posthumously awarded the Victoria Cross.

Initially the attack was successful and most of the lost ground was retaken. However, the Inniskillings had advanced too far and a sunken road to the flank had been overlooked. This was used by the enemy to move around the advancing battalion and a number was taken prisoner, including a section of the 109th Machine Gun Company.

On hearing that some of the guns had been lost to the enemy Lieutenant Walker along with some of his men attempted to go forward, but were driven back by showers of enemy stick bombs. He subsequently observed:

> Some stick bombs fell around us, several on top of the parapet and one or two in front of us in the trench. We had about six men slowly falling back, they had no bombs. One was hit while I was there. I took a squint over the top and saw the Huns throwing many bombs. They had a light machine gun in case we attacked over the open. We threw our few bombs, and that stopped them for a few minutes. When we stopped throwing they came on again. They can throw their stick bombs further than a Mills can be chucked by a normal man. We went on retreating quite slowly. We could have stopped them all right with bombs. Mulholland ran off to get some and finally some reinforcements of the 14th Rifles came up and held the cross-trench, the Hindenburg Line.

This was Major P.D. Mulholland, who was commanding the 109th Machine Gun Company; he was subsequently awarded the Military Cross. Mulholland and Walker then continued to make their way around to the left flank of the position and discovered that two of their gun teams were still intact, despite their exposed position. This was due to having moved into the line during the hours of darkness and being unable to carry out a proper reconnaissance. It was virtually impossible to defend a zigzag trench with a Vickers. Within the gun teams 13 men had been taken prisoner and two men had been killed, Privates George Morley and William Rouse, the latter from Northumberland.

Eventually it became necessary to relieve the battalion and the 11th Inniskillings moved up to take their place. In the last twenty-four hours the 9th Inniskillings had lost all four company commanders and had numerous other casualties. Among the missing was James Edwin Woods of No.8 Company. He was initially listed as missing and would continue to be so until 1919.[14]

During the night of 7 December the 11th Inniskillings had successfully relieved the 9th Inniskillings and, well-supplied with Stokes mortars and rifle grenades, thanks to Lieutenant Vaughan, made ready for a dawn assault. The signal to attack was made at 6:00 am, and the 11th swept forward in a very successful bombing attack on a frontage of 200 yards. The line was straightened out for a length of 300 yards and the Germans driven off the crest of Welsh Ridge. Within the next four hours the Germans launched two counter-attacks, but these were

---

14   An appeal appeared in the local papers on 8 January 1919, when Lieutenant Woods's father (Mr F.W. Woods of Knockbreda, Belfast) requested information.

both beaten off. The trenches on either flank were blocked with barbed wire entanglements and Stokes mortars emplaced to cover both the front and the barricades. By now artillery support was available and a third German attack was broken up by accurate shellfire. Despite utter exhaustion, heavy casualties and an initial lack of artillery support, the men of the 109 Brigade had not only held back strong attacks, but had re-established the line and denied Welsh Ridge to the enemy.

This sector on the night was taken over by 107 Brigade as of 8 December and on the following morning they actually managed to gain some more ground in the Hindenburg System by extending its front to the left. Once the new trenches had been secured they were blocked off using a combination of sand bags and coils of barbed wire. This work was carried out by the permanent brigade works party, under the command of Lieutenant Haig, who had gained the sobriquet 'sandbags' with his successful construction of many similar works. The defences had moved from makeshift to established, with machine gun batteries linked by field telephone to the brigade headquarters in Couillet Wood and on to Highland Ridge.

The 2nd Rifles captured two German prisoners on the night of 6 December, which saw active patrolling by both sides. In this action Second Lieutenant Percy Phillips, from Birmingham, was wounded by a shell splinter in his left leg. One of the prisoners was also wounded and subsequently died. The lieutenant's wound was serious and he was eventually discharged. The 9th Irish Fusiliers (NIH) also brought in a prisoner and from them it was discovered that the enemy had planned an attack for dawn on 14 December. All troops stood to and an hour before dawn all the available British artillery on the III Corps front opened fire. If a German attack had been planned, it did not develop.

Until the division was finally relieved its artillery support consisted of 17 Artillery Brigade, of the 6th Division, and three army field brigades under the command of General Brock. On 14 December the detachments of the 36th Divisional Artillery arrived and took over the guns in situ of two of these brigades.

All were confident that Welsh Ridge was now safe from all but a full dress attack and it seemed that this was in fact what was coming. German artillery was described as very active and enemy aircraft swept up and down the lines every day machine gunning the infantry. The headquarters of the 109 Brigade had moved in Metz on 9 December and found it being bombed both night and day. The German artillery made Havrincourt Wood uninhabitable and sought out any likely targets with accuracy.

To General Nugent it was obvious that the division was in no condition to withstand a new offensive in force. The troops were exhausted, there had been no time lately to get the men clean; uniforms and equipment were engrained with dirt and while the casualty lists were considered high, the number of men reporting sick was enormous. Throat infections, chest infections and infected minor wounds, were all taking their toll. Most of all it was tiredness, so called rest periods were usually taken up with working parties, all of this in the cold and wet of a bitter winter. It was not just the men who were suffering, in the higher ranks the constant strain of command was telling. In the end General Nugent had no option but to report that his division was no longer fit for frontline service.

On 14 December relief for the division came at last, the first to leave the trenches being 107 Brigade, relieved by 189 Brigade of the (Royal Naval) Division. Before the 9th Irish Fusiliers (NIH) left they bombed a German machine gun post, killing one man, driving off the remainder of the crew and bringing back the machine gun as a bonus.

The 36th Division had one more battle to fight to reach its rest area. The wind-driven snow turned into a blizzard, reducing visibility considerably and freezing any exposed skin almost immediately. Those men in charge of the horses and mules did their best to protect their charges; the drivers of motor vehicles could only look forward to spending a long time stuck in snow drifts. The division was to concentrate around the village of Lucheux, described as being small and delightful, not that anyone had a clear view of it through the driving snow. The infantry moved by train and endured a stop-start journey, but at least it was dry. The transport that portion of it that could move, struggled through deep snow and it took double teams of horses to pull the supply wagons, often having to go miles out of their way to avoid the worst of the drifting. Some tracks of the Doullens to Arras Road could not be found so deep were they covered. On top of this there was the confusion of more than one unit moving at a time and the signals company, thinking they were warmly ensconced, were turned out by newcomers with the proper paperwork and had to march a further 50 miles in such conditions.

Eventually all troops reached their allotted quarters and settled down in some degree of warmth and comfort and by Christmas the men, having been supplied with sufficient amounts of alcohol, were in reasonably good spirits.

On 14 December General Nugent wrote to the Adjutant General at GHQ with regard to 109 Brigade:

> Is there any prospect of anything being done to make up the three battalions of Inniskilling Fusiliers in the 109th Brigade of this Division? Their average strength is now under 660, giving a strength of about 350 available for the trenches. They are first-rate fighting battalions and it is a pity to see them dwindling. Would the following suggestions meet with approval:-
> 1. To give the Division two Inniskilling Fusilier battalions, one of which would be a regular battalion, and the other to be broken up to make up the other four battalions of the Inniskilling Fusiliers. The 109th Brigade would then be a homogeneous Brigade of Inniskillings.
> 2. The 14th Royal Irish Rifles, now in 109th Brigade, to be broken up and used to make up casualties in the Royal Irish Rifles battalions in the Division. This battalion should in my opinion be broken up in any case.
>
>   About a year ago, I reported them as totally wanting in military spirit and asked for a CO and a large draft of Englishmen to try to create a fighting spirit in them. You gave me both, and while Cheape was in command they certainly improved, but since he left they have been tried and found wanting. It is significant that the present CO told me two days ago that most of the English draft sent to them a year ago has become casualties. The Brigadier says he cannot trust them and I know that he is right. They are poor stuff, either as worker or fighters, and have been a constant source of anxiety during the past three weeks. I can put this officially if necessary but I would sooner not if it can be done otherwise.

At Little Wood on 25 December, relief of the divisional artillery by the 63rd (Royal Naval) Division Artillery commenced during the evening, full relief was complete the following day. The Ulster Division's guns remained in situ and the men took over 63rd's guns, command passing to the incoming division's CRA at 1:00 pm on Boxing Day. Once this had been completed the Brigades marched to their wagon lines at the Beaulencourt staging area. On 30 December they heard of the German attack that had driven 63rd Division off most of Welsh Ridge.

One man who had failed to recover his health was General Ricardo. Apart from a few weeks commanding the 112 Infantry Brigade, he had served with the division since the beginning, first as commander of the 12th Inniskillings and then 109 Brigade. General Nugent wrote to his wife on 10 December 1917:

> My men are completely exhausted and I don't feel confident about their powers of resistance in case of a big attack. I have had to send General Ricardo home to my very great regret but in this recent fighting I saw he had lost his nerve and looked so old. One can't afford to run risks

in this war and I sent for him and told him he must go home for a long rest. He was quite glad really and owed to being perished.

Brigadier Ricardo would end the war as commandant at the large base of Dieppe. His replacement was another Inniskilling, Brigadier General W.F. Hessey, DSO, who had formerly commanded the 11th Inniskillings and was highly regarded by General Nugent at both battalion and brigade level, despite being handicapped by a hernia injury.[15]

For the remainder of December the division was virtually snowbound and made the best of it. With no shortage of wood for fuel the men were always warm indoors, which was most of the time as training was impossible due to the deep snow. Some musketry training was achieved using a well-maintained rifle range at Lucheux. The divisional artillery, having been relieved by the guns of the 63rd Division on Christmas Day, attempted to make its way to the divisional area, but got no further that Beaulencourt, where it met impassable snowdrifts.

After an all too brief period of rest the division received orders to proceed to the area of Corbie-Boves-Moreuil. Again the infantry moved by troop train, while the dependable horses and to a lesser degree the motor lorries, moved the transport by road travelling via Puchevillers and Contay. The roads were still not totally clear and many of the lorries became stuck in the drifts.

The British Army was extending its right flank ny taking over from the French a much greater length of trenches. In finding the men to fill these new positions there was now a shortage of reserves. The relief of the French divisions was done at a leisurely pace and the division spent five days resting at Corbie where it eventually met up with its artillery. From here it moved slowly forward via Harbonnieres to Nesle, a town surprisingly left undamaged by the German in their retreat. Here divisional headquarters was established on 12 January 1918 and that night 107 Brigade relieved a regiment of the 6th French Infantry Division and consequently coming under the command of the French divisional commander. The following night 109 Brigade took over from another French regiment and at this command resorted to General Nugent. The relief of the French artillery was not completed until 15 January.

Unlike the relief of a British unit the relief of a French unit took a considerable time, as it was not just a matter of signing for stores and ammunition, but actually removing and replacing all bombs, ammunition and suchlike. Given the language barrier, few officers and fewer men of the Ulster Division spoke French, it was surprising how well the relief went. Staff work was meticulous; the reconnaissance of the trenches was thorough, with French guides pointing out all relevant features and landmarks. One officer of an advance party recorded his reception by a French regimental commander; "The most amazing dinner I ever did have in the line! We had course after course of wonderful things, with suitable wines, till it was hard to think that the Huns could be only a thousand yards distant, but that was all they were." He went on to observe that his men were well-treated well by the outgoing poilus who supplied them with generous amounts of food and coffee.

---

15   Perry, *Major General Oliver Nugent and the Ulster Division 1915-1918.*

13

1918

The beginning of the end?

One British officer reckoned that the instinct of self-preservation reached very great proportions: there developed a new spirit of taking care of one's self among the men, which ended, in late 1918, in few rifles being fired, and would, in a few weeks, have meant the cessation of the war, by the frontline troops not refusing, but quietly omitting to do duty.[1] The recorded details within the division and elsewhere speak otherwise. According to the Commonwealth War Graves Commission, 191 men of the British Army perished on New Year's Day. One of these was Private William Hanley from Foxford, County Mayo, serving with the 1st Irish Fusiliers.

The army was still not fully recovered from its time at Cambrai and it was a posture of defence that was adopted. A major German attack was expected, but at what precise location was unknown. On 3 March 1918, the Treaty of Brest-Litovsk was signed between Imperial Germany, her allies and the Russian Soviet Federated Socialist Republic. With Russia removed from the war a large number of German divisions were now able to be transferred to the Western Front. From 1 November 1917 to 20 March 1918, forty-six German divisions arrived from the east, with more to follow. This also saw an increase in both artillery and the much vaunted Lewis gun, a large number of which fell into German hands with the collapse of the Russian Army.

In this, the last year of the war, the tragedy of the Western Front was having a telling effect on the Home Front. On Thursday 21 March Second Lieutenant J.C. Renwick, Royal Irish Rifles, was found in his quarters in Clandeboye Camp, suffering from a gunshot wound to the head. Renwick had served for some sixteen months at the Front and was at Clandeboye recovering from the serious wounds he had received. On being found by a brother officer he had been initially treated by Lieutenant R.G. Lander of the U.S. Medical Corps and was then taken to the Royal Victoria Hospital where he died. His body was returned to his home at Northam-on-Tweed in England for burial, he was 39 years old.

It could almost be said that. at the beginning of 1918, the British soldier on the Western Front was better fed than the working and middle class of Britain and Ireland. The tardiness of the British government in bringing in rationing had caused great suffering to the poorer classes and there were reports of unemployed miners and their families dying of starvation in the north of England. The *Bangor Spectator* of 5 January reported; "Sir Arthur Yapp says; 'At the present moment food is as important as munitions for the purpose of winning the War.' It went on to say that the Urban Council has plots to let and every patriotic man and woman should have one."

Certainly the men of the division were being adequately fed and supplied, thanks to the efforts of the Army Service Corps. While these men faced dangers every time they brought forward supplies, their share of medals and awards was much less than those of the infantry. The award of a Military Cross to Captain Robert Watts was well deserved. A former member of the Queen's University OTC, he was the son of the Reverend J. Watts of Kilmacrenan, County Donegal.

---

1   Holmes, Richard, *Firing Line* (1994).

He had joined the Ulster Division in November 1914 and was promoted to Captain in May the following year. In October 1918, he would add a bar to his MC.

Despite a plethora of men available for the battlefield, Germany was suffering on the home front where food shortages were severe, due to a lack of planning earlier in the war, something all countries, including Britain, had failed to do. By now the Allied blockade was telling and on the home and front lines rations were scarce. The winter of 1916-1917 had become known as the 'Turnip Winter', a result of a failure of the potato harvest, a wet autumn spoiling about fifty percent of the crop. The extreme cold also meant a shortage of coal, not only for homes, but also for the railways, which in turn caused problems in the distribution of foodstuffs, especially in the cities and much was lost during the slow movement of trains. There seemed to be no shortage of turnips and these were distributed widely, being cooked and prepared in many ingenious ways. By now things had only become worse.

Men of the South and North Staffords who crossed the St Quentin Canal.

Another of the same.

The new front line taken over by the division from the French ran from Sphinx Wood about 1,200 yards west of the village of Itancourt, to a point on the St Quentin to Roisel Railway a 1,000 yards west of Rocourt Station, a suburb of St Quentin. The spring thaw had set in and as the division settled into their new home they were greeted with fallen-in trenches and cold, wet mud. Apart from that the Front was quiet and those villages behind the British lines were not completely destroyed and offered some shelter. Some villages, such as Ollezy and Douchy, had been re-occupied by the French, while the town of Ham, Headquarters of the XVIII Corps, was intact and had quite a population.

As usual the Germans had the better observation posts and had noticed the division moving into position. It was not long before they made an attempt at identifying the troops. On the night of 22 January the trenches of both 107 and 109 Brigades, occupying the outpost line, were raided. Between these positions a total of five men became casualties, one of them being taken as a prisoner. When challenged these raiders had replied in English, which had allowed them to get so close before being identified. At the same time a patrol of the 10th Rifles was ambushed and an officer and sergeant taken. After that things seemed to quieten down from the German side for a while, although the division continued to send out patrols to ascertain the strength of the enemy defences.

This was a time of great change within the British Army; the traditional four-battalion brigade was changed to three battalions. This not only caused problems for commanders; they had been handling four battalion brigades for many years and an entire philosophy was based on this organisation. There was also the question of morale, to lose a battalion, particularly in an organisation such as the Ulster Division, even at this stage of the war, was to lose friends, comrades, territorial connections and esprit-de-corps. No longer would the Ulster Division be the Covenanting Army, now its ranks held Ulstermen, Scot, Celt, English and Welsh. The battalion being lost either had its personnel transferred to other units, or were designated as an entrenching battalion, in words of Cyril Falls; "… pitiful, nameless ghosts, robbed of their pride and their traditions."

The official line on these units reads:

> The man who is not young enough or strong enough to fight the Hun with gun or rifle, can still do his bit at the Front with pick and shovel in a labour battalion. Behind the whole of our Front you find units of their Corps, grey haired veterans perhaps with grandchildren at home, young men incapacitated by some physical defect from joining the fighting ranks, men who have already seen hard fighting, but whose wounds now keep them out of the front line; but all cheery hardworking, courageous, determined to the utmost of their ability to give the fighting men whatever help they are capable of.

The division had already received two regular battalions, the 2nd Rifles and 1st Irish Fusiliers, now it was to be joined by the 1st and 2nd Inniskillings from the 29th and 32nd Divisions and the 1st Rifles from the 8th Division. In turn the 10th and 11th Inniskillings and 8/9th, 10th, and 11th/13th Rifles were to be disbanded. From these battalion losses would be made up, with the remainder going on to form the 21st (8th/9th Rifles and 10th Rifles), 22nd (11th/13th Rifles) and 23rd (14th Rifles and 11th Inniskillings) Entrenching Battalions. The 16th Rifles (Pioneers) was reduced, in common with other pioneer battalion, to three companies. As some small compensation the division received the 266th Machine Gun Company, which had arrived from refitting in England on 18 January. It, along with the three existing companies was then formed into the 36th Machine Gun Battalion. This would be commanded by a lieutenant colonel, who would take his orders directly from divisional headquarters. On 7 February Captain (Acting Lieutenant Colonel) Guy de Hoghton, MC, of the King's Own Yorkshire Light Infantry, was appointed as Divisional Machine Gun Commander in the division. He was to be responsible for the discipline and tactical handling of the machine gun companies, but for all other purposes the machine gun companies were to be administered as at present. All this came together on 1 March 1918 when the 36th Machine Gun Battalion officially came into existence.

In a letter to James Johnston, the Lord Mayor of Belfast, dated 28 February 1918, General Nugent explained his decision on the reorganisation of the division. The Mayor had written to General Nugent with a special plea to retain the 14th Rifles:

> In reply to your letter of 9th instant, I regret to say the break-up of the 36th Division in respect of the greater number of its original battalions is already accomplished.
>
> The Division now consists of five Regular North Irish battalions, and five battalions of the original Division.
>
> As General Officer Commanding the Division, I had the most unpleasant duty of selecting two battalions of Inniskilling Fusiliers and four battalions of Royal Irish Rifles for disbandment. I decided that the battalions to remain in the Division should be those which were composed of the men who first came forward to form the Ulster Division. I therefore selected the senior of the three battalions of Inniskilling Fusiliers to remain. In the case of the Royal Irish Rifles, I selected the senior battalion to remain. This was the 15th Battalion, a Belfast Battalion originally raised as the 7th Battalion. The next senior of the original battalions of the Ulster Division would have been the 10th Royal Irish Rifles. This was also a Belfast Battalion and I decided that it would be unfair to the Counties of Down and Antrim that they should have no representation amongst the original units of the Division. I therefore selected the 12th Royal Irish Rifles as the other battalion to remain. The remaining third battalion of Royal Irish Rifles, the Pioneer Battalion, was not affected by the reorganisation of the Division. I

With the arrival of the regular battalions of the Rifles, Inniskillings and Irish Fusiliers, coupled with reinforcements coming from elsewhere in the UK, the mainly Protestant ethos of the Division had gone and all faiths were now being catered for. Here a chaplain from the Royal Munster Fusiliers is saying a prayer over two men who had been killed by a shell. The philosophy of the padres of all denominations was if the men could not go to the church, then the church would go to the men.

have gone into the matter at this length because there is no reason why you should not know the principle on which I acted in naming the battalions which I consider should be disbanded. I need hardly say how deeply I regret the disappearance of so many fine battalions from the Division. The claims of the 14th Royal Irish Rifles to remain in the Division were put to me by the OC, the battalion, but in view of the principles of selection I had decided upon I felt I could not accept his view. As to the point of the reconstitution of the 14th Royal Irish Rifles after the war, I do not think you need anticipate that there would be any difficulty in doing so if it were considered desirable. I greatly regret that I am not able to meet your wishes, and those of the Citizens of Belfast, in respect of the retention of the battalion.

The 1st Inniskillings had received a new commanding officer on 20 January, Colonel J. Norman Crawford, DSO.[2] He took command from Captain (Acting Lieutenant Colonel) J.R.C. Dent, DSO, MC, who had been presented with the French *Croix de Guerre* on 9 December 1917. On promotion Captain Dent went to the South Staffordshire Regiment. He would serve with them until retirement in April 1923.

---

2   *Belfast News Letter*, 10 January 1919.

Within the 9th Inniskillings the Reverend William Fleming joined as Chaplain on 27 January. He had previously been attached to St. Columb's Cathedral in Derry and had been Rector of Learmont from 1914 to 1917. During his time with the battalion he would write a lot of letters to grieving parents, wives and other family members. The same day saw the arrival of Lieutenant W.J. Tipton, RAMC, who would be equally busy of the coming months. There was also a draft of 33 other ranks from the corps reinforcement camp that were much needed. It was also announced that Colonel Peacocke had been awarded a Bar to his DSO, Captain Marshal a Bar to his Military Cross, Second Lieutenant J.B. Tyner was one of five officers to receive the MC and Private J. Alcorn was awarded the Distinguished Conduct Medal, as was CSM J.J. Patterson and CSM G. Belshaw.

On 2 February the 1st Battalion Royal Irish Rifles was told it was to transfer to the 36th Division and would, along with the 2nd Rifles and 15th Rifles, form the 107 Brigade. Again there was some discord within the battalion. Captain Whitfield was far from impressed:

> Definitely settled that the battalion will leave that fine division, the 8th, and go to the 36th Ulster Division – the political division as we know it. The 86th have already joined it I believe. Everyone seems very sick of the move. Heneker made a very nice farewell speech today. I believe he really rather likes us. We had great respect for him and at the same time felt that he had made the division. I never saw a better turned out division in France. They were magnificent and fought very well indeed.

The 2nd Inniskillings arrived with the 109 Brigade on 3 February, having served in France since 1914, being, at various dates, attached to the 4th Division, 2nd Division, 5th Division and 32nd Division. The 1st Rifles were attached to the 107 Brigade.

The 1st Inniskillings joined the 109 Brigade on 5 February. They had landed in France at Marseilles on 18 March, having taken part in the Gallipoli fighting at Cape Helles. Their Commanding Officer, from 29 March 1917, had been Lieutenant Colonel John Sherwood-Kelly VC. A South African by birth Sherwood-Kelly was a veteran of the South African War, having enlisted in the Cape Mounted Rifles at age sixteen, going on to fight against the Mad Mullah in Somaliland and the Zulu Rebellion of 1906. He had been commissioned into the Norfolk Regiment in 1914, seeing service in Ireland. He had served at Gallipoli on attachment to the King's Own Scottish Borderers, where he had earned a DSO. The previous November he had been awarded the Victoria Cross for his actions during the Cambrai battle. Sherwood Kelly was a man capable of heroic deeds that were matched by his explosive temper and rigid discipline towards his officers and men. The previous July he had one of his officers, Lieutenant Alan Lendrum, from Bundoran, County Donegal, placed before a court martial for refusing to supervise a firing squad. This was for the execution of Private Robert Hope of D Company, from Waterside, Londonderry.[3] Lieutenant Lendrum's reason was that he knew the man concerned. This made no difference to Sherwood-Kelly and the lieutenant was found guilty and sentenced to forfeiture of seniority of rank and severe reprimand. Lieutenant Lendrum was then transferred to the 1st Royal Dublin Fusiliers, where he was promoted to captain and subsequently earned the Military Cross and Bar.[4] Sherwood-Kelly himself would face a court martial before the end of his career.[5]

---

3   Served as Hepple.
4   Alan Lendrum was murdered by the IRA in County Clare on 22 September 1920, by being shot in the head during an ambush and not by being buried up to his neck in sand on the beach and left to drown, as legend has it. B.P. Murphy, *The origins and organisation of British propaganda in Ireland, 1920* (Aubane 2006) and special thanks to Kevin Myers.
5   Post Armistice Sherwood-Kelly served in North Russia, where he commanded the 2nd Hampshire Regiment. As a result of improper behaviour in withdrawing his battalion at a crucial time he faced a court martial,

On 22 February the 30th Division, part of the XVIII Corps reserve was positioned between the 36th Division and the 61st (2nd South Midland) Division, taking over the front held by the 36th Division north of the Somme in the Forward System. In the Battle Zone the 36th Division continued to be responsible for a sector north of the Somme, to the rear of the village of Fontaine-les-Clercs. The division's frontage was reduced to about 6,000 yards. The continuing relief of French troops had been ongoing and on the division's right flank was the British 14th (Light) Division of the III Corps, commanded by Major General Victor Couper.

The defence system being employed was one of zones. There was a Forward Zone, a Battle Zone and a Reserve Zone. In the forward zone limited enemy attacks were to be held, while any build up to a major attack would be at best disorganised and fragmented. This zone consisted of a series of redoubts, individual fortifications surrounded by barbed wire and defended by infantry, machine gun and mortars. In the battle zone there were more redoubts and positions for infantry to launch counter-attacks.

All three brigades of the Ulster Division were now in the line. On the right flank was 108 Brigade, on the left 109 Brigade, while the centre was held by 107 Brigade. Each brigade had one battalion in the forward zone, one in the battle zone and the third in reserve. The battalion in the forward zone had two companies in the line of resistance, finding their own outposts, one company held in readiness for any required counter-attack and a fourth company, along with battalion headquarters inside a redoubt.

The battalions allocated to the battle zone were in billets close to their positions. The 108 Brigade was in dug-outs along the railway cutting at Essigny Station, 107 Brigade in the quarries close to Grand Seraucourt, while 109 Brigade was at Le Hamel on the other side of the St Quentin Canal. The supporting artillery was located in two separate groups covering the Forward Zone, with one of the 153 Brigade in reserve. A great deal of labour had been involved in the construction of the redoubts and other defences, which had basically been built from scratch.

In the forward zone the position had been marked out by the French and some wire strung. There was a dire shortage of materials to construct defences, the barbed wire requirement for the Fifth Army was 22,000 tons, but only 7,500 tons had been delivered during January and February. It fell to all units to instigate an intensive salvage operation and recover what wire had been left behind by the French troops and whatever enemy wire was available. Here the first defences were created and communication trenches dug. When these had been completed work immediately began on building the redoubts. The 16th Rifles were heavily engaged here and were also labouring with three companies as opposed to four with the new army organisation. These redoubts were, from left to right, Jeanne d'Arc, Racecourse and Boadicea. Despite the dire shortage of barbed wire the defences were completed, although completed was in fact a misnomer. The majority of the trenches were no more than 18 inches deep, the high command dictating that there would be adequate time to deepen them when it became necessary to occupy them. This is known as applied military logic.

In the battle zone the redoubts were named Station Redoubt, Quarry Redoubt and Ricardo Redoubt. So much time had been spent on these defences that there had been little time left for training and those replacements that had arrived after Cambrai had not been fully integrated into their new units.

On 28 February XVIII Corps Headquarters announced a state of preparation and 153 Brigade deployed its guns south-east of Grand Seraucourt to cover the battle zone, with one section per battery advanced forward to cover the line of redoubts.

---

where he was severely reprimanded, later resigning his commission.

Troops crossing the St Quentin Canal.

On 1 March 1918, 108 Brigade fielded a total of 153 officers and 3,373 other ranks. This included the Trench Mortar Battery, but not the machine gun company, which had moved with the other brigade companies to form No 36 Battalion, Machine Gun Corps.

The Allies were deployed from north to south; First Army, Third Army, Fifth Army and French Sixth Army. Facing them in March 1918, again from north to south, the German Seventeenth Army, Second Army and Eighteenth Army; the Eighteenth, under the command of General der Infanterie Oskar von Hutier, was facing Gough's Fifth Army. The 36th Division was now in the XVIII Corps, along with the 61st, 30th and 20th Divisions. It was to be no picnic.

German platoon-sized patrols were observed approaching all along the divisional position in broad daylight on 4 March. It was assumed that the enemy thought the outposts were abandoned and this was quickly rectified by well-placed bursts from the Lewis guns. From one patrol an officer, a NCO and nine men were taken prisoner. Considerable casualties were caused to the other patrols.

As a result of this enemy activity it was decided to raid the enemy trenches to identify the opposing units, kill as many as possible and bring back a prisoner alive or dead. It is difficult to understand the logic of the prisoner being in the latter condition, but such was the order issued. That night a raiding party from the 15th Rifles left the trenches of the 1st Inniskillings. The party consisted of four officers and 36 men, split into four groups, each man wearing a cap comforter and with face and hands blackened. No regimental badges were worn and weapons were left to the individual, ranging from clubs, bayonets, and pistols, captured German Lugers and privately obtained American Colt .45s, being a favourite along with trench knives. The leading group paid out a white tape as they advanced; this tape was to be followed on the return journey. The Inniskillings would not send out any of its own patrols while the raid was in progress. The war diary of 109 Brigade recorded that the raiding party returned to report the enemy trenches unoccupied.

Aerial reconnaissance showed that old shell holes several 100 yards from the outpost line in the Forward Zone had been excavated in such a manner as to suggest pits for trench mortars. Intelligence sources also confirmed that General Oskar von Hutier was in the line opposite them. Von Hutier came from a long line of soldiers in his family; he had attended the Prussian Military academy, fought on the Marne in 1914, before going to serve on the Eastern Front. Here he presided over a string of victories, including the only successful amphibious assault of the Great War, when his troops captured a number of Russian garrisoned islands in the Baltic Sea.

From 12 March the British began to bombard suspected enemy positions, including valleys and dead ground that could be used as forming up points. There was little reaction from the Germans, with the exception of several individual heavy guns firing and the delivery of some 50 gas shells on the night of 8 March. On the British side there had been rehearsals for the action to be taken on receipt of the message 'man battle stations' and bridges were prepared for demolition, these being the responsibility of the various field companies. As an anti-tank device small mine-fields had been laid throughout the area and the Grugies Valley was peppered with machine gun emplacements to sweep its length with zones of flanking fire. Unlike the Germans the British never did develop a specific anti-tank rifle.

Concern was expressed with regard to the distance between the various redoubts in the forward zone and the lack of men to defend them and be available for any counter-attacks. There was no contact, either by wireless or field telephone, between the various headquarters groups in the redoubts and they were not mutually supporting.

Continued air reconnaissance that was carried out on 15 March discovered that new roads had been built behind Itancourt and from the position known as 'Dovecot' in Essigny. This was considered to be the best observation post in the XVIII Corps front, manned by divisional personnel, a huge increase in enemy road traffic was spotted as of this date.

During the hours of darkness the noise of numerous enemy vehicles, both motorised and horse drawn was heard from 17 March onwards and there was little celebration of St Patrick's Day. Twelve days earlier, 5 March, the Irish Fusiliers had made a spirited attempt at celebrating Barrosa Day, in memory of their victory over the French in Spain on that date in 1811. At this battle, the Irish Fusiliers, then known as the 87th Foot, had captured a French Eagle, screaming their war cay *Faugh-a-ballagh*, this first time this had happened on a battlefield. It is interesting to note that in the war diary of the 1st Irish Fusiliers, the battle is referred to as Barossa.[6] In the ranks of the 16th Rifles, headquartered at Grand Seraucourt, Private GA McBride was killed, the only fatal casualty for the battalion that day.

---

6   1st Royal Irish Fusiliers War Diary, 10 March 1917, apparently the writer was not well versed in the regimental history.

Faugh-a-Ballagh Court, Armagh, a much misunderstood street sign that is often stoned by local youths.

Faugh-a-Ballagh Court, Armagh. Despite the resurgence of Interest in the Great War and Ulster's part, many people remain ignorant of the role played by Irish regiments and of their traditions. Here the war cry of the Royal Irish Fusiliers, first recorded at the Battle of Barrosa in Spain on 5 March 1811, has been defaced by local youths, for reasons known only to them. (Author's photograph)

On the afternoon of 18 March at approximately 2:30 pm, two German deserters came into the divisional lines occupied by 107 Brigade. These men, who came from Alsace Lorraine, belonged to the 414th *Minewerfer* Company of the 204th Division and claimed they wish to desert to avoid the forthcoming battle, which was to begin within a few days. They confirmed that troops were massing behind the lines, St. Quentin was said to packed and numerous artillery pieces were being brought forward and they were hungry. The division's trench mortar batteries fired over 200 rounds into what were considered suspicious shell holes without suffering any retaliation.

In a letter to his wife Wilfred Spender wrote in a forceful manner:

> Germany should be defeated decisively and that fact should be made clear to the German people: Our statesmen have made a great mistake in bewildering the public by talking of Alsace etc., as if these were what we are fighting for. Alsace, the German colonies etc are not worth another year of war, but we have to convince the Huns that their Boschism does not pay or we shall find ourselves in for another war in forty years' time and it would be bad for the morale of the world till the end of time. We have to force the Huns to believe they are defeated and the terms do not matter a hang provided they betoken this.[7]

The British 61st (2nd South Midland) Division, holding the forward zone to the north west of St. Quentin in the area of Ham, launched a raid on the night of 20 March and captured a number of prisoners who, under questioning, stated that the attack would be made the following morning. A bombardment was carried out between 2:30 and 3:00 am, with heavy rolling barrages covering likely forming up points.

21-23 March, Battle of St Quentin

Spring Commences – so does the great Hun offensive, the diary of Drummer Hugh A. Pollock, A Company, 12th Rifles, Thursday 21 March 1918.[8]

The German Seventeenth Army, Second Army and Eighteenth Army, the latter commanded of General Oskar von Hutier, faced Fifth Army's component III Corps, VII Corps, XVIII Corps and XIX Corps.[9] German artillery used in this offensive amounted to 6,473 pieces, of which 2,435 were heavy and 73 were super heavy.[10] There were also 3,532 mortars of various types. This barrage, a mixture of high explosive and gas, opened at 4:40 am on 21 March and stretched from the River Scarpe to the Oise, a distance of 54 miles.

In conjunction with this the Germans deployed *Sturmtruppen* (storm troopers), who moved forward to cut gaps in their own wire to facilitate a speedy advance. These assault detachments had first been observed during the fighting at Verdun and the idea and tactics had been extensively developed since that time. The storm troopers would not stop to reduce every obstacle or defended position, but would sweep on, penetrating deep into the British and French lines, allowing the following troops to overcome any remaining resistance.

At the beginning of March the divisional artillery had been divided into two groups. The centre group, under the command of Colonel Claud Potter DSO, consisted of the 383 Battery, D/91, B/153, A/153 and D/173 Brigades, Royal Field Artillery. The left group, under Colonel Edward Henry Eley, CMG, DSO, was made up of the 463 Battery, C/153, D/232, D/153, B/91 Brigades and 464 Battery, Royal Field Artillery. Now on the morning of 21 March new gun positions were swiftly being reconnoitred by officers on horseback, while those batteries on the eastern bank of the Canal de St. Quentin were ordered to cross by the bridge at Tugny.

Colonel Potter's Centre Group was instructed to cover the front of 108 Brigade, while Colonel Eley's Left Group would cover 107 and 109 Brigades. The right group, commanded by Lieutenant Colonel Erskin, DSO, consisting of the A/91 and C'91 Batteries RFA and the 232 Siege Battery was ordered to cover the front of the 61 Infantry Brigade of the 20th Division. The 36th Divisional

---

7   Baughley (ed), *The Correspondence of Lilian and Wilfred Spender*.
8   Hun was a common name applied to the Germans by the British.
9   *The German Offensives of 1918: The Last Desperate Gamble*, Passingham, Ian, Barnsley, 2008.
10   Terraine, John, *The Smoke and the Fire* (1980).

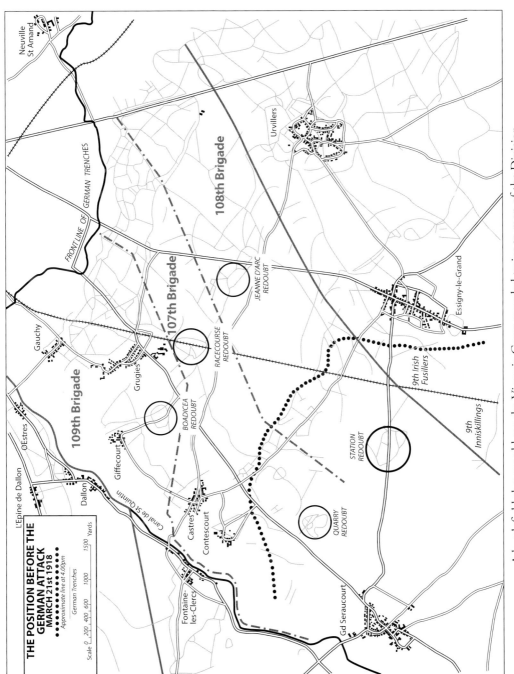

THE POSITION BEFORE THE GERMAN ATTACK
MARCH 21st 1918

● ● ● ● ● Approximate line at 4.00pm
++++++++ German Trenches

Scale 0 200 400 600 1000 1500 Yards

Neuville St Amand

FRONT LINE OF GERMAN TRENCHES

108th Brigade

Urvillers

107th Brigade

JEANNE D'ARC REDOUBT

RACECOURSE REDOUBT

Gauchy

Grugies

109th Brigade

BOADICEA REDOUBT

Essigny-le-Grand

9th Irish Fusiliers

9th Inniskillings

STATION REDOUBT

OEstres

Giffecourt

L'Epine de Dallon

Dallon

Canal de St Quintin

Castres

Contescourt

QUARRY REDOUBT

Fontaine-les-Clercs

Gd Seraucourt

A battlefield that would see the Victoria Cross awarded twice to men of the Division.

Ammunition Column moved from St. Simon to Sommette Eaucourt to the west and established a dump. This order was then cancelled and the column proceeded to Verlaines, further to the west.

The dispositions of the division on the morning of the German attack were as follows. On the right flank was 108 Brigade with the 12th Rifles in the forward zone, the 1st Irish Fusiliers in the battle zone and the 9th Irish Fusiliers (NIH) in divisional reserve. In the centre was 107 Brigade with the 15th Rifles in the forward zone, 1st Rifles in the battle zone and 2nd Rifles in divisional reserve. On the left flank 109 Brigade had the 2nd Inniskillings in the forward zone, 1st Inniskillings in the battle zone and 9th Inniskillings in divisional reserve.

The German bombardment opened at 4:35 am on 21 March, across ground swathed in a thick ground mist.[11] Across the front of the Fifth Army shells from trench mortars by the hundred and every calibre of artillery exploded, a combination of high explosive and gas. The trench mortars seemed to concentrate mostly on the front line system, while a combination of high explosive and phosgene gas came down on the redoubts, the valley to the rear and the trenches of the battle zone and Battery Valley, which ran behind its ridge. These shells were identified as coming from 150mm and 210mm howitzers. Larger calibre howitzers and high velocity guns were used to shell the villages in the rear areas and the bridges across the Canal de St. Quentin. On the redoubts the ration of gas shells gradually decreased until they were all high explosive, no doubt to ensure no gas remained when these positions were stormed by the enemy infantry.

It was five minutes after the opening of the German bombardment before the general staff issued the Man Battle Stations order by field telephone. Given the intensity of the shelling there could be no doubt that this was a major attack. This was confirmed to General Nugent when, at 5:55 am, he received a call from corps headquarters to say that the shelling extended as far south as Moy and over the Third Army front.

For the defenders the breaking dawn brought the difficulty of a thick mist making observation very difficult. While morning mists were not exceptional, this day's was extremely thick and mixed with the smoke of exploding shells reduced visibility at 5:00 am to less than ten yards.

All the battalions in the battle zone made to their positions in good time thanks to both officers and NCOs who knew the ground. The 107 Brigade was in position by 6:50 am, while the 108th and 109 Brigades were in position between 7:00 am and 8:00 am. Communication was another matter and with land-lines being cut on a regular basis most messages were being passed by runners, who suffered from the shell fire and getting lost in the mist.

The Germans also suffered because of this mist, which persisted into the early afternoon. The lack of observation precluded the laying down of a rolling barrage, leaving the advancing infantry without artillery support and communications via landlines was impossible during the move forward. Nor was information from spotter aircraft available as they could not fly in the adverse weather conditions.

The first reports of the enemy having attacked did not reach Grand Seraucourt until 11:45 am and this came from the 30th Division on the left flank. This report stated that the enemy had broken through on either side of Epine De Dallon and Manchester Redoubts and that both redoubts were under heavy shell fire.

At 11:50 am, a similar report was received from 108 Brigade who stated that the enemy had broken through and had been seen in the Grugies Valley.

The 12th Rifles were positioned in the front system of the 108 Brigade and consisted of three companies, A, C and D. Commanding C Company, the counter-attack company, was Captain L.J. Johnston. At about noon the Germans launched a most determined assault using a number of *Flammenwerfer*, a weapon capable of projecting a stream of burning oil to a distance of 20 yards.

---

11   Some sources quote 4:40 am as the opening time.

While initially fearsome in appearance most casualties were caused when men left the shelter of their trench and were shot down with conventional small arms. It was a cumbersome weapon to use, the cylinder, weighing 68 pounds and holding three and a half gallons of oil, was carried by one man, while the projector pipe was carried by a second. These men quickly became prime targets for the defenders.

The next to report in was 107 Brigade who reported at 12:45 to say that the counter-attack company of the battle zone battalion had been observed moving forward, presumably to counter-attack the front line of the battle zone now occupied by the enemy. At 12:50 pm a message was received from the 9th Inniskillings that British artillerymen in Contescourt were blowing up their guns and coming back.

By 1:00 pm, the battle zone on the right flank, on the 108 Brigade front, was still intact as was Racecourse Redoubt. The position became untenable approximately 30 minutes later, when it was reported that the enemy had broken through the front of the 14th Division on the right flank and had captured Manufacture Farm and was attacking Essigny Station.

At 4:05 pm, 108 Brigade was ordered to form a flank from Station Redoubt, which was still holding out, to G.23 Central where they were joined up with the 14th Division who would continue the defensive line as far as Lizerolles. The 9th Inniskillings were placed at the disposal of the brigade for this purpose, while the brigade was ordered to hold as large a portion of this battalion as possible in reserve.

The Ulster Division was then given 61 Brigade of the 20th Division at 4:15 pm and was ordered to man the defences of St. Simon. That evening divisional battalions were formed in all the divisions of XVIII Corps and all trained reinforcements, officers and other ranks were ordered to join. The 36th Division battalion took up its position at Aubigny and divisional headquarters moved from Ollezy to Estouilly.

Captain Hugh Montgomery Baillie, serving in A Company 16th Rifles was killed; he was 25 years old.[12] Baillie and Second Lieutenant Rea had been taken prisoner and were gathered with other prisoners at a road junction some 1,500 yards to the west of Urvillers, on the Essigny–le-Grande to St. Quentin Road (Today the D1). As they were being escorted to the rear Captain Baillie was hit in the head by a bullet.[13] Captain Gordon Alexander Deane of the 1st Irish Fusiliers received a bullet wound to the abdomen and was subsequently taken prisoner. He died as a prisoner of war on 11 April 1918, he was 20 years old. Among those killed here was Corporal Edward James McMenamin from Swinford in County Mayo, serving with the 2nd Inniskillings.

Lieutenant John Barker MC, now serving in the 36th Machine Gun Battalion, was positioned in Boadicea Redoubt, garrisoned by the 2nd Inniskillings, commanded by Lord Farnham.[14] Under Barker's command the guns took a severe toll on the advancing enemy while ammunition lasted.

The 16th Rifles No.1 Company, consisting of nine officers and 150 other ranks, failed to appear at the prescribed rendezvous west of the Somme Dug-outs, having apparently been cut off at Jeanne-D'Arc Redoubt, which they would have helped to defend. All were subsequently reported as missing. Among these was Second Lieutenant Edward Burnside, a former pupil of RBAI and Queen's University. Edward had enlisted in October 1916 and was commissioned in January 1917. His body was recovered after the battle, he was 20 years old.[15]

---

12   The son of Robert and Sara Baillie of 'Ellerslie' Ravenhill Road, Belfast, he had been a member of Fitzroy Avenue Presbyterian Church.

13   Letter to the Baillie family from Second Lieutenant Rea, who was held in a POW Camp at Karlsruhe, Germany.

14   Barker joined the Auxiliary Division Royal Irish Constabulary on 31 August 1920 and was posted to 'K' Company in Cork City. He was wounded on 18 January 1921 and medically discharged on 4 July that year. Barker was recalled to the Colours in January 1940 and served with the South Staffordshire Regiment until 1948.

15   RBAI Archive & *The Terrors* p205.

Second Lieutenant Edmund de Wind was born in Comber, close to Newtownards in December 1883. He attended Campbell College, Belfast and on leaving worked as a clerk in the Bank of Ireland in Cavan. He moved to Canada in 1910 and again went into banking, being employed by the Bank of Commerce. He enlisted in the 31st Battalion (Calgary Regiment) of the Canadian Army in 1914 as a private and arrived in France with the 2nd Division of the Canadian Expeditionary Force in September 1915. He saw action on the Somme and Vimy Ridge before being commissioned in September 1917 and being posted to the 15th Rifles.[16] On this day de Wind was in command of a party in defence of a position known as Racecourse Redoubt. The Redoubt straddled the railway line that ran from Terginer to St. Quentin and was one of 14 redoubts in the area, designed to form a defence that required fewer infantry to defend than conventional trenches. At 4:35 am, the enemy artillery opened fire and continued

Edmund De Wind VC, late of the 15th Rifles.

until 9:40 am, when the infantry began their assault. De Wind, supported by two NCOs, spent seven hours inflicting heavy losses on the encroaching German infantry. On at least two occasions he left the trenches to enemy from the position, all the time under heavy machine gun fire. By 6:00 pm, only a small portion of the redoubt remained in British hands and Lieutenant De Wind, now wounded twice, was fighting alone. A section of infantry came to his aid and he continued to lead an inspired defence until wounded on a third occasion, this time mortally. On his death those men remaining surrendered. These amounted to approximately 30 men, including headquarters staff. The final message from Racecourse Redoubt timed at 11:45 am, read; "At 10:30 am enemy attack developed after heavy bombardment. They are still holding out. Enemy barrage battle zone. No gas.

On 28 June 1919, Edmund De Wind's mother was presented with the Victoria Cross by King George V. It was the day peace was signed at Versailles and five years to the day since Gavrilo Princip had fired his fateful shot in Sarajevo.[17]

Captain L.J. Johnston and his C Company of the 12th Rifles was one of those units cut off in the forward zone. On entering the battle position, they had encountered a German patrol, killing or scattering its members. This, to Captain Johnston, indicated that the Germans had broken through to the battle zone. By 11:00 am, the strong-points defended at A and D Companies had been captured, however, Johnston's Company continued to hold out in Foucard Trench for another four hours. On several occasions the Germans managed to force their way into the trench, only to be expelled in fierce hand to hand fighting, when the shovel and pick axe handle was as effective as the bayonet. Killed serving with the Rifles this day was Second Lieutenant William

16   Doherty & Truesdale, *Irish Winners of the Victoria Cross* and information provided by Keith Haines.
17   See Keith Haines article on Edmund De Wind.

Magookin, who had been awarded the DCM for his actions on 21 November 1915. He was 38 years old and left a widow, Dorothea, at Newport Street, Belfast.

At midday the Germans brought up a flame-thrower, but this was effectively dealt with by quickly shooting down the operator and his assistant. A short time later the persistent fog lifted to reveal the true position on the battlefield. From his position Captain Johnston was able to see German cavalry on the right flank moving through positions that should have been held by units of the 14th Division. To the rear he could see enemy troops swarming over the Jeanne d'Arc Redoubt, which was garrisoned by B Company and battalion headquarters. Then to his front Captain Johnston saw a German supply column of horse-drawn wagons some 300 yards away moving slowly along the St. Quentin to La Fere Road. Although aware of his precarious position Johnson gave the order to open fire and immediately the company's Lewis guns and rifles tore into the column, quickly reducing it to a chaotic tangle of dead and wounded men and horses. Such an action was not to go unnoticed and the enemy immediately attacked the trench from both flanks. Unable to hold back such numbers Captain Johnston immediately ordered a withdrawal to the Lejune Trench, some 500 yards to the rear.

The enemy followed up, showing tremendous tenacity and it was only with great difficulty that they were held at bay. In Lejune Trench C Company was joined by some 120 men from battalion headquarters, who had made their way from Le Pontchu Quarry. With these reinforcements Captain Johnston was able to hold the position until 4:00 pm, when a German tank advanced on to the flank of the position. This was one of four A7Vs that had previously driven the 12th Rifles out of the Quarry and as it manoeuvred into position it was able to bring two of its machine guns into enfilade along the trench. As the bullets from the tank forced the men to keep their heads down a German company attacked the front and made their way into the trench. Within a short time Johnston's command was reduced to some 100 men, many of whom were wounded. Surrender was inevitable. CSM Samuel McKeever, in an unpublished paper, stated he smashed his rifle and threw away the bolt. For his actions on this day Captain Johnston was awarded the Military Cross. The 12th Battalion war diary recorded that 22 officers and 566 other ranks were missing as of 21 March 1918, the most of these being prisoners of war.

During the night of 21 to 22 March all three brigades were withdrawn to the north bank of the St. Quentin Canal, crossing at Hamel and Artemps, the bridge being demolished on completion at 4:15 pm.

Dawn on this the second day of the German attack again saw a dense ground mist obscure the enemy movements. The division's right flank, with the III Corps located also on its right, was located behind the Canal de St Quentin and the situation was relatively quiet. To the north enemy pressure was building and the 1st Inniskillings were involved in fierce fighting in the Battle Zone, but were holding their own. At 2:00 pm, when it was obvious they were outflanked on both sides they were ordered to withdraw inside Ricardo Redoubt. Here they continued to do battle beating off several attacks until the Redoubt was itself surrounded and a fighting withdrawal had to be made by the 9th Inniskillings, who had been defending Aubigny village, back to Happencourt – Fluquieres Line. Ricardo Redoubt was now on its own.

At the headquarters of the 11th/13th Rifles there was an element of confusion. The day was recorded in the journal of Second Lieutenant Culbertson Jackson, formerly Lance Corporal Jackson of the Royal Army Medical Corps and son of the late Reverend Culbertson Jackson of Duncairn Presbyterian Church, Belfast:

> Towards evening of the second day shells began to drop around about our camp. Our CO had received no order as to what he should do and was, I think quite confused regarding what was happening. He decided to send an officer back to corps headquarters, a number of miles down the road, to ask for instructions. The adjutant, coming out of the orderly room,

looking for someone to go on the errant, happened to run into me. So I was provided with a bicycle and given my instructions. Just as I was starting off, there was a hurried order for the men to fall in and men began running for their rifles. It was reported that the enemy had broken clean through and were about to attack us. I decided the best thing I could do was to set out on my errand without further delay! I got a lift, bicycle and all, a great part of the way in one of our lorries and, at length found my way safely to army corps headquarters. After a little delay, a staff captain came out of an inner room and I gave him the colonel's message, asking for instructions. He asked me a number of questions about our position, numbers etc., pondered for a little and then instructed me to report to our colonel that he was to take the battalion forward and line the banks of a canal, which ran in front of our village. As luck would have it, a week or two before this I had overheard a senior officer in conversation state that a soldier when given a message to deliver, had the right to ask for the message in writing. Remembering this, I said, 'Sir may I have this order in writing'. He hesitated and then said 'Perhaps you had better wait and see the staff colonel, who will be out before long'. Presently the staff colonel came and questioned me. Then he gave me instructions to tell my CO to move the battalion to another place, I don't remember where. I asked again for my orders in writing. He didn't wish to take the responsibility on himself and bade me wait a while longer and see the staff brigadier. Finally, he came and, at length I received orders that the battalion was to be marched away back to a big railway junction some 15 miles in the rear. All this gave me a very vivid impression of the utter confusion reigning behind the British lines.

Second Lieutenant Jackson was awarded the Military Cross for his actions later in March, during which he was wounded in the left shoulder and thigh. The London Gazette citation stated:

For conspicuous gallantry and devotion to duty. This officer, with his platoon joined in a counter attack with the division, and fought on till only one sergeant and three men were left. He then retired carrying a wounded man under heavy fire. Then forming a rearguard with twenty men he held the position until his task was finished, when he retired in good order."

In the early hours of 22 March Second Lieutenant Cecil Leonard Knox, 150th Field Company, Royal Engineers, attached to the 36th Division carried out an action that resulted in the award of the Victoria Cross. To deny river crossings to the enemy the Royal Engineers were made responsible for the destruction of some 16 bridges. The 150th Company was split between into two groups, the first under the command of Lieutenant W.M.W. Brunyate, dealt with four bridges in the Artemps area, while Knox dealt with the remainder, ten road and two foot bridges at Tugny further to the south. All bridges were

Second Lieutenant Cecil Leonard Knox, 150th Field Company, Royal Engineers, attached to the 36th Division, carried out an action that resulted in the award of the Victoria Cross.

successfully destroyed, with only one causing any major problems. At one of the steel girder bridges the time fuse failed to detonate the charges. With the enemy already laying down covering fire and troops beginning to cross Lieutenant Knox ran forward on to the bridge and climbed beneath it to access the time fuse. Here Knox lit an 'instantaneous fuse' and as this began to burn, made good his escape as the enemy crossed the bridge. Knox had just made it to a safe distance when the structure exploded. Prior to being commissioned Cecil Knox had been employed as a civil engineer on railroad construction in Edmonton, Canada.

A message was received by General Nugent at noon advising him that a further withdrawal was necessary. The new defence line was to be the Canal de la Somme and towards the south the Canal de St. Quentin. The division, in concert with the 61st Brigade attached, was to hold this position from the current right flank of that brigade as far as the Sommette-Eaucourt. The brigades of the division had all withdrawn by 11:00 pm, when the rearguard passed through Pithon.

During the hours of darkness the 108 Brigade took up positions to defend the Canal bank, from the left flank of the 7th Duke of Cornwall's Light Infantry to Sommette-Eaucourt. The 107 Brigade moved

Cecil Leonard Knox being presented with his VC by the King at Blendecques, HQ of the Second Army, on 6 August 1918.

to Eaucourt and Cugny, while the 109 Brigade moved to Brouchy in support. Patrols from 108 Brigade were unable to make contact with the 30th Division and the 21st Entrenching Battalion was ordered to fill the gap. However, this battalion was unable to complete this move and a company of Royal Engineers along with a number of men under the command of Major Brew, 9th Irish Fusiliers was placed in the line. Meantime a battalion from 109 Brigade was moved forward to hold the northern edges of Aurigny and Brouchy.

Inside Ricardo Redoubt Colonel Crawford and his 1st Inniskillings had held out for most of the day, but now ammunition and water was running low. At 3:00 pm, the colonel sent away a number of walking wounded and all able-bodied men, knowing they would be required elsewhere. Many of these men managed to reach the divisional lines. Those men too seriously injured to be moved and those survivors still able to hold a weapon took their places in the redoubt. With the enemy crowding in on almost all sides the Inniskillings were driven into the trenches at the north-west corner of the redoubt. Here a party of enemy bombers had managed to gain access, but were swiftly attacked and the survivors forced out, Privates Bailey and Conway being mainly responsible for this action. However, courage alone could not hold the Redoubt, the German trench mortars pounded the Inniskillings and as these were well outside the throwing range of the defenders' bombs they could make no reply. At approximately 6:00 pm it was all over and the remaining Inniskillings, along with Colonel Crawford, were taken prisoner.

Saturday 23 March saw the 36th Division and attached units, in position along the Canal de St Quentin and Canal de la Somme. The line began a mile and a half north-west of Jussy and extended to a mile west of Sommette-Eaucourt. Reading from right to left the troops were, 61 Brigade, containing 7th Somerset Light Infantry, 7th Duke of Cornwall's Light Infantry and 1st King's Regiment in support. Then 108 Brigade with 9th (NIH) Irish Fusiliers and 1st Irish Fusiliers, with a composite battalion of details and those men just returned from courses, manning the outposts to allow some rest to the other battalions. Added to this were the men of the 23rd Entrenching Battalion.

All ranks were extremely tired with few men having managed more than a few hours' sleep in the last two days. The withdrawal had been slow and cumbersome with units becoming intermingled with each other and crowds of French civilians. The casualty clearing station at Ham had been evacuated and while lorries and ambulances had taken away the seriously wounded, nurses were seen walking down the Guiscard Road assisting those with less serious wounds and carrying the precious medical supplies.

The 23rd Entrenching Battalion under the command of Major Percy Lewis, a Welshman, had beaten off attempts by the enemy to cross the Canal close to Offoy and had suffered casualties.[18] At the beginning of the war Gerard Ebenezer Fysh had travelled from King's Lynn to enlist as a private in the 14th Rifles, having previously served with the London Irish Rifles. Now four years later he was on a working party in the 23rd Entrenching Battalion, as the former YCVs had become. It was on this mist shrouded morning that he was killed, one of many to die that day.

The line extended for some five miles and given the manpower available could well be described as thinly held. In Sommette – Eaucourt the survivors of the 16th Rifles were busy in constructing a line of strongpoints in event of a further fall back. The 109 Brigade was at Brouchy acting as reserve and during the day casualties were suffered, including Second Lieutenant Joseph J. Fawcett, 9th Inniskillings, from Scotshouse, Clones, County Monaghan, who was listed as missing presumed killed, he had only arrived with the battalion on 21 March, having been commissioned in August 1917. Prior to this he had served in the ranks, being wounded on 1 July 1916.[19]

Nurse Madeline Lyttle.

---

18   Major Lewis, MC, had assumed command on 28 February, succeeding Lieutenant Colonel O.R. Vivian, DSO.
19   Belfast News Letter 1 May 1918.

Second Lieutenant Joseph J. Fawcett, 9th Inniskillings, from Scotshouse, Clones, County Monaghan, listed as missing presumed killed in March 1918. Prior to this he had served in the ranks, being wounded on 1 July 1916. (Photograph courtesy of Patricia Fawcett)

The divisional artillery had suffered losses and found itself attached to various units. The 153 Brigade, referred to as the Potter Group in many accounts, was lending support to the 20th Division and was in action at Bacquencourt during the day, only rejoining the division that evening after a long march. The Erskin Group was located at Aubigny, while the Eley Group was at Brouchy; both were in position to support the division. There was no word from the Heavy Artillery Group and therefore no support could be expected from these guns. The 36th Machine Gun Battalion was so widely dispersed it could not be called upon to act as a cohesive unit, many of its individual guns were still capable of action and detachments were in action with the various brigades.

A report from the 14th Division informed General Nugent that the Germans had crossed the Crozat Canal at Jussy at 3:30 am, but had been successfully counter-attacked by the 7th Battalion of the King's Royal Rifles Corps and driven back. This was to prove only a temporary respite and by 11:15 am the enemy had crossed the Canal de St Quentin at several places, with only the 7th Battalion Somerset Light Infantry holding its position.

Prior to this the 2nd Rifles had been ordered to take up defensive positions east of Cugny and link up with the flank of the 14th Division, which had previously fallen back astride the road between Cugny and Flavy-le-Martel. As the withdrawal continued the 1st Rifles moved up to the right flank of the 2nd and discovered there were no troops on their right. This was quickly filled by a unit of dismounted French dragoons. In the centre of the divisional line running from Sommette-Eaucourt to Ollézy and the positions of the 61st Brigade on the Canals, the positions were held. On the left flank the 9th Inniskillings received a severe shelling and heavy infantry attacks from the north-west that drove them from the village of Aubigny back towards Brouchy. An immediate counter-attack was made, led by the Brigade Major, Captain G.J. Bruce, mounted on horseback. This surprising assault drove the Germans out of the village, the Inniskillings suffering few casualties. The village was to change hands again as the German counterattacked and again the Inniskillings advanced, but this time casualties were heavy and it proved impossible to hold the position as the flank became insecure. Eventually Sommette-Eaucourt fell to the enemy and a short time later Brouchy, now the division had both flanks exposed and the situation looked extremely serious.

The 61st Brigade, under the command of General Cochrane, withdrew from the line at 4: 40pm, a manoeuvre that cost them dearly. On the division's right flank the German attack was renewed with great vigour and soon enemy battalions were observed advancing through Flavy and deploying on either side of the Cugny road. By 5:00 pm Cugny came under fire from enemy trench mortars covering an advance by infantry; they were beaten back by the 2nd Rifles. A gap had appeared between the two battalions and at dusk the Germans were infiltrating through at a steady rate. A number of these Germans met up with part of C Company under the command of Lieutenant R.B. Marriott-Watson MC, on their return to the village at approximately 8:30 pm. The lieutenant spoke to the enemy in German, which gave his men the chance to get close and the enemy were scattered at the point of the bayonet.[20]

It was the turn of the 1st Rifles to be attacked at 7:00 pm, and again the enemy were beaten back. A second attack was made at 7:45 pm, but the line was held. However, at 10:00 pm, an enemy patrol was able to outflank the battalion position as supporting troops fell back in some disarray. Given the situation Lieutenant Colonel MacCarthy-O'Leary had no option but to order a withdrawal. Heffernan William Denis MacCarthy-O'Leary came from County Cork, the son of a military family. He had been wounded earlier in the day and would be wounded again three days later, which would require evacuation to England and the award of a bar to his DSO.

Both Rifles battalions then withdrew, the 1st Rifles going to the high ground at Beaulieu, while the 2nd Rifles made their way to a position astride the Villeselve Road on the western outskirts, a distance of some 300 yards.

With the onset of darkness the divisional line ran from the east of Beaulieu to the western edge of Cugny, then to the railway south-east of Ollĕzy and then along it to the Ollĕzy to Eaucourt road. From here it incorporated the road, including the village of Eaucourt, for 1,000 yards south of Brouchy to the north of Golancourt. Behind this line was positioned a unit of French infantry, who had arrived in a hurry carrying only the ammunition in their pouches and without artillery. The French line ran from Esmery-Hallon, through Flavy-le-Meldeux and Villeselve to Beaumont-en-Beine. General Nugent withdrew his headquarters from Freniches to Beaulieu-les-Fontaines at 6:00 pm, that evening.

Throughout the day all elements of the division had been in near constant action. The 16th Rifles had been attached to the 9th (NIH) Irish Fusiliers and with them had fallen back on the left flank, having performed sterling service. The Divisional Machine Gun Battalion, under the second-in-command, Major Low, although dispersed, had also performed admirably with what-ever unit they had been attached. At Brouchy the clerks and runners of 109 Brigade headquarters had earned a reputation of being excellent fighters. The artillery had served well in supporting all actions and not only that of the division. Two batteries of 91 Brigade, A/91st and C/91st, part of the 20th Divisional Artillery, received a special mention in the report submitted by the CRA. When faced by men of the 109 Brigade and 61 Brigade who had been forced back on the battery positions, the artillery officers acted swiftly to rally the men and prevent a rout. Once order had been restored the artillerymen then assisted in digging trenches in front of the gun positions.

Despite the widespread confusion of the day the supply of rations and other supplies had not failed, with the Divisional Train and Supply Column performing an excellent service. Within 107 Brigade spare picks and shovels were sent to the Rifle Brigade battalions of the 14th Division, then in the area of Cugny. Likewise the divisional medical services had treated and cared for the wounded under the most harrowing circumstances.

The day ended with the battle now well developed into open warfare, the defensive positions and natural obstacles, such as the canals, had been crossed and the ensuing fighting would be in open country, with tactics being hastily amended to suit.

---

20   Second Lieutenant Richard Brereton Marriott-Watson was reported missing believed killed on 24 March 1918. See James Taylor, *The 2nd Royal Irish Rifles in the Great War* (2005).

The expected German attack at dawn on Sunday 24 March did not materialise and it was 10:00 am before the divisional flanks experienced anything like a strong assault. It was disconcerting to discover that enemy troops had penetrated the village of Golancourt during the night, forcing out the defenders. This enemy move threw into total confusion plans that had been made between Brigadier Hessey of 109 Brigade and Brigadier Cochrane of 61 Brigade. A counter-offensive had been arranged to ease the pressure on the left flank and to blunt the pronounced salient that had been formed by the enemy attack. Added to Brigadier Hessey's command for this operation had been a composite battalion under the command of Major Knox, plus 300 more men from Beaulieu, including servants, grooms, orderlies and the personnel from the Signals School. These latter troops were formed into two companies under the command of Captain W. Smyth RE, on attachment to the General Staff and Captain C. Drummond, ADC to General Nugent. In a letter to his wife General Nugent wrote; "I have sent my last men up to support the defence. I have collected even the Officer's Servants and all sorts of odds and ends. Freddie Drummond has gone with them at his urgent request and I sent them off in lorries at 2:00 am this morning.

Major Knox and his detachment were to move via Golancourt and approach Aubigny as closely as possible, using the mist for cover, launching their attack at 8:00 am. Meanwhile the 9th Inniskillings, reinforced by a company of details was to reoccupy Brouchy. Meanwhile General Cochrane had arranged to retake Eaucourt using a force of 100 men of the 284th Army Troops, Royal Engineers, under command of two of his own infantry officers and this was achieved just prior to midnight on 23 March. Contact was made by this force with the 7th Duke of Cornwall's Light Infantry on the railway line where it was crossed by the road between Ollezy to Eaucourt.

The force commanded by Major Knox did not enjoy the same success. On the approach march they came under machine gun fire from Golancourt and were unable to make any headway. The assaults on Aubigny and Brouchy were then cancelled and the companies of details were detached and sent to positions on the left flank of the 9th Inniskillings. The cancellation of these attacks then made the position of the 7th Duke of Cornwall's Light Infantry untenable, with both flanks exposed and at 11:00 am General Cochrane ordered it to retire. This was done, but at a high cost in casualties, the battalion eventually being placed some 1,000 yards west of Cugny, parallel with the Cugny to Eaucourt road.

Closer to Cugny, some 300 yards to the west, was the 2nd Rifles, still holding their position, while behind them, located between Cugny and Montalimont Farm, the 1st Rifles were dug in. This meant that two thin lines of men were positioned back to back with approximately one mile between them, one facing east towards Cugny, while the second faced west towards Golancourt. This was a position that was quickly going to become untenable.

On the right flank of the division confusion reigned as the Germans attacked while French troops were in the process of relieving the remnants of the 14th Division and both forces were driven back. Added to this was the fact that small groups of men from the 14th Division had become intermingled with those of the 36th Division and when the 14th received orders to withdraw gaps were created in the division's lines. These gaps were quickly exploited by German sections armed with light machine guns, troops that were handled with skill by their talented commanders.

Eventually the inevitable occurred and the salient collapsed. On all flanks the men retired towards Villeselve. Here from noon onwards the Germans delivered a heavy bombardment and desperate efforts were made by brigade staff officers to rally the troops in front of the village and get them to man the trenches along with the French. In most cases they were successful. At 3:00 pm the order was given to the French troops to fall back and those men of the division did likewise.

On the right flank Major Richard de Rose of the 2nd Rifles had been wounded and command devolved to Captain Thomas Thompson DSO, who came from Markethill, County Armagh. This force, woefully short of ammunition, had maintained its position throughout the previous night and had as recently as 10:00 am beaten off another enemy attack. Orders were issued to fire only at almost-certain targets only and Captain Thompson deliberately showed himself to the men to encourage morale. This action cost him his life and he was killed by a burst of machine gun fire, as was Lieutenant Marriott-Watson, who had performed so well during the raid on 26 June 1916. Command was now taken by Captain Joseph Bryans who continued to keep a tight hold on his men and the position. Several messages dispatched by runners from the 1st Rifles situated to the battalion's rear, ordering them to withdraw, never got through. On examining the situation Captain Bryans was of the opinion that any withdrawal across open country that lay between Cugny and Villeselve, with the enemy on three sides, was virtually impossible without incurring horrendous losses. An extremely heavy German barrage began just after noon, while machine gun fire and strafing from low flying German aircraft completed the preparations for an attack. At 2:00 pm, the enemy infantry surged forward and despite severe losses in their ranks closed with Captain Bryans' command. The Rifles, their ammunition all but exhausted, leapt from their entrenchments and met the enemy in hand to hand combat, German bayonet against Rifles' swords. Captain Bryans recorded; "Rather than wait for the end, they jumped from the entrenchments and met it gallantly. It was an unforgettable sight. We were overwhelmed, but not disgraced."

Of the six officers present at the onset of the attack, only Captain Bryans and Second Lieutenant Strohm survived to be taken prisoner. In excess of 100 other ranks were killed, among them were Lance Corporal Christopher Wood from Battersea, London, Private Charles Henry Vaughan, who had formerly served with the Army Service Corps and Private Victor Barnes from Whitehouse, Belfast.

General Nugent wrote to his wife;

> I doubt if the whole division could produce more than the equivalent of a full battalion. It has been far the worst battle of the war as far as we are concerned, but if in the end we beat the Germans, it will be worth it. At present he has had matters rather his own way, but then he attacked us in terrific force and with a terrible weight of artillery.

Elsewhere on the battlefield the enemy was pressing hard from the direction of Golancourt and Beaumont-en-Beine and the circumstances were described as 'acute'. The situation was eased by a charge at 3:00 pm, by troops belonging to General Harman's 3rd Cavalry Division that had been assisting to hold the line of the 14th Division throughout the morning. This charge, on horseback, was an example of what could have been achieved elsewhere, had communications worked more swiftly. Under the command of Major Williams of the 10th Hussars, three 50-man troops drawn from three different regiments, 10th Hussar, The Royals and 3rd Dragoon Guards, advanced from the south-west along the road leading to Villeselve, then turned north along a sunken lane leading towards the village of Collezy. Here they came under enemy machine gun fire and took shelter to the south of the village. It was observed that the Germans had ensconced themselves in two small copses approximately 1,000 yards to the north-east and there was firing from at least four machine guns. The cavalry were ordered to charge in the formation known as 'infantry attack', the 3rd Dragoons in the first line, followed by the 10th Hussars, in a loose line, with the Royals in the third line acting as flank guards. The charge was made at a full gallop, the last 200 yards across ploughed ground. The eastern copse was attacked by the 3rd Dragoons and the German broke and ran back into the trees, the Dragoons dismounted and followed, the bullets from a .445 Webley or .303 rifle travelling faster than a German soldier could run, several were killed and 12 prisoners were taken. At the western copse the 10th Hussars and Royals closed with the enemy, a much larger group, and here between 70 and 100 were killed, mostly with the sword, while 94 were taken prisoner, with three machine guns either captured or destroyed. The cost to the cavalry was 73 casualties, of which six were killed.

There was a follow up by infantry, including the division, despite their utter tiredness, but all in all it was nothing more than a delaying action. This did not stop the 1st and 9th (NIH)

Irish Fusiliers of 108 Brigade from entering Villeselve and capture 150 prisoners. However, they were soon forced back by overwhelming numbers to a position about 1,000 yards to the north of Berlancourt. During this time Captain E.L. Rabone, the Brigade Major and Lieutenant G. Deakin, the Brigade Signals Officer, were wounded. The Germans were also taking prisoners, Private Robert T Finnegan of the Royal Army Medical Corps was captured while collecting wounded from the battlefield in a motor ambulance.

The French 9th and 62nd Divisions had orders to withdraw in front of heavy attacks, slowing down the enemy advance, but not allowing their line to be broken. Brigadier Griffith of 108 Brigade rode to Guivry and met with General Gamelin of the French 9th Division, placing his brigade under French command.

As darkness fell white flares soared into the night sky, fired by German reconnaissance patrols for supporting artillery guidance. By 11:00 pm they were in possession of Guiscard. At the same time the 36th Division was placed under command of the French 62nd Division and ordered to withdraw their troops through its line. As the 108 Brigade withdrew the 9th (NIH) Irish Fusiliers remained to act as rearguard, holding positions on the ridge between Guiscard and Berlancourt, while the brigade moved first to Crisolles and then Sermaize. Here there was some time for the men to rest. The 107 and 109 brigades retired to Sermaize and Fretoy-le-Chateau arriving at 2:00 am on 25 March.

Having previously been in action with the 20th Division, the Potter Group (153 Brigade) of the divisional artillery returned and soon all divisional groups were firing defensive barrages on those enemy troops advancing south along the roads from the Canal de la Somme. Shells from the Potter Group fell among enemy troops massing for an attack in the area of the Esmery – Hallon – Golancourt Road, causing severe casualties, while the Erskin Group was in action against near Beines until French and British infantry withdrew through the guns. Then C/91st Battery acted as rearguard covering the retirement until after dark, when they were fortunate enough to be able to extricate the guns after the German had entered Berlancourt. The Eley Group was forced to make three withdrawals. The first as before noon, moving close to Berlancourt, then later at 2:30 pm, to Buchoire, where it provided covering fire for French infantry; and thirdly at 6:00 pm, to the area of Fretoy-le-Chateau. In each case the withdrawal was delayed to the last possible minute.

On the night of 25 March the Erskine Group was placed at the disposal of the 9th French Division, while the Eley and Potter groups were sent to the 62nd French Division, under the control of the 36th Divisional Artillery Headquarters. On his return from leave General Brock assumed command of all groups, while Colonel H.C. Simpson, acting CRA, was allocated to the 62nd French Division as a liaison officer. Further details of the work of the artillery with the French will be found later in this chapter.

An order and current intelligence report was received from the 62nd French Division at 2:15 am on 25 March. The line currently being held ran west of Quesmy, Bethancourt and Freniches to the Canal de Robecourt at Rouy, east of Nesle. The 62nd Division was to check the enemy advance and prevent any crossing of the Canal, with the British batteries remaining under French control. The remaining troops of the 36th Division were to fall back and reform in preparation to assist the 62nd if necessary. The reforming took place along the line of march, which was some 15 miles. The 61st Brigade, now about 500 all ranks, was ordered back to its own division and at Avricourt the men boarded waiting buses. General Cochrane's men would be sorely missed.

At midday, the 36th Division was fully assembled at Avicourt where some food and much needed rest were availed of. The march resumed and eventually the 107 Brigade was billeted at Guerbigny, 108 Brigade at Erches and 109 Brigade split between Guerbigny and Warsy, the latter location also being divisional headquarters. Most troops arrived between midnight and 2:00 am on 26 March, although the 9th (NIH) Irish Fusiliers coming from Guiscard, some 30 miles away, did not arrive until 8:00 am.

Sergeant William McDowall, 12th Royal Irish Rifles, on the left with unnamed sergeant, was the son of Andrew and Mary McDowall and husband of Janet McDowall of Drumalis, Larne, County Antrim. He was killed on 26 March 1918, aged 36 years and has no known grave, being commemorated on the Pozieres Memorial. A former member of the UVF, he had an important part to play in the landing of arms at Larne. See Volume I. (photograph courtesy of Laura Spence)

The Ulster Covenant showing the signature of William Hunter McDowall. (Courtesy of Laura Spence)

An embroidered Christmas card sent from Flanders by Sergeant William McDowall of the 12th Royal Irish Rifles. (photograph courtesy of Laura Spence)

The 'death penny' of Sergeant William Hunter McDowall, 12th Royal Irish Rifles, killed in action 26 March 1918. At the end of the Great War a plaque was given to the next-of-kin of all British and Commonwealth personnel who had been killed during the conflict. As it was made from bronze it was commonly called the 'death penny' and some 1,355,000 were issued, requiring 450 tonnes of bronze. The plaque is approximately five inches in diameter and bears the recipient's name, but no rank, all being equal in death. (Courtesy of Laura Spence)

William Hunter McDowall and family. (Courtesy Laura Spence)

By now the men were thoroughly exhausted and when on the march the regulation halts had been ignored as it was found nigh on impossible to rouse men once they had stopped. The situation was extremely serious as related by General Nugent to his wife:

> It is all a ghastly nightmare, I cannot credit that it is only five days ago that we were holding the trenches just in front of St Quentin. Yesterday was a bad day for the French and British armies. We lost much ground, a great deal of guns and ammunition has been captured. The French have been rushing up Divisions to try and stop the rot, but there is a great deal of confusion and the Germans are giving us no rest. What is left of my Division had terribly heavy fighting yesterday and we had to fall back again in common with the French and British.

Thankfully at Avricourt, some buses not required to transport the 61st Brigade were able to be used to carry the men of the 36th the last few miles.

The confusion continued, retreating columns of infantry and artillery batteries, both British and French intermingled with fleeing civilians, under near constant harassment from long range shelling and air attack. With the French retreating south-west and the British retiring west, it was inevitable that a gap would appear. It occurred late on the evening of 25 March at Roye. The 62nd French Division, ably supported by both the Potter and Eley Groups, fought a delaying action and the Germans were unable to reach Libermont until 4:00 pm, with the Canal not crossed for another two hours. With their flank turned the French was forced to withdraw to the line of the Roye-Noyon Road.

Thus the gap was formed and during the early hours of 26 March the Germans poured through Roye from the north-east, despite a spirited holding action by a French cavalry division that was spread over a front of six miles. As this was happening newly arrived French divisions were due to arrive on the Amiens to Montdidier railway and should the Germans manage to reach these points the result would be disastrous. The only available forces to close the gap were the 30th and 36th Divisions.

At 8:00 am, orders were received by the division to take up a defensive line from l'Echelle St Aurin on the Avre River, where it was to make contact with the French, to the main Amiens to Roye road north of Andechy.

The 108 Brigade was on the left flank and was to link up with the 30th Division. The 109 Brigade was on the right flank, with 107 Brigade acting as reserve in Guerbigny. On the left 108 Brigade was to occupy the woods, but before they could move the Germans had already moved in and established machine gun positions. This prohibited any contact with the 30th Division. On the right flank the German had occupied Andechy before the 109 Brigade got into position.

Throughout the morning small parties of storm troopers worked their way forward probing for weak spots in the divisional line, but accurate fire from the Lewis guns kept them at a distance. Brigadier Griffith ordered the 122nd Field Company to protect the left flank, which they did until at 1:00 pm, when it was noticed that the Germans were increasing the pressure and General Nugent ordered the 107 Brigade to hold the old French line that followed the road from Erches to Bouchoir. Within the remnants of 107 Brigade there was the 121st Field Company, the 16th Rifles, 21st Entrenching Battalion and the men of the brigade's trench mortar battery. Given such a conglomeration it was decided to split the force into three groups, the largest of which was to be the three Rifles battalions, 1st, 2nd and 15th, under the command of Colonel McCarthy-O'Leary. This unit was in position by 4:00 pm and later pushed forward to make contact with the left of 108 Brigade. Lance Corporal George Armstrong from Railway Place Coleraine, Londonderry, was killed. Originally a member of the Cyclist Corps, he died fighting with the 1st Rifles serving in No.9 Platoon of D Company. This company, commanded by Captain L.M. Baly, had been in

Private John Nelson, Army Cyclist Corps, buried in Magherally Presbyterian Church, Garvaghy. (photograph courtesy of Dr Gavin Hughes)

Quarry Redoubt at the beginning of the battle and was last seen in charge of a signal station located in the village of Avricourt when it was overrun.

Casualties among all units were ongoing and in the 16th Rifles a respected officer was lost. Captain William Henry Madden serving in the 16th Rifles came from County Cork and was the son of the Very Reverend S.O. Madden, Dean of Cork. A former member of Campbell College OTC, he was well remembered as a keen sportsman and had fought at the Somme, Messines, Langemarck and Cambrai. He was mortally wounded between 24 and 25 March.

Despite the exhaustion the line held for the next six hours. With limited ammunition and no artillery support each German advance was beaten back. Artillery support, even one 18-pounder battery, would have had ample targets around Andechy, as the enemy formed and reformed for each assault. In the village of Erches 108 Brigade headquarters was forced to move into the open fields behind due to the weight of German shelling. By 8:00 pm the enemy were in the village and so close was the fighting that Brigadier Griffith received a minor wound to his hand as his headquarters staff fought their way clear. Colonel Place, GSO I of the division, was not so fortunate. As he travelled by car from Guerbigny, accompanied by Colonel Furnell of the 1st Irish Fusiliers and Major Brew of the 9th, the vehicle engine was struck by a bullet. As the men dismounted they were attacked by a party of German infantry, Colonel Place being shot in the leg. As he fell another German ran at him and stabbed him with a bayonet, thankfully his issue overcoat was thick enough to protect him for any serious wound. All three officers were taken prisoner, but as they were escorted away a further party of Germans opened fire on the entire group and Major Brew was hit in the chest suffering a severe would. Place and Furnell carried him to the side of the road, but the Germans refused to offer any assistance and he had to be left behind. Major Brew died as a prisoner of war on 6 April; he was 41 years old and left a widow, Annie, of 'Rathlin', Portadown, County Armagh.

Later Lieutenant Cumming led a reconnaissance patrol of six men into Guerbigny to ascertain if it was held by the enemy. It was not, but on returning the patrol was attacked by a German party of five. In the ensuing fight all the enemy were killed.

The remaining men of 108 Brigade took up a line west of Erches and came under the command of Brigadier Hessey, as their own brigade staff had been cut off from them by enemy patrols. By now the Germans had brought forward heavy guns and trench mortars and the British position were under a heavy fire.

At 1:45 am on 27 March a patrol of one officer and two other ranks was sent out by the 121st Field Company towards the village of Erches. Here they lay up some 100 yards from the road and observed a large amount of enemy transport, wagons, limbers, about 20 cavalry, some straggling infantry and one battery of field artillery moving into the village, an ideal target for British or French guns, had any been available.

Situated to the west of the village was Captain Miller's company of the 15th Rifles, and throughout the hours of darkness they were pounded by enemy artillery, with trenches being blown in and many casualties suffered. The company had one Vickers machine gun and as daylight broke it was able to pick out likely targets in and around Erches and much damage was caused. By 8:00 am, the position of this gun had been identified by the Germans who made efforts to bomb their way towards it. Lieutenant Young commanding a small number of men successfully drove them off.

A distance away Captain Densmore Walker of the divisional machine gun battalion, with remnants of several other units, was holding a trench on the Erches to Guerbigny Road. Survivors of his company, armed with rifles, were supported by some men of the 107 Brigade who had one machine gun. Earlier Captain Walker, accompanied by Private Gilmore, a former member of the 14th Rifles, now in the 23rd Entrenching Battalion, had moved into Guerbigny to gauge the strength

Major John George Brew, 9th (North Irish Horse) Royal Irish Fusiliers, died as a prisoner of war on 6 April 1918.

of the enemy. This they were able to do and shortly after returning to his unit the Germans attacked from two different directions. Captain Walker left an excellent account of the action:

Things were looking as black as conceivable. I suppose it would be about 7:30 am when the attack came. We heard shouting straight behind us and saw about a dozen men a mile away, coming towards us in a line.[21] One waved a white flag and they all shouted. Some said they were English and we were relieved; some said they looked like French; and I said that anyway we would fire on them – which we did. They were perfectly good Huns! They took cover when we opened, and then, when we were really interested in them, the real attack came from Erches. He swarmed on to the road and came down the trench. This looked like the finish of it. There was general movement backwards, but Evans prevented the machine gunners from dismounting the one machine gun with the 107 Brigade, and got it into action on the top of the trench. This changed the aspect of things, as the Huns checked. We all got out of our trench (most people with the idea of clearing over the open I fancy) and there we stood for quite a while, our people firing towards Erches, and the Huns hesitating. Seeing this latter tendency, Gilmore and I moved slowly towards Erches, trying to urge the troops to attack, but they were too undecided. Then we saw a Hun in the trench just below us. I fired my revolver

---

21   Cyril Falls assumes these men were advancing from Saulchoy-sue-Davenescourt, into which a number of the enemy had filtered in during the hours of darkness.

at him and he ran back. So we chased him. This settled matters! The Huns turned tail and our men followed. As my particular Hun turned round traverses I got another couple of shots, but didn't bring him down. When we reached the road, which was sunken, the bank came up to his waist and he looked scared horribly but I fired again. I distinctly saw what I thought was a puff of smoke go out from his pack. Anyway he at once went down behind the bank, and Gilmore rushed up with his bayonet. I said 'Leave him', but I don't know whether he did or not. And now I didn't know what to do. Fritz was legging it for Erches hard enough, and by this time indeed they had all reached it. I don't know how big the village was, but we might have rushed it. On the other hand I don't know what had happened on the left, or in what strength the enemy was. At this stage I was delighted to see an infantry officer with an MC come up. I asked him if he thought it was any use trying to go on, and he said it would be better to make a line there.

Eventually Captain Walker and his men were forced to retire. Surrounded in all sides, with the exception of a gap to the north-west and low on ammunition, only three belts remained for the Vickers, they moved out, confident that had played their part in delaying the German advance.

Earlier that morning Major L. Carr, DSO, the GSO of XVIII Corps, arrived at divisional headquarters to take over the duties of GSOI from Lieutenant Colonel Place, who had earlier been taken prisoner. He would stay for only a short time

Many men of the division had been taken prisoner and among them was Lieutenant Morgan Edward Jellett Moore, MC, from Letterkenny in Donegal. He died in a German field hospital from wounds he had received three days before. Moore had been awarded the Military Cross for his actions on the night of 26 June 1916, had been severely wounded on 1 July on the Somme and was subsequently evacuated to England. On returning to service, he was posted to the 2nd Rifles and fought at Ypres and Westhoek in August and at Cambrai in November 1917. He had been mortally wounded at about 4:00 pm on 24 March by the shattering of both legs.[22]

It was at Erches that the enemy broke the line on a major scale. On the right flank, south of the Avre, the French outposts were withdrawn; while 109 Brigade crossed the river, it being impossible to retire along the right bank. This crossing was overseen by the Brigade Major, Captain G.J. Bruce and was carried out in an orderly fashion, with covering fire supplied by successive sections.

North of Erches Captain Miller held his ground until midday when enemy shellfire made his trenches untenable. On his left the remainder of the 1st and 2nd Rifles had fallen back a short distance after they had counter-attacked at 10:00 am and gained some time. In this action Colonel McCarthy-O'Leary had been wounded for the second time.

On the orders of General Withycombe the entire line withdrew to Hangest-en-Santerre since large columns of Germans were observed advancing towards Davenescourt and then moving into the wooded country to its rear. This withdrawal was completed by 5:00 pm. That evening a French division moved up and 107 Brigade was ordered to march back and rejoin the division at Sourdon.

On the morning of 28 March the Germans discovered a gap in the allied lines at Montdidier and by 8:00 am were over two miles west of the town. At 12:30 pm General Nugent received orders from General Debeney, commanding the First French Army. He stated that he was massing artillery at Coullemelle and required all available infantry to cover it. General Nugent wrote to his wife; "I gave them of course and the poor devils who have been fighting for seven days without rest had to drag themselves out to a village called Coullemelle where we took up a position. Fortunately the Germans did not come on and the French drove them back where they had broken in."

22 Taylor, *The History of the 2nd Royal Irish Rifles.*

On the morning of 30 March, after a night spent in the open, cold and wet, the remnants of the division entrained at Saleux to the south of Amiens and moved north to the area of Gamaches, on the coast to reorganise and rest. Prior to the train journey there had been yet more marching. The 9th Inniskillings moved from Coullemelle and stopped briefly at Epagny for a rest and some food. They then continued to Wailly where billets were found for the night. Early the following morning they continued to Saleux where they boarded a train to take them to Eu. From here they marched to Betherncourt-sur-Somme. When Captain Morrison compiled the battalion roll it revealed that from a pre-battle strength of 62 officers and 1,097 other ranks, 23 officers and 464 other ranks had become casualties, a severe butcher's bill for any battalion. While many men had become prisoners of war, many others had been killed. Among the dead were Private William McCord from Moneymore, Londonderry, and Private John Joseph Duff from County Mayo. In the 9th Irish Fusiliers (NIH) Private John Forbes had been killed in an attempt to rescue a fellow private who had been taken by the Germans. Private Forbes was a former member of the North Irish Horse, came from Ahoghill, Ballymena, Antrim, and was 22 years old. Captain Hugh Hogg Beatty, from Dungannon, was killed on 31 March while serving with the 22nd Entrenching Battalion. A former member of the UVF, he had working in Cardiff on the outbreak of War and enlisted in the Welsh Regiment before being commissioned into the Ulster Division. On 16 August he had been wounded while serving with the 11th/13th Rifles.

The Reverend A. Spence MC, on attachment to the 10th Inniskillings, died from a previous gunshot wound to the chest. He had been a patient in a German reserve field hospital at Ham, having been taken prisoner during the offensive. He came from Brookfield, Portglenone, County Antrim, and had been curate at Christ Church, Londonderry.

The divisional artillery was also withdrawn for refitting; however its actions over the last few days of March should not be ignored. At midnight on 24 March the Potter Group was ordered back to new positions. In utter darkness, along narrow rutted roads, horse drawn supply wagons, some motor vehicles and scattered groups of infantry jostled for space as the batteries brought up the rear. This move was accomplished without hindrance despite the enemy following up closely behind and by 4:00 am, all guns were in action. Headquarters had been established in a farm known as Des Fonds Gamets.

Dawn on 25 March revealed that the British infantry had gone and the Potter Group was in the midst of several French batteries. At 7:00 am, firing was heard to the front, although observation was difficult due to the all prevailing mist. When it was ascertained that the enemy were attacking barrages were fired on the Bois de L'Hopital, Freniches to Fretoy le Chateau road and the nearby wood. Repeated attacks were made, especially in front of Libermont and in the Bois de L'Hopital, but without success and at the cost of many casualties. By noon the Germans had managed to force a crossing of the canal north of Libermont near Moyencourt and had advanced on Ercheu. At the same time the French infantry were slowly pressed back through Libermont and the Bois de L'Hopital. By 1:00 pm this retirement had forced the Potter Group to withdraw back to an area immediately west of Beaulieu. Colonel Claud Potter and his battery commanders carried out a mounted reconnaissance of potential gun positions and noted that the village square in Beaulieu was packed with French guns and transport wagons. While a superb target for enemy artillery, it remained shell-free. It would appear that while the German storm troopers were fast on their feet, the artillery moved at a more conventional pace. The Potter Group covered the withdrawal of the Eley Group, before making their move. By 3:00 pm, the guns were again in action and Group headquarters had been established at Bouvresse Farm.

The guns fired to protect the canal gap and enfilade barrages were fired to defend Fretoy le Chateau from the north. As this was happening gun positions further to the rear were reconnoitred near Avricourt and the batteries began withdrawing about 7:00 pm, with the last battery leaving with the enemy within a few 100 yards. The guns again came into action in the vicinity of an ammunition dump at a crossroads and all guns were firing by 10:30 pm. The group headquarters having been established in Avricourt.

The movements and firing of the Eley Group closely followed the Potter Group. A change was ordered by General Brock during the day and C/153rd Brigade and 383rd Divisional Artillery changed from the Potter Group to the Eley Group.

In the 35th Heavy Artillery Group the two 60-pounder batteries were in action west of Ercheu, with the Group headquarters at Solente. Fire was carried out all day in defence of Libermont and the salient, which was heavily attacked. During the afternoon the batteries retired to Margny and took up positions west of the Bois de Champien. The 232nd Siege Battery, under the direct orders of Headquarters 36th Divisional Artillery, bombarded the Bois de L'Hopital and objectives in its vicinity all morning, only withdrawing by sections at midday. The Divisional Ammunition Column and attached units marched at 6:00 pm to Fresniers and established a shell dump.

In the early hours of 26 March orders were received from the 62nd French Division for the withdrawal of all artillery groups during the hours of darkness, with the new positions to be occupied by dawn. The Potter and Eley Groups, along with the 36th Divisional Ammunition Column, moved together, the headquarters having to move rather hurriedly at 4:00 am.

At 9:00 am, the French infantry made a premature retirement on the right flank and all divisional groups had to withdraw rapidly due to their flanks being exposed. The groups moved to a rendezvous at Gury and there came under the command of the 77th French Division. Here they came into action firing on the front covered by Cannectancourt, Thiescourt, Lassigny and Canny-sue-Matz. There was excellent communications between the artillery and the French thanks to the superb work by Lieutenant Colonel Simpson, acting as liaison officer. At this time the 35th Heavy Artillery Group did not come into action, but continued to retire. The 232nd Siege Battery lost touch with the Group during the retirement and could not be recovered and eventually regained its original group, the 93rd Heavy Artillery Group.

For the remainder of the month the 36th Divisional Artillery continued to perform well on all sections of the front and received the thanks of the various French units it served with for their unstinting support.

April 1918

On 1 April 1918, the Royal Flying Corps became the Royal Air Force; this would mean little to the men on the ground, although some humorous quips were recorded concerning the date. In Ulster the local papers reported the award of the Distinguished Conduct Medal to Private J Smith of the Irish Fusiliers; he came from Drumalee in County Cavan and received the medal for the rescue of a wounded officer from the battlefield.

Between 1 and 4 April 1918 the division moved by train from its billets in the Bresle Valley to Ypres. During this time here had been much reorganisation within the division. Those men transferred to the Entrenching Battalions, originally formed in February, were brought back as reinforcements, but did little to alleviate the manpower shortage caused by the March battles. The strength of 108 Brigade was just over 300 men and these were mostly those in the various administrative units, transport etc. The total casualties, dead, wounded and missing, suffered by the division from the opening of the German offensive on 21 March was 7,525 officers and men, the majority being listed as missing in action and would eventually be reported as prisoners of war.

To make up these shortages large drafts of men began to arrive. The vast majority of those received by the division had an average age of 19 and were barely trained. Few came from Ulster or elsewhere in Ireland, but from all corners of the British Isles. The character that had made up the Ulster Division was all but gone.

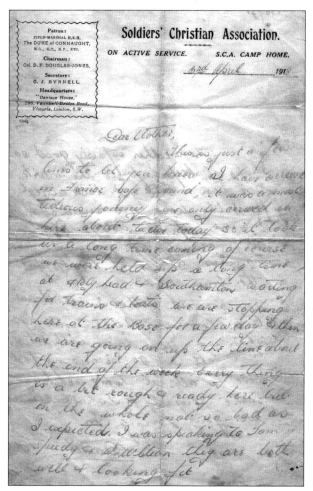

'Dear mother', a letter written home on notepaper supplied by the Soldiers' Christian Association, dated 3 April 1918.

With divisional headquarters now established at Ten Elms Camp close to Poperinghe, on 3 April orders were received for future movement. The new GSOI was Lieutenant Colonel A.G. Thompson, DSO, formerly of the Indian Army; he replaced Major Carr, who had stood in for Lieutenant Colonel Place, taken prisoner in March. As darkness fell on 6 April, the division, less 108 Brigade, moved to relieve the British 1st Division. By the morning of 8 April this had been completed with 107 Brigade in the front line and the 109th in support. Divisional headquarters being located at the Canal Bank a mile to the north of Ypres. A signal received by head-quarters informed them that Lieutenant Colonel Blair-Oliphant, DSO, had died of wounds received in the March battle while commanding the 22nd Entrenching Battalion, having formerly commanded the 11th/13th Rifles. The new front line now held by the division, which included the village of Poelcappelle, was in a deplorable state after the recent fighting and was a virtual waste-land of shell-holes criss-crossed by duckboard walkways interspersed with some pill boxes. In the rear areas things were slightly better, with adequate huts for the men and even an officer's club in ruined Ypres. However, any thoughts of rest and recreation were short lived.

Battle of the Lys

The Battle of the Lys is also known as the Fourth Battle of Ypres, the Third Battle of Flanders, the Lys Offensive, or if you are Portuguese, *Batalha de La Lys*. It began on 9 April and lasted for 20 days. The German intention was the capture of Ypres and the forcing of British forces back to the Channel ports, and they named their attack Georgette, being part of the Second Ludendorff offensive.

The German opening bombardment began on 7 April and the enemy troops moved west up the valley of the River Lys, hitting the Allied lines between Gapaard in the north and Givenchy in the south. Here the Portuguese Corps was pushed back losing approximately 7,500 men, killed, wounded and taken prisoner. Armentieres was captured and the enemy advanced towards the vital railway junction at Hazebrouck. By nightfall on 10 April the Germans were in Estaires, some ten miles to the west of Armentieres. The mademoiselle was far from pleased.

The involvement of the Ulster Division in this battle was restricted to General Griffith and his 108 Brigade, as part of the II Corps reserve. They were deployed in support of the British 19th Division. The remainder of the 36th Division was not directly attacked, but took part in the British withdrawals around Ypres.

The 108 Brigade had travelled from Herzeele via narrow gauge railway and arrived in Poperinghe at 11:00 am on 9 April. At noon the following day Brigadier Griffith received orders to move immediately to Kemmel in conjunction with C Company of the 36th Machine Gun Battalion, all being transported by motor-bus. Included in his force was a draft of 255 reinforcements who had been allocated to the 1st and 9th (NIH) Irish Fusiliers.

The infantry were loaded on to buses and, travelling via the village of La Clytte, reached Kemmel at 4:15 pm, where it came under the command of the 19th (Western) Division. This division, along with the 9th (Scottish) Division, had been fighting strongly in defence of the Messines Ridge.

Brigadier Griffith established his headquarters in the Kemmel Chateau and prepared to integrate his men into the Kemmel defences. In the early hours of 11 April the brigade was ordered to move up to the Messines Ridge to provide support for the South African Brigade of the 9th (Scottish) Division. The South Africans had earned an enviable reputation during the March offensive when they had made a determined defence at Gauche Wood near Villers Guislain, followed by a fighting withdrawal to Marrieres Wood close to Bouchavesnes. Here they stood totally unsupported, fighting until there were about 100 men of all ranks remaining, only surrendering when they had run out of ammunition.

In deploying his brigade Brigadier Griffith put the 1st Irish Fusiliers on the Messines to Wytschaete Road, located 500 yards north of Messines to the area of Pick House. The 12th Rifles were on the Spanbroek Ridge providing support, while the 9th Irish Fusiliers were occupying the old British front line on the Wulverghem to Messines Road. Casualties suffered during this move were 11 other ranks wounded and seven reported as missing.

A quiet morning was interrupted by a succession of messages to say that the Germans were advancing north of Ploegsteert. Brigadier Griffith then received a secret warning order at 2:15 pm to the effect that should the Germans capture Hill 63; the entire line would have to carry out a pivoting manoeuvre on the Spanbroek Ridge and its prolongation east of Wulverghem, where a junction would be made with the 25th Division. As a result of this brigade headquarters moved to Daylight Corner where telephone communication was established, while a small number of signallers and runners, under the brigade signalling officer, remained at North Midland Farm as a forward report centre.[23]

The enemy bombardment came down in the afternoon and at 3:30 pm the Germans launched their attack against the crest road between Pick House and 4 Huns Farm. On the left flank the South Africans were pushed back and the 1st Irish Fusiliers had their line ruptured. An almost immediate combined counter-attack by the South Africans and Fusiliers restored the position, causing the enemy heavy casualties. Fatal casualties to the Irish Fusiliers included Captain Gordon Alexander Deane from Loughgall, County Armagh, and Lance Sergeant Harry Taylor of C Company, who came from Ash Vale, Aldershot.

A telegram was received from Major General D. Jeffreys, CB, CMG, commanding the 19th (Western) Division: "Heartiest congratulations to 108 Brigade and R.I. Fusiliers and South Africans on their fine success."

---

23   Brigade War Diary, 11 April 1918.

However continuing pressure on the left flank forced the line to be refused from the road towards Hell Farm. A further German assault at 7:00 pm, although strongly pressed was held by the Irish Fusiliers, despite the high percentage of raw recruits in the ranks.

During the night the warning order previously received by Brigadier Griffith had to be carried out and the Ridge was abandoned, with the exception of the northern part, still defended by the 9th Division in and around Wytschaete. About midnight brigade headquarters had moved back into the dug-outs on the southern side of Kemmel Hill. By dawn on 12 April the withdrawal had been completed, but there was no contact with the left flank of the 25th Division. This was rectified by withdrawing the right flank of the 9th (NIH) Irish Fusiliers for approximately 200 yards. From the positions of the 9th (NIH) Irish Fusiliers the enemy was seen massing at about 11:20 am in the area of La Petite Douve Farm. Supporting artillery fire was brought down on them and no attack developed. With an annoyance being caused by bursts of machine gun fire and occasional snipers the enemy attempted to push forward patrols from time to time, but each of these was attacked and driven back by counter-patrolling or accurate Lewis gun fire. And so it continued for the remainder of the afternoon, but then at 6:40 pm a short but heavy German bombardment fell, and the enemy attacked along the Wulverghem to Messines Road and also to the south of it. The 9th (NIH) Irish Fusiliers had their left flank broken, but this was almost immediately rectified by a counter-attack by the reserve company led personally by Colonel Pelly, supported by a party of men from the 12th Rifles commanded by Major Holt Waring. In the 12th Rifles, A Company, which had been in local support, was moved to the right flank to strengthen the Irish Fusiliers line that by now was very thin. The 1st Irish Fusiliers, well under strength, was formed into one company and attached to the 9th Division. By 8:25 pm, the situation was reported as having been restored and all was quiet. The right flank of the Brigade was in touch with the 25th Division, while on the left flank the South Africans were holding firm.

That night at 10:12 pm, Colonel Pelly reported that the 25th Division had fallen back and he had lost touch with it. He was also receiving enemy machine gun fire from the right and consequently was swinging back his right flank. From brigade headquarters Captain V.B. Rogers went up the line to ascertain the situation more accurately. So far the action had cost the loss of five officers killed, six wounded and one missing. There were also three other ranks killed, 109 wounded and 145 missing.

Despite sending out patrols just after midnight on 13 April, the 9th (NIH) Irish Fusiliers were unable to make contact with the 25th Division and at 2:00 am some Royal Engineers and infantry from 57 Brigade were sent forward to fill the gap thus created on the right flank of the Fusiliers. Captain Rogers returned to brigade headquarters at 4:00 pm and reported that the Fusiliers had failed to find 25th Division. It later transpired that a gap of some 1,000 yards had developed between the two units and a battalion from the 178th Infantry Brigade, on attachment to the 19th Division, was sent forward to fill this gap and restore the situation. It arrived at 6:00 am, just as the enemy launched an attack against the front held by the 12th Rifles east of Wulverghem. They had been using the early morning mist for cover, advancing in short rushes, and had reached to within 150 yards of the line when the mist lifted. At that range the rifles and Lewis guns took a terrible toll, even the rawest recruit was able to hit a man sized target at that range. The battalion's Lewis guns were particularly well sited, having been placed by Captain Walker in old positions he had previously held prior to the Battle of Messines in 1917.

By 8:15 am another large group of enemy were reported massing for an attack against the Wulverghem to Messines Road and in the valley south of it. Artillery support was called for, but it was then reported that small arms fire had already dispersed the attack and this was cancelled.

A report from the 25th Division received at 9:10 am told that the Germans had occupied Neuve Eglise and a battalion from the 178 Brigade was sent forward to counter-attack and assist the 25th Division. For the 108 Brigade the remainder of the morning passed in a relatively peaceful state.

In the afternoon, about 2:00 pm, groups of the enemy were observed working their way forward under cover of the old camouflage screens on the Messines to Wulverghem Road in an attempt to enfilade the 12th Rifles, while at the same time other parties were bombing their way up the disused trenches. In each case counter-attacks drove them off when they then suffered heavy casualties from the Lewis guns.

Another telegram was passed on via Major General G.D. Jeffreys of 19th Division:

> 9th Corps Commander wishes to congratulate all ranks on the magnificent fighting qualities which they are displaying under very arduous conditions against heavy odds. Reinforcements are coming up to our assistance and the enemy has suffered very heavy losses in his attempt to break through the British Armies. The Royal Air Force today crashed forty-seven enemy aeroplanes of which thirty-nine were on this battle front.

For the brigade a further 13 other ranks were killed, 59 wounded and 16 were reported as missing. One officer was wounded.

In the early hours of 14 April the 7th Sherwood Foresters from 178 Brigade relieved the 9th (NIH) Irish Fusiliers and 1st Irish Fusiliers in the front line. These two battalions then moved to Kemmel Shelters for some relief, while the 12th Rifles remained in the line. The stay at Kemmel was brief, at 11:45 am orders were received from the 19th Division that a battalion was to be sent to the Kemmel defences, while a second to provide close support to the front line. So it was that the 9th (NIH) Irish Fusiliers went to the defences, while the 1st Fusiliers moved forward to the Beehive Dugouts opposite the Kruisstraat Cabaret. At 6:00 pm it was confirmed that the enemy had occupied Neuve Eglise and at 10:30 pm that night orders were received from the 19th Division that the line was to withdraw west of Wulverghem during the night.

At 1:30 am on the morning of 15 April the 12th Rifles refused their flank, pivoting on a point just west of Wulverghem where it joined up with the 178th Infantry Brigade west of the village, and they continued the line in a westerly direction. The line north of the Rifles stayed unchanged and their outposts remained out until 2:30 am to cover the withdrawal, which was completed without incident. Brigade headquarters was relocated on the northern slope of Kemmel Hill.

This move was carried out just in time as at 5:30 am an intense enemy bombardment of various calibres fell on the front line, a line that was very exposed and groups of the enemy were able to break through in the area of the junction of the 12th Rifles and the 178 Brigade. The left and centre of the 12th Rifles was forced to withdraw a few 100 yards and seek cover in an old communication trench known as Kingsway, that provided an element of cover and a good field of fire. The 1st Irish Fusiliers, at company strength, was sent forward as reinforcements and, joined by parties from the Rifles, counter-attacked, they were unable to restore the situation, but did prevent any further enemy advance. During the counter-attack Major Holt Waring, from Waringstown, County Down, was killed, he was 41 years old. From Castlebar, County Mayo, Lance Corporal Michael O'Callaghan was killed, he was 18 years old.

The 9th (NIH) Irish Fusiliers were brought back from the Kemmel defences about 9:30 am and were moved forward to a support position about Spy Farm and Regent Street dug-outs. Colonel Kelly was then ordered to push forward platoons to join the right of the line in Kingsway and this was carried out successfully by two platoons from C Company under the command of Captain Thomas Crosbie, MC. Later in the day Captain Crosbie's position was attacked and partially surrounded, being forced to withdraw after suffering heavy casualties, mostly in wounded. Among those killed was Private Percy Harris, a 33 year old from London and Captain Crosbie, who was mortally wounded and died later that night in the dressing station on Kemmel Hill. The captain had earned his Military Cross while on a raid at Havrincourt the previous November and would posthumously be awarded a Bar for his action at St. Quentin several weeks earlier.

Second Lieutenant Culbertson Jackson was wounded in the left shoulder and right thigh on 15 April, while serving with the 11th Rifles. He recalled the incident in his journal:

> Suddenly I was confronted by a strong continuous line of thick barbed wire. The Germans had advanced during the night and in the mist had erected this quite unknown to us! I caught a glimpse of a couple of startled men in the trench beyond rushing to pick up their rifles and before we realised fire was opened on us. My batman was hit and fell to the ground. I tried to lift him, then saw he was unconscious and perhaps dead; so I slipped back into the mist, followed by a volley of shots. I was a bit nervous coming back, as I thought our fellows might fire at me. Later I found that they had seen us all the time, but under heavy fire. The next day the bombardment of our lines increased. I was with my platoon in the front line, the shelling was continuous and we had little protection. Once I was blown off my feet by the blast of a shell into the arms of my platoon sergeant. Picking ourselves up we discovered that one of the men beside us had been killed. At length another shell exploded behind me. It seemed as if a stick had hit me in the back of the thigh, otherwise I felt no pain at all. It turned out afterwards that a big fragment of shell had embedded itself in my leg, missing my artery by a quarter to half and inch according to the doctor in hospital, who treated the wound.

Captain Harold Hardy, who resided at Helen's Bay, County Down, was killed. He came from the town-land of Ballygrot, Bangor, and had originally enlisted in the 13th Rifles. On amalgamation of the battalions he transferred to the 12th Rifles.

On orders issued by 19th Division at 2:15 am on 16 April, the remnants of the brigade commenced a withdrawal covered by fire from four machine gun outposts, to a position about Clydesdale Camp and were placed in reserve. The brigade headquarters was located near the crossroads at La Clytte, firstly in Fairy House and later at Scherpenberg. The withdrawal was carried out successfully, but the 12th Rifles suffered from enemy shelling, losing ten men killed, 15 wounded and one missing. Among the dead were Lance Corporal Henry Murray, from Liscard, Cheshire, and Private Archibald Connolly from Banbridge, County Down.

The Germans were now carrying out what was known as area bombardments, concentrating all their available artillery on one half square mile of territory for half an hour and then switching the batteries to another. This was an extraordinary noxious and demoralising experience, depriving men of sleep or rest and forcing them to change position frequently. The re-supply of ammunition and rations is often disturbed as a quiet location suddenly becomes the centre of a raging inferno.

Elsewhere on the battlefield the village of Wytschaete had fallen to the enemy, only to be retaken by a superb counter-attack by the 26th (Highland) Brigade of 9th (Scottish) Division. Unfortunately it could not be held due to its exposed position and the line was withdrawn to the former British trenches of 1917. Passchendaele and Poelcappelle were also lost, as was Bailleul. The Germans had advanced elsewhere and in one village, Westoutre, the villagers had to abandon their homes under enemy shell fire.

On a brighter note the French were sending help. Their forces hurried north and the vanguard had already arrived on the right flank of the 9th Division. Their field artillery, each gun towed by a lorry also carrying the detachment, was in position along the hills of the Scherpenberg, Mont Rouge and Mont Vidaigne. When Cyril Falls wrote "Black as was the night, there was, if as yet no faintest light of dawn, the paler grey on the horizon which is its herald ..."

It was not only poetic, but accurate. The brigade received further orders at 8:15 pm on 17 April. Such were its losses, its strength was approximately 400 rifles, it was to form a composite battalion and report to Major Baines of the 2/5th Sherwood Foresters, at or before 4:00 am the following day. Colonel Kelly formed the 1st and 9th (NIH) Irish Fusiliers together, adding a Lewis gun detachment from the 12th Rifles and under his command proceeded with his orders. They moved to Kemmel Hill and here stopped at the foot of the northern slope, where they remained for most of the day. During this time they came under heavy shell fire, suffering about 70 casualties. Among the dead was Captain Charles Despard, DSO, MC, from the 6th (Inniskilling) Dragoons and on attachment to the 9th (NIH) Irish Fusiliers. He was 37 years old and came from Malone Park, Belfast; he has no known grave. Despard was the last remaining captain with the battalion. At 8:30 pm Colonel Kelly received orders from the 19th Division to withdraw, the French having taken over the Kemmel defences.

The 108 Brigade then moved by march route to Hospital Farm and Siege Camp, located between Poperinghe and Elverdinghe, where they rejoined the 36th Division at 5:30 am, on 19 April. For the second time in a month the Brigade had been cut to pieces. The 12th Rifles had suffered approximately 1,500 casualties. Considered to have been practically destroyed in the March battle, it had within ten days entered another battle and proved it still had fighting quality. This is even more remarkable when the youth and inexperience of the rank and file are taken into consideration. Again the IX Corps Commander sent a message to the troops under his command;:

> The C. in C. has just been at Corps HQ. He would have liked to see all ranks now fighting on the 9th Corps front, and tell each one of them of his personal appreciation of the magnificent fight they have made and are making. He would like to shake hands with each individual and thank him for what he has done. He has no time for this, but has asked me to give everybody this message.

What the survivors thought of the corps commander's message is not recorded. To continue with the history of the division we must go back in time. When 108 Brigade left to fight alongside the 9th Division on 10 March, the remainder of the division had its front line east of Poelcappelle, with its headquarters on the Canal Bank. It was on this day that Field Marshal Haig decided to withdraw the II Corps to its Battle Zone, which was to all intents and purposes the old British front line of 1917. The right flank of the division was situated just in front of the village Wieltje, well familiar to those who had fought here the previous year. There was an outpost line maintained along the Steenebeek.

This withdrawal was absolutely essential and had to be performed with some haste. By 11 April the Germans were approaching the Forest of Nieppe, and Passchendaele with Poelcappelle now created a salient equal to if not greater than Ypres. The heavy artillery was to retire first, carrying with them as much ammunition as possible. That which they had to leave behind was tipped into waterlogged shell holes. There was an extensive programme of demolition carried out by the Royal Engineers, with every dug-out or pill-box destroyed by explosives at the last possible moment. Craters were blown at important road junctions, and light railways, laid at such a considerable cost in lives and effort, were torn up or otherwise demolished. On the division's front most of the demolition was carried out by the 122nd Field Company, assisted by parties of infantry and under the command of Major W. Smyth, well known for his exemplary behaviour during the March battles while acting as an attaché to the divisional staff. Under Smyth's direction the field company dammed the Steenebek in an attempt to make it a more formidable obstacle and began the construction of a new line behind it. The 150th Field Company prepared ten bridges across the Ypres Canal for demolition, but by a narrow margin this act was averted.

On the night of 11 April the withdrawal of the heavy artillery began. Three days later they were in position to cover the battle zone. The field artillery also moved back, but left a number of guns in position to fire during the hours of darkness to deceive the enemy. On the night of 15 April, with the rear positions now complete the remaining battalions manning the outposts withdrew, firing the demolitions as they retired. The British Army was now abandoning ground it had previously won with much blood and sacrifice over several months.

The Belgian Army was extending its front and on the night of 17 April, the 4th Belgian Division relieved the 30th Division on the left flank of the 36th Division. On issue of Brigade Order No.232 the Belgians also took over the position held by the 2nd Rifles of 107 Brigade, this relief being completed by 1:00 am on the morning of 18 April. At 11:00 am, a patrol from the 1st Rifles captured two runners belonging to the German 458th Infantry Regiment. The cost to the Rifles for this prize was three other ranks killed and six wounded.[24] Information gathering was an expensive business. The following week passed relatively quietly, the infantry showing a degree of aggression in their patrolling and several prisoners were taken, but always at a cost.

Divisional headquarters was withdrawn from the Canal Bank to Border Camp, located in woodlands north of the Vlamertinghe to Poperinghe Road. For a couple of days the Steenebeek became the line of resistance, with outposts situated on the eastern bank. However, Kemmel had fallen and the Germans were attacking north of it and General Plumer ordered a further withdrawal. The new line of resistance was to be the Ypres Canal although this was never a place of battle; an outpost line some 2,000 yards to the east of it was the main area of contention. Not that there was much of this. The German troops to the immediate front remained unaggressive. They had suffered a heavy defeat from the Belgians further to the north a few days before and the Lys Battle had now died down. The lines to the rear were greatly improved and British dispositions altered to provide a greater strength in the event of any attack.

This second withdrawal of the division was evidently anticipated by the enemy who followed up closely. An officer and two men of the 458th Infantry Regiment of 31st *Landwehr* Division were taken prisoner when they came forward a little too far.

The Germans took possession of Juliet Farm, Canopus Trench and a pillbox on the night of 27 April, all without meeting any resistance, despite 107 Brigade having responsibility for the defence in this area. It appeared this incursion occurred as the 1st and 2nd Rifles were involved in carrying out a relief and 15th Rifles occupied the Canal defences. By 6:00 am all moves had been completed and 1st Rifles were re-established in Canopus Trench and the pillbox had been retaken together with a machine gun and five prisoners.

---

24   This claim with regard to 1st Royal Irish Rifle casualties, originating from a letter by an unnamed officer, is not substantiated by either the battalion war diary or the recent (2002) regimental history by James Taylor.

14

First Battle of Kemmel

The principal function of a wartime navy is command of the seas to ensure freedom of passage whilst denying the same to the enemy. In order to have this superiority it is necessary to remove such obstacles that stand in the way. One such obstacle to the Royal Navy during the Great War was the German High Seas Fleet. If destruction was not possible, then 'forced inactivity' would do just as well; the Battle of Jutland, fought on St. George's Day, 31 May 1916, was instrumental in the latter. Never again were major units of either Navy to meet in battle on the high seas. However, there remained a severe thorn in the side of Britain and that was attacks by German U-boats operating from the Belgian coast. On 22 April the British launched operation Zo, more familiarly known as the Zeebrugge Raid, in which a force of ship and men attacked the port in order to block the egress of U-boats. Argument continues to this day as regards its success, or not.

On land, the first tank versus tank action, as opposed to the first tanks in action, was fought at Villers-Bretonneux on 24 April 1918. While the Germans only ever built 21 A7V tanks in the course of the entire war, they used 14 of them in this action. They were opposed by three British tanks, two female and one male Mk IVs, the former armed with machine guns, the latter with two 6-pounder guns. In the ensuing melee all three British tanks were knocked out, as was one of the A7Vs, while two others were forced to retire due to the arrival of seven British Whippet tanks.

On 2 April the 1st Rifles received a reinforcement draft of four officer and 160 other ranks from the 10th and 14th Rifles. One of these was Second Lieutenant Frederic Homer Lewis, aged 24 years, from the Shore Road, Belfast. Just over three weeks later he was dead. The battalion moved into the Pilkem trenches on 22 April to relieve the 15th Rifles and suffered casualties soon after. The Reverend W.H. Hutchinson, the Presbyterian chaplain to the battalion wrote to the lieutenant's father:

> It is with profound sorrow that I write to acquaint you with the death of your son, Second Lieutenant F.H. Lewis, which occurred yesterday from enemy shell fire. Since your son came to this battalion he endeared himself to his fellow officers as anyone ever did. His loss is deplored and we grieve with you for one who was the truest of comrades, the bravest of soldiers, and the best and most charming of men. I know that any words of mine must seem weak to assuage a grief so deep as yours, yet if the thought that in his life and death he revealed a spiritual kinship to One who laid down His life for the sins of men; that he offered his life upon the altar of sacrifice for righteousness and humanity; that he did not fall or shame his kith and country. If the sympathy of officers and men – if they have any comfort – we offer them.

Captain Archibald Taylor observed:

> With the greatest regret I have to render to you on behalf of Lieutenant Colonel Hunt, DSO, and my brother officers our sympathy to the sad news I have to convey. Your son was killed on

30 April by shell fire when on outpost duty in the front line. He so recently being appointed to this battalion, rather few of us really know him, but that he did at his post proved he did all a man could do when his back is to the wall.[1]

On 29 April the Germans launched an attack from the south of Meteren to Voormezeele against the French Detachment des Armees du Nord and the British Second Army. Everywhere it was completely and bloodily repulsed, much to the surprise of the enemy. This attack marked the failure of the German northern offensive. The tenacity of the troops on the flanks, such as the 55th Division on the right and the 9th Division on the left, had confined and narrowed the thrust. The almost straight line of hills, Kemmel, the Scherpenberg, Mont Rouge, Mont Vidaigne, Mont Nor, Mont Kokereele, Mont des Cats and Cassel, had proved to be an impassable barrier in the later stages of the battle. Only Kemmel fell, the remainder were well defended by French artillery that poured death and destruction on the enemy below. A short time earlier General Ludendorff had attacked Amiens, but had been pushed back by determined counter-attacks and by the timely capture of Villers-Bretonneux by the Australian Corps.

There were further German offensives and more ground was gained by them, most notably close to Rheims where they were able to cut the main Eastern Railway and came close to Paris at Chateau-Thierry. However, there were the death throes of the Imperial German Army and the end was drawing closer.

The following six weeks were relatively quiet for the division, with the exception of a dug-out close to Juliet Farm. Around this position, a former signal testing point for overhead wires, there was near constant bombing and raiding. In these exchanges the Germans usually came off the worst, the troops appeared to be of lower quality and were not that adept at hand to hand fighting. In seven different actions during the month of May 14 German prisoners were taken. So indeterminate were the two lines that on one evening a German supply wagon loaded with rations drove into a divisional outpost and was captured intact. The quality of the food was barely edible.

Across the entire British front the situation had become very serious, so much so that Field Marshal Haig issued an Order of the Day, which has since entered the tradition of the British Army:

To all ranks of the British Forces in France:

> Three weeks ago today the Enemy began his terrific attacks against us on a 50-mile front. His objects are to separate us from the French, to take the Channel ports and destroy the British Army.
>
> In spite of throwing already 106 divisions unto the battle and enduring the most reckless sacrifice of human life, he has yet made little progress towards his goals.
>
> We owe this to the determined fighting and self-sacrifice of our troops. Words fail me to express the admiration which I feel for the splendid resistance offered by all ranks of our Army under the most trying circumstances.
>
> Many amongst us now are tired. To those I would say that victory will belong to the side which holds out longest. The French Army is moving rapidly and in great force to our support.
>
> There is no other course open to us but to fight it out! Every position must be held to the last man: there must be no retirement. With our backs to the wall, and believing in the justice of our cause, each one of us must fight on to the end. The safely of our homes and the freedom of mankind alike depend on the conduct of each one of us at this critical moment.

---

1   *Belfast News Letter* 8 May 1918 and Taylor, *The 1st Royal Irish Rifles in the Great War*.

Whilst there may have been a feeling within the rank and file that the Germans were almost finished and it was simply a matter of sticking it out, there was still some hard fighting to do. Early in May the divisional artillery, in conjunction with all other artillery units, received a number of Indian personnel for employment in the Divisional Ammunition Column. The former members of the column were then sent for training as artillerymen. The shortage of men was telling in all units and on all fronts.

On 6 May General Nugent was relieved of his command and posted to India where he assumed command of the Meerut Division, a post he held until his retirement in 1920. Nugent was one of only two original New Army commanders still in France and policy was that these men should be replaced by younger officers. Nugent's replacement was Major General Coffin, VC, ten years his junior.

From Dragon Camp, Ypres, General Nugent he wrote to his commanding officers within the division:

> As I cannot come round and see all the Units of the Division to wish them good-bye, I must say what I can on paper. I want you to tell them how much I appreciate the splendid work they have done during the two and a half years that I have had the honour and pleasure of commanding the Division. They have never failed to reach a high standard of performance. They have shown at all times a high sense of duty and conscientious thoroughness in the discharge of it. I know they will do their duty as thoroughly in the future as they have done in the past. I should like to have had the opportunity to thank all your Officers personally for their work and to have told them how I appreciate it but I can only ask you to do it for me. I wish you all good luck in the future. I know you and your men will not fail.

The division's new commander was Major General Clifford Coffin VC. Born in Blackheath, London, in 1870, the son of Lieutenant General Sir Isaac Campbell Coffin, he had been educated at Haileybury College and the Royal Military College at Woolwich. Coffin had served in the South African War and had been awarded the South African Medals for 1901 and 1902 and clasps for Paardeberg, Dreifontein, Relief of Kimberley and Transvaal when serving with the Royal Engineers; he had also been mentioned in despatches. As a brigadier general commanding the 25th Infantry Brigade he was awarded the Victoria Cross for his actions during Third Ypres:

> … when his command was held up in attack owing to heavy machine gun and rifle fire, Brigadier-General Coffin went forward and made an inspection of his front posts. Although under the heaviest fire from both machine guns and rifles and in full view of the enemy, he showed an utter disregard of personal danger, walking quietly from shell-hole to shell-hole giving advice and cheering his men by his presence. His gallant conduct had the greatest effect on all ranks and it was largely owing to his personal courage and example that the shell-hole line was held.

Coffin was presented with his Victoria Cross on 2 January 1918 by George V at Buckingham Palace; His Majesty presented General Haig with his Field Marshal's baton the same day.

William McIlveen, a clerk in the Iron and Steel Depot of Harland and Wolff, had enlisted on the day war was declared and first served in the 14th Rifles. He was an exceptional soldier and on being promoted to Company Sergeant Major with the 15th Rifles had already been awarded the Distinguished Conduct Medal and Bar. Courage and efficiency seemed to be a family trait, his brother Jack had enlisted in 1915 and by the time he was commissioned as a Second Lieutenant in late 1918, had been awarded the Military Medal and Medalle Militaire. On 6 May, his 26th

Birthday, CSM McIlveen was shot and killed by a single bullet from a German sniper. He is buried in Canada Farm Cemetery.[2]

By May 1918, General Gough had changed his opinion of the Ulster Division since August the previous year when both he and Haig had sought scapegoats for the failure at Langemarck. The local papers published the following:

> General Sir Hubert Gough, KCB, KCVO, in a letter to the lord Mayor of Belfast (Alderman James Johnston JP) pays a striking tribute to the work of the Ulster Division during the retreat from the neighbourhood of St. Quentin. Sir Hubert refers 'to the very gallant conduct of the Division in stemming the tide of the immense German attack that was launched against them on 21 March and subsequent dates. The fighting of the Ulster Division, as indeed of all the divisions in the Fifth Army against the greatest odds hurled on any body of troops throughout this great war, was magnificent. The main features of the situation to which the whole Fifth Army, including the Ulster Division, was exposed are known to everyone, I believe, and give some idea of what those odds were, namely fourteen infantry divisions against forty German divisions on the 21st, reinforced by some eight to ten more divisions during the subsequent two days. I cannot speak too highly of the splendid calmness and doggedness with which my fellow-countrymen met and fought this storm, and though many laid down their lives, their splendid tenacity saved the British Empire and the kingdom of France by permitting the arrival of reserves. The corps commander has penned an order thanking all ranks of the Division for the fighting spirit they have displayed and reminding them that further deeds of gallantry will be required of them in the coming months.

As part of a series of changes within the Army as a whole, Brigadier Griffith of 108 Brigade was relieved on 21 May 1918, and posted to command the 20th Training Reserve Brigade in the UK, later renamed to the 1st Training Brigade of the Machine Gun Corps, who trained recruits for that corps.[3] His replacement was Brigadier General E. Vaughan, DSO. Vaughan had begun his military career with the Manchester Regiment in November 1888 and had served with their 1st Battalion in the opening stages of the War in South Africa. During the course of the campaign he was appointed as Adjutant of the 2nd Johannesburg Mounted Rifles and was awarded the brevet of major for distinguished service, was wounded on two occasions and mentioned in despatches on an equal number of occasions.

In the 107 Brigade General Withycombe was replaced by Brigadier General E.I. de S. Thorpe, DSO. Apart from an absence of three months, March to June 1917, when command devolved to Brigadier General F.J.M. Rowley, former Middlesex Regiment and later commander of 56 and 138 Brigades, Withycombe had led the 107 Brigade from October 1915 to date. Edward Ivan de Sausmarez Thorpe, had been born in 1872 at Madras, India, he had attended Sandhurst and been commissioned into the Bedfordshire Regiment as a second lieutenant. He had taken part in the Niger Expedition in 1879 and on promotion to major had command the 1st Battalion Bedfordshire Regiment in 1914, being further promoted to lieutenant colonel the following year.

The first days of June came as a most welcome relief. The defence of the front line was handed back to the 12th Belgian Division and the 36th moved to a comfortable wooded area between Poperinghe and Proven, being designated as being part of the II Corps Reserve. Acting in this roll it was ready, if necessary, to support the right flank of the Belgian Army. From the division, one brigade, two field companies and two companies of the pioneers were placed at the disposal of the

---

2   Somme Archive 1994/522.
3   Brigade War Diary; Information provided by Bedfordshire Regiment Museum.

II Corps for work on the rear defences. It was rumoured that the belts of barbed wire stretched unbroken from Ypres to Calais. Between Ypres and Poperinghe, a distance of six miles, there were no less than four well-defended lines; the Brielen defences and the Green, Yellow and Blue Lines. Behind Poperinghe were more works. The troops assigned to work on these defences were relieved periodically, the other units carrying out training. Within the divisional artillery there was one section per battery in positions prepared for defence of the Blue Line, in the event of another major German attack, which still seemed probable.

With the exception of those few cold days at Christmas resting in the snow, this was the first the time the men of the division had the opportunity to properly relax. The new recruits, mostly in their late teens, grew strong under the influence of good food, exercise and life in the open under pleasant conditions. For many this was the only time in their lives that they enjoyed four meals a day. Their physical fitness increased swiftly under steady training and there was ample sport in the form of football, cricket, running and boxing, with the Belgians taking part on many occasions and often winning.

Cyril Falls, in his history of the Ulster Division, states that 'men recovered quickly from its effect' when referring to the influenza pandemic that swept not only the battlefields, but the entire globe in 1918. The divisional death toll, excluding supporting units, was 91 Rifles, 20 Inniskillings and 33 Irish Fusiliers. These deaths were not all the result of sickness, in the 15th Rifles Private George Forrester was killed on 15 June. He had been a former carpenter and a signatory to the Ulster Covenant.[4] In the late afternoon of 21 June 1918, Captain M.H. Browne MC of the 108th Trench Mortar Battery, died during a training exercise at 22 Corps School. He was in the process of conducting anti-aircraft practice on the range with live ammunition and had fired three rounds successfully when the fourth exploded in the barrel of the weapon. He was killed instantly, while three other men subsequently died of their wounds. Maximilian Herbert Browne was born in 1896 and was the son of George Burrowes Browne of Lisnamaul, Ormeau Road, Belfast. He had been educated at RBAI and was a former member of Queen's University OTC.[5] As the men attending this class came from other units it has proved impossible to trace if all who died were from the division. In the 1st Inniskillings six men died on 2 June due to enemy shelling. This makes 11 deaths to either accident or enemy action, far short of the 144 listed on the Commonwealth War Graves website at the time of writing.

There were rumours that some German divisions had been rendered almost incapable of taking the field. Post-war research showed that the sickness struck the German and Austrian troops before the Allies. As the total number of deaths worldwide was between 20,000000 and 40,000000 people this rumour is quite believable. Half of the deaths suffered by American troops in France were due to influenza.

On 1 July the Divisional Horse Show was held at Proven, in what was described as beautiful weather and surroundings. Sadly for the division the neighbouring Belgian Cavalry Division, according to Falls 'descended like wolves on the fold, and took almost all the prizes in the jumping events.

At home in Ulster a memorial screen that had been placed in the grounds of the City Hall, in Belfast had attracted a large number of visitors. Many had laid wreaths and among them was one from Lisburn No. 6 District, L.O.L., while a second from No2 Ballymacarrett Women's Orange Lodge carried the inscription, "In memory of the Ulster Division in the honour and glory of God

---

4   The Living History of East Antrim, Community Support and Development Partnership, *We Will Remember Them*.

5   From the R.B.A.I. Archives, he is buried in Esquelbecq Military Cemetery, Nord, France, grave III.A.3. Number of dead 'other ranks' is confirmed as three by the brigade war diary.

Private Joseph Totten had enlisted in the11th Royal Irish Rifles in May 1915 and was wounded twice during his war service. On 8 August 1917 he was shot in the face, while on 27 July 1918 he received further gunshot wounds to his face, right arm and thigh. It was most likely on this latter occasion that a bullet lodged in his wallet, ripping the photograph of his brother James that was inside.

The photograph of James Totten, ripped by a bullet. The Totten and Orr families were linked by marriage and contributed a fair number of men to the war. Herbert Totten from Ballydolly, Stoneyford, County Antrim, had enlisted in the 11th Rifles on 15 June 1915, only to be discharged on 26 October following when it was discovered he was under age. Lieutenant Richard John Orr from Ballyrenan, Downpatrick, County Down, had served with the 177th Overseas Battalion (Simco Forrsters) of the Canadian Expeditionary Force, he had transferred to the Royal Flying Corps and was killed in action on 9 August 1918. Lieutenant William James Orr, also from Ballyrenan, enlisted in December 1915 and served with the 60th Siege Battery of the Royal Garrison Artillery, transferring to the Supplementary Reserve in March 1919 and relinquishing his commission on 1 April 1920. Such service was not rare among Ulster families during the Great War and earlier.

Memorial to the 14th Royal Irish Rifles in Belfast City Hall. (Author's photograph)

and those brave and dear ones who have fallen for King and Country at the Battle of the Somme, 1916, and since then." A meeting had been held in the Central Hall of the Belfast Technical Institute to honour the memory of Private William McFadzean, VC and those former pupils who had made the supreme sacrifice. The headmaster, Mr W.J. McCracken, stated that since the declaration of war 150 former pupils had joined His Majesty's forces and of these one had been awarded the Victoria Cross, while four others had earned the Military Cross and 24 had been killed.

After being defeated at Kemmel the French had made a good defence at Locre, considered to be the vital gateway to the valley between the Scherpenberg and Mont Rouge, and were now being relieved by British troops along the line of hills. After spending three days around Cassel in reserve to the French XVI Corps, the division relieved the 41st French Division on the northern outskirts of Bailleul. General Coffin established his divisional headquarters at Terdeghem, with an emergency command post on the Mont des Cats at 8:00 pm on 7 July. General Coffin took command of the sector at 3:00 am the following morning. Apart from desultory shelling there was little to report in the divisional war diary, apart from 11 July when a Portuguese prisoner having escaped from the Germans entered the divisional lines.[6]

---

6   Germany declared war on Portugal on 9 March 1916. Portuguese troops subsequently saw action in France

The new divisional sector was at the north-west corner of the great salient created by the Lys offensive. The divisional front ran from Fontaine-houck, a hamlet north-east of Meteren, which was still in German hands, to the high ground south of the Croix de Poperinghe, about a mile and a half north of Bailleul. From the line of hills the division had a good view of the German positions and all daylight movement and gun flashes could be noted for future reference. The many abandoned farms provided the men with fresh potatoes and green peas, which could be picked quite close to their positions, after the time spent at Ypres it was a most agreeable location.

There was a limited amount of shelling as the German batteries were easily observed and counter-battery fire was most effective. Instead the Germans resorted to night bombing from aircraft. The most common aircraft used was the Friedrichshafen G.IIIa. Fitted with two Mercedes engines and with a crew of three it could carry a bomb load of 2,200 pounds. Casualties from these raids were not that heavy, but should have been lower. Unfortunately the men were very careless when it came to following hedges to hide their tracks and confining most of their movement to the hours of darkness. While both the French and Germans had learnt this lesson to their cost, the British soldier never did.

Meteren was captured by the 9th Division on 19 July, the 36th Divisional Artillery providing supporting fire.

At 1:00 am, on 22 July a raid was launched against Shoddy Farm by elements of the 9th (NIH) Irish Fusiliers. A reconnaissance had been carried out two nights previously by Lieutenant Colonel Forde Captain Murphy of B Company, which had lasted for seven hours and was successful in locating the enemy positions and estimating the strength as approximately 70 men and five machine guns. Numbers involved were three platoons from B Company, commanded by second Lieutenants Reynolds, Leahy and Ratcliffe and one platoon from D Company. The purpose of the raid was to identify the defenders, believed to be a unit of the 186 Infantry Regiment, which was part of the 112 Infantry Brigade, kill the defenders and locate further enemy positions. There were three objectives, a small post some 100 yards north of Shoddy Farm, the Farm itself, which had been converted into a strongpoint including the cellars and a position 100 yards south known as Soot Farm. As midnight approached the leading platoon of A Company left the trenches and moved to secure the rendezvous point. A short time later the other platoons followed. The covering barrage was supplied by the four batteries, Lieutenant Colonel Claud Potter's 153 Brigade of the divisional artillery. The guns opened fire at 1:00 am and Captain Murphy led the raiders forward over open ground to the enemy wire. Here Second Lieutenant Leahy successfully cut the required gap as fire from the Lewis guns kept the Germans below their parapet. The raiders poured into the trench moving quickly north and south, clearing the way with bombs and rifle fire. Two German light machine guns were captured; one personally by Captain Murphy who killed the two gunners with his revolver. When the Germans managed to launch a distress flare the order was given for the raiders to withdraw. On crossing no man's land they were hit by machine gun and artillery fire, losing men, including the man carrying one of the captured machine guns. Second Lieutenant F.J. Elliott McFarland, MC, 9th Irish Fusiliers, was a former pupil of Belfast Royal Academy. His father was serving as a lieutenant colonel in the RAMC, while a brother, the Reverend L.W. McFarland had been awarded the Military Cross when serving in the Army Chaplain's Department. Initially reported as missing, it was later determined that he was killed during this raid.[7]

The 2nd Rifles had established their headquarters at Kopje Farm on 23 July, with two companies deployed forward, the right company around Haute Porte Farm, the left around Salvo Farm, the counter-attack company was around Risky Farm, while the reserve company was at Runaway

---

and Africa.
7   See Metcalf, Nick, *Blacker's Boys* (2012) for a full account of this raid.

Farm. On 29 July a patrol was sent out from Haute Porte Farm to ascertain the identity of the enemy units opposite the battalion. A force of four other ranks, led by Lieutenant Walkington, assisted by Second Lieutenant Stewart left at 7:00 pm. Dolway Walkington, from Belfast, had been commissioned in September 1914 and had suffered injuries and sickness throughout most of his service. However, this would not be a bar to him winning the Military Cross. James Noel Greer Stewart also came from Belfast and had previously served as a stoker aboard HMS *Vivid*. He had then served as a private in the North Irish Horse and later with the Royal Flying Corps. He joined the battalion as a second lieutenant in October 1917. Like Walkington, he too would earn the Military Cross. The patrol had crossed some 500 yards of open ground when they came across a farmhouse and discovered it was held by a squad of 12 enemy soldiers. The patrol rushed the position and in the ensuing melee four of the Germans were killed, two wounded and four taken prisoner, with two others escaping. Taking the time to bomb a small dug-out, the patrol then withdrew, coming under fire from a German machine gun alerted by the bombing. .

As the patrol crossed no man's land a burst of enemy fire came very close and as the men took cover two of the prisoners attempted to escape, but were quickly shot as they ran away. The remaining prisoners were either killed or wounded during further bursts of enemy machine gun fire. Two of the Germans who were wounded and survived were found to belong to the 10th Company, 3rd Battalion, 88th Infantry Regiment of the 56th Division. The patrol suffered no casualties. This action had been observed from the German lines and also where the patrol returned to. The following day at 4:00 pm, 'Haute Porte Farm' was hit by a heavy barrage of enemy artillery that lasted for an hour. Among the casualties was Lieutenant Edwin Morrow, from Portrush, County Antrim, who lost the sight of an eye. Among the dead were Private William Smyth, Private Stanley Collins, a 19 year old from Ashford in Kent, Sergeant Robert Gibson from Banbridge, Down, Private David McIlroy, from Belfast and Private Samuel Clarke from Sandy Row, Belfast. It would appear that the German 56th Division knew how to hold a grudge.

A very wet day was recorded in the war diary. Such were the conditions that the 1st Inniskillings moved into the line to relieve the 2nd Battalion on 27 July. During the change over the enemy delivered a heavy barrage beginning at 11:30 pm, causing five deaths and numerous wounded, this despite poor visibility.

A reconnaissance patrol, led by Lieutenant Hughes left the lines at 6:00 pm on 1 August and captured four enemy soldiers belong to the 118th Infantry Regiment. Constant patrolling was a necessity to dominate the various sectors of the battlefield and to maintain fresh intelligence on whom or what was occupying the enemy trenches.

George V visited the divisional area on 6 August and at Oxelaere, a small village on the slopes of Cassel Hill, he presented Lieutenant Knox of 150th Field Company RE with the Victoria Cross. This was in recognition of his actions the previous March.

The division was now part of British Second Army and as such did not take part in the early counter-offensives. The first of these had been the Battle of Tardenois that had begun on 18 July. Here the salient created by the German advance to Chateau-Thierry had been retaken, with the enemy pushed back, many prisoners taken and much equipment seized. This battle had been fought by mostly French troops, supported by four British divisions. The second blow was delivered on 8 August when the Fourth British and First French Armies began an advance down the Amiens to Roye Road. Reports to the various headquarters told of a weakening of enemy resistance and what appeared to be a breakdown in discipline. On 21 August the British Third Army and later the First Army, launched more attacks across the old Somme battlefield and again approached the Hindenburg Line.

Within the divisional area there had been various local offensives planned to recapture what little good ground the German still held. As previously mentioned the 9th Division had taken

Meteren and at the end of July the 1st Australian Division had captured Merris. On 18 August the 9th Division had gone on to take the Hoegenacker Ridge, south-east of Meteren.

It was now the turn of the 36th Division to improve its position. The first move was made on 22 August, when the 15th Rifles, on the right flank, advanced for a quarter of a mile on a front of half a mile. In the ensuing action Mural Farm and Wirral Farm were taken along with 22 prisoners and two machine guns. This attack had been all the more successful due to a ruse using the Livens Projector. The demoralising effect of this weapon had been effectively seen in the past and the Germans were very familiar with it. However, should it have been used in its conventional role, to deliver gas, it would also have made the ground untenable for the attacking British troops. Therefore the drums launched against the enemy positions were filled with a liquid that had the smell of gas, but without the effects. Many of the enemy fled the position, while others were found wearing their respirators and therefore being at an immediate disadvantage.

The early part of the month saw a series of fierce raids as the division attempted to identify the enemy on the far side of the wire. On the night of 11 August a patrol from the 9th (NIH) Irish Fusiliers consisting of two officers and 32 other ranks, moved across no man's land towards the now familiar position known as Shoddy Farm. As the patrol neared the Farm bombs were thrown from it and a strong party of enemy charged the patrol from the rear. The Irish Fusiliers fired on this group and then counter-charged with fixed bayonets. Casualties were inflicted on the enemy, but at a cost of two men killed, two wounded and one missing believed a prisoner. The two men killed were Privates William Brown and Andrew Pepper, both from Bloomfield in Belfast. Before the War William Brown had been an Assistant Librarian in the Central Library, Belfast. Newspaper reports have indicated that Private Brown was mortally wounded, dying a short time later.

On the left flank of the division an attack was prepared on 24 August against enemy positions on the Haagedoorne to Dranoutre Road, on a frontage of approximately a mile. This would be by 108 Brigade and the units involved were the 1st and 9th (NIH) Irish Fusiliers. The previous evening the Fusiliers had moved from their support position on Mont Noir and both it and the 1st Battalion were in position by 3:00 am. Zero was at 7:00 am and the supporting artillery opened up a terrific barrage against the German rear positions, while the Trench Mortars fired on selected targets. At zero plus two minutes the attacking troops were clear of the front line and going forward in a steady manner. At 7:30 am a heavy enemy barrage fell on the Brigade front line and lasted for about 45 minutes. On reaching their objectives the Fusiliers quickly consolidated their line. The attack was a success and came as a complete surprise to the enemy, many being killed before they could emerge from their dug-outs. Those machine gunners who opted to fight it out had to be killed as few choose to surrender. The strongest German positions were found between Soot Farm and La Bourse Farm. Here the enemy suffered heavy casualties and those who attempted to withdraw were shot down by rifle and Lewis gun fire. Fifty-seven prisoners and 11 machine guns were captured. While the afternoon passed quietly there was a strong artillery barrage at 7:05 pm, quickly followed by a smoke screen laid between Bailleul and the Brigade lines. An assault group of some 350 men was spotted assembling at the Asylum on the Bailleul to St. Jans Cappel Road and SOS rockets brought down a protective barrage. The attack spread to the left and the enemy advanced in two waves, but were broken up after only approaching about 40 yards by concentrated Lewis gun, artillery and fire from the Vickers machine guns.

The British lines were now only 1,000 yards from Bailleul and the town defences had been pierced in several places. However, there was to be no fight for possession of the town, as using skilful leadership and superb discipline the enemy withdrew during the hours of darkness a short time later.

15

Advance in Flanders

During the night of 26 August 1918, near Mametz, Captain James Henry Fletcher, DSO, MC, serving with the 36th Field Ambulance, earned a Bar to his DSO. With the assistance of another officer, he crawled out into no man's land, under heavy enemy machine gun fire and dragged to shelter two wounded stretcher bearers. Having dressed their wounds, Fletcher then crawled back for assistance and organised two squads of stretcher bearers to bring the men to safety. While doing this he discovered two more wounded men and also brought them in. Captain Fletcher, who was acting as a lieutenant colonel at the time, came from Killeshandra in County Cavan. It should be noted that despite its number this Field Ambulance did not serve with the Ulster Division.

On 30 August 1918, the headquarters of the 2nd Inniskillings was located at Shoddy Farm north of Bailleul. The first day of September was a balmy day and Lieutenant Colonel Knox, 11th Inniskillings, was talking to some of his staff when the area came under shellfire. Splinters from the blast severely wounded Knox and the Brigade Major RA, Major H.F. Grant Suttie, DSO, MC. The same blast mortally wounded the Intelligence Officer of 109 Brigade, Second Lieutenant J.J. Fox, a 30 year old from Dublin. James Joseph Fox died of his wounds the following day; he had only been married the previous December. A further tragedy for the brigade was when the Divisional Train, located close to St Jans Cappel, was bombed by enemy aircraft. The detonation of a single bomb killed five men, wounded a further nine and killed no less than 50 valuable horses, besides injuring some 20 more. To the men the death and injury of so many horses was always a most distressing sight in a war filled with distressing sights.

Troops of the division entered Neuve Eglise on 1 September. After dusk 108 Brigade passed through 109 Brigade, which then moved into reserve with divisional headquarters located at Mt Noir. At 3:00 am, the following day, 108 Brigade passed through 109 and all units reported relief completed successfully. There was now greater resistance from the enemy and there was some stiff fighting before Neuve Eglise and the old GHQ line was cleared of the enemy. The advance continued slowly with the Germans having to be winkled from each position. In one attack on 4 September, against what was described as a chemical factory, the 1st Irish Fusiliers suffered several casualties. Private Charles Mclean recalled several years after the event: "There was a chemical factory and our artillery shelled it for about an hour and we went over the top and the Germans were lying everywhere and we only lost about four men. A fellow called Rice and another went to get water and a machine gun got them and then our artillery blasted the machine gun." The battalion after-action report lists Privates H. Rice, M. Masterson, Andrew Little and James Hewitt, killed on 4 September.

On the night of 5 to 6 September 107 Brigade suffered a number of casualties from a sustained German gas attack during their relief of 108 Brigade. This relief was followed by an attack to capture and consolidate a line that included the Douve crossing, Hanbury Support, Boyle's Farm and Crater inclusive. On the right flank of the division the 31st Division was to attack from Douve Crossing to Irish Farm, while on the left flank the 30th Division would hold its ground.

The 2nd Rifles were engaged in an attack near the village of Boeschepe on 6 September and almost on the border between France and Belgium. The objective was the capture of part of the German defensive line. From divisional headquarters Brigade Order No.33 was issued and handed

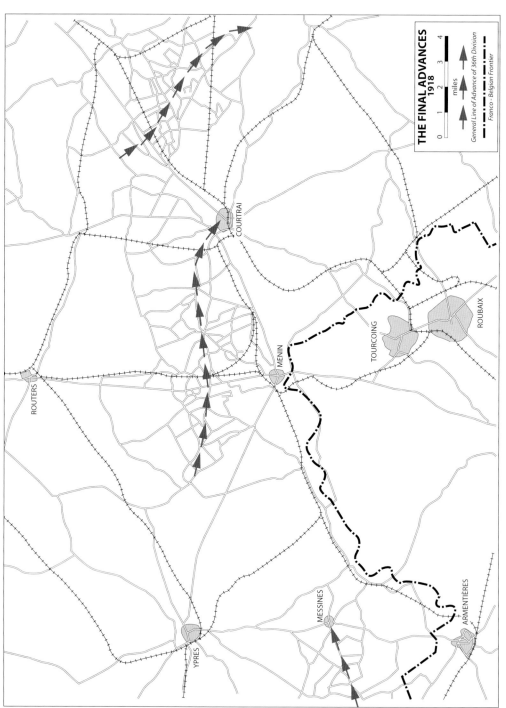

THE FINAL ADVANCES
1918

miles
0 1 2 3 4

General Line of Advance of 36th Division

Franco - Belgian Frontier

COURTRAI

ROUTERS

MENIN

TOURCOING

ROUBAIX

YPRES

MESSINES

ARMENTIÈRES

The Divisional battlefield during the last 100 days.

personally to Lieutenant Colonel Bridcutt of the 2nd Rifles. This directed 107 Brigade to carry out an attack to capture and consolidate the line incorporating the crossing over the Douve at U.7.b.6.3, the road junction at U.7.b.6c.96 and Banbury Support, Boyle's Farm and the Crater at U.1.a.35.1C., inclusive.

At the same time the 31st Division on the right flank was to attack and hold a line from the crossing over the Douve at U.7.b.6.6 through Irish Farm at U.7.d.6.6. The 30th Division on the left flank would not advance. Within the brigade the attack was to be carried out by the 2nd Rifles with one company from the 1st Rifles attached. The order of attack was with three companies in the front line, A, B and C, 2nd Rifles and two acting as reserve, D Company 2nd Rifles and D Company 1st Rifles. The first line was to consolidate the line captured, while the second, support, line was to consolidate the line King Edward Trench from Wulverghem to Messines Road southwards, U.1.c.1.4. to U.1.c.25.5C and then southwards to the Douve River. A strong advance post with Lewis guns was to be established in Gabion Farm at U.1.d.9.1., once consolidation had been achieved D Company of the 2nd Rifles was to rejoin its parent battalion prior to dawn on 7 September. Artillery support was to open fire at Zero, which was 4:00 pm and at Zero plus five minutes was to creep forward at the rate of 100 yards in three minutes. After reaching the objective a stationary protective barrage was to be kept at 250 yards in front of the objective. This supporting fire was to cease at Zero plus 92 minutes. Two companies from the 36th Machine Gun Battalion would also lend support and cooperate with the Artillery. Their S.C.S. lines would search the Douve and Steenebeek Valleys and the valley running north east towards U.2.cent., after the objective was captured.

By 3:30 pm, the troops were in position as follows; in the firing line were A, B and C Companies, while in support the two D Companies were concealed behind bushes on or near the jumping off point. This force consisted mainly of 18 and 19 year olds, command by officers that were no more than a year or two older. Second Lieutenant William Eaton, from Manchester, had been commissioned from the ranks and only the previous November had been before a court martial on a charge of drunkenness. He had been sentenced to be dismissed, but this had been commuted to forfeiture of seniority. He was 22 years old and was believed to have served in one of the Machine Gun Companies.

Lieutenant W.F. 'Fred' Hunter from Belfast was a former University student and member of the OTC. The *Belfast News Letter* of 13 June 1917, reported he had been wounded, most probably at Messines. Lieutenant Visto Clive Young, from Holywood, County Down, was 23 years old and had been commissioned in 1915. A member of C Company, he also had faced a court martial the previous May on a charge of disobedience and leaving his post. He had been sentenced to be cashiered, but this had been commuted to a severe reprimand. Second Lieutenant William MacPherson, from Bangor, County Down, was another graduate from the OTC and had worked for a time in the linen industry. He was commissioned in August 1917 and was renowned as 'hard working and a first class shot'. On this night he was an acting captain in command of B Company.

At the scheduled time the artillery barrage opened and those troops not exactly in their places moved from their concealment to get ready for the barrage lifting. The barrage lifted as per the time-table and the troops moved forward in small worm-like columns picking their way through the undergrowth and uncut wire, moving steadily forward until their objectives were reached. Here battle outposts were pushed forward as near as possible to the standing barrage line, the troops consolidating Hanbury Support Trench. Sergeant Herbert Higgins was a scout and during the action he provided much valuable information from his various reconnaissance patrols. In the latter stages of the action he fell victim to a gas shell, but remained on duty. So different from the Somme, as now the men were trained and had gained the experience necessary for such an advance.

As darkness fell patrols were sent out to make contact with the enemy and they were found holding a length of trench at U.d central. There was also a considerable amount of machine gun fire coming from the direction of The Crater, Mortar Farm and the trench system at T.6b. Second Lieutenant Eaton was killed, while Lieutenant 'Fred' Hunter was wounded while leading his platoon on an assault against an enemy machine gun position. The position was taken, the crew killed and the gun captured. Hunter's wound was serious and would eventually lead to his leaving the army. Lieutenant Young was also wounded, but A Company suffered a large number of deaths, including Private James Kavanagh from Dublin, who was 17, Private George Baldwin from Worcester, who was 18, Lance Corporal Thomas Ferguson from Larne, Antrim, who was 19, Private George Cobourn, aged 19 from Bethnal Green, London and Private J. McCandless from Newtownards, who was 18 years old.[1] James McCandless had worked in the Ulster Print Works in Newtownards prior to enlisting on 26 July 1917 at 17 years of age.

Many of the men wounded were hit in the back and this, not unnaturally, gave the impression that the Rifles were being surrounded. To counteract this D Company, 1st Rifles, was ordered to form a defensive flank between the support and front line and this was carried out very professionally under the command of Captain P.J. Cullen.

On the right flank all objectives were quickly taken, with the exception of Gabion Farm, which took over an hour to secure. This was mainly due to the difficulty in identifying the exact spot, but once this had been done a post was established and handed over on relief. On the left flank Boyle's Farm and The Crater were given as an objective and this was taken. However, on examination of the ground the company commander on the spot decided it would be better to hold the trench system that ran some 30 to 40 yards west of the Farm and Crater. On later examination by Colonel Bridcutt this move was confirmed as the correct thing to do on the grounds that the men had been shot at from the left rear, chiefly from the trenches in T.6.b and that from the new position Boyle's Farm was denied to the enemy. Casualties had been heavy enough for such a minor action. Second Lieutenant Eaton and 18 other ranks had been killed, with three other officers and 148 other ranks wounded. Lieutenant Hunter received the Military Cross, as did Second Lieutenant McPherson, while Sergeant Higgins was awarded the Distinguished Conduct Medal.

In the 109th Field Ambulance the men performed their duty in the usual fashion and Private William Campbell earned an MID for driving his motor ambulance through severe shell fire while removing the wounded from the battlefield near Neuve Eglise.[2]

On the night of 13 September Brigadier Thorpe, commanding 107 Brigade, accompanied by General Brock, was carrying out an inspection of the brigade's posts on Hill 63 and the sentry posts north of it. As the men moved along Winter Trench they approached one such post and were challenged by the sentry. For some reason Brigadier Thorpe did not respond and in keeping with standing orders the sentry opened fire hitting the brigadier in the arm and causing a serious wound that saw part of his elbow being blown away. Brigadier Thorpe was forced to relinquish command as a result of his wound and Lieutenant Colonel Robert Harman MacKenzie, MC, RE, took immediate command of the brigade, until a replacement was found. The replacement was General Brock, who after almost two and a half years of leading the divisional artillery, now made a seamless change to leading the brigade, which he would do until the Armistice. Brigadier Thorpe returned to command his regiment, but not until after the war and for the remainder of his life suffered extreme pain from his wound.

---

1   Another casualty was Private Robert Shaw who, at the time of this writing, has been accepted by the CWGC, for inclusion on the Ploegsteert Memorial, but has yet to have his name inscribed.

2   Certificate issued on 9 February 1919.

Within the divisional artillery General Brock was succeeded as CRA by General Hawkes, DSO. Corlis St. Ledger Gillman Hawkes came from Passage West in County Cork. He had been privately educated prior to enlisting in the Militia, being appointed to the Limerick City Artillery in 1889. Four years later he was with the Royal Field Artillery and saw service in the South African War, gaining the King's Medal with six clasps. He would command the divisional artillery until the Armistice.

Lieutenant Colonel L de V Fitzgerald, of the Irish Fusiliers and now commanding the 2nd Inniskillings was killed at 3:00 pm on 16 September when a shell burst in the doorway of the Officers' Mess. The second-in-command, Major Gordon Miller Forde DSO, MC, was wounded, as was Second Lieutenant E.M. Phillips, the Intelligence Officer. Major Crawford assumed command of the battalion, but was subsequently relieved by Major A.E. Gallagher DSO, a former Royal Munster Fusilier officer, who had previously served with the 7th Royal Fusiliers. It should be noted that Major Forde, DSO, MC, had been awarded a Bar to his MC for his actions at Messines.[3]

The 107 Brigade was located at Mont Des Cats on 18 September and was carrying out training. There was a visit to Brigade Headquarters from the local Mayor and orders had been received to move the following day to Steenvoorde.

Fifth Battle of Ypres 1918

The end of September saw three divisions of the British Army placed under the command of the King of the Belgians, one of which was the 36th Division. It was with some secrecy that the division moved from its location on the Messines Ridge and moved to a new position between the 9th and 29th Divisions in the Ypres Salient. The II Corps attack saw the 29th Division on its right flank and the 9th Division on its left. The left flank of this division rested on the Zonnebeke Road at Mill Cott, with beyond this the 8th Belgian Division. The 36th Division was held in Corps Reserve and had orders to hold in readiness to move forward if necessary to exploit any success gained by the attacking divisions.

On the morning of 28 September the three Divisional Artillery Brigade Groups were located as follows. The 107 was at P Camp Area 28/A.15, the 108 Brigade at Vlamertinghe and the 109th at Dirty Bucket, Area 28/A.30. The 153 Brigade was supporting the 9th Division, while 173 Brigade was in support of the 36th Division, both assisting in the 'creeping barrage' supporting the forthcoming infantry attack.

The Corps artillery opened fire at 2:30 am, with Zero being at 5:30 am. This was a far cry from earlier attacks and the following 'creeping barrage' contained a large number of smoke shells. While resistance from the enemy proved to be light, with the exception of several determined strong-points, the terrain was no easier than at the previous battle at Ypres. Despite the heavy rain the attack was a complete success. The Belgian infantry, not having suffered from preceding defeats and being fresh, attacked with great determination, fighting as they were on their own territory. The Frezenberg Ridge, the obstacle that had thwarted so many assaults, was carried by the 9th Division in just over an hour's fighting. By nightfall the 29th Division had captured Gheluvelt and had advanced to the Menin Road a mile to the east. The Belgians had taken Zonnebeke and had made contact with the 9th Division on the Broodseinde Ridge. Added to this the 9th had also sent one of its brigades to successfully capture the village of Becelaere.

---

3   His brother Lieutenant Kenneth Rowley Forde, 3rd Buffs hailed from Kilcronaghan, County Londonderry and was killed on 24 July 1915.

Men sheltering in a ruined building, note the cartoon drawn on the wall and that a bunker has been constructed in the floor.

With things going so well it was noon before the II Corps ordered the 36th Division forward with the brigades in echelon. The men of 109 Brigade entrained and were carried forward by light railway to Potijze, arriving at 3:00 pm. From there the Brigade marched to the area of the Bellewaarde Lake. At noon the 108 Brigade was ordered east of Ypres and later in the afternoon the 107 Brigade was also sent to Potijze. However, such had been the speed and success of the initial attack that on arrival here they were ordered to remain on board the train and subsequently moved another three miles before darkness fell. By 11:00 pm they were in position at 'Hell Fire Corner'. Divisional headquarters was then established in the old dug-outs of the Ypres Ramparts and was up and running by 2:00 pm.

At 5:00 pm, orders were issued to the 109 Brigade to take up a position between the 9th and 29th Divisions, running from Judas Farm North and Judge Cross Roads. From there they were to prepare to advance at dawn and capture Terhand. Artillery support was to be provided by the 153 Brigade, RFA, which had earlier been under the command of the 9th Division. Given the state of the ground it was 24 hours before the guns were in a position to fire.

The 109 Brigade was to pass through 27 Brigade then in Becelaere, which would then follow up. Within the 109th the attack formation would see the 2nd Inniskillings on the right flank, the 9th Inniskillings on the left and the 1st Inniskillings in support. It had been planned for a dawn assault, but a combination of heavy rain, bad roads over unknown ground and enemy air attacks during the night caused a postponement until 9:30 am.

At 9:30 am, on 29 September, the 109 Brigade advanced to capture the town of Terhand, north of the Menin Road. The order of attack was the 2nd Inniskillings on the right flank, the 9th Inniskillings on the left and the 1st Inniskillings in support. The advance moved quickly across relatively open ground until early afternoon when the 2nd Inniskillings were held up for a while by machine gun fire. The main enemy resistance came from such fire with individual machine gun nests dug in to hedgerows and buildings, each one to be winkled out by combined assaults using bombers covered by fire from the Lewis guns. Due to the state of the roads to the rear artillery support was still not available and it was left to the infantry to press on with attacks regardless of casualties.

By 3:45 pm, the village of Terhand had been entered by the 2nd Inniskillings and the 9th Inniskillings had reached the outskirts of Dadizeele to the east, which was then taken and consolidated by the 9th Division. Enemy resistance in Terhand had been severe, the troops fighting from house to house and it had not been cleared until 5:00 pm. It was during the capture of Terhand that the Inniskilling Fusiliers added another Victoria Cross to their already impressive total. The right flank of A Company of the 9th Inniskillings was brought to a halt by accurate machine gun fire from several different positions. As the men went to ground Lance Corporal Ernest Seaman, a Lewis gunner, rushed forward firing from the hip and capturing two machine guns, killing an officer and two crew

Major Joseph M McBride, 27 Brigade Royal Field Artillery, from Bangor, County Down, killed on 23 April 1917, he was 31 years old.

men, while taking another 12 crewmen prisoner. Later in the action he again charged a machine gun position and again was successful in its capture, but was killed almost immediately afterwards. Lance Corporal Seaman came from Norwich and had left England for a better life in Canada. On the outbreak of war he had returned and enlisted in December 1915. Considered as being of relatively poor physique he served in the Forces Canteens until the later war manpower shortage lowered the medical requirements and saw him posted to the Inniskillings. Ernest Seaman has no known grave and is commemorated on the Tyne Cot Memorial. His Victoria Cross was gazetted after the armistice on 15 November 1918.

At this time each battalion had one section of machine guns and one Stokes mortar attached and CQMS Thomas Clay, from Lambeg, Antrim, was serving in the Trench Mortar Battery of the 9th Inniskillings. He was killed during the attack. In a letter to CQMS Clay's mother Captain C.W. Milne observed:

Your son has been a very good soldier, and a great favourite with everybody, and all his chums wish me to convey to you an expression of their sincere sympathy. It will be some comfort to you at this time to know he made the supreme sacrifice in the service of his country. I deeply regret his death, and I hope you will derive some comfort from these few lines.

By the end of the day the 9th Division had advanced for some three miles on the left flank, while the 29th Division had been held up at Becelaere. The German positions were defended by wire, which in places had already been pierced. However, nature also played a part in the defences. The embankment of the main road acted as a natural barrier, with Hill 41 being the key to the entire position. This hill rose to 60 feet above the surrounding countryside and was topped with several farms complete with outbuildings, which had been strengthened with concrete. With the current lack of supporting artillery this was a difficult position to attack.

The 108 Brigade, supported by D Company of the 36th Machine Gun Battalion, had been on the move since 5:30 am on 30 September, the order of advance being 9th (NIH) Irish Fusiliers on the right flank, 12th Rifles on the left and 1st Irish Fusiliers in reserve. They also had trench mortars and machine gun sections attached. At 7:30 am the Brigade passed through the lines of 109 Brigade and advanced towards the Menin to Roulers Road, maintaining the same formation.

Within 109 Brigade there had been considerable action against German machine gun positions. Private William Hynes of the 9th Inniskillings had earned the Distinguished Conduct Medal when he had assisted the acting company sergeant major to drive off an enemy machine gun from a distance of some 50 yards, by killing two of the crew and wounding several others. Private Hynes had then held the abandoned position for the following four hours while being exposed to enemy machine gun fire and warding off two German counter-attacks.

In the 108th Trench Mortar Battery Second Lieutenant James Bailey Young, formerly of the North Irish Horse, came under fire from a farm some 250 yards away. Despite being in the open he immediately ordered his mortar into action and proceeded to shell the enemy-held buildings. When the base plate of the weapon broke Bailey stood up and held the mortar steady until all his ammunition was exhausted and in the meantime having knocked out a German machine gun position. He then organised his crew into an infantry section and led them into action protecting an exposed flank against an enemy counter-attack. After several hours' fighting, he was eventually wounded and evacuated. Young was subsequently awarded the Military Cross.

The attack on Hill 41 was launched on 1 October at 6:15 am and almost immediately heavy resistance was encountered. In 108 Brigade the 12th Rifles the leading elements were held up by enemy machine guns and the battalion commander, Lieutenant Colonel William Goodwin was forced to bring forward his reserve company, leading them personally in the assault that secured the capture of Twig Farm, 22 Germans and several heavy machine guns. Still under machine gun fire from a nearby wood, Goodwin quickly reorganised his forces and drove the enemy from the woods, capturing several more machine guns, but still unable to advance forward. For this action Goodwin was awarded a bar to his DSO. A soldier of the 12th Rifles who died was Private Robert Regan, who served in C Company. A former member of the YCV and 14th Rifles, his death was described in a letter home to his parents Thomas and Harriet Regan living at Bowtown, Grey Abbey, by the Reverend J. Hubert, the battalion padre:

> Your son's company was ordered to attack a position which was strongly held by the enemy, and in the advance your son was unfortunately hit in the chest by a machine gun bullet, and died almost instantaneously. We buried him close to the town of Dadizeele, in Belgium, and erected a cross at the head of the grave with his name, regiment and date of death upon it, so that the spot can be easily located. I cannot tell you how I and all the officers and men sympathise with you in your tragic bereavement. We feel we have lost not only one of our finest soldiers, but also one who by his bright, cheery, and unselfish disposition made himself a general favourite, and his place in the ranks and our hearts will be hard to fill.

In conjunction with this attack by 108 Brigade, 109 Brigade had been ordered to make a flanking attack on the Hill from the north, but they were unable to make any headway as a consequence of extremely heavy machine gun fire from the railway in the village of Dadizeelehoek. At 11:30 am and again at 6:40 pm, the enemy made two determined counter-attacks against the British line, but both were driven off after the Germans appeared to suffer heavy casualties. During the night the 107 Brigade and 109 Brigade relieved the 108 Brigade in the line, the latter being

German prisoners being marched to the rear, the official escort was one man per seven prisoners.

withdrawn into the divisional reserve. In 107 Brigade, Lieutenant Colonel John Henry Bridcutt DSO, commanding the 2nd Rifles, was killed in action some 150 yards from the position known as Carlton House.

Lieutenant Robert Chambers of the 9th Inniskillings came from Fintona, County Tyrone, and was in charge of the battalion's transport. From 28 September until 5 October, he worked tirelessly with his men to bring forward rations, water and ammunition. On numerous occasions he personally led forward trains of pack mules along narrow muddy and frequently shelled and machine gunned tracks. Never once did he fail to deliver the supplies, much to the gratitude of the men in the trenches. His was a well-deserved Military Cross.

On 8 October the local papers carried news of the death in action of Captain G. J. Bruce DSO, MC and bar, formerly of the 13th Rifles and then currently acting as Brigade Major of 109 Brigade, who died on 2 October 1918. George James Bruce had been an original member of the division; he had been mentioned in despatches for his actions on 1 July and awarded the Military Cross on 11 August prior to the action at Langemarck, adding a bar to his MC at Cambrai. He was also awarded the Distinguished Service Order for his leadership at Aubigny the previous March. His brother, Major R. W. V. Bruce served with the 17th Lancers.

Private William Jones, a former member of the Welsh Regiment and presently serving in the 36th Machine Gun Battalion, was killed on 8 October, he came from Holyhead in Wales. With increasing frequency the casualty lists reveal men from outside not only Ulster, but Ireland.

For two weeks the 9th (NIH) Irish Fusiliers had spent time and effort in consolidating their positions and bringing forward their reserves, all the time under near continuous German shell-fire. At dawn on 10 October a party of 30 other ranks under Second Lieutenant Darling MC formed up around Twig Farm. At 10:00 am, under cover of an intense artillery barrage and smoke screen, they rushed Goldflake Farm, capturing 14 prisoners, three machine guns and killing about ten of the enemy. A position about 100 yards south-west of the farm was consolidated. The enemy barrage was extremely heavy, the first such volume of fire that had been experienced for some time. Fusilier casualties were one killed and two wounded. At about 5:50 pm, the enemy counter-attacked heavily on Goldflake, Mansard and Twig Farms. The garrison in Goldflake Farm withdrew after inflicting very heavy casualties on the enemy, who were caught in the flank on the road. The garrison of Mansard Farm was surrounded, but managed to fight their way back. The enemy succeeded in reaching Twig Farm but was stopped by a small party which still held out in front of the farm. The enemy was finally cleared from Twig Farm by a counter-attack. Mansard and Goldflake Farms remained in German hands. Lieutenant Colonel Philip Edward Kelly DSO was killed during the day by a shell. Kelly came from Westport in County Mayo and had previously served at Gallipoli where he was severely wounded. On returning to duty he had arrived in France in June 1917 and been again wounded in March 1918. Further casualties for the day were two officers and 25 other ranks. The battalion was relieved by 12th Royal Irish Rifles and on relief moved into brigade reserve in vicinity of Pease Corner.

Battle of Courtrai

As the advance continued, so did the casualties. Lieutenant Arthur Patterson, from Ramelton, County Donegal, serving in the 109th Trench Mortar Battery, was killed on 14 October 1918; he was 32 years old. The following day the 2nd Rifles attacked Gulleghem and Private Walter Gudgeon's platoon was held up by the interlocking fire of two German machine guns. Gudgeon, a Lewis gunner, immediately ran to a firing position in the roadway and proceeded to engage both enemy positions, by firing short controlled bursts. The Lewis then suffered a stoppage, which Gudgeon calmly cleared before once again firing on the enemy. Such was the accuracy of this fire that both enemy gun teams were forced out of their positions and the platoon was able to continue its advance. For his actions Private Gudgeon was awarded the Distinguished Conduct Medal. The Inniskillings were also in action at Gulleghem. The 109 Brigade was attacking north of the town and had encountered strong resistance in the area of Jago Farm. Here the 9th Inniskillings had halted as the support battalion had not gotten into position. By 10:00 am the advance had continued and the Inniskillings advanced through the village of Heule. The platoon led by Lieutenant T. J. Adams was stopped by machine gun fire and went to ground. Taking half his platoon the lieutenant made his way along a hollow and was able to outflank the German position. The ensuing assault saw the capture of 13 enemy machine gunners and their weapons. For this action Lieutenant Adams received a bar to his Military Cross.

The divisional artillery continued to play its part. During the advance one battery from each brigade was constantly in close touch with the battalion in the line. These batteries undoubtedly rendered valuable assistance with their forward guns in neutralising machine gun nests and enabling the infantry to deal with points of resistance. Major R.R. Sharp, DSO, MC, RFA, commanding A Battery of the 173 Brigade carried out a very successful shoot on a German 77mm field gun battery, which was causing considerable damage to the attacking troops. Using the church tower in Moorseele as an observation post, which was practically in the front line at the time, Major Sharp was able to register hits on the gun detachments and ammunition stores. He was also able to prevent enemy horse teams from withdrawing the guns to a safe distance, thus allowing the infantry to capture them in the subsequent advance.

For a front line officer life on the battlefield was either fatal or, if he survived, worthy of reward. Adequate demonstrations of the latter were to be found among the Royal Engineers of the division. The 122nd Field Company was in action at Courtrai. Here, on 16 October, command was in the hands of Captain William Smyth, MC, from Burtonport, County Donegal. The bridging of a river under fire is a dangerous task at the best of times, in daylight doubly so. It was the courage and behaviour of Captain Smyth that allowed communications via his bridge across the canal until nightfall that allowed the infantry to successfully withdraw. Smyth was awarded a Bar to his Military Cross. Assisting Captain Smyth was Second Lieutenant John Joseph Aloysius Fagan, who spent most of the day conveying orders to the men and assisting where needed. Later in the afternoon he was hit in the left leg by a burst from an enemy machine gun. For his actions he was awarded the Military Cross.

In the 121st Field Company Second Lieutenant Wallace Achison Delahey was responsible for reconnoitring the River Lys for potential crossing points. This he did with the utmost profession-alism and at great danger to himself. It was thanks to his copious notes and accurate sketch maps that the subsequent operation was a success.

The 150th Field Company carried out a reconnaissance of the Lys during the day, responsi-bility for this was given to Lieutenant William Waddingham Brunyate. Despite accurate enemy machine gun fire he traversed the length of the divisional sub-sector and located possible crossing places and enemy strong-points. The accuracy of his reconnaissance undoubtedly saved many lives on the actual crossing. He was awarded the Military Cross.

On the night of 19 October the 121st Field Company was engaged in bridging the River Lys to the south of Oyghem. In command was Major Harold Gooch, MC, a former teacher at the Municipal Technical Institute, Belfast. Initially a ferry was put in place and despite the heavy shelling and machine gun fire supplies were taken across the river. Regardless of heavy and contin-uous casualties this ferrying operation was followed by a completed bridge, which allowed the attacking infantry to cross at the precise time. Major Gooch was constantly on the move both encouraging and assisting his men where necessary, for his actions he was awarded the DSO. Assisting Major Gooch was Lieutenant Thomas Kenneth Knox, MC. Earlier in the day Lieutenant Knox had managed to bring forward the bridging material and keep it concealed from enemy eyes. That night he too was conspicuous by his actions at the crossing and as a result earned a bar to his Military Cross. Thomas was the brother of Lieutenant Cecil Knox, VC, of the same unit.[4]

The crossing had been supported by fire from the divisional artillery and on the night of 21 October 153 Brigade crossed the river, while 173 Brigade was held in divisional reserve to the west, but was still able to take part in the barrage supporting the general advance on 22 October.

A casualty to the 15th Rifles on 20 October was Private Ernest Bruce, MM. Private Bruce had first served with the 14th Rifles and had previously been wounded in action. One of the many men of the division who was a member of the Orange Order, he was a member of Derriaghy LOL No.135 and had been an apprentice draughtsman with Harland and Wolff prior to enlisting, he was 22 years old.

In the 150th Field Company Lieutenant Alan Ferrier had commanded during the successful bridging operation across the River Lys that had begun for this Company on 9 October. Despite his sappers suffering many casualties the bridge was maintained for the use of the infantry and field artillery. Even though he had gone almost a week without adequate rest, his continued cool-ness and leadership had kept his company in a good state of morale. He was awarded the Military Cross.

---

4   The Knox brothers were highly-decorated for their service. In addition to Cecil Knox, Lieutenant Colonel James M Knox, Royal Warwickshire Regiment, had been awarded a bar to his DSO, whilst another brother, Lieutenant Roland Knox RE, was killed in December 1915.

The Victoria Cross memorial at the Ulster Tower.

Private Patrick McHugh, 9th (NIH) Irish Fusiliers, from Clanmorris, County Mayo, was killed on 21 October. By now the Ulster Division was recruiting from all counties in Ireland as well as the remainder of Great Britain.

On 25 October, the 1st Inniskillings were held up at Ingoyghem by strong enemy resistance and had suffered numerous casualties from heavy machine gun fire. On his own initiative, Private Norman Harvey rushed forward and in a brief, but bloody skirmish, killed some 20 enemy soldiers and captured two machine guns. Later in the day Harvey's company was held up by another enemy strong-point and once again Harvey made a lone attack and forcing the enemy to retreat. After the onset of darkness Harvey carried out a reconnaissance of the enemy line and returned with valuable information. Throughout the day he had been observed limping from a sprained ankle and according to his platoon sergeant seemed to bear a charmed life.[5] For his actions on this date Private Harvey was awarded the Victoria Cross.[6] In the ranks of the 36th Machine Gun Battalion Private Edward Jones was killed, he came from Holyhead, Wales.

According to the 108 Brigade war diary 26 October was the last day on which the brigade saw action. The casualties noted were one officer killed and five wounded, 11 other ranks killed, 33 wounded and 15 missing in the 12th Rifles. Three other ranks wounded in the 1st Irish

---

5   Arthur, Max, *Symbol Of Courage*, London (2005).
6   During the Second World War CQMS Norman Harvey VC, served with No199 Railway Workshop Company, Royal Engineers. He died on 16 February 1942 and is buried in Khayat Beach War Cemetery.

Fusiliers, two officers wounded, seven other ranks killed, 37 wounded and four missing in the 9th (NIH) Irish Fusiliers, while the 108th Trench Mortar Battery had no casualties. These figures do not agree with what is listed on the Commonwealth War Graves Commission website.

Private Charles Grundie 9th Inniskillings, from Disraeli Street, Belfast, died of gas poisoning in No.29 General Hospital on 27 October, he was 33 years old. He had been previously wounded on two occasions and had in excess of four years' service. Prior to his enlistment he had worked on Queen's Island as a plumber. His brother John was a sapper with the Royal Engineers, while his brother-in-law Driver John Kielty was with the Army Service Corps. His widow, Annie Grundie, resided at Disraeli Street, Belfast. He is buried in Etaples Military Cemetery. On this date the battalion was relieved in the line by the 2nd North Lancs of the 34th Division. The Inniskillings marched back to billets in the Hulste area arriving at about 12:50 am the following morning.

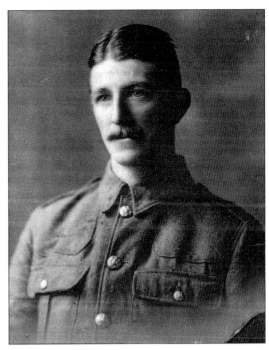

Private Charles Grundie, 9th Royal Inniskilling Fusiliers. On occasions his name is rendered as Grundy. (Courtesy of Carol Walker)

On the same day the divisional artillery was relieved and withdrew from the line. During the recent operations casualties to personnel were described as slight, but casualties to horses were rather severe. As darkness fell the 101st Brigade of the 34th Division relieved the two exhausted brigades in the line and they then marched back to the area around Courtrai. For the infantry of the Ulster Division the war was over.

The Artillery and Trench Mortar Batteries would fight a little longer. When the 34th Division forced the crossing of the Escaut Canal during the first week of November, it was supported by the Divisional Artillery and the three Trench Mortar Batteries. It is possible that the 108th Battery fired the last round in the war, the other two having exhausted their ammunition. Divisional headquarters along with the 107 Brigade moved to Mouscron on 2 November. Here training and reorganisation was carried out as drafts of reinforcements arrived. Billets were comfortable and rations plentiful and the men were soon ready for another spell in the line. They would not be required. For the 36th (Ulster) Division the Great War was over. As of 11 November 1918, the War Diary of DADOS recorded "Nothing unusual occurred."

At home the local press carried various notices; Second Lieutenant John Wylie, Irish Rifles, the son-in-law of Mr R.M. Gray, an auctioneer of Royal Avenue, Belfast, wounded. Private James Bingham, Motor Transport Company, son of Mr R. Bingham, Donacloney, died of pneumonia. Throughout the winter months the local newspapers continued to carry notices asking for information on men missing in the recent battles. One such was placed by the family of Lieutenant James Edwin Woods of the 9th Inniskillings. The first appeared on 8 January and on succeeding days: "Missing since 6th December, 1917 at Cambrai. Any information about him would be gratefully received by his father, Mr F.W. Woods, Knockbreda, Belfast."

The notice appeared for several days, just one of many. Lieutenant Woods had been killed on 6 December and has no known grave.

LOL 862 in January 1919.

This is not peace.
It is an armistice for twenty years
Maréchal Ferdinand Foch

The Great War was over, but still men of the division continued to die. On 25 February 1919, Private Albert Connolly of the division's Army Service Corps, died of pneumonia; he came from Ballygowan and was 22 years old. Private Connolly had come to France in October 1915 and was employed as a despatch rider with the 110th Field Ambulance. On the same day Lieutenant Frank Farrell, anxious to get back to his work at the Textiles Testing House in Belfast, succumbed to trench fever and pneumonia. He had been demobilised on 12 February at Oswestry, but became ill on the journey home, dying shortly after arriving at Victoria Barracks, Belfast. He was buried in the City Cemetery two day later, his coffin carried on a gun carriage and a firing party was supplied from the Northumberland Fusiliers. Second Lieutenant H. De Vine of the 10th Rifles died on 17 February, his widow lived on Achill Island, County Mayo.

John Ramsey, 11th Royal Inniskilling Fusiliers, died in April 1933.

16

Going Home

In the wake of Hell
I hear them coming:
Fireside judges damning what I'd done.
So little said of why they paid their taxes:
For me to win a War, and I have won.[1]

The local papers of 9 April 1919 carried the news that Ulster Division no longer existed as a unit of the British Armies in France, the process of demobilisation having gone on steadily for many weeks. The GOC, Brevet-Colonel (T/Major General) Clifford Coffin, VC, CB, DSO, was appointed as a brigade commander in the Army of the Rhine. It was reported that he had led the Division with signal success in the final advance in Flanders, in which the 36th proved itself, in the words of the Corps Commander, Lieutenant General Sir Claud Jacob, 'one of the best fighting divisions in the Army'. Those troops of the division remaining in France were under the command of Brigadier General Philip Levenson-Gower, CMG, DSO, the former commander of 49 Brigade, 16th (Irish) Division.

Homecoming parade, Belfast city centre 1919. The men are marching to the front of the City Hall, going in the opposite direction to the farewell parade of 1915.

---

1   With the permission of Maureen Browne, Ards Writers.

(Left) A Certificate of Employment in the name of Private George Burns of the 8th Royal Irish Regiment, but typical of those issued to men who had their peacetime apprenticeship interrupted by military service. Burns had been an apprentice linen napper. (Right) Certificate of transfer to the Army Reserve on demobilisation in the name of Lance Corporal William Gamble, of the Royal Irish Rifles.

A fair degree of cynicism had settled on the people of Ulster by the end of the war. Fortunes and careers had been made by a few as the many had suffered. The following poem, which appeared in the *Bangor Spectator* on 22 June 1918, appeared to sum up public opinion:

> I knew a man of industry,
> Who made big bombs for the RFC,
> And pocketed lots of L.s.d.
> And he (thank God) is an O.B.E.

> I know a woman of pedigree,
> Who asked some soldiers out to tea,
> And said "Dear me" and Yes I see"
> And she (thank God) is an O.B.E.
> I know a fellow of twenty-three,
> Who got a job with a fat M.P.,
> Not caring much for the infantry,
> And he (thank God) is an O.B.E.

I have a friend, a friend and he,
Just holds the line for you and me,
And keeps the Germans from the sea,
And fights without the O.B.E.
"Thank God", he fights without the O.B.E.

The *Belfast News Letter* of 16 June 1919, reported that four battalions of the Ulster Division, reduced to cadres, would arrive in Belfast that day. For men returning home there was at time a vast difference between other ranks and officers.

Major Percy B. Lewis, MC, 14th Rifles, relinquished his commission on account of ill-health caused by wounds received on 23 March 1918. He returned to his pre-war employment wit the Ocean Accident and Guarantee Corporation, Ltd, Belfast. Having previously served with the Gloucestershire Hussars, he had joined the Young Citizen Volunteers some 18 months before the outbreak of war. On the formation of the Ulster Division had had obtained a commission in the 14th Rifles and had served continuously with the battalion from September 1914, with the exception of a period in 1916, when he was Transport Officer of the 109 Brigade. He was awarded the Military Cross for conspicuous gallantry in action in the winter of 1916 and assumed command of the battalion 28 February 1918, in succession to Lieutenant Colonel Vivian, DSO. He led the battalion at St Quentin on 23 March and was wounded on that day. On returning home Major Lewis was quoted as saying he hope the old YCV men would be keen enough to carry on the organisation again. The son of the late John H.B. Lewis and Mrs T. Morgan Jenkins, of Cardiff, he had married in June 1915, Miss Ethel Gunning of Cedar Grove, Creagh, Belfast.

The Belfast newspapers reported the following;

> Brigadier General George William Hacket Pain, CB, General officer Commanding the northern District, Irish Command, was appointed a knight Commander of the Most Excellent order of the British Empire (K.B.E.) for valuable service rendered in connection with the war. Sir George Hacket Pain, who has a distinguished record of service to his credit, is a well-known and popular figure in military and social circles in the North of Ireland. He was the first Brigade commander of the 108th Brigade, Ulster Division, which he took to France in October 1915. Subsequently he commanded the 15th (Reserve) Brigade of the Belfast district and since 1916 he has been G.O.C. on the Northern District.

Other officers preferred to retire from public life to enjoy the peace they had earned at such a high price. Some did not see it. Lieutenant Colonel Peacocke of the Inniskillings resigned his commission and returned to his home at Skevenish House, Innishannon, in the Bandon River Valley, where he lived with his widowed mother. On the evening of 31 May 1921, Warren Peacocke was working in the garage at his home when he was approached by two armed and masked men. He was shot in the stomach and mortally wounded, dying the following morning. The fatal shot was fired by Tom Kelleher, a member of the Irish Republican Army. Justification for the killing was that Peacocke was either an informer, or had been commanding a paramilitary gang that had murdered IRA members and their sympathisers. One week after the killing the Peacocke family home was one of a number burned down in the area by a 'flying column' commanded by Tom Barry.

Some men lived a lengthy and eventful life after the war, but history in Ireland has an equally long memory. Lieutenant, later Captain Norman Stronge, of the 15th Rifles, who had earned the Military Cross, later became The Right Honourable Sir Norman Strong, MC, PC, JP, and Speaker of the Northern Ireland House of Commons. He was murdered, along with his son, by the Provisional IRA at his home, Tynan Abbey, County Armagh, on 21 January 1981.

Appendix I

Prisoners of War

The Geneva Convention regarding the treatment of prisoners of war begins:

> Prisoners of war are in the power of the hostile government, but not of the individuals or corps who capture them. They must be humanely treated. All their personal belongings, except arms, horses, and military papers, remain their property.

The Convention goes on to cover such things as accommodation, faith, work, clothing and mail. However, this agreement had been drawn up with earlier conflicts in mind. By 1918, Germany held almost 2,500,000 prisoners, of French, Russian, British and other nations. As the war progressed the allied blockade caused shortages in all areas and feeding prisoners became a low priority. The experiences of Ulster Division prisoners seemed to vary.

On release from prison camp Colonel Place, the former GSO I, was awarded the CMG for his services with the Ulster Division and as Brevet Lieutenant. The authorities in Whitehall considered he had some potential and Colonel Charles Otley Place, CMG, DSO, received an appointment at the War Office as a GSO I.

Private J. Read, No.1717, 12th Rifles received a personal hand-written letter from the King commenting on his release from prison camp in 1918 and the hardships he had undergone. It made him feel so much better[1]

On 22 November 1918 the *Belfast News Letter* reported that Second Lieutenant Stanley Hunter, 8th Rifles, of Eglantine Avenue Belfast, had returned home from Holland. He had been taken prisoner on 28 November 1915 and had been held as a prisoner of war until the previous April when he was transferred to Holland for internment. He claimed that the Germans "…could not have treated us much worse."

This officer had three brothers in service, Lieutenant W. Fred Hunter, MC, Rifles, Lieutenant Harold Hunter, Inniskillings and the Reverend. W. Johnstone Hunter, Chaplain to the Forces.

Private James Cope had been held listed as missing for over two years. In September 1918, his sister Mrs Birrell of Killycomaine Lodge, Portadown, received a post card informing her he was a prisoner of war and in service had been gassed twice and wounded three times. On 8 January 1919, a reception was held in the Town Hall, Cavan for returning prisoners of war. Bedecked in the flags of the allied nations and with the catering prepared by the County Cavan Women's Patriotic Association, all present enjoyed an evening that was both moving and entertaining. The toast to 'The King' was proposed by the Right Honourable Thomas Lough, HML, County Cavan, chairman of the Reception Committee. Proposing the toast of the evening, he said that they were all proud of the men from County Cavan who had answered the call of King and Country, and that evening's entertainment was only an initial effort, as a committee had been formed on a broad basis to give recognition to all belonging to the country who had served in any capacity in the Great War. He suggested that a tablet be erected in every parish church in the County recording the names of those who had

---

1   Somme Museum Archive.

Die deutsche Verteidigungs-Offensive im Westen.

Men of the Royal Irish Rifles taken prisoner during the March 1918 offensive. (Photograph courtesy of Aribert Elpelt)

made the supreme sacrifice, as the dead heroes should never be forgotten. Colonel Farnham replying to the toast, which was honoured with enthusiasm, said it should be remembered always that it was largely due to the gallantry of the men who died that the cause of military domination and brutality had been finally overcome, and freedom and liberty established in the world. This was met with thunderous applause throughout the hall. Sergeant Major Hamilton and Sergeant J.J. McGuinness of the Royal Irish Fusiliers also responded and Captain Henry Kennedy replied to the toast of 'His Majesty's armed forces'. With that the evening's entertainment got under way and was thoroughly enjoyed by all.[2]

The *Belfast Evening Telegraph* of 11 January 1919 reported the following men had died as prisoner-of-war in Germany: Privates Robert Skillen, Rifles, Gertrude Street, Belfast; John Dickson, 12th Rifles, Mill Street, Newtownards; and James Hunter, Rifles,

A soldier of the Royal Inniskilling Fusiliers found at Pozieres.

2   *Belfast News Letter,* 9 January 1919.

Eglington Street, Portrush. Private Robert McKay, No.19107, had been born in Greyabbey in 1884, the son of Robert and Jane McKay and had been a member of St Saviour's Church. He had been taken prisoner in March 1918 and died on 15 April, being interred in Tyne Cot Cemetery, Belgium. Second Lieutenant Stanley Woods Maxwell served in B Company of the 12th Rifles and had been captured on 1 July 1916, after having been wounded in the leg. At first thought to have been killed in action, his mother, of Cliftonville Avenue, Belfast, had been informed by letter on 8 July 1916, that he was a prisoner of war in Germany and suffering from a broken leg. Sadly Lieutenant Maxwell died of his wounds on 27 July 1916. Private Alexander Moore, No.18495, of the 11th Rifles died of sepsis in the German Garrison Hospital at Düsseldorf, on 26 May 1918; he came from Lisburn, Antrim and was 23 years old. Lieutenant John Barker spoke little of his time as a prisoner of war. One particular remark was remembered by his son, when he was told how the Lieutenant had observed two fellow prisoners fighting over a dead sparrow. *Sergeant William Donnan, No.41872, 1st Irish Fusiliers, was captured on 21 March 1918. Private Ashley Albert Milne was also captured on this date. He was sent to Camp 5260 and worked in a salt mine. He died on 19 July 1918. His brother John was seriously wounded at Havencourt Wood and evacuated to hospital in England. Another brother, Earnest, had previously been sent home due to illness. Their father served in France until the end of the War. They lived in Roden Street, Belfast.* Lance Corporal James Riddell Taylor had been wounded in the leg at the Battle of the Somme on July 1, 1916.

The *Belfast News Letter* reported on July 28, 1916:

> Mr. Alex Taylor, Donegall Street, Belfast, yesterday received a postcard from his son, Lance-Corporal J. R. Taylor (YCV), stating that he is wounded and a prisoner of war in the Festungs Lazaret (Prison Hospital), Kaiserin Augusta School, Cologne. Lance-Corporal Taylor was shot in the knee during the advance on the 1st inst, and when his comrades retired they had reluctantly to leave him behind in a dug-out – indeed, he insisted on them doing so rather than imperil their own safety. He says that he is well treated, and that there are 'a number of the lads here'. Six weeks is the usual period allowed for receiving news from prisoners of war, and in the case of Lance-Corporal Taylor word has come through unusually quickly.

Private Ashley Albert Milne,
Royal Irish Rifles. Men are
not like that now.

The *Belfast News Letter* reported on 3 January that Mr Alexander Taylor had received word that his son had died in a Swedish internment camp on 22 December 1918. He had been released after the Armistice and sent to Sweden en-route for England. Before the war he had worked for Messrs. Lindsay Bros. Ltd., Donegall Place, he was 31 years old.

```
                          COPY.

      NOT  FOR  PUBLICATION  IN  THE  PRESS.


      Knowing how very anxious you must be about 17706
Sergeant R. GILCHRIST who is posted as "missing" in the
Casualty lists of the battalion since 21st. March, 1918
this circular letter has been prepared to tell you all
we ourselves do know at the moment.   He was with his
Unit in the front line Area when the German attack was
launched.   The morning was misty rendering visual
observation impossible, and owing to the heavy shell fire
communication with the front line was very difficult to
maintain, so that we have but little reliable information
as to what actually hapened.   None of the officers in the
line at the time came back and only a very few of the
other ranks.   Apparently they repelled several enemy
attacks holding on to their positions with great gallantry
and courage.   Later in the day the enemy threw very heavy
forces against the troops on our right flank pressing
them back and in this way managed to get behind the
position our men were holding, cutting them off.   As a
result most of them are, we believe, prisoners of war, and
we must wait, in the absence of other reliable information
until the lists of those who were taken prisoner are
published.   The part played by the division in the great
battle has been most warmly praised by the Higher
Command and the exploits of this battalion have been
specially referred to.   This, we trust, will be some
comfort to those whose hearts are torn with anxiety and
suspence to know that their beloved played such a worthy
and heroic part in the day of the Empire's need and trial.
We believe that those at home will meet the days of weary
waiting with patience and in the same spirit of endurance
and courage as their men met the might of the enemy and
hurled it back.   We assure you of our deepest sympathy
and share with you in your anxienty and with a view to
helping you we have prepared this letter and are sending
it to the relatives of all our "missing" men as far as
their addresses are known.



                          (Sgd) GEORGE THOMPSON. Major
In the Field              Commanding 12th. R.I.Rifles.
8th April 1918.
```

A note from Major George Thompson concerning Sergeant Gilchrist, who was reported as missing in action and was found to be a prisoner of war.

Corporal William A. Fleming, MM, of the Inniskillings and the son of Mrs Fleming of Rose Cottage Sariggan, Dungiven, arrived home at the end of December 1918; he had been a prisoner of war for nine months. During his captivity he was held at Mannheim, in Baden and worked in a jam factory. He described in great detail the havoc caused by allied aircraft that bombed and strafed the factory and other military targets during repeated air raids.

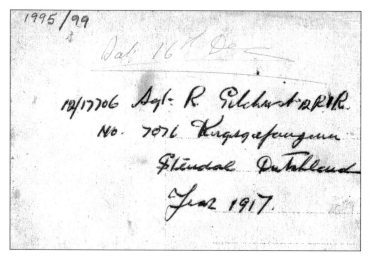

Sergeant R. Gilchrist, 12th Royal Irish Rifles, on the left, who was a prisoner of war, he had originally been reported as missing in action.

Postcard addressed to Sergeant R Gilchrist 12th Royal Irish Rifles, and dated 16 December 1917.

Royal Inniskilling Fusiliers, group photograph 'SOMME'

"Greater love hath no man than this that a man lay down his life for his friends." (John 15 v13)

Appendix II

A Note on Casualties

While much is made of casualties in the various battles especially those suffered on 1 July 1916, the men did not stop dying at the conclusion of the war. Many of those men suffering severe gunshot and shrapnel wounds endured for many months and years before succumbing, one being Private Charles James Mills, from Newcastle Street, Ballymacarret, Belfast. A member of the 108th Field Ambulance, who died on 24 January 1919, he was 24 years old. Men who had been gassed, continued to die from those effects for many years, Lance Corporal Albert Edward Truesdale died in 1948 of complications caused by gas in March 1918.

A sampler dedicated to the Division.

Belfast City Hall, the Cenotaph.
(Courtesy of Carol Walker)

The Ulster Tower stands some seventy feet high and was the first official war memorial to be erected on the Western Front. It is a replica of Helen's Tower, which stands in the Dufferin and Ava Estate at Clandeboye, County down, which had been built in 1867.

Appendix III

Honours & Awards

Nine men of the Ulster Division were awarded the Victoria Cross, while seventy-one earned the Distinguished Service Order, with a further 459 gaining the Military Cross, some on more than one occasion, as the manuscript shows. There were 173 awards of the Distinguished Conduct Medal, 1,294 of the Military Medal, again many on more than one occasion and 118 of the Meritorious Service Medal. A total of 312 foreign awards were also made. These brief biographies of the Victoria Cross recipients are listed in chronological order. On 2 April 1919 the *Belfast News Letter* reported the numbers of awards made and quoted eight of the Victoria Cross, this was due to the award made to Edmund De Wind not being gazetted until 15 May 1919.

Private William Frederick McFadzean, No18278. 14th Royal Irish Rifles

Born in Lurgan, County Armagh on 9 October 1895, the son of William and Annie McFadzean. The family later moved to Belfast settling in the Creagh area. Billy, as he was popularly known, attended Mountpottinger National School where he was not the best of students and his record there shows in excess of thirty reprimands. This was followed by time at the Trade Preparatory School of the Municipal Technical Institute, before becoming an apprentice with Spence Bryson and Company, a local linen manufacturer, where he was paid £20 per year. Standing six feet tall, Billy was extremely fit and keen on all games, playing rugby for Collegians Rugby Football Club. In 1912 he joined the Young Citizen Volunteers, and on 22 September 1914 he became a member of C Company of the 14th Royal Irish Rifles.

The local papers of 13 July 1916 carried an account of his action, including letters from Captain James McKee and Second Lieutenant James Marshall of the 11th Rifles. Second Lieutenant Marshal stated that his brother, Corporal David Marshall was standing close to Private McFadzean at the time and is forever grateful for the heroic self sacrifice that was shown.

General Nugent wrote to his wife on 25 July 1916:

> I recommended a man today for the posthumous conferring of the VC for almost the finest act of self-sacrifice I have ever read of. He was giving out bombs just before the attack on the 1st of July to a number of our men in a trench. He was walking along the top giving them out of a box. He slipped and the box fell out of his hand into the trench and the jar set off the fuzes in two of the bombs. The trench was full of men. Without a second's hesitation the man jumped down into the trench and threw himself down onto the bombs and covered the burning bombs with his own body. He was blown to pieces, but he saved the lives of all the men in the trench. He knew what he was doing as he was a bomber. His name was W.J. McFadzean, 14th R I Rifles. It was a sublime act and he will get the VC for it I am certain.

Private William McFadzean has no known grave and is commemmorated on the Thiepval Memorial Pier and Face 15A and 15B.

10. Victoria Crosses

During World War One, the men of the Ulster Division received almost 2500 awards for gallantry, including 9 Victoria Crosses.

Cpt. Eric Norman Frankland Bell
9th Battalion Royal Inniskilling Fusiliers

Lt Sgt.Geoffrey St.George Shillington Cather
9th Battalion Royal Irish Fusiliers

2nd-Lt. James Samuel Emerson
9th Battalion Royal Inniskilling Fusiliers

Pte Norman Harvey
1st Battalion Royal Inniskilling Fusiliers

2nd-Lt Cecil Leonard Knox
150th Field Company Royal Engineers

Pte William Frederick McFadzean
14th Battalion Royal Irish Rifles

L/Cpl. Ernest Seaman
2nd Battalion Royal Inniskilling Fusiliers

Pte Robert Quigg
12th Battalion Royal Irish Rifles

2nd-Lt. Edmund de Wind
15th Battalion Royal Irish Rifles

The 36th (Ulster) Division recipients of the Victoria Cross.

Captain Eric Norman Frankland Bell, 9th Royal Inniskilling Fusiliers

Bell was born on 28 August 1897 at Alma Terrace in the town of Enniskillen, the son of Edward and Dora Bell. Captain Edward Bell was at the time a quartermaster with the 2nd Battalion Royal Inniskilling Fusiliers. In 1901 the family moved to England, residing at Seaforth, Lancashire. Here Eric Bell attended school and later went to Liverpool University to study architecture. On the outbreak of war Captain Bell rejoined the Inniskillings and was appointed as adjutant of the 9th Battalion. His two brothers also joined the Inniskillings, Eric being posted to the 9th like his father, while his brothers served in other Inniskilling battalions. Eric Bell has no known grave and is commemorated on the Thiepval Memorial. His Victoria Cross was presented to his family by the King at Buckingham Palace on 29 November 1916.

Captain Bell's Victoria Cross was presented to the Regimental Museum by the family in February 2001. The VC had been in New Zealand for almost 70 years in the possession of some of Eric Bell's kin. In June 2000, Air Marshal Sir Richard Bolt, stepson of the owner of the Cross, made an approach via the British Embassy in New Zealand to Headquarters Royal Irish Regiment and thus began the journey to Enniskillen. It was on display at a Dinner Night in the Regimental Depot Mess and on Thursday, 15 February 2001, the Regimental Colonel, Colonel Stewart Douglas OBE, handed over the Victoria Cross to Viscount Brookeborough, patron of the Regimental Museum in Enniskillen.

Private Robert Quigg, 12th Royal Irish Rifles

Robert Quigg was born at Corkkirk, close to the Giant's Causeway in County Antrimon 28 February 1885. His father Robert, worked as a guide and boatman at the Causeway and was kept busy, especially during the summer months with the large number of visitors to the site. Quigg attended the local National School, where he was described by the headmaster, Mr David McConaghy, as a diligent and reliable pupil. He became a member of the Orange Order, becoming a member of L.O.L. 1196 and on leaving school he went to work on the farm of John Forsyth at Turfahun and later for the Macnaughten family on their estate at Dunderave. He became a member of the UVF in January 1913 and was made commander of the Bushmills Volunteers, UVF. On the outbreak of war he enlisted in the 12th Battalion, Royal Irish Rifles (Mid Antrim Volunteers) and became batman to Sir Harry Macnaughten, a subaltern in the battalion, a common arrangement at this time. When the division left the Somme area Lady Macnaghten wrote to Private Quigg's mother; "I hear from Major Hamilton that your son, Private Robert Quigg, has behaved magnificently, going out in the face of danger seven times to try and find Sir Harry. He brought a wounded man back each time. All are very proud of him."

Private Quigg was presented with his Victoria Cross by the King on 8 January 1917 at York Cottage on the Sandringham Estate. On returning to County Antrim Lady Macnaghten made him a gift of a gold watch in memory of his attempts in recovering her son from the battlefield. Robert Quigg retired from the army in 1926 with the rank of sergeant and died on 14 May 1955 at Ballycastle. He is buried in Billy Parish Churchyard. His Victoria Cross and the Russian award of the Order of St George are held by the Royal Ulster Rifles museum, Belfast. There is a statue to Quigg VC in the square at Bushmills and several wall murals exist, one at the Creagh estate, Belfast.

Lieutenant Geoffrey Shillington Cather, 9th Royal Irish Fusiliers

Geoffrey Cather was born at Streatham Hill, London on 1 October 1890, of Irish parents. He was educated in England, attending Rugby school amongst others but spent most of his school

The first group visit by the
Royal British Legion to the
Ulster Tower in 1928.

The Ulster Tower
at Thiepval.

holidays in County Armagh. He served in the 1/28th Battalion, The London Regiment (Artists Rifles), as a private and in 1912 began to work as an executive with the Tetley Tea Company. From 1912 to 1914, he worked in the Company's New York office. When the war began Cather enlisted in the 19th (2nd Public Schools) Battalion of the Royal Fusiliers and was later offered a commission in the Royal Irish Fusiliers. He has no known grave and is commemorated on the Thiepval Memorial. The local press reported on 2 April 1917:

> The Victoria Cross awarded to the late Lieutenant Geoffrey Shillington Cather, of the Royal Irish Fusiliers, was handed to his mother by his Majesty the King, at Buckingham Palace on Saturday. Lieutenant Cather was a grandson of the late Mr. Thomas Shillington of Tavanagh House, Portadown, and a nephew of Captain D. Graham Shillington, Ardeevan, Portadown. His mother resides at West Hampstead, London. In the official account, given at the time the announcement was made of the awarding of the coveted distinction, it was stated that from 7:00 pm until midnight Lieutenant Cather searched 'no-man's-land' and brought in three wounded men. He continued his search next morning and while engaged in rescue work he was killed. His operations were carried out in full view of the enemy, and under direct machine gun fire and intermittent artillery fire. He received his commission in Royal Irish Fusiliers (County Armagh Volunteers) in May 1915.

Second Lieutenant James Emerson, 9th Royal Inniskilling Fusiliers

The *Belfast News Letter* reported on 5 April 1918 that Brigadier General George William Hacket Pain, CB, General Officer Commanding the Northern District, Irish Command, visited Drogheda on Wednesday for the purpose of presenting the Victoria Cross won by the later Second Lieutenant J.S. Emerson, Royal Inniskilling Fusiliers, to the deceased officer's mother Mrs Emerson of Collon. The Mayor (Mr W.T. Skeffington) presided at the interesting ceremony.

James Samuel Emerson was born in Collon, Drogheda in County Louth on 3 August 1895, the son of John and Ellen Emerson. He has no known grave and is remembered on the war memorial of the Church of Ireland parish church at Collon and on the Cambrai Memorial at Louveral, he was 22 years old.

Second Lieutenant James Emerson VC was a keen violinist pre-war. (Courtesy of John Emerson)

Second Lieutenant Edmund De Wind, 15th Royal Irish Rifles

On 30 June 1919, the *Belfast News Letter* reported the following:

> At the investiture held at Buckingham Palace on Saturday his Majesty the King handed to Mrs. De Wind, of Comber, County Down, the Victoria Cross posthumously awarded to her son, Second Lieutenant Edmund De Wind, 15th Battalion Royal Irish Rifles. Mrs. De Wind was accompanied by Miss De Wind and Mrs. J.G. Allen. On the same occasion Captain Robert Watts, MC, Royal Irish Rifles, of Ardnagreena, Circular Road, Bloomfield,

Louverval Military Cemetery.

Comber War memorial was dedicated in 1923. The *Newtownards Spectator* reported the following: "At 3:00pm, all businesses in the town closed as a parade of ex-servicemen marched into the town, led by the Comber Amateur Flute Band. Among those present were Lord and Lady Londonderry and Viscount Castlereagh, the service was led by Canon Manning, who had served with the 13th Rifles. The Memorial was unveiled by Mrs Hind, the widow of Lieutenant Colonel Lawrence Hind,1/7th Battalion Sherwood Foresters, who was killed on 1 July 1916. A German field gun was also placed in the Square in memory of Edmund de Wind VC." (Author's photograph)

was decorated by the King with the Military Cross and Bar in recognition of his gallantry on the western front.

Edmund de Wind as the youngest son of the late Arthur Hughes De Wind, C.F., and Margaret Jane De Wind of 'Kinvara', Comber, County Down, where he was born on 11 December 1883. Educated at Campbell College, Belfast, he later became a clerk in the Bank of Ireland in Cavan, before emigrating to Canada in 1911. Here he was employed by the Bank of Commerce in Edmonton and proved to be a willing and conscientious worker. He was also a keen sportsman, excelling at hockey and cricket. Showing an interest in the Home Rule question and activities of the Ulster Volunteer Force, he enlisted in the Army in 1915, joining the 31st Battalion, Second Canadian Contingent, serving with a machine gun section. He saw action at both St Eloi and on the Somme, before being granted a commission in the 17th Battalion of the Royal Irish Rifles on 26 September 1917. After the award of the Victoria Cross was made Comber received a captured German artillery piece in recognition of his bravery. In Canada Mount De Wind in Alberta was named in his honour.

Second Lieutenant Cecil Leonard Knox, 150th Field Company, Royal Engineers

Born in Nuneaton, Warwickshire on 9 May 1888, Knox was trained as a civil engineer. Knox was decorated by the King in France on 6 August at the village of Oxelaere. *The London Gazette* 4 June 1918 carried the following:

> On the 22 March 1918 twelve bridges at Tugny France were entrusted to this officer for demolition, and all of them were successfully destroyed. In the case of one of the steel girder bridges, the destruction of which he personally supervised, the timing fuse failed. Without hesitation Second Lieutenant Knox ran to the bridge, under heavy fire and machine gun fire, and while the enemy was still on the bridge, tore away the fuse and lit the instantaneous fuse, to do which he had to get under the bridge. This was an act of the highest devotion to duty, entailing great risks, which as a practical civil engineer he fully realised.

Knox died on 4 February 1943, as the result of a bicycle accident at Buck's Hill, Nuneaton.

Corporal Ernest Seaman, No42364 2nd Royal Inniskilling Fusiliers

The officer commanding A Company of the battalion recorded the following:

> He was one of the best soldiers whom I have ever met, an excellent soldier in every sense of the word, and very keen in his duties. He always volunteered to help in any extra work that had to be done, no matter how dangerous and difficult, and for his constant devotion to duty and gallantry in voluntarily attending his wounded comrades under heavy fire, I recommend his being awarded the Military Medal.

Ernest Seaman was born on 15 August 1893 at Derby Street, Heigham, Norwich, Norfolk, the son of the late Harry Seaman and Mrs. Palmer of the King's Inn, Bungay Road, Scole, Norfolk, his mother having remarried on the death of his father. Corporal Seaman, he was promoted some fifteen days before his death, has no known grave and is commemorated on the Tyne Cot Memorial, Belgium.

Corporal Seaman's award of the Victoria Cross was gazetted on 15 November 1918 and presented to his mother, Mrs Sarah Palmer, in the ballroom of Buckingham Palace on 13 February 1919. At the time of writing the medal is held by the museum of the Royal Logistics Corps.

Private Norman Harvey, 1st Royal Inniskilling Fusiliers

Norman Harvey was born on 6 April 1899, the son of Charles William and Mary Harvey of Newton-le-Willows, Lancashire. He was educated at St Peter's Church of England School and then worked for a time with Messrs. Randal, a High Street business, prior to being employed by Messrs. Caulfields' in the town. He enlisted in the South Lancashire Regiment in November 1914, aged 15 years, being wounded the following year in France. Two years later he received a more severe wound and was evacuated to hospital in England. On learning his true age the military authorities refused to allow him to return to France and he was sent on a series of courses until he had reached 18 years of age, when he was sent back to France being posted to the 1st Inniskillings with the service number 42954.

Private Harvey earned his Victoria Cross on 25 October 1918, despite his citation, dated 6 January 1919, claiming it was on 20 October. On 15 May 1919, accompanied by his sister, he was decorated with his award in the Quadrangle of Buckingham Palace by the King.

The people of Newtown-le-Willows gave him a rousing reception and presented him with an illuminated address and £100 in war bonds. At the beginning of 1919 he was promoted to lance corporal, being demobilised the same year and getting married. His wife was Norah Osmond, who had served as a member of the Queen Mary Auxiliary Corps during the war. He worked for a railway company between the wars and on the outbreak of the Second World War he served with the Royal Engineers, holding the rank of sergeant. He died on 16 February 1942, the result of an accident near Haifa in Palestine, while attached to the 199 Railway Workshop Company, Royal Engineers, holding the rank of CQMS. He is buried in Khayat Beach War Cemetery, Haifa, plot A, row A, grave 4.

Within the Ulster Division the following awards were also earned:

Distinguished Service Order 71
Military Cross 459
Distinguished Conduct Medal 173
Military Medal 1294
Meritorious Service Medal 118
Belgian and French awards 312

Appendix IV

Tributes

Messages of tribute to the Ulster Division from
The Corps Commander.
The Divisional Commander.
The Commanding Officer of the Ulster Volunteer Force.
Sir E. Carson.
The Lord Primate.
The Bishop of Down.
The Bishop of Clogher.
Belfast.
Lieut.-General Sir T. L. N. Morland, K.C.B., DSO, commanding the Army Corps in which the Ulster Division was serving, has issued the following order.

> The General Officer Commanding the Corps wishes to express to the General Officer of the Division and all ranks his admiration of the dash and gallantry with which the attack was carried out, and which attained a large measure of success under very unfavourable conditions. He regrets the heavy and unavoidable losses sustained, and feels sure that after a period of rest the Division will be ready to respond to any call made upon it.
>
> G. WEBB, Brigadier-General, D.A. and Q.M.G.

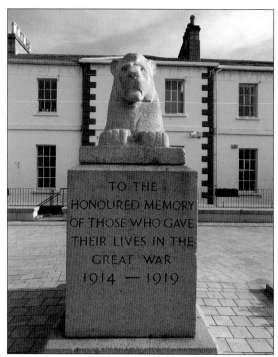

The War Memorial in
Newcastle, County Down,
believed to be the only one
in Ireland bearing a lion.
(Courtesy of Nigel Henderson)

A plaque attached to the war memorial at Magherally Presbyterian Church, showing some fascinating detail open to much debate as to its significance. The wording around the plaque reads; All they had hoped for – all they had they gave – to save mankind themselves they scorned to save. Lest we forget. (Courtesy of Nigel Henderson)

'Ulster Forever' an embroidered card.

The General Officer Commanding the Ulster Division has issued the following special order:

The General Officer Commanding the Ulster Division desires that the Division should know that in his opinion nothing finer has been done in the war than the attack by the Ulster Division on July 1st. The leading of the company officers, the discipline and courage shown by all ranks of the Division will stand out in the future history of the war as an example of what good troops, well led, are capable of accomplishing. None but troops of the best quality could have faced the fire which was brought to bear on them, and the losses suffered during the advance. Nothing could have been finer than the steadiness and discipline shown by every battalion, not only in forming up outside its own trenches, but in advancing under severe enfilading fire.

The advance across the open to the German line was carried out with the steadiness of a parade movement under a fire from front and flanks which could only have been faced by troops of the highest quality. The fact that the objects of the attack on one side were not obtained is no reflection on the battalions that were entrusted with the task. They did all that men could do, and in common with every battalion in the Division, showed the most conspicuous courage and devotion.

On the other side the Division carried out every portion of its allotted task in spite of the heaviest losses. It captured nearly 600 prisoners, and carried its advance triumphantly to the limits of the objective laid down. There is nothing in the operations carried out by the Ulster Division on July 1st that will not be a source of pride to all Ulstermen. The Division has been highly tried, and has emerged from the ordeal with unstained honour, having fulfilled in every particular the great expectations formed of it. Tales of individual and collective heroism on the part of officers and men come in from every side, too numerous to mention, but all showing that the standard of gallantry and devotion attained is one that may be equalled but is never likely to be surpassed. The General Officer Commanding the Division deeply regrets the heavy losses of officers and men. He is proud beyond description, as every officer and man in the Division may well be, of the magnificent example of sublime courage and discipline which the Ulster Division has given to the Army. Ulster has every reason to be proud of the men she has given to the *service of our country. Though many of our best men have gone, the spirit which animated them remains in the Division, and will never die.*

Rally The Flag embroidered postcard.

The following orders of the day have been issued by General Sir George Richardson, K.C.B., G.O.C., Ulster Volunteer Force:

1. The General Officer Commanding wishes to take this opportunity of recording an appreciation of the gallantry of the officers and men of the Ulster Division. Perhaps it may serve as a solace to those on whom will fall the heaviest burden of sorrow, and that it will help to sustain them in the knowledge that duty was nobly done, and that the great warm heart of Ulster goes out to them in affectionate sympathy and takes an unfathomable and unforgettable pride in every man of them.

2. Perhaps more especially the officers and men UVF offer their heartfelt sympathy to the relatives of those who fell on the 1st July, 1916. They were put to the supreme test, and history will claim its own record.

3. For those who fell in the service of their King, the Empire, and the glory of Ulster, we mourn, but we have no regrets. We are proud of our comrades. Our path of duty is clear. Every effort must be made to fill up the casualties in the Division, and maintain the glorious lead given by the brave men of Ulster.

4. The attack of this Division is already talked of outside the Division as a superb example of what discipline, good leading and magnificent spirit can make men capable of performing. Much was expected of the Ulster Division, and nobly they have fulfilled expectation.

5. I will quote from a letter received – "There was never a sign of falter. On the right two battalions of the 108th, the 109th and the 107th swept over four successive lines of German trenches, capturing nearly 600 prisoners and reaching the objective laid down for them absolutely on the stroke of the hour fixed as the time they might be expected to get there. On the left the 12th Royal Irish Rifles made a magnificent effort, but were swept away by machine gun fire. They did all that men could do. The 9th Royal Irish Rifles went to them, and succeeded in getting into the German trenches, and were held up there by weight of 'munition and machine guns."

6. It fills me with pride to think how splendidly our men were capable of performing.

7. On the 30th September, 1915, His Majesty the King was graciously pleased to say to the Ulster Division :-" I am confident that in the field you will nobly uphold the traditions of the fine regiments whose name you bear."

   This mandate has been faithfully obeyed with a heroism and devotion that will establish a rich record in the annals of the British Army, and conveyed to us by the war cry of Ulster – No Surrender."

Ulster Special Service
Force badge.

GEO. RICHARDSON, Lt.-General, G.O.C., UVF
Sir E. Carson has issued the following message to the Ulster people:

> I desire to express, on my own behalf and that of my colleagues from Ulster, the pride and admiration with which we have learnt of the unparalleled acts of heroism and bravery which were carried out by the Ulster Division in the great offensive movement on July 1st.
>
> From all accounts that we have received they have made the supreme sacrifice for the Empire of which they were so proud, with a courage, coolness, and determination, in the face of the most trying difficulties, which has upheld the great tradition of the British Army. Our feelings are, of course, mingled with sorrow and sadness at the loss of so many men who were to us personal friends and comrades; but we believe that the spirit of their race will at a time of such grief and anxiety sustain those who mourn their loss and set an example to others to follow in their footsteps.

His Grace the Lord Primate of All Ireland, who was in Dungannon holding a visitation of the clergy of the rural deaneries of Dungannon, Aghalo, and Tullyhogue, has given us the following message to the people of Ulster –

> All Ireland is proud of the noble gallantry of the Ulster Division. I have lived amongst these officers and men for the greater part of my life, and I expected nothing else. They are of the stock from which our heroes come and to whom our Empire owes so much – unconquered and unconquerable.
>
> Today our hearts are bowed with woe for their relatives at home who have been so grievously bereaved. For many years to come the gallantry of these sons of Ulster will be an inspiration to fresh generations of Irishmen.
>
> I spent a considerable time with them last January in France, and I can testify to their patience and pluck, as well as to their chivalry and courtesy. Oh! the wild charge they made! Their services for honour and truth, after they have passed on into the near presence of God, will never be forgotten.

The Right Reverend Dr D'Arcy, the Bishop of Down, in a message, says:

> The 1st of July will for all the future be remembered as the most glorious in the annals of Ulster. Terrible indeed are the losses sustained. Many of our noblest and best young men, to whom we looked for help and leadership in the time to come, have given their lives in the service of their country and for the welfare of humanity. But our deep sorrow is permeated by the sense of the joyful exultation at their splendid heroism. They have proved themselves worthy of the grandest traditions of their race. They have, indeed, surpassed all records of ancient chivalry. Wherever Ulstermen go they will carry with them something of the glory of the great achievement of the 1st July. The spirit of willing sacrifice for the sake of those great ideals of liberty and progressive humanity which belonged to all that is best in the British race, and which has inspired Ulster throughout all her recent struggles, was never more magnificently exhibited.

The war memorial in Banbridge, County Down, one of the few in the United Kingdom and the only one in Ireland showing celebration. (Courtesy of Dr Gavin Hughes)

A close up of the Banbridge statue, helmet raised to celebrate peace, but bayonet still fixed. (Courtesy of Peter Morton)

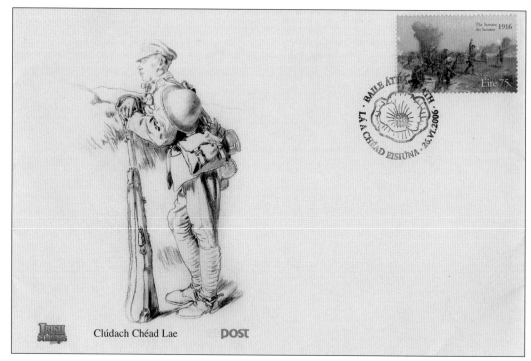

On 26 June, 2006, An Post issued a stamp to mark the 90th Anniversary of the Battle of the Some. The stamp is based on the painting by JP Beadle, the original of which hangs in Belfast City Hall, while the sketch of the soldier is by Sir William Orpen RA, entitled 'South Irish Horse: A Dubliner resting on his way to the Arras Front'.

The Right Reverend Dr Day, the Bishop of Clogher writes:

> I most heartily join with the Lord Primate, the Bishop of Down and others in offering my congratulations to the Ulster Division on the record of their noble deeds at the front in taking a prominent part in the great offensive which was begun on July 1st by the united forces of France and England. While we regret the heavy roll of casualties with which their great achievements were carried out, and sincerely sympathise with the sorrowing relatives of those who have fallen in the cause of their King and country, the "order of the day " issued by General Nugent is a testimony to valour and determination which may well rouse the admiration of everyone who is associated with Ulster.

Appendix V

Reserve Battalions

Six reserve battalions (17th, 18th, 19th and 20th Royal Irish Rifles, 12th Royal Inniskilling Fusiliers and 10th Royal Irish Fusiliers) of the Division were also raised. The 36th Division was the only Irish Division to have its own reserve formations and these battalions did much to provide reinforcements of the service battalions. The 18th Rifles, under the command of Colonel RG Sharman Crawford, CBE, played a part in the Easter Rising of April 1916.

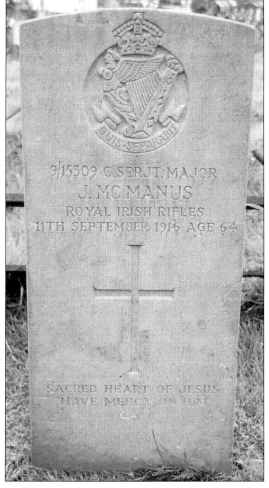

The headstone of Colour Sergeant McManus in (Milltown) RC Cemetery, Belfast. (Photograph courtesy of Nigel Henderson)

Company Sergeant Major John McManus, 18th Royal Irish Rifles, who died on 11 September 1916, aged 64, surely one of the oldest men to serve. He was the husband of Hannah McManus of Mayorca Street, Belfast, and held the Long Service and Good Conduct Medals. (Photograph courtesy of Nigel Henderson)

Appendix VI

Trench Dictionary

Contemporary Trench Dictionary courtesy of the *Belfast News Letter* of 31 August 1918:

ADS – Advance Dressing Station
Aerial Torpedo – Species of trench mortar bomb
Ammonal – High explosive used in bombs
Barrage – Concentrated shell fire on a section of the line
Big Stuff – large shells
Buckshee – Superfluous, extra, not required
Caterpillar – Powerful tractor engine for hauling heavy guns
CCS – Casualty Clearing Station
CT – Communication trench
Compree – Soldier's French for 'Do you understand?'
Consolidate – Strengthen and prepare for defence a captured trench
Crump – Name for a German 5.9 shell so called from sound of exploding
Digging In – making trench in captured position
Dixie – Iron coking pot with handle
Dud – Shell which has failed to explode
Dump – Store of ammunition, rations, or engineering material
Elephant Dug-out – Dug-out braced by heavy steel ribs
Emma-gees – Machine guns
Five-nine – German heavy shell
Four by two – Piece of flannel, four inches by two used for cleaning rifles
Gas Gong – Empty shell case or triangle of iron used for warning in case of gas
Getting a Sub – Receiving an advance of pay
Gippo – Bacon grease, gravy, soup
Going in – and Going out – Entering and leaving the trenches
Got the Crown – promoted to sergeant major
G.S. Wagon – 4-wheeled wagon driven by ASC
Iron Rations – Tin of bully beef, two biscuits and tin containing tea, sugar and Oxo, only to be used in extreme emergency
Mad Minute – Firing fifteen rounds for the rifle in a minute
Mills – Favourite British hand-grenade
Minnie – Short for Minewerfer; German high powered trench mortar bomb
Napoo – Soldier's French for 'Done, no more – Equivalent to 'Fini'
Nose cap – point of shell which unscrews and contains device and scale for setting time fuse
O.Pip – Observation post used by artillery
Pip-Squeak – Small shell
Pull-Through – cord with weight at one end and lop at the other for oily rag (four by two) used in cleaning rifle
RAP – Regimental Aid Post

Ricoc – Ricochet

Rifle Grenade – Bombs on end of rod for firing from a rifle

SAA – Small arms ammunition

Salvo – Battery firing all guns simultaneously

Seventy-five – French field gun, can fire 30 shells a minute

Skrim-shank – To slack or pretend to be ill

Smoke-bomb – Used for clearing Germans out of dug-outs

Stand-to – Time about dawn and dusk when all men in trenches keep on alert in case of enemy attack. After half an hour the 'stand down' leaving only sentries on watch

Strafe – Extra heavy outburst of artillery or rifle fire

Taking over – occupying billets or trenches about to be vacated by another unit

Toot-sweet – *Toute Suite* – Soldier's French for 'Hurry Up', 'Get a move on'

TNT – high explosive

Tin-hat – Steel helmet

Too-Emmas – Trench mortars

Waders – Waterproof boots reaching to thigh used in wet trenches

Wangle – To secure your ends by blarney, bluff or deception e.g. to wangle leave or wangle light duty

Wave – line of troops going over the top

Whiz-bang – Small German shell

Wind-up – Getting nervous or apprehensive about enemy shell fire or attack

Win – To pinch or pick up a thing that does not belong to you. Scrounging is another name for the same thing

Winkle – to clear the enemy out

Appendix VII

Angels of Mons

Since the time of the Great War the story of angels appearing at Mons and saving the British Army has attained mythic status. The legend has existed for more than 80 years, yet there is no official evidence to support the stories. In the various archives of the British Army there is no proof as to any supernatural intervention during the retreat in August 1914. Over the years there have been many stories and theories and it would seem that there are still a number of people who firmly believe that divine intervention by an angelic host saved the army from destruction.

Did the "Angels" give sustenance to the British or terrify the enemy? The one fact not in dispute is that on 23 August 1914, the Germans were abruptly checked in their advance and recoiled in some disorder towards the right flank allowing the remnant of the British forces to continue their retreat.

From that time rumours have constantly circulated regarding the incident, but just what did happen that hot summer day in 1914. In his book *Angles A to Z* Matthew Bunson observed:

> One of the most famous episodes of angelic intervention [was] the supposedly widely reported descent of an angelic army in August 1914, which came to the aid of the British forces against the Germans in Mons. . . The angelic host's assistance could not have come at a more propitious moment as the British were being driven back by the relentless German advance.

Another version, apparently verified by German prisoners, described a band of ghost-like archers led by a tall figure on a shining white horse that led the British during an assault on German trenches, while another told of three angelic beings seen by the British, hovering in the air over German lines, providing a source of deep inspiration for them. Added to this were stories that soldiers claimed to have seen St. Michael the Archangel, the Virgin Mary and even Joan of Arc.

None of the eyewitnesses, however, who later asserted having viewed the Angel came forward in 1914 and had his name recorded in any log or document. British Army veterans who later told of seeing the Angel were suspect and few who fought at Mons survived the war.

One would think that had something sensational been witnessed by the men of a particular battalion or company it would be would be recorded somewhere. In the histories of the regiments involved in the fighting at Mons there is no mention of any events that could be construed as a distraction or an intervention to the action. The units that suffered the most casualties on the 23 August, the 4th Royal Fusiliers and the 4th Middlesex did not record any peculiar events whatsoever. Nor did such regiments active in the battle or retreat such as the Royal West Kents and the 2nd King's Own Scottish Borderers record anything but the trials and tribulations of the battle.

Nevertheless, something occurred on that date to cause many men to put pen to paper in letters, diaries and journals. The British press soon took up these writings and by 1915 the public accepted that an anomalous event had occurred at Mons.

It would appear that the nature of the apparition was angelic rather than saintly or spectral. As a result of this those in the trenches and family at home came to believed in a stereotyped legend of the 'Angel of Mons' whose timely appearance showed that God was providing support for the opponents of the Kaiser's hordes, something that was encouraged by both government and church.

Over the years little has changed and historians who have studied Mons have incorporated the legend of the Angel of Mons into their writings up to the present day. Trevor Wilson and Martin Gilbert mention the phantom in their works. Daniel David in his book, *The 1914 Campaign* states: "Some beleaguered soldiers reported being rescued by angels and ghostly bowmen."

Arch Whitehouse mentions in an earlier work, *Heroes and Legends of World War One* that after the battle a detachment of the Coldstream Guards being the last to withdraw, lost their way in the Mormal Forest. They had dug in to make a last stand when an angel appeared as a dimly outlined female figure. She was described as tall and slim, wearing a white flowing gown. The Guardsmen followed the glowing figure across an open field to a hidden, sunken road and were to escape. No explanation is given as to why the guardsmen should follow such a figure; perhaps they had not seen a woman for a while!

Lyn MacDonald's seminal work, *1914*, includes an account by Captain Arthur Osbon of the 4th Dragoon Guards, a cavalry unit that was involved in the retreat from Mons. He thought that the threatening Cimmerian skies reminded him of Milton's description of legions of dark angels driven by St. Michael to the plains of Hell, vividly descriptive, but hardly relevant to succouring angels.

Either something unusual happened during the battle, in the subsequent retreat or, the legend has a source divorced from the battlefield. The Angel of Mons remains elusive. Eighty years of historical and scientific investigation have left a situation where many reputable sources point to events at Mons, while others treat the Angel as a phenomenon created on the home front.

Suggestions as to what the soldiers saw vary from source to source. Some say that what appeared in the sky were unusual cloud formations, vapour trails from aircraft, or possibly aircraft themselves.

The early morning of 23 August started out with mist and rain, but this cleared around 10:00 am to fair weather with a prevailing westerly wind. There was a warm August sun later in the day, an Ascoli, a stifling August heat and hot sunshine. No weather report mentions unusual cloud formations.

The Royal Flying Corps was active over the battlefield scouting for the enemy and searching for German artillery batteries. The men who comprised the BEF would be accustomed to military aircraft and would not be likely to confuse aircraft or their vapour trails with ethereal phantoms. There are many War Diary entries that confirm the sight of friendly aircraft raised the morale of the troops on the ground.

It has been suggested that during the hours of darkness the Germans used an airship equipped with powerful searchlights. It is feasible that this could have been confused with an angelic host, but none of the later supposed sightings make reference to an event during the hours of darkness.

23 August was a Sunday, was it possible that the idea of forthcoming help had been born during a church service held that morning? Church bells were ringing early and the inhabitants of the villages near the canal were seen in their best attire going to worship. But none of the British unit histories mentions a church parade by the troops at Mons. There is much detail about rations, accommodation, and uniform state, but there is no mention of worship during the day.

On 26 August, Smith-Dorrien's Second Corps, cut off from Haig's Corps, chose to fight a rear-guard action at Le Cateau. In this action the exhausted soldiers of Dorrien's Corps inflicted heavy casualties on the German First Army and still managed to escape. Despite Le Cateau being fought on the anniversary of the Battle of Crecy where victory was won by English archers, no link has ever been made with 'angels'.

In September 1914, the writer Arthur Machen published a short story called 'The Bowmen'. This was a fictional account of a phantom English Army led by St. George marching from Agincourt to relieve their modern counterparts on an unidentified battlefield. 'The Bowmen' was published in September 1914 in the London Evening News. Machen was an author of mildly supernatural stories and a sometime member of a society known as 'The Hermetic Order of the Golden Dawn'.

The Kaiser and Hindenburg meet at the Belgian town of Spa, after the latter's return from success on the Eastern Front.

A quote from Machen states 'The snowball of rumour was set rolling until it was swollen to a monstrous size.' Machen claimed that, "In the popular view shining and benevolent supernatural beings are angels. I believe, the Bowmen of my story have become 'the Angels of Mons." Unfortunately for Machen his story was published after the supposed happenings in Belgium, so was Machen influenced by the rumours coming from France?

Since the end of the Great War the legend has continued to fester in the minds of both the public and historians. Numerous explanations have been offered from both British and German sources.

In February 1930, the following appeared in a New York newspaper; Colonel Friedrich Herzenwirth, who was described as a former member of the Imperial German Intelligence Service, explained that 'angels' really had appeared at Mons. Apparently German aircraft equipped with enormously powerful cinema projectors had used the clouds as a giant screen. The concept was to create panic among the British troops, but had instead created the opposite effect. Counter propaganda in its purest form! Subsequent investigation proved that both the officer and idea were nothing more than a hoax.

So what was the reason for the heroic stand that stopped the Germans in their tracks on that day? Medical evidence would seem to offer the most logical answer.

The army was in full retreat, men marched along roads that were different in construction from those they were used to in Britain and excessive weariness was caused. The distances marched were long, starting at first light and continuing on into the evening, the march quite often interrupted by shelling or the need to fight a rearguard action. There was a shortage of food and water was scarce. During the night little shelter was to be found and troops were forced to sleep outdoors with only their groundsheets and greatcoats for shelter. To alleviate this hunger the troops consumed ripe apples and pears from the numerous roadside orchards.

So we have a combination of extreme exhaustion, immense stress from combat, dehydration and hunger. The latter assuaged by fresh ripe fruit from the orchards. This fruit not only slaked hunger and thirst, but also provided the body with an energy boost from the natural sugar content.

The evidence points to a dire shortage of food water and rest prior to 23 August. If on the evening of 25 August the men concerned had 'dined' on the local fruit they would have gained the energy required for the battle the following day. With regard to 'angels', extreme exhaustion will cause hallucinations, that state where a person suffers errors in perception afflicting some sense organ to such an extent that the person imagines they perceive something for which there is no foundation. For example, a person may fancy he hears himself called during perfect stillness, or may see lights in pitch darkness. Illusions are misinterpreted sensations e.g. the person may constantly mistake articles of furniture for figures of a friend or animal. Both errors occur in sane people and may indicate some slight brain derangement, due to sleeplessness, overwork, feverishness or other cause. They are usually however, a symptom of insanity.

On the night of 26 August 1914 it would only take one man to say he had seen an 'angel' or 'angels' to have the story spread like wildfire among men who were in a similar mental state. And these were soldiers who were in dire need for something to bolster their flagging morale. With the BEF in retreat and the situation as desperate as it was this 'grasping at a straw' was the only alternative to defeat and who else but an 'angel' would come to the aid of a Christian army?[1]

On 19 August 1914, Kaiser Wilhelm allegedly issued an Order of the Day which read in part: "my soldiers to exterminate first the treacherous English; walk over Field Marshal French's contemptible little Army." This led to the men of the British Expeditionary Force proudly labelling themselves the "Old Contemptibles". However, no evidence of the famous Order of the Day was ever found in the German archives after the war, and the former Kaiser denied having given it. An investigation conducted by General Frederick Maurice traced the origins of the Order to the British GHQ where it apparently had been concocted for propaganda purposes.

---

1   Moreno, Amanda & Truesdale, *Angels and Heroes* (2004).

Appendix VIII

Annotated 36th (Ulster) Division Orders of Battle

All numbers quoted are War Establishment, in reality as the months passed there would have always been less, both in manpower and animals. At the heading of each battalion the title is given in full. In the manuscript the battalion titles are abbreviated. The division was to consist of a headquarters, three infantry brigades and supporting units, including machine guns, mortars, supply train and medical services. Training camps were established at Ballykinlar, Newcastle, the Clandeboye Estate near Bangor and Newtownards, all in County Down. To the west of Ulster there was Finner Camp in County Donegal. Those officers who came to the division from the regular army generally had followed a similar path. They would have been educated at a good school, usually followed by Sandhurst and then active service in the Sudan, India and/or the war in South Africa against the Boer Republic.

Brigades & Battalions

Apart from original commanding officers, any attempt to list other officers, such as seconds-in-command or company commanders in any sort of chronological order is almost impossible due to the rapid changes and promotions, especially after General Nugent took command. The Western Front was also a place where promotions, transfers and death came quickly. There are certain exceptions and these have been listed.

107 Brigade

Raised in the City of Belfast, the 107 Brigade did its training at Ballykinlar and was initially commanded by Brigadier General G.H.H. Couchman, DSO, CB. George Henry Holbeche Couchman had been commissioned into the Somerset Light Infantry, rising to the rank of colonel. He had served with the Mounted Infantry on the Burmese Expedition of 1885-1887, where he was twice mentioned in despatches and awarded the Distinguished Service Order. He again served in Burma in 1891 and while there was awarded a Bronze Medal from the Royal Humane Society for rescuing a man who was drowning. Fond of the outdoor life, keen about sports and a fine shot, he undertook survey work while serving in Burma, India and Bengal, eventually serving in the Army Intelligence Branch, in which he served as Deputy Assistant Quartermaster General and later as Assistant Adjutant General. On being promoted to brevet lieutenant colonel he was given command of the 2nd Battalion of the Somerset Light Infantry, a position that he held for the following four years. Prompted to colonel he was subsequently given command of the South Western Brigade (Southern Command) in June 1910. He retired from the army in January 1914, after 36 years' service. He had led a UVF command in Belfast, which in turn gave him command of the 107 Brigade. With a serious shortfall of junior officers Couchman promoted young men who had attended a Belfast grammar school and when this did not harvest enough officers, he

Officers of the Royal Irish Rifles.

then promoted men from the working class areas of the city, who had neither military nor UVF experience, but came recommended by other officers or politicians, this would in turn lead to dire repercussions in France. The Brigade Major was Major J.T. Scriven, however he relinquished his commission in January 1915 and was replaced by Captain F.P. Grant of the Indian Army, who had originally been posted to the Service Squadron of the Inniskilling Dragoons at Enniskillen.

8th Royal Irish Rifles (East Belfast Volunteers)

Formed from the Willowfield Battalion of the UVF, which had, on paper the strength of 1,358 officers and men in May 1913, it was originally commanded by Colonel H.T. Lyle, DSO, on transfer from the 12th Rifles. Lyle was the son of the late James Acheson Lyle, JP, of Portstewart. Lyle had acted as a magistrate for Antrim and his home was in Derganagh, Ballycastle. His second-in-command was Major P.T. Chute, DSO, from Glenfield, County Kerry and formerly of the Cheshire Regiment and Royal Munster Fusiliers. Chute was a veteran of the Burmese Expedition of 1885 to 1889 and the South African War, serving at the actions of Lindley, Bethlehem and Wittebergen, subsequently being awarded the DSO and twice mentioned in despatches.

9th Royal Irish Rifles, (West Belfast Volunteers)

On its formation this battalion was commanded by Lieutenant Colonel G.S. Ormerod, late of the 3rd Battalion Royal Munster Fusiliers, the London Gazette showing his appointment as 30 September 1914. George Sumner Ormerod had served in Burma and South Africa and was aged 60 years. A keen sportsman, he was an avid cricketer and a member of the Middlesex County Cricket Club. The second-in-command was Major Frank Percival Crozier, attached to the battalion as of 4 September 1914. Crozier, the son of an officer, was born in Bermuda in 1879, but spent his early childhood in Ireland, being raised by an aunt in Castlerock, County Dublin. Despite a period serving with the Middlesex Rifle Volunteers, plans for a military career were thwarted due to his lack of height and weight, so he went to Ceylon to become a tea planter. It was here he began to drink heavily before becoming a reformed alcoholic. He travelled to South Africa in 1900 and served as a Corporal in Thornycroft's Mounted Infantry, before obtaining a commission in the Manchester Regiment, receiving the Queen's South African Medal with seven clasps. As a result of dishonoured cheques Crozier resigned his commission in June 1908 and was declared bankrupt the following year. After some time farming in Canada, he returned to the United Kingdom and became involved with the UVF, eventually commanding the West Belfast Battalion. Crozier was given command of the Special Squad that provided security for the Unionist leadership. Having been commissioned into the Royal Irish Fusiliers, Crozier transferred and was appointed as second-in-command of the 9th Rifles. He would gain some notoriety post-war as an author of sorts. Colonel Ormerod became ill in France and was sent back to England. He recovered, but did not return to France and until 1919 commanded a reserve battalion and a prisoner of war camp. Major Crozier, on promotion, took command of the battalion.

10th Royal Irish Rifles, (South Belfast Volunteers)

Commanded by Colonel Herbert Clifford Bernard, a veteran of the Indian Army, having served with the 45th Rattrays Sikhs and later in the Burmese War of 1885-1891, he was gazetted to the battalion as of 14 October 1914. Bernard had been born in Cheltenham the son of a naval officer, Robert Bernard, MD, RN, who had been Deputy Inspector of Hospitals and Fleets. Bernard had been educated at Llandovery College, Wales and had attended Sandhurst. He was gazetted to the 67th (Hampshire) Regiment in 1884 and the following year joined the Indian Army. Bernard married Ina Hoff of Melbourne in 1898, she died ten years later. He commanded the 45th (Rattray's) Sikhs from 1909-1914, when he retired from the Army. Despite his age, he was fifty in 1914, his experience was welcome in this new division of Kitchener's New Army. Officers from far outside the Province were also appointed. The Indian Army supplied Captain J. Hardcastle from the 46th Punjabis, Captain E.P. Grant from the 25th Cavalry Frontier Force, who went to the 6th Service Squadron Inniskilling Dragoons and Lieutenant H.W. Seton from the 9th (Gurkha) Rifles to the 9th Irish Fusiliers.

15th Royal Irish Rifles, (North Belfast Volunteers)

This battalion was initially commanded by Lieutenant Colonel George Higgenson Ford-Hutchinson DSO, who had been commissioned into the Connaught Rangers in May 1885. Ford-Hutchinson was born in October 1861 at Stranocum, Antrim and had been educated at Monaghan Diocesan School, Foyle College, Londonderry, and Trinity College, Dublin, before entering Sandhurst. He had seen service in the Sudan, fighting at Dongola, Atbara and Khartoum in 1882, where he was mentioned in despatches and awarded the DSO, presented to him by Queen Victoria at Windsor in December 1898. He then went on to serve in the South African War seeing action at Ladysmith and Colenso and was later taken prisoner for a time. He had commanded the 1st Connaught Rangers from 1910-1914, retiring in July 1914, only to be recalled to command the 15th Rifles. His second-in-command was Major C. Jackson.

108 Brigade

On being recruited from the counties of Antrim, Down, Armagh, Cavan and Monaghan, the 108 Brigade trained at Clandeboye in Down. The commander was Brigadier George William Hacket Pain, CB. Hacket Pain had been commissioned into the Queen's Royal Regiment in 1875 and served in both Egypt and the Sudan. He had then served in the South African War with the 2nd

Battalion Worcestershire Regiment. Hacket Pain had taken command of the battalion in February 1900 when Colonel Charles Coningham was killed. Following this, he successfully led the force that captured Boer General Prinsloo and 4,000 of his men in July of the same year. In June 1901, he held the town of Heilbron after a fierce action and was considered to be a fearless and gallant soldier, loved and respected by all ranks and had the confidence of both his peers and men. For his actions in South Africa he was made CB, and appointed Governor of Bloemfontein.[1] Hacket Pain had retired from the Army with the rank of Colonel in 1912 and became chief of staff to the UVF.

11th Royal Irish Rifles, (South Antrim Volunteers)

The 11th Rifles were commanded by Lieutenant Colonel H.A. Pakenham, the son of General T.H. Pakenham, CB, of Langford Lodge, Crumlin, a veteran of the Crimean War where he had been twice wounded while serving with the Grenadier Guards; while a grand-uncle, Edward Pakenham had served with Wellington in the Peninsula and was later killed at the battle of New Orleans. Hercules Arthur Pakenham had been commissioned into the Grenadier Guards in 1883 and served in the Sudan Campaign of 1885. Prior to the Great War he had served as an MP, and performed military and political duties in Canada, India and Australia. He had the reputation of being a very fast speaker, much to the chagrin of reporters. Major Blair-Oliphant was the second-in-command of the battalion. Philip Laurence Kington Blair-Oliphant, born in 1867, was the head of the Kingston-Blair-Oliphant family of Ardblair, Blairgowrie, Scotland, a family that traced their roots back to Sir William Oliphant, who defended Stirling Castle against the English in 1303. Blair-Oliphant was the son of Philip Oliphant Kington Blair-Oliphant and Henrietta Yaldwyn, of Ardblair Castle, Blairgowrie, Perthshire, and the husband of Geraldine Blair-Oliphant. He was educated at Harrow and entered the Army in 1888, being commissioned in to the Rifle Brigade. He was promoted to the rank of Lieutenant in 1891 and in June 1895 was gazetted as Captain. He retired in 1902, having married the previous year Laura Bodenham, of Elmhurst, Hereford. He came to Lisburn and joined the UVF, being attached to the 1st Lisburn Battalion, where his experience and strict discipline, but charismatic leadership soon made the battalion proud to serve under him. On the formation of the 11th Rifles, he was promoted to major and accepted the post of second-in-command.

12th Royal Irish Rifles, (Central Antrim Volunteers)

The battalion was initially commanded by Lieutenant Colonel R.C.A. McCalmont, MP. Educated at Eton, he had joined the Army in 1900 and saw service in the South African War with the 6th Royal Warwickshire Regiment. On the formation of the Irish Guards in 1902 he was gazetted as a second lieutenant, becoming a major by 1910. He had retired from the Army in 1913 to become Member of Parliament for East Antrim. McCalmont had commanded a battalion of the Antrim Regiment of the UFV prior to being given command of the 12th Rifles. In April he was appointed to command the 1st Battalion Irish Guards. Command of the Rifles then devolved to Lieutenant Colonel George Bull, DSO, of Downshire House, Newry, County Down. Bull had previously served with the Royal Irish Fusiliers, being wounded with them in 1915 and had been mentioned in despatches by Viscount French and awarded the DSO. The second in command was Major Claude George Cole-Hamilton, DSO, appointed from the Reserve of Officers. He was formerly a captain in the 4th Rifles and had served in South Africa as commander of a mounted infantry

---

1   Diary of Captain C.F. Wodehouse, Worcestershire Regiment, killed at Neuve Chapelle 1 March 1915.

Men of the Royal Irish Rifles, three wearing wound chevrons.

Newtownards war memorial today. Tardiness on behalf of the local authorities caused a number of ex-servicemen to build a memorial from snow in March 1924. As a result four of them were arrested and charged with obstruction, being fined 2/6d plus 2d costs. Despite the public outcry it was not until 26 May 1934 that today's memorial was unveiled by the Marquis of Londonderry.
(Author's photograph)

company, earning an MID and the DSO. In 1912 he had been appointed as Chief Constable of Breconshire and had been living for some time in South Wales.

13th Royal Irish Rifles, (1st County Down Volunteers)

Commanded by Colonel William Henry Savage from Cushendall in County Antrim, he had formerly served in the Indian Army and was on the point of retirement when approached to command a battalion of the UVF. Major Holt Waring, formerly serving with the North Irish Horse, was the second-in-command and would later command the battalion. C Company was commanded by Major Robert D. Perceval-Maxwell, who would also later command the battalion. He had previously served with the North of Ireland Imperial Yeomanry. Perceval-Maxwell had family retainers follow him into the division. His butler from Finnebrogue House, Downpatrick, served as Private Henry Walker, he was wounded on 1 July. Private John Doherty, the footman, was killed on the same day. Both men had been members of the Inch Company UVF. Perceval-Maxwell's son, Lieutenant J.R. Perceval-Maxwell, serving with the King's Royal Rifle Corps, was also wounded in action.

The war memorial at Moy, County Armagh. (Author's photograph)

9th Royal Irish Fusiliers, (Armagh, Monaghan and Cavan Volunteers)

The Armagh, Monaghan and Cavan Volunteers were organised under their commanding officer, Lieutenant Colonel Stewart W. Blacker, formerly of the Royal Field Artillery and a well-respected figure in the local community. Blacker had served on the North West Frontier, had been wounded in action and received a mention in despatches for his service in the South African War. He had retired from the Army in 1903 and was a staunch member of the Orange Order. The Armagh Volunteers became the 9th Battalion Royal Irish Fusiliers and were soon nicknamed Blacker's Boys. The battalion contained a high number of farmers and owing to responsibilities on the farm, recruiting volunteers was harder and took much longer than other battalions. Blacker arguably, raised the best battalion in the division in terms of both discipline and combat effectiveness.[2] Second-in-command of the battalion was Major Audley Pratt, the son of Joseph Pratt, DL, former High Sheriff of Cavan; he had served with the 1st Battalion, Royal Scots in the South African War and been mentioned in despatches. The padre was the Reverend Francis Johnston Halahan, AchD, who would become the senior chaplain of the division and later a recipient of the Military Cross.[3]

109 Brigade

Recruited from Tyrone, Londonderry, Donegal and Fermanagh, including one Belfast battalion, the 14th Rifles, the brigade trained at Finner Camp in Donegal and was commanded by Brigadier T.E. Hickman, CB, DSO. Thomas Edgecumbe Hickman was born in 1859, one of six children to Sir Alfred Hickman Bt, a major Black Country industrialist and Conservative MP for Wolverhampton West. Hickman was commissioned into the 36th Regiment of Foot, later the 2nd Battalion, Worcestershire Regiment from the Militia, in February 1881, aged 22. Hickman spent most of his early military service attached to the Egyptian Army and earned the nickname Hickman Bey. He also took part in the South African War and when peace was declared he was appointed as GOC Middleburg District, Cape Colony, from 1902-08, after which he went on half pay. Hickman retired from the Army on 4 April 1914 and had devoted his time to being Unionist MP for Wolverhampton South since 1910. He took a great interest in Irish affairs and became President of the British League for the Defence of Ulster and Inspector General of the Ulster Volunteer Force.

Private James Culbert, a fifer with the Royal Irish Rifles.

Hickman had served as second-in-command to General Kitchener at the Battle of Handoub in January 1888, when units of the British-trained Egyptian Army attacked the stronghold of Osman Dinga (Today rendered as Uthman Diqna). It was here that Hickman had to take command when Kitchener was hit in the jaw by a bullet that caused a near fatal wound. Consequently, it was Hickman that Kitchener, now Secretary of State for War, sought out when he wanted the Ulster

---

2   Bowman, *Irish Regiments in the Great War, Discipline and Morale.*
3   *London Gazette,* 18 October 1917.

Officers and men of the Royal Inniskilling Fusiliers.

Volunteers for his New Army. In turn Hickman was granted the rank of brigadier general and given command of 109 Brigade, despite him being 55 years old and a sitting M.P. Described by many as a competent soldier, he nevertheless believed in the maxim that any fool can be uncomfortable, so he took his butler with him to France to act as batman. Hickman would hold this command until he was replaced by Brigadier General Reginald Gauntlett Shuter, DSO.

9th Royal Inniskilling Fusiliers, (Tyrone Volunteers)

Commanded by Colonel Ambrose St. Quentin Ricardo DSO. The Ricardo home was in Gloucestershire and Ricardo had become a director of Herdmans Ltd, on the death of his father. He had been commissioned into the Inniskillings in 1888 and was promoted to Captain in 1897 and had seen service on the North West Frontier during the following year. Ricardo was twice mentioned in despatches for his service in the South African War and awarded the DSO. He retired from the Army in 1904 and subsequently became involved in the organising of the UVF. He rejoined the Army in 1914. The majority of the battalion had been members of the Tyrone Regiment of the 5th Ulster Volunteers. In October 1913 a permanent camp was established at Baronscourt, the home of the Duke of Abercorn since 1612. Here the stables were converted into barrack rooms, with a post office and telegraph office. There were drill parades, lectures and a firing range was provided.

10th Royal Inniskilling Fusiliers, (Derry Volunteers)

The UVF Headquarters in Derry was located on Hawkin Street and it was from here that the first group of volunteers marched to Finner Camp in Ballyshannon. The battalion was commanded by Lieutenant Colonel Ross Acheson Smyth who came from Londonderry and it was to him that credit was due for the initial instilling of discipline and morale within the Battalion. Smyth was born on 3 September 1862 and been commissioned into the Royal Irish Regiment in May 1885. He saw action during the Chin-Lushai Expedition of 1889-90 and served with the Mounted

Infantry in the South African War, where he was wounded. For his services in South Africa, he was mentioned in despatched and awarded the brevet of major. He also received the Queen's medal with five clasps, before retiring on half pay in 1903.[4] The Colonel lost his son John Ross Smyth killed in action in October 1914.[5] In March 1915, Captain F.G. Kunhardt, late of the 74th Punjabis, was appointed as second-in-command. Among the battalion's officers was Eton-educated Lieutenant Charles Norman Lockhart Strong, the son of Sir Charles Strong 7th Baronet, of Tynan Abbey, Armagh, who would do well while serving with the battalion. A and B companies consisted mostly of men recruited from Derry City, while C Company consisted of men from Coleraine, Limavady and the country districts, with D Company recruiting from the smaller villages and rural districts of the County.[6] Not all members of the UVF who enlisted served in the Ulster Division. Thomas Boston from Mount Pottinger, Belfast, served as adjutant with the South Derry Volunteers, UVF, before joining the Inniskillings. He later transferred to the 10th Battalion of the Machine Gun Corps where he served as a lieutenant, seeing action in the Middle East. He died of pneumonia on Christmas Day 1918 and is buried in Cairo War Memorial Cemetery.

11th Royal Inniskilling Fusiliers, (Donegal and Fermanagh Volunteers)

Raised at the beginning of September 1914 from the Donegal and Fermanagh Volunteers, the battalion moved into Finner Camp on 20 September. The first commanding officer was Lieutenant Colonel William Francis Hessey, who had been commissioned into the Inniskillings in 1890 and was a veteran of the South Africa War, having been adjutant of the 1st Battalion. While in South Africa he had been wounded at Colenso on 15 December 1899, but had recovered in time for the actions at Vaal Krantz, the Tugela Heights and the relief of Ladysmith. After service in South Africa, Hessey had been adjutant of the OTC at Durham University, from where he also gained his BA. He had officially retired from the Army in 1913, holding the rank of major. The second-in-command was Major the Earl of Leitrim, who had formerly served in the 9th Lancers and had seen service in South Africa with the Imperial Yeomanry. While there he had been taken prisoner with Winston Churchill while on a reconnaissance aboard an armoured train. Held in a prison in Pretoria both he and Churchill subsequently escaped, making their way overland for some 300 miles to Portuguese territory. The adjutant was Captain R.L. Moore, formerly of the 3rd Hussars. With difficulties in recruiting locally, Fermanagh and Donegal being primarily farming country, men were sought elsewhere. A large number of men volunteered from Tyneside.

14th Royal Irish Rifles, (Young Citizen Volunteers of Belfast)

This battalion was formed from the ranks of the Young Citizen Volunteers of Belfast, a mostly middle class organisation that had been formed in September 1912. All men between the ages of 18 and 35 were eligible for membership, with a minimum height of five feet and on the proviso of credentials of good character. While the membership was largely Protestant, there were also Catholics, Jews and Quakers.[7] The battalion was first commanded by Lieutenant Colonel Robert

4   *Belfast News Letter,* 7 July 1916.

5   Second Lieutenant John Ross Smyth, 2nd Battalion Royal Irish Regiment, killed on 20 October 1914, he has no known grave, commemorated on the Le Touret Memorial panel 11 & 12.

6   Much argument arises from the naming of Derry/Londonderry. Its use is taken from an account written by Lt. Colonel FSN Macrory, DSO.

7   The Quakers served as medical orderlies and stretcher bearers. Other Quakers from Ulster served with the Friends' Ambulance Unit, which was founded as the Anglo-Belgian Ambulance Unit, with over 1,000 members seeing service in France and Belgium.

Peel Dawson Spencer Chichester, formerly a major with the Irish Guards, and a man who suffered from persistent problems with his lungs, making it necessary to be absent on sick leave from October 1915 until September 1916. Major H.R. Bliss, 3rd Royal Irish Regiment, became acting commanding officer for three months until Major Llewellyn, from the 9th Inniskillings, took temporary command. The battalion began recruiting on Monday 14 September 1914, when their office opened at the Old Town Hall in Victoria Street, Belfast, with a stream of men appearing throughout the morning and afternoon for medical examinations. In the evenings a magistrate was on hand for the swearing-in process, which was not done on an individual basis, but in groups of twenty or more. Colonel Chichester always addressed his men as Young Citizens and set a high example in obtaining billets, food, uniforms and generous leave for his men, a standard that many other battalions were unable to emulate. Chichester's servant (batman) was Private McCoubrey, an ex-Irish Guardsman who was so proud of his former regiment that he continued to wear its cap badge for some time. The adjutant was Captain Robert Bentley, who had served as Adjutant of the YCV. The battalion's first parade had been held in Davidson's Yard on the Ravenhill Road, Belfast. The YVC had consisted of eight companies, lettered A to H, and on this parade each man was permitted to pick his own company so as friends could be together. As a regular army battalion only had four companies some amalgamation was necessary, therefore E-F became C etc. Those men who had been non-commissioned officers in the YCV generally carried their ranks into the 14th Battalion. Second Lieutenant H. Hanna, a former member of the Officers Training Corps, had a loud clear voice for issuing drill instructions and struck a dashing figure in his neat civilian clothes and straw hat. To assist him with the drill movements were several veterans of the war in South Africa, who acted as Senior NCOs on these parades. There was also a pay parade where an allowance was made for the men's use of their civilian clothes.[8] Again, there was difficulty in recruiting and approximately 17 percent of the men came from others parts of Ireland, while it is estimated 25 percent were from England, Scotland and Wales. During the first year of its existence the battalion contained five officers and 98 other ranks who were Roman Catholic.

16th (Pioneer) Battalion Royal Irish Rifles (2nd County Down Volunteers)

The 16th Rifles were divisional pioneers and not attached to any particular brigade. To give an idea of the work carried out by the pioneers the following may serve as an example: In order to construct a reserve trench of 1,800 yards in length, it required 5,036 bags of cement, 19,384 bags of shingle and 9,692 bags of sand. Considering the number and length of trenches the amount of material required throughout the war was enormous. In 1914 a British division required 27 railway wagons of supplies, food, ammunition, fodder and equipment, to survive for a week. By 1916 the same division required 50 wagons, mostly due to the increase in ammunition and munitions being used. The railway lines and sidings that brought these supplies to the Front were built by the pioneer battalions under the direction of the Royal Engineers. In construction sandbags were used by the million. They were widely used in the Crimea and can be traced back to the early 18th Century. It has been wrongly assumed by some writers that when men are described as advancing carrying sand bags that these are full of earth or sand! This is not the case, empty sand bags were carried forward and filled where and when necessary to help fortify captured enemy positions. In October 1915 the UVF sent the Ulster Division 20,000 sandbags. Sir George Richardson wrote to General Nugent to say that there was a loving thought in every stitch.[9] Likewise with barbed wire, when coils of barbed wire were taken forward, it was for the same reason. In waterlogged

---

8   DSCF 9059 & 9071.
9   Letter from General Nugent to his wife, 31 October 1915.

parts of the Front the fortifications consisted of breastworks, built up high to the front, with just a shallow trench dug behind, due to the drainage being so difficult. These breastworks were made of millions of tightly-made sandbags laid one upon the other, packed well together. Every eight yards there was an island traverse, a great mound of earth and sandbags strengthened by revetting, round which the trench would wind. This was to localise the explosion of enemy shells or prevent an enemy who might reach the flank being able to shoot down the length of a trench. There were communication trenches back every few yards and innumerable succeeding lines for the main army. The whole network extends in most places for three or four miles. The dug-outs were all in lines, but mostly along the communication trenches.

Work such as this was carried out by the pioneers of the division, who also went by the nickname 'The Terrors' and were recruited mostly in the Lurgan area of County Down, with their headquarters being in Brownlow House, Lurgan. The first commanding officer was Lieutenant Colonel Charles Gilbert Carnegy MVO, and its establishment was to be 1,139 officers and other ranks.[10] The first man to enlist in the battalion was John McAvoy of Maryville Street, Belfast, who had given up his job as an apprentice motor mechanic. By January 1915, this strength stood at about 700. The role of the pioneers was more than just manual labour; each member of the battalion was a fully trained infantryman and many had other skills, such as railway engine driver. It would appear that Colonel Carnegy never actually took his post and command of the battalion was in the hands of Major John Leader. Leader had been commissioned into the Bedfordshire Regiment in 1896 and had been a captain by 1902. He had served in China and the South African War, seeing action in the Orange Free State, Cape Colony and at Colesberg; he was also a fluent speaker of German and Japanese. His second-in-command was Major Robert Gardiner who excelled at teaching the men foot drill and basic military discipline, such as not spitting on parade. The local papers carried a report on 24 September 1915 that Major Alexander Gordon Lind, formerly of the 58th Vaughan's Rifles (Frontier Force Indian Army), had been appointed as second-in-command. However, there is no further documentation regarding this officer in any of the war diaries and it must be assumed he did not take up the post.

The battalion adjutant was Captain W.J. Allen, formerly a local JP and highly placed member of the Orange Order. He supervised the intake of new recruits and the administration of discipline. Allen would eventually become second-in-command of the battalion and finally its commanding officer. Recruiting for the pioneers began in January 1915, with almost weekly full page advertisements appearing in the likes of the *Bangor Spectator* and *Newtownards Chronicle* throughout January, February and March. If a man was already a member of the UVF, his company commander issued him with a free travel warrant for the train journey to Lurgan from anywhere in the Province. The battalion seemed, on occasion, to be a bit less selective in its recruits. Thomas Davis, Old Hillsborough Road, Lisburn, had originally tried to enlist in the 11th Rifles, but was debarred due to his age. As an ex-soldier he was anxious to do his bit in the conflict and therefore made his way to Lisburn, where a combination of losing a few years of his age, his obvious experience and the shortage of recruits, saw him enlisted in the pioneers. Davis was soon promoted to sergeant and was wounded in June 1916, returning home for convalescence. His son, also Sergeant Davis, served with the 14th Rifles.

The battalion consisted of four companies with a War Establishment of 1,139 all ranks. Each company was commanded by a captain and consisted of approximately 180 men. No.1 Company, Captain Shepherd, No.2 Company, Captain W.R. White, No.3 Company, Captain Chase and No.4 Company, Captain Knox. In February 1915 a number of men from the battalion were sent to Dublin to acquire skill and working knowledge of railway engine driving. The Field Service

---

10   *Belfast New Letter,* 4 January 1915.

Pocket Book (1914) includes no reference to pioneer battalions, however that relating to the War Establishment (India) did. It would appear that the need for pioneers in Kitchener's New Armies emerged as the first clashes occurred in France and Flanders. The men received the normal infantry training and had to be in the peak of physical fitness. They received an extra 2d per day for their prowess in railway and road construction; the digging and constructing of field defences, stringing of barbed wire, bridging and demolition. They were also required to construct huts and encampments, often at short notice. Their duties were little short of the work carried out by the Royal Engineers field companies. The main difference was that the Battalion carried out all this work by hand as they had no access to mechanical aids. It takes a special kind of courage to work with pick and shovel while under shell and machine gun fire. *Captain Hugh Montgomery Baillie was one of the original members of the UVF and had been a squad leader, section commander and half company commander. Pre-War had had been apprenticed to Carson and McDowell Solicitors, Belfast, before enlisting in November 1914. In January of the following year he had been granted a commission in the 16th Rifles.* On arrival at Seaford, Captain Knox, Lieutenant WR White and Second Lieutenants Kemp, Maxwell and Swan had attended and passed the machine gun course at Aldershot. On many occasions when the division was out of the line the battalion would continue to serve elsewhere with other units and by the War's end held the record for seeing more action that any other battalion of the division. In India a pioneer battalion had an authorised allocation of camp followers, no such dispensation was granted to the Terrors.

Divisional Units

An infantry division must be supported in the field, be fed, transported, receive medical care and be re-supplied with ammunition, uniforms and equipment. Those units responsible for the 36th Division were as follows.

Stone of Remembrance at Connaught Cemetery.

48th Mobile Veterinary Section

The Army Veterinary Service was founded in 1796 as a direct result of public concern that more horses were being lost to poor handling and care as opposed to enemy action. Public outcry and debate in Parliament led to the Committee of General Officers authorising the formation of the Army Veterinary Service to 'improve the practice of Farriery in the Corps of Cavalry'. John Shipp of the 87th Regiment and 11th Light Dragoons was the first veterinary surgeon and as he had been commissioned on 25 June 1796, this date remains as the Foundation Day of the present Royal Army Veterinary Corps, John Shipp Day.

The formation of the Army Veterinary Department in 1880 saw most of the veterinary officers placed under the Department's direction, although the officers remained under the direct control of their parent regiment. The Army Veterinary School was created at Aldershot that same year and when this was merged with the Artillery School there was a vast improvement in the skills and military application in good horse management. In 1890, Colonel John Lambert was appointed as Director General and in 1903 the Army Veterinary Service saw all officers, with the exception of some cavalry units, serving under the one badge. This organisation also provided a source of other ranks to assist the surgeons, as previously these had been supplied at the discretion of the regiment. During the Great War the AVS would treat some 2.5 million animals, the majority on the Western Front and would see almost 80 percent returned to duty, an outstanding achievement in battlefield conditions.

One of the most important, if not vital animals was the horse and the Ulster Division, despite being an infantry division, still required a large number of horses to carry out its duties in the field. The official War Establishment for an infantry division, as per 1914, was 5,592 horses and mules. Of these 1,471 were riding horses, 3,350 were draught horses, 644 were heavy draught horses and 127 were pack animals. These animals were not only required to carry officers and dispatch riders, but also to pull carts, wagons, ambulances and the attached artillery pieces.

The care of horses required a degree of skill and affection, something that often had a detrimental effect on morale. Horses can sleep either standing up or lying down. They will sleep standing up due to the fight or flight instinct. Better to be on your toes and ready to run away from the hunter. They will sleep lying down when relaxed and in what they consider to be a safe environment. Horses are very easily spooked, sometimes all it takes is a fluttering piece of paper in the hedge that they haven't spotted before and they'll jump to the other side of the road. There was many an officer who got on a horse he was unfamiliar with, only to find it bolting out of sheer terror at the first sound of the artillery. Not all officers were financially able to bring their own mounts to France. Horses are real herd animals, very sociable and have a definite pecking order. A horse employed in hard work needed approximately 20 pounds of hay a day and about three to four of extra food like barley, bran or mixed grains. They have a passion for apples, carrots, bread, turnips and parsnips as treats. In the summer time however they can do fantastically well on just grass alone. They also drink water in large quantities. If they are working very hard they will get through a set of iron shoes in about four to five weeks. These horses enjoyed their work, were strong boned and had a calm temperament, not at all like thoroughbred racing horses who act like royalty. The bonds that would have been built up between each horse and his rider or handler would often have been very strong. A great horse will be incredibly loyal and many horses recognised familiar footsteps before their handler was in sight; they quite often whinny when their riders or handlers left them for other tasks. In the winter conditions of the Western Front many horses suffered from a condition called mud fever. It particularly occurred on horses with white socks or stockings on their legs. It is a bacterial infection. The bacteria lives in the ground, but it really only occurs in the winter time when a horse is out in sloppy, muddy conditions. It doesn't cause any fever, more of a nasty skin rash that results in tiny little scabs

A Section of the Divisional Engineers.

that have to be kept dry to heal up. In the summer time, the flies probably caused a great degree of annoyance and they would have stood head to tail swishing their tails to get rid of them. Some cavalry regiments cropped the horse's tails to keep them tidy, therefore giving them no means of swatting flies from each other's faces during the summer months. To the handlers the loss of a horse was felt as strongly, if not more so, than the loss of a fellow soldier. As of 8 April 1915, Major C. Rose was appointed as Assistant Director of Veterinary Services within the division. It is to the eternal shame of the British Government that at the end of the War those horses and mules that had survived were sold for slaughter. It was decreed that the cost of bringing them home as too expensive.

Royal Engineers

The maintenance of railways and roads was the responsibility of the Royal Engineers, as were the supply of fresh water and the construction of bridges. They also operated the railways, both narrow and broad gauge, piloted canal barges, erected and repaired telephone lines, dug trenches, constructed strongpoints and artillery positions. On the outbreak of the War there were 1,056 officers and 10,394 other ranks serving as Regulars and in the Special Reserve, as well as a further 513 officers and 13,127 other ranks with the Territorial Force. By the end of the War the establishment had increased twelvefold. As the War progressed the Royal Engineers would take on such tasks as tunnelling and gas companies.

121st & 122nd Field Companies Royal Engineers

Commanded by Colonel H. Finnis CSI, as of April 1915, the 121st and 122nd Field Companies recruited in Belfast and initially trained at Clandeboye, prior to moving to Antrim on 11 November 1914. However, due to a shortage of men with an element of mechanical training recruits were sought elsewhere, both within Ireland and from the north-east of England. A party of men remained in Clandeboye to assist in the erection of huts. In January 1915, it was decided to increase the two Field Companies by 75 men each, making their establishment 305 all ranks. Captain Rupert Stanley was posted to A Company as of 3 October 1914, post-war the Rupert Stanley College, Belfast, would be named in his honour. Temporary Major Clarence Craig joined the Company in 1916; he resigned his commission on 28 December 1917 and was granted the honorary rank of Major. Lieutenant M.J.D. Kerr was sent to the School of Military Engineers at Chatham for a course of instruction in May 1915.

150th (Field) Company Royal Engineers

With a War Establishment of 305 all ranks, this unit was initially based in Antrim. Mr J.L. Peacocke, CE, originally from Norfolk, was employed by Newtownards Council and was commissioned into the Royal Engineers about March 1915 and made his way to Antrim, after a brief soiree. Also here was Second Lieutenant W.L. Shaw. In March 1915, Lieutenant A.W. Stark Christie was transferred from the 109 Brigade to the Divisional Engineers, later joined by Lieutenants W. Smyth and E.A.T. Dillon. Eventually all officers attended courses of instruction at Chatham. On 4 May 1915, Lance Corporal E. Driscoll and several others were sent to Dublin on a railway transport course. From Dean's Hill in Armagh came Second Lieutenant Michael Richard Leader Armstrong, a former student at Trinity College, Cambridge, who had earned his BA in Mechanical Science. The Armstrong School in Armagh would eventually bear his name. Driver W. Holmes was a former member of the Malone and Balmoral Battalion of the South Belfast Regiment, Ulster Volunteer Force and a member of the Malone Darts Club. He has the dubious honour of being the first member of the Field Company to become a casualty on 16 October 1915, he was sent to hospital in Bristol. The Balmoral area of the city had a fine recruiting record, from the Golf Club 36 members had enlisted up to August 1915.

A leave pass issued to Corporal W. Thompson of the Divisional Signal Company.

Divisional Signal Company

Recruited in Belfast, mainly from men who worked in the shipyards, it consisted of 346 officers and men with 40 vehicles and 120 horses and mules. Its equipment was of the latest design, with the field telephones better than those supplied to the Regular Army. These had been brought with them from UVF stores. After a time spent at Newtownards, the Signals Company then moved by rail to Downpatrick to continue training.

Army Service Corps (Royal Army Service Corps as of Army Order 362, 1918) & Divisional Train

During the Great War the Army Service Corps carried out a wide range of duties, which expanded as the War progressed. It was organised at the company level, each fulfilling a specific role and controlled at divisional, corps or army level.

In 1914, the British Expeditionary Force numbered 120,000 men and 53,000 horses. On a weekly basis this force required 900,000 pounds of meat, 1,375,000 pounds of bread, 210,500 gallons of petrol and 1,500,000 pounds of horse fodder. By 1918, manpower had increased to 3,000,000 men and 500,000 horses consuming 16,870,000 pounds of meat, 22,000,000 pounds of bread, 3,000,000 gallons of petrol and 8,250,000 pounds of horse fodder.

These supplies were shipped across the Channel to ports in France and from there by train to a Divisional Railhead or Advance Supply Depot. Here trucks would carry the supplies to a Divisional Refilling Point and from here horse drawn wagons took them to the forward dumps where Quartermasters oversaw supplies.

Each army division had its own transport, usually horse-drawn; this was known as the Divisional Train and provided the main means of transporting supplied to the various brigades and artillery batteries. It theoretically comprised of 26 officers and 402 other ranks of Army Service Corps personnel, who again theoretically, had 387 horses, 125 wagons, 17 carts and 30 bicycles. These were organised into a headquarters and four Horsed Transport Companies, one per brigade and one for the divisional headquarters and attendant troops. The Train always moved with the division. In the 36th Division 251, 252, 253 and 254 Companies of the Army Service Corps were formed at Enniskillen in November 1914. The division also had a certain amount of motorised transport allocated to it, although this was not under its direct command. The 379 Divisional Supply Column Company was formed in July 1915 and consisted of five officers, 337 other ranks and 45 3-ton lorries, 16 30cwt lorries, seven motorcycles, two cars and four other assorted trucks for the workshops and stores of the Supply column itself.

Dumps and stores of ammunition were the responsibility of the Motor Transport Companies known as Ammunition Parks. These units handled all types of ordnance from small arms ammunition, mortar bombs, grenades, shells for field guns and included the handling of the larger calibre shells that required special equipment to move them. The 380 Motor Transport Company of the 36th Division was formed in July 1915. The ASC also drove ambulances, operated Heavy Repair Shops (the forerunner of the Royal Electrical Mechinical Engineers of the Second World War), bridging and pontoon companies and the ASC Remounts Service.

On 27 November 1914, the *Belfast News Letter* announced that Annadale Hall had been taken over for the accommodation of the Divisional Train ASC. The mansion had recently been the scene of a Suffragette fire, but an early discovery had resulted in minimal damage being caused. An advertisement in the local papers appeared on 30 November 1914, asking for recruits to the Army Service Corps, much needed were carpenters, wheelers, coopers, farriers, saddlers, collar makers, harness makers, shoeing and jobbing smiths, shoemakers, tailors, drivers, bakers, and butchers. Drivers were especially required and when judged proficient were to receive and extra 6d per day, making a total of 1s 6d per day. Drivers were especially difficult to recruit, given that so few young men were capable of driving at that time and had little interest in doing so.

Major J.M. Harrison assumed command of the unit as of December 1914, and was promoted to lieutenant colonel. Harrison, from Newcastle-on-Tyne, had seen previous action in West Africa and the South African War. In January 1915 headquarters was located in Carlton House, 364 Ormeau Road and the following officers were know to have been attached to the corps at that time; Captain C. Blakiston-Houston and Lieutenants William Hunter, Robert Cowzer, Harold C. Robinson and A.J. Cussans. There was also the 8th Auxiliary Horse Transport Company, 225th Company (Ulster) ASC, under Captain J. Gilman, MT, ASC.

Lieutenant R.J. Cowzer, came from Bangor, Down and worked as a stockbroker with Messrs. Josias Cunningham & Co. of Belfast. A former member of the UVF, he had been commissioned into the Army Service Corps in September 1914, accompanying the 107 Brigade to Ballykinlar. Promoted to captain he would do sterling service in France, seeing to the feeding of some 6,000 men and 5,000 horses and mules. In August 1916 he succeeded Major English VC, as senior supply officer for the division. In 1917, he was promoted to major and awarded the Military Cross, an award made for continious service up to and including March 1918.

Major William John English, VC, had been born in Ireland, educated in England and at Campbell College, Belfast. In 1900 he travelled to South Africa and enlisted as an 'other rank' in the Scottish Horse, a locally raised unit, he was 17 years old. The following year he was commissioned as a lieutenant in the 2nd Scottish Horse and saw action against the Boers. On 3 July at the small settlement of Vlakfontein, English and five of his men were holding the right flank of a position while under attack from a Boer commando. With two of his men killed and almost out of ammunition English ran to the next position in the line, across some 15 yards of open ground, and obtained both ammunition and water. For his actions he was awarded the Victoria Cross, receiving it in person from King Edward VII in July of the following year. He later served with the 2nd Dragoon Guards, and in 1906 was commissioned into the Army Service Corps. A veteran of three wars, South African, The Great War and the Second World War, he died of a cerebral haemorrage on board ship near Egypt while serving with the Royal Ulster Rifles on 4 July 1941. He is buried in Maala Cemetery, Aden. On his death his medal group was bequeathed to his former school, Campbell College.

6th Inniskilling Dragoons

The service squadron of the 6th Inniskilling Dragoons had been largely raised from the Enniskillen Horse of the UVF, which had in turn been raised by William Copeland Trimble, a prominent Fermanagh Unionist and editor of *The Impartial Reporter* newspaper. The original unit had been raised to provide a mounted escort for Sir Edward Carson's visit to that town in 1912. Trimble was not offered a command within the Dragoons, no doubt due to his lack of military experience and advanced age.[11] In November 1914 Trimble presented the Squadron with a trained Drum Horse and the loan of a drum saddle and drums. Major Strettel, commanding the Squadron, hoped they would have both time an opportunity to make use of them before going overseas.[12] In January 1915 a section of Military Police arrived from Aldershot and with a number of men from the Dragoons were posted to the Divisional Train as provost guards.

---

11   Bowman, *Irish Regiments in the Great War, Discipline and Morale.*
12   *Belfast News Letter,* 28 November 1914.

36th Cycling Company

> We got the train down to Enniskillen. Some of us got to go at a riding school, but there were fellas gettin' on the horse facing the tail! Some fella in charge would make a noise and they'd make a movement! So the man says, 'You, you and you' to the ones that was able, and those ones got working the horses. The rest of us was the Cyclin' Corps. We went up to Magilligan. Then the Corps was cut down, so we came down to Belfast and were told a new unit was being formed in Lurgan.

From the memoirs of Private Tommy Jordan, of Ballynafeigh, Belfast, later 16th Rifles.

The Cyclist Company attracted men who had not only been keen cyclists pre-War, but also contained those men who were unable, or unwilling, to handle horses. On 10 December 1914, a meeting was held in the Old Town Hall, Belfast, at 8:00 pm, with the object of forming a cycling company to be attached to the division. The meeting, presided over by Mr. R.S. Osborne, chairman of the Ulster Centre of the Irish Cyclists Association, was addressed by Lieutenant Colonel James Craig, MP, AAQMG of the division. Many of those who attended were there at the behest of Mr. T.C. Brown, of the West Belfast Regiment, UVF, who had been actively engaged for some time in promoting such a unit. It was stressed that members of the unit should be active men of skill and intelligence. Lieutenant W.H. Warman also addressed the audience and told them that while the war in South Africa had not been suitable for cyclists, the roads being far and few between, both French and Belgian cyclists had proved to be very effective in the present conflict. On 7 November the King had signed a Royal Warrant calling into existence a Regular Army Cyclists Corps, which would be as distinctive as the Royal Flying Corps or the Army Service Corps. Lieutenant Colonel James Craig spoke of the need for cyclists; the abnormal frontage of their troops in the War required that there be quick communications throughout the divisions that were engaged. In order to ensure that everything worked as they would wish it to do it was necessary to have a large number of smart cyclists. He emphasised the word 'smart', because they wanted the very best type of men they could get. They initially asked for a small force of 260 men. Headquarters for the corps was to be the Homes of Rest at Bangor, also know as the 'Cripples Institute'. At the close of the meeting several members of the audience came forward to enlist. The first four being Samuel Mark from Carnmoney, John Wills, Isabella Street, Belfast, R. Dickson, Summer Street and J. Smyth, Townsend Street. Recruiting for the Cyclist Company was not initially encouraging and by 16 December 1914, only 16 men had enlisted for a suggested establishment of 271.[13] However, a total of 250 cyclists being the War strength of the company had not been reached by end of December 1914. It was announced that the authorities would provide a complete outfit, including bicycle, for each rider accepted. By 11 January 1915, the corps still required 200 men and free railway warrants were offered to induce men to travel from anywhere in Ulster to enlist, while the phrase 'bad teeth no bar' appeared on recruiting posters! Headquarters was now at Carlton House, 364 Ormeau Road. On 25 February 1915, the corps suffered its first casualty when Private J. McClelland Nelson died in the Military Hospital, Donegal Road. He is buried in the Magherally Presbyterian Churchyard, Down.

By 7 March 1915, the 80 men of the corps who had enlisted so far, arrived in Enniskillen after their recruiting ride across the Province from Bangor. An initial recruit was Robert Lytle, he had first enlisted in the 13th Rifles, but while training at Clandeboye he had succumbed to a kidney infection. As a result of missing out on initial training Robert was transferred to the Cyclist Corps. However, his health did not improve and he was discharged in May 1915, as being unfit for further

---

13   *Belfast News Letter.*

military service. He moved to America for his health, but died in California in September 1917. As the company prepared for the move from Seaford to France it was commanded by Lieutenant W.H. Warman of the 12th Rifles. Educated in part at Worcester College, Oxford, the Captain took a great interest in the men and prompted their resettlement on farming land after the War. He would retain command until his transfer to the Machine Gun Corps (Heavy) Branch in 1917.

Divisional Artillery

At the beginning there was much discussion regarding the formation of divisional artillery and it was 'reluctantly decided'[14] that this unit should not be raised in Ulster. It was pointed out that the Ulster Volunteer Force had no artillery and consequently no partially trained force on which to draw. It was also thought that it would take too long to train the required detachment and this would in turn delay the departure of the division to France. With Ulster and Ireland as a whole not having a Territorial Force, men would have to be trained from scratch, it taking considerably longer to train a Gunner than an infantryman. However, there did exist the Antrim Royal Garrison Artillery, then part of the Special Reserve and responsible for the manning of the heavy guns ensconced at Grey Point Fort and across Belfast Lough at Kilroot. There were also the former members of the Tyrone and Donegal Artillery, which had only been disbanded in 1909, with a number of Royal Artillery officers still resident in Ulster, including the redoubtable Fred Crawford.[15]

The Divisional Artillery was eventually raised some six months later from men recruited in the London area, the first recruits signing up on 5 May 1915, when 60 men assembled at Victoria Street, London. Both 153 and 154 Brigades were formed by the British Empire League, with strong support from General Sir Bindon Blood, and were recruited mainly from the Croydon, Norbury and Sydenham areas of the city. Born near Jedburg in Scotland, Bindon Blood was a descendant of the infamous Colonel Thomas Blood who had attempted to steal the Crown Jewels in 1671, while Colonel Holcroft Blood had commanded the artillery at the battle of Blenheim on behalf of the Duke of Marlborough.[16] Blood attended the Royal School, Banagher, Queen's County (today County Offaly), Queen's College, Galway, and the Addiscombe Military College. He was commissioned into the Royal Engineers in 1860, as a Temporary Lieutenant in charge of signaling and pontoon bridge construction in India, and also served for a time in

Captain George Gibson Lyttle, medical officer.

---

14   Falls, *The History of the 36th (Ulster) Division*.
15   Information provided by Timothy Bowman.
16   Falkner, James, *Marlborough's Battlefields* (2008).

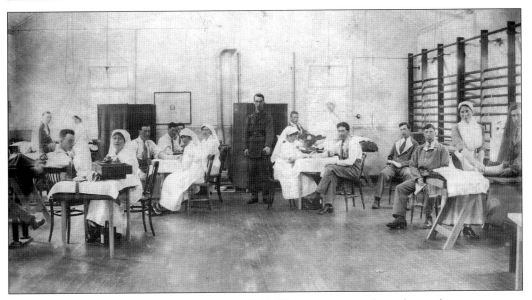

Captain George Gibson Lyttle, RAMC, on duty in a military hospital.

Zululand and South Africa. Promoted to Captain in 1873, he served on the North West Frontier. In 1879 he returned to Africa for service in the Anglo-Zulu War. He went on to fight in the Second Afghan War and the Battle of Tel-el-Kiber. By 1882 he was a Brevet Lieutenant Colonel. In 1883, Blood married Lady Charlotte E. Colvin, second daughter of Sir Auckland Colvin, a distinguished Indian administrator. Blood then returned to India and took command of the Bengal Sappers and Miners in 1885. After seven years he reached the rank of Brigadier General, serving at Rawalpindi, and later with the Chitral Relief Force. He then commanded in turn the Malakand Field Force and the Buner Field Force, relieving the garrison during the Siege of Malakand in 1897. At the end of this command he was promoted to Major General. In 1901, Lord Kitchener requested Blood for service in South Africa, where he was stationed in the Eastern Transvaal. In November 1907 he retired to England, where he continued to lead a very active life. He was made Colonel Commandant of the Royal Engineers in 1914 and gave his support to raising recruits for the Great War.[17]

The 172nd and 173rd Brigades were formed with men from the north-east of London with assistance from the Mayors of East and West Ham. These two brigades operated as separate entities until, in July they, along with the Divisional Ammunition Column, moved to Lewes in Sussex, where the serious training really began.

Command of the Divisional Artillery initially went to Colonel H.A. Brendon. Herbert Algernon Brendon had been commissioned into the Royal Artillery in 1881 and retired in 1912 at the age of fifty. The following year he was recalled and appointed as CRA of the Highland Division (TF) with the rank of colonel and retained this position on the outbreak of War. Sir Henry Rawlinson described him as a 'solid, slow, stupid man',[18] and he was appointed as CRA of the Ulster Division in August 1915. He did not accompany the guns to France and in 1916 he was superseded by Brigadier General Henry Jenkins Brock. Brock been commissioned into the Royal Artillery in 1889 and had served in South Africa, where he was severely wounded. He had served as Adjutant

---

17   *Who's Who* and *Dictionary of National Biography.*
18   Information provided by Dr John Bourne.

of the Royal Horse Artillery until December 1901 and subsequently commanded the Colonial Light Horse, taking part in operations in the Transvaal, Orange Free State and Cape Colony. On the outbreak of war, he commanded the 42nd Battery, RFA and accompanied them to France. He was a lieutenant colonel by 1914 and was appointed as CRA of the Ulster Division Artillery from 1915-1919 and was described as a competent Gunner officer.[19]

Not all of the Divisional Artillery was comprised of Englishmen. Major Robert Lloyd Thompson, from Bertha House, Strandtown in Belfast, and past pupil of Campbell College, served in C Battery of the 173rd Brigade and had enlisted in the Royal Field Artillery in 1912. He would subsequently be awarded the Military Cross.

The majority of artillery pieces that saw action on the Western Front belonged to the Royal Field Artillery (RFA), which had come into being on 1 July 1899. The RFA was the largest arm of the Royal Artillery and was equipped with medium calibre guns and howitzers that were deployed for action on and close behind the trenches and were considered to be reasonably mobile. The main tactical unit of the RFA was the brigade, consisting of a headquarters and four batteries. The brigade was commanded by a lieutenant colonel, assisted by a captain or lieutenant, fulfilling the rolls of adjutant who controlled administration and orderly officer, who saw to transport and stores. There was also a commissioned officer from the Royal Army Medical Corps and one from the Army Veterinary Corps, horses and mules being the main source of moving the battery. Each 18-pounder required six horses to pull it. Other ranks within headquarters consisted of 22 men under the command of a sergeant major. These various ranks acted as signallers, telephonists, medical orderlies, batmen and grooms. These ranks and roles were usually repeated within the four batteries within the brigade.

The 36th Divisional Artillery consisted of four brigades, 153rd, 154th, 172nd and 173rd Brigades, along with a Divisional Ammunition Column. The first three Brigades consisted of three batteries each of four 18-pounder field guns and one battery of four 4.5-inch howitzers. The 18-pounder had a range of 7,000 yards and could fire eight 18-pound shells every minute utilising a detachment of six men on the gun and a further four as ammunition carriers. The 4.5-inch howitzer also had a range of 7,000 yards and was capable of firing four 35-pound shells per minute, again with a detachment of six men. The fourth brigade consisted of three four-gun 18-pounder batteries. By this time, May 1915, the Brigade Ammunition Column had been abolished and replaced with a Divisional Ammunition Column, which had been increased in proportion. Ammunition for the brigade, depending on whether it was 18-pounder or howitzer was 176/108 rounds at the battery position, 126/44 within the Divisional Ammunition Column, 150/80 at the Divisional Ammunition Park, 472/520 in reserve, giving a total of 1,000/800 per gun or howitzer in the field. It must be stressed that this was a minimum number of rounds per gun, it was usually more. However, by the same token, as the war continued the number of men and horses usually decreased due to casualties. To move the detachments and guns required 2,880 officers and men and 2,000 horses and mules. In the Royal Artillery the men who operate the guns are known as detachments, they are called "crews" in the Royal Navy.

The guns and howitzers were capable of firing various types of ammunition. High explosive was generally used against entrenchments and fortifications, shrapnel was used against infantry and smoke shells provided cover for attacks and withdrawals, while star-shells provided illumination during the hours of darkness. There were also gas shells delivering the various types of gas. For the cutting of barbed wire shrapnel was used as it was found that high explosive simply lifted the wire into the air and then dropped it down into the resulting shell hole, most of the time, therefore recreating a barrier.

19   Perry, Nicholas *Major General Oliver Nugent and the Ulster Division 1915-1918.*

Trench Mortar Batteries

The War Establishment for a Trench Mortar Battery, known to signallers as the "Too-Emmas", was eight mortars in two sections of four each. In personnel this amounted to a captain, three subalterns and 46 other ranks. These comprised of two sergeants, eight corporals or lance corporals and 32 privates. Each officer also had a batman. A mortar detachment consisted of a corporal and four privates. Each section of four mortars was commanded by a subaltern, the third subaltern was responsible for the supply of ammunition, rations and other sundries. All detachments were recruited from the infantry and not the Royal Artillery. The mortar is an ancient weapon, its first recorded use was by the Turks at the Siege of Constantinople in 1453, it t found a new lease of life in the Great War and since then has never looked back. By definition a mortar is a short metal tube that is designed to launch a projectile in a high arc, greater than 45 degrees, towards the enemy, an ideal weapon for trench warfare. Another advantage of the weapon was the fact that the detachment could remain in cover to operate it and its light construction meant it could be moved from position to position with relative ease. At the beginning of the war only Germany had a ready supply of mortars, mainly due to observations made by German military representatives during the Russo-Japanese War of 1904-05. Both France and Britain were taken completely by surprise, the British having totally ignored the weapon in their last major conflict, the South African War. While the German had the *Minenwerfer* (mine thrower), it was not until the later part of 1914 that the British were able to introduce a crude weapon in the shape of a smooth-bore four inch diameter pipe lacking both sights or a recoil system. It was not until January 1915 and the invention of the Stokes mortar that British troops were issued with a weapon that surpassed any fielded by the enemy.[20] This mortar consisted of a 3-inch diameter tube fitted with a base plate to absorb recoil

and was supported by a bipod. It was simply a matter of dropping the ten pound bomb down the tube where it impacted with a fixed firing pin, which ignited the firing cartridge and thus propelled the bomb towards the enemy. The Stokes could fire 22 bombs per minute out to a range of 1,200 yards, its minimum range being dictated by the angle of the tube. It must be noted that "minimum" range was not necessarily 'safe' range and it was possible to launch a bomb that fell so close it could injure the firers.

It was said that the trench mortars required the command of a peculiar type of artillery officer, resolute, hard bitten, perhaps often careless and unconventional, but capable in great moments of the most splendid courage lightly worn and taken for granted between comrade and comrade. Captain Eric Norman Frankland Bell was one such officer. The son of Captain E.H. Bell, Quartermaster of the 2nd Inniskillings, he was born in Enniskillen in 1895, the youngest of four children. When

Temporary Captain Eric Norman Frankland Bell VC, killed in action on 1 July 1916, while commanding 109th Trench Mortar Battery.

20　AFC Stokes, later Sir Wilfred Stokes KBE.

his father was posted to England, Eric was educated in Liverpool and attended the School of Architecture at Liverpool University. He was commissioned in the Inniskillings in September 1915, being appointed to the 9th Battalion the following November, where his father was serving as Adjutant. When the Battalion went to France in October 1915, Bell had transferred to the 109th Trench Mortar Battery. From Ramelton in Donegal came Arthur Henry Patterson, who was commissioned into the Inniskillings as a lieutenant and later served in the 109th Battery. Also from the north-west came Second Lieutenant Colin Craig, the son of the late Mr. G.C. Craig, Under Sheriff of Derry. From the Young Citizen Volunteers Private Edward Bowman volunteered, as did Second Lieutenant W.B.M. Thorpe. He had served as a midshipman on the Belfast ship *Rathlin Head,* owned by the Ulster Steamship Company Ltd. He had obtained a commission in the 17th Rifles at Ballykinlar in August 1915 and transferred to the Trench Mortar Company in May 1916.

There was also Second Lieutenant M. Jackson. He was the son of the late Reverend W.J. Jackson, of Duncairn Presbyterian Church. His brother was Lieutenant Sinclair Jackson, Royal Fusiliers, who would win the Military Cross at Salonika, while another brother, Culbertson, was serving as a lance corporal in the RAMC attached to the division.

Another volunteer from the YCV was Second Lieutenant R.A. O'Neill. He was a former pupil of RBAI and had served in the South African War with the Imperial Yeomanry. He had been commissioned into the 14th Rifles and later transferred to the Trench Mortar Battery as did Second Lieutenant C.H.H. Orr. From the 8th Rifles came Lieutenant I.A. Grove-White, the son of a solicitor, he would eventually be promoted to command the 107th Trench Mortar Battery at Messines in June 1917.

Machine Gun Corps

Ordnance historian Ian V. Hogg describes an action that took place in August 1916, during which the British Army's 100th Company of the Machine Gun Corps fired their ten Vickers guns continuously for 12 hours. Using 100 new barrels, they fired 1,000,000 rounds without a single breakdown. It was this absolute foolproof reliability which endeared the Vickers to every British soldier who ever fired one.[21]

At the beginning of the war all infantry battalions were equipped with a machine gun section comprising of two Maxim guns, which was increased to four in February 1915. The section consisted of a subaltern and 12 other ranks and each gun could deliver 500 rounds per minute, equivalent to the firepower of some 40 trained infantrymen. Each gun team had a limber, drawn by a single horse or mule, for carrying ammunition. As with the Trench Mortars, it was a subaltern of a particular character that did best in the Machine Gun Companies. In signalling parlance the machine guns were referred to as 'Emma Gees', after the initials MG. A machine gunner was paid 1s 6d per day and those recruits with an engineering background, however vague, were much sought after.

With the formation of the Machine Gun Corps in October 1915, the Maxim was replaced by the Vickers Mk I. The Vickers machine gun was a water-cooled .303 inch calibre (7.7 mm) machine gun produced by Vickers Limited and was formally adopted by the Army on 28 November 1912. It required a six to eight-man team to operate: one to fire, one to feed the ammunition, while the remainder had to help carry the weapon, its ammunition and spare parts. The weight of the gun itself varied based on what was attached, but was generally 25 to 30 pounds, with a 40 to 50 pound tripod. The ammunition boxes for the 250-round ammunition belts weighed 22 pounds

---

21   Hogg, Ian V., *Machine Guns: 14th Century to the Present* (2002).

each each. In addition, it required about 7.5 imperial pints of water in its cooling jacket. The heat of the barrel boiled the water in the jacket and the resulting steam was taken off by a rubber tube to a condenser container, which had the benefits of not giving away the gun's location and enabling re-use of the water, which was very important in desert conditions. The cooling system, though cumbersome, was very effective, and enabled the gun to keep firing far longer than air-cooled weapons. The loader sat to the gunner's right, and fed in cloth belts of ammunition into which the rounds had been placed. The weapon would draw in the belt, pull each round out of the belt and into the breech, fire it, and then drop the brass cartridge out of the bottom, to gather in a pile of spent brass underneath the weapon, while the cloth belt would continue through the mechanism. It fired the standard .303 inch cartridges as used in the standard Lee Enfield service rifle. The gun had a cyclic rate of fire between 450 and 600 rounds per minute. Theoretically it could fire 10,000 rounds per hour, with the barrel being changed every hour, which took two minutes in the hands of a trained team. Firing the Mark 8 cartridge it could be used against targets at a range of approximately 4,500 yards, or 2.56 miles.

The drill for preparing a Vickers was, the No.1 released the ratchet that held the front legs of the tripod so that they swung forward, both pointing outwards, these were then secured by tightenign the ratchet handles. From a sitting postion he removed two metal pins from the head of the tripod. Then the No.2 placed the gun in position on the tripod and the No.1 then replaced the metal pins to hold the gun. The No.3 brough forward an ammunition box holding 250 rounds in a canvas belt and inserted the brass tag-end of the belt into the feed block on the right-hand side of the gun. The No.1 then grabbed the tag-end poking through the left side, jerked it through further and at the same time pulling back the cranking handle twice, which completed the loading operation.

In action at the beginning of the War the machine guns were deployed in depth in the trenches. With the later introduction of the Lewis gun, the Vickers were moved further back to provide indirect fire against enemy positions at ranges up to 4,500 yards. This plunging fire was used to great effect against road junctions, trench systems, forming up points, and other locations that might be observed by a forward observer, or zeroed in for future attacks, or using map and compass. They could also provide a box barrage around a certain point to prevent the enemy from sending in reinforcements. Eventually all machine guns would be linked by field telephone to battalion headquarters to increase efficiency. Those guns issued to the cavalry were carried on pack horses, while the infantry were supplied with "pack animals", more often than not a mule.

Many myths grew up around the new weapons. It was said that on prolonged firing when the water boiled it was sometimes used to make tea. While such water would be tainted with oil and grease, it was used, but rarely. Again it was said that when there was a shortage of water urine would be used, preferably after tea had been brewed.[22] The more modern phrase "The whole nine yards" is supposed to come from the length of an ammunition belt for a Vickers. In fact a fully loaded belt measures just over six yards and two feet. However, a Browning .50 calibre machine gun of Second World War vintage and later uses a metal linked belt of 350 rounds, which measures out at nine yards to 351 rounds, perhaps this is where the saying came from? Some sources trace it back to 1908!

It has also been stated that the machine gun killed more than any other weapon, this is also a myth. Statistics show that those men who died of bullet wounds, from rifles, machine guns or pistols, account for 38.98 percent, the artillery accounted for 58.51 percent. The concept that the machine gun was the prime killer of the Great War is based in the myth of literature, not historical research.

---

22   Corporal John Young, 12th Machine Gun Company, correspondence.

On 2 September 1915, a definite proposal was made to the War Office for the formation of a single machine gun company per brigade, by withdrawing the guns and required crews from the battalions. Therefore a machine gun company was now comprised of four sections each of four guns and a company headquarters, a total of 16 machine guns. During the Great War eight members of what would become the Machine Gun Corps were awarded the Victoria Cross.

107th Machine Gun Company

The 107th Machine Gun Company was formed at Forceville and joined the Ulster Division on 18 December 1915. Lieutenant Albert Stewart came from Belfast and was a former pupil of RBAI and a member of the UVF. Pre-war he had been well known as a rugby player, winning three international caps. A former chartered accountant, he was commissioned as a second lieutenant into the 10th Rifles and on promotion to lieutenant joined the Machine Gun Company. Lieutenant Geoffrey Evian Sanderson came from Northumberland, living at Eastfield Hall in Warkworth. He was a member of the Masonic Order, being attached to the Isaac Newton Lodge.

108th Machine Gun Company

The 108th Machine Gun Company was formed at Ribeaucourt and joined the Division on 26 January 1916. A former member of the company was Captain James Samuel Davidson, of 'Seacourt' Bangor. He was the son of Samuel Davidson, the founder and owner of the Sirocco Engineering Works, Belfast. Educated at Campbell College and RBAI, James worked for his father as a manager pre-war and coming from a wealthy family was able to indulge in various hobbies and pastimes. He was a member of the Ulster Reform Club and Royal North of Ireland Yacht Club, as well as being an active member of the 1st Battalion, North Down Regiment, UVF. He was commissioned into the 13th Rifles, and given his engineering background was soon transferred to the Machine Gun Company, when, after being promoted to captain, he became Brigade Machine Gun Officer. Private Hugh Wilson, of Abbey Street Bangor, had worked as a gardener to the Davidson family and had also been a member of the UVF. He had also enlisted in the 13th Rifles and then transferred to the Machine Gun Company, as batman to Captain Davidson.

Second Lieutenant William Turner Richardson had been commissioned into the 18th Rifles in March 1915, later transferring into the 12th Rifles. From Dublin, he was a keen sportsman and for many years was a member of the Old Wesley Football Club, as well as being an excellent golfer and tennis player. Pre-war he had worked in the Midland Great Western Railway at Broadstone in Dorset. Second Lieutenant W.P. Vint, came home from working in South America and joined the 11th Rifles in June 1915, before transferring to the machine gun company. He was the grandson of Jonathan Vint of Willowfield, Belfast. Lieutenant James Dermot Neill came from Cultra, County Down, and had been educated at RBAI, followed by time spent in Switzerland and Germany. He was a former member of the UVF and had been commissioned into the 13th Rifles. Another of those with mechanical abilities he, in conjunction with James Davidson, had been instrumental in the forming of the 108th Machine Gun Company. His younger brother Robert Neill had been killed in May 1915 at Fromelles while serving with the 5th Rifles.

109th Machine Gun Company

The 109th Machine Gun Company was formed at Fienvillers under the command of Captain W. McConachie and joined the division on 25 January 1916. William McConachie had been commissioned into the 10th Inniskillings in October 1914, before transferring to the Machine Gun Corps. Among the officers was Lieutenant Holt Montgomery Hewitt, a former member of

D Company UVF, who was the son of James Hewitt of Mornington Park, Bangor. He had two brothers also serving, Ernest, a Lieutenant with the King's Own (Royal Lancaster) Regiment, and William, a Second Lieutenant, was serving with the 9th Inniskillings. One of his brothers, Lieutenant Ernest Henry Hewitt of the King's Own (Royal Lancaster Regiment) was killed on 15 June 1915, at Festubert, and is commemorated on the Le Touret Memorial. Second Lieutenant Andrew Chichester Hart came from an old Derry family, tracing his ancestors back to 1613, with his great-grandfather being the military governor of Londonderry from 1820-1832. Andrew had been commissioned into the 11th Inniskillings on the formation of the division before transferring to the Machine Gun Company in early 1916. Lieutenant Gilbert Colclough Wedgwood was 22 years old and came from Bloomfield, Belfast. He was a past pupil of Methodist College and had originally obtained his commission with the 14th Rifles prior to transferring to the Machine gun Company. His brother, Second Lieutenant Philip Wedgwood, served with the 16th Rifles, while a third brother, George, served in the Royal Navy.

Pre-war Alfred Owens of University Street, Belfast, had been a keen sportsman having played for the Ulster Cricket Club and Malone Rugby Club. An original member of the YCV and later the 14th Rifles, he had been promoted to Sergeant and transferred to the Machine Gun Corps. Lance Corporal William Robert Gardner Kennedy came from Coleraine and was a former member of the Bann Rowing Club, he was 19 years old.

Royal Army Medical Corps (RAMC)

The stretcher-bearers, denoted by an armband bearing the letters "SB", had their efforts largely ignored by those who had never seen them in action. The number of lives they saved was immeasurable, the reward from a "grateful nation" meagre:

> A feature of every report, narrative or diary I have read has been a tribute to the stretcher bearers. All ranks, from Generals in command to wounded men in hospital, are unanimous in their praise. I have watched a party from the moment when the telephone summoned them from their dug-out to the time when they returned with their wounded. To see them run light-heartedly across fire-swept slopes is to be privileged to witness a superb example of the hero in the man. No braver corps exists, and I believe the reason to be that all thought of self is instinctively flung aside when the saving of others is the motive.

From the third Despatch of General Sir Ian Hamilton, Commander-in-Chief of the Mediterranean Expeditionary Force, printed in the Third Supplement of the *London Gazette* of 6 January 1916.

The philosophy of saving lives on the battlefield often resulted in many cases of more lives lost in the recovery of one man. The answer to this conundrum is of course that the effort of recovery adds to the morale of the unit as a whole if each man believes that his comrades will do their utmost to save him. Hence the biblical verse: "Greater love hath no man than this that a man lay down his life for his friends." (John 15 v13).

The men of the RAMC would have to treat both battlefield wounds and disease as the war progressed. In the opening battles records show that artillery fire caused 60 percent of wounds, followed by rifles and machine guns causing 35 percent, with bombs and bayonets causing five percent. This last figure would rise as the war went on and the bomb became a primary weapon in trench fighting. There would also be gas, a completely new type of warfare using firstly chlorine and then mustard gas. While gas did not kill large numbers it did incapacitate and deaths from this continued for many years after the war ended. The high numbers of 'shell shock' cases were initially treated in a haphazard and ill-informed fashion, but treatment improved over time as it became better understood.

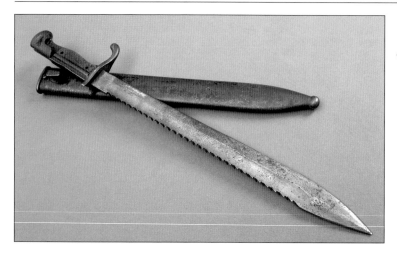

Bayonet as issued to engineers, the serrated edge was used for cutting tree branches.

The Divisional RAMC units were recruited and initially sent to Clandeboye, the Assistant Director Medical Services (ADMS) Colonel F.J. Grieg, an officer recalled from retirement. Colonel Grieg would not serve in France, but continue to train medical personnel within Ulster. He was promoted to Temporary Colonel on 4 July 1915.

As well as horse drawn vehicles, the RAMC elements of the division were the first to be fully equipped with motor vehicles, with public subscription enabling the provision of the most modern of motor ambulances. The *Ballymena Observer* reported in April 1915 that an appeal for £500 from the general public resulted in a collection of £250 in one week. Approximately half of what it cost to provide a motor ambulance of the best quality. The paper also stated; "As we said in last week's appeal, the scheme has got nothing whatever to do with any political party or religious denomination. It is for us all, masses and classes, and all must take a pleasure in its promotion."

While most of the fundraising was done within the Province, assistance also came from elsewhere. The Constitutional Club, London, collected subscriptions from its members valued at £1 each and quickly raised enough to purchase a vehicle, most of these cost in the region of £550 each and were built by Messrs. Charles Hurst Ltd, a local coach builder to specific War Office requirements:

The chassis is a 20 hp Wolseley special long wheel-base (11ft 8in.), four detachable wheels and one spare wheel and tyre being included. The petrol tank is of especially large capacity, and in addition eight gallons are carried in a box separately on the step. The body has been specially approved of by the War Office. The four stretchers are arranged with a passage up the centre with the attendant's seat at the front end of the passage, the attendant thus having a complete view of the patients and full control of the stretchers, and being at the same time in immediate communication with the driver. In this respect the machine constitutes a great advance on the earlier ambulances in which there was no centre passage, the wounded being attended from outside when the canvas sides of the vehicle were rolled up. The machine can be instantaneously converted into a waggonette to carry ten passengers, the stretchers being neatly folded away. An extension over the driver and a windscreen are also provided. The lighting is by acetylene and oil, this being preferred by the War Office to electric light. Over and above these numerous conveniences have been provided for the comfort of the wounded. On the side is a large box divided into compartments intended for blankets, pillows and equipment, and in another compartment is a Primus stove for preparing hot soup, etc. Two large Thermos flasks are carried inside. Behind the attendant's seat is a large specially constructed water tank

for carrying drinking water. The whole of the interior is illuminated by a self-contained acetylene hand lamp which can be detached for looking for wounded in the field. The machine is
one of a large number of ambulances being built.

On 28 January 1915, the first two ambulances, of 21 promised to the War Office by the Ulster
Committee, left Belfast for the drive to the Field Ambulance depot in Newry. These two vehicles
had been built with funds raised in Portadown and Newry, by Mr. John Collen DL and Mr. T.P.
Willis respectively. On the way the ambulances would stop at Lisburn, Portadown, Armagh and
Banbridge, where recruiting would take place. In command of the ambulances, which, it was
stressed, were 'on loan' to the division, was Lieutenant W.S. Gibson, Quartermaster, Royal Army
Medical Corps. The disappointment can be imagined when these magnificent vehicles were then
taken from the division by order of the War Office and sent to a Motor Workshop in Croydon.
From here they were taken to France by other units.[23]

A report in the *Belfast News Letter* on 18 November 1914 recorded that despite the St. John's
Ambulance Association recognising the UVF first aid certificates as a guarantee of proficiency,
the men belonging to the Lurgan medical corps were not satisfied with this and decided to submit
themselves for the St. John's First Aid examination. Twenty-four of the 25 candidates passed and
Dr Gray, the examiner, noted the remarkable degree of aptitude demonstrated by the majority.

There were three field ambulances, 108th, 109th and 110th and despite the similarities these
were not numbered after the Brigades. After a suitable number of men had been recruited they
were then moved to the Training Establishment at Newry. Here the 109th and 110th Field
Ambulances were accommodated in the Linenhall Barracks, formerly the White Linen Hall, while
the 108th was billeted in the Town Hall and Ulster Volunteer force Hall. The White Linen Hall
had been built in 1783 for the promotion of linen exports from Down and Armagh and thus
by-pass the dealers in Dublin. With changing patterns in trading the Hall became redundant and
was then purchased by the Government in the early part of the nineteenth century. Here there was
accommodation for 600 men and a fully equipped hospital with 30 beds. As well as the medical
orderlies and doctors of the Field Ambulances, each battalion had its own medical unit, and the
men who formed the various battalion bands received the full infantry training and were then
further trained to act as stretcher-bearers in time of battle. Quakers were among the group known
as 'c objectors', quite a few are listed on the nominal roll of the 14th Rifles, and they served as
stretcher-bearers on the battlefield, therefore running no less a risk to being killed or wounded.
In November 1915 Lieutenant Colonel Frank Irvine, DSO, was appointed as commandant of the
Training Establishment. An experienced officer, he had been educated at Methodist and Queen's
College, Belfast and served in the South African War from 1899 to 1902. On the outbreak of
war he had served with the 2nd Division and had been a prisoner of war for a short time before
escaping.

Casualty evacuation was an organised affair, as much as was possible in a battlefield situation.
The wounded man was first taken by the stretcher-bearers to the Regimental Aid Post (RAP),
usually a dug-out or some other form of shelter close to a communications trench. Here he received
first aid, had his wounds assessed and was issued with a tag. This tag bore the man's name, regiment, the nature of his wound and information on the inoculation for lockjaw; should it be given,
had it been given and the name of the doctor who administered the treatment. From the R.A.P.
he was taken to the Advanced Dressing Station (ADS), which could be over a mile to the rear. In
some instances it was possible to use wheeled stretchers or avail of a trench tramway. On reaching

---

23   Becke, Major A.F., *Order of Battle of Divisions: Part 3B* (1945) and Frank Fox, *The Royal Inniskilling Fusiliers
    in the Great War* (1928).

the ADS, the wounded man had his injuries re-dressed and morphia administered if necessary, was fed if required and given a soothing cigarette.[24] From here the motor ambulances carried the man to the Main Dressing Station (MDS), where surgery would be carried out if needed. If the man required any further treatment or major surgery he was taken by motor ambulance to a hospital train, which took him to a base hospital, or in the case of a "Blighty" wound, back to England. A 'blighty' wound was one that required the man to return to the UK for treatment, from the Arabic word Beladi, meaning "my own country". This was considered by many men to be a lucky wound.

As per the War Establishment a Field Ambulance contained ten officers and 224 other ranks and was commanded by a lieutenant colonel. It consisted of three sections, each a self-contained unit comprising of doctors, stretcher-bearers, a cook and "washerman". There was also attached a sergeant, ten drivers and four officers batmen, supplied by the Army Service Corps. In early 1915 a Sanitary Section was added, with the responsibility of providing clean water, cooking facilities, de-lousing etc.

At Newry the 40th Casualty Clearing Station was also raised and served in both France and Salonika. From October 1915 until the Armistice in November 1918, the British Salonika Force suffered approximately 2,800 deaths in action, with 1,400 men being wounded and a further 4,200 suffering from sickness. The campaign resulted in little success for the Allies and certainly nothing of any importance until the last two months of fighting. The local conditions and geography ensure that many men constantly suffered from malaria and a dire shortage of roads and railways meant that these had to be specially built.

In common with other units of the Ulster Division and within the Army as a whole the Field Ambulances depended a lot on horses. As per the War Establishment each Field Ambulance had 14 horses for riding and 52 as draught animals. For these there were 23 wagons, three water carts, three forage carts, six general service wagons, then ambulance wagons and a cook's wagon. They also had a bicycle. Eventually many of the ambulance wagons were replaced by motor ambulances and a workshop to maintain these vehicles was added to the divisional strength. In 1916, this was transferred to the Supply Column.

108th Field Ambulance

In December 1914, the 108th Field Ambulance was stationed at Newry and was commanded by Major A. Pearce. In May of the following year command devolved to Lieutenant Colonel R.F.M. Fawcett, DSO. Fawcett was a regular army officer who had served in the South African War, being awarded the Queen's medal and four clasps. Among his medical officers was Lieutenant J.L. Dunlop from Bangor, County Down, and Lieutenant William Russell, MB, from Ballynahinch, later to be awarded the Military Cross.[25] The Quartermaster was Lieutenant John Tewkesbury, his commission dating from 11 November 1914.

109th Field Ambulance

Lieutenant Colonel W.S. Dowman, RAMC, was posted from Eastern Command to duty with the division and was appointed to command the 109th Field Ambulance at Newry. He had seen action in the South Africa War, including the Relief of Ladysmith. His Quartermaster was Lieutenant Stephen Charles Chester Roberts, he would later serve with the Army Ordnance Corps. Lieutenant S.P. Rea was attached to the 13th Rifles as their Medical Officer in April 1915. Dr. Frank P

---

24   Falls, *The History of the 36th (Ulster) Division*.
25   *London Gazette* 19 October 1917.

Montgomery was a well-known Queen's University and Irish fullback and was placed on attachment to the unit as of August 1915. Lieutenant W.W. Dickson, MB, was commissioned into the Ulster Division and posted to the Field Ambulance.

Not all members of the Field Ambulance died as a result of enemy action. Private John Edmund Mullarchy, a former clerk from Arklow, had enlisted at Cavan in January 1915, going to France in October. During January he had become ill showing all the symptoms of having suffered a stroke. He was discharged on 24 July 1916 as being medically unfit for further military service and died on 25 August, aged 44. He left a widow, Mary, who lived in Middleton, County Armagh.

110th Field Ambulance

Captain J Ewing took command as of 24 March 1915 and had the following officers available for service immediately; Lieutenants J. Duffin, R.B. Jackson and John Henry O'Neill. Among the other ranks was Robert Doggart from Newtownards, he had joined the Army on 28 September 1914 and was posted to the 110th Field Ambulance for training, first at Clandeboye and later in Newry.

The *Bangor Spectator* of 8 October 1915 reported that the following men had volunteered for the RAMC; Alexander Davidson, Robert Davidson and Joe Brown. It would seem that the more mature men served in England as opposed to going to France. John O'Neill who lived at Victoria Road, Bangor, was one of those who served in England. His son, Private John O'Neill, served with the 12th Rifles and would be killed on 1 July 1916. George Absolom of Killiney, Bangor, was rated as being too old for front line service and served in England throughout the War. Two of his sons served, Gunner D Absolom fought in South West Africa under General Botha, while Lance Corporal Leo Absolom served with the 13th Rifles.

76th Sanitary Section RAMC

The Sanitary Section was responsible for the provision of clean drinkable water, cooking facilities, billets and washing and delousing stations within the Division. It was staffed by a subaltern, his batman, two sergeants, two corporals and 20 privates. This unit was formed at the end of September 1915 and commanded by Captain J Davies. Major responsibility of the Section was the provision of latrines. The latrine was the name given to a trench toilet. These were usually pits, four to five feet deep, dug at the end of a short sap. Each company had two sanitary personnel whose job it was to keep the latrines in good condition. In many units, officers gave out sanitary duty as a punishment for breaking Army regulations.Before changeover in the trenches, the out-going unit was supposed to fill in its latrines and dig a new one for the incoming units. There was also the question of horses. The division had almost 6,000 horses within its organisation, each one of which would deposit a degree of waste per day, which had to be disposed of. This was achieved by burying, burning or passing on to the nearest willing French farmer.

Army Chaplains Department

The Army Chaplains Department was 120 years old when the Great War began. Initially comprising of only Church of England padres, it had by the beginning of the 20th Century grown to encompass Roman Catholic, Wesleyan, Jewish and other denominations. In August 1914, when the British Army sailed for France the Department has just over 100 serving chaplains, an adequate number to cover the 65 required by the original BEF. Four years later some 3,500 had served in all theatres of the War, ministering to the needs of men and women of all denominations overseas. There are no exact figures, but it is believed that between a 170 and a 180 died or

The Somme Museum, Newtownards, County Down.

The Ulster Tower at Thiepval, redolent with poppies and bathed in July sunshine.
(Courtesy of Carol Walker)

were killed on active service. The number with the letters MC after their name is extraordinary. A wartime quote sums up the role of the chaplain "If the men can't go to church then the church must go to the men."

A large number of church ministers were attached to the Ulster Division, initially, give the make-up of the division there were mostly Church of Ireland and Presbyterian. Eventually most faiths would be represented including those of the Catholic Church.

The Reverend John Redmond joined 36th Division on 11 May 1917, serving in 109 Brigade. He had served in Egypt before being posted to the 31st Division in France in May 1916. In July 1916, he would work with a casualty clearing station treating many of the wounded of that Division. On joining the Ulster Division he was the Church of Ireland padre to the 9th and 10th Inniskillings.[26] He observed in his journal:

It is most encouraging to see the very large proportion of men who turn out. Sometimes the service is held in a large factory, when we have the looms and machinery all around; or in a large ward of what, in ordinary times, is a civilian hospital, but now a billet for our troops. The latter has suffered considerable from shellfire. Every window in that large room is broken, so there is no scarcity of fresh air. Again, we meet in a farmyard, in the centre of which is a sort of pen or enclosed place for calves etc. As the service goes on these animals make themselves heard. On another occasion it is a barn and the men sit on the straw or hay; but sometimes we are fortunate enough to get a more suitable place as, for instance the lecture hall of the large public hall, the seats rising in tiers, so that every man can see and hear well. When it is a band service for a regiment the bandsmen generally form a choir, which is a great help to the service. The bandsmen of the regiment act as stretcher bearers when in the trenches and they perform many deeds of heroism, most of which went unnoticed.

26   Somme Museum Archive.

Bibliography

National Archives (Kew)

A&Q Branch October 1915-June 1919 WO 95/2493
Commander Royal Artillery WO 95/2494-0554-0877
Deputy Assistant Director Ordnance Services WO95/2495
Divisional Cyclist Company WO 95/2496
107 Infantry Brigade WO 95/2502
108 Infantry Brigade WO 95/2504
109 Infantry Brigade WO 95/2508-2509
Divisional War Diary WO 95/2491

Other

Ireland's Memorial Records
Rev. Culbertson Jackson, MC, BSc Great War Reminiscences
Presbyterian Church in Ireland Roll of Honour
Redmond Papers, Somme Archive

Museums & Libraries

Border Regiment & King's Own Royal Border Regiment, Carlisle
Downpatrick Museum
North Down Museum, Bangor, County Down
Royal Inniskilling Fusiliers Museum, Enniskillen
Royal Irish Fusiliers Museum, Armagh
Royal Ulster Rifles Museum, Belfast
Somme Museum, Newtownards
Gloucestershire Police Museum
PSNI Museum, Belfast, N. Ireland
Library & Archives, Canada
Library Headquarters, Ballynahinch
Newtownards Library
National Museum of Ireland, Collins Barracks, Dublin
National Library of Ireland
Jersey Museum, St. Helier, Channel Islands

Books & Articles

Arthur, Max, *Symbol of Courage* (London, 2004).
—— *Last Post* (London, 2005).
Barnett, Correlli, *The Sword Bearers* (London, 1963).
Beach, James (ed) *The German Army Handbook of 1918* (London, 2008).
Beatty, Jack, *The Lost History of 1914* (London, 2012).

Bowman, Timothy, *Irish Regiments in the Great War, Discipline and Morale,* (Manchester, 2003).
—— *Carson's Army, the Ulster Volunteer Force 1910-22* (Manchester, 2007).
Brown, Malcolm, *The Imperial War Museum Book of the Somme* (London, 1997).
—— *The Imperial War Museum Book of the Western Front* (London, 2001).
Buffetaut, Yves, *The 1917 Spring Offensives* (Paris, 1997).
Bujak, Philip,'*Undefeated', The Extraordinary Life and Death of Lt. Col. Jack Sherwood Kelly VC, CMG, DSO* (Devon, 2008).
Canning, W.J. *Ballyshannon, Belcoo, Bertincourt* (Antrim, 1996).
—— *A Wheen of Medals* (Antrim, 2006).
Cherry, Niall, *Most Unfavourable Ground* (Solihull, 2005).
Clark, Alan, *The Donkeys* (London, 1961).
Clarke, P.J. & Feeney, Michael, *Mayo Comrades of The Great War, 1914-1919* (Ballina, 2006).
Coombs, Rose, *Before Endeavours Fade* (London: 2006).
Coppard, George, *With A Machine Gun to Cambrai,* (London, 1969).
Corbett-Smith, A, Major, *The Retreat From Mons* (London, 1916).
Cornish, Paul, *Machine Guns and the Great War* (Barnsley, 2009).
Corns, C & Hughes-Wilson, J, *Blindfold and Alone* (London, 2005).
Corrigan, Gordon. *Mud, Blood and Poppycock* (London, 2003).
Cron, Hermann, *Imperial German Army 1914-1918, organisation, Structure, Orders-of-Battle* (Solihull, 2001).
Crozier, F.P. *A Brass Hat in No Man's Land* (London, 1930).
Crutchley, C.E. *Machine Gunner 1914-1918* (Folkestone, 1975).
Cuttell, Barry, *One Day on the Somme* (Peterborough, 1998).
Denman, Terence, *Ireland's Unknown Soldiers, the 16th Irish Division in the Great War, 1914-1918* (Dublin, 1992).
Doherty, Richard & Truesdale, David, *Irish Winners of the Victoria Cross* (Dublin, 2000).
Doherty, Richard, *The North Irish Horse, a Hundred Years of Service* (Staplehurst 2002).
Dudgeon, Jeffrey, *Roger Casement: The Black Diaries* (Belfast, 2002).
Dungan, Myles, *Irish Voices from The Great War* (Dublin, 1995).
Edmonds, Brigadier General Sir James, Miles, Captain Wilfred, et al, *Military Operations France and Belgium* (London, 1922-48).
Falls, Cyril, *The History of the 36th (Ulster) Division* (London 1922).
Farrar-Hockley, Anthony, *Death Of an Army* (New York, 1997).
Feeney, Michael, *Remembering Mayo's Fallen Heroes* (Castlebar, 2008).
Fitzpatrick, D, *Politics and Irish Life: Provincial Experience of War and Revolution, 1913-1921* (Cork. 1998).
Fox, Frank, *The Royal Inniskilling Fusiliers in the Great War* (London, 1928).
Gilbert, Martin, *Somme, The Heroism and Horror of War* (London, 2006).
—— *VCs of the First World War, The Final Days* (Stroud, 2000).
—— *VCs of the First World War, Spring Offensive 1918* (Stroud, 1997).
—— *VCs of the First World War, The Somme* (Stroud, 1994).
Gray, Randall, *Kaiserschlacht 1918* (London, 2004).
Grayson ,Richard S, *Belfast Boys* (London, 2009).
Groom, Winston, *A Storm in Flanders* (London, 2003).
Haines, Keith, *Somtyme in Chyvachie in Flaundres, Edmund De Wind VC.*
Hayward, James, *Myths & Legends of the First World War* (Stroud, 2002).
Heathcote, T.A. *The British Field Marshals 1736-1997* (Barnsley, 1999).
Holmes, Richard, *Shots From The Front* (London, 2008).
Holzer, Hans, *The Habsburg Curse* (Folkestone, 1974).

Horne, Charles F, (ed) *Source Records of the Great War Vol. V* (London, 1923).

Hughes, Gavin, *The Hounds of Ulster* (Bern, 2012).

Jeffery, Keith, Field Marshal Sir Henry Wilson: A Political Soldier (Oxford, 2006).

Johnson, Nuala C, *Ireland, the Great War and the Geography of Remembrance* (Cambridge, 2003

Johnson, J, *Stalemate* (London, 1995).

Johnston, J.H. *1918, The Unexpected Victory* (London, 1997).

Johnstone, Tom, *Orange, Green and Khaki* (Dublin, 1992).

Kane, James S, *Portadown Heroes* (Newtownabbey, 2007).

Keegan, John, *The Face of Battle* (London, 2004).

Kenyon, David, *Horsemen in No Man's Land* (Barnsley, 2011).

Kitchen, Martin, *The German Offensive of 1918* (Stroud, 2001).

Lewis, Geoffrey, Carson: *The Man Who Divided Ireland* (London, 2005).

Liddle, Peter H. *The 1916 Battle of the Somme, A Reappraisal* (London, 1992).

Liddell Hart, B.H. *History of the First World War* (London, 1970).

Lundy, Derek, *Men that God Made Mad* (London, 2007).

Luxford, J.H. Major, *With the Machine Gunners in France and Palestine* (Auckland, 1923).

Macdonald, Lyn, *To The Last Man, Spring 1918* (London, 1999).

McNab, Chris, *Twentieth-Century Small Arms* (Rochester, 2001).

McWilliams, James, & Steel, R. James, *Amiens, Dawn of Victory* (Oxford, 2001).

Mace, Martin & Grehan, John, *Slaughter on the Somme 1 July 1916* (Barnsley, 2013).

Mallinson, Allan, *1914 Fight The Good Fight, Britain, The Army & The Coming Of The First World War* (London, 2014).

Marix Evans, Martin, *1918 The Year of Victories* (London, 2002).

—— *Battle of World War 1* (Devizes, 2004).

Maurice, R.F.G., Major. *Tank Corps Book of Honour* (Eastbourne, 2009).

Metcalf, Nick, *Blacker's Boys, 9th Royal Irish Fusiliers 1914-1919* (Woodstock, 2012).

Middlebrook, Martin, *The First Day on the Somme* (Middlesex, 1971).

—— *The Kaiser's Battle* (Worcester, 1978).

Moore, Steven, *The Irish on the Somme* (Belfast, 2005).

Moore, William, *See How They Ran: The British Retreat of 1918* (London, 1970).

Moreno, Amanda & Truesdale David, *Angels and Heroes* (Armagh, 2004).

Murphy, B.P., *The Origins and Organisation of British propaganda in Ireland 1920* (Aubane, 2006).

Myers, Kevin *Ireland's Great War* (Dublin, 2015).

Newell, Richard, *Tandragee Remembers* (Armagh, 2009).

Nicholson, CMG, DSO, WN, *Behind The Lines: Administrative Staff Work in the British Army 1914-1918* (London, 1939).

O'Carroll, Declan, *Finner Camp, A History* (Dublin, 2007).

Oldham, Peter, *Pill Boxes on the Western Front* (Barnsley, 2011).

Oldham, Peter, *The Hindenburg Line* (Barnsley, 2000).

O'Neill, H.C. *The Royal Fusiliers in the Great War* (London, 1922).

Orr, Philip, *The Road to The Somme* (Belfast, 2008).

—— *Ballykinler Camp, the First Seven Decades, 1900-1969* (Down, 2012).

Orr, David R, & Truesdale, David, *The Rifles Are There, 1st & 2nd Battalions the Royal Ulster Rifles in the Second World War* (Barnsley, 2005).

Palazzo, Albert, *Seeking Victory on the Western Front: The British Army and Chemical Warfare in World War One* (Nebraska, 2002).

Parkinson, Alan F, *Friends In High Places* (Belfast, 2012).

Passingham, Ian, *The German Offensives of 1918* (Barnsley, 2008).

Pegler, Martin, B*ritish Tommy 1914-18* (Oxford, 1996).

Perret, Bryan, *For Valour*, London, 2003

Perry, Nicholas (ed), *Major General Oliver Nugent and the Ulster Division 1915-1918* (Stroud, 2007).

Pope, Stephen & Wheal, Elizabeth-Anne, *The Macmillan Dictionary of The First World War* (London, 1995).

Potter, John, *Scarce Heard Amid the Guns* (Belfast, 2013).

Redmond, William, *Trench Pictures From France* (Belfast, 2007 reprint of 1918 edition).

Reitz, Deneys, *Trekking On* (London, 1947).

Richardson, Neil, *A Coward If I Return, A Hero If I Fall* (Dublin, 2010).

Robbins, Simon, *British Generalship on the Western Front 1914-18: Defeat into Victory* (London, 2005).

Schama, Simon, *A History of Britain* (London, 2002).

Sheffield, Gary & Bourne, John, *Douglas Haig, War Diaries and Letters, 1914-1918*, (London, 2005).

Sheldon, Jack, *The German Army at Passchendaele* (Barnsley, 2007).

—— *The Germans at Beaumont Hamel* (Barnsley, 2006).

—— *The German Army on the Somme 1914-1916* (Barnsley, 2007).

—— *The German Army at Vimy Ridge 1914-1917* (Barnsley, 2008).

—— *The German Army at Cambrai* (Barnsley, 2009).

Shooter, W.A. Lieut. Col. *Ulster's Part in the Battle of the Somme* (Belfast, 1966).

Steel, Nigel & Hart, Peter, *Passchendaele The Sacrificial Ground* (London, 2000).

Stokesbury, James L. *A Short History of World War I* (London, 1981).

Strachan, Hew, *The First World War* (London, 2003).

Taylor, James, *The 1st Royal Irish Rifles in the Great War* (Dublin, 2002).

—— *The 2nd Royal Irish Rifles in the Great War* (Dublin, 2005).

Terraine, John, *Douglas Haig, The Educated Soldier*, London, 1963

Terraine, John, *The Smoke and the Fire: Myths and Anti-Myths of War 1861-1945* (London, 1980).

Thompson Robert & Beattie, Keith, *Hero of Messines Ridge 1917: The Story of Private John Meek MM and Major William Redmond* (March, 2005).

Thompson, William A.R., *Burke's Medical Dictionary* (London, 1981).

Totten, Andrew, *The Tenth: A Century of Scouting at the 10th Belfast* (Belfast, 2009).

Truesdale, David (ed) *Young Citizen, Old Soldier* (Solihull, 2012).

Turner, Alexander, Cambrai 1917 *The Birth of Armoured Warfare* (Oxford, 2007).

Van Emden, Richard, *The Soldier's War* (London, 2008).

Walker, Stephen, *Forgotten Soldiers, the Irishmen Shot at Dawn* (Dublin, 2007).

Wallace, Richard T. *The World War One Rolls of Honour, Ballynure Presbyterian Church and Ballynure Methodist Church* (Newtownabbey, 2014).

White, Stuart N, *The Terrors, 16th (Pioneer) Battalion, Royal Irish Rifles* (Belfast, 1996).

Whitehead, Ralph J, *The Other Side of the Wire Vol.2* (Solihull, 2013).

Winter, Denis, *Haig's Command* (London, 1991).

Newspapers & Magazines

Armagh Gazette
Bangor Spectator
Battle Lines
Belfast News Letter
Belfast Evening Telegraph
Cityweek

Daily Mail
Down Recorder
Irish Soldier
Irish Times
London Gazette
Lurgan Mail
Newtownards Chronicle
Portadown News
Straits Times
Norwich High School Magazine
The Cyprus Gazette

Unpublished Sources

Hughes Gavin, 'Remembering and Forgetting Old Battles', Trinity College Dublin, 8 May 1914.
Skinner, Robert, 'Kitchener's Camps at Seaford', Archaeological Report (2010).

Somme Association Veteran Interviews

Adams, Hugh James
Allen, William
Bell, Leslie
Brazil, Billy
Caldwell, George
Christie, Jack
Collins, W.E.
Colvill, James
Currie, Harry
Fyvie, William
Getty, Jessie
Gibson, Billy
Grange, R.T.
McBride, George
McFadzean, Billy (nephew)
Pollock, Thomas
Proctor, P.
Trimble, Jack
Wallace, Sam
Williamson, William

With special thanks to the following individuals and organisations:

Clare Ablett
Pamela Agnew
John Richard Barker
Ian Bartlett
Dr. Keith Beattie
Roy Black
Dr Timothy Bowman

Mary Bradley
Leanne Briggs
Maureen Browne
Ronnie Brown
Capt. Donal Buckley
Jason Burke
David Cargo
Niall Cherry
Katrina Clydesdale
Gordon Corrigan
Lyn Cropton
Heather Curran
Richard Doherty
Leah Donnelly
Stuart Eastwood
Alison Finch
Douglas Ford
Jim Fraser
Patricia Fawcett
Steve Fuller
Matt Gamble
Pat Geary
Gerald Gliddon
Rebecca Gordon
Prof Richard Grayson
Sharon Gregg
Keith Haines
Rosemary Hamilton
Jeanetta Harper
Nigel Henderson
Dr. Gavin Hughes
Barbara Janman
The late Prof. Keith Jeffrey
The late Noel Kane
Paul Kerr
Michael LoCicero
Leanne Macey Lillie
C. Macquigg
Pat McCarthy
Tommy McClimmonds
Jim McDowell
Heather McGuickin
Sylvia McRoberts
Clare McWhirter
Walter Millar
Sandra Millsopp
Heather Montgomery
Ian Montgomery
Steven Moore

Amanda Moreno
Dr. Gerald Morgan
Kevin Myers
Dr. Kathy Neoh
Bob O'Hara
Philip Orr
John Potter
Pamela Rea
Gemma Rees
Elizabeth Rice
Steve Roberts
Andrew Robertshaw
Cameron Robinson
Rev. James Rogers
Leslie Simpson
Danielle Smith
Laura Spence
Prof Sarah Alyn Stacey
Sharon Tate
James Taylor
F. Glenn Thompson
Nathan Truesdale
Elizabeth Walker
Richard Wallace
Maeve Watt
Kate Wills
Donna Wilson
Neil Wilson
The late Tom Wylie
John Young
Mike Young

Special thanks to Hazel Martin, Sharon Tate and Dr Kathy Neoh, for all their support over what has been a difficult time.

Index

INDEX OF PEOPLE

INDEX OF PLACES

INDEX OF MILITARY FORMATIONS & UNITS

Armies

Corps

Divisions

Brigades

Regiments & Battalions

INDEX OF GENERAL & MISCELLANEOUS TERMS